The Archaeology of Tribal Societies

edited by

William A. Parkinson

INTERNATIONAL MONOGRAPHS
IN PREHISTORY

Archaeological Series 15

ISBN 1-879621-34-7 (Paperback)
ISBN 1-879621-35-5 (Library Binding)

Library of Congress Cataloging-in-Publication Data

The archaeology of tribal societies / edited by William A. Parkinson.
     p. cm. -- (Archaeological series ; 15)
Includes bibliographical references.
  ISBN 1-879621-34-7 (pbk. : alk. paper) -- ISBN 1-879621-35-5 (lib. bdg. : alk. paper)
  1. Tribes. 2. Villages. 3. Social structure--Cross-cultural studies. 4. Social archaeology. I. Parkinson,
William A. II. Archaeological series (Ann Arbor, Mich.) ; 15.
  GN492.5 .A73 2002

2002153770
CIP

This book is printed on acid-free paper. ∞

International Monographs in Prehistory
P.O. Box 1266
Ann Arbor, Michigan   48106-1266
U.S.A.

Table of Contents

Continued on next page...

Table of Contents *(Continued)*

List of Contributors

Michael Adler — Department of Anthropology, Southern Methodist University, Dallas TX 75275-0336

David G. Anderson — Southeast Archaeological Center, National Park Service, Tallahassee, FL 30210

Ofer Bar-Yosef — Department of Anthropology, Harvard University, Cambridge, MA 02138

Daniella E. Bar-Yosef Mayer — Peabody Museum, Harvard University, Cambridge, MA 02138

Donald J. Blakeslee — Department of Anthropology, Wichita State University, Wichita, KS 67260

Peter Bogucki — School of Engineering and Applied Science, Princeton University, Princeton, NJ 08544

Robert L. Carneiro — Division of Anthropology, American Museum of Natural History, New York, NY 10024

David Cheetham — Department of Anthropology, Arizona State University, Tempe, AZ 85287

Jeffery J. Clark — Center for Desert Archaeology, Tucson, AZ 85705

John E. Clark — Department of Anthropology, Brigham Young University, Provo, UT 84602

Severin M. Fowles — Department of Anthropology, University of Michigan, Ann Arbor, MI 48109

Michael Galaty — Department of Sociology and Anthropology, Millsaps College, Jackson, MS 39210

Sarah A. Herr — Desert Archaeology, Inc., Tucson, AZ 85716

Lawrence H. Keeley — Department of Anthropology, University of Illinois at Chicago, Chicago IL 60607

Claire McHale Milner — Department of Anthropology, The Pennsylvania State University, University Park, PA 16802

John M. O'Shea — Department of Anthropology, University of Michigan, Ann Arbor, MI 48109

William A. Parkinson — Department of Anthropology, Florida State University, Tallahassee, FL 32306

Elsa M. Redmond — Division of Anthropology, American Museum of Natural History, New York, NY 10024

Dean Snow — Department of Anthropology, The Pennsylvania State University, University Park, PA 16802

Richard W. Yerkes — Department of Anthropology, Ohio State University, Columbus, OH 43210

Preface and Acknowledgements

In 1877, Lewis Henry Morgan made the insightful observation that "It is difficult to describe an Indian tribe by the affirmative elements of its composition." As I send off this volume to the press, I have a very good idea of what he was writing about.

The 'germs of thought' that inspired this publication were sown during a graduate seminar on *Scale and Boundaries in Middle-Range Societies* taught by Robert Whallon and John O'Shea at the University of Michigan in 1997. Several of the theoretical concepts that were discussed and developed in that class provided the initial impetus for writing this book on tribal societies, as well as several other publications, Ph.D. dissertations, and 'preliminary papers.' I personally owe a great deal of gratitude to everyone who participated in that seminar not only for the opportunity to exchange ideas with them in the halls of the Museum of Anthropology and at the Brown Jug, but also for the collegial support they have provided me over the years.

Like most good things in archaeology, the publication of this edited monograph took a considerable amount of time and involved a wonderful team of individuals who each contributed their own innovative ideas, harsh criticisms, and invaluable support to produce what I hope is a book that—like the structural organization of tribal societies—will be something more than the sum of its parts. The ideas that underlie the majority of the chapters that make up this volume originally were presented in a symposium Severin Fowles and I organized at the 64ᵗʰ Annual Meetings of the Society for American Archaeology in Chicago, IL, in 1999. In that symposium—'The Archaeology of Tribal Societies'—Sev and I tried to bring together some of the best archaeologists in the world to comment on the notion of tribe from their own theoretical perspective, and also to present substantive information from their own research contexts that would help us reassess and reevaluate the tribal concept in anthropological archaeology. Michael Adler, David Anderson, Ofer Bar-Yosef, Daniella Bar-Yosef Mayer, James Brown, John Clark, Lawrence Keeley, and Dean Snow all graciously agreed to participate in the symposium and have been on board from the beginning. I want to thank them each for their continual patience and level-headed guidance in helping this book evolve and develop.

The success of the SAA symposium encouraged us to expand the geographic and temporal scope of the edited volume to include ethnographic and ethnohistoric contributions, as well as additional archaeological contributions from different parts of the world. The end result, we hoped, would be more representative of the holistic nature of anthropological discourse, and also would provide specific examples of how different processes within tribal societies are accessible to anthropologists via different research methodologies, be they archaeological, ethnohistoric, or ethnographic. To help achieve this, Donald Blakeslee, Peter Bogucki, Robert Carneiro, Jeffery Clark, David Cheetham, Michael Galaty, Sarah Herr, John O'Shea, Claire McHale Milner, and Elsa Redmond all kindly made outstanding contributions to the cause. I thank them for the enthusiasm with which they took on the task of participating in the volume and for how carefully they considered my own ideas, no matter how under-baked.

Robert Whallon—first as an instructor and later as a publisher—has been very supportive of this task from its inception and has provided invaluable help and support along the way. I would like to thank him for his patience and guidance as this project finally found its way to completion.

I also am deeply indebted to Severin Fowles, who has been a fantastic colleague and close friend since before that graduate seminar held all those years ago. Sev was a co-organizer and co-chair of the SAA symposium in Chicago, and his ideas and influences have continued to permeate throughout the pages of this book and through my own research. Sev wrote the theoretical framework for the volume (Chapter 2), and the volume would not be complete without his very substantial contributions. I owe him a very special thanks for his continued help in bringing this volume to fruition and for helping me to learn how to be a professional colleague and a dear friend at the same time.

In the years that have passed since this edited volume initially was conceived, I have had the good fortune to interact with several different colleagues at four different universities—the University of Michigan, the University of Cincinnati, Ohio State University, and Florida State University. While these years have been wonderful for fine-tuning my ideas about tribal social organization, they have been less than ideal for my wife, Betsy, who has been forced to find a new position in each new town. To her I owe the biggest thanks of all.

William A. Parkinson
Tallahassee, Florida
December 2001

1. Introduction: Archaeology and Tribal Societies

William A. Parkinson

Do tribes exist? Or are they chimeras, imaginary compounds of various and, at times, incongruous parts, societal illusions fabricated for diverse reasons, but once created, endowed with such solid reality as to have profound effect on the lives of millions of people? The question is practical, because it does have consequences in daily life, and theoretical, because the notion of tribe has played a vital role in various social sciences, perhaps most conspicuously in anthropology.

This is how Morton Fried began his seminal work entitled, *The Notion of Tribe* (1975). In the decades since Fried posed this simple question—'Do tribes exist?'—anthropologists still cannot agree on its answer. Fried's own conclusion was that tribes are an aberrant form of social organization that occur only in very specific secondary social contexts (see also Fried 1968).

Most cultural anthropologists—following Fried's lead—have abandoned the concept entirely. As Elisabeth Colson (1986:5) began one article:

> I do not know what is meant by 'Tribal Societies.' 'Tribe' and 'tribal' are slippery terms despite various attempts to pin them down so that they could be used analytically, 'tribe' has been used with reference to the whole span of human groups, with perhaps the exception of the nuclear family. *The Tribe On The Hill* which Jack Weatherford published in 1981 is about the United States Congress with its associated staff and penumbra of lobbyists.

Colson's explicit disdain of the tribal concept should resonate with anyone who has turned on a television recently, only to find so-called 'reality' programs about 'tribes' of attractive, scantily-clothed, urbanites competing with each other in extreme environments for large cash prizes. The Cleveland Indians have been referred to by their loyal fans as 'the tribe' for years, and a recent *New York Times Magazine* contained a piece that used the term to refer to a close-knit group of unmarried friends who find solace in each other in the absence of a spouse. Of course, the term also has a very specific legal definition in the halls of the United States government (see Beinart 1999; Sterritt et al. 1998).

Like Elisabeth Colson, many anthropologists, because of the semantic and analytical problems associated with the term 'tribe', have abandoned it in favor of more descriptive—and usually multi-hyphenated—phrases such as 'small-scale, semi-sedentary, trans-egalitarian societies'. But given the long—albeit rather jaded—history of the tribal concept within the discipline (see, for example, June Helm's [1968] edited volume, *The Problem of Tribe*), we should consider the possibility that there may be something salvageable in the concept before we discard it entirely. Even Dr. Colson's quote, cited above, is from an article entitled "Political Organizations in Tribal Societies." Thus, despite the fact that the *term* has come to acquire—and always may have had—a variety of different technical and colloquial definitions, the *concept* of tribe, as Fried himself noted, has "played a vital role in various social sciences, perhaps most conspicuously in anthropology" and deserves to be revisited before it is banished forever from our analytical arsenal.

The present volume represents an attempt at doing just this. Using information derived from ethnographic, ethnohistoric, and archaeological sources, the various authors who have contributed chapters to this volume each have made an attempt to assess the utility (or futility) of the concept in the wide variety of different socioenvironmental contexts in which they work. The end result is a volume that can itself be viewed as a collection of ethnographers', archaeologists' and ethnohistorians' perceptions of what the 'tribe' concept means and, much more importantly, how they believe the concept can be employed to learn about human social variability in various prehistoric and historic contexts.

The common thread that ties together the various contributions to the volume is the theoretical proposition that although the tribal concept finds its historical roots in the ethnographic branch of

1

anthropological discourse, it may be a concept that is better approached using information derived from the archaeological—rather than the ethnographic—record. Specifically, the authors were urged to consider whether the long-term perspective available to archaeologists allows them to track subtle changes in social organization that ethnographers are seldom at liberty to witness given the inherently short-term nature of the information at their disposal. Thus, the volume attempts to explore the utility of retaining the tribal concept and redefining it in such a manner that it may be useful for comparing social trajectories in a cross-cultural framework (see Fowles, this volume, Chapter 2). In doing so, we hope to build upon the work of our colleagues who in recent years have tried to retool cultural—or in Flannery's (1995) terminology, social-evolutionary frameworks to focus upon social processes that operate at many different temporal, geographic, and social scales (see, for example, Carneiro 1996; Drennan 1991; Feinman 2000; Neitzel and Anderson 1999; Spencer 1997).

Why 'Tribe'?

The word *tribe* is one of several arbitrary, operational definitions used by anthropologists to facilitate cross-cultural comparison (Bernard 1994; Kuznar 1997). Other examples of operational definitions include the terms *culture, band, society,* etc. The use of such discipline-specific terminology is a necessary evil within the social sciences, wherein the unit of analysis is seldom clearly defined. Regarding this problem, the late Marvin Harris (1979:15) noted that:

> A strong dose of operationalism is desperately needed to unburden the social and behavioral sciences of their overload of ill-defined concepts, such as status, role, group, institution, class, caste, *tribe*, state, and many others that are part of every social scientists' working vocabulary. The continuing failure to agree on the meaning of these concepts is a reflection of their unoperational status and constitutes a great barrier to the development of scientific theories of social and cultural life. (my emphasis)

The 'strong dose' of operationalism suggested by Harris was never taken, and anthropologists concerned with cross-cultural analysis currently find themselves inundated with a plethora of ill-defined terms which each seem to acquire their own definition depending upon the specific context within which they are employed. Nowhere is this

problem more apparent than dealing with the term *tribe*.

The term 'tribe' is used throughout this book not because we wish to rekindle the polemic debate surrounding the supposedly inexorable process of sociocultural evolution (e.g., Band-Tribe-Chiefdom-State [for example, Service 1971]), but rather because the term has a long history in cross-cultural anthropology, and because it denotes a form of social organization generally understood to refer to a wide range of social systems that regularly exhibit some degree of institutionalized social integration beyond that of the extended family unit, or band. Nevertheless, some are bound to find the use of the term anachronistic, since it has come to be replaced by even more ambiguous phrases, such as 'middle range society' (e.g., Feinman and Neitzel 1984). This latter moniker attempts to place tribes somewhere *Between Bands and States* (Gregg 1991), as one book title puts it, and emphasizes the transitional and more ephemeral nature of tribal social systems.

But is precisely this tendency—to view tribes as ephemeral *ad hoc* social constructions—that has resulted in the creation of a number of appellations, such as 'tribelet' (e.g., Bocek 1991), 'rituality' (e.g., Yoffee et al. 1999), and 'transegalitarian societies' (e.g., Owens and Hayden 1997), which frequently apply to only a few historically particular contexts and have no more utility in comparative cross-cultural analyses than does the tribal concept. Although cases occasionally arise when it is necessary to create new terms within the discipline, such neologisms have begun to run rampant within the field, and it is now necessary to begin reassessing their utility. To this end, the research presented in this volume represents an attempt at stressing not the historically particular characteristics of tribal social systems, but their lasting—albeit somewhat elusive—processual similarities, several of which are only accessible via the diachronic perspective of archaeological inquiry.

The remainder of this chapter briefly outlines the development of the tribal concept within ethnography and discusses the various characteristics that have come to be associated with tribal societies in that context. Several of these characteristics derive from models that were dependent upon the synchronic information contained in the ethnographic record—models that were unable to account for social processes that occurred over temporal durations of several decades or centuries.

The following chapter by Severin Fowles then discusses how the tribal concept has been translated into the diachronic context of archaeological research during the last half of the twentieth century and suggests that it is necessary to shift the subject matter "from types of entire societies to types of cultural processes or historical trajectories."

A Brief History of Tribe

Since the time of Morgan the concept of tribe has been plagued by the tendency of earlier generations of anthropologists to generate attribute lists that attempt to pigeonhole societies into different classificatory groupings. Early attempts at such classificatory schemes were based upon unilineal evolutionary paradigmatic approaches (see also Spencer 1896; Tyler 1871), wherein 19th century European civilization was envisioned as the ultimate predestined form of social organization to which all societies were inevitably progressing (see Trigger 1990). Several of the characteristics that initially were attributed to tribes within this teleological context continue to plague more recent formulations of the concept, and must be recognized if we are to arrive at an operational definition of the concept.

Morgan's (1851, 1877) initial social typology placed human societies into three developmental 'stages' through which he believed all societies necessarily passed—Savagery, Barbarism, and Civilization. Each of these stages was indicated by a particular technological repertoire, and was associated with a particular subsistence strategy and political form. This error—to group together societies based upon a plethora of characteristics which are understood to be intimately intertwined—was perpetuated throughout the following century in the works of various influential authors, such as White, Service, and Sahlins (see Feinman and Neitzel [1984] for an excellent discussion of the problems with 'typological approaches'). Nevertheless, Morgan's initial discussion of tribal society set the terms for the way in which both the term and the concept would be employed during the next century.

Morgan used the term tribe to refer to linguistically homogeneous cultural units:

> Each tribe was individualized by a name, by a separate dialect, by a supreme government, and by the possession of a territory which it occupied and defended as its own. The tribes were as numerous as the dialects, for separation did not become complete until dialectical variation had commenced. Indian tribes, therefore, are natural growths through the separation

of the same people in the area of their occupation, followed by divergence of speech, segmentation, and independence. (Morgan 1995 [1851]:93)

Morgan envisioned tribes as forming due to a gradual outflow, or budding-off, of groups from a hypothesized geographic tribal center. Over time, these emigrants would acquire distinct cultural traits and, eventually, linguistic differences, thus creating new tribes (see Morgan 1851:95).

Morgan cites as a causal factor in the formation of tribes "a constant tendency to disintegration." This notion persists in even some recent archaeological discussions of tribes, which are commonly understood as regionally-integrated systems that develop out of a quagmire of disaggregated bands (e.g., Braun and Plog 1982). In addition, it is important to note that the principle of segmentation already was present in Morgan's initial formulation of the concept as an anthropological classification of society.

Durkheim's (1893) tangential contribution to the topic also stressed the principle of segmentation, or mechanical solidarity, to distinguish less economically complex societies—what later came to be referred to as bands and tribes—from those societies that exhibit organic solidarity, or economic specialization—chiefdoms and states. Although Durkheim was concerned explicitly with the development of the division of labor, his basic classificatory scheme carried with it the assumption that changing economic strategies occurred hand-in-hand with particular political forms. As Lewis Coser notes in his introduction to *The Division of Labour:*

> Durkheim was, by and large, beholden to a structural explanation of moral phenomena. The essential differences between types of society were to be sought on the structural or morphological level. The causal arrow in the analysis of social phenomena went largely from productive relations and structural linkages between people to moral or legal systems of thought. (Coser 1984:xviii)

In Durkheim's work, the concept of segmentation— in the guise of mechanical solidarity—was combined with Marxist structural principles wherein different economic infrastructures produce different forms of superstructures. This basic structuralist concept of segmentation as being characteristic of less economically complex societies heavily influenced not only the pre-war British structuralists, but also the work of later writers, such as Steward, Sahlins, and Service (see below).

During the early decades of the last century, several British anthropologists began working with tribal societies in different parts of the world, bringing a functional-structuralist perspective to the discipline. Influenced by French sociologists writing at the turn of the century, such as Henri Hubert and Emile Durkheim, members of the British school proposed an ethnographic method that combined a focus upon structure and function. This functionalist perspective lead Radcliffe-Brown to a methodology that was cross-cultural in nature, and which focused upon each culture as an adaptive and integrative mechanism (see Radcliffe-Brown 1948:ix). The functional aspect of this perspective was based, in large part, upon Durkheim's concept of 'solidarity' (see Harris 2001:516 for additional discussion).

Radcliffe-Brown delineated Andaman social structure as consisting of independent and autonomous small communities, each "leading its own life and regulating its own affairs."

> These local groups were united into what are here called tribes. A tribe consisted of a number of local groups all speaking what the natives themselves regarded as one language, each tribe having its own language and its name. The tribe was of very little importance in regulating the social life, and was merely a loose aggregate of independent local groups. Within the local group the only division was that into [nuclear] families. These were the only social divisions existing among the Andamanese, who were without any of those divisions known as 'clans' which are characteristic of many primitive societies. (Radcliffe-Brown 1948:23)

Each of the tribal units occupied a particular territory, and spoke a different dialect. As was the case with Morgan, Radcliffe-Brown defined a tribe an essentially linguistically homogeneous region that was associated with a particular territory.

E. E. Evans-Pritchard, a student of Radcliffe-Brown's, also assumed an explicitly structuralist perspective of tribal societies in his work *The Nuer* (1940), in which he wrote:

> The largest political segment among the Nuer is the tribe. There is no larger group who, besides recognizing themselves as a distinct local community, affirm their obligation to combine in warfare against outsiders and acknowledge the rights of their members to compensation for injury. (Evans-Pritchard 1940:5)

Nuer tribes had no common organization or central administration, although they sometimes formed loose federations. In this formulation, a tribe was defined in terms of a group which was recognized by its member: as constituting a coherent unit, particularly for the purposes of warfare and homicide retribution. Within the various tribal groupings of Nuer society, Evans-Pritchard noted several structural subdivisions:

> A tribe is divided into a number of territorial segments and these are more than mere geographical divisions, for the members of each consider themselves to be distinct communities and sometimes act as such. We call the largest tribal segments 'primary sections', the segments of a primary section 'secondary sections', and the segments of a secondary section 'tertiary sections'. A tertiary tribal section consists of a number of villages which are the smallest political units of Nuerland. A village is made up of domestic groups, occupying hamlets, homesteads, and huts. (Evans-Pritchard 1940:5)

Each of these various structural sections formed part of a segmentary system, "by reference to which it is defined, and, consequently the status of its members, when acting as such towards one another and to outsiders, is undifferentiated" (Evans-Pritchard 1940:4). Like his mentor, Radcliffe-Brown, Evans-Pritchard envisioned these segments as integrating at various levels, each level determining the structural 'distance' between the members of different segments.

While the British structural-functionalist perspective proved extremely useful for describing social relations within static cultural contexts, it inevitably failed to formulate the significant sociocultural laws it had proposed to produce. Harris attributed this failure to the structural-functionalist tendency to allot social structure a central, primary, role to the expense of subordinating other techno-economic parameters (see Harris 2001:524).

The structuralist concepts of segmentation and integration figured largely into Steward's argument that societies should be approached in terms of varying levels of sociocultural integration (see Steward 1955). This idea carried over, in somewhat modified form, into the work of Sahlins and Service (1960). Initially, Steward intended the concept not as a component in cultural evolutionary theory, but as a tool for cross-cultural comparison. During this brief time, the tendency to lump together various political, economic, and social attributes became temporarily uncoupled. In Steward's view, a particular structural characteristic—the level of integration—was used as the primary unit of societal analysis. It was only later, when the concept was co-opted by Sahlins and Service (1960), that particular levels of integration became equated with particular stages of cultural evolution and were again associated with specific economic, ideological, and political criteria.

Steward (1931) proposed the concept of levels of integration primarily as a tool for cross-cultural analysis as an alternative to what he called the traditional assumptions about tribal societies (Steward 1955:44). This traditional view was based upon three fundamental aspects of the behavior of members of tribal societies, which Steward rejected. He outlined these aspects in the following manner. First, tribal culture was a construct that represented the ideal, norm, average, or expectable behavior of all members of a fairly small, simple, independent self-contained, and homogeneous society. Second, tribal culture had a pattern or configuration, which expressed some overall integration. Finally, the concept of tribal culture was understood to be essentially relativistic—meaning that the culture of any particular tradition was seen to be unique in contrast to cultures of other traditions. Steward (1955:46) suggested that while this conceptualization of tribal culture had been a tool useful for analysis and comparison, it was of little utility in dealing with culture change. In place of this normative perspective, Steward proposed the concept of levels of sociocultural integration.

Steward initially intended the concept of levels of sociocultural integration to be used as a methodological device:

> The cultural evolution of Morgan, Tylor, and others is a developmental taxonomy based on concrete characteristics of cultures. The concept of levels of sociocultural integration, on the other hand, is simply a methodological tool for dealing with cultures of different degrees of complexity. It is not a conclusion about evolution. (Steward 1955:52)

He argued that the concept "provides a new frame of reference and a new meaning to pattern; and it facilitates cross-cultural comparison" (Steward 1955:52).

Steward built upon Redfield's (1941, 1947) distinction between folk societies and urban societies, noting that by establishing an empirically-based typology of integrational levels, it would be possible to examine the incorporation of smaller (what he called 'simpler') societies into larger sociocultural systems, "...and to make generalizations about processes which go beyond what Redfield derived from the process of urbanization"

(Steward 1955:53). To this end, Steward defined three basic integrational levels: the nuclear family, folk societies (or multifamily sociocultural systems), and states. He conceded that there are probably several levels of sociocultural integration between these three, but that "these are qualitatively distinctive organizational systems, which represent successive stages in any developmental continuum and constitute special kinds of cultural components within higher sociocultural systems" (1955:54). Steward suggested that the concept of sociocultural levels should be used as an analytic tool in the study of changes within particular sociocultural systems, which each consist of parts that developed at different times and which continue to integrate certain portions of the culture.

Service (1971) built upon Steward's concept of levels of integration, but reincorporated an explicitly evolutionary component to its initial formulation. Despite the various critiques of his now (in)famous *Band-Tribe-Chiefdom-State* model (e.g. Fried 1968), the strength of Service's model lies in its focus upon the structural integration of societies:

> If the general evolution of society consists, as some have said, of not only a multiplication of groups but also of an increase in specialization into economic and political parts, ritual units, and the like, then tribes have advanced over bands only in the sense of multiplication and integration of parts. This is why the present book chooses as the discriminating criterion of stages the *form of integration*. At each level the integration of parts is carried out differently. (Service 1971:132, original emphasis)

Within this scenario, the defining characteristic of tribal social organization is the structured organization of segmentary units of a similar scale, usually lineages or groups of lineages (bands), via some integrative institution. According to Service, this institution usually takes the form of a pan-tribal sodality, which crosscuts lineages and unites groups of bands into tribes. As Service (1971:100) notes:

> A tribe is of the order of a large collection of bands, but it is not *simply* a collection of bands. The ties that bind a tribe are more complicated than those of bands and, as we shall see, the residential segments themselves come to be rather different from bands. (original emphasis)

This contention—that tribes are essentially social segments integrated via some sort of pan-tribal institution—reiterates Steward's contention that it is necessary to focus upon levels of integration as a primary criterion for typological classification. But whereas Steward attempted to apply the concept (of levels of integration) as a methodological tool for cross-cultural investigation, in Service's formulation the degree and manner of integration had itself become the typological indicator. Thus, the level of integration—initially intended as a methodological tool—had become, perhaps inevitably a 'conclusion about evolution'.

Also inherent in Service's concept of tribe is a certain degree of fragility, and a tendency towards disunity:

> Considering the lack of institutional political means of unity and the absence of organic solidarity, and considering such grave sources of disunity as feuds, it seems remarkable that a tribe remains a tribe. It seems sensible to reaffirm that *external* strife and competition *among* tribes must be the factor that provides the necessity for internal unity. (Service 1971:104; original emphasis)

While the concept of levels of sociocultural integration, as Service used it, provides a method useful for classifying different societal forms, it suffers from a static quality that does not account adequately for the degree of dynamic flexibility documented in the archaeological record. That is, even the roughly-hewn forms of social integration that Service employs suffer from the fact that they are themselves static idealizations of dynamic phenomena. Although Service's model allows for a certain range of variability within each of his forms of social integration (e.g., lineal and composite tribes), it does not account for the basic fact that the social structures, which themselves define the different evolutionary stages, inherently allow for a certain degree of integrative, or 'organizational flexibility' (see Fowles, this volume, Chapter 2; Fowles and Parkinson 1999; Parkinson 1999:44-47). Because this flexibility may not be expressed within the short-term perspective inherent to the ethnographic record, it is a characteristic that can only be actively explored using the diachronic information contained in the archaeological record.

Marshall Sahlins also subscribed to a version of the basic *Band-Tribe-Chiefdom-State* evolutionary scheme and distinguished between bands and tribes in the following manner:

> A band is a simple association of families, but a tribe is an association of kin groups which are themselves composed of families. A tribe is a larger, more segmented society. Without im-

plying this as the specific course of development of tribes, we may nonetheless view a tribe as a coalescence of multifamily groups each of the order of a band. (Sahlins 1961:324)

In Sahlins' view, tribes consist of economically and politically autonomous segments that are held together by their likeness to each other (i.e., by mechanical solidarity) and by pan-tribal institutions, which crosscut the primary segments. For Sahlins (1961), the segmentary lineage system is a substitute for the fixed political structure that tribal societies are incapable of sustaining.

Sahlins built upon Steward's notion of levels of integration by linking varying levels of organization with sectors of social relations. Within this 'sectoral model', "relations become increasingly broad and dilute as one moves out from the familial navel" (Sahlins 1968:16). Sahlins understood cooperation and social interaction to be most intense at the tribal 'core'—the homestead and hamlet. Thus, the degree of integration decreases as the level of organization increases, and degrees of sociability diminish as fields of social relation broaden. In his own words:

> The model before us is set out in social terms. But more than a scheme of social relations, it is an organization of culture. The several levels of organization are, in the jargon of the trade, levels of sociocultural integration; the sectors, sectors of sociocultural relations. Functions are regulated by levels of organization, and transactions by sectors of relation. (Sahlins 1968:16)

Within Sahlins' holistic approach, tribes can subsume an astonishing array of different societal arrangements, from segmentary tribes to chiefdoms (see Sahlins 1968:20). He envisioned many intermediate arrangements between these two ends of the tribal spectrum. These include: conical clans, segmentary lineage systems, territorial clans, dispersed clans, and local cognatic descent groups.

In addition to trying to blur the line between different social classifications, Sahlins also attempted to decouple the relationship between social forms and economic practices, "while it is true that most tribesmen are farmers or herders, thus cultural descendants of the Neolithic, not all are. The Neolithic, then, did not necessarily spawn tribal culture. What it did was provide the technology of tribal dominance" (Sahlins 1968:3).

Fried's visceral reaction to the *Band-Tribe-Chiefdom-State* model, and to Service and Sahlins in particular, was based upon his paradigmatic assumption that social classification should be based upon the differential access to status positions available to individuals in different societies. This led to his tripartite classificatory system of egalitarian, ranked, and stratified societies. Since Fried understood both bands and tribes to be essentially egalitarian in nature, he saw no need to subdivide egalitarian societies into two discrete groups. In a series of articles (e.g., Fried 1968) and a book (Fried 1975), he launched a series of attacks upon the concept of tribe, arguing that tribes tend to occur only in secondary contexts, "as a consequence of the impinging on simple cultures of much more complexly organized societies" (Fried 1975:10).

Fried's critique deserves careful consideration, not least because it constitutes the inception of the replacement of the term tribe by much more cumbersome phrases, such as 'middle-range societies'. This is unfortunate, for Fried's arguments seem to augment, rather than discredit the concept of tribe as a construct useful for cross-cultural analysis.

For example, Fried's contention that tribes form only when less complex societies are affected by more complex ones, seems to beg the question: why do certain societies turn into tribes when they come into contact with states and empires, and others do not? Fried's inability to answer this simple question exposes the Achilles heel of his entire argument, which is based upon the untenable position that tribes exist only as discretely-defined cultural units, a notion explicable by his dependence upon the ethnographic record. When viewed solely through the short-term perspective available through ethnography, the distribution of tribes across the globe would certainly seem to correlate with those regions which were heavily influenced by historical state-level societies: North America, New Guinea, South America, etc. Nevertheless, a closer look at the archaeology of these same regions would reveal that several tribes had emerged prior to contact, and indeed prior to the indigenous development or impact of state-level societies in these regions. Furthermore, even in the same areas where Fried argued that contact produced tribal systems, he fails to explain why certain societies, such as the Shoshone of California, or the Australian hunters and gatherers, never developed into tribal units, but remained un-integrated bands.

Fried's formulation of tribal society suffers from a static quality that precludes the possibility for tribes to assume a variety of different configurations throughout their ontogeny. The reason why tribes emerged in some instances of Western contact, and not in others, must have something to do

with the structure of their social relations prior to contact. Some societies exhibited certain structural features—such as sodalities—that allowed them to organize into more, and more complex, integrative units than other societies. These included tribes. Other societies lacked the structural mechanisms necessary to integrate into these more complex units—these were bands. The structure of social relations prior to the time that societies were impinged upon by more complex ones necessarily determined the trajectories these societies assumed after contact. Fried's inability, or unwillingness, to accept this basic fact can be attributed, at least in part, to his overreliance upon the ethnographic record, which because of its short-term perspective was limited in its ability to track trajectories of change that occur on a much longer diachronic scale.

This tendency—to construct classificatory systems based exclusively upon ethnographic and ethnohistoric examples—resonates throughout all of the models discussed above. Despite this fact, certain threads permeate each of the models, suggesting the existence of some ethnographic patterns that need to be considered while formulating an archaeologically useful notion of tribal social trajectories.

Attributes Associated with the Tribal Concept in Ethnography

This brief overview of the development of the tribal concept in ethnography reveals several attributes that frequently have been associated with the tribe concept. These include:
1. The concept of segmentation, or 'mechanical solidarity',
2. A tendency towards entropy, or disunity,
3. The idea that tribes exist only as discrete entities, with well-defined social and geographic boundaries, and
4. The idea that tribes are somehow 'transitional' between less complex social forms, such as bands, and more complex forms, such as chiefdoms and states.

Of these attributes, perhaps the only one that should be retained in an attempt to operationalize an archaeological definition of tribal social processes is the concept of segmentation. The rest of the characteristics can be attributed to the skewed temporal perspective offered through the information contained in the ethnographic record—the primary data source for most of the models presented above.

Segmentation

Perhaps the most pervasive characteristic associated with tribal systems in both ethnographic and archaeological contexts is the idea that they are segmented (see Fowles, this volume, Chapter 2, for an extensive discussion of segmentation). As noted above, the idea that tribes can be characterized by segmentary forms of organization can be traced back to Morgan (1851). Durkheim (1984) associated the term with mechanical solidarity, which later authors, such as Sahlins and Service, used to characterize bands and tribes, economically and politically (see also Kelly 1985). This notion carries over into archaeological approaches to tribal societies. Although different authors argue the degree to which mechanical solidarity—as it refers to the redundancy created by a lack of economic specialization between different social segments practicing the domestic mode of production (see Sahlins 1972)—can vary within tribal systems, there is some general consensus that social segments of roughly similar scale and composition replicate themselves at varying levels within tribal societies. The precise manner in which this integration occurs varies considerably within different tribal societies, but as a general rule it must involve at least some regular integration beyond the extended family unit, or band. Several of the papers in this volume address the nature of integration within tribal social trajectories directly (see Redmond, Chapter 4; Fowles, Chapter 5; Adler, Chapter 9), and a good deal of my own research has been dedicated to developing a methodology for modeling integration over the long-term (Parkinson 1999, and this volume, Chapter 18).

Tendency towards disunity

In contrast to the relatively useful idea that tribes are segmented, the notion that tribes tend towards disunity seems to be a vestigial characteristic that has been perpetuated by historical developments within the discipline. In Morgan's initial formulation of the tribal concept, he argued that the reason tribes were segmented was because they were constantly fissioning. This basic notion carried through in the work of Sahlins and Service who saw entropy not as a causal feature in the evolution of tribes, but as the unfortunate result of a lack of centralization. In their view, tribes were plagued by external strife and it was only through constant competition with each other that they managed to sustain any degree of cohesion.

Warre was allotted a primary, central role.

While there does seem to be a tendency for tribes to develop in groups, perhaps indicating some sort of interdependent relationship between them (see, for example, Braun and Plog 1982), the nature of these relationships, and in particular the nature of intra- and inter-tribal aggression, seems to vary widely (see Keeley 1996, and this volume, Chapter 17). At times, aggression in tribal societies consists essentially of intra-tribal feuds, occurring between family units (e.g., the Yanomamö; Chagnon 1983), at other times, it consists of all-out warfare between highly organized confederacies (e.g., the Iroquois, see Snow 1994; see also Ferguson and Whitehead [eds.] 1992, for several examples). While there may, in fact, be some social logic behind these changing patterns of aggression, their existence should not lead us to presuppose a tendency towards disunity. Rather, it is more productive to envision different mechanisms that facilitate fission, at times, and fusion, at other times. This more accurately represents what happens within tribal trajectories, especially when they are viewed from the long-term diachronic perspective of the archaeological record (see, for example, Snow, Chapter 6; Herr and Clark, Chapter 8).

Tribes as discrete entities

Another ethnographic fiction that has been perpetuated by the misrepresentation of tribal systems is the notion that tribes exist exclusively as discrete entities with very well-defined social and geographic boundaries. While some tribal societies certainly do exhibit clear boundaries, others appear as smears across the archaeological landscape, with few discernible internal or external boundaries. The segmented nature of tribal systems, combined with their tendency to fission and fuse given different social and environmental conditions, results in a social picture that assumes discrete boundaries at only isolated moments in time. The tendency of different segments within the system to constantly renegotiate their relationship with each other can preclude the formation of established social boundaries over the long term, usually resulting in a complicated archaeological picture with fuzzy lines approximating the borders between different prehistoric 'groups'. The chapters by O'Shea and McHale Milner (Chapter 11), Blakeslee (Chapter 10), Anderson (Chapter 13), Clark and Cheetham (Chapter 14), Bar-Yosef and Bar-Yosef Mayer (Chapter 15) and myself (Parkinson, Chapter 18) all address the nature of scale and boundary formation in different contexts, and suggest that the nature of boundaries within tribal social trajectories are in constant (or near constant) states of flux, and can be expected to vary at temporal scales that exceed the purview of ethnographic research. As these studies demonstrate, however, despite their diachronic fluctuation, such boundaries frequently do leave behind material remnants that make them accessible archaeologically.

Tribes as transitional social forms

A final characteristic associated with tribes based upon ethnographic cases is the notion that they are transitional (read *ephemeral*) formations that exist evolutionarily or geographically between bands and states. The idea that tribes are a stage on the evolutionary ladder dates back to Morgan's (1851) unilineal stages of Savagery, which subsumes both bands and tribes, and Barbarism, which subsumes both tribes and chiefdoms. This basic idea was rephrased by Sahlins (1961) and Service (1971), both of whom were heavily influenced by Steward's notion of multilinear evolution, and by the concept of sociocultural levels of integration. Service considered tribes to be transitional between bands, which are segmented and disintegrated, and chiefdoms, which are centralized and ranked. Sahlins, on the other hand, used the term tribal to refer to the range of evolutionary forms that exists between bands and states, including chiefdoms. Within this scenario, tribes are distinct from civilizations primarily because the former are in a Hobbesian condition of war, "Lacking specialized institutions of law and order, tribes must mobilize the generalized institutions they do have to meet the threat of war. Economics, kinship, ritual, and the rest are so enlisted" (Sahlins 1968:12-13). Within the tribal form, Sahlins distinguished between segmentary tribes and chiefdoms:

> The segmentary tribe is a permutation of the general model in the direction of extreme decentralization, to the extent that the burden of culture is carried in small, local, autonomous groups while higher levels of organization develop little coherence, poor definition, and minimum function. The chiefdom is a development in the other direction, toward integration of the segmentary system at higher levels. A political superstructure is established, and on that basis a wider and more elaborate organization of economy, ceremony, ideology, and other aspects of culture. (Sahlins 1968:20)

As discussed earlier, Sahlins suggested that many intermediate arrangements stand between the most advanced chiefdom and the simplest segmentary tribe.

Unlike Service and Sahlins, who argued that tribes should be considered evolutionary stages between bands and states, Fried contended that tribes develop only in secondary contexts when band societies are impinged upon by much more complex societal forms. In this case, tribes were seen not as transitional entities on an evolutionary ladder, but as entities that develop in geographically transitional environments. While their views varied dramatically, all three evolutionary models were based not upon long-term processes documented in the archaeological record, but on synchronic, ethnographic examples.

This focus upon the short-term perspective available through the ethnographic record has resulted in the placement of tribes as transitional, ephemeral formations that occur between bands and states, evolutionarily and geographically (see Gregg 1991:1). An archaeological perspective of tribal social trajectories would suggest, rather, that tribes were a dominant social form on the planet for several thousand years following the end of the Pleistocene. The chapters by Galaty (Chapter 7), Anderson (Chapter 13), Clark and Cheetham (Chapter 14), and Bar-Yosef and Bar-Yosef Mayer (Chapter 14) all address the varying temporal lengths tribal trajectories persisted in different parts of the world. In addition, other chapters in the volume, such as those by Carneiro (Chapter 3), Redmond (Chapter 4), Fowles (Chapter 5), Adler (Chapter 9), and Keeley (Chapter 17) all address the variable nature of leadership and political hierarchy within tribal social trajectories, thus providing a framework that allows these processes to be modeled at varying temporal scales (see Fowles, Chapter 2).

Towards an Archaeology of Tribal Social Trajectories

The last thirty years have witnessed the near abandonment of the tribe concept in ethnology in favor of, on the one hand, a tendency towards historical particularism with the analytical emphasis placed upon the cultural variables that distinguish one society from another. On the other hand, this trend has been accompanied by a tendency in archaeology to employ classificatory schemata that basically employ social types that roughly correlate with what previously had been called 'tribes', such as 'middle-range' or 'transegalitarian' societies. Ultimately, the burden of exploring cross-cultural comparisons between tribal societies falls upon the shoulders of archaeologists, who, with their long-term perspective are capable of identifying and differentiating social processes that occur at temporal scales not accessible to ethnographers or ethnohistorians. Conversely, as several of the papers in this volume demonstrate, ethnographers and ethnohistorians frequently have access to more subtle social processes that are nearly invisible within the long-term view of prehistoric archaeology. But it is only through the profitable combination of both perspectives that we can ever hope to arrive at an anthropological understanding of what it means 'to act tribally' (see Fowles, this volume, Chapter 2).

The remainder of this volume constitutes an initial attempt to redefine and operationalize the tribal concept as a tool for cross-cultural comparison in anthropology and anthropological archaeology. In the following chapter, Severin Fowles discusses how the tribal concept has been translated from its synchronic ethnographic origins into the diachronic realm of archaeology. He then outlines an approach to studying tribal social processes that calls for analysis at multiple temporal scales. The next chapter, by Robert Carneiro, discusses the relationship between the concepts of autonomous villages and tribal societies, and describes the general characteristics of autonomous villages. Together, these three chapters comprise the theoretical framework of the volume.

The next section of the book consists of ethnographic and ethnohistoric perspectives on tribal social organization. Elsa Redmond uses ethnographic information to examine the two temporal dimensions of a Jivaroan war leader's career. Severin Fowles, Dean Snow and Michael Galaty draw from ethnohistoric evidence to discuss the social organization of societies in Africa (Fowles, Chapter 5), northeastern North America (Snow, Chapter 6) and southeastern Europe (Galaty, Chapter 7).

The third section of the book is comprised of archaeological approaches in New World prehistoric contexts. Sarah Herr and Jeff Clark (Chapter 8) discuss the role of mobility in the prehispanic southwestern United States, and Michael Adler (Chapter 9) considers how we might best use our anthropological perspectives the creation, use, and abandonment of public (ritual) architectural space within Pueblo communities. The chapters by Don Blakeslee (Chapter 10), John O'Shea and Claire

Milner (Chapter 11), Richard Yerkes (Chapter 12), and David Anderson (Chapter 13) focus on the Great Plains, the Great Lakes, the Ohio Hopewell, and the southeastern United States, respectively. John Clark and David Cheetham (Chapter 14) then synthesize an impressive amount of information to explore the tribal foundations of prehistoric Mesoamerica.

The final section represents archaeological approaches to studying tribal social organization in the Old World. The chapters by Peter Bogucki, Lawrence Keeley, myself, and Ofer Bar-Yosef and Daniella E. Bar-Yosef Mayer examine prehistoric tribal societies in the Neolithic of Northern Europe (Bogucki, Chapter 16; and Keeley, Chapter 17), the Copper Age on the Great Hungarian Plain (Parkinson, Chapter 18), and in the Pre-Pottery Neolithic of the Near East (Bar-Yosef and Bar-Yosef Mayer, Chapter 15).

While these diverse contributions by no means exhaust the wide range of variability that has been exhibited by social trajectories throughout the world, they nevertheless provide several insights into the various social processes that have, over the years, had a profound and very real effect on the lives of millions of people—they are neither chimera, nor societal illusions, but societies our predecessors chose to call 'tribes'. They deserve our attention as well.

References Cited

Beinart, Peter
1999   Lost Tribes: Native Americans and Government Anthropologists Feud over Indian Identity. *Lingua Franca* May/June:32-41.
Bernard, Russell
1994   *Research Methods in Anthropology: Qualitative and Quantitative Methods*. Sage, Thousand Oaks, CA.
Bocek, Barbara
1991   Prehistoric Settlement Pattern and Social Organization on the San Francisco Peninsula, California. In *Between Bands and States*, edited by Susan A. Gregg, pp. 58-88. Southern Illinois University, Carbondale, IL.
Braun, David, and Stephen Plog
1982   Evolution of "Tribal" Social Networks: Theory and Prehistoric North American Evidence. *American Antiquity* 47:504-527.

Carneiro, Robert L.
1996 Cultural Evolution. In *Encyclopedia of Cultural Anthropology*, edited by D. Levinson and M. Ember, pp. 271-277. Henry Holt, New York.

Chagnon, Napoleon
1983 *Yanomamö: The Fierce People*. Holt, Rinehart and Winston, Inc., Chicago.

Colson, Elizabeth
1986 Political Organizations in Tribal Societies: A Cross-Cultural Comparison. *American Indian Quarterly* X:5-20.

Coser, Lewis
1984 Introduction. In *The Division of Labor in Society*, Emile Durkheim, pp. ix-xxxi. The Free Press, New York.

Durkheim, Emile
1984 [1893] *The Division of Labor in Society*. The Free Press, New York.

Drennan, Robert D.
1991 Cultural Evolution, Human Ecology, and Empirical Research. In *Profiles in Cultural Evolution: Papers from a Conference in Honor of Elman R. Service*, edited by A. T. Rambo and K. Gillogly, pp. 113-135. Anthropological Papers No. 85. Museum of Anthropology, University of Michigan, Ann Arbor.

Evans-Pritchard, E. E.
1940 *The Nuer*. Oxford University Press, New York.

Feinman, Gary
2000 Cultural Evolutionary Approaches and Archaeology: Past, Present, and Future. In *Cultural Evolution: Contemporary Viewpoints*, edited by Gary M. Feinman and Linda Manzanilla, pp. 3-12. Kluwer Academic/Plenum Publishers, New York.

Feinman, Gary, and Neitzel, Jill
1984 Too Many Types: An Overview of Sedentary Prestate Societies in the Americas. *Advances in Archaeological Method and Theory* 7:39-102.

Ferguson, R. B., and Whitehead, N. L. (editors)
1992 *War in the Tribal Zone*. School of American Research, Santa Fe, NM.

Flannery, Kent V.
1995 Prehistoric Social Evolution. In *Research Frontiers in Anthropology*, edited by C. R. Ember and M. Ember, pp. 1-26. Prentice Hall, Englewood Cliffs, NJ.

Fried, Morton
1968 On the Concepts of "Tribe" and "Tribal Society". In *The Problem of Tribe: Proceedings of the 1967 Annual Spring Meeting of the American Ethnological Society*, edited by June Helm, pp. 3-22. University of Washington Press, Seattle.
1975 *The Notion of Tribe*. Cummings, Menlo Park, CA.

Gregg, Susan A. (editor)
1991 *Between Bands and States*. Occasional Paper No. 9. Center for Archaeological Investigations, Southern Illinois University at Carbondale, IL.

Harris, Marvin
1979 *Cultural Materialism*. Random House, New York.
2001 *The Rise of Anthropological Theory: A History of Theories of Culture*. Updated edition. AltaMira Press, Walnut Creek, CA.

Helm, June (editor)
1968 *The Problem of Tribe: Proceedings of the 1967 Annual Spring Meeting of the American Ethnological Society*. University of Washington Press, Seattle.

Keeley, Lawrence H.
1996 *War Before Civilization*. Oxford University Press, New York.

Kelly, Raymond C.
1985 *The Nuer Conquest: The Structure and Development of an Expansionist System*. University of Michigan Press, Ann Arbor

Kuznar, Lawrence
1997 *Reclaiming a Scientific Anthropology*. AltaMira, Walnut Creek, CA.

Morgan, Lewis Henry
1964 [1877] *Ancient Society,* edited by Leslie White. Belknap Press, Cambridge, MA.
1995 [1851] *League of the Iroquois*. JG Press, North Dighton, MA.

Neitzel, Jill E., and David G. Anderson
1999 Multiscalar Analyses of Middle Range Societies: Comparing the Late Prehistoric Southwest and Southeast. In *Great Towns and Regional Polities in the Prehistoric American Southwest and Southeast*, edited by Jill E. Neitzel, 243-254. Amerind Foundation New World Studies Series 3, University of New Mexico Press, Albuquerque.

Owens, D'Ann, and Hayden, Brian
1997 Prehistoric Rites of Passage: A Comparative Study of Transegalitarian Hunter-Gatherers. *Journal of Anthropological Archaeology* 16(2):121-161.

Parkinson, William A.
    1999   The Social Organization of Early Copper
            Age Tribes on the Great Hungarian Plain.
            Ph.D. Dissertation, University of Michi-
            gan, Ann Arbor.
Radcliffe-Brown, A. R.
    1948   *The Andaman Islanders*. The Free Press,
            Glencoe, Illinois.
Redfield, Robert
    1941   *The Folk Culture of the Yucatan*. Univer-
            sity of Chicago Press, Chicago.
    1947   *Tepozlan, a Mexican Village: A Study of
            Folk Life*. University of Chicago Press,
            Chicago.
Sahlins, Marshall
    1961   The Segmentary Lineage: An Organiza-
            tion of Predatory Expansion. *American
            Anthropologist* 63:322-345.
    1968   *Tribesmen*. Prentice-Hall, Englewood
            Cliffs, NJ.
    1972   *Stone Age Economics*. Aldine, New York.
Sahlins, Marshall D. and Elman R. Service (eds.)
    1960   *Evolution and Culture*. University of
            Michigan Press, Ann Arbor.
Service, Elman
    1971   *Primitive Social Organization: An Evo-
            lutionary Perspective*. Second Edition.
            Random House, New York.
Snow, Dean
    1994   *The Iroquois*. Blackwell, Cambridge, MA.
Spencer, Herbert
    1896   *Principles of Sociology*. D. Appleton and
            Co., New York.

Spencer, Charles
    1997   Evolutionary Approaches in Archaeolo-
            gy. *Journal of Archaeological Research*
            5:209-264.
Sterritt, Neil J., Susan Marsden, Robert Galois,
Peter R. Grant, and Richard Overstall
    1998   *Tribal Boundaries in the Nass Water-
            shed*. UBC Press, Vancouver.
Steward, Julian
    1937   Ecological Aspects of Southwestern So-
            ciety. *Anthropos* 32:87-104.
    1951   Levels of Sociocultural Integration: An
            Operational Concept. *Southwest Journal
            of Anthropology* VII:374-90.
    1955   *Theory of Culture Change: The Method-
            ology of Multilinear Evolution*. Univer-
            sity of Illinois Press, Urbana, IL.
Trigger, Bruce
    1990   *A History of Archaeological Thought*.
            Cambridge University Press, New York.
Tyler, Edward B.
    1871   *Primitive Culture*. J. Murray, London.
Yoffee, Norman, Suzanne Fish, and George
Milner
    1999   Comunidades, Ritualities, Chiefdoms:
            Social Evolution in the American South-
            west and Southeast. In *Great Towns and
            Regional Polities,* edited by J. Neitzel,
            pp. 261-272. Amerind Foundation, Dra-
            goon, AZ.

2. From Social Type to Social Process: Placing 'Tribe' in a Historical Framework

Severin M. Fowles

Introduction

The search for cross-cultural patterning in human organization is a central and distinguishing aim of an anthropological approach to social theory. As a consequence of this lofty goal, however, much of anthropology has of necessity wedded itself to the use of typologies in the course of comparative studies. Whether of particular historical processes, social relations, or entire societies, types of some sort or another are a requisite first step, necessary evils that bring order to the infinite shades of empirical experience and offer an initial rationale for comparing certain social contexts rather than others. But first-round typologies almost always sow the seeds of their own undoing, or at least their own redoing, for the process of cross-cultural comparison is nothing if not a continuous challenge of a type's utility. Only so much variability can be accommodated before utility turns to futility and the type is placed into question.

Such has been the fate of the notion of tribe.

Early on, in the proto-typology days of colonialism, almost all non-European societies—from small Australian aboriginal groups to complex African states—were freely labeled 'tribal.' In the middle of the 20th century, however, 'tribe as other' began to give way to a more refined notion of tribe as a stage of general cultural evolution. Marshall Sahlins helped sculpt tribe into a transitional social form that bridged the gap between simple hunter-gatherer bands and complex states, while Elman Service further whittled the concept down by separating out tribes ('properly so called') from chiefdoms. In so doing, the tribal type had finally received a clear anthropological rendering. "A tribe is a segmental organization," wrote Sahlins:

> It is composed of a number of equivalent, unspecialized multifamily groups, each the structural duplicate of the other: a tribe is a congeries of equal kin group blocs...[and] as a whole is normally not a political organization but rather a social-cultural-ethnic entity. It is held together principally by likenesses among its segments (mechanical solidarity) and by pan-tribal institutions. (Sahlins 1968:190-191)

Clarity, however, is often a double-edged sword. Grouping together all social contexts that appeared to more or less rely on segmentary structures and pan-tribal institutions or sodalities as their primary means of sociopolitical cohesion led to some unsatisfying bedfellows with widely diverse economic practices, social relations, and scales of organization. Rival typological schemes proliferated (see Feinman and Neitzel 1984). By the time that Morton Fried (1975) hammered his own nail into the concept's coffin, Service (1971:157, 1975) was already relinquishing 'tribe' in favor of Fried's looser, more versatile stage of 'egalitarian society'. Furthermore, strong critiques of the neoevolutionary agenda itself soon resurfaced in ethnology as tides again turned toward a historical particularism more akin to Boas than to Morgan or White. By the 1980's, movements toward a more relativistic and politicized ethnology left the entire endeavor of generalization from an evolutionary standpoint to be abandoned as ethically suspect. Archaeology, which could not do without some sort of comparative evolutionary framework, was left to pick up the pieces on its own.

Throughout the 20th century, 'tribe' has been defined and redefined time and again in anthropology, colonial politics, and popular culture and in its travels has accumulated tremendous baggage. Given this, it has been tempting to follow Steward and Faron's (1959:17, 21) lead and take the position that "the term tribe, thus having no clear meaning, will be generally avoided." To do this, however, would be to dodge a central problem. Whereas the other neoevolutionary social types have—to a much greater degree—been the focus of refinement, reevaluation, and, at times, rejection in archaeology, 'tribe' has received comparatively little attention. At the end of the 20th century one can openly argue about chiefdoms or hunter-gatherer bands; 'tribe', however, must be hidden behind quotation marks or aliases.

But it is not this essay's intention, nor that of the volume as a whole, to dwell on critiques of the tribal type and the neoevolutionary framework in which it is set. Rather, the initial goal is to evaluate the ways in which the notion of tribe—developed from ethnographic contexts and with a particular evolutionary agenda—has been translated into the diachronic context of archaeological inquiry. Traditionally, this translation process has proceeded in a fairly straightforward middle-range manner, the goal being to establish the material correlates of a 'dynamic' and ethnographic tribal context as they would appear in the 'static' archaeological record. In this essay, however, I will follow the lead of Upham (1990a, 1990b) and others in arguing that such a methodology needs to be rethought. Without diminishing the importance of ethnographic analogizing, one must acknowledge that, in an important sense, the ethnographic record is the more 'static' of the two, limited as it is to the observation of short-term events. Just as a day in mid-summer will not serve as a model for an entire year, neither can a purely ethnographic model of tribal society stand for an archaeological one. Long-term history (archaeological or otherwise) has its own dramas and storylines played out on different stages.

The second goal of this and the other essays in the present volume, therefore, is to explore archaeological alternatives to the short-term models of tribal society. In this search one cannot, of course, do away with typologies altogether—the nature of cross-cultural comparison depends upon them—but one can shift the subject matter from *types of entire societies* to *types of cultural processes or historical trajectories* (cf. Barth 1967; Friedman 1982; Upham 1990b, Mills 2000). As many have emphasized, what, how, and how quickly aspects of a social context change (as well as what does not change) are questions more amenable to archaeological data than is inquiry into the structure of a social context at one point in time. More importantly, if distinctive historical patterns of change can be identified cross-culturally, then these patterns may potentially be used as an alternate means of breaking into the study of sociopolitical evolution. In this essay, I elaborate on this central notion and the ways in which it directly applies to the problem of the tribal type. In doing so, an alternate typological framework is developed that distinguishes

three temporal scales (intra-generational, multi-generational, and long-term) at which different trajectories of change might be productively compared.

Archaeological Translations of The Ethnographic Tribe

But before doing so, it is useful to first briefly review how the ethnographic model of tribal society has been used in archaeology, how it has been translated. What is meant—explicitly and implicitly—when an archaeological context is labeled tribal? This question can be answered on a number of levels and below I review three answers that have particularly wide currency in the literature. The first and most explicit answer involves a structural model of tribal society. The second adopts a more informal trait-list approach. And the third is fully impressionistic, although it very likely is the most accurate representation of how 'tribe' and 'tribal' are used archaeologically.

The structural model of tribal society

If asked to define a tribe, many archaeologists would probably more or less still accept Sahlins' definition, quoted above, and maintain that an archaeological tribal context is one in which relatively equal and functionally independent kin-based social segments cohered into larger communities by means of certain distinctively tribal principles of organization. Haas (1990:172) for example, emphasizes the economic autonomy of segments in his model of tribal society, and both Braun and Plog (1982) and Habicht-Mauche (1993) explicitly describe tribal units as integrated into larger social entities by means of "cross-cutting pan-residential institutions." These two central concepts—segmentary structure and crosscutting sodalities—are the pillars that hold up the formal tribal edifice and deserve to be considered in some detail.

Like so many concepts in anthropology, the ancestry of the concept of segmentation can be traced back to the publication of *Ancient Society*. Morgan's (1974 [1877]) early description of historic Iroquois society as an aggregate of roughly equivalent and equal kinship groups that united at different levels to face periodic challenges was one of the first segmentary models of a tribal organization. Combined with Durkheim's[1] (1893) consideration of mechanical solidarity, Morgan's model set the stage for the later reformations of segmentary structures in British social anthropology during the 1940's and 50's (Fortes and Evans-Pritchard 1940; Fortes 1953; Barnes 1954; Bohannan 1954; Smith 1956). The neoevolutionary emphasis on tribal segmentation that has been adopted by most archaeologists grew out of these earlier studies and really did little more than clarify the basic form of the model. In Sahlins' (1961, 1968) classic discussions, for instance, segmentation was used to refer both to an equivalency of basic social units (or 'primary segments') and to the manner in which these basic units manage to form collectivities in the absence of permanent and institutionalized positions of leadership. In short, when a perceived need for group action or decision-making arises, primary segments are understood to voluntarily band together into larger second-order segments which can then join forces into third-order segments, and so on until the necessary scale of organization is met. The resultant decision-making hierarchy is largely consensus-based, situational, and unstable. The most powerful examples of segmentary principles are to be found in lineage systems, which naturally take on many of these characteristics; however the principle is not limited to kinship alone. Johnson's (1978, 1982) more recent thinking on sequential hierarchies has placed renewed emphasis on the use of segmentation as a general organizational principle in all manner of consensus-based decision-making contexts.

If segments and the individuals within them are the building blocks of the neoevolutionary model of tribal society, then the social institutions that overlap them are considered to be a form of social mortar or glue. For Service (1962) in particular, the critical aspect of tribal institutions or sodalities such as clans, age-grades, and religious societies is that their memberships cross-cut one another in such a way that individuals find themselves more or less enmeshed in a web of relations, obligated to maintain at least an appearance of civility toward other individuals in their "social-cultural-ethnic entity" or tribe. The result is not a world without tensions and dispute, but it is one in which the lines of fission inherent in segmentary systems are thought to be temporarily neutralized. Kroeber's early study of Zuni society provides one of the classic examples of such a tribally integrated system. In describing Zuni social groups he notes:

> Four or five different planes of systematization cross cut each other and thus preserve for the whole society an integrity that would be speedily lost if the planes merged and thereby inclined to encourage segregation and fission. The

clans, the fraternities, the priesthoods, the kivas, in a measure the gaming parties, are all dividing agencies. If they coincided, the rifts in the social structure would be deep; by countering each other, they cause segmentations which produce an almost marvelous complexity, but can never break the national entity apart. (Kroeber 1917)

Clear ethnographic examples of this principle have also been discussed in Brazil (Gross 1979) and South-Central Africa (Gluckman 1965:110-112), to mention but a few.

Taken together these two organizational principles are the heart of a structural model of tribal society, which if evoking a feeling of timelessness undoubtedly does so for two primary reasons. First, though the model no longer holds currency in ethnology, it has been well curated for nearly forty years in archaeological research in close to its initial form. Frequently used terms such as 'middle range', 'kin-based' or 'autonomous village' society have arisen to replace 'tribe' during this time, but they have so far offered little more than semantic alternatives that do little to change the manner in which we understand the social contexts so labeled (but see Carneiro, this volume). Second, the structural model does not make explicit reference to time. On one hand, this timelessness simplifies the transportation of the model between ethnographic and/or archaeological contexts. On the other, it is unavoidably ahistorical and demands that we view a tribe—once an archaeological context can in fact be considered a tribe—as a structure frozen in time until the point at which it is no longer a tribe and the structure begins to thaw (see Upham 1990a).

Be that as it may, if this model is what is really meant when an archaeological context is described as tribal, then we must ask whether or not the evidence used to support such a position is adequate. With respect to a segmentary principle, the strongest and undoubtedly the most widely cited evidence is architectural. Consider the case of the prehistoric Puebloan villages of the American Southwest where a great deal of research has revealed countless examples of clear architectural segmentation that presumably had a basis in a similarly segmented social organiztion (Adler, this volume; Steward 1937; Varien and Lightfoot 1989:76). Household units that in one time period were constructed as isolated hamlets came to be used as recognizable building blocks of large villages in other periods. The resulting architectural hierarchy has suggested to many that decision-making in the prehistoric Pueblos rose up through the residential units by consensus (Johnson 1989).[2]

Research along these lines has been productive and is bolstered by Johnson's (1978, 1982) more theoretical consideration of the underlying logic of information processing within such systems. However, two cautions can be raised with respect to this approach. First, the segmentary structure reflected architecturally in archaeological contexts may well have been of a different nature than those in the ethnographically derived tribal model discussed earlier. A village that existed for a mere decade, for example, would have far exceeded the period of unified action involved in the examples of segmentary lineage systems discussed by Sahlins. At the very least, our understanding of the correlation between architectural and decision-making structures may be incomplete, especially in those cases for which we have no support from direct historical evidence. Second, it must be acknowledged that 'tribal' segmentary principles may at times be difficult to distinguish archaeologically from the equally situational decision-making structures of more 'band-like' groups (e.g., Johnson 1978) or from the conical clan structures of some chiefdoms (Sahlins 1968:24-25, 49-50).

As for evidence of overlapping social institutions, the typical data cited are even more equivocal. Very few archaeological analyses of tribal contexts actually offer such evidence at all, and those that do typically focus upon mortuary data, using the presence of overlapping patterns of associated artifacts as a material signature of overlapping memberships in sodalities. But leaping from skeletons bedecked in arrows to 'arrow societies' is at best tenuous. And even if solid archaeological evidence of cross-cutting sodalities is found, one must still acknowledge that memberships in various groups overlap in almost *all* known societies, including our own. In tribal contexts, such groups are thought to simply bear a greater burden with respect to social integration.

Perhaps then, the structural model—seductive though it may be—is not exactly what is meant when an archaeological context is described as tribal.

The tribal trait-list

Worth considering next are the more casual, but also more tangible, criteria used by many archaeologists to define tribal contexts. When distilled to an essence, these criteria are frequently summed up in the following trait-list, or something

very close to it: sedentary, non-hierarchical (or egalitarian), and small-scale. Regarded loosely, these adjectives characterize a good many social contexts that one would be tempted to consider tribal, and they deal in variables archaeologists are accustomed to measuring. But these casual criteria have not been proposed as a formal definition of tribal society for good reason. Indeed, a less cavalier investigation of the criteria brings to the fore recent reevaluations of each that must be addressed.

A stark contrast between 'sedentary' and 'nomadic', for instance, has been found to drastically misrepresent most non-industrial societies (Kent 1989). As Sarah Herr and Jeffrey Clark (this volume, Chapter 8) point out, the dividing line drawn by neoevolutionists between band-level hunter-gatherers and tribal societies tended to emphasize the emergence of a commitment to agriculture, with increased sedentism being one of the most structurally significant implications of that commitment. Robert Carneiro's (this volume, Chapter 3) impressive synthesis of much ethnographic and archaeological data reemphasizes this general point, that on some level we cannot ignore the reality that agriculture and increased sedentism were critical preliminaries to more complex social forms in much of the world. Herr and Clark's central argument, however, is that by over-emphasizing sedentism the equally important elements of mobility in such systems tend to be ignored. Their work reveals that tribal mobility continues to play a significant structural role over time as it directly affects patterns of intergroup conflict, land tenure, sociopolitical inequality, and religion. As a result of this realization, many archaeologists have resorted to the use of such terms as 'semi-permanent sedentary', 'short-term sedentism', or 'deep sedentism'. Each qualification highlights the observation that many important social dynamics emerge when we view sedentism and mobility as relative concepts figured on a shifting scale.

Much research has also been devoted to complicating the concept of egalitarianism. It is now no longer accepted that the traditional group of 'egalitarian societies' did in fact lack forms of ranking, hereditary leadership, and privileged control of such things as ritual knowledge and land. Elsa Redmond's (this volume, Chapter 4) discussion of Jivaroan war leaders and Fowles' (this volume, Chapter 5) discussion of Tonga prophets provides two concrete ethnohistoric examples of how unbalanced power relations are often found to exist within certain spheres of a society rather than others.

During times of warfare or religious crisis, in particular, otherwise 'egalitarian' or tribal societies may temporarily take on structural qualities more similar to chiefdoms. Privileging one structural pose—in other words, one configuration of social relations—rather than another in analytic models seriously misrepresents by over-simplifying the dynamics present within such historical/social contexts.

In many ways, 'small-scale' is the thorniest of the three criteria commonly attributed to tribal contexts. Individuals and social groups more often than not interact on very different economic, religious, political, and military levels, and to define a social or organizational scale based upon one such sphere would be limiting at best. Even with respect to one manner of social interaction—for instance, political decision-making—scale is an elusive variable that often shifts dramatically from moment to moment as the types of decisions change. Furthermore, archaeologists face the special problem of having to construct their own boundaries in order to make scalar estimates, and all too often the latter are drawn to accommodate preconceived notions of tribal scale rather than the patterning within the archaeological record itself. Lekson's (1999) recent efforts to throw away such preconceptions and vastly enlarge the scale of the Chacoan system in the American Southwest reveal how problematic this issue of drawing a boundary around a 'tribe'—or even around a network of social interaction, for that matter—can be. Given these challenges, the 'small' of small-scale says very little.[3]

If there remained any lingering hope that a trait-list approach might still be used as a means of social classification, Feinman and Neitzel's (1984) ambitious ethnographic review of New World 'middle-range' or 'intermediate' societies during the mid-1980's should have ended all such optimism. Even keeping in mind the problems and inconsistencies of the ethnographic data they employed, their study clearly indicated both (1) that continuous, non-modal variation is to be found in nearly every social attribute that has been used to differentiate types from one another, and (2) that very few of these variables can be shown to correlate even loosely with one other. They concluded that trait-list approaches are simply incapable of dealing with significant amounts of variability. In Chapter 17, Lawrence Keeley also offers a complementary critique, noting the degree to which the classic tribal type overlaps with both the band and chiefdom types.

On an even more basic level, however, it should also be clear that reducing ongoing systems to particular states also demands that we ignore the reality that all individuals and social groups are, in an important sense, warehouses of organizational options. As Salzman puts it:

> [t]he crucial fact, often overlooked or de-emphasized, is that every society provides alternatives—*institutionalized alternatives*—for many if not all major areas of activity: alternative organizational forms, alternative productive activities, alternative value orientations, alternative forms of property control. This results in fluidity and variability as people switch back and forth between activities, between organizational forms, and between priorities. (Salzman 1980:4)

By ignoring this central point, trait-list approaches have done much to block entry into dealing with historical dynamics among tribal or any other sort of social contexts.

Impressions of Tribe

Barring other definitional options, it is probably not misconstruing matters to fess up to the fact that what we really mean when we call a social context tribal is frequently something much more impressionistic. To begin with, the term commonly signifies that the social context in question is big, but not too big. A number of attempts using ethnographic data have been made to specify precisely how big is too big (Naroll 1956; Carneiro 1961, 1967, 1987; Chagnon 1983). While these studies have met with some success in identifying broad scalar thresholds that probably speak to some biological aspects of human information processing (Johnson 1982; Kosse 1990, 1996), it remains the case that the scale of decision-making at any particular time is only very loosely correlated with other aspects of human social life.

Second, the label typically signifies that no solid evidence of elites—such as elaborate burials or large, specially constructed residences—has yet been uncovered. While the use of negative evidence may feel unsatisfying, this criterion is indeed essential to the tribal ideal given that in almost any archaeological context presently considered tribal, the discovery of one or two truly 'elite' burials (e.g., in an elaborate mortuary complex surrounded by preciosities and a crew of sacrificed attendants), would be enough for most scholars to bump the case in question up from a tribe to a chiefdom—regardless of other evidence to the contrary.

In short, when employed casually, 'tribe' or 'tribal' do a better job of indicating what the social phenomenon in question is not—not too big, not too small, and not too centralized or chiefdom-like. Which is to say that the 'tribe as other' perspective of the early 20th century has not entirely disappeared. Tribe has overtly come to assume the middle-range in the continuum of human social forms, a theoretical empty space betwixt, between, and only loosely bounded by its sibling evolutionary types (cf. Gregg 1991). Morgan's (1974:103) late 19th century sentiment, in this sense, continues to hold currency: "It is difficult to describe an Indian tribe by the affirmative elements of its composition" (see also Steward 1963:44, footnote 3).

Recognition of the various problems with the structural, trait-list, and impressionistic translations of the ethnographic model of tribal society, however, has not yet led to the development of substantially more satisfying typological alternatives with which to enter into the cross-cultural analyses so central to anthropological understanding. Michael Adler's chapter (this volume, Chapter 9), for example, takes a critical look at how archaeologists in the American Southwest have recently sought to characterize prehistoric Puebloan groups using the dual processual model developed by Blanton et al. (1996) in Mesoamerica. As Peregrine (2001:37) and others have recently emphasized, the corporate and network strategies distinguished in this model "*do not* define societal 'types' nor do they define a unilineal evolutionary trend," and it is in this way that many have found the model to hold promise (Mills 2000). While this may be true within theoretical discussions of the model, we must acknowledge that describing a society as dominated either by corporate or network strategies immediately places that society within a very definite typological classification. Thus both early Basketmaker pit house settlements of the American Southwest and the Classic Maya have been classified as societies dominated by "network" strategies, while the later Puebloan village communities and Teotihuacan have both been classified as societies dominated by "corporate" strategies. To be sure, the dual processual model does realign traditional typological relationships in novel ways; however it remains to be seen whether our understanding of individual societies will be enhanced by the new cross-cultural typology that has been constructed.

Realignments in a similar vein have, of course, been attempted previously. One need only look back to Southall's (1956) development of the segmentary state model to understand the Alur followed by the concept's subsequent application by other scholars to a range of social contexts elsewhere in the world. The segmentary state was defined as "one in which the spheres of ritual suzerainty and political sovereignty do not coincide" (Southall 1988:52), and thus there were certain structural similarities between leadership in such societies and segmentary tribes (or, as Fortes and Evans-Pritchard [1970:13] referred to them, "Group B" societies). Segmentation came to be thought of as a social and political strategy that could be analyzed across societies that were traditionally thought of as fitting into very different social types. The problem, however, was that all social contexts have some segmentary characteristics and, consequently, the extremely broad comparisons that resulted from the cross-cultural study of segmentary contexts only offered limited insight.

As Adler (this volume, Chapter 9) notes, the recent archaeological interest in dual-processual, heterarchical, and other models is, ultimately, symptomatic of modern desires to break apart the essentialism of classic neoevolutionary types. This, then, is our principle problem. Given that we can perceive a group of archaeological social contexts that feel similar enough to merit detailed comparison, how and on what level can we best go about learning from the differences and similarities within that group? Along what course might we continue to explore evolutionary processes through cross-cultural comparisons without lapsing into a heavy-handed essentialism? The answer to these questions undoubtedly involves a move beyond straightforward translations of ethnographic models. Though we may be attracted by the readiness of such models, the data with which we work are often not so accommodating. Qualitatively more historical, archaeological remains speak in terms of archaeological time (Smith 1992) and resist being treated as the residue of a suspended ethnographic moment. Because of this, archaeologists more often than not deal in historical trajectories rather than in societies, per se. With respect to the problem of tribal society, we therefore stand to profit from an analytic framework that reflects this reality and concerns itself less with characterizing the political, ideological, or economic qualities of a society—in other words, with what a tribe is—and more with what happens over time in tribal contexts.

In the remainder of this essay I explore this position of 'tribal is' as 'tribal does'—that a framework based upon types of trajectories or processes as opposed to total societies is a productive change of focus.

Towards the Study of Tribal Trajectories

Enough work has been devoted to the search for particular characteristics with which to clearly demarcate tribal versus other forms of organization. Enough work has also been devoted to exploring the shortcomings of this approach. As noted above, the essays in the present volume represent an attempt to build from a different starting point: a desire to compare trajectories of change rather than to compare the synchronic attributes of idealized societies. In a way, the search for particular tribal characteristics is akin to asking 'what color is a chameleon?'—it simply poses the wrong question. One must instead investigate the variability of colors over time and space and from there ask how and why these colors change. The ultimate goal of this sort of questioning is an understanding finally of how and why the very patterns or rhythms of change may have themselves evolved. In tribal studies such an approach is particularly relevant, for the critique of the tribal type has emerged not only from the observed variability between contexts that one would be tempted to label tribal (Feinman and Neitzel 1984), but even more powerfully from the observed organizational variability that is exhibited within particular social contexts as they developed over time.

Consider, for example, Fried's (1968, 1975; see also Kroeber 1955; Berndt 1959; Helm 1968) influential rejection of the notion of tribe in the 60's and 70's. On one level, Fried argued that crystallized tribal collectivities may have only ever existed as secondary phenomena in the context of contact between states and decentralized egalitarian groups. The subtext of this argument, however, is that if historical data can show that the socially bounded tribes of the colonial world had been unbounded, unmobilized, and fluid prior to European contact, then to talk about tribe as an autonomous developmental type of society is misleading. But does it really come as a surprise that individuals and groups changed their behaviors and organized themselves differently in a substantially changed sociopolitical context? The more interesting question, it seems, is why some indigenous groups mobilized (or were able to be mobilized) into 'tribes' while other groups (many in Australia and Africa, for example) did not—or were not able to—centralize and in some cases even became more loosely

bounded (a process that has been described as 'detribalization' or 'devolution', Berndt 1959). Also in need of explanation is why some large prehistoric 'tribal' social formations did emerge from or cycle between smaller ones in relative isolation from chiefdoms or states (see Fried [1968:12] and Sahlins [1961:326], as well as O'Shea and Milner, this volume, Chapter 11, and Parkinson, this volume, Chapter 18).

Ultimately, we must realize that what ethnologists rejected was the idea that the relatively sharp political/ethnic boundaries between modern 'tribes' had a temporal reality beyond that inscribed into them by more complex societies. Well-bounded and stable tribes, they concluded, were simply secondary products of colonialism. Fair enough. But if archaeologists were too quick to impose the synchronic tribal model of ethnology onto its diachronic data, it would be equally premature to immediately accept the ethnologists' subsequent critique. Indeed, the very malleability of social boundaries in such contexts over time is what many archaeologists have found to be *most* characteristic of the tribal type (Fowles and Parkinson 1999). Perhaps this is the natural outgrowth of the archaeological need to determine social boundaries through patterning in material remains rather than through the use of tribal names created, or at least rigidified, by state governments. If one does not have labels such as Chimbu, Kalinga, or Nuer with which to contend, one need not become preoccupied with whether or not these labels actually reflect meaningful social units. Perhaps this position also stems from the fact that the end goal of archaeological investigations into tribal contexts is almost never a characterization of particular 'tribes' per se. More often, for example, one finds conclusions drawn about various 'phases' within the historical trajectory of a given region (see, for example, O'Shea and Milner's, this volume, Chapter 11, discussion of the Juntamen Phase in the Upper Great Lakes, and Blakeslee's, this volume, Chapter 10, discussion of the Nebraska Phase on the Central Plains).

Regardless, archaeological engagement with the problem of tribal society has shifted the focus of the debate in an important direction, a point that can be clearly seen in many of the chapters in the present volume. Snow's (Chapter 6) examination of migration and ethnogenesis among the historic Penobscot, for instance, might be directly contrasted with Fried's (1968:6) discussion of the shifting nature of ethnic identity. Ethnicity in tribal contexts, Fried emphasized, was malleable and easy altered to fit the politics of the moment. Thus he concluded that 'tribes' do not exist in any important ethnic sense. Far from being grounds for a complete rejection of the tribal concept, however, Snow's study reveals that that it might instead be worth viewing a certain amount of flexibility in ethnic identification as highly *characteristic* of tribal groups, as something that an archaeology of tribal society must accept as a necessary background to its investigations.

Indeed, if one examines the ethnographic and ethnohistoric records with sufficient care, it becomes clear that the critique of the notion of a rigid or stable tribe was truly the critique of straw men. Consider, for example, Oliver's (1968) discussion of the American Plains where the congregation of the buffalo into large herds in the late summer and autumn led many native groups to aggregate during the summer and disperse in the winter. Such a yearly alternation between aggregation and dispersal demanded that society be organized at a variety of levels. Thus Oliver concluded that the True Plains groups, such as the Teton Dakota, alternated yearly between a "band-level" sociopolitical organization governed by local hereditary leaders and a "tribal" organization governed by temporarily chosen warriors (1968:256, see also Carneiro 1967:241). Such a situation also existed in many Central Brazilian societies, for which Gross has documented a yearly shift between nomadic foraging groups and villages of up to 1,400 people. Rather than viewing the two seasonal organizations as elements within a single social structure, Gross importantly concluded that it was best to view these groups as having two distinct social structures that are implicated at different times of the year (Gross 1979:333). His sentiment mirrors Gearing's (1958:1149) important observation that resulted from a study of Cherokee ethnohistory: "In a word, a human community does not have a single social structure; it has several."

Elsa Redmond's (Chapter 4) ethnohistoric analysis of the development and social role of Jivaroan war leaders also brings attention to this central point, however with an emphasis on the overlap between 'tribal' and 'chiefly' organization, classically defined. She reveals that one might profitably consider Jivaro groups as chieftaincies headed by powerful chiefs during war, but as more decentralized and egalitarian during times of peace. The Jivaro clearly have different organizational strategies that they employ selectively as the larger sociopolitical context changes, and it would therefore be inaccurate to paint one picture of Jivaro society. Rather, the society must be discussed as comprised of a set of strategies—both egalitarian and hierarchical—over time.

The inherent inaccuracy of descriptions in which social groups are characterized as having a single state—a state which has, of necessity, been stereotyped from an aggregate of observed behaviors—is a problem also addressed by Barth (1967). Barth noted that social change tends to be either dramatically misrepresented or not represented at all when we do not clearly distinguish between (1) the elements of a formal social system that may be continuously preserved and (2) the organizational options within that system that may change with ease and without significant ramifications to the underlying nature of the system itself. The objective, he argued, should rather be to characterize a social context "as a statistical thing, as a set of frequencies of alternatives" (see also Meggitt 1979:122; Smith 1960:148).

Such are the observations that anthropologists have made over the limited historical purview of ethnographic fieldwork. Archaeologists and historians engaged in the analysis of longer segments of social trajectories have, of course, encountered much greater temporal variability in organizational strategies. As Upham (1990b) nicely summarized, confrontation with such variability has played a large role in the late 20th century shift in archaeology from the use of stage-based evolutionary frameworks to more processual frameworks of continuous change. The contrast between these approaches might be viewed schematically as graphs of organizational structure versus historical time. Figure 1, for example, represents the neoevolutionary use of ideal-typic social models to characterize the process of general evolution. This is the classic stage-based approach that is theoretically conceptualized as a sort of stepping from one level of sociopolitical integration to another. Figure 2, on the other hand, represents what Upham describes as a more processual approach in which organizational variation is considered to be continuous and ever-changing, with few, if any, clear boundaries between broad social types.[4] Thus, when those who have adopted such a model are compelled to engage in cross-cultural comparison they typically prefer to refer to societies that fall within a middle-range of organizational variability, rather than within a social type, per se.

While the continuous change model (Fig. 2) has refocused attention on historical process and in this sense is consistent with the goals of the present volume, two strong objections must be

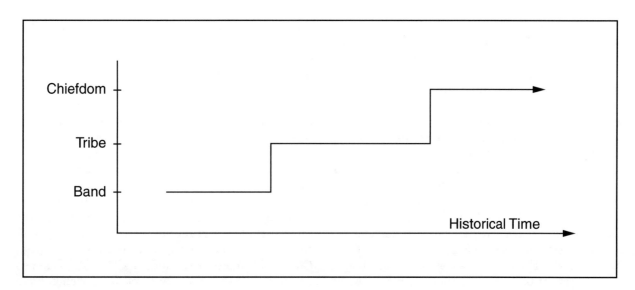

Fig. 1. Stage-based or ideal-typic model of general evolution.

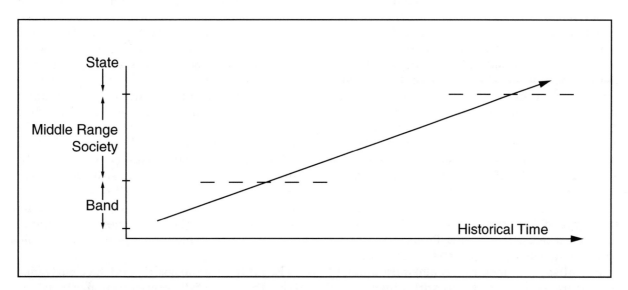

Fig. 2. Continuous model of evolution. Social types are arbitrarily defined as
ranges of organizational variability.

raised. First, nearly all proponents of the model use Feinman and Neitzel's (1984) study of non-state organizational variability in New World ethnography and ethnohistory to substantiate their position. Feinman and Neitzel's study and others like it, however, are not based upon cross-cultural analyses of diachronic patterns of change. Rather, they are compilations of ethnographic snapshots, the utility and accuracy of which has already been questioned above. Such data do not, therefore, directly speak to the question of whether or not the evolution of any *particular* society will follow patterns of continuous or discontinuous organizational change over time.

More importantly, however, the continuous change model does little better than the stage-based or ideal-typic model in acknowledging our central observation that societies are bundles of organizational options that are drawn upon to meet changing needs over time. If ethnologists have been able to document cyclical temporal patterns that vacillate between 'band' and 'tribal' levels of organization over the course of the year, or between 'tribal' and 'chiefdom' levels as societies shift in and out of

21

times of warfare, then a study of tribal trajectories should at least attempt to incorporate such realities. Indeed, once one accepts the position that tribal contexts must be viewed as a set of ever-shifting structural poses over time, the problem then becomes to explore the nature, underlying structures, and different trajectories of these shifts.

To do this, it may prove useful to follow Friedman's (1982) lead and conceptualize historical trajectories as evolving through relatively cyclic patterns of change (see also Parkinson, this volume, Chapter 18). Figure 3 offers a picture of what such a model might look like graphically using the same basic axes of organizational form versus historical time as used in Figures 1 and 2. Of particular note in Figure 3, however, is that typologies of social organization—whether expressed as an idealized single organization or a certain organizational range—have been eliminated in favor of a typology of patterned historical change. That a social context may at one moment in time be structured in classically 'tribal' fashion but at another appear more like a 'band' or a 'chiefdom' is therefore not only unproblematic, but expected. Much more important are the qualities of the organizational dynamic in time, the shape and tempo of the trajectory as it shifts between organizational forms. The ultimate challenge is to explore whether or not such a dynamic might be used to better characterize and compare those societies—or, at least, a useful subset of those societies—that we impressionistically label as 'tribal'.

Adoption of a comparative framework founded upon types of historical trajectories, however, carries with it certain conditions, foremost of which is that one develop a heightened concern with the temporal scale of inquiry. (Pre)history undoubtedly operates at many levels with different processes only coming into focus at different degrees of magnification. In an interesting approach to the subject, Donald Blakeslee (this volume, Chapter 10) uses fractal imaging as a metaphor with which to better appreciate this quality. As he suggests, there is a sense in which it is useful to view the archaeological record as having fractal qualities with patterns over the shorter terms always embedded within patterns over longer terms. However, at each scale of inquiry, the nature of the questions as well as the data relevant to those questions will vary.

Such observations have always been influential in defining processualist approaches toward understanding social change (e.g., Bailey 1981; Binford 1986; Butzer 1982; F. Plog 1974) and they

have taken on new significance with the growing archaeological interest in historiography—especially that of the *Annales* school—during the past fifteen or so years (e.g., Barker 1995; Bintliff 1991; Hodder 1987; Knapp 1992; Preucel and Hodder 1996:14). But our ability to deal with processes at these different scales is also central to much contemporary debate in archaeology, as well. Many who have embraced agency approaches, for instance, have taken the position that prehistoric archaeologists can deal effectively with the short time span of individuals and individual events, and that any understanding of long-term processes must include the repercussions of human motivations as they develop over that time span (e.g., Clark and Blake 1994; Hodder 2000). Those not so enamored with agent-centered approaches have tended toward Binford's (1986:27) position that:

> the observations by ethnographers and historical figures, while perhaps documenting something of the internal dynamics of cultural systems, cannot be expected to be necessarily germane to an understanding of a much slower and larger-scale process of change and modification

—a position not entirely different from Marx's (1991:15, orig. 1852) contention that although individuals "make their own history," the production process is always conditioned to a large degree by the inherited social circumstances over which the individual has no control (see also Lévi-Strauss 1963:23). At issue in such positions are not only the appropriate temporal scales of analysis, but also the relative privileging of one scale or another with respect to explanatory power (see Peebles 1991:114).

Regardless of the position taken, clearly identifying the scale of the processes under investigation and their potential relations to processes operating at other scales can only help matters. An example of an impressive analysis along these lines—albeit one based upon ethnohistoric and ethnographic data—is Friedman's (1979) classic discussion of Kachin groups and the evolution of the Asiatic state, in which three temporal scales are effectively juggled. In that work, competition between individuals and families in a particular agrarian context is presented as the short-term engine that has driven the Kachin through cycles of successive *gumsa* or egalitarian social formations and *gumlao* or ranked social formations. Friedman suggests that this mid-level cycling was, in turn, enough to propel the Kachin towards a major systemic contradiction as each mid-level cycle

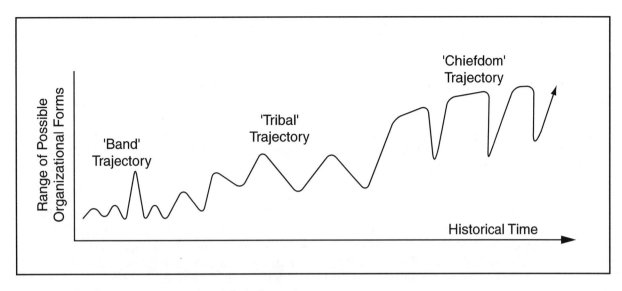

Fig. 3. ZzzEvolution as types of social trajectories.

added to the degradation of the local ecological setting. The result was a systemic contradiction that was sufficiently severe to bring about the development of an Asiatic state. Whether or not one takes issue with Friedman's discussion on empirical grounds, he nevertheless offers an integrated historical model that is sensitive to issues of temporal scale and succeeded in relating one scale to another (see also other explicitly Marxist analyses by Kristiansen [1982], Bender [1990], and Parker Pearson [1984] that work along similar lines).

Ultimately, however, we must be cautious that one totalizing model is not permitted to colonize all of our levels of analysis. Braudel's central insight was that explanation must be permitted to vary with temporal scale. The point at which models—Marxist or otherwise—come to be universally applied in law-like form is the point at which we cease to explain or provide insight into social phenomena (Braudel 1980:50). As a consequence of this heightened concern with temporal scales, therefore, a comparative framework founded upon types of historical trajectories necessitates that we be receptive to a more eclectic use of models as we attempt to weave the various scales of inquiry into a fuller understanding of particular contexts. It may simply be impossible to satisfactorily explain processes occurring over certain temporal scales using certain theoretical approaches. It is in this sense that Brumfiel's (1994) pragmatic suggestion that archaeologists must entertain both agent-centered and system-centered approaches gains further relevance. A full understanding of systems or

structures—from those of the long-term to those of the short—must undoubtedly consider the context of their actual construction and perpetuation, in the actions and multifarious goals of individuals over historical time. But the converse is equally true. Inquiry into individual actions and goals—in prehistory, in particular—would be little more than a tacit reification of untested philosophical positions on human nature in the absence of a sensitivity to the larger inherited structures within which individuals maneuver. The analytic coin in this sense must have at least two faces.

These concerns must be kept in mind as we move from a comparative framework dealing in ethnographic-based models toward a more historical one. Tribal studies of the past two decades have already begun this movement as emphasis has been increasingly placed upon problematizing the process by which regionally integrated 'tribal' systems come about (Braun 1977; Braun and Plog 1982; Creamer and Haas 1985; Haas and Creamer 1993; Plog 1990; Saitta 1983; Voss 1980, 1987). The archaeological use and redefinition of the term 'tribalization' to describe this process highlights the tension that persists in our attempts to translate an ethnographic model of tribal society into archaeological time. Already, in this sense, tribe is being transformed from state to process (Haas 1990). Nonetheless, the subject matter overtly remains the becoming or emergence of a particular organizational state.

What is called for, it seems, is continued work in the same spirit as past tribalization studies, but without the emphasis on particular end states.

Movement through successive formations must itself become the central subject of interest and the basis of a typological system.

A Comparative Framework for the Study of Tribal Trajectories

Toward this end, it may be useful to recognize three rough temporal scales at which different historical processes can be thought of as operating: 1) intra-generational, 2) multi-generational, and 3) long-term. Such a tripartite scheme will feel familiar, for it echoes others of long-standing, in particular Braudel's (1972, 1980) *event-conjoncture-longue durée* framework (see also the temporal frameworks in Bailey [1981] and Butzer [1982]). But these similarities are partly superficial. Below I offer descriptions and discussions of these scales that have emerged from thinking about the specific sort of data with which archaeologists tend to deal.

Intra-generational processes

At one end of historical time are those short-term events and processes that occur within the duration of individual lifespans (up to about 25 or 30 years). Intra-generational processes are, by definition, limited to the duration of a human's lifetime. Thus, when individuals participate in such a process, they are much more likely to be cognizant of the effects of their actions given that the whole of the process can be directly experienced. As a result, explanations of intra-generational processes must contend with the intentions of individuals at a much deeper level than explanations of longer-term processes.

Dealing effectively with intra-generational processes demands fine chronological control and often a wide diversity of data about brief periods of time. Because of this, such processes are the traditional domain of ethnographic and ethnohistoric studies. This is not to say, however, that prehistoric archaeologists are incapable at operating at such a level. Indeed, archaeological data does tend to be highly personal (Hodder 2000). Each artifact in some manner is the record of a short-term sequence of behaviors by an individual or small group. The problem is that most of these data are only indirectly relevant to our broader anthropological questions at the intra-generational level and must be used creatively to say anything at all. Nonetheless, intra-generational processes are at least an aim of much archaeological work.

Examples of intra-generational processes that are of particular relevance to archaeological studies include:
(1) Seasonal settlement mobility.
(2) Village fission-fusion cycles.
(3) Periodic shifts of organization between times of peace and times of war.
(4) The ascendancy of leaders by achievement.
Among these and the many others that could be listed, the typically frequent shifts in settlement location in many tribal trajectories is a problem given special attention in the present volume.

In Chapter 12, for example, Richard Yerkes builds a case for viewing the Ohio Valley Hopewell as highly mobile peoples who supplemented a predominantly hunting and gathering economy with low-level cultivation. Large-scale ceremony at major earthwork centers and elaborate patterns of regional trade were strategies that evolved to maintain a wide network of social ties between otherwise autonomous local groups, but these strategies, he argues, did not curtail the frequent, intra-generational settlement relocations that were necessitated by the economy. Consequently, Hopewell domestic settlements in the Ohio Valley have been found to be ephemeral, with thin middens, little to no architecture, and no evidence of substantial storage features.

John O'Shea and Claire Milner (this volume, Chapter 11) develop an elegant model of tribal organization in the Juntunen Phase of the upper Great Lakes that depends upon the existence of a similar settlement dynamic. Their analysis focuses upon the material indicators of the group boundaries (e.g., shrines, burial mounds, and natural landmarks) that structured Juntunen Phase social interaction. O'Shea and Milner suggest that 'band'-level boundaries marked the territories within which groups relocated seasonally in order to exploit different natural resources. In most years, the scale of interaction and decision-making was thus relatively small. During periodic times of resource scarcity, however, multi-band organizations emerged as large groups of people descended on a few resource-rich areas. Such episodic aggregations were characterized by intense interaction and a correspondingly high degree of ritual and ceremonialism.

In both the Hopewell and Juntunen Phase cases, large population aggregations did periodically occur, though only in ritualized contexts and for relatively brief periods of time. As O'Shea and Milner point out, these occasional aggregations ensure that the regional community has a predictable structure for the community members. However, the underlying dynamic was governed by frequent settlement relocations that had the effect over time of enhancing decision-making autonomy at a small-scale. Community members retained an ability to 'vote with their feet' to a significant degree. As many have suggested, the leisure to respond to social conflict with mobility rather than the institutionalization of strong positions of leadership has undoubtedly played a critical part in keeping many tribal groups 'tribal' over the long run (Kent 1989; Trigger 1990).

As noted above, a unifying aspect of all intra-generational processes is that they are solidly within the realm and perception of individuals. Whether the movement of one's camp, the soliciting of supporters, or the slitting of throats is involved, the actions are calculated and can analytically be attributed to the initiative of particular persons. As such, intra-generational processes are frequently most appropriately understood and modeled in terms of agent-centered approaches.

Multi-generational processes

When a process extends beyond the individual's lifetime and becomes multi-generational, one can no longer simply speak in terms of the agency of the individual in the same manner. Multi-generational processes necessarily result from the composite decisions of multiple individuals. They mark an important movement away from those just described because in order to surpass the actions and goals of an individual, they must in some way become entrenched in a social context and be inherited by the following generation(s) of individuals. Inasmuch as this is true, the nature of explanation must tend more toward the structural. Individuals do indeed witness parts of these processes and may be keenly aware of their place within the longer sequence of events. However he or she might seek to influence those events during their lives, the individual can nonetheless only affect the trajectory of the total process to the degree that he or she is able to change the inheritable structures within which the process is taking place. The complex interplay of structure and agent thus comes to the foreground in a dramatic manner during the analysis of multi-generational processes.

Due to the time span involved, it is rare that an ethnographic project is able to operate effectively at the multi-generational level (cf. Foster et al. 1979), at least in the absence of complimentary ethnohistoric documents from which to build. For archaeologists and ethnohistorians, however, this temporal scale tends to be the goal of much research particularly when regional chronologies are achieved that utilize periods of 150 years or less. Correspondingly, the sorts of processes involved are familiar subject matter to prehistorians. Included among the many multi-generational processes frequently considered are:

(1) The development of religious traditions.
(2) The entrenchment of leadership in a particular lineage or social group.
(3) The assimilation of immigrant groups.

Regarding the latter, Sarah Herr and Jeffrey Clark (this volume, Chapter 8) focus on what they rightly emphasize are migration *processes*—rather than events—in the American Southwest that necessitated sequential periods of social reorganization over multiple generations. By drawing on a number of examples from across the Puebloan world, they reveal the complex relationship between the context of migration and the organizational shifts that result. In their Grasshopper Plateau and Tonto Basin cases, immigration into previously occupied regions at times resulted in the coresidence of groups who purposely maintained markedly distinct traditions and social identities, especially in the generation directly following movement into an area. At times, it appears that immigration introduced a new element of hierarchy as the 'latecomers' were forced to live on the margins where they had more restricted access to land, religious authority, and social positions of prestige. In contrast, Herr and Clark also consider an interesting example from the Silver Creek Drainage in which migrants moved into a previously unoccupied frontier. In this case, a different process was initiated in which the 'firstcomers' attempted to attract followers and to develop their own system of prestige over time through the construction and use of Great Kivas. In each example, the organizational changes triggered by migrations became part of the social structure inherited and elaborated on by successive generations.

In most tribal contexts, though, significant social inequalities—however they are introduced—are difficult to maintain over the long-term. This is the theme of Fowles' consideration of leadership among the historic Tonga of south central Africa in Chapter 5. Fowles uses ethnographic and ethnohistoric data to argue that would-be Tonga leaders did exploit religion in their efforts to accrue social power and that over time some kin-groups were able to solidify relatively strong positions of influence and prestige. As inequality bred increasing resentment, periodic 'egalitarian rebellions' ensued, initiated by those who were being disempowered. He concludes that such multi-generational cycles of leadership—not an actual state of equality—is what results in the particular brand of 'egalitarianism' so frequently associated with tribal society. It is through such rebellions that an ethic (if not a practice) of equality comes to be written into social organizations over time.

Understanding multi-generational processes such as those discussed above necessitates a shift in theoretical focus. Just as discussions of kinship lineages must involve a greater emphasis on structure in contrast to discussions of the individuals within those lineages, so do multi-generational processes demand that we move beyond solely agent-centered approaches. Why certain social relations, behaviors and ideas are inherited or discarded by a group over time raises questions of social reproduction and cultural transmission (Boyd and Richerson 1985) and leads to new concerns with historical contingency, social adaptation (cf. Braun 1991), and more generally with the structures that underlie individual action.

Long-term processes

At the far end of historical time are those processes that occur over the long-term (hundreds or thousands of years), generally beyond the precise record-keeping and active experience of the individuals and groups involved. As such, there is little opportunity for the individual to be truly aware of his or her actions within the larger process. Actions performed in the hopes of fulfilling shorter-term goals may be imbedded within long-term processes that have a life of their own in the sense that they are not truly propelled by 'goals' at all. In Marxist terms, such processes are frequently viewed as the unforeseen consequences of human action. To a much greater degree, it may be useful to deal with these processes in analyses on a structural level.

Long-term processes are the traditional domain of archaeological inquiry, for the necessary chronological purview to understand such processes tends to be very great. As such, an appreciation of the long-term is considered by many to be one of archaeology's principle contributions to the human sciences (Hodder 1987). Long-term processes that are often a focus of research include:
(1) Shifts in subsistence strategies.
(2) Cycles of aggregation and dispersal.

(3) The development of a group ethnic identity.
(4) The development of increasingly regional social networks.

That the nature of explanation must shift as research turns to address such processes is clearly shown in William Parkinson's (this volume, Chapter 18) consideration of settlement changes between the Late Neolithic and Early Copper Ages on the Great Hungarian Plain. To understand these long-term processes, Parkinson adopts an explicitly structural perspective, and through a careful analysis of shifting patterns of integration and interaction he concludes that the same basic segmentary structure was perpetuated in this context during both time periods—a combined length of some one thousand years. The introduction of pastoralism, he argues, elicited a shift in the structural arrangement of those segments but did little to affect the underlying—or, in his words, latent—structural potential of the society's tribal adaptation. Parallels to this case have been found in other contexts as well (e.g., Dean 1970), suggesting that such long-term cycles represent a truly cross-cultural tribal pattern. Importantly, Parkinson emphasizes that it is precisely this ability of tribal societies to shift through organizational forms with ease that makes them adaptive over the long-term.

In addition to change within a certain range of organization, however, the long-term is also, of course, the level at which one typically considers the *evolution* of a trajectory out of what we might consider a tribal dynamic and into a dynamic of some other sort. In their major synthesis of Mesoamerican data, for example, John Clark and David Cheetham (this volume, Chapter 14) raise the very interesting observation that only a relatively small segment of the developmental history of this part of the world can appropriately be considered tribal. Institutionalized social ranking, they conclude, emerged a mere four centuries or so after settlement patterns shifted toward sedentary agricultural villages. From a long-term evolutionary perspective, then, Mesoamerican tribal trajectories must be viewed as having been relatively unstable and transitory.

Explanation at multiple temporal scales

Parsing analyses into multiple temporal scales, of course, accomplishes little if no effort is ultimately made to consider the manner in which the processes operating at these scales interrelate. Longer processes are of course of necessity constituted out of shorter ones, and shorter processes are always embedded in longer ones. By drawing attention to the relative brevity of the Meso-american tribal phase, for example, Clark and Cheetham effectively challenge research to explore the shorter-term dynamics that may have driven the speedy emergence of institutionalized social ranking.[5]

Indeed, as the reader will note, all of the chapters in the present volume already integrate these scales to the degree permitted by their data; in most cases the phenomena under discussion could not be understood otherwise. Peter Bogucki's (this volume, Chapter 16) consideration of household cycles in the Brześć Kujawski Group, for example, emphasizes the flux of prestige and status over time as Neolithic immigrants settled and established a tribal social context in northern Poland. He uses as his starting point a theoretical consideration of the potential variability in wealth that might be expected both between and within longhouse households over time. Whereas from the perspective of the long-term, the Brześć Kujawski Group is best described as a more-or-less egalitarian society in which power and wealth did not accrue in the hands of any one lineage or social group, the intra- and inter-generational processes of change reveal a somewhat different scenario. Accumulation of wealth was clearly a preoccupation of households, so much so that Bogucki suggests that we view them as characterized by an 'ideology of accumulation'.

Perhaps the most characteristically 'tribal' aspect of this situation, however, was that the copper, shell, worked bone, etc. that an individual or household was able to procure during one generation does not appear to have been passed on to the next. Instead, they were buried in large amounts with the deceased in a manner similar to that discussed by Mauss (1990) as the conspicuous destruction of wealth. In this practice, we find a familiar contrast between a conscious ethic of accumulation on an intra-generational level by individuals and households that was held in check on an inter-generational level by burial rites that had the effect of taking wealth out of circulation. Bugocki is thus able to use the complex burial data as a window into the waxing and waning of the economic standing of households from one generation to the next.

To consider a second example, Michael Adler's essay (this volume, Chapter 9) investigates the leadership strategies employed in the aggregated Puebloan villages of the Taos District, New Mexico. Rather than seeking to outline a general structure for the society in these villages, Adler concerns

himself initially with the short-term patterns of rise and fall among ritually based social groups through time. In the course of this study, the Picuris notion of "sponsorship" emerges as a central mechanism of leadership. Sponsorship, as Adler documents, is a type of social control and leadership in which a degree of decision-making power is temporarily vested in the representative of a sodality or social group only so long as that group serves the interests of the community as a whole.

In the case of Picuris Pueblo, for example, Adler reveals that the eldest male of a ritual society might control access to a kiva only so long as the principle ceremony held therein was the responsibility of that society. Should the ceremony cease to be practiced for whatever reason, the society would no longer hold a unique right to leadership, and the operation of the kiva would revert back to the community as a whole. Adler points out that on a multi-generational level this form of leadership tends to place a limit on the degree of power that any one ritual society might develop, a situation that he is also able to document in the construction, maintenance, and abandonment cycles of kivas at the prehistoric village of Pot Creek Pueblo. Over the long-term, such dynamics result in the familiar ambiguity and fluctuations of leadership that typify what we think of as 'tribal' social traditions.

David Anderson's (this volume, Chapter 13) deft synthesis of over 4,000 years of tribal variability in the Southeastern United States provides a final example of how one might attempt to juggle multiple analytic scales and diverse theoretical approaches. From the perspective of the long-term, Anderson reemphasizes Braun and Plog's (1982) suggestion that the emergence of regional tribal networks can be viewed on a general level as a form of risk minimization strategy to buffer stresses introduced either through population increase, environmental change, or a combination of the two. In order to understand how this general adaptation developed, he focuses in upon shorter processes, in particular on the development of mound-building traditions.

Anderson notes, for instance, that the earliest large-scale constructions during the Middle Archaic appear to have been produced by peoples that were ritually integrated into regional communities, but were not yet politically centralized in any archaeologically observable way. Over time, however, group construction projects in many areas came to be more closely associated with the burial of relatively high status individuals, a structural shift that undoubtedly played a critical role in the development of increasingly regional social networks. Ultimately to understand how and why this shift took place, Anderson further suggests that archaeologists need to look with yet greater resolution at the repeated developmental sequences of individual mounds and mound groups. It is at this short-term level that one can begin to question why individuals and social groups may have consciously chosen to participate in group construction projects during their own lifetimes.

Of course, the data required to satisfactory explore many temporal scales simultaneously is only rarely available in archaeological contexts. But as a discipline, archaeology is expertly accustomed to the task of working with patchy and incomplete datasets. It is out of this reality that creative modeling invariably begins.

Conclusion

As a neoevolutionary type, 'tribe' was intended to be used as a concept that could be stretched over the long-term to describe a cross-cultural stage of 'general evolution' within the variable, particular trajectories or 'specific evolution' of individual social contexts (Sahlins 1960). There may yet be important work to be undertaken towards these ends, however in the present volume this traditional typological approach has been laid to the side. Instead, emphasis has been placed on a comparative typology of historical processes at multiple temporal scales. By its nature, much of a society's organizational dynamic tends to elude ethnographic observation and so did not enter into the classic ethnographic literature on evolutionary typologies. Given this, the study of tribal trajectories has become a problem of social theory for archaeologists and historians.

Useful typologies must work upwards from the specific to the general. In this spirit, the case studies included in this volume begin at the specific level by considering individual historical trajectories of change at a variety of temporal scales. On one hand, this approach highlights the variability between the social contexts that, for better or for worse, have been considered tribal or middle-range. Robert Carneiro begins this task in the following chapter by distilling from the world ethnographic database a synthesis of the array of social organizations that have contributed to our modern sense of the tribal—or, following his model, 'autonomous village'—type. The succeeding chapters extend our understanding of tribal variability by considering fluctuations in the organization of particular 'tribal'

societies through time. More than simply confounding our impressions of what a tribe is, these case studies offer a comparative database with which to explore the possibility of a typology of historical trajectories and to develop new generalizations in those areas in which generalization is warranted. Ultimately, it is these sorts of studies that may lead to a fuller understanding of what—if anything—it means to act tribally.

Notes

[1]See Middleton and Tait (1958:8, footnote 1) for a succinct description of the difference between Durkheim's mechanical solidarity and later British notions of segmentary systems.

[2]See also Marcus and Flannery (1996) for a discussion architectural segmentation at the site of San José Mogote during the 'tribal' phase of development in the Valley of Oaxaca.

[3]See Trigger (1978:156-157) for a review of past attempts in ethnology to establish the scalar limitations of tribal society. Carneiro (1967), Kosse (1996), and Feinman and Neitzel (1984) also tackle the problem of scalar organizational thresholds with their own cross-cultural databases.

[4]One might reasonably critique this contrast by arguing that both models were really subsumed within the neoevolutionary framework through the differentiation between 'general' and 'specific' evolution (Sahlins 1960). Continuous change (Figure 2), in this sense, should be thought of as a characteristic of specific evolution, or the development of a particular society along a historical trajectory. Change between idealized social types (Figure 1), on the other hand, should simply be thought of as a heuristic model with which to understand and compare cases of specific evolution. While valid, this critique does not directly affect the argument developed in the essay.

[5]This challenge has, of course, already begun to be met in Mesoamerica though analyses by Clark and Blake (1994), Blake and Clark (1999), and Marcus and Flannery (1996).

Acknowledgments

An earlier version of this paper was carefully read by Bill Parkinson, Norm Yoffee, Ellen Morris, David Anderson, John Clark, and Graciela Cabana, all of whom provided very valuable commentary. Thanks are also extended to John O'Shea and

Robert Whallon in whose seminar and under whose guidance the original thoughts in this paper were formulated.

References Cited

Bailey, G. N.
  1981 Concepts, Time-scales and Explanations in Economic Prehistory. In *Economic Archaeology: Towards an Integration of Ecological and Social Approaches*, edited by A. Sheridan and G. Bailey, pp. 97-117. British Archaeological Reports, International Series 96. BAR, Oxford.
Barker, Graeme
  1995 *A Mediterranean Valley, Landscape Archaeology and* Annales *History in the Biferno Valley*. Leicester University Press, New York.
Barth, Fredrik
  1967 On the Study of Social Change. *American Anthropologist*. 69(6):661-69.
Bender, Barbara
  1985 Emergent Tribal Formation in the American Midcontinent. *American Antiquity* 50(1):52-62.
  1990 The Dynamics of Nonhierarchical Societies. In *The Evolution of Political Systems*, edited by Steadman Upham, pp. 247-263. Cambridge University Press, New York.
Berndt, Ronald M.
  1966 [1959] The Concept of the 'Tribe' in the Western Desert of Australia. In *Readings in Australian and Pacific Anthropology*, edited by I. Hogbin and L.R. Hiatt, pp. 26-56. Cambridge University Press, New York.
Binford, Lewis R.
  1986 In Pursuit of the Future. In *American Archaeology Past and Future*, edited by D.J. Meltzer, D.D. Fowler, and J.A. Sabloff, pp. 459-79.
Bintliff, John, editor
  1991 *The* Annales *School and Archaeology*. Leicester University Press, London.
Bohannan, Paul
  1954 The Migration and Expansion of the Tiv. *Africa* 24:2-16.
Blake, Michael and John E. Clark
  1999 The Emergence of Hereditary Inequality: the Case of Pacific Coastal Chiapas. In *Pacific Latin America in Prehistory*, edited by Michael Blake, pp. 55-73.

Blanton, Richard E., Gary M. Feinman, Stephen A. Kowalewski, and Peter N. Peregrine
  1996 A Dual-Processual Theory for the Evolution of Mesoamerican Civilization. *Current Anthropology* 37:1-14.
Braudel, Fernand
  1972 *The Mediterranean and the Mediterranean World in the Age of Philip II*, translated by Sian Reynolds. 2 vols. New York, Harper and Row.
  1980 [1958] History and the Social Sciences: the *Longue Durée*. In *On History*, translated by Sarah Matthews, pp. 25-54. University of Chicago Press, Chicago.
Braun, David P.
  1977 Middle Woodland - (Early) Late Woodland Social Change in the Prehistoric Central Midwestern U.S. Unpublished Ph.D. Dissertation, Department of Anthropology, University of Michigan.
  1991 Are There Cross-cultural Regularities in Tribal Social Practices? In *Between Bands and States*, edited by Susan A Gregg, pp. 423-444. Center for Archaeological Investigations, Occasional Paper No. 9.
Braun, David and Steve Plog
  1982 Evolution of "Tribal" Social Networks: Theory and Prehistoric North American Evidence. *American Antiquity* 47:504-25.
Brown, James
  1985 Long-Term Trends to Sedentism and the Emergence of Complexity in the American Midwest. In *Prehistoric Hunters and Gatherers*, edited by T.D. Price and J.A. Brown, pp. 201-31. Academic Press, New York.
Brumfiel, Elizabeth M.
  1994 Factional Competition and Political Development in the New World: An Introduction. In *Factional Competition and Political Development in the New World*, edited by Elizabeth M. Brumfiel and John W. Fox, pp. 3-13. Cambridge University Press, Cambridge.
Butzer, Karl W
  1982 *Archaeology as Human Ecology*. Cambridge University Press, Cambridge.
Carneiro, Robert L.
  1967 On the Relationship Between Size of Population and Complexity of Social Organization. *Southwestern Journal of Anthropology* 23:234-243.

1987   Village Splitting as a Function of Population Size. In *Themes in Ethnology and Culture History*, pp. 94-124. Archana Publications, Sadar, India.

Chagnon, Napoleon A.
1983   *Yanomamö, The Fierce People*. Third Edition. Holt, Rinehart and Winston, New York.

Clark, John E. and Michael Blake
1994   The Power of Prestige: Competitive Generosity and the Emergence of Rank Societies in Lowland Mesoamerica. In *Factional Competition and Political Development in the New World*, edited by E. Brumfiel and J. Fox, pp. 17-30. Cambridge University Press, Cambridge.

Colson, Elizabeth
1962   Residence and Village Stability among the Plateau Tonga. In *The Plateau Tonga of Northern Rhodesia*, edited by Elizabeth Colson, pp. 172-206. Manchester University Press, Manchester.

Creamer, Winifred and Jonathan Haas
1985   Tribe Versus Chiefdom in Lower Central America. *American Antiquity* 50:738-54.

Dincauze, Dena F. and Robert J. Hasenstab
1989   Explaining the Iroquois: Tribalization on a Prehistoric Periphery. In *Centre and Periphery*, edited by T.C. Champion, pp. 67-87. Routledge, New York..

Dobres, Marcia-Anne and John Robb
2000   Agency in Archaeology, Paradigm or Platitude? In *Agency in Archaeology*, edited by Marcia-Anne Dobres and John Robb, pp. 3-17. Routledge, New York.

Eckholm, Kajsa
1980   On the Limitations of Civilization: The Structure and Dynamics of Global Systems. *Dialectical Anthropology* 5:155-66.

Feinman, Gary M., Kent G. Lightfoot, and Steadman Upham
2000   Political Hierarchies and Organizational Strategies in the Puebloan Southwest. *American Antiquity* 65(3):449-70.

Feinman, Gary and Jill Neitzel
1984   Too Many Types: An Overview of Sedentary Prestate Societies in the Americas. In *Advances in Archaeological Method and Theory* 7:39-102.

Flannery, Kent
1983   Divergent Evolution. In *The Cloud People, Divergent Evolution of the Zapotec and Mixtec Civilizations*, edited by Kent V. Flannery and Joyce Marcus, pp. 1-4. Academic Press, New York.

Fletcher, Roland
1992   Time Perspectivism, *Annales*, and the Potential of Archaeology. In *Archaeology, Annales, and Ethnohistory*. edited by A. Bernard Knapp, pp. 35-49. Cambridge University Press, New York.

Fortes, Meyer
1953   The Structure of Unilineal Descent Groups. *American Anthropologist* 55:17-41.

Fortes, Meyer, and E.E. Evans-Pritchard, editors
1940   *African Political System*. Oxford University Press, London.

Fowles, Severin and William Parkinson
1999   Organizational Flexibility: An Archaeological Notion of 'Tribe'. Paper presented at the 1999 Society of American Archaeology Meetings in Chicago.

Fried, Morton
1968   On the Concepts of "Tribe" and "Tribal Society". In *Essays on the Problem of Tribe*, edited by June Helm, pp. 3-20. Proceedings of the 1967 Annual Spring Meeting, American Ethnological Society. University of Washington Press, Seattle.
1975   *The Notion of Tribe*. Cummings Publishing, Menlo Park, CA.

Friedman, Jonathan
1979   *System, Structure, and Contradiction in the Evolution of "Asiatic" Social Formations*. National Museum of Denmark Social Studies in Oceania and Southeast Asia No. 2. Copenhagen.
1982   Catastrophe and Continuity in Social Evolution. In *Theory and Explanation in Archaeology, The Southampton Conference*, edited by Colin Renfrew, Michael J. Rowlands, and Barbara A. Segraves, pp. 175-96. Academic Press, New York.

Gearing, Fred
1958   The Structural Poses of 18th-century Cherokee Villages. *American Anthropologist* 60:1148-56.
1962   *Priests and Warriors*. Memoirs of the American Anthropological Association 93.

Gluckman, Max
1965   *Politics, Law and Ritual in Tribal Society*. Aldine Publishing Co., Chicago.

Gregg, Susan A., editor
1991   *Between Bands and States*. Center for Archaeological Investigations, Occa-

sional Paper No. 9. Southern Illinois University.

Gross, Daniel
1979 A New Approach to Central Brazilian Social Organization. In *Brazil, Anthropological Perspectives, Essays in Honor of Charles Wagley*, edited by Maxine L. Margolis and William E. Carter, pp. 321-342. Columbia University Press, New York.

Haas, Jonathan
1990 Warfare and Tribalization in the Prehistoric Southwest. In *The Anthropology of War*, edited by Jonathan Haas, pp. 171-89. Cambridge University Press, Cambridge.

Habicht-Mauche, Judith A.
1990 Pottery Styles, Ethnicity, and Tribalization in the Northern Rio Grande Valley. Paper Presented at the Annual Meetings of the A.A.A., New Orleans.

1993 *The Pottery from Arroyo Hondo Pueblo, New Mexico.* School of American Research Press, Santa Fe.

Helm, June, editor
1968 *Essays on the Problem of Tribe.* American Ethnological Society. Proceedings of the 1967 Annual Spring Meeting. University of Washington Press.

Hodder, Ian
1987 The Contribution of the Long-Term. In *Archaeology as Long-Term History*, edited by Ian Hodder, pp. 1-8. Cambridge University Press, New York.

Hodder, Ian, editor
1987 *Archaeology as Long-Term History.* Cambridge University Press, New York.

Hodder, Ian
2000 Agency and Individuals in Long-Term Processes. In *Agency in Archaeology*, edited by Marcia-Anne Dobres and John E. Robb, pp. 21-33. Routledge, New York.

Johnson, Gregory
1978 Information Sources and the Development of Decision-Making Organizations. In *Social Archaeology: Beyond Subsistence and Dating*, edited by C. Redman et al., pp. 87-112. Academic Press, New York.

1982 Organization Structure and Scalar Stress. in *Theory and Explanation in Archaeology: The Southampton Conference*, edited by C. Renfrew, M.J. Rowlands, and B. A. Segraves, pp. 389-421. Academic Press, New York.

1989 Dynamics of Southwestern Prehistory, Far Outside—Looking In. In *Dynamics of Southwestern Prehistory*, edited by Linda Cordell and George Gumerman, pp. 209-62. Smithsonian Institution Press, New York.

Kent, Susan
1989 Cross-cultural Perceptions of Farmers as Hunters and the Value of Meat. In *Farmers as Hunters, The Implications of Sedentism.* edited by Susan Kent, pp. 1-17. Cambridge University Press, New York.

Knapp, A. Bernard, editor
1992 *Archaeology, Annales, and Ethnohistory.* Cambridge University Press, New York.

Kosse, Krisztina
1990 Group Size and Societal Complexity: Thresholds in the Long-Term Memory. *Journal of Anthropological Archaeology* 9(3):275-303.

1996 Middle Range Societies from a Scalar Perspective. In *Interpreting Southwestern Diversity: Underlying Principles and Overarching Patterns*, edited by Paul R. Fish and J. Jefferson Reid, pp. 87-96. Arizona State University Anthropological Research Paper No. 48. Tempe.

Kristiansen, Kristian
1982 The formation of Tribal Systems in Later European Prehistory: Northern Europe, 4000-5000 B.C. In *Theory and Explanation in Archaeology, The Southampton Conference.* edited by Colin Renfrew, Michael J. Rowlands, and Barbara A. Segraves, pp. 241-80. Academic Press, New York.

Kroeber, A.L.
1917 Zuni Kin and Clan. *Anthropological Papers.* American Museum of Natural History. 18(2).

1955 The Nature of the Land-Holding Group. *Ethnohistory* 2:303-314.

Lekson, Stephen H.
1990 Sedentism and Aggregation in Anasazi Archaeology. In *Perspectives on Southwestern Prehistory*, edited by Paul Minnis and Charles Redman, pp. 333-40. Westview Press, Boulder.

Lévi-Strauss, Claude
1963 *Structural Anthropology*, translated by Claire Jacobson and Brooke Grundfest Schoepf. Basic Books.

Marcus, Joyce and Kent V. Flannery
  1996 *Zapotec Civilization: How Urban Society Evolved in Mexico's Oaxaca Valley.* Thames and Hudson, London.
Marx, Karl
  1991 [1852] *The Eighteenth Brumaire of Louis Bonaparte.* International Publishers, New York.
Mauss, Marcel
  1990 [1950] *The Gift, The Form and Reason for Exchange in Archaic Societies,* translated by W.D. Halls. W.W. Norton, New York.
Meggitt, M.J.
  1979 Reflections Occasioned by Continuing Anthropological Field Research Among the Enga of Papua New Guinea. In *Long-Term Field Research in Social Anthropology,* edited by G.M. Foster, T. Scudder, E. Colson, and R.V. Kemper, pp. 107-126. Academic Press, New York.
Mills, Barbara
  2000 Alternative Models, Alternative Strategies: Leadership in the Prehispanic Southwest. In *Alternative Leadership Strategies in the Prehispanic Southwest,* edited by Barbara Mills, pp. 3-18. University of Arizona Press, Tuscon.
Morgan, Lewis Henry
  1974 [1877] *Ancient Society,* edited by E.B. Leacock. Peter Smith, Gloucester, Mass.
Naroll, Raoul
  1956 A Preliminary Index of Social Development. *American Anthropologist* 58(4): 687-715.
Oliver, Symmes C.
  1968 [1962] Ecology and Cultural Continuity as Contributing Factors in the Social Organization of the Plains Indians. In *University of California Publications in American Archaeology and Ethnology.* 48(1):13-18, 46-49, 52-68.
Parker Pearson, Michael
  1984 Economic and Ideological Change: Cyclical Growth in the Pre-State Societies of Jutland. In *Ideology, Power, and Prehistory,* edited by D. Miller and C. Tilley, pp. 69-92. Cambridge University Press, New York.
Peebles, Christopher S.
  1991 *Annalistes,* Hermeneutics and Positivists: Squaring Circles. In *The* Annales *School and Archaeology,* edited by John Bintliff, pp. 108-124. New York University Press, New York.

Peregrine, Peter N.
  2001 Matrilocality, Corporate Strategy, and the Organization of Production in the Chacoan World. *American Antiquity* 66(1):36-46.
Plog, Fred T.
  1974 *The Study of Prehistoric Change.* Academic Press, New York.
Plog, Stephen
  1990 Agriculture, Sedentism, and Environment in the Evolution of Political Systems. In *The Evolution of Political Systems,* edited by Steadman Upham, pp. 177-199. Cambridge University Press, New York.
Preucel, Robert and Ian Hodder
  1996 Process, Structure and History. In *Contemporary Archaeology in Theory,* edited by Robert Preucel and Ian Hodder, pp. 205-219. Blackwell Publishers, Cambridge, Mass.
Redmond, Elsa
  1998 Introduction. In *Chiefdoms and Chieftaincy in the Americas,* edited by Elsa Redmond, pp. 1-17. University Press of Florida, Gainesville.
Rogers, Rhea J.
  1995 Tribes as Heterarchy: A Case Study from the Prehistoric Southeastern United States. In *Heterarchy and the Analysis of Complex Societies,* edited by R.M. Ehrenreich, C.L. Crumley, and J.E. Levy, pp. 7-16. Archeological Papers of the American Anthropological Association No. 6.
Sahlins, Marshall D.
  1960 Evolution: Specific and General. In *Evolution and Culture,* edited by Marshall Sahlins and Elman Service, pp. 12-14. University of Michigan Press, Ann Arbor.
  1961 The Segmentary Lineage: An Organization of Predatory Expansion. *American Anthropologist* 63:332-45.
  1966 [1963] Poor Man, Rich Man, Big Man, Chief: Political Types in Melanesia and Polynesia. In *Readings in Australian and Pacific Anthropology,* edited by I. Hogbin and L.R. Hiatt, pp. 159-179. Cambridge University Press, New York.
  1968 *Tribesmen.* Prentice-Hall, Englewood Cliffs, NJ.
Saitta, Dean J.
  1983 On the Evolution of "Tribal" Social Networks. *American Antiquity* 48:820-24.

Salzman, Philip, editor
  1980 *When Nomads Settle: Process of Sedentarization as Adaptation and Response.* Praeger, New York.
Service, Elman R.
  1962 *Primitive Social Organization.* Random House, New York.
  1971 *Cultural Evolution, Theory in Practice.* Holt, Rinehart and Winston, New York.
  1975 *Origins of the State and Civilization.* W.W. Norton and Company, New York.
Smith, Michael E.
  1992 Braudel's Temporal Rhythms and Chronology Theory in Archaeology. In *Archaeology, Annales, and Ethnohistory,* edited by A. Bernard Knapp, pp. 23-34. Cambridge University Press, New York.
Smith, Michael G.
  1956 On Segmentary Lineage Systems. *Journal of the Royal Anthropological Institute* 86:39-79.
  1960 Kagoro Political Development. *Human Organization.* 19(3):137-149.
Southall, Aidan
  1956 *Alur Society: A Study in Processes and Types of Domination.* Heffer, Cambridge.
  1988 The Segmentary State in Africa and Asia. *Comparative Study of Society and History* 31:52-82.
Steward, Julian
  1937 Ecological Aspects of Southwestern Society. *Anthropos* 32:87-104.
Trigger, Bruce G.
  1978 *Time and Traditions.* Columbia University Press, New York.
  1990 Maintaining Economic Equality in Opposition to Complexity: An Iroquoian Case Study. In *The Evolution of Political Systems,* edited by Steadman Upham, pp. 119-145. Cambridge University Press, New York.
Upham, Steadman
  1990a Decoupling the Processes of Political Evolution. In *The Evolution of Political Systems,* edited by Steadman Upham, pp. 1-17. Cambridge University Press, New York.
  1990b Analog or Digital?: Toward a Generic Framework for Explaining the Development of Emergent Political Systems. In *The Evolution of Political Systems,* edited by Steadman Upham, pp. 87-115. Cambridge University Press, New York.
Varien, Mark and Ricky Lightfoot
  1989 Ritual and Nonritual Activities in Mesa Verde Region Pit Structures. In *The Architecture of Social Integration in Prehistoric Pueblos,* edited by William D. Lipe and Michelle Hegmon, pp. 73-88. Occasional Paper No. 1. Crow Canyon Archaeological Center. Cortez, Co.
Voss, Jerome A.
  1980 Tribal Emergence During the Neolithic of Northwestern Europe. Unpublished Ph.D. Dissertation, Department of Anthropology, University of Michigan.
  1987 Prehistoric Tribalization in Northwestern Europe. In *Polities and Partitions, Human Boundaries and the Growth of Complex Societies,* edited by K.M. Trinkaus, pp. 29-60. Arizona State University, Anthropological Research Papers No. 37.

3. The Tribal Village and Its Culture:
An Evolutionary Stage in the History of Human Society

Robert L. Carneiro

From the end of the Paleolithic to the onset of chiefdoms, human beings throughout the world lived in small, simple, autonomous villages. While these villages varied widely in culture, there was nonetheless a broad underlying similarity in the way in which those who resided in them made their living and conducted their lives. The period involved here, that generally equated archeologically with the Neolithic, was one of village self-sufficiency, both political and economic. It was a period which represented a *universal stage* in socio-cultural development. Preceding it were the hunter-gatherer bands of the Paleolithic. Following it, came a form of society consisting of large multi-village polities ruled by a powerful chief. In some parts of the world, such as the ancient Near East, the autonomous village stage lasted but a few millennia before giving way to it successor. In other parts, like New Guinea and Amazonia, it exists to this day.

Frequently—as in the title of this book—the autonomous village stage is labeled *tribal*. I hesitate to use this term for the form of culture I wish to describe because 'tribe' has a variety of different meanings, and has been the subject of much controversy. Thus, before proceeding further, it may be useful to present some of the background to this controversy and to see how it will affect the treatment of village cultures which is to follow.

Conceptions of the Tribe

In 1955 Kalervo Oberg proposed a typology to characterize successive levels of culture in South and Central America. The three lowest of these levels, as Oberg designated them, were (1) homogeneous tribes, (2) segmented tribes, and (3) politically organized chiefdoms. Much impressed by this typology, and seeing that the categories Oberg had proposed merely as *types* were in fact evolutionary *stages,* Service set forth his own typology, the now

famous sequence of *Band, Tribe, Chiefdom,* and *State* (Service 1962).

While Service perceived the tribe as having a number of forms which were "adapted ...to varying local circumstances," he nevertheless saw tribal society as having "general characteristics as a level or stage in evolution ..." (Service 1962:111). Many of these characteristics, especially those having to do with kinship and marriage, Service recognized as being retentions from an earlier band type of society into a village type. But the tribe was something beyond mere villages. The essence of it, according to Service, was not the internal culture of each village, but the external means by which several villages were linked together. And, unlike the chiefdom, these means were not political:

> ... tribes are not held together by the dominance of one group over others, nor are there any other true or permanent political-governmental institutions. Presumably a great many societies of tribal potentialities merely fissioned, but those that became tribes all had made certain social inventions that had latent integrating effects. *To ask what these are is to ask what a tribe is.* (Service 1962:112-113; emphasis mine)

Service then went on to enumerate the structural features which had permitted villages to establish closer relations with one another, thus forming a tribe:

> The means of solidarity that are specifically tribal additions to the persisting band-like means might be called *pan-tribal sodalities....* Probably the most usual of pan-tribal sodalities are clans, followed by age-grade associations, secret societies, and sodalities for such special purposes as curing, warfare, ceremonies, and so on. (Service 1962:113)

Not long after the appearance of Service's four stages of social evolution, the scheme was criticized by Morton Fried (1966). Fried's principal objection centered on the stage of "tribe," which he argued should not be considered a universal stage in socio-political development. On the contrary, Fried believed it was only a response to the dislocation and disruption undergone by aboriginal societies as a result of European contact. Service (1968:167) readily accepted Fried criticism, and recanted, deciding to "abolish" the tribe as a general stage in his typology of socio-political evolution. Indeed, he went a step further, truncating his evolutionary sequence by collapsing it from four stages to three, and renaming them: (1) Egalitarian Society, (2) Hierarchical Society, and (3) Archaic Civilization (Service 1968:167).

But the world did little note nor long remember Service's emendation of his own sequence. In fact, Service himself showed signs of having recanted his recantation, because three years later, in the revised edition of *Primitive Social Organization,* he retained the 'tribe' as a stage in his evolutionary sequence, noting only that "the law and order imposed by colonial power could have the effect of restricting or even reducing the territories controlled by the tribal kin group without otherwise disturbing the tribe" (Service 1971:126).

In his book *Tribesmen,* published in 1968, Marshall Sahlins did not hesitate to embrace the concept of tribe. In fact he stretched its meaning to the maximum. Tribes, he wrote, "represent a certain category of cultural development, intermediate in complexity between the mobile hunters and ... gatherers and early agrarian states such as the Egyptian and Sumerian" (Sahlins 1968:vii). So broad was Sahlins conception of the tribe that the category of chiefdom was submerged within it. But for Sahlins the tribe was more than just a *category.* It was a *stage*: "Tribes occupy a position in cultural evolution. They took over from simpler hunters; they gave way to the more advanced cultures we call civilizations" (Sahlins 1968:4).

To Sahlins, as it was to Service, the essence of the tribe was the overarching set of structures which enabled autonomous local communities to establish close ties with other communities, thus forming a wider network of social relations. Accordingly, he wrote:

> The constituent units of tribal society ... make up a progressively inclusive series of groups, from the closely-knit household to the encompassing tribal whole. Smaller groups are combined into larger ones through several levels of incorporation. The particular arrangements vary, of course, but the scheme might read some-

thing like this: families are joined in local lineages, lineages in village communities, villages in regional confederacies, the latter making up the tribe. (Sahlins 1968:15)

Sahlins (1968:21) also pointed out the transient nature of much of tribal organization:

> Certain groups may ally for a time and a purpose, as for a military venture, but the collective spirit is episodic. When the objective for which it was called into being is accomplished, the alliance lapses and the tribe returns to its normal state of disunity." A related feature of tribal organization was the attenuation of cohesiveness as one proceeded toward the outer limits of the tribe: "The social system... becomes weaker where it is greater: the degree of integration decreases as the level of organization increases, and degrees of sociability diminish as fields of social relation broaden. (Sahlins 1968:16)

We see, then, that the essence of the tribe as depicted here consists of the supra-village links or ties between communities—the "pan-tribal sodalities" of Service. But it is important to emphasize that the building blocks from which the tribe is built are *villages*. Furthermore, the usual condition of these villages is one of economic self-sufficiency and political autonomy. Accordingly, it seems fitting to devote the lion's share of our treatment of "tribal culture" to the constituent units that make it up. Then, after having done so, we will be in a better position to examine again those supra-village links which, for certain occasions and under certain conditions, tie villages together to form a tribe. These tribal ties can then be examined to discover what means they provide for taking the next great evolutionary step, namely, the formation of chiefdoms. At this point, the autonomous village has been surpassed, and a categorically new form of socio-political structure has been created.

Autonomous Village Culture

Accordingly, this paper will describe the general features of autonomous village-level culture. In this description, I will emphasize its most widespread characteristics but will also indicate its variant forms. The result will be a picture familiar to anyone who has ever delved into a classic "tribal" ethnography, a picture of a distinctive, cohesive, and well-adapted mode of life which at one time was shared by the ancestors of us all.

While this culture is most typical of the mode of life associated with the Neolithic, it must be kept in mind that many of its elements had already come into being during the preceding Paleolithic period. They formed part of a body of culture traits invented by nomadic foragers over the course of hundreds of thousands of years, and bequeathed by them to their Neolithic heirs.

These pre-Neolithic culture traits, which I call *substratum traits*, were ones that did not require a settled mode of life or an agricultural subsistence in order to arise. We know this because most if not all of them are found among contemporary hunters and gatherers, such as the Yahgan of Tierra del Fuego, the !Kung San of the Kalahari Desert, and the aborigines of central Australia. I list several of these traits here to give some idea of their nature and to impart some small notion of how many of them there are:

> food taboos
> puberty rites
> hunting magic
> cordage
> basketry
> fire making
> body painting
> shamanism
> trade
> warfare
> marriage
> kinship terms
> sexual division of labor
> origin myths
> polygyny
> infanticide
> cremation
> personal souls
> belief in spirits
> an afterworld
> soul loss theory of disease
> witchcraft
> musical instruments
> constellations named
> omens
> numeration

We shall meet many of these traits again in the course of our survey of autonomous village culture.

The Roots of the Neolithic

The rise of settled village life is usually associated with the coming of the Neolithic. In point of fact, though, the first settled villages occurred earlier—during the preceding Mesolithic period in northern Europe, and the Archaic period in the eastern United States. With the decline of big game hunting in Europe, bands of foragers settled down along the coast, and began to rely more heavily on fish as their main source of protein. In North America, a similar shift took place, with riverine resources becoming increasingly important to subsistence. The relative inexhaustibility of fish (compared to that of game) permitted small groups of people who still lacked agriculture to settle securely in one locale.

Originally, the Neolithic period was defined by the presence of ground stone tools, especially axes, which replaced, or at least supplemented, chipped stone tools. Stone axes were the implements which early Neolithic farmers used to fell the forests in order to clear their garden plots. However, it wasn't long before archeologists came to see that agriculture and pottery were even more important than ground stone tools in providing the hallmarks for this period. Agriculture and pottery thus joined stone axes to form the great triumvirate of traits diagnostic of the Neolithic. That having been said, we are now ready to begin our survey of this form of culture.

Village Size

Settled village life, in contrast to a nomadic band existence, was one of the fundamental features of the Neolithic. Along with the expansion of sedentism, the Neolithic saw an increase in community size. A typical Paleolithic band ranged in size from about 20 to 50 persons, and the earliest agricultural villages were probably not much larger. However, Neolithic subsistence, which was based on agriculture, permitted villages to grow significantly in size. A population of 80 to 100 may perhaps be considered typical for early Neolithic villages, but in time, and in certain favored habitats, villages attained a much larger size. A population of several hundred became possible, and in some areas, such as the Southwestern United States, villages sometimes exceeded a population of 1,000.

On the average, though, following the coming of the Neolithic, community size probably only doubled or tripled. However, the increase in the total *number* of communities was much greater than the increase in their average *size*. In fact, villages proliferated greatly. I once estimated (and it was little more than a wild guess) that around 1000 B.C. the number of autonomous villages reached a maximum of about 600,000, the largest number there have ever been at any one time (Carneiro 1978:213). After that, while the sheer number of villages continued to increase, they were being absorbed into chiefdoms and states more quickly than they arose, so that the total number of *autonomous* villages existing in the world as a whole actually declined.

Constraints on Village Size

The size an autonomous village can attain is limited at both ends of the scale. At the lower end, a village may contain as few as 15 persons, but apparently no fewer. When its population threatens to fall below this level (as happened in the case of the Nafukuá in the Upper Xingú region of Brazil), a village finds it difficult to carry on its customary activities, and is likely to join with another village in order to remain above the minimum viable size. Accordingly, when the Nafukuá fell perilously close to this level, they moved in with the neighboring Matipú.

But if the minimum viable size of a village in the Upper Xingú can be as low as 15, this figure is possible only because there is no warfare in the region. Where warfare is present, a village's minimum viable size may be substantially larger. Napoleon Chagnon (1968:40) reports for the Yanomamö of southern Venezuela, among whom warfare is endemic, that minimum village size is around 80. Below this figure, a village would be unable to muster enough fighting men to adequately defend itself against attack.

Warfare, in fact, may be an important factor in leading a village to grow substantially larger. The Kayapó of central Brazil, who until recently were markedly warlike, had villages as large as 600 or 800. And there is evidence to suggest that in seeking military advantage, several Kayapó villages in the past had coalesced into one. The same may have happened in the case of Acoma and other Pueblo villages of the Southwest.

Turning to the upper end of village size, it is safe to say that autonomous villages almost never exceed a population of 2,000, and rarely approach it. Generally speaking, even when it is considerably smaller than this, a growing village has a tendency to fission. If arable land is freely available, and if no strong, overarching political controls exist to keep a village united, then whenever internal strains and stresses reach a certain point, a hostile confrontation may take place between dissident factions, and if the argument between them cannot be resolved, one of the factions will hive off and establish a village of its own.

Village Splitting

Village splitting is a very interesting phenomenon. It has occurred in the life history of practically every autonomous village ever studied, yet it has received virtually no theoretical attention. Basically, village splitting involves two elements which operate in opposite directions: *internal pressure* and *external constraints*. The former is largely the result of an increase in population. The bigger the village, the greater the pressure for it to split. I once speculated that this pressure is proportional, not to the first power of the population, as one might suppose, but to the *square* of the population (Carneiro 1987:100). If this conjecture is true, then a village of 200 persons would not be twice as likely to split as one of 100 persons, but rather, *four* times as likely.

The external constraints that serve to put a brake on village splitting are mainly of two sorts. As I have noted, as long as there is plenty of arable land available, a dissident faction will find it relatively easy to split off and found a new village of its own. But if the surrounding area has become increasingly filled in, and thus land for a new settlement is less readily available, then the village is more likely to patch up its differences and remain intact.

As mentioned above, war is an important determinant of village size. A Yanomamö village may remain at a size larger than its residents find comfortable but which may nevertheless be tolerated because of the advantage that having a large number of warriors confers on the village.

Less obvious factors, such as accusations of witchcraft, may also affect village size. When I revisited the Kuikuru in the Upper Xingú in 1975, I found that about a third of its residents had moved out of the village and into that of the neighboring Yawalapití out of fear of witchcraft allegedly being practiced by a man in their home village.

Settlement Patterns

With regard to settlement pattern, two questions readily arise: What kind of locale does a village choose to settle in? and, How long will it remain there? The principal factors at work in determining the answer to the first question are subsistence requirements, defensibility, and accessibility to water. The interplay of these three factors, along with a few others like being close to clay for pottery making, and other raw materials, determines the location of the site. For almost all autonomous villages, the site chosen must be within or close to arable land. If the group still relies heavily on hunting, then being near game, whose availability is usually more limited than that of arable land, may be the paramount consideration.

These same factors also play a role in determining how long a village can stay in one spot, and, when it does move, how far it will have to go. In forested areas of the world, the prevailing mode of agriculture is slash-and-burn, and since this type of cultivation rapidly depletes the soil, a large reserve of standing forest must be close by if the village hopes to remain in the same locale for very long. If this is not the case, swiddeners may have to pull up stakes and move some distance away where there is an ample amount of forest for their gardens. However, if human settlement is dense throughout a region, relocation within it may prove difficult. The result may be that gardening practices must be modified, and that swiddeners might have to get along with less productive land under bush fallow rather than the forest fallow they previously preferred.

Agricultural demands, though, may not be the most decisive factor in causing a village to move. Among many Amazonian groups who rely heavily on hunting, such as the Amahuaca of eastern Peru, depletion of the game in surrounding forests is a weightier factor in deciding when to move a village. The Amahuaca's cornfields yield harvests large enough to allow a community to remain sedentary several years, but their reliance on hunting is such that in order to stay abreast of the game, they must move their villages well before their agriculture would require it.

Where warfare is intense, villages may be forced to move more often than otherwise in order to keep at a relatively safe distance from enemy attack. The effect of war on the frequency of village movement may, however, be less direct. The fear of enemy raids forces some Amazonian groups to clear their gardens close to the village, thereby reducing the area of land they can safely cultivate. Exhausting available land more quickly thereby, such a village may be forced to relocate sooner.

Village Types

In terms of basic settlement layout, there are two types of villages. The more common type is the nucleated village, often circular in ground plan, with dwellings distributed around a central plaza. In some parts of the world, like certain areas of New Guinea, the "hamlet" type of village tends to

predominate. Here, the houses are distributed irregularly over the landscape, generally at some distance from one another. Hamlets are usually smaller than nucleated villages. A third type of village layout is linear, with dwellings strung out in a line, especially when the residents choose to live along a major river.

Where warfare is a constant threat, village nucleation is the rule since a concentration of its warriors renders a village less vulnerable to attack. The opposite strategy, though, is sometimes employed. The Amahuaca live in small, dispersed communities deep in the forest, and avoid their enemies by frequent relocation of their hamlet-type settlements.

Houses and House Types

The houses of autonomous villages vary greatly in size and shape; less so in building materials. The beehive-shaped hut typical of hunter-gatherers is replaced by a larger, sturdier, more durable dwelling usually holding several nuclear families. Among some Amazonian societies, such as the Tukano and the Witoto, the *maloca* or communal house may be large enough to hold the entire community.

In floor plan, the circular shape of the beehive-shaped hut tends to be replaced by an oval or rectangular ground plan. Poles and thatch are the basic building materials, the pole framework being lashed together with vines. In northern climes, where palm leaves for thatching are not available, alternate materials such as bark or straw may be used for roofing. In much of Mesoamerica, as well as in certain parts of Europe, houses were made of wattle-and-daub. And in arid areas where rain was not a threat to wash away the walls, adobe brick was used in house construction.

The care expended on building a house generally reflects the length of time its occupants expect to occupy it. The Amahuaca, who don't plan on staying in a house more than a year or two, build their dwellings rapidly and flimsily. In fact, a man and his wife are able to erect a house in three days. On the other hand, the Indians of the Upper Xingú, who may live in a house for 20 years, build it sturdily, with a strong understructure of heavy house posts lashed firmly together. However, the thatching of such a house may have to be replaced every few years when it becomes infested with vermin and threadbare.

In addition to dwellings, several other types of structure may be found in a tribal village. A men's house, such as the famous *tambaran* of New Guinea, may occupy the center of the village. Such a structure serves as a clubhouse, where men gather to talk and work, away from the eyes of the women. The men's house may also serve to store ceremonial paraphernalia, such as sacred flutes, or to perform ceremonies, especially if women are forbidden to witness the proceedings.

The men's house may also be a kind of bachelors' quarters, as is the case among such tribes as the Masai of east Africa and the Kayapó of central Brazil, who use it as a place to raise boys away from their mothers, and train them in the martial arts they will pursue as warriors when they grow up.

Other kinds of structures may be found as well, such as cooking sheds, menstrual huts, sweat lodges, *kivas,* and the like.

Subsistence

Agriculture is almost synonymous with autonomous village life. In forested areas, the system of cultivation almost universally employed is that of slash-and-burn. Patches of forest are cut down at the end of the rainy season, the fallen trees allowed to dry out during the dry season, and then burned just before the ensuing rains. The burning is usually incomplete, and the crops are planted between the logs and stumps that remain, giving a swidden its typical messy appearance. Reasonably good crops can be harvested for two or three years, but by then the fertility of the soil has noticeably declined and weeds are becoming a problem, so the garden plot is usually abandoned and a new one cleared.

Root crops are the staple of most swidden cultivators in the tropics: manioc in Amazonia, taro, yams, and sweet potatoes in the Pacific. In much of Mesoamerica, maize was the staple, with beans and squash supplementing the diet. In the Near East and in temperate Europe, grains such as wheat, barley, and oats were the principal crops.

Preparing the Fields

Aboriginally, felling the trees in the process of clearing a garden was done with the stone axe. It was a long and arduous task. Axes soon became dull and had to be resharpened, sometimes being ground down to the nub before being discarded. Digging sticks were used for planting, and in some areas hoes were employed to till the ground. These sometimes had stone blades, but in eastern North America they were often made from a deer scapula attached by thongs to a wooden handle. The plow does not form part of the technology of swidden cultivators, but it was found among a number of peoples in prehistoric Europe as well as in contemporary Asia, regions where villages were relatively permanent and domesticated draft animals were available to provide the necessary traction.

Land Tenure

Slash-and-burn agriculture exerts a decisive influence on the prevailing system of land tenure. Since swiddens are abandoned after only a few years of cultivation, and the land is useless until it regains its fertility some 15 or 20 years later, there is little point in retaining permanent ownership of it. The form of land tenure among swiddeners, therefore, is generally one of *usufruct*, with a family exercising ownership rights over a plot of land only so long as they have it under cultivation. When a plot is abandoned, the land reverts to common ownership. Once the forest has regenerated and the soil beneath it can once again be profitably tilled, the plot can be recleared and planted by anyone who wants to.

Hunting

Once a Neolithic mode of subsistence was established, hunting, while then subordinated to agriculture, still continued to be practiced. The game animals hunted varied widely. Large animals were sought as long as they were available, but as the density of human occupation increased, big game animals were either killed off or driven away, and hunting was reduced to the taking of smaller species. To draw the game nearer, animal cries are imitated, often with great skill and effectiveness, and tracking is also expertly done.

Hunting is most often carried out individually, since a group of hunters moving together in the forest tends to reveal their presence and scare away the game. Exceptions to this occur, however. When herd animals, like the white-lipped peccary, are being hunted, having a good many men cooperate in the chase may increase its chances of success.

The bow-and-arrow is the weapon of choice among most Neolithic hunters, superseding the spear and the *atlatl* of their Paleolithic forebears. In certain parts of the world, though, the bow is supplemented, or even replaced, by other weapons. A prime example of this is provided by the blowgun in Amazonia and Southeast Asia. The effectiveness of this weapon against arboreal game depends on the use of a powerful poison like *curare*, a muscle relaxant, which causes a wounded animal to fall readily out of the trees.

Fishing

For many villages, fishing makes an important contribution to the diet. Since fish are much harder to deplete than game, villages which rely on fishing rather than hunting for their protein (like those of the Shipibo of eastern Peru) are often able to grow large and to remain completely sedentary. Not having to move periodically has the added benefit of allowing agriculture to be developed more fully.

Bows and arrows are used for fishing as well as for hunting, but a variety of other devices are also employed. Among them are harpoons and fish traps, some of which may be set into weirs. The most productive fishing method of all, though, is by poisoning the quiet waters of a lagoon or the dead arm of a stream with a vine such as *barbasco*. The narcotic sap of this vine is extruded by pounding cuttings of it in the water. A ton or more of fish may be taken during a successful fish poisoning expedition.

Domesticated Animals

Most agricultural villages have no domestic animals other than the dog. Significant exceptions, though, do occur. In Melanesia, pigs are commonly raised for food, and in addition play an important role during ceremonies, being killed and eaten in large numbers at that time. Cattle were significant in the Neolithic economy of prehistoric Europe, and continue to be so among many tribes of east Africa. There they supply not only meat, blood, and milk, but also serve as a symbol of wealth. Goats are also raised for consumption in this part of the world.

Political Organization

Autonomous communities usually have a leader or headman. This leader was formerly referred to as a chief, but by convention, the word "chief" is now generally reserved for the powerful political leader of a multi-village chiefdom. The lesser designation of "headman" is meant to convey the notion that the political leader of an autonomous village usually has rather limited authority.

In characterizing the power of a typical Amazonian headman, the ethnologist John M. Cooper is said to have remarked, "One word from the chief, and everyone does as he pleases". And this apt phrase has been quoted many times over. A Kuikuru headman, for instance, when he gives orders at all, gives them "into the air," hoping someone will follow them. Were he to give an order directly to a particular individual, the latter would be more likely to turn around and walk away than to obey. Being regarded as purely human, a typical village headman lacks the supernatural power attributed to a paramount chief. Thus he has none of the aura which gives special weight to the commands of a prominent chief in Polynesia.

The often modest status of a village headman may be reflected in his economic position. The headman of a Lengua village in the Paraguayan Chaco, for example, is likely to be the poorest man in the village since, if he happens to acquire some material possession which someone else lacks, he is expected to part with it.

Chiefly redistribution, once regarded as the principal avenue for a paramount chief to acquire real power, is no longer thought to play that role. Indeed, at the autonomous village level, where redistribution is most characteristic, it serves more as a leveling device than anything else. For example, when a Shavante hunting party in central Brazil returns home, the headman redistributes the catch evenly among all the families in the village, keeping no more than an equal portion for himself. While this may enhance the esteem and affection in which he is held, it adds nothing appreciable to his authority.

Under certain conditions, though, a village headman may temporarily acquire powers well beyond those he ordinarily enjoys. This occurs in times of emergency, especially war. Tribal warfare usually requires—or at least benefits from—centralized leadership and direction. And by taking control of a war party, a headman adds a considerable measure to his ability to command. The well-known "Big Man" of Melanesia is most often thought of as an economic entrepreneur, which he is, but before Australian colonial authorities put a damper on intervillage fighting in New Guinea, the Big Man was, in many cases, a feared war leader as well.

Among some tribes of the Guianas in South America a separate war leader existed, distinct from the regular village headman. In the case of the Yanomamö, though, the two functions are carried out by the same individual. And since his power tends to be significantly augmented during wartime, he is not above instigating a war raid on an enemy village as a means of enhancing his authority.

The size of a village also affects the power of the headman. A larger village, which requires stronger controls and direction, is likely to have a more powerful leader than a smaller one.

Occasionally, the village headman is also a shaman, in which case his supernatural powers, added to his political ones, are likely to gain him greater respect, and probably also a measure of fear.

Law and Order

The criminal justice system prevailing among autonomous communities is not, as a rule, highly developed. One way of stating this is to say that at this level of culture there is generally only *civil* law but no *criminal* law. That is, offenses are not ordinarily regarded as crimes against the society as a whole, but only against a particular individual or his kin. And it is a particular individual, rather than some agent acting in the name of the society, who, having ascertained the identity of the guilty party, metes out punishment.

In a society bound together by ties of kinship, as autonomous villages assuredly are, the notion of collective responsibility and individual retribution are deeply ingrained. Thus if an offense is committed by a member of a particular kin group, such as a clan, all members of that clan may be held liable. By the same token, the victim himself (or a relative) is free to "take the law into his own hands" and avenge himself on the offender on behalf of his clan. In short, then, in most tribal societies self help is generally resorted to, and there are thus no legal institutions worthy of the name.

That does not mean, of course, that most autonomous villages lack any sort of mechanism for punishing violations of tribal norms. Likewise, there are generally means of resolving serious disputes when they arise. If a theft occurs among the Elgeyo of Kenya, a council of elders decides who is guilty of the crime and levies a fine of one goat against the offender. Fines are indicative of a society capable of taking corporate action, and therefore they are commonly levied in societies where the village headman, or a council of elders, exercises more than minimal authority.

If an offense is considered particularly heinous or disruptive to the society, drastic steps may be taken. Murder, especially if it is thought to have been carried out by witchcraft, calls forth a swift and decisive response. Once the culprit is identified, someone acting with the tacit approval of the village may play the role of executioner. I knew a Kuikuru who, having gained the general acquiescence of the village, took it upon himself to execute a man who people believed had killed a number of infants through sorcery.

If an offense is considered serious, but nevertheless falls short of being a capital crime—as, for example, a flagrant case of incest—the persons responsible may be ostracized, or even expelled from the community.

Sometimes the disturbance within a village involves a dispute between factions rather than an outright crime. In this case, some form of duel may take place to try to settle the matter. Among the Yanomamö and the Kayapó, club fights serve this purpose. Violent though they may be—and serious injuries often result from such duels—they are at least a form of *controlled* violence rather than out-and-out, no-holds-barred mayhem. Duels of this sort may result in a temporary lowering of tensions within a village. But if the dispute is deep-seated and fails to be settled by a duel, it may erupt again, in which case one of the dissident factions may leave the community and start a new village elsewhere. Indeed, many an autonomous village has begun life after just such a split (Carneiro 1987:96-97).

Segmentation

The threat of fission is ever present in autonomous villages, especially as they grow larger. The tendency to split may, however, be counteracted in part by the formation of structural sub-units within the society. In his famous book, *Tristes Tropiques,* Claude Lévi-Strauss (1964:230) called the Bororo of south-central Brazil "a society whose complexities seem to spring from a delight in complication for its own sake...." Yet this increase in complexity may not be as puzzling or irrational as it appears. Underlying the development of an intricate, even puzzling social structure, a perfectly intelligible process may be at work. Lineages, clans, moieties, and age grades—that is, societal sub-units of the type so often found in autonomous villages—may be thought of as imparting a kind of *cellular structure* to the society, thus making it better able to hold together in the face of divisive tendencies than if it consisted of merely a single amorphous, undifferentiated aggregate.

A variety of ways exist in which a society may create sub-units within itself, and assign membership in them to everyone in the village. Most societies created such segments through use of the principle of unilineal descent. Distinct social segments could not readily be formed if membership in them were to be assigned bilaterally—the reason being that kinship relations, when traced bilaterally, ramify outward from Ego in every direction. Thus they could hardly form the basis of an easily distinguishable and cohesive social unit.

By contrast, if membership in a social unit is reckoned *either* in the male line *or* the female line, the result is an identifiable, discrete social segment with readily ascertainable boundaries and manageable size. The most common such segment, which societies around the world have created over and over again, is the *clan*. But the unilineal clan is not the smallest social segment above the nuclear family. The smallest such segment (apart from the extended family) is the *lineage*. The lineage is the backbone of a clan, being composed of kinsmen related through the male line (patrilineal) or the female line (matrilineal). The lineage is always the precursor of the clan. It is formed, almost automatically, when there is a unilocal rule of post-marital residence, either matrilocal or patrilocal, which brings together and aligns persons who are related through either males or females. As an example, a lineage structure (patrilineal, in this case) characterizes the Yanomamö, who usually occupy relatively small villages of 100 persons or less, and who have not "graduated" to a full-blown clan structure.

Over time, though, as the number of descendants of the founder or senior head of a lineage grows, the lineage naturally increases in membership and expands in scope. Within a few generations, all knowledge may be lost of who the founder of the lineage actually was, and before long, a legendary figure may be assigned that role. With its founder thus enshrined in a mythical past, and its membership growing in size and crystallizing in structure, the lineage reaches the point at which it warrants being called a clan. After even more generations (as among the Siuai of the Solomon Islands), a clan may be thought of as having, not a human founder at all, but an animal as its totemic ancestor, whom clan members hold sacred and are forbidden to kill or eat.

Clans do not arise as single entities; they always form and grow in multiples. Thus a good-sized village may have half a dozen clans. And as clans continue to grow in size, and the village in which they started splits and splits again, the same set of clans may eventually be represented in more than one village.

The most common function of the clan is to regulate marriage. Almost by definition, clans are exogamous units which thereby create a mutual dependence among their members since they must seek a spouse in a clan different from their own. Clans sometimes have other functions too. In a large settled village, clans may be land-owning units, the clan elders parceling out land for garden plots among its members as the need arises. Clans may also perform various rituals and ceremonies specific to them. Some well-established clans may be said to have a *corporate structure*, with distinct leadership and designated functions.

Another form of social unit is much like the clan in some respects but not in all. This is the *moiety*, one of two equivalent divisions into which an entire village may be divided. Membership in a moiety is usually assigned unilineally, but this is not always the case. Within a Kayapó village, for instance, moiety membership is sometimes based on whether one lives in the eastern or western side of the village, or whether he was born during the rainy season or the dry season. Almost any dichotomous principle will do to establish a system of moieties. The important thing is that it divide the village into more or less equal halves, and that everyone be assigned to one or another of them.

When moieties are exogamous, they serve to regulate marriage, just as clans do, but they often have other functions as well. For example, Kayapó moieties provide opposing teams for such competitive sports as field hockey and log racing. And they also have complementary and reciprocal functions, such as burying each other's dead. Now, each moiety is of course perfectly capable of burying its own dead, but by assigning this function to the opposite moiety, an artificial but nonetheless useful dependence is created between them. And this dependence operates to integrate the village and counteract the divisive forces which are always at work within it, especially if the village is a large one.

Finally, as a further instance of segmentation, we can cite the formation of age grades. These segments tend to arise in militaristic societies such as the Masai of east Africa and the Kayapó of central Brazil. A system of age grades creates a series of cohorts of young men who, as boys, were trained together in the men's house, and as adults, form the warrior class of the society.

Division of Labor

Virtually all autonomous villages have a subsistence economy in which each family produces and consumes its own food. In such a society, no great accumulation of property is possible, and there is little in the way of craft or service specialization. In activities involving the obtaining of food, the division of labor along sex lines is universal. Men hunt and fish, women gather, prepare and cook the food, and raise the children. Within the category of agricultural pursuits, though, the participation of the two sexes varies considerably. Although the line of demarcation is not nearly as clear-cut here as in, say, hunting, there is nonetheless a rather striking correlation to be noted. At least in Amazonia, I have found virtually no exception to the rule that if hunting, or warfare, or both are important male activities, then it is the women who tend the gardens and harvest the crops. However, if neither hunting nor warfare is important, then the men will do the bulk of the agricultural labor. The one exception to this rule is that in clearing a tract of forest to make a garden plot, the men invariably do the heavy work of felling the trees.

The Possibility of a Surplus

Whether swidden cultivators can produce a true surplus of food was, for a long time, much debated. It now seems clear, though, that with relatively little extra effort swiddeners are *technically* capable of producing a good 15 or 20 percent more food than they need for their own consumption. This can be inferred from the fact that when villages become incorporated into states, and are subject to a regular system of taxation, a surplus of this magnitude is usually wrung out of them to fulfill their tax obligations.

As long as villages remain autonomous, however, neither the economic incentives nor the political coercion necessary to generate a surplus of food appears to exist. We must distinguish, though, between a surplus over the full yearly cycle of cultivation and that produced over shorter periods of time. Seasonal surpluses can, in fact, be regularly produced. After a good harvest, a Trobriander's yam hut may be filled to overflowing with tubers which will take weeks to consume. During the dry season, a Kuikuru family will harvest thousands of manioc tubers which, once processed into flour, will last them through much of the ensuing rainy season.

With a crop more easily storable than tuberous roots, even more of a seasonal surplus can be accumulated. Thus, with maize as their principal crop, an Amahuaca family can pick and store 25,000 to 30,000 ears of corn at harvest time, enough to last as much as a full year.

Leisure Time

The relatively high productivity of swidden agriculture, coupled with the moderate labor demands it entails, means that tribal villagers relying on it usually have a considerable amount of time left over after subsistence. Some of this time may be spent relaxing or loafing, but much of it is spent in a variety of other pursuits, from ceremonial performances, to arts and crafts, to body decoration. One need look only at the layer upon layer of ornaments on the person of an Amazonian Indian or a New Guinea native to see hundreds of hours of labor congealed into ostentatious display.

But here a caveat must be entered. The old saying that "men work from sun to sun, but women's work is never done," holds true of the primitive world just as it does of Western societies—at least in so far as women's work is concerned. But in the primitive world, men usually do have more disposable time left to them after finishing their subsistence chores than do their counterparts in industrial societies. In fact, on the average, a Kuikuru man spends only about 3 hours a day on subsistence.

Specialization

Full-time craft specialists are all but unknown among tribal societies. The itinerant blacksmiths of east Africa are the only exceptions that come readily to mind, and their origin is clearly post-Neolithic. Part-time specialization, though, is more common. Among the Kuikuru, the making of canoes, stools, and sacred flutes, for example, is limited to only a few men in the village.

Specialization by sex, though, is extremely common if not universal. Women are almost always the potters in the primitive world. It is they whom archeologists have to thank for providing the most widespread and enduring evidence of Neolithic culture left in the ground for their spades to unearth. And women are generally the weavers, too, wherever that craft is practiced as a domestic art. The making of baskets is not so clearly assigned to one sex or the other, even within the same region, like Amazonia. Here some types of baskets are made by the men, others by the women.

Property

With no powerful chiefs to exact tribute, and with almost every adult having to engage in subsistence, there is little opportunity for anyone in a tribal village to amass a significant amount of wealth. To be sure, some men are more highly skilled or more industrious than others, and they generally have more and better possessions. The wealthiest man in the village is likely to be the shaman, who functions mainly as a curer. He is the principal (if not the only) service specialist in the community, and is well paid for his work—even handsomely if he manages to effect a particularly difficult cure.

In tribal Africa, where cattle are a visible token of one's wealth, building up a large herd through careful breeding or shrewd dealing may raise a man well above his fellows in terms of the property he owns. And, as among most societies, prestige comes with wealth. Rarely, though, is a person's status so much higher than that of anyone else in the village, either in material possessions or in social standing, that any real class distinctions can be said to exist.

Inheritance

One reason for the lack of accumulation of wealth in primitive societies is the general failure of property to be transmitted from one generation to the next. It is a striking fact that at this level of culture the inheritance of goods is all but lacking. Why should this be? Two principal reasons can be offered. First, there is a great reluctance among the living to claim ownership of objects that belonged to the dead. This is so since the deceased's soul, which has now become a malevolent ghost, is easily angered and quick to wreak vengeance on those of the living who may have displeased it. And secondly, as a Kuikuru once solemnly informed me, a good person does not want to be constantly reminded of his late lamented father or mother, as he would be if he held on to their possessions. Thus, among tribal peoples far and wide, at a person's death his property is generally either buried with him or destroyed.

A great threshold in economic evolution was crossed when, instead of being thus disposed of, a dead man's property began to be passed on to his surviving kin. When this point was reached, eco-

nomic considerations can be said to have begun to seriously rival supernatural ones in the native view of things. This step, in its incipient form, can be seen in a few tribal societies. The Kuikuru, for instance, do not transmit material possessions through inheritance, but do pass down the ownership of *piquí* fruit trees from father to son. And among the Flathead of Montana, the prohibition against inheritance was sometimes circumvented when a seriously ill man, in anticipation of death, conveyed his property to his son before he died.

Trade

Within autonomous villages, material objects are often exchanged. Such exchanges may occur when someone lacks an item and someone else has a spare and is ready to trade. Or exchange may be based on the slight amount of craft specialization that occurs in some villages, in which case a person may produce more of a certain item than he needs for himself, and is quite ready to trade the surplus items to others.

Trade *between* villages, in contrast to that *within* them, is based largely on village specialization in the making of a variety of items. This in turn may depend on differences in the kinds of raw materials available to each village. The Kuikuru, for instance, make a kind of shell necklace called an *uguká* from a certain species of land snail which is found in their territory, but not in that of the Kamayurá to the north. The latter, for their part, make particularly fine bows from the wood of the *majafi* tree, which does not grow near the Kuikuru village. The two groups exchange these two items even-up, one *uguká* for one *majafi* bow.

In northern Amazonia, a marked degree of village specialization exists in various kinds of artifacts. One group specializes in making blowguns, another in the manufacture of *curare*, a third in the hollowing out of dugout canoes, and a fourth in turning out manioc graters. Through trade, sometimes over long distances, each village is able to gain access to the specialized products of the others.

In some parts of the world elaborate patterns of intertribal exchange have been established. The Trobrianders and other islanders living off the east coast of New Guinea participate in a highly formalized series of exchanges called the *kula* ring. One group of islanders sails clockwise in their canoes, exchanging necklaces with their trading partners on the islands they visit. The other group of islanders sails counter-clockwise, supplying their trading partners with cowrie shell armbands.

Medium of Exchange

When trade is frequent and involves the exchange of a variety of products, the rudiments of money may be dimly discerned. Initially, some decorative item, such as an *uguká* necklace, or a wampum belt, or a string of dentalium shells—something that is particularly valued and commonly traded—may become a standard by which the value of other objects is measured. Thus, among the Kuikuru one bow, one hammock, one stool, and one pot are all said to be equivalent in value to one *uguká*.

It is a short step from an object's serving as a standard of value to its becoming a medium of exchange, being freely traded for a variety of other goods, as is the case with the *uguká*. But the final step in the evolution of money, in which an object no longer has intrinsic aesthetic or ornamental value, but is used only for buying and selling, is well beyond the tribal level of economics.

Kinship

As indicated earlier, kinship is the armature around which autonomous communities are organized, as well as the glue that holds its members together. Villages make up true kinship networks, binding people together and prescribing many of the forms of interpersonal behavior that regulate their lives. Reciprocal obligations between certain sets of kinsmen are common, as, for example, a pattern of gift giving between brothers-in-law among the Kuikuru.

Every one of the 145 persons in the Kuikuru village employed a kinship term for everyone else, even though he might not be able to trace the actual genealogical connection between them. The behavior of persons toward one another may not always be governed by kinship rules, but at least these rules establish a well-recognized set of expected interactions among relatives.

Marriage

Smaller villages tend to have a rule of local exogamy, but as villages grow larger, this rule is relaxed, and endogamous marriages become, first permissible, and then common. In the Kuikuru village, which, as just mentioned, had 145 residents, some 70 percent of marriages were endogamous.

Cross-cousin marriage is extremely widespread among village communities. Where a rule of local exogamy prevails, a man must seek a wife in another village. Since under this rule cross cousins ordinarily live in different villages, their marriage serves to strengthen the ties between their respective villages. At marriage, the groom must often pay a bride price to his father-in-law. In east Africa, the usual bride price—the *lobola*—consists of several head of cattle. Among the Kuikuru, a groom is supposed to give his parents-in-law various shell necklaces and waistbands, but if he does not own such items, this obligation may be commuted to that of bride service. In that case, the groom helps his father-in-law clear and plant his manioc gardens.

In an exogamous community with matrilocal residence, the customary residence rule may be waived in the case of a headman, thereby obviating the necessity of his having to move out of his natal village to find a wife.

Regardless of what type of marriage may be contracted, it is never simply a union of two individuals. It is also an association between two families. If one spouse dies, the levirate and sororate, very commonly practiced in primitive societies, not only provide widows and widowers with new spouses, but also restore the affinal link between families temporarily broken by the death.

While the roughly equal sex ratio in all societies dictates that most marriages will be monogamous, polygyny is also generally permitted. A polygynous man will usually have no more than two or three wives, but among a few large tribes, such as the Tupinambá, a powerful chief might have as many as a dozen.

Population Control and Demographic Growth

In addition to the widespread post-partum taboo on sexual relations between husband and wife, population limitation occurs in tribal societies through the practices of abortion and infanticide. The latter, it should be noted, is invariably a private family matter; the opinion of the rest of the community is not sought, nor is its permission required.

Female infanticide is sometimes said to be a way in which a village consciously seeks to hold its population below carrying capacity. However, while this may be an *effect* of this form of infanticide, it is not likely to be its *cause*. Population limitation within a village is the result of an aggregate of separate individual actions, not of a concerted societal policy.

Over the course of centuries, the average annual rate of population growth among tribal peoples is very low—something on the order of 1/10 of one percent. However, for smaller populations and over shorter periods of time, this rate may be substantially higher. For example, for the Shamatari, a Yanomamö sub-group, Napoleon Chagnon (1974:129) found that over the last century they had increased from one village to 17, and, assuming an initial population for the parent village of about 200, and given their current population of some 2,700, the average annual rate of growth of the Shamatari has been about 2 percent.

Death and Disposal of the Body

Despite how fast a village may be growing, death, of course, inevitably overtakes every one of its members. And for the survivors, a death is always an occasion for lamentation and concern. On the one hand, there is much grieving for the deceased, but at the same time there is an abiding dread of the dead man's ghost. No matter how beloved he was in life, he is greatly feared in death. Accordingly, a solemn ceremony takes place which not only allows the survivors to mourn, but also helps ensure that the ghost of the deceased will not linger around the village and haunt the living.

The ways of disposing of a corpse are legion. Burial and cremation are the principal ones, but each of these in turn has a number of variants. For example, there may be secondary urn burial, in which the skeleton of the deceased, once the body has been cremated, is disarticulated, and the bones placed in a pot for final burial. There is also the striking ritual of funerary endocannibalism. As practiced by the Amahuaca and the Yanomamö of Amazonia, the body of the deceased is cremated, the bones ground into powder, mixed with banana drink, and imbibed by the dead man's close relatives. In this way, it is believed, the remains of the dear departed become incorporated into the bodies of its surviving kinsmen.

Religion and Mythology

Ritual practices surrounding the disposal of a corpse bring us to the subject of religion. The religious beliefs of most tribal peoples center around a bewildering variety of supernatural beings. Few such societies can be said to believe in a single "high god." Rather, most of them believe in a profusion of "bush spirits." These spirits are often associated with particular animals, especially noxious or dangerous ones, such as poisonous snakes or jaguars. However, when drawn for the benefit of the ethnographer who wants to know what they look like, these spirits often turn out to be represented as anthropomorphic.

Bush spirits are widely regarded as malevolent, and while they can be seen and interrogated with impunity by the shaman, should an ordinary person suddenly come face to face with one of them, he will surely sicken and quite possibly die. Some of these spirits are more distinctive and well defined than others, as is true of the *kachinas* of the Hopi, who have special powers and designated functions.

Another class of supernatural beings is that of culture heroes. During the time they walked on earth, these mythological figures were conspicuous for their creative acts, giving rise to the prominent features of the earth, such as rivers, lakes, and mountains, and to phenomena like night and day and the seasons of the year. They also bestowed the gift of fire on mankind as well as instructing people how to hunt, how to plant, how to mate, and the like. Some culture heroes are thought of as master artificers, who taught human beings all manner of arts and crafts. But then, after making the world ready for human habitation, they rose into the sky to become the sun, the moon, or various planets and constellations. And there in the heavens these culture heroes continue to reside, remote and aloof, still observing life on earth but no longer taking any part in it.

The sky is also the location where most tribal peoples place the afterworld. Generally speaking, it is conceived of as a village (much like the one people dwell in here on earth) where departed souls go after death. Unlike the heaven or hell of "civilized" societies, the afterworld of most tribal peoples is not a place where virtue is rewarded and evil punished. More often than not, a soul's fate is determined, not by how it lived but by how it died. For example, in addition to the regular village of the dead, where most souls are destined to go, the Kuikuru believe there is a special village in the sky for the souls of those who died by poisoning, and another one for those who died a violent death.

Witchcraft and Magic

Returning to the world of the living, we find that one of the greatest sources of anxiety in life—a concern which repeatedly disturbs the tranquility of a village—is the fear of witchcraft. The belief in witches and a dread of them is universal in primitive society. The great irony is that witchcraft is much more often alleged than actually practiced. Thus the most disruptive fear among tribal peoples is one of their own creation.

Magic is also universal in village societies, and in the form of exuvial or sympathetic magic, is the instrument by which witchcraft is most commonly thought to be practiced. Accusations of witchcraft are generally leveled at persons who are disliked or regarded as antisocial. Thus, at the same time that witchcraft is disruptive of people's lives, the fear of being thought a witch also serves to make a person adhere more closely to the norms of his society, and thus promotes the integration of the village.

Another way of fostering compliance with social norms is through the operation of taboos. While breaking a taboo often acts only against the transgressor himself, it is sometimes said to result in an outcome damaging to the entire community, thus adding pressure on individuals not to violate it.

Shamanism

At the center of much supernatural belief and practice in tribal villages is the shaman, an all but universal figure in such societies. The shaman is primarily a curer. With the aid of spirits which he can freely summon and interrogate through the taking of drugs like tobacco or *ayahuasca*, incessant drumming, or some similar way of inducing a trance, the shaman is able to effect a cure. The two most frequently cited causes of ailments in primitive societies are the loss of a person's soul and the presence of an intrusive object within his body. By means of an impressive performance, the shaman contrives to recover a lost or stolen soul, while intrusive objects are either sucked or drawn out of a patient's body by skillful sleight of hand.

A shaman may carry out a number of other tasks as well. He may be asked to find lost or stolen objects, and is thought to be able to foretell the future and to identify witches. He may also help defend a village by directing sorcery against its enemies. Thus, through his magical power, a Yanomamö shaman is said to kill the souls of infants in enemy villages. A shaman, then, is not only a figure who commands respect within his village, but one who is also likely to elicit fear.

Nevertheless, a shaman's life is not altogether secure and serene. There are occupational hazards to worry about. So well versed is he in controlling the dangerous forces of the supernatural that he is

often a prime candidate for suspicion when someone in the village is thought to have died from witchcraft. In that case, all of his powers may not be enough to prevent his being killed in an act of retaliation by an angry relative of the deceased.

Ceremonies

The social life of a tribal village is enlivened by the performance of a variety of ceremonies. Often these ceremonies are said to be owned by, or at least associated with, particular spirits who may in some cases be impersonated during the ceremonies themselves, as occurs, for example, among the Hopi. Some are performed for a specific reason, such as bringing rain, ensuring a good harvest, or for marking a particular occasion, such as the winter solstice. Other reasons may be purely secular and recreational, with the ceremony being performed with no other objective than the enjoyment of the participants and onlookers.

Another class of ceremonies are those which serve to mark changes in the life cycle. The Kuikuru have a ritual called *tipoño* in which prepubescent boys have their ears pierced and their names changed. But more common—in fact well nigh universal in primitive societies—are puberty rites, which often involve the seclusion of the initiate. This is the case in the Upper Xingú in central Brazil, where a pubescent boy or girl may be expected to remain inside a partitioned section of the house for a year or even longer. In many parts of the world, puberty rites involve some sort of ordeal— a test of courage, hardihood, and endurance, after the successful conclusion of which the boy or girl is regarded as an adult. In the Guianas, a particularly rigorous puberty rite is the ant ordeal, the initiate being subjected to having a mat, with stinging ants trapped within it, placed against his chest, the expectation being that he will endure the pain of dozens of stings without flinching.

Some peoples, especially in west Africa and New Guinea, have men's secret societies in which adult males are made privy to arcane knowledge forbidden to the rest of the community. In a few cases, what the initiates are told, after a prolonged and arduous series of tests, is that the closely guarded secret of the society is—*that there is no secret!*

Intervillage Relations

While most ceremonies among autonomous communities are performed within the village for the enjoyment of its residents, some are *inter*village in nature, and may be designed to, or at least have the effect of, bringing neighboring villages closer together. One such ceremony is the *kuarup*, or feast of the dead, of the Upper Xingú. This ceremony cycles among the nine villages of the region, being performed in a different one every year. Its stated purpose is to commemorate those members of the chiefly line of that village who have died since it last hosted the ceremony. Decorated posts are erected for each person being memorialized, and the men of the visiting villages take turns dancing around the posts and performing certain rituals. By dawn of the next day, the commemorative part of *kuarup* is over. Then follow intervillage wrestling matches from which will emerge a champion wrestler of the whole region, a distinction which a man will bear proudly throughout his life.

The formal part of *kuarup* having concluded, informal trading begins among friends of the various villages. At the same time, any girl of the host village who is near the end of her puberty seclusion is trotted out for all the young bucks from the visiting villages to behold and admire. Girls are now at their most marriageable, and betrothals may be arranged at this time. Although animosities between members of different villages may surface during the wrestling phase of *kuarup,* the net effect of the ceremony is to cement the bonds of friendship that exist among the villages.

Warfare

Relations between neighboring villages are not always so peaceful, however. Indeed, warfare between adjacent villages is not uncommon. Nor are kinship ties necessarily a barrier to warfare any more than propinquity is. The initial causes of war at the tribal level may be such familiar occurrences as murder, witchcraft, and wife stealing. Yet many war raids stem from causes long since forgotten. All that may be retained is the sense that the contending villages are "traditional enemies," between which there is a recurring cycle of revenge killings.

Intervillage "wars" are often little more than raids or skirmishes in which only a few men take part, rather than mass conflicts in which the entire body of adult males of both villages are arrayed against each other. As a rule, war raids take the form of pre-dawn surprise attacks, followed by a quick retreat, and result in relatively few casualties. Occasionally, though, warfare becomes a more serious and deadly business in which heads are lopped off and brought home as trophies. Associated with intense tribal warfare among some

societies is the practice of cannibalism, the bodies of slain enemies being brought back to the village to be cooked and eaten. A more benign effect of war, however, is the frequent capture of women as wives.

The effect of warfare among autonomous communities is generally the dispersal of villages rather than their aggregation. On occasion, though, smaller, weaker villages which have been the repeated victims of raiding, may coalesce into a larger village for the purpose of mutual defense. More common than outright coalescence, though, is the formation of military alliances in which the villages cooperate in time of war but still retain their separateness and autonomy. These alliances are usually transitory, lasting no longer than the duration of hostilities. And when these coalitions reform at a later date, they may well involve a different set of villages. Nonetheless, as we will see shortly, in these alliances, ephemeral as they may be, lie the seeds out of which will grow wider, stronger, more permanent alliances, leading ultimately to the emergence of chiefdoms.

Travel and Transport

The swift movement of raiding parties is facilitated in some parts of the world by the use of watercraft. For probably the whole of the Paleolithic, human travel and transport was entirely on foot. With the coming of the Mesolithic/Archaic period, however, and certainly with that of the Neolithic, canoes make their appearance. The ground stone axe, the distinctive tool of the Neolithic, made possible the hollowing out of large tree trunks which served as the hull of dugout canoes. Before that, however, there were probably bark canoes, made from the thin outer layer of the birch tree in northeastern North America, and the inch-thick bark of the *jatobá* tree in lowland South America.

Canoes made long range travel possible, and in a region like Amazonia, with hundreds of navigable rivers, they enabled people to disperse widely over the entire basin.

Ethnographic Analogy and Archaeological Reconstruction

This is a volume by archaeologists for archaeologists. What, then, is a chapter on ethnology by an ethnologist doing here? The answer is that anthropology is a unitary science, and that ethnologists and archaeologists have the same ultimate goal: the presentation and interpretation of a culture (or cultures) as fully as it can be done. In this joint endeavor, ethnologists enjoy an advantage over their archaeological brethren. The cultures they work with are alive and intact functioning systems, and ethnologists are able to study them in intricate detail. Archaeologists, on the other hand, deal with cultures that are no longer living, breathing entities. They have died, and have left behind them only a very partial material record of what they were like when they were flourishing societies. The archaeologist, then, is faced with a severe challenge. He must try to reconstruct an extinct culture from the small fragments of it still left in the ground.

Faced with this difficult task, the archaeologist is obliged to seek whatever help he can. His published reports are only in part *observations*. To a large extent what he can say about his extinct cultures are *inferences*. And in drawing these inferences his foremost ally is, unavoidably, the ethnologist. The vast corpus of published writings by ethnologists provides, in exhaustive detail, information covering the full gamut of existing cultures. How can the archaeologist not avail himself of this treasure trove of fact and theory?

There is general agreement that living and extinct cultures are not totally separate and distinct entities. They were both produced by human beings who, at least over the last 30,000 years or more, were essentially like those living today. And the conditions under which extinct cultures were created were much like those still found somewhere in the world today. Thus the archaeologist, by studying the ethnographies of living societies, can derive a fair notion of what elements of culture that are archaeologically unrecoverable, were associated with those elements that are in fact recoverable.

To be sure, there is rarely a strict one-to-one relationship between, say, a trait in settlement pattern and one in kinship structure, or between burial practices and soul beliefs. But ethnology provides at least some *suggestion* of what goes with what, of the *range* of manifestations that can be expected to have occurred within a given aspect of extinct cultures. And by availing himself of this knowledge, the archaeologist can broaden his horizons and add immeasurably to his arsenal of interpretive devices. He can, in short, be much better able to put flesh on the bones of his archaeological discoveries.

Nevertheless, the extent to which the archaeologist may draw on ethnographic analogy, and indeed even the *validity* of doing so, remains a matter of dispute within the profession. Let us look briefly at some of the arguments that have been raised in this regard.

A leading archaeologist of an earlier period, V. Gordon Childe (1946:250), made it clear that "[t]he ethnographers' picture of a contemporary savage [hunter and gatherer] or barbarian [agricultural village] society can with due reserve be used to supplement the archaeologists' picture" of extinct societies at the same general level of culture. And this attitude was retained, and indeed reinforced, with the coming of the "new archaeology." As Robert Dunnell (1980:77), noted, "If one thing is clear about the new archaeology it is that it was intended to be explicitly modeled on sociocultural anthropology ...."

But not all archaeologists welcomed this development. William Longacre (1970:136), for example, asserted, with what strikes me as a touch of wounded pride: "The role of ethnographic analogy in [archaeological] interpretation has been called into serious question lately, especially with respect to the interpretation of behavioral and organizational phenomena. It we *base* our interpretation on the ethnographic present, then we are saying we have nothing to learn from the past."

And has pride become hubris when Norman Yoffee (1993:67) asserts: " ... the logic of the urban implosion and subsequent political explosion in Uruk [in ancient Mesopotamia] cannot begin to be accounted for through a series of ethnographic analogies masquerading as social evolutionary theory. What is needed is archaeological analyses of these archaeological data and the confidence that appropriate theory can be constructed by archaeologists to do the job"?

Well, I would argue just the opposite. There is no such thing as archaeological theory as a separate and distinct entity, isolated and insulated from outside contamination. What there is, or should be, is *anthropological* theory, in which archaeologists and ethnologists are full and trusting partners, setting aside petty jealousies, neither one claiming exclusivity or dominance. Only then can further progress be made toward a fuller and deeper understanding of extinct cultures.

Ethnographic Analogy Put to Use

The preceding pages have presented a broad survey of what autonomous village culture, yes, *tribal* culture, is like as seen through the eyes of an ethnologist. One of the principal differences between ethnologists and archaeologists is that ethnologists study a living culture *synchronically,* at essentially a single point in time, whereas archaeologists generally study a culture *diachronically,* as it changed over time. The present-day archeologist, unlike what was often the case half a century ago, is not content to present a mere chronological succession of projectile points or ceramic styles. He looks at the changes in forms and features observable in the archaeological record as a *process.* And, as argued above, he needs to have some notion of the *dynamics* of that process. Here the ethnologist, and the ethnohistorian, again come to his assistance.

Let us take a concrete problem: the origin of the chiefdom. From an examination of grave goods, settlement patterns, architecture, and the like, an archaeologist may be able to infer, with some degree of confidence, that he is in the presence of a chiefdom. But *how* did this chiefdom come to be? Specifically, by what process was a groups of autonomous villages welded into a multi-village polity? The artifacts and features the archaeologist has unearthed will not give him the answer to that question. He must turn to other sources of information—to ethnographic and ethnohistorical accounts—in order to be able to form a coherent and convincing notion of how this, as well as other chiefdoms, arose.

The ethnological and ethnohistorical record bearing on the origin of the chiefdom is scattered but illuminating and persuasive. From it can be gleaned innumerable examples of how chiefdoms functioned, and, with a close examination of the evidence, how they arose. Elman Service and others have complained that no Western observer ever actually *saw* a chiefdom emerge from among a group of autonomous villages. Even if true (and I've always regarded this as an overstatement), written records exist of cultures at every gradation in the process of political evolution, from tiny villages to full-fledged chiefdoms. These accounts serve as 'still frames' which, when carefully collated and conjoined, come very close to revealing a detailed moving picture of the actual historical process of chiefdom formation.

The above is an example, not only of the use of ethnographic analogy, but, more broadly, of the application of the *comparative method.* One or a few ethnographic examples may not yield an answer to an archaeologist's question. But many such examples, examined together, are likely to shed considerable light upon it. Now, let me anticipate the usual criticism. Just because the comparative method may have been used uncritically in the past, does not mean that it cannot be used with

critical acumen and valid results today. There is every reason to believe that through its careful and judicious use, an archaeologist should be able to supplement and enrich the knowledge his unaided spade has provided him.

Tribal Organization

Early in this chapter, when citing the discussions of Service and Sahlins of the nature of the tribe, we saw that tribal structure was not something totally distinct and removed from that of autonomous villages. Rather, it was something *superadded* to it. This structure consisted of the means by which villages reached out beyond their borders and linked up with related neighboring villages. Now, the question may be raised, How many of these links do there have to be, and how close a bond must they forge, for a 'tribe' to be formed? This is a central question, and not an easy one to resolve.

To indicate the difficulties involved, take, for example, the Upper Xingú region of central Brazil. Nine Indian villages are located in this region, representing three different language families, Carib, Arawak, and Tupí-Guaraní. Yet despite the large linguistic gulf that divides them, these nine villages are alike in many respects. They intermarry, they exchange specialized items in trade, they compete in sporting events, and they hold joint ceremonies, the sorts of activities which Service labeled 'pan-tribal sodalities'. Yet Amazonian ethnologists who work in this area never refer to these nine Xinguano villages as constituting a tribe.

Let us look at another Amazonian example. Neighboring Yanomamö villages frequently intermarry, invite each other to feasts, and form military alliances. Yet these links are not of such a nature as to make the ethnographers who have studied the Yanomamö refer to the village associations thus formed as a tribe.

So where do we draw the line between 'autonomous village' and 'tribe'? Although this answer may seem to be an evasion, perhaps it is unnecessary to do so. Perhaps we can settle for some such summary statement as the following: 'Autonomous villages', as dealt with in this chapter, are never fully autonomous. They do not live in complete isolation and independence of each other. There is always some degree of contact and association between adjacent villages, and this association varies along a continuum. It may be minimal and sporadic, or it may be frequent, intimate, and prolonged. Somewhere along the line—at a point each observer is free to choose for himself—enough of a bond may exist among a collection of villages for them to be referred to as a tribe.

As noted above, tribal structure is something superadded to the culture of autonomous villages. It does not *subtract* from that culture. Indeed, it merely *adds* to it. Thus, the picture of autonomous village culture painted above can also be said to be that of *tribal culture*.

The Transition

I have made it a point to emphasize that autonomous village culture represents a *stage* in sociopolitical evolution. The very notion of a stage implies that a different form preceded it, and that a different form is to follow. So it was with the autonomous village. I would like now to review, in brief compass, the career of the autonomous village, from its inception to its replacement by a more evolved form of society.

With the coming of agriculture, the band of Paleolithic times was replaced, in most parts of the world, by the village as the basic unit of human settlement. As a social and subsistence unit, the village endured for millennia. Indeed, in a few places it still survives. And not just in New Guinea and Amazonia. A village of *fellahin* in modern-day Egypt, for example, is much the same today as it was in pre-pharaonic times. Agricultural villages have thus long remained the basic food-producing units of human society. What they have lost—never to be regained—is their political autonomy.

The important question in studying social dynamics—important to ethnologists and archaeologists alike—is how autonomous villages lost their individual sovereignties and became incorporated into larger multi-village chiefdoms. The transition could not have been an easy one to make, since it took several thousand years to achieve.

History and ethnography bear witness to the fact that no political entity, be it a band or a village, a chiefdom or a state, ever willingly gives up its sovereignty. It has to be coerced into doing so—either by outright conquest or by intimidation. And the instrument of coercion *par excellence* is, of course, war. It is in war that we find the one mechanism powerful enough to overcome local autonomies and weld separate villages into larger political entities.

The wars which actually achieved this transcendent step are seldom recorded in written history, since the participants in them were generally preliterate societies. Nevertheless, instances of such wars can be found in a few accounts dating from a time when Europeans were first becoming acquainted with the non-Western world. For example, chiefdom formation was described, if only sketchily and without appreciation of its full importance, among the Caribs of northern Venezuela and the Tupinambá of the coast of Brazil. Villages of these societies, which fought fiercely and frequently among themselves, often formed intervillage alliances of the kind described above. Ordinarily, such alliances were forged during wartime, only to break up again when hostilities ceased. However, in the two regions just cited, these alliances sometimes endured beyond the end of hostilities, continuing on into peacetime.

It seems to have been through the agency of a particularly strong war leader that such alliances were able to endure. The power that such a leader gained during a successful military campaign evidently proved strong enough so that he could not be forced to relinquish it at war's end. Military success brought the war chief wealth and prestige, to be sure, but more important, it also served to establish him as the permanent political leader—the paramount chief—of a newly-formed, multivillage polity. This political entity, in which several subordinate villages were ruled over by a single powerful leader, was the *chiefdom* (Carneiro 1998).

The creation of chiefdoms was not, however, always a permanent evolutionary step. During their early days especially, chiefdoms not infrequently fragmented back into their constituent units, namely, autonomous villages. But a large enough number of chiefdoms survived disintegration and established themselves more or less permanently to have created a genuine new stage in socio-political development.

In many respects, autonomous villages were thereby transformed. Politically, the village was no longer a *whole*, but now formed only a *part* of a new, more inclusive whole. As a subordinate unit, it was no longer able, without interference, to determine its own affairs. No longer, for example, could it move its location freely whenever it wished. It first had to seek permission from the paramount chief (Carneiro 1987:98). Moreover, the members of a village were now subject to the demands of the paramount chief for tribute or taxation. And in addition to this, the village was generally expected to provide a contingent of warriors whenever the chief chose to go to war.

Beneath all these changes, though, most of the features that characterized community life at the autonomous village stage remained essentially the same. The multitude of culture traits that Neolithic villages had inherited from their Paleolithic forebears they in turn passed on to their more highly evolved descendants. No doubt, by the time they were transmitted to chiefdom-level cultures, many of these traits had been greatly elaborated and even transformed. Nonetheless, in many cases, the earlier tribal-level forms of these traits were still clearly distinguishable.

It is these widespread and enduring features of autonomous village culture that I have sought to describe and emphasize. They marked a great and universal era of human history. As such, they deserve to be recognized as representing an important and in some cases indelible part of our cultural heritage.

References Cited

Carneiro, Robert L.
  1978 Political Expansion as an Expression of the Principle of Competitive Exclusion. In *Origins of the State,* edited by Ronald Cohen and Elman R. Service, pp.205-223. Institute for the Study of Human Issues (ISHI), Philadelphia.
  1987 Village Splitting as a Function of Population. In *Themes in Ethnology and Culture History, Essays in Honor of David F. Aberle*, edited by Leland Donald, pp. 94-124. Folklore Institute, Archana Publications, Meerut, India.
  1998 What Happened at the Flashpoint? Conjectures on Chiefdom Formation at the Very Moment of Conception. In *Chiefdoms and Chieftaincy in the Americas,* edited by Elsa M. Redmond, pp. 18-41. University Press of Florida, Gainesville.
Chagnon, Napoleon A.
  1968 *Yanomamö, The Fierce People.* First edition. Holt, Rinehart and Winston, New York.
  1974 *Studying the Yanomamö.* Holt, Rinehart and Winston, New York.

Childe, V. Gordon
  1946 Archaeology and Anthropology. *Southwestern Journal of Anthropology,* 2:243-251.
Dunnell, Robert C.
  1980 Evolutionary Theory in Archaeology. In *Advances in Archaeological Method and Theory,* edited by M. Schiffer, 3:35-99. Academic Press, New York.
Fried, Morton H.
  1966 On the Concept of 'Tribe' and Tribal Society. *Transactions of the New York Academy of Sciences,* Series II, Vol. 28, pp. 527-540.
Oberg, Kalervo
  1955 Types of Social Structure Among the Lowland Tribes of South and Central America." *American Anthropologist* 57:472-487.
Lévi-Strauss, Claude
  1964 *Tristes Tropiques.* Translated from the French by John Russell. Atheneum, New York.
Sahlins, Marshall D.
  1968 *Tribesmen.* Prentice-Hall, Inc., Englewood Cliffs, N.J.
Service, Elman R.
  1962 *Primitive Social Organization; An Evolutionary Perspective.* First edition. Random House, New York.
  1968 War and Our Contemporary Ancestors. In *War: The Anthropology of Armed Conflict and Aggression*, edited by Morton Fried, Marvin Harris, and Robert Murphy, pp. 160-167. The Natural History Press, Garden City, N.Y.
  1971 *Primitive Social Organization; An Evolutionary Perspective.* Second edition. Random House, New York.
Yoffee, Norman
  1993 Too Many Chiefs? (or, Safe Texts for the '90s). In *Archaeological Theory: Who Sets the Agenda?,* edited by Norman Yoffee and Andrew Sherratt, pp. 60-78. Cambridge University Press, Cambridge.

4. The Long and the Short of a War Leader's Arena

Elsa M. Redmond

Introduction

The saying – "I was born to die fighting" (Harner 1972:170) – epitomizes the life's purpose and trajectory of individual Jivaroan tribesmen in Amazonia. From the time in a Jivaroan boy's childhood when his father begins reciting the history of hostilities and killings of his ancestors and exhorting him to take up the lance and seek blood revenge, the individual tribesman views the pursuit of warfare as his sacred duty. His motives and lifelong aspirations would seem to derive from a clear-cut case of tit for tat: a raid on an enemy household triggers a counterraid or ambush against his settlement, which calls for a revenge raid, and so forth. By undergoing rigorous training to become a warrior and an adult, and by participating in a sequence of raids and carrying out multiple killings, the warrior seeks to redress wrongs committed against his kinsmen and acquire the status of a renowned warrior, who is sought out as the leader of intersettlement and intertribal war parties.

As Fowles (this volume, Chapter 2) points out in his discussion of what it is like to act tribally, individual actions can only be understood in the context of the larger inherited structures within which individuals maneuver. The intensity with which Jivaroan tribesmen of eastern Ecuador and Peru have waged intertribal warfare against groups "that speak differently" (Harner 1972:183; Fig. 1), is fueled by the spirits of their ancestors, "the ancient ones" (*arútama*), who lived and fought in the mythical past. No self-respecting warrior will walk the path to war without consulting them and obtaining their supernatural energy. Some of the most renowned Jivaroan war leaders attribute their success in warfare—and their longevity—to their divinatory encounters with the ancient ones who inhabit an invisible, supernatural realm, yet one which the Jivaroans consider the "real" world (Harner 1972: 134-135).

In this chapter, then, I will examine the two temporal dimensions of a Jivaroan war leader's career. The first is his lifetime's pursuit of warfare during which he gains the training, experience, authority, and standing to command raiding parties and to host the post-war feasts. As a distinguished killer, war leader, and host he will achieve the status of big man or chieftain (Redmond 1998b) and will wield considerable authority in the village and region at large. The other dimension of a war leader's pursuit of warfare extends back to the distant past of the primordial *arútama*, from whom the aspiring war leader acquires the soul power that makes it possible for him to avenge the death of his kinsmen and obtain the enemy's soul power through killing and headtaking. By seeking the counsel and power of these ancient warriors (Brown 1985:53; Karsten 1935:448), the war leader is filled with the confidence to go to war and the desire to kill. According to the Jivaroan view of human agency (Hendricks 1991:54), "without direct contact with spiritual beings, there can be no harnessing of power for human use in goal-directed actions" (Hendricks 1991:55). Hence, war leaders who encounter the ancient ones and obtain their soul power are accorded the unquestionable authority to command a raiding party, the most highly organized all-male task group in Jivaroan (Achuar) society (Kelekna 1981:212-213). As their war deeds and tally of heads accumulate, so does their soul power, their social standing and their renown.

The epilogue of a renowned war leader's trajectory is his attempt to pass on his accrued power and position to his eldest son. Under certain conditions, that power and position will be transmitted to the following generation, thereby setting the stage for the development of permanent hereditary leadership.

The Beginning of War

The exploits of the primordial ancestors who created Jivaroan culture are related in a body of myths that the Aguaruna and other Jivaroan groups refer to as "ancestor stories" (Brown

1985:48). The basic tenet of these ancestor stories is that the earliest ancestors emerged from the clutch of cannibalistic forest monsters with the help of certain culture heroes and acquired knowledge—both practical and visionary knowledge—about fire, horticulture, pottery, the blowgun, hunting, and all other aspects of Jivaroan life, including warfare (Brown 1985:48-50; Kelekna 1981:99-118; Pellizzaro 1990:43-48).

Many of the ancestor stories derive from the sacred origin myth or "earth story," which the re-

nowned war leader Anguasha of the Yaup' river drainage recounted to Matthew Stirling in 1931 (Stirling 1938:123). The myth relates the creation of the earth and the birth of the first Jivaroan, Uñushi, firstborn son of Etsa, the sun, and Nantu, the moon. Uñushi married a woman by the name of Mika and after establishing their own household the couple traveled down the river in a canoe and a son was born to them, Ahimbi the water serpent. During their travels, Uñushi became angered by his wife's incestuous relationship with

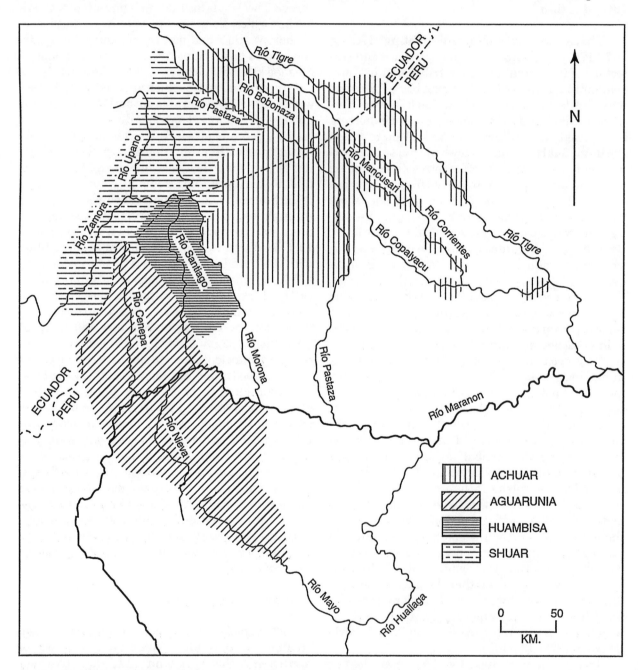

Fig. 1. Map of Jivaroan groups (redrawn from Brown 1985:27 by Bridget Thomas).

Ahimbi. Uñushi sought revenge. He accused Nantu, the moon, of consenting to his wife's adultery; so enraged was Uñushi that he assaulted Nantu with a lance and threw her into a pit and buried her. When Nantu managed to escape, she related her ordeal, which prompted the killing and taking of Uñushi's head, and the unleashing of a war among the offspring of Uñushi, Mika, and Ahimbi. So violent was the war that it brought about a great storm with lightning, thunder, rain, and hurricane-force wind. At the height of the storm a bolt of lightning struck the earth and a powerful Jivaroan warrior armed with a lance and a shield appeared. This was Masata. Masata visited the warring factions, the originators of the different Jivaroan groups, and encouraged them to seek blood revenge. He incited them by telling each group that the warrior who killed the most would become powerful and would be a great war leader. "This was the beginning of war" (Stirling 1938:129).

Lessons in Warfare

A Jivaroan boy's first exposure to warfare is at the age of six or seven years, when he begins entering the male section of the house in the early morning to be instructed in a solemn litany of war lessons by his father (Kelekna 1981:93,135). The great Shuar war leader of the Upano river drainage in the 1930s and 1940s, Utitiája, described his early lessons in some detail:

> And every morning, since before I can remember, he sat me down in front of him, even before we ate food, and told me what I must do when I grew up. He told me who our enemies were, who had killed my brother, his father, his brother. Each time he told me exactly how they died and who had caused their deaths. He had avenged his father by killing the man....
>
> ...he told me that my most solemn duty would be to take blood revenge against those who had killed members of my family. I can still see him, serious, stern, speaking softly but with great force. If I did my duty and fulfilled all obligations to the spirits of my dead family, I would have good wives, good hunting, and long life. If I failed my crops would spoil and my aim become poor because the spirits of my relatives would be unhappy and would bother me. (Cotlow 1953:238-239)

The father repeats the hour-long war recitation every morning for a period of more than five years, until he detects that his son is thoroughly inculcated in the need to become a warrior (Stirling

1938:51). Moreover, the morning litany includes the admonition to bathe in the sacred waterfall and seek and encounter the *arútama* before going to war. Accordingly, as early as the age of six years, but usually between ten and twelve years of age, a boy begins accompanying his father to a sacred waterfall to bathe by day, to fast, to drink green tobacco water, and by night to await the *arútama* in a lean-to. The Shuar consider the boy's encounter with an *arútam* to be the most important of all his childhood experiences; his very life is believed to depend upon it (Descola 1996:304; Harner 1972:91, 136).

The boy learns about existing hostilities by listening to the men's discussions at their gatherings in the early morning and in the evening; the men discuss the most recent raids, the stratagems they have used, and the enemies they have killed, sometimes in the company of visiting allies (Kelekna 1981:57, 93; Cotlow 1953:239). As young as six or seven years old and by the time he is ten years old a boy accompanies his father on a raid for the first time, mainly to observe raiding tactics and gain experience in war and bloodshed. A father will have his son approach the corpse of a slain enemy and thrust his lance into it or fire at it with a shotgun. Utitiája remembered being handed the lance by his father for this purpose, "so that I would come to know the feel of it and learn how hard I must thrust. He wanted me to do this, also, so I would not be afraid, so I would become accustomed to blood" (Cotlow 1953:239; Harner 1972:113; Kelekna 1981:93, 213). A Jivaroan boy's early lessons in the art of warfare include the tactical aspects of raiding and killing, the strategic significance of building alliances, but also the supernatural dimension of seeking the counsel and power of the *arútama*. Thus indoctrinated, a seven-year-old Huambisa boy that Lewis Cotlow befriended in 1940 stood up straight and with his eyes flashing related his greatest wish: "most of all I want to be a great warrior when I grow up so that I can avenge my father's death and take many Aguaruna heads" (Cotlow 1953:49).

Becoming an Adult

A youth pursues his apprenticeship in warfare by accompanying his father on raids and carrying provisions, guarding canoes, and scouting for the raiding party. He hones his marksmanship in hunting, wrestles with his peers, and participates in ceremonial wrestling matches at the opening dances of victory feasts. He is warned by his father to avoid having sex during his adolescence for fear of becoming weak (Cotlow 1953:239; Harner 1972:89, 92-93; Hendricks 1993:157; Karsten 1935:342; Kelekna 1981:135; Up de Graff 1923:256).

When the youth reaches puberty at the age of fifteen or sixteen years he undergoes a series of initiation rituals that are designed to test some of his developing qualities as a warrior and to mark his transition to manhood. His father hosts a great feast for the men that lasts three days, during which the young warrior is given repeated doses of tobacco juice or tobacco smoke on an empty stomach. At the tobacco feast's conclusion, he sips the hallucinogenic *maikiua* drink (from the juice of the bark of *Datura arborea*), which is not only the most potent of all the hallucinogens taken by Jivaroans, but is also the hallucinogen reserved for warriors. The young warrior must sip *maikiua* from a cup offered to him either by the oldest man of his family, or sometimes by two facing rows of assembled warriors, beginning with the oldest warrior. When a youth was asked if he knew why he was drinking *maikiua*, he responded, "it is in order that I may become a real man and a brave warrior and that I may be able to marry" (Karsten 1935:240-241, 439; Harner 1972:137).

Often the initiate takes *maikiua* only after he has travelled into the forest to a sacred waterfall, where the *arútama* or the ancient warriors may be encountered (Harner 1972:136; Pellizzaro 1990:167). These ancient warriors dwell in a great house in the lower sky where strong winds, lightning, and thunderstorms are generated, but they wander in the form of breezes above the surface of the earth and scatter the spray of the waterfall, which serves as a point of interface between the human world and the hidden world (Brown 1985:53-54; Harner 1972:134, 136; Pellizzaro 1990:9, 167). Here the youth levels a clearing or "path" (Descola 1996:299) for the *arútama* and erects a lean-to shelter called a "dreaming hut" together with his father or with an elder or shaman. By day he fasts and strides in the waterfall's curtain, aided by a wooden staff that he prepares for the occasion. By night he drinks tobacco water and sips *maikiua*; after an initial phase of excitation, the youth will enter a deep slumber, during which the *arútama* might appear in his dreams. They are fantastic animal specters of jaguars, serpents, caimans, condors and eagles, but they can also appear in the form of great balls of fire, shaking trees, human heads and dismembered bodies. Moreover, the *arútama* are accompanied by hurricane-force winds and deafening roars. The dreamer must summon his courage and strike

the apparition with his staff or touch it with his hand, at which point his mission is accomplished. The specter vanishes in a reverberating explosion, but a faceless ancestor (Marcus 1998:19)—or as the Achuar say "whose face has no name" (Descola 1996:114)—with a resonating voice will appear to him and bestow his prophecy:

> I am your ancestor.
> Just as I have lived a long time,
> so will you.
> Just as I have killed many times,
> so will you. (Harner 1972:138-139)

At that moment the youth acquires the *arútam*'s prophecy and power (Brown 1985:53-54, 167; Descola 1996: 302-303; Karsten 1935: 439, 447-451; Kelekna 1981:126).

Other initiation rituals involve venturing into the forest, killing a tree sloth and preparing a trophy from its head. The use of the sloth for this head-taking ritual is appropriate, since the sloth is a living descendant of Uñushi, the first Jivaroan to have suffered this fate (Karsten 1935:298; Stirling 1938:72, pl. 33). The father of the young headtaker will host mock victory feasts, after which the youth is entitled to wear the cotton and feather-tasseled headband, the badge of an adult man (Harner 1972:93). At the conclusion of the initiation rituals and his encounter with an *arútam* the young man can marry (Descola 1996:304; Karsten 1935:241).

After these defining experiences, the young warrior is prepared for war, for making his transition to adulthood. Harner (1972:139, 151-152) has described the effects of acquiring an *arútam*'s power. The person feels a surge of power, self-confidence, and invincibility. His forceful bearing and speech reflect his newly acquired power. Above all, he is "seized with a tremendous desire to kill" (Harner 1972:139). Having successfully encountered and killed a charging jaguar during his visionary quest at puberty, the great Utitiája recounted how he felt:

> I felt wonderful, of course, as anyone would who knew that he would be successful in achieving the most important thing in life. I was happy.
> I felt strong—strong enough to kill a real jaguar, to kill real enemies. (Cotlow 1953:240)

The young warrior begins participating in raids led by his father, father-in-law, or related war leaders, in the hope of killing an enemy and thereby becoming an adult. On his first raid, seventeen-year-old Utitiája succeeded in killing and taking the head of the man who had killed his father, an achievement he attributed to the *arútam*'s prophecies on the eve of that raid (Cotlow 1953:241). When the renowned Jivaroan war leader of the Makuma river drainage, Tukup', recounted his life story to Janet Hendricks in 1982, he emphasized the criteria for become an adult male in Shuar society. Tukup's transition to adulthood began with the visionary experiences of "seeing" and acquiring the knowledge and power of an *arútam*, after which he began fighting to avenge the killing of his father when he was nineteen years old (Hendricks 1993:144, 151). With his first killing of an Achuar enemy, which Tukup' described in detail, he avenged his father's death. The act of killing transformed him into an adult:

> And then
>
> then having killed,
>
> indeed with that I too became an
>
> adult. (Hendricks 1993:152-153)

On becoming an adult a young man carves his own wooden stool to sit on in the men's section of the house. Achuar men decorate their hollowed log stool with a lug that represents the head of the anaconda and believe that the stool rests on the four feet of the jaguar (see Fig. 2; Descola 1996:143, 283; Harner 1972:93; Karsten 1935:96; Kelekna 1981:48, 117). Their stools denote their manhood, their entry into the arena of war, and their participation in the affairs of adult men.

Following the Path of War

The young Jivaroan warrior follows the path of war by participating repeatedly in head-taking raids against enemy settlements located as far as a six days' journey on foot. The preparations for war begin when the male members of an aggrieved household who wish to avenge the death of a kinsman retreat to a dreaming hut in the forest for the purposes of drinking *maikiua* and awaiting the *arútama*'s prophecies about the raid they wish to mount. Only if the *arútama*'s responses are favorable do they pursue their plans for a revenge raid (Karsten 1935:279). A renowned warrior agrees to lead the raid. The *arútama*'s revelations and all subsequent preparations for an upcoming raid must be kept secret by the participating warriors, and nighttime discussions must be guarded (Descola 1996:304; Karsten 1935:279-280; Pellizzaro 1990:254).

In the final days before the raid, the warriors are summoned to the site of the pre-war rituals by the sacred signal drum. This 5-foot-long hollowed log drum (Fig. 3) is designed after the anaconda (*Eunectes murinus*), one of the warring protagonists in the Jivaroan origin myth and among the most powerful and dreaded *arútama*. The drum's handles represent the head and tail of this water serpent and the pattern of diamond-shaped sound

Fig. 2. Wooden stool decorated with the head of the anaconda and supports that represent feet of the jaguar (redrawn from Descola [1996:43] by Bridget Thomas).

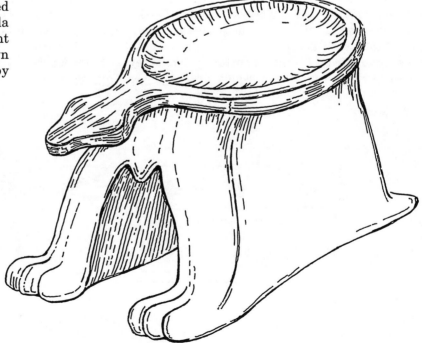

holes and undulating slots depict its distinctive markings (Stirling 1938:92, 126-129; Karsten 1935:110, 375-376, 448, 490-492). The warriors arrive individually bearing lances which they thrust at the host as they engage in a ceremonial dialogue with him. By means of this stylized, aggressive greeting, the speakers inform each other of their identity, their possession of *arútam* power, and their common purpose (Harner 1972:184; Hendricks 1993:86-87; Karsten 1935:283-284). The 6 to 8-foot-long lances (Fig. 4) made from the *chonta* palm (*Bactris, Giulielma, Iriartea*) that in the past were tipped with points made from the leg bones of the jaguar are imbued with supernatural power and are often decorated with the markings of the *arútama* whose power they contain. So powerful is the lance that when any Jivaroan Shuar goes out at night he is armed with one (Stirling 1938:52, 86; Pellizzaro 1990:257). Moreover, "carrying the lance" is a Jivaroan expression for going to war (Hendricks 1993:151).

The assembled warriors perform lineups, lance-wielding exercises and war chants on the final nights before the raid. In their war chants the warriors most frequently identify themselves with jaguars and anacondas, two greatly feared predators, and make claims of preying on the enemy (Descola 1996:301,391-393; Harner 1972:41). Much manioc beer and tobacco are consumed at these pre-war rituals, which infuse the members of the war party with strength, courage and confidence for the upcoming raid. Indeed, Cotlow (1953:143) described a soon-to-depart party of 25 Shuar warriors as tense, excited, and overstimulated. On the evening before an attack they decorate their faces and bodies with designs of black paint *Genipa americana* (Figs. 4-6) that denote the *arútama* they have experienced and the consequent *arútam* power

they have acquired (Karsten 1935:280, 288, 492-95; Kelekna 1981:209).

The raiders file out of the village silently and pitch lean-to shelters at overnight camps along the path to war. Silence is observed by the members of the war party. At the final overnight camp they receive their combat instructions from the war leader, who also incites them by revealing the auspicious *arútam* he has encountered in his dreams. Each warrior in turn reveals the *arútam* he encountered, the declaration of which prepares him for the early morning attack (Brown 1985:167; Harner 1972:140).

The raiders dress for war with monkey-fur caps, hair wrapped into pigtails, fine toucan-feather crowns, feather-tufted bamboo ear-tubes, necklaces of jaguar teeth, pectoral or dorsal strands of oilbird (*Steatornis caripensis*) bones, and belts of anaconda skin or human hair (Figs. 7-8) (Karsten 1935:89-93). They apply black face and body paint; the black spots or circles on their faces can represent "*pangi* (anaconda)'s spots" or "the mouth of the jaguar" (Descola 1996:295; Karsten 1935:492). The warriors' insignia derive from the stealthy jaguar and the great anaconda—the two predators they readily identify with, the human scalp, and the cave-dwelling, nocturnal oilbird that repels intruders with aggressive behavior and deafening screams (Descola 1994:75; Snow 1961:27, 34). These ornaments signal the warriors' bravery, their possession of *arútam* power, and imbue them with invincibility. Their insignia will also be used for recognition by the members of the war party during the actual raid (Harner 1972:frontispiece; Karsten 1935:66-67, 288-289, 426-429; Stirling 1938:100-102).

Under the cover of darkness the raiding party approaches to within ten meters of the enemy

Fig. 3. Hollowed-log signal drum that is patterned after the anaconda (redrawn from Karsten [1935:fig. 2] by Bridget Thomas).

household and waits for the moment to attack anyone emerging from the house. Before the introduction of the shotgun in the 1850s, Jivaroan warriors fought with the wooden lance and were armed with a round shield of wood or hide (Fig. 4). Like the lance, the shield contained the properties of the empowering *arútama*—especially the anaconda—that were portrayed in the painted designs on its face (Harner 1972:205; Karsten 1935:264-266; Stirling 1938:87, plate 28).

Thus empowered and filled with anticipation, the raiders await the signal from the leader of the war party before storming the household (Redmond 1994:5-8). The raiders' objectives are to seek blood revenge by killing as many of the inhabitants as possible and taking their heads as trophies. Only if there is time will the raiders ransack and set fire to the settlement before retreating "swiftly and silently" (Cotlow 1953:234) from enemy territory. Up de Graff accompanied an Aguaruna-Antipas raid against a Huambisa settlement in 1899 and described the lance-thrusting attack and its aftermath. The raiders immediately set to work severing the heads of the dead and dying victims with stone axes, bamboo knives, sharpened clam shells, and *chonta*-wood machetes, and departed with 11 Huambisa heads slung over their shoulders (Up de Graff 1923:259-260).

Once outside enemy territory the raiders stop along the way home from war to prepare the head trophies (*tsantsa*). The first post-war rituals are celebrated by the victors at the trophy-processing camp, situated along a river (Redmond 1994:10-11). The heads are placed face upwards on large leaves or shields in the middle of the circle of warriors. Each warrior who has killed and taken a head is designated the master of the head; his first ritual act is to sit down on top of the head and receive a blast of tobacco juice in his nose. This is the first of many observances practiced by the headtaker to thwart the avenging soul (*muisak*) of the victim whose head was taken from harming him. The avenging soul that is contained in the head must be prevented from seeing or emerging from the mouth, which is sealed shut with *chonta* pins and palm-fiber stitches. The headtaker will abstain from bathing, eating many animal foods, having sex, and other activities that might make him vulnerable to the revengeful soul of his dead enemy. Following the tobacco inoculation, the killers skin the heads and often throw the skulls into the river—intended as a gift to *pangi*, the anaconda (Harner 1972:143-145, 187; Karsten 1935:294-295; Up de Graff 1923:261-263).

Fig. 4. Jivaroan warrior carrying *chonta*-palm lance and wooden shield decorated with the undulating body and markings of the anaconda (adapted from Stirling [1938: pl. 28] by Bridget Thomas).

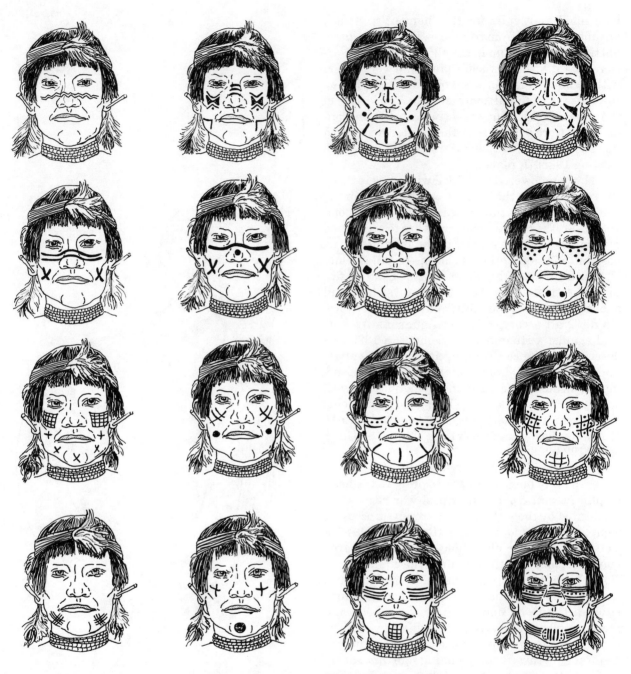

Fig. 5. Face-painting designs worn by Jivaroan warriors that denote the *arútama* they have encountered and the power they have acquired therefrom (adapted from Stirling [1938: fig. 5] and Karsten [1935: pl. XIV and figs.18-19] by Bridget Thomas).

The head skins are heated to boiling in large, ceramic cooking jars filled with water. The cooking jars are made secretly "under auspicious lunar conditions" (Up de Graff 1923:263) and are used solely for this purpose. Once the head skins are removed for drying and further shrinking by filling them with heated sand and pebbles and rubbing their exteriors with heated stones and char-coal—so that the revengeful *muisak* within the head cannot see out—the cooking jars are also cast into the river (Up de Graff 1923:264). The headtakers continue to shrink, seal, and decorate their head trophies at camps along the journey home. Peruche, the Shuar war leader on the Paute River in 1945, recounted his observances during this interval of time before the victory feasts are concluded:

Fig. 6. Ceramic cylinder seals formerly used by Jivaroan warriors to adorn their bodies with black rolled-out concentric circles and snake-like designs. From Macas, Ecuador; 2/3 actual size (redrawn from Karsten [1935: fig. 9] by David Kiphuth).

We must be very careful that the spirit of my enemy does not harm me for his spirit lives in his head, above all in his hair…I do many things to conquer the spirit and make it obey me, help me. We stick the *tsantsa* on a lance in the ground, the lance I killed my enemy with. We dance around it and thrust our lances at it, frightening the spirit, showing how we killed. (Cotlow 1953:124)

This lance-thrusting dance is intended to subdue the avenging soul of the decapitated enemy.

Upon the victors' return, they celebrate the first *tsantsa* feast at the host's house. The first victory feast is designed to protect the headtakers by painting their bodies with black *Genipa* paint, receiving tobacco-juice infusions, and performing lance-thrusting dances aimed at their impaled head trophies, which are displayed before their fellow kinsmen for the first time. Any young raider who

hasn't yet married seeks a bride at this feast. Significantly, women participate in the night-long circle dances wearing belts of snail-shell and dried-seed rattles and reciting chants, which are intended to contain the dead enemy's *muisak* but also to begin to appropriate the power of the head trophy. The enemy's *muisak* is especially powerful and coveted if the killed enemy was a renowned warrior who amassed much *arútam* power during his life (Drown and Drown 1961:100; Harner 1972:146-147; Karsten 1935:297, 304-306; Pellizzaro 1990:203).

After the victory feast, the killers immediately retreat to a dreaming hut at a waterfall, where they bathe, take tobacco water, the hallucinogenic drink *natém* (from the vine *Banisteriopsis*), and await any *arútama* to appear in their dreams, in order to acquire new *arútam* soul power (Harner 1972:140-141; Kelekna 1981:127; Pellizzaro

Fig. 7. Jivaroan warriors wearing monkey-fur caps, face paint, pigtails, tassels of toucan and parrot feathers, beetle wings, and human hair, as well as belts and multicolored cotton wristbands. Photograph taken by William Bell Taylor in Ecuador (1907-1909), Neg. No. 125199. Courtesy of the Department of Library Services, American Museum of Natural History.

1990:216). The killers continue their purification observances and are wary of encountering in their dreams the soul of a deceased enemy disguised as a forest animal who is seeking revenge for the recent death of a kinsman (Harner 1972:150; Karsten 1935:308).

It is not until the final *tsantsa* feast, celebrated a year or more later, that the killers emerge from ritual seclusion. They receive haircuts, black body paint, and are dressed in new loincloths and belts and bedecked with crowns of toucan feathers, ear tubes, oilbird pectoral ornaments, and other finery. Their wives weave them new multicolored wristbands that signal their newly acquired *arútam* power and seal its pathway (Descola 1996:310). The headtakers display their *tsantsa* hanging from their necks (Fig. 9). The head trophies have received their final grooming, including the removal of the

Fig. 8. Back view of Jivaroan warriors wearing capes of toucan and parrot feathers (left) and oilbird leg-bones (right). Photograph taken by William Bell Taylor in Ecuador (1907-1909), Neg. No. 125990. Courtesy of the Department of Library Services, American Museum of Natural History.

chonta pins and palm-fiber stitches from the mouth and the tying of long cotton cords from the lip holes. Rafael Karsten, who observed the great victory feast celebrated at the Achuar settlement of Chiwiasa on the Upper Pastaza River in August 1917, learned that this final victory feast was sometimes referred to as "the eating of the *tsantsa*." Formerly, the headtaker ritually consumed the *tsantsa* before

hanging it from his neck by swallowing a token of skin from the neck of the *tsantsa* (Karsten 1935:317, 360-361; see also Hendricks 1993:18). This ritual act of "eating his enemy" was the culminating moment of the headtaker's appropriation of the head-trophy's power. The feared *muisak* power seized from his enemy is transformed into a useful, beneficial force that will promote his family's ma-

Fig. 9. Jivaroan warrior at a victory feast, wearing his head trophy and wristbands (drawn from Karsten [1935: pl. XXVIII] by David Kiphuth).

terial well-being; it is for this reason that his wives, who are the family's principal cultivators, participate in the circle dances at the victory feasts. To the renowned war leader and taker of more than 50 heads, Anguasha, the head trophy was a sign that the maker had fulfilled his sacred duty to his ancestors, who would be pleased and would bestow him with good fortune and good crops (Kelekna 1998:168-69; Redmond 1998:72; Stirling 1938:40, 75). Utitiája, who was known to have taken 59 heads, expressed his feelings of triumph at the final *tsantsa* feast:

> You have triumphed over your enemy by killing him. You now triumph over his evil spirit and make it a good spirit to help you more. And you tell the souls of the people you loved that they can stop wandering unhappily. Those are all splendid things to feel. It seems as if you are soaring high like the condor. (Cotlow 1953:242)

At the same time that the headtaker promotes his family's well-being he acquires enormous prestige and builds his network of alliances by hosting this final and largest victory feast. Ironically, hosting the final victory feast results in the utter depletion of his family's resources brought by supplying food and drink for some 125 guests for six days (Harner 1972:190-193).

From Warrior to War Leader

When his black body paint wears off, the warrior resumes his normal life. Yet he wishes above all to "set off on the path" (Descola 1996:304) and "see" the future, by seeking a new *arútam*, which initiates the next round of acquiring *arútam* soul power and of wanting to kill. By participating in many raids the warrior accumulates both experience in intertribal warfare and *arútam* power. When he has killed three or four persons the warrior becomes a *kakáram* or "powerful one." The *kakáram* is respected and feared as an outstanding killer, he is considered mentally and physically strong, and above all, he is deemed invincible (Descola 1996: 305-6; Harner 1972:112-115, 140-142, 183; Kelekna 1981:128; Pellizzaro 1990:215). Accordingly, a *kakáram* will be asked to lead war parties.

The assembled warriors for an allied raid elect a *kakáram* as their war leader, who will plan and command all aspects of the upcoming raid. Beginning some months before the raid he will recruit warriors on a household-to-household basis. The war leader will prepare for the anticipated victory feast by arranging for a respected elder to serve as master of ceremonies and overseeing the construction of a large house that will be the site of both the pre-war ceremonies and the expected victory feast (Harner 1972:183-84). His preparations include repeatedly taking *maikiua* and *natém* to encounter and receive the augury of the *arútama*. If the answer is auspicious, and he hears an eagle's call overhead in the morning, the war leader proceeds with his final plans, which must be kept secret. He dispatches scouts into enemy territory to reconnoiter the target settlement's defenses. With his forceful calls-to-arms and his promises of victory, this war herald, as the Achuar refer to him, continues to motivate and recruit warriors for the raid (Descola 1996:290, 294; Drown and Drown 1961:77-78; Hendricks 1988:223; Karsten 1935:282; Pellizzaro 1990:192-193).

On the eve of the raiders' departure the war leader alone sounds the signal drum to summon the members of the war party to his house. He delivers his exhortation to fight during his face-to-face dialogue and lance exchanges with each of the arriving participants. The warriors stand in rows to perform the menacing lance exercises and accompanying war chants, led by the war leader, who sounds the sacred anaconda drum as a means to communicate with the *arútama* (Karsten 1935:110-11; Stirling 1938:53). Indeed, while the warriors imbibe manioc beer and tobacco water, the war leader takes *natém* or *maikiua*. The significance attached to the war leader's dreams is pivotal in his momentous decision to launch the raid:

> Well, those who dream badly
> indeed they are to die. Hendricks 1993:164)

But if the *arútama* proclaim victory, as in the following dreams, the outcome is promising:

> I dreamed of the boa, I saw the
> boa,...
> I dreamed of the boa because I
> was to kill a great one. (Hendricks 1993:254)
> I have had good dreams; I won't be killed, but
> will return with the heads of my enemies.
> (Karsten 1935:286)

At dawn the warriors dress for war, ready their provisions, and file out of the house in silence. Just before departing the warriors unwrap and discard the wristbands that have signalled their possession of *arútam* power, confident that they will be victorious (Descola 1996:310). The war leader is the last to leave and the only one to make any parting words before he shuts the door behind him. His wooden stool is left turned on its side during his absence (Descola 1996:69).

Throughout the trek to war the raiders maintain strict silence and obedience to the war leader. Once in enemy territory the raiders walk aside the trail in single file, each stepping in the footprints of the person ahead. Scouts are sent to crisscross the trail and forest ahead. The war leader's knowledge of the terrain, trails, settlements and customs of the target settlement's inhabitants is crucial to the raid's success. At the last overnight camp the war leader voices his instructions for the early morning raid to his warriors. He leads the round of divinatory dream declarations:

> Take courage and don't fear, for I dreamed this night that I saw the great eagle and the toucan. They told me that we are going to take a soul. You are not going to die; you are going to be victors and to kill your enemies. (Karsten 1935:287)

The war leader's knowledge about the future has the effect of "creating order where there had previously been uncertainty" (Brown 1985:165), and inciting his warriors to carry the lance in a matter of hours.

As the raiders encircle the target settlement and take up their attacking positions it is the war leader who decides when to attack. He must weigh the need to wait for the inhabitants to emerge from the fortified household against the ambivalence of his warriors. There are many circumstances that can arise at the target village prior to the attack that call for ad hoc decision-making by the war leader, as to whether or not to abide by the decision reached earlier to target a particular individual for killing or to pick off whomever emerges first, or to wait for the chance to storm the house when all the inhabitants can be entrapped (Hendricks 1993:259-260). Should barking dogs alert the enemy of the raiders' presence the war leader might have to call for a retreat; often, however, he will instruct his raiders to loop back through the forest "as silently as jaguars" (Cotlow 1953:146) and resume their attacking positions. The leaders of allied war parties numbering 50, or 200 or more warriors, will have to negotiate with the leaders of the member groups and deploy the large-scale allied fighting forces strategically (Redmond 1994:4, 124). Under the command of its leader, the raiding party is thus a hierarchically differentiated, highly effective fighting force (Kelekna 1981:213).

In the aftermath of a victorious raid the war leader presides over any on-the-spot discussions about which victims' heads cannot be taken because they happen to be relatives of members of the war party. Although the war leader acts no

differently from his fellow warriors during the ensuing looting spree of the raided settlement, he has first choice when it comes to abducting female captives. The war leader also announces that the first victory feast will be celebrated at his house and dispatches the youngest warriors home with the news (Cotlow 1953:149; Descola 1996:174; Drown and Drown 1961:98-99; Stirling 1938:56).

In the process of leading war parties, killing and headtaking, and hosting victory feasts, a *kakáram* acquires experience in the tactics of warfare and in the building of alliances with the villagers of his neighborhood and beyond in the region. He can count on the active support of half a dozen warriors of his generation and a dozen or more younger warriors, whom he addresses as "my sons" (Descola 1996:178, 291). He also accumulates *arútam* power with aplomb and becomes a *ti kakáram* or a "very powerful one" (Descola 1996: 305; Harner 1972:115). By the time he achieves this status a war leader might well be commanding allied war parties for other war leaders who submit to his authority, and will be gaining renown on a supraregional, intertribal scale. The leadership such *ti kakáram* wield over the communities of a region and beyond, especially in times of war, can be considered a chieftaincy, which is characterized by its centralized and hierarchical structure (Redmond 1998a:3; Redmond 1998b:70-78). Sometimes the territory comprising the alliance of settlements under the authority of such a war chieftain will bear his name (Descola 1981:627; Redmond 1994:126-127).

Utitiája attained the status and authority of a war leader on the Chupientsa River by thirty-five years of age. By waging intensive intertribal warfare, within three years he was already becoming the war chieftain of the entire Upano river drainage. Indeed, by the age of fifty years, Utitiája was recognized as the greatest warrior and headtaker of all by an illustrious Shuar war leader who lived several days' travel downriver (Cotlow 1953:128; Redmond 1994:126, 1998b:74). When Utitiája was fifty-six or fifty-seven years old, he was asked about his career and great success as a warrior. Utitiája attributed his continuing success in warfare to two factors. First was his training by his father, who had lived until Utitiája was thirteen years old. A *kakáram* himself, Utitiája's father had taught Utitiája his lessons as a boy, and versed him in tactics by having Utitiája attend discussions with allies and tag along on actual raids. In Utitiája's words, "he gave me some of his strength and brains. He trained me well" (Cotlow 1953:242). The second and most important factor was the visionary knowledge Utitiája had acquired from the *arútama*:

> But the main reason is that before any war or raid I always drank *nateema* or *maikoa* and through my dreams learned from the Old Ones whether my plans could succeed or not. If they said no, I postponed the raid. If they said yes, I went ahead, knowing that I was absolutely certain to win. (Cotlow 1952:242-243)

Utitiája attributed part of his success as a war leader to the rigorous training he received at home and in war by his father, from whom he inherited his strength and his brains. Jivaroans consider the brain to be the repository of practical knowledge (Hendricks 1991:61), which served as the vehicle for Utitiája's early lessons and lifetime's experience in warfare. But it was the visionary knowledge that Utitiája obtained from the *arútama*, knowledge which Jivaroans hold in their heart (Brown 1985:19, 49) and which enable them to think well, that Utitiája considered most important. As Hendricks (1991:61) learned, "the knowledge obtained through contact with the supernatural world in visionary experiences gives an individual a deeper understanding of the causes of events and the ability to use this knowledge in goal-directed action." It is the war leader's mastery of both the tactical and the supernatural dimensions of warfare that invests him with the presumed invincibility and authority to influence the actions of others.

One reason for the inextricable link between these two dimensions of a tribal war leader's trajectory may be the legitimizing power of the first ancestors and their exploits in the cosmological origins of many tribal societies. Their legitimizing power derives from the simple notion of primacy (Helms 1998):

> Primacy is universally revered. The first-born child, the first animal of the season killed, the first fruits of a crop, the first menstruation, the first inhabitants to arrive, the first ancestors—all have special merit and the powers of freshness. The first are the beginnings of a sequence, and are hence the primary sources of power. (Goldman 1975:49, cited by Helms 1998:78)

Those tribal leaders who attain privileged access to their cosmological forefathers will be accorded a share of that ultimate primacy and power. Their contact with the first ancestors legitimizes their authority as they conduct diverse economic, social, or political activities—including warfare. Whatever activity they direct is validated as well since it is viewed as necessary for reproducing the original status quo (Helms 1998:74). Hence, Jivaroan war leaders who are renowned killers and headtakers and who encounter the ancient ones and obtain their soul power are accorded the unquestionable authority to command a raiding party. Their war deeds, but especially their accrued *arútam* power sanctify their authority and facilitate their command over others.

The Heritability of a Chieftaincy

By the time a war leader is deemed very powerful and is wielding the authority of a chieftain, however, he will be over forty years old and an elder (*uunt*) (Kelekna 1981:97). When he reaches the age when he no longer leads war parties, he can continue to accumulate power and influence the actions of others in other ways. Many war leaders seek shamanic power as they grow older and are sought out as diviners and as curing and bewitching shamans (Redmond 1998b:90-92). Certain older war leaders, renowned for their long and distinguished careers, their visionary knowledge, and especially for the *arútam* power they exude, serve as master (*wea*) of the victory feasts. So prominent and powerful is a *wea* that as he presides over a headtaker's final observances, leading him by the hand, and injecting him periodically with tobacco juice, the *wea*'s palpable power can be transmitted to the headtaker (Harner 1972:183,193; Hendricks 1993:6; Karsten 1935:301-305, 318-319, 328-367; Siverts 1975:665). The transmission of ritual knowledge and power to the headtaker is evident at the feast's conclusion when the *wea* declares, "What I have done now you may also do later when you grow old" (Karsten 1935:364).

Above all, the aging war leader will seek to pass on his knowledge and *arútam* power to his eldest son. The primacy of the firstborn male child begins at birth. Jivaroans express a distinct preference for having sons, especially their firstborn. There is male primacy in naming boys for celestial bodies and renowned ancestors—indeed, for renowned warriors (Harner 1972:83; Kelekna 1981:124-25, 157-58). Moreover, the newborn is administered a mild hallucinogenic drink to empower him with an *arútam* soul and enhance his survival (Harner 1972:84). It is with this same sense of urgency that a father will take his young son to a dreaming hut in the forest to encounter *arútama*; the son's acquisition of an *arútam* soul is considered critical to the boy's survival—and to the father's as well (Harner 1972:136, 224). It is not too long before the father takes his son along on raids.

The importance of this bloodline is expressed in some of the war chants uttered by warriors when they assemble for a raid:

> To my son also I have said:
> "My son, my son,
> Make you strong, make you brave!
> ...Presently I will be engaged in fighting!
> All right, may my enemy come, may he come!
> And may he take my life if he can!
> If he kills me,
> my sons will certainly see (that it will be avenged)." (Karsten 1935:285-286)

By exhorting his son to become a *kakáram* and knowing that his son will assume his sacred duty to "see" and avenge his death, a warrior prepares himself for combat and accepts his fate.

When the son of a great war leader becomes a full-fledged warrior in his own right, he will serve as his father's deputy. He remains in his father's household after marriage because he is exempt from the post-marital period of matrilocal residence (Descola 1996:178). He will be dispatched to canvass the households of a dozen or more neighborhoods to recruit warriors for his father's war party, which will prove to be an exercise in the art of ceremonial dialogue, arm-twisting, and building alliances. He will be asked to sound the sacred signal drum, to greet visitors, and to stand in for his father on ritual occasions. During a raid the son will act as his father's buddy, not only to shield him from being the target of the enemy's counter-attack, but also from any assassination attempt by another member of the raiding party (Cotlow 1953:124-125; Harner 1972:183-185; Zikmund and Hanzelka 1963:269-271).

In time an aging war leader will dispatch his son to lead war parties in his stead. And as a war leader becomes infirm, his son will often be chosen war chieftain in his own right by the participating warriors or by a shaman who will perform divination by drinking *natém* to obtain the *arútama*'s counsel (Descola 1996:348; Karsten 1935:267, 282; Cotlow 1953:47). The son's bloodline weighs heavily in his selection:

> The Jibaros have absolute faith in the heritability of prominent qualities and ascribe extraordinary importance to education and the power of example. The son of a great chief, they say, must necessarily also become an able warrior because he is, as it were, a direct continuation of his father, has received a careful education for the deeds of war, and has always had the good example of his great father before his eyes. (Karsten 1935:267)

The eldest son (or oldest surviving son) is favored for being his father's son and the graduate of his great father's individual training.

Paradoxically, as an elderly war leader becomes physically decrepit his accrued *arútam* power instills fear in his enemies and provides him with a certain measure of resistance from enemy attack. Indeed, Tukup' recounted matter-of-factly that a revenge raid had failed to kill the desired enemy when he emerged first from the enemy household because that individual had killed well and had dreamed well, which made him invincible (Hendricks 1993:269-270; Descola 1996:305). On his deathbed a renowned chieftain will advise his son of his last wish: for his son to acquire some of his own *arútam* souls, that is, those born at the moment of his death and equivalent in number to the number of *arútam* souls he had acquired during his life. When he dies the newly-created souls leave his body in a detonation and go to their abode in the lower sky, generating lightning, thunder, and strong winds (Brown 1985:53-54, 167; Descola 1996: 306, 379; Harner 1972:142-143, 168; Karsten 1935:381-382, 412). In an effort to fulfill his wish the deceased war leader is accorded special funerary observances. His body is dressed, adorned, and seated on his stool, facing the doorway of his house—"in the posture of a host receiving visitors" (Descola 1996:378), and propped up against the central post, which is referred to as the ritual post because it serves as the *arútama*'s pathway (Pellizzaro 1990:59). A cylindrical palisade of *chonta* staves erected around the seated body prevents it from toppling. The funerary accompaniments include his lance, jars of manioc beer, his drinking cup, and bowls of manioc, meat, and fish. The wooden staff that the deceased used in his encounters with the *arútama* is inserted through a small hole in the front of the palisade, far enough to touch the deceased's chest, the site of his heart, and the repository of his visionary knowledge (Hendricks 1991:61). Upon the war leader's death, his family abandons the house, which is transformed into the family's mausoleum (Redmond 1994:15).

Having erected dreaming huts several hundred meters from the house in the four cardinal directions, the son returns to the house at night in total darkness to touch the staff leading to his father's chest and declare "I am your son, Father" (Harner 1972:169). Following this ritual visit the son goes to the dreaming hut to the north, where he drinks tobacco water and awaits an *arútam*. He will repeat the ritual visits throughout the night, going in turn to the southern, eastern, and western dreaming huts until he encounters one of his father's *arútam* souls. Sometimes the son will encounter the *arútam* in the house itself. After two nights the deceased war leader is buried in the usual manner: in a hollowed-log coffin, together with his lance and other accouterments. In 1940 Cotlow observed the funerary treatment accorded a Huambisa chieftain on the Santiago River; his body lay in a hollowed-log coffin that was suspended on end from the ritual post of his house—unlike the horizontal resting position of ordinary warriors—together with his lance, blowgun, quiver of darts, gourd of poison, and vessels of food and manioc beer. Family members would replenish the food and drink for a period of two years. By that time, the deceased's *arútam*, which was expected to be a jaguar because he had been such a distinguished war leader and headtaker, would reach maturity and be able to care for himself (Cotlow 1953:9-11; Stirling 1938:113-114). Should a son successfully encounter one of his father's *arútam* souls, and a jaguar at that—as we've seen was the outcome of Utitiája's *arútam* quest—he would be empowered and would achieve great deeds during his life (Cotlow 1953:240).

A son's own success in warfare often determines whether or not he will inherit his father's chieftaincy. Chumbika, the son of the Huambisa chieftain in the upturned log coffin observed by Cotlow, confided to Cotlow that his older brother, who was already distinguishing himself as a brave warrior and headtaker when he met his untimely death, should have succeeded to his father's chieftaincy. But as an experienced warrior and headtaker himself, Chumbika was old enough to assume the position of chieftain (Cotlow 1953:46-47). In the case of Antún Tsamahén, an Aguaruna war leader on the upper Marañón River, he was favored—over his older brothers—to inherit his father's chieftaincy because he had distinguished himself in warfare (Siverts 1972:17).

A war leader's concern for nurturing his son's interest in warfare from early childhood and honing his skills as a warrior and headtaker is just one way in which a war leader seeks his son's succession to his chieftaincy. For almost from the moment of his son's birth, a war leader inoculates him with *arútam* power and prepares for his son's induction into the *arútam* cult (Kelekna 1981:32). The chieftain oversees his son's initiation rituals and appraises his acquisition of *arútam* soul power. At his death, he seeks to have his son acquire one of his own *arútam* souls. By training, testing, and empowering his son, through "example, obser-

vation, and the personal transmission of techniques of symbolic control and supernatural powers" (Taylor 1981:662), a chieftain enhances his eldest son's chances of inheriting his chieftaincy. The ascribed qualities embodied in the eldest son of a war chieftain will be sought after, especially under conditions of escalating warfare (Redmond 1994:128; 1998b:78). Accordingly, the father's chieftaincy will transcend the short-lived nature of most positions of leadership achieved by Jivaroan tribesmen and pass to his eldest son. It is fitting that the Jivaroan Shuar adopted the Quechua term, *curaca*, which the Inka had used to designate local hereditary native rulers in the fifteenth century, for referring to these war chieftains. The title of *curaca* or hereditary lord, stems from *curac*, the Quechua word for eldest son (González Holguín 1989:55-56). In the immediacy of war the eldest son of a deceased *curaca* is perceived as the direct continuation of his great father and as the next best war leader. The need for permanence in times of war will pave the way for a lineage of hereditary war leaders to emerge (Goldman 1970:xvi, cited by Helms 1998:109).

Summary

Jivaroan tribesmen like Utitiája in 1949 and Tukup' in 1982 continued to uphold their sacred duty as warriors despite their adoption of many Western customs. At any moment they would—and Utitiája did—shed their Western trappings and carry the lance to avenge the death of their kinsmen (Redmond 1998b:74-77). Their lifelong aspirations and successes as warriors and renowned war leaders were shaped by the two temporal dimensions of their arena. Their rigorous training and ardent pursuit of warfare throughout their adult lives reaped the victories they had sought so cunningly. But both tribesmen emphasized that their success in warfare derived from the visionary quests they had made to their cosmological origins. They had acquired the *arútam* power of warriors of preceding generations, reaching far back in time to the primordial Masata of their sacred origin myth, who had appeared in *arútam* form to incite the founding Jivaroans to war. That access to their cosmological origins through the quest for *arútam* soul power enabled both men to "see" the outcome of their upcoming raids and to tailor their actions. Their obvious success as war leaders could be measured in their wide-ranging alliances and victories, their multiple trophy heads and wives, their bountiful gardens and hunting grounds, and last but not least, their long lives.

What more could any tribesman ask for? To bequeath some of that bounty to his firstborn and to become a jaguar spirit of the sort that might appear as an *arútam* to future generations of warriors and intone the following revelation:

> Just as I have lived a long time,
> so will you.
> Just as I have killed many times,
> so will you. (Harner 1972:138-39)

Conclusions

There are three conclusions I would like to draw from this examination of the temporal dimensions of a Jivaroan war leader's pursuit of warfare. The first is the different "structural pose" assumed by Jivaroan tribesmen in times of peace and times of war, making it difficult, if not inaccurate, to present a single picture of Jivaroan tribal organization. Fred Gearing (1958) proposed the notion of structural pose in his study of the sequence of organized groups that eighteenth-century male Cherokee villagers assumed throughout the year. The sequence consisted of the task groups and decision-making bodies that formed in times of relative peace, and the villagers' structural pose in wartime. When the village council declared war a new order of village leadership went into operation that was hierarchically ranked and differentiated. The hierarchical war organization facilitated the rapid chain of command necessary for waging warfare expeditiously and successfully. At the conclusion of war, the war organization disbanded and male villagers resumed their peacetime relations.

For Jivaroan tribesmen, times of relative peace are still punctuated by feuding and intervillage raids. Male household heads will agree in nightlong discussions to launch a raid. A war leader will be elected, who will recruit warriors from neighboring communities, enlist the services of an elder to serve as master of the victory feasts and oversee the construction by members of the raiding party of a large house for the post-war feasts, command the raid, and host the final victory feast. At the conclusion of the final victory feast the war leader will have increased his supernatural power and renown at the cost of impoverishing his family. When his black body paint wears off and he resumes his normal life, the war leader and his family will have little to consume as they wait for their exhausted manioc gardens to recover. Hence the hosting of the final victory feast serves to level any accumulation of material wealth that might ac-

company the war leader's increasing renown and accrued supernatural power.

As the frequency of intervillage and intertribal warfare intensifies, however, and is waged in the form of monthly raids, and even repeated daily attacks (Redmond 1994:4,15-16,129), Jivaroan war leaders are too engaged in war to observe their month-long post-war period of ritual seclusion, and to prepare for and celebrate the victory feasts. Moreover, through his leadership of allied war parties the prominent war leader builds a widening network of intervillage alliances and obligations, and reaps material rewards therefrom (Redmond 1998b: 70). Accordingly, the same conditions that allow the war leader to keep his gardens' harvest for his family's well-being enable him to amass external sources of wealth.

As the leader of allied war parties, the war leader commands not only his own warriors but also negotiates with the leaders of the allied war parties, and commits the large-scale, allied fighting forces to a common course of action. In time, the leaders of other war parties being mounted by warring communities in the larger region will seek his proven experience and perceived power and submit to his authority. Under conditions of escalating warfare, Jivaroan tribesmen frequently will yield to the centralized and hierarchical regional authority of a war chieftain, whom they designate a *curaca* or ruler. Moreover, there are recorded instances of Jivaroan *curacas* deferring to the leadership and hegemony of an especially strong *curaca* (Redmond 1994:126). This form of centralized political leadership that aspiring tribesmen can achieve I have designated a chieftaincy, wherein the chieftain wields authority beyond his village and exercises hierarchically differentiated leadership over a group of villages in the manner of a chief (Redmond 1998a: 3-4). In times of war the group of villages that make up a regional chieftaincy might even bear the name of the chieftain (Redmond 1998b: 71). Conditions of intensive warfare favor a structural pose that centers on the emergence of a strong regional leader, the war chieftain, whose centralized leadership can extend over many villages in a region.

Secondly, this appraisal of both the tactical and supernatural dimensions of a tribal war leader's trajectory emphasizes the importance of his accrued supernatural power. An aspiring war leader who is successful in his visionary quests and acquires the *arútam* power and prophecy of ancestral spirits is especially empowered to lead others in risky intervillage and intertribal raids. The visionary knowledge he obtains from the supernatural world, together with his accrued *arútam* power make him confident of undertaking a dangerous mission, but most importantly, make him appear invincible in the eyes of fellow tribesmen. In his public personae he assumes a commanding presence and conveys a palpable authority that sets him apart. A renowned war leader is perceived as having an enhanced understanding of causality and the necessary foresight and acumen that can allay the fears of his warriors, incite them to war, and achieve victory. Moreover, his encounters with cosmological ancestors vest him and his ventures with legitimacy and moral authority. His accrued supernatural power earns him the ritual sanctity and the unquestionable authority to command a hierarchically differentiated fighting force, to make critical on-the-spot decisions, and to influence the actions of others in general. The heightened authority of renowned war leaders is a remarkable achievement given their tribal social context that values personal freedom, consensus-based decision-making, leadership by example that has been characterized as "one word from him and everyone does as he pleases" (Sahlins 1968:21), and village autonomy.

Finally, the need that warring tribesmen may have for the centralized and hierarchical leadership of chieftains can be guaranteed by electing the eldest son of a deceased chieftain to the position. It is the very ascribed qualities possessed by the eldest son of a renowned war chieftain that are sought by tribesmen in times of war to assure permanence and prosperity. Those ascribed qualities are the product of the son's birthright, as well as his training and visionary quests under his father's tutelage. Additionally, certain advantages accrue to him as his father's deputy, most notably his exemption from the usual post-marital period of matrilocal residence and service to his wife's natal household. Regardless of his birthright, however, the son must also achieve his own measure of success in the pursuit of warfare and the acquisition of *arútam* power before he can be elected war leader and succeed to his father's position. The son's inheritance of his father's chieftaincy depends upon his ascribed qualities as well as his own achievements. Both achieved and ascribed statuses can be said to exist in tribal societies, which have been characterized as egalitarian societies. As shown here, the sons of chieftains become members of a privileged but "submerged" social rank (Young 1971:63).

The point that needs to be raised in any discussion of the role that achieved versus ascribed statuses may assume in the leadership dynamics of temporary chieftaincies and the development of more permanent chiefdoms is that while both exist in the pool of the qualities of leadership variability among tribal societies, when ascribed characteristics of leadership offer the greatest selective advantages in terms of material and reproductive benefits to a tribal society in a particular historical instance (Braun 1990:79-82), those ascribed characteristics of leadership will likely be selected and replicated by succeeding generations. We have seen how certain ascribed characteristics of leadership are sanctified by the emergent leader's birthright and privileged access to cosmological sources of power that bestow him with the legitimacy to command fellow tribesmen. When ascribed qualities of leadership make the intergenerational transfer of centralized authority more efficient and speedy, and less prone to disruption (Johnson 1978:101), they will be favored, selected, and even replicated by succeeding generations, especially in dire situations that call for greater efficiency and centralized decision-making (Braun 1990:70). I have shown how conditions of chronic warfare are precisely the sort of urgent situation that would favor ascribed qualities of leadership in the form of the eldest son of a renowned chieftain being elected his successor. In time the temporary chieftaincy that emerges to serve the needs of warring tribesmen has the potential to be considered so advantageous and beneficial that it will be institutionalized and made permanent in the form of the hereditary chiefdom, wherein a lineage of hereditary leaders who by their birthright and legitimized authority will rule over the member communities of their polity in perpetuity.

Acknowledgments

I would like to thank Bill Parkinson and Severin Fowles for inviting me to contribute to this volume and giving me the opportunity to reappraise Jivaroan war leaders by learning to think with my heart. Bernardo Urbani and Dr. Carlos Bosque kindly provided me with references about the oilbird. David Kiphuth and Bridget Thomas prepared the figures.

References Cited

Brown, M. F.
1985   *Tsewa's Gift: Magic and Meaning in an Amazonian Society*. Smithsonian Institution Press, Washington, D.C.

Braun, D. P.
1986   Selection and Evolution in Nonhierarchical Organization. In *The Evolution of Political Systems: Sociopolitics in Small-Scale Sedentary Societies*, edited by S. Upham, 62-86. School of American Research. Cambridge University Press, Cambridge.

Cotlow, L.
1953   *Amazon Head-Hunters*. Henry Holt, New York.

Descola, P.
1994   *In the Society of Nature: A Native Ecology in Amazonia*. Cambridge University Press, Cambridge.
1996   *The Spears of Twilight: Life and Death in the Amazon Jungle*. The New Press, New York.

Drown, F. and M. Drown
1961   *Mission to the Head-Hunters*. Harper and Row, New York.

Gearing, F.
1958   The Structural Poses of 18th Century Cherokee Villages. *American Anthropologist* 60(6):1148-1157.

Goldman, I.
1970   *Ancient Polynesian Society*. University of Chicago Press, Chicago.
1975   *The Mouth of Heaven*. John Wiley and Sons, New York.

González Holguín, D.
1989   *Vocabulario del la Lengua General de Todo el Peru Llamada Qquichua o del Inca* (1608), edited by R. Matos Mendieta. Editorial de la Universidad Nacional Mayor de San Marcos, Lima.

Harner, M. J.
1972   *The Jívaro: People of the Sacred Waterfalls*. Doubleday/Natural History Press, Garden City, New York.

Helms, M. W.
1998   *Access to Origins: Affines, Ancestors, and Aristocrats*. University of Texas Press, Austin.

Hendricks, J. W.
1991   Symbolic Counterhegemony among the Ecuadorian Shuar. In *Nation-States and Indians in Latin America*, edited by G. Urban and J. Sherzer, 53-71. University of Texas Press, Austin.
1993   *To Drink of Death: The Narrative of a Shuar Warrior*. The University of Arizona Press, Tucson.

Johnson, G. A.
1978   Information Sources and the Development of Decision-Making Organizations. In *Social Archeology: Beyond Subsistence and Dating*, edited by C. L. Redman et al., 87-112. Academic Press, New York.

Karsten, R.
1935   *The Head-Hunters of Western Amazonas*. Societas Scientiarum Fennica. Commentationes Humanarum Litteratum VII (1). Centraltryckeriet, Helsingfors.

Kelekna, P.
1981   *Sex Asymmetry in Jivaroan Achuara Society: A Cultural Mechanism Promoting Belligerence*. Ph.D. dissertation, University of New Mexico. University Microfilms, Ann Arbor.
1998   War and theocracy. In *Chiefdoms and Chieftaincy in the Americas*, edited by E. M. Redmond, 164-188. University Press of Florida, Gainesville.

Marcus, J.
1998   *Women's Ritual in Formative Oaxaca: Figurine-Making, Divination, Death and the Ancestors*. Memoirs of the Museum of Anthropology, No. 33. University of Michigan Museum of Anthropology, Ann Arbor.

Pellizzaro, P. S.
1990   *Arutam: Mitología Shuar*. Colección 500 Años 22. Ediciones ABYA-YALA, Quito.

Redmond, E. M.
1994   *Tribal and Chiefly Warfare in South America*. Memoirs of the Museum of Anthropology, No. 28. University of Michigan Museum of Anthropology, Ann Arbor.
1998a The Dynamics of Chieftaincy and the Development of Chiefdoms. In *Chiefdoms and Chieftaincy in the Americas*, edited by E. M. Redmond, pp. 1-17. University Press of Florida, Gainesville.
1998b In War and Peace: Alternative Paths to Centralized Leadership. In *Chiefdoms and Chieftaincy in the Americas*, edited by E. M. Redmond, pp. 68-103. University Press of Florida, Gainesville.

Sahlins, M. D.
1968   *Tribesmen*. Prentice-Hall, Englewood Cliffs, NJ.

Siverts, H.
1972 *Tribal Survival in the Alto Marañon: the Aguaruna Case.* IWGIA Document 10. Copenhagen.
1975 Jívaro Head Hunters in a Headless Time. In *War, Its Causes and Correlates*, edited by M.A. Nettleship, R. D. Givens, and A. Nettleship, 663-674. Mouton Publishers, The Hague.

Snow, D. W.
1961 The Natural History of the Oilbird, Steatornis caripensis, in Trinidad, W.I. Part 1. General Behavior and Breeding Habits. *Zoologica* 46:27-48.

Stirling, M. W.
1938 *Historical and Ethnographical Material on the Jívaro Indians.* Bureau of American Ethnology Bulletin 17. Smithsonian Institution, Washington, D.C.

Up de Graff, F. W.
1923 *Head-Hunters of the Amazon.* Herbert Jenkins Ltd., London.

Young, M. W.
1971 *Fighting with Food: Leadership, Values and Social Control in a Massim Society.* Cambridge University Press, Cambridge.

Zikmund, M. and J. Hanzelka
1963 *Amazon Headhunters.* Artia, Prague.

5. Inequality and Egalitarian Rebellion, a Tribal Dialectic in Tonga History

Severin M. Fowles

Introduction

During the early historic period, 'Batonga' was the name that emerged to describe a group of dispersed cattle herders and agriculturalists living on the Batoka Plateau and surrounding regions in what is today modern Zambia (Fig. 1). According to the earliest written documents, the term Batonga (or Tonga in the remainder of the paper) was loosely translated as those who were political 'independents' (Livingstone 1865:220). By their very name, the Tonga of the late 19th and early 20th century associated themselves with a notion of self-autonomy and of dispersed power in the absence of strong centralized chiefs. They were, in this sense, highly egalitarian in dogma, actively asserting equality rather than taking it for granted. This is not to say, however, that all Tonga were in fact equal, nor that gender and age differences alone were the sole sources of inequality. As discussed below, leaders of varying status, power and authority were present. It is the task of this paper to examine the existing ethnographic and ethnohistoric evidence for both the various types of Tonga leadership as well as the impacts of individual leaders on the historical trajectory of the Tonga social context as a whole.

In doing so, this paper follows the general re-evaluation of the nature of tribal egalitarianism that has been underway on a number of fronts in anthropology during the past twenty or so years (e.g., Flanagan 1989; Paynter 1989; Whiteley 1988; Brison 1989; Price and Feinman 1995; Blake and Clark 1999). This reevaluation has been brought about, in part, on empirical grounds as tribal ethnographies and historic documents are reread to expose the social inequalities that at times failed to be sufficiently emphasized in earlier writings. However, the reevaluation has also been stimulated by recent theoretical shifts toward more agent-based approaches to social theory, in which the self-interested goals of individuals are given caus-

al priority over the goals of the group or social system. Agency models have sensitized anthropologists to the reality that, even on those occasions when a relatively high degree of social equality is the end result of a set of practices, equality itself is very rarely the personal goal of the practitioners involved, a trend that has not been without influence in the study of African societies (van Binsbergen and Schoffeleers 1985). As one of the best studied tribal societies in south-central Africa, the early historic Tonga provide an interesting case in which to consider not only such shifts in thinking about tribal egalitarianism, but also how the concept of tribal egalitarianism articulates with the historical framework advocated by the present volume.

The analysis begins by establishing the historical position of the late 19th/early 20th century Tonga within the long-term patterns of change in south central Africa generally. The focus then shifts to the ethnographic evidence for events occurring within a much shorter time span: the careers of Tonga leaders and the effects of those careers on multi-generational traditions of leadership vested in particular matrilineal groups. In the concluding sections, the implications of the Tonga case for the problem of tribal egalitarianism more broadly are considered.

The Long-Term Setting: Geographic and Historical Background

Data on the Tonga are to be found in traveler's accounts, Tonga oral tradition and 20th century governmental reports; however the bulk of current knowledge comes from the extensive ethnographic work of Elizabeth Colson and others during the 1940's, 50's, and 60's. This analysis focuses on developments in Tonga society during the first half of the 20th century, the period just prior to the major British development projects that significantly altered local settlement patterns. As Colson (1968)

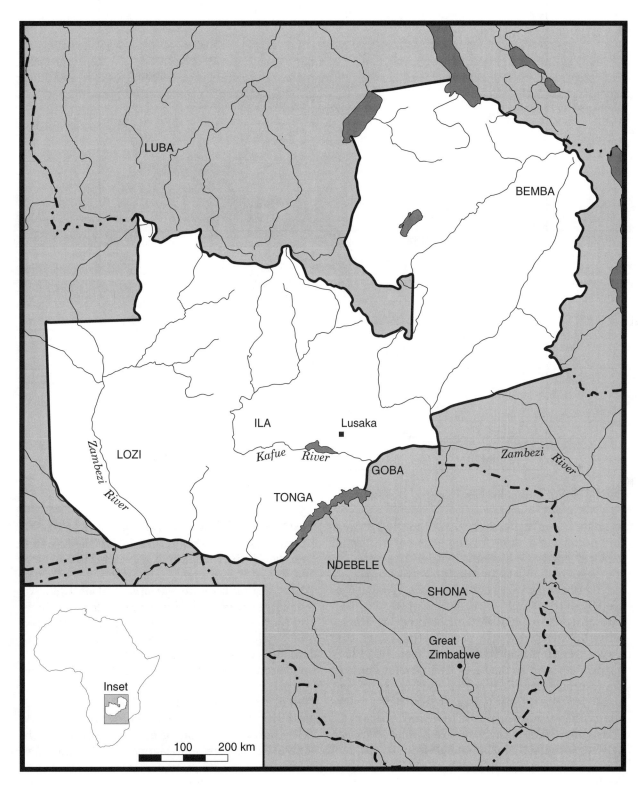

Fig. 1. Tongaland and its environs.

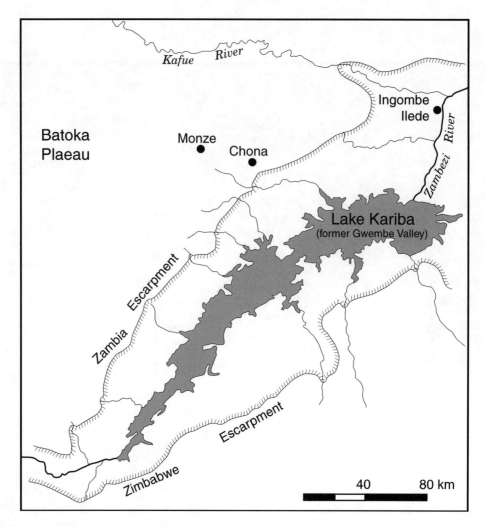

Fig. 2. Major Tonga areas discussed in the text.

has noted, it is misleading to refer to the Tonga of this period as a 'tribe' in the sense of an actual political entity. While the British attempted to create such an entity for administrative purposes during the early years of colonialism, 'Tonga' was used by native Zambians to define an ethnic group with blurred and ever shifting boundaries. Physically, linguistically, and socially the Tonga displayed few significant differences from neighboring peoples such as the Ila or Goba, and it appears that ethnic unity really only arose later in the colonial period as ethnicity came to be used to determine access to natural resources (Lancaster 1974). Consequently, data on these closely related groups will be periodically included below to fill out portions of the discussion for which the Tonga data are lacking.

As a social context, Tongaland occupied[1] two principle ecozones in south-central Zambia: the large, open Batoka Plateau to the northwest and

the Gwembe Valley to the southeast (Fig. 2). The Batoka Plateau is a region of relatively fertile soils bounded by the perennial Kafue River to the north and by the Escarpment country to the southeast. While rainfall is highly variable (Colson 1968:97), the plateau was conducive to the traditional slash-and-burn strategies that required relatively frequent field and residence moves but did little to deplete the soils over the long term. Prior to the introduction of corn by the British, sorghum and bulrush millet were the two principle crops of the Tonga. Equally important, however, was the compatibility of the plateau region with large-scale cattle herding. As among many groups in south-central Africa, the maintenance of large numbers of cattle was of great importance to most Tonga both for their economic benefits and due to the centrality of cattle to the native system of prestige. Particularly interesting is the fact that Tonga men primarily herded cattle that they held on loan from others, leaving their own herds to also be dispersed as temporary loans to acquaintances over a wide area. This practice reduced the risk of disease and theft to any one man's property while creating a geographically broad network of social ties that could be drawn on in other spheres of social life (Colson 1962:122-171).

The relative agricultural and herding success experienced on the Batoka Plateau made it a place of refuge for groups in the Gwembe Valley to the southeast during periods of stress. In the late 19th and early 20th centuries, the Gwembe Valley was also home to a substantial Tonga population that was connected to the plateau through economic and kinship ties. Economic life in the Gwembe Valley differed somewhat from the plateau. Agriculture focused on yearly-replenished floodplain fields, fishing received greater emphasis, and large-scale cattle herding was rendered difficult by the lack of grazing land and the presence of the tsetse fly. During the late prehistoric and early historic periods, the Gwembe Valley periodically received immigrants from the south and east, resulting in some of the largest population densities in Tongaland. Rainfall in the valley, however, was both limited and unpredictable, so much so that periodic famines were a way of life along the Zambezi's banks. During such famines, the Valley Tonga tended to migrate north to draw off the resources of those on the Escarpment and Plateau with whom they could claim some sort of basis for social obligations (Reynolds 1968:6, 78).

Despite the different ecological settings of the Valley and Plateau Tonga, both groups were characterized by similar social structures and roughly comparable settlement patterns. Both were matrilineal societies in the sense that inheritance and most social obligations were traced through one's mother's line more frequently than through one's father's. Matrilineages were important corporate groups, though they tended to be residentially dispersed over a number of different neighborhoods. Individual settlements were thus typically composed of members of a number of different kin groups, reducing the potential power of headmanship significantly—a point discussed at greater length below. Settlements were typically small and rarely housed much more than 100 people; however, in some regions—especially in the valley and on the margins of the Kafue Plain where population pressures were greatest—dense clusters of households grew to include many hundreds of individuals (Colson 1962:214; Reynolds 1968:10). Colson (per. com. 2000) notes that Tonga 'villages' may

have been much more ephemeral social units prior to British-imposed regulations that all Tonga reside in a village of at least 10 taxpayers. Neighborhood communities, on the other hand, almost certainly had a greater social relevancy arising out of the common use of community shrines. Residential mobility between villages and neighborhoods tended to be high, and economic specialization within and between settlements was limited. Based upon these observations, the Tonga would appear to fit comfortably into certain classic social typologies as an 'acephalous', 'big man', 'egalitarian' or 'tribal' society.

But as is the case with all social contexts, the early historic Tonga were the product of a particular historical trajectory, and the features of Tonga social life cannot be satisfactorily explored unless one is mindful of this fact. For present purposes, the story of the Tonga commenced some time during the first millennium AD as the initial Iron Age settlers entered Zambia (Fagan 1967, 1970; Phillipson 1978). It was at this point that the characteristic mixed farming and herding adaptation was first established throughout the region, replacing a previously dominant and widespread hunting and gathering tradition. The Tonga appear to have emerged out of this generalized adaptation as a recognizable social tradition by the early second millennium, an event marked archaeologically by the rapid appearance of a distinctive ceramic style on the Batoka Plateau (Phillipson 1968). General ceramic continuity after the 12th century suggests that the Tonga occupation of the plateau was temporally deep and that no major replacement by another cultural group occurred subsequent to the initial Tonga Diaspora (Smaldone 1979:10; Fagan 1970:216-17; Oliver and Fagan 1975:100-101).

During the hundreds of years that the Tonga occupied the Batoka Plateau they never developed a long-term pattern of centralized political leadership and chose instead to remain relatively dispersed, economically unspecialized, and politically decentralized. Neighboring groups, however, constructed very different social formations out of the same basic economic adaptation. As early as the 14th century AD, a complex, probably Shona-speaking political center with extensive trade relations developed at Great Zimbabwe to the south (Garlake 1973); and in the Zambezi Valley, at the eastern edge of Tongaland, the trade center of Ingombe Ilede was constructed, at which clear evidence of elite burials has been found (Phillipson and Fagan 1969). By the beginning of the 15th century, a large and highly centralized regional polity known as the Mwene Mutapa Confederacy had also developed just to the southeast (Abraham 1962). More recently, during the 18th and 19th centuries, the Lozi, descendent Shona, and Ndebele are but a few of the surrounding groups that continued the trend toward centralization and established polities with three or more tiers of political control, formal armies, and stratified systems of inequality (cf. Vansina 1968).

Why the Tonga did not follow a similar evolutionary path cannot be explained by any natural deficiencies in the ecology of Tongaland. A great deal of potential for political centralization probably did exist. Possibilities for craft specialization, monopolization of trade, and the domination of groups on the plateau over their frequently dependent kin in the valley, however, all went largely unexploited during the early historic period (Colson 1968:103-110, Saha 1994:13). In fact, the Tonga held a number of attitudes that appear designed specifically to have prevented any such possibilities. Craft specialization and formal trade in ceramics, for example, appear almost to have been consciously avoided when one considers the implications of the Tonga conviction that "a promised pot will break during firing" (Colson 1968:104). While this is not to say, of course, that exchange did not occur, it does highlight a social attitude in which relationships based upon debt and economic obligation were avoided.

One might also have expected the Tonga to centralize as a defensive response to the presence of nearby powerful kingdoms. Throughout the 19th century, the Tonga suffered significant losses as aggressive neighbors such as the Kololo, Lozi, and Ndebele raided their settlements for cattle and slaves. When faced with such raids, however, existing evidence suggests that the Tonga dispersed rather than aggregating. The famed traveler and missionary David Livingstone—the first European to make sustained contact with the Tonga— traveled across the Batoka Plateau in 1855 and found them to have already been severely weakened by aggressors to the west and south. By the time of his visit, the Makololo, Chikunda, and Ndebele had all been making significant incursions into Tonga country (Livingstone 1899:76, 448, 475; Colson, per. com. 2000). Livingstone's informants told him that the land had previously been more densely settled with larger villages but that recent raiding had led most to disperse into small homesteads for defensive purposes (1899:451, 455, 476). A similar reaction has been noted historically among other Southern Bantu groups (Huffman 1986:293) who also lacked either the desire or the organizational capability to mobilize the populace. But the Tonga were not only influenced by such aggressors through direct raiding. Refugees escaping from Luba control in the north and Shona domination in the south and east appear to have filtered into Tongaland on numerous occasions in the late prehistoric and early historic periods, and to have become assimilated into local cultural patterns (cf. Lancaster 1971:456-7, 1974, 1981:13-17; van Binsbergen 1981:131; Colson 1970). Some Lozi leaders, ousted by the Makololo in the mid-19th century, also escaped to the Tonga area. In this sense, the appellation 'Tongaland' is somewhat of a misnomer; the region was and remains a complex ethnic mix of peoples who immigrated from a variety of locales (Colson, per. com. 2000). It was not until the British-imposed peace at the turn of the century that such externally derived stresses upon Tonga social life were relaxed.

It would be impossible to extract from the existing data an image of what Tonga society would have been like had it existed in isolation. Such a situation never existed in prehistory. However, the Tonga *were* politically independent of their more centralized neighbors, and although they suffered the raids of these neighbors, we can assess the effects of this stress in the same way that we might assess the effects of a drought or the spread of disease on a group's organization. When we do, certain aspects of Tonga life have an undeniable flavor of having been reactionary—not the least of which was the Tonga dogma of egalitarianism. The Tonga staunchly defended the independence of each individual and household in their society, an attitude summed up in the Tonga saying: "Any man may call himself a chief, but that does not mean that I will obey him" (as quoted in Colson 1958:31). Households were thought to be political equals and to have the right to move at will and to follow whomever they pleased, a freedom which would have been given enthusiastic emphasis by refugees fleeing from highly stratified societies as well as by locals struggling to defend themselves from surrounding dictators. Ironically, then, their interaction with surrounding complex societies appears, on one level to have encouraged rather than discouraged the maintenance of an egalitarian ethic among the Tonga (see also Smith and Dale 1968 for a similar situation among nearby and closely related Ila groups).

Lancaster (1974) has collected some of the most convincing evidence to suggest that the early historic Tonga ethnic identity may have been born of rebellion to surrounding, strongly hierarchical societies. The following oral history excerpts were recorded among the Gwembe Tonga and are deserving of somewhat lengthy quotation:

> The Tonga had lived a long time in Southern Rhodesia [Zimbabwe] along with the Karanga (Shona)…there was some kind of trouble and then as the Tonga had done something wrong the Tonga separated from the Shona. Before that they had lived together and spoken each other's languages. But after the trouble things began to change and it was said "the Tonga are no good because they complained against their chief." They did in fact rebel against their chief in Southern Rhodesia. When they rebelled against Mambo they came north and crossed the Zambezi in many places from Livingstone to Feira (Vila). This was a movement of many separate groups over a long period of time…The Tonga of Zambia never had any real chiefs or paramounts except Mambo south of the Zambezi whom they ran from so they could be free people. So they were called Tonga, which means grunters, dissatisfied people who complained and rebelled against their chief. (as quoted in Lancaster 1974:723)

Tongaland emerged in the late prehistoric periods as somewhat of a rebel sanctuary, a 'no-chief's land' filling the interstices between neighboring complex societies. Tonga identity was consciously reactionary and it is likely that particular patterns of leadership and egalitarianism within the society were equally so.

The historical context in which their society was set may help to explain certain Tonga attitudes toward social life, however it opens questions of how the Tonga egalitarian ethos actually manifested in the social sphere. Furthermore, we may also question how Tonga individuals sought their own self-interested goals *despite* this ethos, in other words we may look for the differences between ideology and outcomes as discussed by Flanagan (1989:248). These, of course, are the sorts of questions that have been central to contemporary reevaluations of tribal egalitarianism generally. In the remainder of the paper, we will turn to consider these issues in greater depth.

Tonga Egalitarianism in Practice

To say that the Tonga asserted an egalitarian principle does not necessarily imply anything about the actual degree of equality in their social relations as practiced. In most cases, however, the term 'egalitarian society' is used in Fried's (1967) sense to refer to contexts in which the dominant social inequalities are based solely on differences of gender, age and personal ability. Accepting the broad definition of social inequality "as social differentiation accompanied by differential moral evaluation" advocated by Kelly (1993:473), our analysis of Tonga egalitarianism may proceed by considering (1) a few of the major socially defined positions or categories in the Tonga world, and (2) the privileges and prestige—or, conversely, social stigma and lack of privilege—associated with those positions.

Social differentiation within the kin group

The basic decision-making unit in Tonga society is the matriline. Tonga matrilines were not land-holding groups, but they did share bridewealth and inheritance obligations and congregated regularly for such occasions as funerals, girl's puberty rites, vengeance or offense, etc. (Colson 1962:23). As such, they were the principal institution with respect to the mobilization of people and/or wealth. The matrilineal group itself was seldom composed of over 40 adults, and these individuals tended to be scattered over a wide area in a number of different neighborhood groups (Colson 1977:123).

Given the importance of the matriline, it is interesting to note that the matrilineal group was not internally ranked in any way and that all members were considered equally related and equally deserving of all the privileges of group membership (Colson 1962:22-25; Gluckman 1965:95-6).[2] For example, at the death of an individual, all members of the deceased's matriline were thought to have equal inheritance rights. In other words, the Tonga did *not* have segmentary lineage systems similar to those discussed by Sahlins (1961, 1968) and others (Fortes and Evans-Pritchard 1940; Fortes 1953; Smith 1956). Was this lack of internal segmentation a conscious move to avoid the development of conical clans and the leaders that accompany them? Perhaps. Indeed it is telling that Tonga in the middle of the 20th century even commented that segmentary lineage systems *couldn't* work in their social context (Colson 1968:139).

Regardless, there do appear to have been systemic deterrents to the use of kinship to institutionalize decision-making inequality—even at the level of the kin group. Kinship leaders did exist, and when those leaders were able to attain significant wealth (typically assessed by the size of their cattle herds) they became the focus of particularly large matrilineal groups. The enlargement of a kin group around a wealthy individual did not, however, always result from that individual's active recruitment of new kin members. Rather, it was frequently a repercussion of the unwillingness of existing members to split off and form a separate matriline, an action that would significantly reduce their chances of inheriting a portion of a leader's wealth (Colson 1962). Indeed, upon the death of the wealthy individual, claims would be made upon the inheritance from relatives near and far, and that wealth would not exist intact to support the authority of a single new kin leader.

At a more fundamental level, even when an individual did manage to amass wealth, social prestige, and a large group of dependent kin, the costs of these accomplishments were great. The 'bigger' a Tonga big man or woman became, the more that individual was obliged to take on the economic responsibility of the kin group. The carelessness of one bad seed in a leader's extended family, for example, might indebt that leader financially or make his village vulnerable to raids/attacks in the name of compensation. Given this reality, the degree of social prestige that came with leadership was likely of little consolation. Interestingly, in her account of the history of the Nampeyo neighborhood on the Tonga Plateau, Colson (1991) reports a number of instances in which there was no one willing to inherit the position and responsibility of a kin-based leadership position, even though this position was the most prestigious in the neighborhood. Here, we find that leadership and prestige among the Tonga wss similar to that among many other 'tribal' societies. Leadership positions of some sort inevitably existed, and some of these positions were accompanied by significant social valuation. However, such prestige—and not any significant material or economic perks—was typically the sole reward for agreeing to take on the heavy burden of representation.

Kin-based leadership was therefore limited and costly. While an individual might expect to accrue prestige through his/her age, charisma and personal wealth over time, the prestige tended to be fleeting and it dispersed at the death of the individual into the undifferentiated body of the matriline.

Social differentiation within the village

Unlike the matrilineal group, villages in Tonga society did have formally recognized positions of leadership. Villages tended to be small (no larger than 500 people in most cases) and relatively dispersed throughout the landscape (Colson 1968; Selous 1888:216; Livingstone 1899:554). Each, however, had a headman, and this position was clearly one of some importance worth competing over. Headmen or would-be headmen actively sought to recruit followers, especially during the early years of village growth when a headman's own sons were immature (Colson 1962:204).[3] Personal charisma was by far the principle means through which this was accomplished, and there are no recorded examples of the use of outright coercion to build a following. There were, of course, cases in which headmanship was 'inherited' from a matrilineal relative. In such cases, however, inheritance was still always subject to village consensus, such that the new official's position was still earned through his or her personal qualities and past record. In this regard, Tonga headmen were similar to the big men of New Guinea (Meggitt 1973; Strathern 1971) or the 'chieftains' of the Americas as defined by Redmond (1998).

Whereas the New Guinean big men maintained their position by indebting their dependents through competitive feasting, however, Tonga headmen held little means of building social debt. Only those villagers whom the headman had acquired as slaves through purchase or raiding tended to be highly dependent, and this due principally to the fact that they had been separated from their own local kin base. Other village members followed the headman in the same way as they would a kin leader—on a tentative basis, granting him seniority as the right due any individual willing to accept the risks of representing the village in the larger social arena (e.g., Colson 1991:13). There were also few material benefits to headmanship. Headmen appear not to have had significantly more wives than non-headmen and they received no tribute. A strong statement of the limited power of the position was recorded by Colson in the 1940's, during which time she noted that a disgruntled villager displeased with his/her headman was freely permitted to shift allegiance to the headman of another nearby village without having to physically move to that other village (Colson 1968:119). While colonial restrictions on movement were probably partly responsible, such remarkable freedom of allegiance indicates again that native Tonga positions of leadership were relatively ineffectual.

Indeed, a headman's power was also limited by the relatively high residential mobility required by the swidden agriculture of the Tonga (Colson 1962:21; Barrie 1968:71-8). This was especially true on the Batoka Plateau where soils were quickly depleted and a frequent desire to move closer to the ever-distant fields was felt. Villages tended not to persist more than a generation, during which time the composition of the group fluctuated widely.

Another factor that held the power of headmen in check was that beer—in addition to being the accepted form of offerings to ancestral spirits— was also the primary incentive used when mobilizing work parties or other forms of non-kin based social collectivities (Colson 1967:11; Colson and Scudder 1988). Despite its ritual and social importance, beer had certain properties that limited the degree to which it could be used by leaders to compete for prestige and to build a fund of power. First, beer had to be the product of a man's wife. Men were not able to brew beer themselves, and therefore it was only through marriage that men gained the ability to make offerings to the spirits. The result of this situation was that marriage and the appropriation of a wife's labor were critical and limiting elements in a man's competition in the ritual and social sphere. Second, beer had to be consumed immediately after it was brewed, lest it sour. As a valued product, it therefore could not be saved or used to generate a surplus.

In sum, then, the position of headman carried with it little potential for true social power. Prestige alone was the perquisite of the headman and this was obtained only through negotiation and hard work.

Social differentiation within the neighborhood

Successful and aggressive headmen, nonetheless, were not limited to competition at the village level, but also frequently sought to develop a position of leadership and authority within the surrounding community. The neighborhood, or *cisi*, was an indigenously recognized, albeit loosely bounded social collectively that joined together for initiation ceremonies and to solicit the spirits for rainfall. Such neighborhood communities tended to be composed of 4-8 villages and between 400-800 individuals who were led by either "unofficial leaders" (Colson 1958:27, 1977:121) or a succession of local chiefs.

Competition for preeminence within neighborhood communities—as at the village level—was still largely a matter of personal charisma. Howev-

er, the historic documents reveal that many of the ambitious Tonga leaders were experimenting with different means to enhance their social influence. Livingstone, in the 1950's, for example, encountered a number of Tonga 'chiefs' along the Zambezi who were in the habit of keeping dozens of human skulls (the victims of successful raids) on spikes outside their residences (Livingstone 1865:328, 335; 1899:74, 454). The same practice was noted among related Ila groups by Smith and Dale (1968:24). Implicit within this kind of behavior of course was the use and/or threat of force as a means of empowerment. And in another social or historical context, such threats might have helped form the foundation for chiefly leadership over a broad region. However, the Tonga had had enough of chiefly bullies and, consequently, only indulged such aggrandizing individuals so far.

Ultimately, the only moral imperative that could be mustered to legitimize a particular individual's eminence in a neighborhood emerged out of the actual history of immigration into a region. As in many other tribal contexts throughout the world, the first individuals to arrive in a given area were viewed by the Tonga as having a certain amount of de facto authority (Colson 1958, 1962:92; Barrie 1968:11). As a neighborhood was settled over time, a crude ranking of the matrilines thus emerged based on the order of arrival. However, the relatively high settlement mobility necessitated by Tonga swidden agriculture left this rationale for leadership with only limited short-term effect.

When an ambitious individual did achieve a chiefly position in a Tonga neighborhood there were, again, very few material perks. The chief might play a role in distributing land to newcomers or be consulted on local matters of importance, but no Tonga chiefs received tribute or were able to delegate their own daily agricultural or herding chores to others. Indeed, it appears to have been the case that chiefs worked harder than others in the community. As one Ila man described the same situation in his related community: "Chiefdom is serfdom" (Smith and Dale 1968 vol. 1: 307). As a result, the tendency for chiefly positions to be handed down matrilineally was of little consequence in terms of the institutionalization of inequality. And even given this tendency toward matrilineal inheritance, the choice of a chief remained one of consensus based upon a particular person's achievements and social standing. "A chief does not beget a chief" (Smith and Dale 1968 vol. 1:304) - the chiefly role very much remained an achieved status.

Differentiation within the ritual order

Ultimately, it is probably most accurate to say that the real Tonga individuals with significant, socially legitimate power were those who had *died* and entered the spirit world. As in many other preindustrial societies, the Tonga believed that events in this world were deeply affected by the spirits or shades of the deceased. It is safe to say, in fact, that Tonga society might be viewed as having been a set of mini chiefdoms, were one to view the deceased as the chiefs.[4] Indeed, the deceased were viewed as being concerned with building up a large following within the kin group (Colson 1962:41), they passed harsh judgment on those that displeased them, and they were considered to be deserving of tribute in the form of beer and/or iron offerings on important occasions. But, of course, the spirit world could not speak for itself. Spirits needed mediums or prophets to articulate their wishes, and it is within these positions among the living that the most interesting potential for the development of institutionalized inequality can be explored.

There were a number of minor types of spirits in Tonga cosmology, but two main types were clearly of greatest importance to social life. The first was anchored in kinship and was comprised of the *mizimu*, spirits of deceased individuals directly ancestral to a particular matrilineal group. Such ancestral spirits demanded constant offerings from their matriline, but were powerless with respect to other kin groups. The second type of spirit, known as *basangu*, was not rooted in any one kin group, but rather influenced the ecological world at large. The *basangu* were generalized spirits that affected certain aspects of the total community life—rainfall in particular. Access to each type of spirit by members of the society was different and had particular ramifications for both leadership potential and the distribution of power.[5]

The *mizimu*, for example, could only be accessed by members of a given kin group. Consistent with the undifferentiated nature of the Tonga matriline, all adults of the group had relatively equal rights to approach their ancestral spirits, however in many cases propitiations would have to be made by the individual who had inherited that *mizimu's* spirit on behalf of the concerned family member. Each individual was further viewed as having his or her own guardian *mizimu* that was closely entwined with that individual's life. Guardian *mizimu* were inherited through the taking of a particular family name. When an average individual died, their guardian *mizimu* might then be inherited by others (the particulars of such inheritance varying somewhat throughout Tongaland). At the death of important individuals in the community with many surviving children, however, the Tonga believed that they themselves became new *mizimu*, and so it became possible for the living to directly inherit the spirit of the recently deceased during funeral proceedings. *Mizimu* of important individuals inherited in this manner were thought to imbue an individual with many of his or her personal qualities, to the point that the distinction between the personalities of the living and the deceased became blurred (Colson 1962) and a form of extended spirit possession resulted. As one Tonga individual commented, for example:

> Ndaba was an important man with many followers. Before I was born, his *muzimu* came and said that I could be called by his name. Now it is easy to see that I am indeed Ndaba, for I too have become an important man with many people who depend on me. (as quoted in Colson 1962:13)

This tradition of *mizimu* inheritance is particularly interesting to consider with respect to the problems of Tonga leadership and succession. As anthropologists, we are accustomed to imagining a categorical difference between leadership positions that are 'achieved' versus those that are 'ascribed'. The former are considered to be earned through one's personal abilities and therefore to be typical of egalitarian systems. The latter are considered typical of societies with institutionalized inequalities in which positions of power are inherited. *Mizimu* inheritance, however, was really a hybrid of these two pathways to leadership, given that what one presumably *inherited* was the charisma and other personal qualities which enabled an individual to *achieve* a certain position of prestige and influence. The *mizimu* provided both a means and an ideological justification for the inheritance of a degree of social power, while still couching that power in the overriding achieved or egalitarian ethic. Ultimately, however, the influence of a *mizimu* was focused on a single matrilineal group and its patrilineal extensions, referred to together as a *lutundu*. And given the typical Tonga mixture of matrilineality and patrilocality, this group tended to be both dispersed over a large area and difficult to mobilize politically.

The *basangu*, on the other hand, were generalized spirits that could potentially influence all the matrilines in a region. As ecologically influential spirit agents, their potential use in power struggles among the living was greater. The *basangu* influenced the Tonga communities through their ability to send sickness and famine, but their most significant power rested in their control of rain (Colson 1962, 1977; Smith and Dale 1968 vol. 2:141). Importantly, while the *mizimu* were thought to be the domain of particular matrilineal groups, the *basangu* were viewed as spirits to whom the total community had the right to appeal. The Ila—a closely related group living immediately to the north of the Tonga—held similar beliefs about the spirit world, and they contrasted the *basangu* with the *mizimu* at the start of the 20th century as follows:

> The divinities of the community [*basangu*] are common property, there is no man who can claim them as his own. The divinities of men [*mizimu*] are not assimilated; a man who is not your relation does not join you in making offerings to your divinities; he would be doing wrong. But it is otherwise with the communal demigod [*basangu*]: none refrains from calling upon him; he belongs to all. In a household there are various divinities [*mizimu*]; a husband prays to his, a wife prays to hers; but as members of a community they all pray to one and the same demigod [*basangu*]. (as quoted in Smith and Dale 1968, vol.2:180-1)

Theoretically, then, the *basangu* spirits both affected all and were accessible to all.

The Tonga conceptions of the *basangu*, in this sense, reiterated their basic egalitarian ethic. Spirits of greater influence in the natural world and in community affairs were believed to be open to every member of society, through the petitioning of a spirit's shrine or medium. No one matrilineal group could monopolize access to the *basangu* nor use them to legitimize that group's privilege over any others in the community. Only those spirits that were ineffectual in greater community life (i.e., the *mizimu*) could be dominated by a particular group. Here also is another element of the greater Tonga structure that may have been consciously constructed in order to avoid the development of any sort of divine kingship or ritual basis for elite rule.

It is, therefore, particularly interesting to note that, in practice, this *ethic* of equal access to the *basangu* was not precisely followed. For instance, *basangu* were thought to reside in tangible shrines either constructed or at least maintained by the living. As home to the spirits that control the weather, rain shrines—which ranged from small constructed huts to natural features like a spring or old tree (Barrie 1968:23)—were loci of power. Unlike matrilineal obligations that were dispersed and over-lapping over a wide area, ritual obligations to a rain shrine were localized such that anyone living within a certain radius of a shrine was beholden upon that shrine's spirits, irregardless of their matrilineal or clan affiliations. Indeed, Colson (1962:87) found the shrines to be the clearest indicators of the supra-village neighborhood groups. Each shrine was maintained by a shrine custodian, a position that was passed down matrilineally. However inheritable, the social position of the shrine custodian was merely that: a custodian, without the power necessarily to direct ritual or make demands on the community at large.

In contrast to the custodian who had only weak ties to the *basangu*, another group of individuals was generally believed to be the direct representatives of important spirits, and it is here that we see the strongest signs that access to the *basangu* may not always have been equal. Prophets in Tonga society were either men or women who had been visited and possessed by a spirit, becoming the medium through which that spirit made its wishes known. Prophets and the shrines they established were especially influential as institutions to which appeals could be made in times of ecological hardship. Prophets were considered the 'rain-makers' in society. Given their role, it is not surprising to find that the most influential prophets in Tongaland were based in the Escarpment region where rainfall was both more abundant and predictable (Colson per. com. 2000). Environmental patterns, in this sense, were loosely translated into social patterns through the role of the prophet, and the Escarpment prophets at times gained wide regional recognition.[6]

Nonetheless, the prophet was merely a temporary vehicle for a *basangu* and did not, in theory, have any power of his/her own that could be passed down. Furthermore, each was competing with many other prophets for the attention of a community of followers. No prophet, therefore, could deviate far from public opinion to exert his or her own agenda. Colson (1977:124) notes that Tonga prophets "vie with each other for recognition and their influence fluctuates enormously even within a short period of time. Each neighborhood, and indeed each homestead, appears to have the option of choosing which prophet it will patronize on any particular occasion." The situation that resulted was a sort of free market in which ritual consumers were able to keep the prophets' profits (e.g., prestige, control over the structure of ritual, etc.) to a minimum.

The special relationship between the prophets and the *basangu* made it almost inevitable that, while representing the latter, the former would on occasion become influential leaders in society. Early historic evidence from nearby groups suggests that they may have even held brief but significant amounts of social power. Smith and Dale (1968 vol. 2:141) also reported for instance that:

> As the mouthpieces of the divinities they [the prophets] are legislators of the community and, generally speaking, they receive a great deal of credit. Sometimes the message they deliver is harmless enough, sometimes it is distinctly good, but sometimes it is noxious. The word of the prophet is sufficient to condemn to death for witchcraft a perfectly innocent man or woman. And such is the extraordinary credulity of the people that often they will destroy their grain or their cattle at the bidding of a prophet.

While Colson did not find such a degree of power among Tonga prophets of the 1940's and 50's, Livingstone's (1963) experiences in the mid 19th century do suggest that this situation was probably also the case in Tongaland prior to the solidification of British rule.

Regardless, the openness of spirit mediumship in Tonga society clearly did heavily restrict a prophet's ability to both accrue and maintain social power. Anyone could conceivably be possessed by any of the *basangu*, and in the case of a spirit that was viewed as especially potent, it was common for many prophets across the region to be possessed by that same *basangu* (Colson 1969). The influence and prestige of individual prophets tended therefore to be fleeting. Prophets had important social roles during times of ecological crisis and in some cases even received material gifts. However, such importance largely disappeared once either (1) conditions improved and the prophet was no longer needed or (2) bad conditions continued or worsened such that the petitioner's lost faith in the efficacy of the prophet and his or her spirit.

Finally, it must also be noted that formal mediumship was not the exclusive means by which an individual might exhibit a special relationship with the spirit world of the community. Important leaders in Tonga society were also frequently considered to be powerful medicine men, who—through the production and use of special medicines—were able to affect the world in ways that directly benefited the community. For example, one well-known neighborhood leader in the mid 19th century, Chief Chona Mupati, was able to protect his people from

Lozi and Ndebele raids with his medicine and so became an important historical figure in his region. Even though Chona Mupati was never possessed by *basangu* directly, he was venerated "because he dreamed and so was like someone who is entered by *basangu*" (Colson 1991:9). Inasmuch as the use of medicine was also associated with a connection to the *basangu*, the medicine man and the prophet appear to have been conceived in terms of the same, or at least a very similar, social role. Ultimately, we must also face the reality that as the British formalized chiefly rule in Tongaland, they simultaneously exerted pressure to dissociate ritual from political power, a pressure that was noted by Tonga leaders themselves (e.g., Colson 1991:48). The persistent bond between mediumship and political rule throughout the early historic period, therefore suggests a very strong relationship indeed.

Regional Rain-Shrine Cults as Historical Paths Towards Centralization and Institutionalized Inequality

There is "a deep-seated tendency among the Tonga to equate rain rituals with political integration." (Colson 1968:161)

As we have just seen, the Tonga cosmological system included two major types of spirits—one closely tied to the immediate concerns of the matriline and a second tied to the ecological and social concerns of a geographically based community. These two types of spirits controlled the affairs of different social groups and so led to the existence of two distinct avenues toward social power for would be leaders. Each avenue in turn had its own structural limitations that put a ceiling on the fund of power that might be accrued by a particular individual and his or her successors over time. The cosmological system thus tended to discourage the emergence of strong, centralized leadership while simultaneously reinforcing the social cohesion that resulted from the cross-cutting of matrilineages and neighborhood groups. Individuals competed for power but rarely were able to develop a deep support base.

On one hand, the early historic Tonga cosmological order—like the social system in general—may have been constructed and manipulated over time in reaction to and as a rejection of the cosmological hierarchy present in the systems of religiously-based leadership among some surrounding states. Much anthropological effort has gone into documenting the ways in which institutionalized inequality was frequently legitimized in hierarchical African societies through the manipulation of ritual. Given a widespread model of inequality employed in surrounding complex societies, one must consider the degree to which aggrandizing individuals may have strove to institute this model within early historic Tonga society.

On a cosmological level, the *basangu* spirits represented a latent potential for centralization through their ability to influence the ecology of a region. However, because they were not directly tied to a particular matrilineal group, any prophet might claim to be possessed by a *basangu* from anywhere in Tongaland or beyond. The central problem for a would-be chief, then, was how to gain privileges and legitimate rights of unique access to the regional power of certain *basangu*, to whom everyone (and not just his or her matrilineal group) was beholden. Here the exceptions in Tonga leadership become very interesting as opposed to the norms discussed above. A number of recent researchers have, in fact, challenged Colson's portrayal of the Tonga's decentralized politics, pointing to certain exceptional shrine cults as evidence of incipient political centralization at a regional level (e.g., O'Brien 1982, O'Brien and O'Brien 1996, Werbner 1977:xvi, van Binsbergen 1981). In the remainder of this chapter I will turn to examine what light these seemingly anomalous cases may shed on the historical development of Tonga society as a whole.

The problem of the Monze rain cult

In doing so, one case in particular emerges as the most influential in the recent reevaluation of Tonga egalitarianism—that of the Monze cult centered on the Batoka Plateau. The term Monze (as in the case of other shrine cults) has been used to refer on one hand to a particular Tonga *basangu*, but also to the prophets who were the mediums of that spirit as well to the overriding cult that surrounded the spirit's shrine. The first reference to the cult comes from Livingstone in the 1850's. While traveling across the plateau, Livingstone passed through the region inhabited by Monze, whom he reported was "considered the chief of all the Batoka [i.e., Tonga] we have seen" (1899:475). Monze's village was located near a hill from which Livingstone also noted that there was a good view of the surrounding territory, and it is tempting to view this as the seat of regional leadership.

Such early references have been used by some to argue that the high egalitarianism recorded by Colson and others in the mid-20th century was the result either of British control or of an anthropological interest in theoretically contrasting the 'simple and egalitarian' with the 'complex and inegalitarian' African societies. Both the traditional egalitarian and the more recent hierarchical interpretation of Tonga society have been suggested based upon what is essentially the same data, suggesting the problem is not entirely an empirical one. Rather, it appears to be in part a matter of perspective—dependent upon whether one focuses on general patterns or on the exceptions to those patterns. With respect to the goals of the present volume, the problem can be rephrased by instead posing the following questions: (1) in which domains or aspects were the Tonga egalitarian or inegalitarian, and (2) in what ways did these opposing principles manifest over time in Tonga history. To answer these questions we must look more closely at the social role of prominent prophets such as Monze throughout the early historic period.

By most accounts, the Monze cult began in the first half of the 19th century[7] when the initial Monze moved onto the plateau where he was possessed and became a highly successful prophet (Colson 1969:74). Monze appears to have developed authority based upon his ability to make rain and heal in the manner of other Tonga prophets—coming to be known among British missionaries as the "wizard of the north" (Saha 1994:53). Using oral histories recorded both by themselves in the 1970's and 80's and by Jesuits in the early 1900's, the O'Briens (1996) have summarized some of the probable events in the development of the cult after this initial prophet. Following the death of the first Monze, they report, "the people [of his village] dispersed because there was no chief." Then another man, known as Mayaba (see also Saha 1994:25), was brought into the region of the initial Monze and married into the local community.

> Mayaba...was penetrated by the rainbow in his house, then he became a prophet, the people came to acclaim him as such, then Mayaba declared "I am Monze who went to heaven." Then the rain fell in abundance. ("The Old Monze" file, as quoted in O'Brien and O'Brien 1996:530)

Mayaba, thus, became possessed by Monze who by that time had become a viable *basangu*. Especially significant is the fact that this was not possession by a generalized spirit, but rather by one that would have had a recognized association with a particular matrilineal group.

After Monze Mayaba, a succession of other prophets continued the tradition of Monze mediumship, each building off of their predecessor's renown (O'Brien and O'Brien 1996:532). Why the Monze prophets were considered to be so effective throughout this period can, in part, be explained by their advantageous geographic position. For example, when Livingstone entered the region in the 1850's, the Tonga traveling with him noted when scaling the escarpment that "no one ever dies of hunger here" (Livingstone 1899:458). All the major rain shrines were on the escarpment, a region characterized by high precipitation. And Monze's village was in an area of particularly plentiful rainfall (Livingstone 1899:477), an observation that undoubtedly would have made a strong impression on the Tonga, given the highly variable rainfall on the Batoka Plateau generally. The more predictable rainfall along the escarpment would have stood as visible testimony to the efficacy of the *basangu* who were based there—Monze included. The Monze prophets also appear to have developed their positions of influence on occasion through their organization of the Tonga in opposition to the incursions of neighboring groups. In at least one recorded case, the Monze cult was central in an attempt to ally the Tonga with Ndebele to fend off the Lozi whose raids had been intensifying during the late 19th century (O'Brien 1983:26, see also Colson 1950).

The O'Briens (1996:532) note that the most interesting development in the Monze cult from a structural perspective, however, was associated with the reign of Monze Ncete at the start of the 20th century. While we cannot fully assess the regional significance of the cult during this period, Fr. Moreau described Monze Ncete as a "fairly big chief" in 1902 (as quoted in Saha 1994:52), who was 'big' enough at least to be viewed as a rebellious threat to the British South Africa Company (Saha 1994:43). Ncete appears to have been chosen by the Monze matrilineal group to become the successor of the former prophet. He was taken into a hut, symbolically taking over the 'chieftaincy'. Only after accepting this position was Ncete then possessed by the Monze *basangu*. As the O'Briens observe, this formal inheritance clearly represents a shift away from an emphasis on the Monze prophet as medium of an important spirit and toward an emphasis on Monze as an institutionalized social position, only secondarily legitimized through its ties to the spirit world. Nonetheless, Ncete did ultimately become known as a great healer in times of sickness (Saha 1994:26).

Clearly Monze and his matrilineal group were relatively important leaders in Tonga society, but how much power did they actually have? It is difficult to find tangible examples of Monze's power in the existing literature. There was, however, one point in the early 20th century when Monze moved his village 20 miles into another preexisting neighborhood community. At the arrival of Monze, the community gave up its existing rain ritual and local ritual leadership in order to follow that of Monze (Colson 1968:152). This development is particularly interesting because it runs counter to the general Tonga pattern that ritual leadership is properly due to the first to arrive in an area (Colson 1958:30-31), and it suggests that the cult had the power and authority to supplant local ritual traditions—at least in nearby neighborhoods.

O'Brien (1983) has further pointed to one event 1903 that he takes as evidence of the emergence of significant political power. During this period, the British South Africa Company had just taken formal control of Tongaland and the Tonga were at risk of being placed by the British under the leadership of the neighboring Lozi kingdom. In an effort to assert that he was in fact a legitimate ruler of his people, Monze Ncete took it upon himself to collect the British-imposed tax, ostensibly in order to travel to England to petition for his right to leadership over the Tonga people (see also Saha 1994:26). While this plan was ultimately foiled by the Lozi, Monze Ncete had enough clout to collect 623 pounds sterling (a sizeable sum of money from the people in his district) and this, by itself, does suggest that he possessed a certain degree of regional authority (O'Brien 1983).

It was also the case that throughout the 20th century delegations from other Tonga regions on the Plateau and in the Gwembe Valley, as well as from surrounding peoples such as the Ila, Sala, and Lozi, recognized the potency of the Monze cult and came to its shrine to ask for rain. In the 1940's Colson (1968:154) found that "[t]he floor of the Monze shrine [was] covered with hoe-blades paid as fines" by such groups for offences made during rain rituals or harvest ceremonies (see also O'Brien and O'Brien 1996:533). While at this time the Monze shrine was composed simply of a small structure called a *kaanda*, it was physically the largest such shrine in Tongaland (Colson 1968:156). Furthermore, the shrine itself did not merely house the Monze spirit, but also appears to have included the physical graves of past Monze prophets (Saha 1994:53). A final statement of the regional importance of the Monze cult came when the British institutionalized leadership or 'chiefly' positions for the newly defined governmental districts. Monze was formally established as chief of his district, and when the British further lumped all the Tonga into a single, large administrative unit, Colson (1968:96) notes that "Monze [was] recognized, with many reservations, as senior chief."

On the surface, this picture of the early historic Monze cult is at odds with the highly egalitarian system discussed at the start of the paper. In the late 19th century, the Monze referred to by Livingstone was clearly a male ritual leader who had great influence at least in the region surrounding him. And he had significant social power inasmuch as his pronouncements caused other Tonga to engage in activities in which they would not otherwise have engaged.

But Monze was not an individual prophet who had simply been possessed one day by a *basangu* in the normative fashion discussed in the previous section. Livingstone's Monze was part of a large kin group that took active roles in the ritual leadership of the region. Indeed, in Livingstone's writings both Monze's wife and sister appear at times to have held equally influential leadership roles. For example, while brandishing a battle-axe in a clear show of force, Monze's wife formally greeted Livingstone along side her husband at their first meeting. And when Livingstone again set upon his travels following the visit, it was Monze's sister who ordered ahead that there might be food for the European in more distant villages.[8] The important point is that the Monze shrine-cult—as an institution—appears not to have been the soul domain of an individual 'Monze', but rather of a kin group, all of whose members had an investment in the renown and influence of the cult.

There are also a number of indicators that the influence of the cult may not have been as uniform and widespread as some have suggested. For example, the Monze shrine never came to be viewed as the paramount shrine hierarchically related to a series of local, lesser shrines (Colson 1962:87), as was the case among some neighboring peoples (e.g., Garbett 1967; Bourdillon 1982). While considered to be especially potent, it does not appear to have been structurally different from any other. Gluckman (1965:116) also questions Monze's power given his apparent inability to protect the traveler and hunter Selous (1893) from a neighboring group of Tonga who were out to get him. Furthermore, while Livingstone does note the regional influence of the cult, it is also true that Monze was not the only 'chief' in the 1850's on the Batoka

Plateau (e.g., Livingstone 1865:220). Regarding the mid-1900's, Colson makes note of Monze's influence as well, but also highlights the rival importance of a female prophet known as Chibwe from the 1940's to the 1960's (Colson 1958:34). Numerous other regionally significant prophets have been documented during the 20th century both within Tongaland proper and among neighboring groups (Werbner 1977).

Even if Monze was but one among a number of shrine cults that served a wide regional population during the early historic period, the interesting questions still remain. How did the cult and the leaders within it manage to attain and hold onto a degree of ritual seniority for a number of generations, given the underlying egalitarian ethic of the society as a whole? How did the mediumship of a particular *basangu* become tied to a matriline to create a relatively institutionalized position of ritual leadership? At the largest level, the analytic challenge is to understand how one might resolve the largely egalitarian system encountered by Colson with the suggestions of institutionalized religious (and at times more strictly political) leadership positions such as that of Monze.

To understand the multi-generational development of ritual leadership in historic Tonga society, we must first look to the careers of individual leaders. Luckily, Colson (1969) has described the path towards *basangu* mediumship in some detail.

The historical effects of prophets

A prophet or spirit medium's career began with an initial possession experience, over which the individual was not considered to have any direct control. This experience might occur during childhood or as an adult. In Tonga thought, possession was an act of agency by a *spirit*, and the living prophet was not considered deserving of any special respect simply based upon the fact that he or she had become a receptacle for that spirit agent. When an individual was first possessed by a *basangu*, members of the local community assembled to clap in appreciation for the spirit's visit and to hear what predictions and/or demands the spirit had come to make. In addressing the community, the new prophet took on the role of a public resource through which community members might seek counsel with the controlling spirits in times of ecological hardship. The prophet might also at this time demand the construction of a local shrine to house his or her spirit if none was already in existence (Colson 1968:157).

Over the course of the prophet's life, then, he or she competed with other local prophets for the attention of the surrounding community. Demands—ostensibly from the spirit world—for ritual modification or for greater attention to the local shrines would be made to alleviate poor weather patterns. As noted above, success as a religious leader in this competition was based almost entirely on the accuracy of predictions and on the efficacy of the proscriptions demanded. By necessarily grounding a prophet's reputation in the vagaries of the local and regional weather patterns, limitations were undoubtedly set on the public's potential confidence in the powers of a prophet and his *basangu*. As noted earlier, this achievement-based model did tend, however, to privilege those prophets living in the Escarpment region where rainfall was highest.

Furthermore, even if the rains came as needed and a prophet's reputation were to grow, it was not necessarily always the case that his or her social prestige would grow accordingly. Colson notes that "[p]eople are very clear that they respect spirit rather than medium. It is only when they are concerned with the former that they are prepared to clap before the latter" (Colson 1969:77). This sentiment, in essence, preserved the high egalitarian ethic despite the obviously critical role of the prophet as 'rain-maker' in Tonga society. In most instances, the prophet lived no differently than any other Tonga individuals and (s)he was not considered to be endowed with special powers. Rather, the prophet was simply a vehicle through which the powerful spirits expressed their desires.

Nevertheless, in some cases it is clear that a significant degree of social prestige did develop despite this egalitarian attitude. The case of Monze 'the great rain-maker', introduced earlier, is the most frequently noted example among the Tonga. Among the closely related Ila, Smith and Dale (1968 vol. 2:147-50) also describe the path by which the prophet Mupumani gained regional renown and importance in 1913. Mupumani grew in popularity through a series of natural occurrences that dovetailed nicely with his messages, a happy outcome that probably did encourage an underlying notion that he himself had certain powers. Other examples might be included (e.g., Lancaster 1981:16). This situation, however, also had its flip side. Just as ecological happenstance might boost a religious leader's power, so too might a major drought or some other calamity destroy a leader's reputation. Prophets, therefore, tended to wax and wane in influence and popularity throughout their life span depending on their particular mix of charisma, luck, and social perceptiveness.

When a prophet died, the rain shrine (s)he had set up might continue to function, and in such cases the prophet's matrilineal group would assume the custodianship duties of the shrine. The death of a successful prophet, however, was also an occasion for the institution of a second shrine, the latter as a home for the spirit of the prophet himself, for in dying the prophet brought into existence a new *basangu* (see Colson 1991:22). As a *basangu*, the prophet then became one of the forces that affected the natural world and might potentially possess other individuals throughout Tongaland and beyond. This, then, was the basic life trajectory of the prophet. In order to address the question of how a cult such as that controlled by the Monze matrilineal group could develop and perpetuate over multiple generations, however, we must investigate what potential for inheritance existed in this system.

With respect to the problem of inheritance, it is particularly interesting to find that Colson has made note of cases in which a shrine established for a deceased prophet is merged into the shrine of the *basangu* for whom that prophet was a medium. At such shrines, "both *basangu* will be appealed to at the same time and place" (Colson 1968:157). The structural significance of such a situation is that it appears to have created an avenue by which kin groups could gain a degree of privilege in regional religious decision-making. Indeed, when a successful prophet died, (s)he entered the spirit world in two forms. On one hand, the prophet became a *mizimu* or ancestral spirit of a particular matrilineal group. As a *mizimu*, the deceased prophet both continued to affect the lives of his or her relatives and might act as the guardian spirit for particular individuals within the kin group who also stood to inherit the prophet's powers. On the other hand, an important prophet also brought into existence a *basangu* or generalized spirit that had the potential to affect any and all matrilineal groups throughout Tongaland. In a sense then, the death of an important prophet held the potential to combine the inheritability of the matrilineally based *mizimu* with the community influence and power of the generalized *basangu*.

This situation becomes even more complicated as we turn to consider the structural implications of the coalescence of the shrine of the deceased prophet with that of his former *basangu*. In such cases, it appears that the distinction between the powers of the two spirits blurred, and the surviving matrilineal group of the deceased prophet suddenly obtained a basis for linking itself with not only the *basangu* of the prophet, but also with the *basangu* who had possessed that spirit during his or her lifetime. Colson (1968:157) notes that the Monze rain shrine was one case in which such a ritual coalescence occurred. Given this, the confusion that exists in the literature over what and who the term 'Monze' represents begins to make some sense. Monze was at once (1) an original and powerful prophet of the early 19th century, (2) the *basangu* who possessed that prophet, (3) the *mizimu / basangu* of that prophet, and (4) the successive ritual leaders who inherited and were potentially possessed by the *mizimu / basangu* of the prophet. Together, these elements comprised a cult with regional influence whose power was based at the Monze shrine. Members of the matrilineal group had a vested interest in promoting the ritual importance of the shrine cult because through it their status in society at large was enhanced. Over time, the prestige of each successive Monze appears to have accrued within the cult itself resulting in a form of feedback loop.

Other examples following this pattern can also be noted, not only in other Tonga neighborhoods (e.g. Colson 1991), but also among neighboring peoples. The Goba—a closely related group living along the Zambezi just to the east—also maintain in their oral history that a powerful and well known female prophet known as Kasamba was asked by warring groups along the Zambezi to migrate down from the Batoka Plateau and bring peace through her ritual leadership. Kasamba was apparently successful in this task and after death her rain shrine and *basangu* continued to be used as a center of power through which succeeding leaders sought to legitimize their social positions (Lancaster 1981:16-7). In this case, we find once again that a successful prophet's career might have multigenerational resonance and that the leadership of a prophet was at times solicited to influence the greater political world. This tradition has been noted in the general region throughout the historic period and was dramatically seen in the role of Shona prophets during the Zimbabwe struggle for liberation in the latter half of the 20th century (Lan 1990).

The processes by which political centralization and institutionalized inequality developed and amplified over time in south-central Africa were probably variable. The cases of Monze and other Tonga prophets, however, reveal that the merger of generalized spirits with specific ancestors may

have been one route by which individuals and kin groups sought to institutionalize their right to rule.

Discussion

Leadership cycles and egalitarian rebellions

Had the British not intervened, might Monze or one of its rival cults have developed into something more akin to the divine kingship found elsewhere in Southern Africa (Netting 1982)? Might the Monze matrilineal group have succeeded in enhancing their ritual authority with some sort of institutionalized political authority in a manner comparable to the way Polynesian elites solidified and legitimized their political rule through a monopolization of *mana* (Goldman 1970)? While recent accounts of the Monze cult during the early colonial period might lead one to this conclusion, it is important to remember that accounts of the past tend to reflect the political goals of the present. Colson (1996) makes clear, for example, that many Tonga in the late 20th century have desired to invent for themselves a history of strong chiefly rule that would elevate their own past to the same level as that of the centralized and strongly hierarchical groups elsewhere in Zambia. The histories of chiefs such as Monze based upon the modern accounts must take this problem into consideration.

At a deeper level of analysis, however, it also appears that Tonga cosmology was in fact consciously structured so as to block exactly the possibility of significant ritually-based inequality. Consider, for example, the very different case of the Bemba among whom powerful chiefs passed on both their own personal qualities as well as their supreme ecological influence to a successor. There, chiefly power was both inherited and naturalized— very different from the pragmatic attitude of the Tonga who acknowledged a prophet's efficacy only after seeing some semblance of 'proof' in the material world. Richards (1970:98) notes that Bemba leadership operated under the concept that a chief's "ill health or death, his pleasure or displeasure, his blessings or curses [would necessarily] affect the prosperity of the people."

But such an intricate and *de facto* connection between the position of the leader and the ecological world was essentially prohibited by Tonga cosmology. While not dissimilar notions of power and inheritance did exist, they were importantly bifurcated into two separate spheres: the *mizimu* and the *basangu*. As noted above, *mizimu*, because they were directly ancestral to matrilineal groups, were the spirits that could be inherited specifically within a kin group. However, the influence of the *mizimu* was also restricted to that kin group, effectively prohibiting their use in the larger political sphere. The *basangu*, on the other hand, did have regional ecological influence but might potentially possess an individual from any matrilineal group. In theory, no *basangu* could be monopolized by an elite among the living.

The posturing of the Monze matriline and its assent to a position of regional leadership in ritual and (to some degree) politics, however, provide an intriguing example of how some individuals creatively navigated through the cosmological structure in such a manner as to raise the status of themselves and their matrilineal group. These aggrandizers successfully found—and to a point were able to exploit—egalitarian 'loop-holes', merging matrilineal inheritance with the geographically based power of the *basangu* to open a pathway toward centralized inequality. The potential of this particular pathway rested in its superficial concordance with the structure of Tonga life. It neither curtailed the residential mobility that was critical to the Plateau Tonga's economic adaptation, nor did it immediately violate the egalitarian ethic that underwrote many of the Tonga's actions. Prophets—however influential—were still considered to be mere vehicles through which the powerful spirits passed. Unlike the Bemba, the Tonga 'chief' may have been associated with powerful agents, but (s)he was not considered to be in possession of significant personal power over the environment.

Van Binsbergen (1981) has further noted that while the Ila and Tonga have historically avoided the institutionalization of strong political inequality, this was not due to an absence of attempts along those lines. Strong leaders from the Luba/Lunda region to the north appear to have periodically entered the region with the intent to build and establish control over centralized polities among the local groups. However, these attempts either ended in the expulsion of the would-be conquerors or their assimilation into the more egalitarian Tonga/Ila social matrix (van Binsbergen 1981:130-2). It is not that the Tonga preferred local kings. They simply would not put up with any at all.

Undoubtedly there were points at which ritual leaders within Tonga society also attempted to advantage themselves economically. Smith and Dale (1968:305-7), for instance, note that among the Ila some prophet/chiefs were permitted to personally keep the livestock, hoes, and other offerings given to the *basangu* at a particular shrine as compensation for ritual transgressions, such as fighting during the period surrounding the rain festival. Given the small step between such payments and a form of ritually sanctioned tribute, it is likely that some Tonga leaders periodically had aspirations toward a more exploitative leadership role. The tie to the spirit world and the 'powerful medicine' thought to be controlled by many of the more important chiefs may have been exploited to legitimize such claims.

Disputes over leadership positions and attempts to take advantage of others materially were indeed ever present in Tongaland (e.g., disputes recorded in Colson 1962:102-121, 1991). While it may yet be appropriate to describe the Tonga as egalitarian, this is not because each individual simply respected the rights of all others and acted accordingly. Examples such as the Monze chieftainship discussed above attest to the fact that at least some Tonga were quite willing to assume leadership positions in those domains and during those historic periods when they could get away with them. Rather, Tonga egalitarianism was more of an elaborate stalemate within a society in which each individual or matrilineal group was quick to protest any abuse or lack of respect done unto them. Witchcraft accusations, village desertion, simple insubordination and the like, were means that individuals had at their disposal with which to counter those who would attempt to control them from within the society.

Such protests may be contrasted with what Gluckman (1965:137) referred to as 'rebellions' among more highly centralized societies with powerful chiefs. Gluckman noted that in the latter contexts it is common for paramount chiefs to be repeatedly challenged and overthrown, creating a distinctive pattern of chiefly flux over time. Importantly, however, these patterns typically do not involve structural modifications in these societies. Almost never do such rebellions take the form of popular uprisings to challenge the *position* of the chief. Instead, they represent efforts by incumbents to insert themselves into leadership roles that themselves remain largely unchanged—substitutions merely of the fillers of positions rather than any sort of structural change to the system itself. The resulting cyclical pattern of competition and overthrow may be indicative of chiefdoms and kingdoms in many parts of the world as much archaeological and ethnohistorical research has revealed.

On the other hand, the periodic lower-level rebellions among the Tonga and, I suspect, many other tribal societies were of a qualitatively different nature. Egalitarian rebellions in such societies were *structural corrections* that reasserted egalitarianism when this ethic has been broached. Challengers, of course, would always be hidden in the brush awaiting their turn, but they would have to build their own petty empires from the ground up. There was no established position of de facto authority for the upstart to simply assume.

We might therefore imagine the trajectory of Tonga society as vacillating over time. As leadership tended toward centralization and inequality became institutionalized under leaders such as Monze, the stage was periodically set for egalitarian revolts which ushered in greater political equity (at least in principle) for a period of time, brief though it may be. Such trajectories appear to have been present on a number of levels. (1) Individual headmen pushed the limits of control within their local communities bringing about village or community fission as former members 'voted with their feet'. These cycles appear to have been a nearly ever-present short-term drama that in Tonga society had very little intergenerational effect. (2) In some cases, however, strong ritual leaders were able to build off of their matrilineal predecessors to further their own fund of power on a regional level. As long as the rains (or their warnings of no rain) held, certain shrine cults and the leaders associated with them might develop a wide following and begin to reap benefits, both moral and, to a degree, material. It is clear that such shrine cults at times did maintain their reputation and regional influence for multiple generations. (3) Finally, over the long term, we must also acknowledge that the Tonga social context itself appears to have developed as a broad-based egalitarian rebellion of sorts in which a number of south-central African peoples sought refuge from the strongly centralized and exploitative power in nearby kingdoms.

The Tonga in comparative perspective

The latter suggestion having been made, it should be clearly stated that the intent of the present analysis is not to simply reiterate Fried's (1968, 1975, see also Whitehead 1992) position that 'tribal society'—traditionally conceptualized—better describes a series of secondary reactions to the presence of the state than it does the evolutionarily prior 'tribes' that may have led towards state development. There has been, of course, an assump-

tion in anthropology generally that to understand the potential steps in social evolution one must look to those societies that are in some sense 'pristine' or 'traditional'. Working under such a paradigm, the Tonga would hold little relevance to an evolutionary discussion of tribal society due to their long history of interaction with the more centralized polities that surrounded them.

But such a position is both highly limiting and logically suspect. As Leach (1989) has emphasized there is not—nor has there ever been—any social formation that can legitimately be described as 'traditional'. All societies are responses to a complex mix of social, ecological, and historical pressures. Just as it would be absurd to argue that the Natufian societies of the Levant became non-traditional after the domestication of plants, or that the Paleo-Indian of the New World became non-traditional as they confronted the rapid extinction of the megafauna herds, so too would it be wrong to *a priori* dismiss the Tonga from theoretical consideration because of a few aggressors next door. In every case, whether the impinging force is environmental, technological, or social, the nature of the response is the subject of interest.

A more important point with respect to the present volume is that the dynamics that drove Tonga history must have been present on some level during the social evolution of non-state contexts throughout the world. The egalitarian ethic so central to our intuitive definition of band and tribal-level societies (i.e., those societies thought to be structurally most similar to the starting points of social evolution) is, of course, inherently reactionary. There could not have been a rationale for *dogmatically* asserting social equality either during our evolutionary beginnings or in more recent non-state social contexts if significant social inequality were not previously (or simultaneously) known and feared.

On this point, it is also interesting to find that similar problems are currently being debated in the anthropology of tribal societies in other parts of the world. In discussing Hopi ethnography and ethnohistory, for example, Whiteley (1998:82) has recently grappled with the problem of why this 'tribal' group has long been described as egalitarian by some and highly stratified by others. He concludes that those who would view the Hopi as egalitarian are ignoring 'religious' power in favor of an analysis based in material inequalities. Plog (1995) tackles this same problem in the Southwestern literature more broadly, concluding that from a diachronic perspective Pueblo societies must be viewed as having "*both* egalitarian and hierarchical aspects," each of which appear to have manifested more strongly at certain periods over time (see also Brandt 1994; McGuire and Saitta 1996; Feinman et al. 2000; Mills 2000; Adler this volume, Chapter 9).

Both the Tonga and the Pueblo data further suggest that periodic ritual leadership may be exploited as a powerful source of potential inequality in societies in which unmediated economic and political inequalities are not tolerated. Such ritual leadership also reveals that the contention that 'tribal' or simple stateless societies are organized principally by kinship relations—a contention of long-standing in anthropology (Maine 1954; MacIver 1947)—is inaccurate. Many different and potentially opposed ethnic groups in south-central Africa were known to use the same shrine cult from time to time, creating a ritual community that overlapped smaller political boundaries. The Monze shrine, for example, was used by numerous groups including Lozi leaders who were simultaneously busy raiding Tonga communities for their cattle. In the Puebloan world, the regional Chaco 'cult' of the 11th and 12th centuries may have originated along a similar trajectory in which the ritual community grew to a scale far larger than any definable political community.

That the Chaco cult appears to have developed a measure of strongly centralized leadership during the century prior to its demise (or, at least, decentralization) may also be a sign that the cult had pushed beyond the bounds of tolerable social inequality. Just as early historic Tonga egalitarianism may be read as a long-term popular rebellion against the inequality of surrounding complex societies, so too might the prehistory of the Puebloan world be viewed in part as a response to the internal development of a hierarchical system centered on Chaco. Indeed, as more tribal contexts are examined from a historical standpoint, much classically 'tribal' socio-political organization will very likely prove to be nested in larger historical trajectories involving constant drives toward inequality punctuated by periodic egalitarian rebellions.

Conclusion

Of all the traits in the trait-list approach to the definition of tribal society, egalitarianism has, perhaps, the deepest roots. Differences of gender, age, or natural ability may be permitted to introduce 'low-level' social inequalities, but communi-ty-level leadership positions in tribal contexts have come to be viewed as necessarily grounded in consensus and democratic representation. In so doing, egalitarianism becomes roughly equated with a measure of on-the-ground decision-making *equality*, and the stage is set for this trait-list definition of tribe to be up-rooted each time a presumably 'tribal' group can be demonstrated to have indulged in a relatively high-level of decision-making inequality. Thus we also find in the archaeology of many parts of the world a recent tendency to question whether this or that 'tribal' society was, in fact, a chiefdom or even a state (e.g., Creamer and Haas 1998, Malville n.d.).

Beyond the obvious limitations to such an overly typological approach, the more specific problem has been clear for some time: egalitarianism does not necessarily imply equality in any given social sphere. Egalitarianism is an ethic or sentiment that at times may merely be a façade hiding significant underlying inequalities. Furthermore, *it is an ethic that is inherently reactionary, implying that significant decision-making inequality has been previously known and rejected,* and that it also continues to pose a social threat. In this sense, egalitarianism implies the historical presence of both experienced inequalities at the community level and an at least superficial equality born out of social rebellion. Realistically, this dialectic between the periodic attainment of significant decision-making inequality followed by egalitarian rebellion is what we should expect to find in *all* social contexts over time on some level as leaders overstep their bounds or experiment with the limits of their control. Distinguishing 'tribal' variants of this dialectic may depend on our ability to identify (1) the periodicity of egalitarian rebellions, (2) the threshold beyond which an individual or faction cannot step without eliciting outward social opposition, and perhaps most importantly (3) whether or not the rebellions have the net effect of reestablishing greater social equity.

Notes

[1] Throughout the paper the past tense will be used when describing the early historic Tonga despite the fact that the modern Tonga still inhabit much of the same region and have maintained a number of precolonial practices.

[2] An exception must be made for a few parts of the Gwembe Valley in which a segmentary lineage system was present (Colson 1967:69).

[3] British institutionalization of the position of the headman probably enhanced its desirability (Colson per. com. 2000), but the manner in which headmanship was competed over can be taken as indicative of native modes of competition and posturing.

[4] Hopgood (1950:68) suggests, in fact, that when one also considers the position of the Tonga notion of God (or Leza), the cosmological system itself might be viewed as one with hierarchically ordered chiefly offices.

[5] These two types of spirits have been described for the closely related Ila peoples by Smith and Dale (1968) as 'personal and family divinities' and 'communal divinities' respectively.

[6] This same ecologically driven pattern is also found to a degree among related groups to the south of the Zambezi River in Zimbabwe (Alexander and Ranger 1998).

[7] O'Brien and O'Brien (1996), however, have reviewed oral history documents in the Jesuit Archives in Lusaka which, they suggest, indicate an early 18th century origin for the cult.

[8] Colson (per. com. 2000) notes that although Monze's wife would have of necessity belonged to a different matrilineal group, she may have been assuming the role of a ritual wife or may have been a slave assimilated into the matriline of her owner/husband.

Acknowledgments

This paper is based entirely on published material on the Tonga and in particular on Elizabeth Colson's major ethnographic studies during the 1940's, 50's and 60's. Many thanks are extended to Dr. Colson both for her prolific publication record and for her time taken to discuss the problem of Tonga egalitarianism with an archaeology student of the American Southwest. The paper has also benefited from a close reading by Ray Kelly who in particular helped contextualize the Tonga material within the larger anthropological corpus of work on egalitarian politics and power relations.

References Cited

Abraham, Donald P.
1962 The Early Political History of the Kingdom of Mwana Mutapa. In *Historians in Tropical Africa*. International African Institute, Salisbury.

Alexander, Jocelyn and Terence Ranger
1998 Competition and Integration in the Religious History of North-Western Zimbabwe. *Journal of Religion in Africa* 18(1):3-31.

Bourdillon, M. F. C.
1982 Freedom and Constraint Among Shona Spirit Mediums. In *Religious Organization and Religious Experience*, edited by J. Davis, pp. 181-94. A.S.A. Monograph 21. Academic Press, New York.

Blake, Michael and John E. Clark
1999 The Emergence of Hereditary Inequality: the Case of Pacific Coastal Chiapas, Mexico. In *Pacific Latin America in Prehistory*, edited by Michael Blake, pp. 55-73.

Brandt, Elizabeth A.
1994 Egalitarianism, Hierarchy, and Centralization in the Pueblos. In *The Ancient Southwestern Community: Models and Methods for the Study of Prehistoric Social Organization*, edited by W. H. Wills and Robert D. Leonard, pp. 9-23. University of New Mexico Press, Albuquerque.

Brison, Karen J.
1989 All Talk and No Action? Saying and Doing in Kwanga Meetings. *Ethnology* 28(2):97-115.

Colson, Elizabeth
1948 Rain Shrines of the Plateau Tonga of Northern Rhodesia. *Africa* 18(3):272-283.

1949 *Life Among the Cattle-Owning Plateau Tonga: The Material Culture of a Northern Rhodesia Native Tribe*. Rhodes-Livingstone Museum, Livingstone.

1950 A Note on Tonga and Ndebele. *Northern Rhodesia Journal* 2:35-41.

1951 Residence and Village Stability Among the Plateau Tonga. Human Problems in British Central Africa. *Rhodes-Livingstone Journal* 12:41-67.

1958 *Marriage and the Family among the Plateau Tonga of Northern Rhodesia*. Manchester University Press, Manchester.

1962 *The Plateau Tonga of Northern Rhodesia*. Manchester University Press, Manchester.

1967 (1960) *Social Organization of the Gwembe Tonga*. Manchester University Press, Manchester.

1968 (1951) The Plateau Tonga of Northern Rhodesia. In *Seven Tribes of British Central Africa*, edited by E. Colson and M. Gluckman, pp. 94-162. Oxford University Press, London.

1969 Spirit Possession Among the Tonga. In *Spirit Mediumship and Society in Africa*, edited by John Beattie and John Middleton, pp. 69-103. Africana Publishing Corporation, New York.

1970 The Assimilation of Aliens Among the Zambian Tonga. In *From Tribe to Nation in Africa: Studies in Incorporative Processes*, edited by R. Cohen and J. Middleton, pp. 35-50. Chandler Publishing Company, Scranton.

1977 A Continuing Dialogue: Prophets and Local Shrines Among the Tonga of Zambia. In *Regional Cults*, edited by R.P. Werbner, pp. 119-40. A.S.A. Monograph 16. Academic Press, London.

1980 The Resilience of Matrilineality: Gwembe and Plateau Tonga Adaptations. In *The Versatility of Kinship*, edited by L. S. Cordell and S. Beckerman, pp. 359-374. Academic Press, New York.

1991 *The History of Nampeyo*. Kenneth Kaunda Foundation, Lusaka, Zambia.

1996 The Bantu Botatwe: Changing Political Definitions in Southern Zambia. In *The Politics of Cultural Performance*, edited by D. Parkin, L. Caplan, and H. Fisher. Berghahm, Oxford.

Colson, Elizabeth and Thayer Scudder
1988 *For Prayer and Profit, The Ritual, Economic, and Social Importance of Beer in Gwembe District, Zambia, 1950-1982*. Stanford University Press, Stanford.

Creamer, Winifred and Jonathan Haas
1998 Less Than Meets the Eye: Evidence for Protohistoric Chiefdoms in Northern New Mexico. In *Chiefdoms and Chieftaincy in the Americas*, edited by E. M. Redmond, pp. 43-67. University Press of Florida, Gainseville.

Fagan, Brian M.
1967 *Iron Age Cultures of Zambia*. Chatto and Windus, London.

1970 The Iron Age Sequence in the Southern Province of Zambia. In *Papers in African Prehistory*, edited by J.D. Fage and R.A. Oliver, pp. 201-22. Cambridge University Press, New York.

Feinman, G. M, K. G. Lightfoot, and S. Upham
2000 Political Hierarchies and Organizational Strategies in the Puebloan Southwest. *American Antiquity* 65(3):449-70.

Flanagan, J. G.
1989 Hierarchy in Simple "Egalitarian" Societies. *Annual Review of Anthropology* 18:245-66.

Fortes, Meyer
1953 The Structure of Unilineal Descent Groups. *American Anthropologist* 55:17-41.

Fortes, Meyer and E. E. Evans-Pritchard, ed.
1940 *African Political Systems*. Oxford University Press, London.

Fried, Morton
1968 On the Concepts of "Tribe" and "Tribal Society". In *Essays on the Problem of Tribe*, edited by J. Helm, pp. 3-20. American Ethnological Society. Proceedings of the 1967 Annual Spring Meeting. University of Washington Press.

1975 *The Notion of Tribe*. Cummings Publishing, Menlo Park, Ca.

Garbett, G. K.
1967 Prestige, Status and Power in a Modern Valley Korekore Chiefdom, Rhodesia. *Africa* 37:307-26.

Garlake, Peter S.
1973 *Great Zimbabwe*. Thames and Hudson, London.

Gluckman, Max
1965 *Politics, Law and Ritual in Tribal Society*. Aldine Publishing Co., Chicago.

Goldman, Irving
1970 *Ancient Polynesian Society*. University of Chicago Press, Chicago.

Hopgood, Cecil R.
1950 The Idea of God Amongst the Tonga of Northern Rhodesia. In *African Ideas of God*, edited by E. W. Smith, pp. 61-74. Edinburgh House Press, London.

Huffman, Thomas N.
1986 Archaeological Evidence and Conventional Explanations of Southern Bantu Settlement Patterns. *Africa* 56(3):280-98.

Kelly, Raymond C.
1993 *Constructing Inequality: The Fabrication of a Hierarchy of Virtue Among the Etoro*. University of Michigan Press, Ann Arbor.

Lan, David
1990 (1985) *Guns and Rain, Guerrillas and Spirit Mediums in Zimbabwe*. University of California Press, Berkeley.

Lancaster, Chet S.
1971 The Economics of Social Organization in an Ethnic Border Zone: The Goba (Northern Shona) of the Zambezi Valley. *Ethnology* 10:445-65.

1974 Ethnic Identity, History, and "Tribe" in

the Middle Zambezi Valley. *American Ethnologist* 1:707-30.

1981 *The Goba of the Zambezi.* University of Oklahoma Press, Norman.

Leach, Edmund

1989 Tribal Ethnography: Past, Present, Future. In *History and Ethnicity*, edited by E. Tonkin, M. McDonald, and M. Chapman, pp. 34-47. Routledge, New York.

Lewis, I. M.

1968 Tribal Society. In *International Encyclopedia of the Social Sciences*, Vol. 16., edited by D. Sills, pp. 146-51. The Macmillan Co. and The Free Press.

Livingstone, David

1865 *Expedition to the Zambesi and its Tributaries; and of the Discovery of the Lakes Shirwa and Nyassa.* John Murray, London.

1899 (1858) *Missionary Travels and Researches in South Africa.* Ward, Lock, and Co. Ltd., New York.

1963 *Livingstone's African Journal 1853-1856.* Chatto and Windus, London.

MacIver, Robert M.

1947 *Web of Government.* The Macmillan Co., New York.

Maine, Sir Henry

1954 *Ancient Law.* Dutton, New York.

Malville, J. McKim

n.d. Chaco as an Emergent Segmentary State. http://www.Colorado.EDU/Conferences/chaco/state.htm

McGuire, Randall H. and Dean J. Saitta

1996 Although They Have Petty Captains, They Obey Them Badly: the Dialectics of Prehispanic Western Pueblo Social Organization. *American Antiquity* 61:197-216.

Meggitt, M. J.

1973 The Pattern of Leadership Among the Mae-Enga of New Guinea. In *Politics in New Guinea*, edited by R. M. Berndt and P. Lawrence, pp. 191-206. University of Washington Press, Seattle.

Mills, Barbara J.

2000 Alternate Models, Alternate Strategies: Leadership in the Prehispanic Southwest. In *Alternative Leadership Strategies in the Prehispanic Southwest*, edited by B. J. Mills, pp. 3-18. University of Arizona Press, Tuscon.

Netting, Robert McC.

1972 Sacred Power and Centralization: Aspects of Political Adaptation in Africa. In *Population Growth: Anthropological Implications*, edited by B. Spooner, pp. 219-44. The MIT Press, Cambridge, Massachusetts.

O'Brien, Dan

1983 Chiefs of Rain - Chiefs of Ruling: A Reinterpretation of Pre-Colonial Tonga (Zambia) Social and Political Structure. *Africa* 53(4):23-41.

O'Brien, Dan and Carolyn O'Brien

1996 The Monze Rain Festival: The History of Change in a Religious Cult in Zambia. *The International Journal of African Historical Studies* 29(3):519-41.

Oliver, Roland and Brian M. Fagan

1975 *Africa in the Iron Age.* Cambridge University Press, New York.

Paynter, Robert

1989 The Archaeology of Equality and Inequality. *Annual Review of Anthropology* 18:369-99.

Phillipson, David W.

1968 The Early Iron Age in Zambia. *Journal of African History* 9:191-211.

1978 *The Later Prehistory of Eastern and Southern Africa.* Heinemann, London.

Phillipson, David W. and Brian M. Fagan

1969 The Date of the Ingombe Ilede Burials. *Journal of African History* 10:199-204.

Plog, Stephen

1995 Equality and Hierarchy, Holistic Approaches to Understanding Social Dynamics in the Pueblo Southwest. In *Foundations of Social Inequality*, edited by T. D. Price and G. M. Feinman, pp. 189-206. Plenum Press, New York.

Price, T. D. and James A. Brown, editors

1995 *Foundations of Social Inequality.* Plenum Press, New York.

Redmond, Elsa M.

1998 Introduction. In *Chiefdoms and Chieftaincy in the Americas*, edited by E.M. Redmond, pp. 1-17. University Press of Florida, Gainesville.

Reynolds, Barrie

1968 *The Material Culture of the Peoples of the Gwembe Valley.* The University Press, Manchester.

Richards, Audrey

1970 (1940) The Political System of the Bemba Tribe—North-Eastern Rhodesia. In *African Political Systems*, edited by M. Fortes and E. E. Evans-Pritchard, pp. 83-120. Oxford University Press, New York.

Saha, Santosh C.
1994 *History of the Tonga Chiefs and Their People in the Monze District of Zambia.* Peter Lang, New York.

Sahlins, Marsall D.
1961 The Segmentary Lineage: An Organization of Predatory Expansion. *American Anthropologist* 63:332-45.
1966 (1963) Poor Man, Rich Man, Big Man, Chief: Political Types in Melanesia and Polynesia. In *Readings in Australian and Pacific Anthropology*, edited by I. Hogbin and L.R. Hiatt, pp. 159-179. Cambridge University Press, New York.
1968 *Tribesmen.* Prentice-Hall, Englewood Cliffs, NJ.

Selous, Frederick Courteney
1893 *Travel and Adventure in South East Africa.* R. Ward and Co., London.

Smaldone, Joseph P.
1979 Historical Setting. In *Zambia, A Country Study*, edited by I. Kaplan. The American University, Washington, DC.

Smith, Edwin W. and Andrew Murray Dale
1968 (1920) *The Ila-Speaking Peoples of Northern Rhodesia.* University Books, New York.

Smith, Michael G.
1956 On Segmentary Lineage Systems. *Journal of the Royal Anthropological Institute* 86:39-79.

Strathern, A.
1971 *The Rope of Moka, Big-Men and Ceremonial Exchange in Mount Hagen, New Guinea.* Cambridge University Press, London.

van Binsbergen, Wim
1981 *Religious Change in Zambia.* Kegan Paul International, Boston.

van Binsbergen, Wim and Matthew Schoffeleers
1985 Introduction: Theoretical Explorations in African Religion. In *Theoretical Explorations in African Religion*, edited by W. van Binsbergen and M. Schoffeleers, pp. 1-49. KPI, Boston.

Vansina, Jan
1968 *Kingdoms of the Savanna.* University of Wisconsin Press, Madison.

Werbner, Richard
1977 Introduction. In *Regional Cults*, edited by R.P. Werbner. A.S.A. Monograph 16. Academic Press, London.

Whitehead, Neil L.
1992 Tribes Make States and States Make Tribes: Warfare and the Creation of Colonial Tribes and States in Northeastern South America. In *War in the Tribal Zone*, edited by R. B. Ferguson and N. L. Whitehead, pp. 127-150. School of Amercian Research Press, Santa Fe.

Whiteley, Peter M.
1988 *Deliberate Acts: Changing Hopi Culture Through the Oraibi Split.* University of Arizona Press, Tuscon.
1998 *Rethinking Hopi Ethnography.* Smithsonian Institution Press, Washington.

Woodburn, James
1982 Egalitarian Societies. In *Man* 17:431-51.

6. The Dynamics of Ethnicity in Tribal Society: A Penobscot Case Study

Dean Snow

Introduction

Archaeology needs to find a useful definition of tribal societies, one that neither misrepresents by oversimplification nor depends upon exhaustive elimination of everything they are not. Most archaeologists would accept a general definition of tribes as "small-scale, sedentary, and non-hierarchical societies." But this really does misrepresent by oversimplification. And such a definition is only slightly more useful than one that defines tribal societies as all those that are both more complex than band societies and less complex than chiefdoms.

More precise definition is possible. Fowles (this volume, Chapter 2) and Parkinson (this volume, Chapter 1) observe that that tribes are organized according to segmentary principles, and that they are integrated by pan-residential social institutions. These are two tribal means of ensuring that a group will be able to organize and sequentially reorganize itself in a multitude of social arrangements. They are organizational characteristics that endow great flexibility. Looked at over time tribal societies are also seen to fragment and recombine at a range of spatial and temporal scales.

One can add that while tribal societies tend to be based on kinship, their segmentary nature and frequent migratory episodes often bring groups together that do not share common descent. In these cases clan designations and implied fictive kinship often come into play.

Penobscot Case Study

I turn now to the example of the Penobscot nation of Maine, which was a sovereign autochthonous tribal society three centuries ago. It still exhibits some tribal features, although circumstances have changed dramatically. It is still small scale and sedentary. Its members resist hierarchical organization, although elected political leadership has long been required by Maine. The Penobscots persist as a corporate group, albeit one that is embedded within a larger state society with a multitude of economic, social, religious, and political linkages with many other groups. Penobscot leaders have long been mindful that group identity depends upon several things. One of these is outside recognition of the Penobscot nation as a legitimate entity. In this case recognition by the State of Maine and by the United States are both important. Federal recognition is framed specifically in terms of Penobscot legitimacy as a 'tribe' as intended by Article I, Section 8, Paragraph 3 of the Constitution of the United States.

But Penobscot group identity also depends upon internal recognition of particular individuals as tribal members. If membership were defined too narrowly the tribal roll could shrink to extinction over time. If it were defined too broadly the tribe could grow rapidly, outstrip its resources, and risk losing group cohesion.

Social groups vary considerably in how they define membership. A celibate religious order, like the Shakers, does not allow for endogenous growth through biological reproduction, and must recruit all new members from the outside. A fecund religious group, like the Hutterites, might allow only endogamous biological reproduction and ban recruitment and intermarriage altogether. Tribal societies maintain membership practices that range widely between these extremes.

It is useful to remember that all societies experience turnover. New members are admitted and current members depart. Admission of new members involves biological reproduction or recruitment from outside. The latter can be anything from a passive acceptance of refugees to coercive recruitment of captives. On the other hand, existing members are lost through death or departure, and the latter can involve anything from voluntary emigration to expulsion. How a society balances these factors determines whether it increases or decreases in size. It also determines the proportions of various heritages in the evolving population.

The Iroquois nations of the seventeenth century maintained their numbers in the face of epidemics and warfare by allowing for adoption on a large scale. Foreigners were adopted both individually and as groups. Adoption was sometimes coerced, sometimes voluntary. In most cases the descendants of the adoptees were considered full members of the adopting nation within three generations, and links to source populations were lost. In the twentieth century the Iroquois nations have tended to allow only endogenous growth, and matrilineal descent has been the rule. Endogamy has not been required, but while the children of a member woman and a nonmember man have been accorded membership, the children of a member man and a nonmember woman have not. The current effects of these practices include slow population growth and slow growth in fractions of foreign background when compared to the Penobscot case.

Penobscot practice was to allow easy adoption of men and women in the nineteenth century, so long as they were of American Indian descent. This became more restrictive in the twentieth century, particularly with regard to the adoption of men. However, any child was and is considered a member so long as one grandparent was a member. No gender preference conditioned this principle. Generally speaking, Penobscot practice has allowed for fairly rapid growth. Like many small national societies, the Penobscots have experienced difficulty finding suitable mates within the group, so intermarriage with outsiders has been common. Thus many nonmembers have migrated into the reservation community. However, it is also the case that the children of successive intermarriages have ever smaller fractions of Penobscot biological heritage, and they are likely to lose their identities as Penobscots. Members who do not live in or near the reservation at Old Town, Maine, and who reckon their descent from only one or two great-grandparents are likely to appear on the inactive list these days. Many such people have disappeared from the tribal rolls over the years.

I argue that this kind of dynamic group membership turnover is typical of tribal societies. While some tribes might successfully maintain strict rules of endogamy, most do not. Moreover, migration by individuals, families, or larger subsets of the tribe is a common occurrence. Outsiders are allowed in by adoption, or might even be actively recruited. Current members might drift away or even be expelled for various reasons. Two tribal groups might merge into one, or one might split into two or more independent groups. Thus demographic dynamism that goes far beyond the processes of birth and death is a common characteristic of tribes. Despite these processes (and often while denying them) tribal societies maintain their continuity over time. The Penobscot case provides a good example of how this works.

Genealogical data that I have compiled for the Penobscots going back to the middle of the nineteenth century suggests that the fractions reported in the 1900 census generally underestimated the amount of earlier intermarriage with Euro-Americans and other Indian communities. As a general rule, most people know some details about their grandparents, but even in societies where oral tradition is important knowledge about great-grandparents is usually sketchy. In 1900 many Penobscots had lost track of earlier exogamous marriages, and the fractions given to census takers underreported it. But this is precisely how tribal groups maintain continuity of identity over time, even in the face of frequent exogamy.

Of those identified as Penobscots in 1900, 70 (27%) were listed as having 100% Penobscot heritage. But many of the 70 either did not know or chose to not report the details of their ancestry. For example, Peter M. Nicola's grandfather, Tomer Nicola, was an Abenaki (specifically Norridgewock) man who married a Huron woman before settling at Old Town. Peter's father, Joseph M. Nicola, considered himself to be Penobscot and that is how his ethnicity was reported by Peter in 1900. Peter's mother and maternal grandparents were all Penobscots, so he reported himself as 100% Penobscot. But had Peter computed his ethnicity based on his grandparents' rather than his parents' identities, he would have reported that he was half Penobscot, a quarter Norridgewock (or Abenaki), and a quarter Huron. There are several other contemporaneous examples of this process of ethnic simplification with the passage of generations, a process with which most Americans should be personally familiar.

At the other end of the identification scale in the 1900 census, there are 30 people (11% of the sample) that were listed as ethnic Penobscots even though they had no Penobscot heritage at all. Six of these 30 had one Euro-American parent and a few more had a Euro-American grandparent, but all of them had at least 50% Indian heritage of some sort. That qualified them to be considered adopted Penobscots.

Thus of 269 people living on the Indian Island reservation at Old Town, Maine in 1900, 97% were ethnic Penobscots. But if we recompute their aggregate fractional ethnicity based on parental ethnicities and fractions of European admixture reported in the census data we get the percentages shown in Table 1. The case of Peter Nicola and several others tells us that even these figures must overstate the Penobscot fraction and understate all others. Tribal societies constantly reinvent and reconstitute themselves in this way, creating solidarity and group cohesion in the face of turnover that constantly brings in new blood.

Frank Speck (1940) was interested in this phenomenon when he did his field work among the Penobscots in 1915 (Table 2). He missed a few marriages and he dealt only with cases where the married couples were still living on Indian Island. People who married outside the tribe and left the reservation were apparently not considered at all.

Sixty percent (81) of the 134 marriages in Speck's sample involved Penobscots marrying non-Penobscots, either other Indians or people of Euro-

pean extraction. Precise computation was beyond Speck's capabilities, and it remains a complex and time-consuming problem even with modern computers. His solution was to examine surnames as a means of measuring non-Penobscot inputs to the Indian Island population. This is a reliable way to measure change in the composition of the population so long as the number of in-marrying males is about equal to the number of in-marrying females. The reason for this is related to the Hardy-Weinberg law of genetic equilibrium, which is explained in any good introductory course in biological anthropology. Consider, for example, a case in which a man has two grandparents that are Penobscot and two that are Euro-American. It does not matter which two have either of those identities, for the individual is half Penobscot in any case. Now suppose that the man marries a woman who also has two Penobscot and two Euro-American grandparents. Their children will all also be half Penobscot. Surnames generally pass patrilineally. So long as males and females have married into the population in equal proportions, there is a 50% chance

Table 1. Fractional aggregate identity on Indian Island in 1900.

Ethnic Identity	Aggregate Percentage
Penobscot	60.9%
Euro-American (incl. Canadian)	21.1%
Micmac	0.6%
Abenaki (incl. Norridgewock)	1.3%
Malecite	5.5%
Passamaquoddy	10.2%
Huron	0.4%
Mohawk	0.2%

Table 2. Penobscots in three generations prior to 1915.

Penobscot Marriages with:	No. Marriages
Penobscot	53
Euro-American (incl. Canadian)	29
Micmac	4
Abenaki (incl. Norridgewock)	4
Malecite	14
Passamaquoddy	30
Huron	0
Mohawk	1

that the children will have a Penobscot surname. Thus for the population as a whole, the proportion of Penobscot surnames is a reasonably good indicator of the aggregate fraction of Penobscot genetic heritage. Counts of non-Penobscot surnames in any year are a reasonably good measure of cumulative inputs from other ethnic groups as of those years.

A list compiled in 1942 (Proctor 1942) recorded twenty marriages between Penobscots and Euro-Americans among people then living on Indian Island. Ten were cases of Penobscot men marrying Euro-American women and ten were cases of Penobscot women marrying Euro-American men. Thus males and females were marrying into the Penobscot tribe in about equal numbers. There is currently little reason to think that an imbalance in these proportions might have invalidated the use of surnames as a means to measure the effects of intermarriage over time.

Another way to show the relationship between Penobscot intermarriage and surnames is shown as a matrix in Table 3. Say that we have a population of 100 Penobscots, 50 men and 50 women. Now say that half of each group marries within the tribe and the other half marries outside. Finally, stipulate that each marriage produces two children. Although our 100 fictional Penobscot parents have merely reproduced themselves, their combined marriages produce 150 children because of the non-Penobscot inputs. Two-thirds of the children, a hundred of them, are half Penobscot, half something else. Fifty of the children, the third of them with non-Penobscot fathers, will have non-Penobscot surnames. The children's' generation is, in the aggregate, 66.6% Penobscot and 33.3% non-Penobscot, a ratio that is reflected exactly in their frequency of non-Penobscot surnames.

Changes in the proportions occur for two reasons. First, additional inputs through new intermarriages will change the proportions. Second, stochastic variations in such a small sample will have some effects. Some families will have only daughters and surnames will disappear over time. Others will have many sons and their surnames will proliferate even if they are not unusually fertile. The surnames of inmarrying females will not be preserved, but these will be balanced in the aggregations by those of inmarrying males.

Table 4 shows the fractional ethnicity of the Penobscot nation at ten-year intervals (census data are not available for 1890, 1910, or 1930). These are aggregate figures for all living and enrolled Penobscots at these dates. Fractional ethnic backgrounds of individuals would vary widely from these aggregate figures. Nevertheless, Table 4 shows that the Penobscots have incorporated many intermarriages. While non-Penobscot men have not often been adopted as members, their children carry their surnames. Thus by 1960 more than half of all Penobscots had European surnames. Only a quarter had traditional Penobscot surnames by 1960.

The genetic effects of this admixture have not been studied, but it is safe to assume that there has been a substantial amount of gene flow. For present purposes, it is enough to point to this case as one that is probably typical of tribal societies. The Penobscot tribal roll ranged between 275 and 459 in the nineteenth century. While it might be ten times higher now, it is still so small that young people are likely to look outside the tribe for suitable marriage mates. The effects shown in Table 4 are thus both unavoidable and common in tribal societies. Ironically, the process is often vigorously denied by tribal spokespeople because

Table 3. Matrix of Penobscot marriages.

	50 Penobscot Men	50 Non-Penobscot Men
50 Penobscot Women	25 Marriages 50 Children	25 Marriages 50 Children
50 Non-Penobscot Women	25 Marriages 50 Children	n.a.

Table 4. Penobscot fractional ethnic heritages as indicated by surnames.

	Penobscot	Abenaki	European	Malecite	Passamaquoddy	Other Indian	Total
1860	58.6%	6.8%	9.6%	14.1%	9.2%	1.7%	100%
1870	62.0%	6.6%	10.3%	10.5%	8.6%	2.0%	100%
1880	59.5%	3.4%	11.5%	15.8%	8.9%	1.0%	100%
1900	50.0%	5.1%	21.0%	11.6%	10.9%	1.5%	100%
1920	41.0%	3.5%	31.1%	11.5%	12.7%	0.2%	100%
1940	30.4%	3.0%	43.8%	10.3%	12.3%	0.2%	100%
1950	29.3%	4.0%	47.6%	7.2%	11.7%	0.2%	100%
1960	24.9%	3.6%	51.3%	7.5%	12.5%	0.1%	100%
1970	23.9%	3.4%	54.6%	6.4%	11.7%	0.0%	100%

it is regarded as a threat to traditional identity, group cohesion, and continued recognition by outsiders.

All human groups constantly reinvent themselves as populations. Individuals make choices about their ethnicity, for to do otherwise results for nearly anyone in a crazy quilt of fractional affiliations. The processes I have described here have to be assumed for all middle-range societies, and our analytical procedures must take account of them.

Great Lakes Tribal Societies in the Colonial Period

Applying the principles drawn from the Penobscot case more broadly to the tribal societies of the Great Lakes region during the colonial period allows me to make some more general points regarding the archaeological study of such societies. Figure 1 shows the Great Lakes region as depicted in *The Atlas of Ancient America* (Coe et al. 1986). This is a traditional but oversimplified depiction of the distribution of tribal societies in the region. I can be as sharply critical of it as I wish because I was responsible for the maps and text in this part of the atlas. As depicted here, each of the tribal territories is well bounded and areas of no-man's-land are allowed to exist only where our knowledge is incomplete. I produced this map from prototypes published by various other scholars. Like them I showed eighteenth-century distributions in the west as if they were contemporaneous with seventeenth-century ones farther east, and sixteenth-century ones along the coast.

Figure 2 shows a somewhat more realistic view of known data from the same Great Lakes region. It is based upon a tribal distribution map produced by David Anderson (1991) for the year AD 1540. To it I have added site clusters for the Northeast that his study did not include. Specialists will notice that a few may still be missing. Nevertheless it is more realistic than Figure 1. Note that it differs from Figure 1 in two important ways. First, it applies uniformly to the year 1540 and second there are many buffer zones between tribal community clusters.

I have found in my own work that even Anderson's refined approach aggregates data too much to allow one to see the dynamic patterns of evolving tribal societies. If we wish to examine tribal societies archaeologically in an even more realistic way, we must further disaggregate the data to the community (site) level. I have developed a GIS data base with over 2000 communities, each of which has an ethnic identifier, a founding date, and an abandonment date. Some of them have names and other attached data.

Figure 3 shows the same region and its known native communities in a particular year, AD 1600. I have produced an electronic animation that starts with this frame and advances for the following 200 years at ten-year intervals. Here there is space for only six of them. Figures 4 to 8 show the region in AD 1640, 1680, 1720, 1760 and 1800 respectively. A dynamic map animation with frames at one-year intervals is possible and would be better, but this is feasible only with electronic publication. I have shown migratory events as arrows. These usually occurred as unique one-year events, so only a small percentage of them appear on the maps shown here. American Indian villages are shown as round dots. European forts and posts are shown as squares but European communities are not shown at all. All symbols are color coded for ethnicity on the electronic versions of these maps.

101

Fig. 1. Traditional representation of Great Lakes tribal distributions (after Coe et. al. 1986).

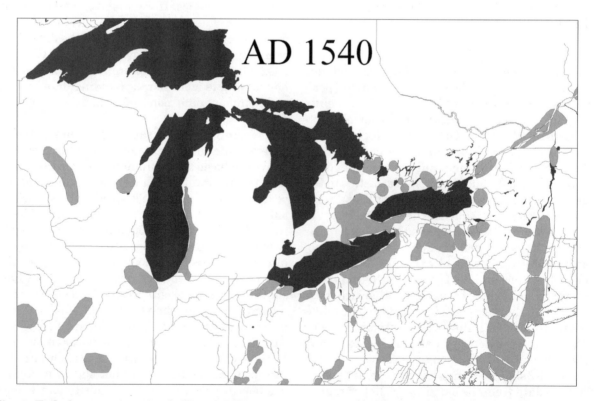

Fig. 2. Tribal cores areas in the Great Lakes region around AD 1540 (after Anderson 1991).

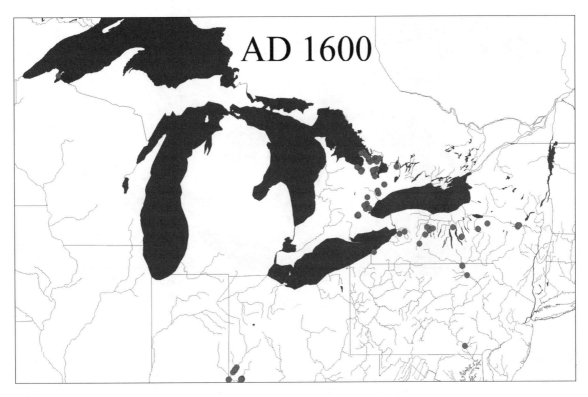

Fig. 3. Known tribal communities in the Great Lakes region around AD 1600 (after Tanner 1987, with corrections). Round dots = American Indian villages.

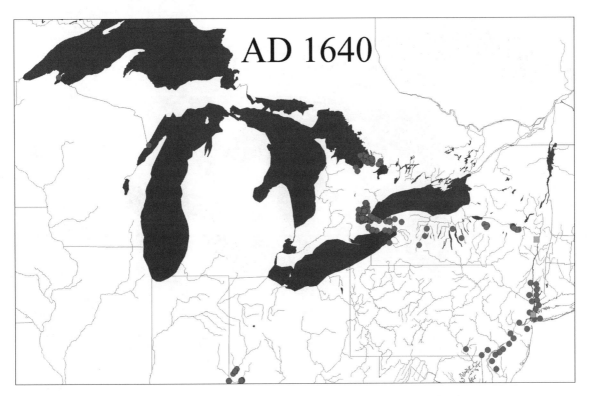

Fig. 4. Known tribal communities in the Great Lakes region around AD 1640 (after Tanner 1987, with corrections). Round dots = American Indian villages. Squares = European forts and posts.

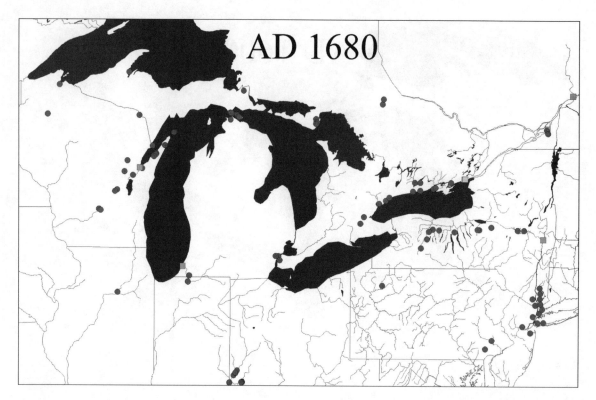

Fig. 5. Known tribal communities in the Great Lakes region around AD 1680 (after Tanner 1987, with corrections). Round dots = American Indian villages. Squares = European forts and posts.

Fig. 6. Known tribal communities in the Great Lakes region around AD 1720 (after Tanner 1987, with corrections). Round dots = American Indian villages. Squares = European forts and posts.

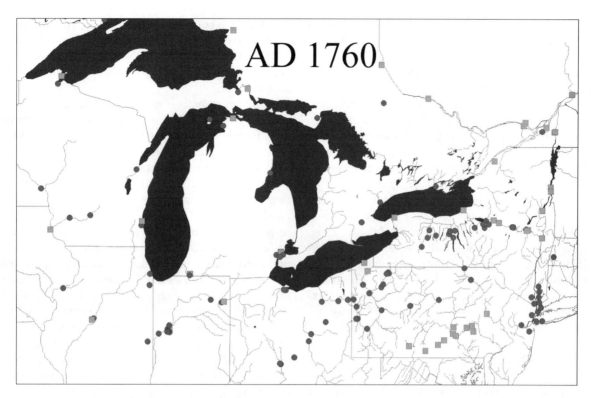

Fig. 7. Known tribal communities in the Great Lakes region around AD 1760 (after Tanner 1987, with corrections). Round dots = American Indian villages. Squares = European forts and posts.

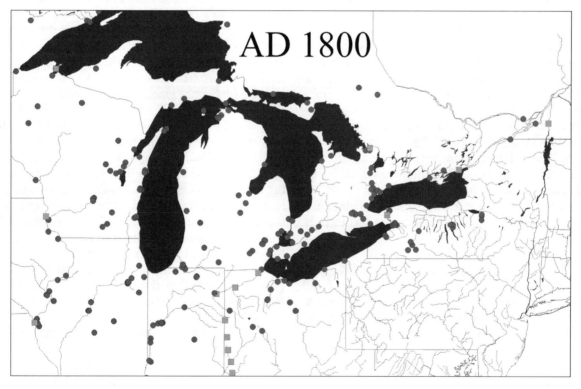

Fig. 8. Known tribal communities in the Great Lakes region around AD 1800 (after Tanner 1987, with corrections). Round dots = American Indian villages. Squares = European forts and posts.

The figures suggest that to the extent allowed by our data, we should endeavor to reduce the use of phases, complexes, and other essentialist categories if we are to more fully understand the dynamics of prehistoric demography and ethnogenesis. Their use was necessary before computers made data management easy, but it risks oversimplification if the goal is regional analysis. While inclusive taxons are still useful for the supplementary description of data sets, they are not analytically useful as replacements for data.

Nor should we expect that classifications drawn from different data domains will map on to each other neatly. Classifications drawn from historical linguistics, ceramic analysis, and settlement patterns might map on to one another or they might not. Instances were they do not map on to one another ought to be of particular interest, not inconsistencies that have to be explained away but informative departures from expectations.

Temporal Data Disaggregation

Just as the a priori aggregation of spatial data impedes analysis, so too does temporal aggregation. Period designations were invented in the first place to facilitate cross dating based on index types. That need was made obsolete by radiocarbon dating and other absolute dating techniques, yet the period designations persist. Independent dating techniques have long since reversed the logic of the pre-radiocarbon paradigm. While it was once necessary to assume that similar objects found at different sites were probably the same age, homologous rather than merely analogous, such cross-dating exercises should no longer be carried out except as means to achieve first approximations. Independent dating of similar remains at different sites entails an epistemological reversal, such that one now can reasonably ask questions about the clines between the age of an object in one place and the dates of similar objects elsewhere rather than assuming contemporaneity.

I am mindful that there are many data sets that have inherent limitations that make some amount of data aggregation unavoidable. Thus I am advocating only the disaggregation of data to the extent allowed by those limitations. For example, the site distributions in specific years shown in Figures 3-8 are possible only if we know or can approximate both the founding dates and the abandonment dates of components. Such maps can be generated only if each site shown is independently dated with enough precision to allow the assignment not just of a mean date but a probable range of occupation between beginning and ending dates. This is admittedly an easier task when the sites are relatively recent and historically documented as these are.

Fortunately, it is not necessary to require the ±1 year precision found in the data set that generated Figures 3-8. I have used a similar data set of over 800 Iroquoian sites, some of them over a millennium old, to generate a series of maps and a dynamic animation (Snow 1996). In this case a particular site might be assigned an occupation range of AD 1300-1350. However any criticism based on the admittedly correct observation that I could not possibly know the founding and abandonment dates that precisely is misplaced. Indeed I cannot, but that is not the point of the dynamic model generated by this and several hundred other sites of similar type. The point has to do with the overall dynamic pattern of site occupations and abandonments, which shows important general trends over the course of a millennium even though the dating of specific cases, especially early ones, is always approximate.

Ethnogenesis

Even without the detail provided by color coding and maps redrawn at one-year intervals, one can see from Figures 3-8 that the Great Lakes region was culturally very dynamic over the course of the two centuries from AD 1600 to 1800. There is no reason to believe that this dynamism was unique to North America in the contact period. Indeed, Fried's (1967) well-known general discussion of tribes and ethnicity is consistent with this picture. One can deal with the complexity of precontact population dynamics as most archaeologists did in the 1970s and 1980s, that is by defining it *a priori* as irrelevant to archaeological problems of scientific interest. However, I argue that the realistic solution of problems involving the complex interactions of human demography, historical contingency, technology, cultivation, sociopolitical evolution, and environmental adaptation requires that tribal fissioning, fusion, intermarriage, and migration be at least assumed as background noise.

If one traces that dynamism through the decades in the Great Lakes case, one can clearly see the cycles of fission and fusion that attended the relocation of tribal communities. John Moore's (1987, 1996) work on Cheyenne ethnogenesis shows clearly that a simple dendritic model borrowed from

106

biology seriously misrepresents the origins of tribal societies. The approach I am using here overcomes that problem and others of our own making. It also identifies some new and difficult problems. American Indian communities in this 200-year period were as often as not multiethnic. Language switching was common. It is unlikely that these confounding processes were unique to the contact period, however convenient it might be to assume so.

Thus we must substitute a rhyzotic model of ethnogenesis for a dentritic one using the principles advocated by Moore (1994). Dendritic models work well in biology because of the nature of genetically-determined inheritance. They even work reasonably well in linguistics, because languages typically do not blend easily. Thus biological (and often linguistic) populations can fission, but after enough time and differentiation they cannot fuse again. Some branches survive and experience further branching while others become extinct. A branching model serves well in such cases.

Implications for Archaeology

Dendritic models have often been misleading when applied in archaeology, even (or perhaps particularly) when they are only implicit. The post-1600 histories of tribal societies in North America reveal frequent migrations, the frequent merging of multiethnic communities, the frequent fissioning of communities, and frequent language switching. Tanner's (1987) Great Lakes atlas documents many examples. These realities make a mockery of dendritic models when applied to cultural evolution, yet it remains tempting to try to map the archaeology of tribal societies on to the branching trees reconstructed by historical linguists. Among other failings, the approach fails to take into account language switching, which Moore's work has shown was common in tribal societies on the Great Plains and in the Southeast (Moore 1987; Pers. Comm.). There are many other examples as well. One well documented case is that of the Kuuvaum Kaniagmiut of Alaska. This society is identified today as IÒupiaq Eskimo but records show that they were Koyukon-speaking Athapaskans in the early nineteenth century. The language (and ethnic) switch took plnãe in as little as two decades, between about 1860 and 1880, and probably involved only a single bilingual generation (Burch, et al. 1999).

If we use the tools we have at hand to disaggregate our data and date our assemblages, and if we

deal realistically with the processes of ethnogenesis, we will come closer to realistic representation of the evolution tribal societies at regional scales. Models derived from cases like those discussed here better represent the archaeological past and provide us with more precisely defined conceptual tools. We will never be able to replicate something like the Penobscot case from the archaeological record, and the details of the Great Lakes regional case are unlikely to be equaled archaeologically. Even the Northern Iroquoian case that I have published elsewhere (Snow 1996) is likely to remain a rare example of what can be done with enough fine-grained spatial and temporal data. However, temporal and spatial aggregation of archaeological data need no longer proceed beyond that shown in Figure 2. Our understanding of the archaeological past is substantially improved by an appreciation and accommodation of the nature of tribal societies.

References Cited

Anderson, D. G.
  1991   Examining Prehistoric Settlement Distribution in Eastern North America. *Archaeology of Eastern North America* 19:1-22.
Burch, E. S., E. Jones, H. P. Loon and L. D. Kaplan
  1999   The Ethnogenesis of the Kuuvaum Kaniagmiut. *Ethnohistory* 46(2):291-327.
Coe, M., D. Snow and E. Benson
  1986   *Atlas of Ancient America.* Facts on File, New York.
Fried, M.
  1967   *The Evolution of Political Society: An Essay in Political Anthropology.* Random House, New York.
Moore, J. H.
  1987   *The Cheyenne Nation: A Social and Demographic History.* University of Nebraska Press, Lincoln.
  1994   Putting anthropology back together again: The ethnogenetic critique of cladistic theory. *American Anthropologist* 96:925-948.
  1996   *The Cheyenne.* The Peoples of America. Blackwell Publishers, Cambridge.
Proctor, R. W.
  1942   *Report on Maine Indians Prepared at Request of Legislative Research Committee.* Maine State Legislature.

Snow, D. R.
1996   GIS Applications in North America. In *The Coloquia of the XIII International Congress of Prehistoric and Protohistoric Sciences*, edited by I. Johnson, pp. 159-168. vol. 1 Theoretical and Methodological Problems. A.B.A.C.O. Edizioni, Forli, Italy.

Speck, F. G.
1940   *Penobscot Man*. University of Pennsylvania Press, Philadelphia.
Tanner, H. H. (editor)
1987   *Atlas of Great Lakes Indian History*. University of Oklahoma Press, Norman.

7. Modeling the Formation and Evolution of an Illyrian Tribal System: Ethnographic and Archaeological Analogs

Michael L. Galaty

The Illyrians, broadly defined, were an early European 'ethnic' group, occupying wide portions of the Balkan peninsula (Fig. 1), of whom we know very little, besides that which was recorded about them by various ancient—particularly Roman—authors. Their archaeological remains have been studied by scholars in several Balkan countries, such as Bosnia, Croatia, Montenegro, and Albania, where it is argued that the Illyrians were the ancestors of modern Albanians. Archaeological research in Albania, though, is nearly always of a cultural-historical sort, highly and expertly descriptive, but lacking any kind of theoretical grounding. That being the case, various anthropological theoretical frameworks might profitably be put to work in Albania, especially those relating to the study of so-called 'middle-range' societies, as defined in this volume. More specifically, a 'tribal' model can be brought to bear on the seemingly intractable 'Illyrian' question: Who were they, and what can we say about the organization and evolution of their social and political systems? Furthermore, can a tribal model be applied in southern Albania to help us better understand the interaction of Greek colonists and indigenous Illyrians?

In one of the last articles he published before passing away, "The Ethne in Epirus and Upper Macedonia," Nicholas Hammond argued, as he had done before, that when ancient authors referred to *ethne* (i.e. tribes), what they were describing were societies that were tribally, not necessarily ethnically, defined. In this sense, a group was considered to be non-Greek because its form of political and social organization was different from that of the Greek, based primarily on kinship (i.e. clan-based) affiliation rather than citizenship. Until recent times, a tribal society operated in northern Albania, and aspects of this society may have Illyrian antecedents. As a result, analysis of the northern Albanian tribes may serve to illuminate ancient Illyrian tribal institutions, and at the same time help to tighten Hammond's definition of ancient *ethne*. Furthermore, understanding the evolution of the Illyrian tribal system requires an appreciation for processes of colonization that directly affected Illyrian peoples, particularly along the eastern coast of the Adriatic in pre- and proto-historic times. Employing an explicitly comparative methodology, the colonization of Virginia by the English can be contrasted with that of Illyris by Greeks, thereby using the Algonquian response to colonialism, recorded in some detail by the English colonists, as an analog for the Illyrian experience of Greek colonization, known almost exclusively through archaeology.

The Definition of Tribe

Archaeologists are currently in the midst of redefining what is meant by the term 'tribe' (e.g., Feinman and Neitzel 1984). Whereas the term had been nearly driven out of the anthropological lexicon, it is now being rehabilitated, primarily by archaeologists, who continue to find the idea of tribal societies useful (see Parkinson, this volume, Chapter 1). So, what do we mean when we say that a society is 'tribal'? As Severin Fowles writes in Chapter 2 of this volume:

> …[W]hen employed casually, 'tribe' or 'tribal' do a better job of indicating what the social phenomenon in question is not—not too big, not too small, and not too centralized or chiefdom-like …Tribe has overtly come to assume the middle-range in the continuum of human social forms… (p. 18)

As traditionally understood—based on the so-called 'structural' model (Fowles, this volume, Chapter 2, p. 14)—tribes are also, besides being small and egalitarian: 1) 'segmented', though mechanisms exist to combine social segments into larger units, when necessary, so that, 2) segments are cross-cut by overlapping webs of social obligation designed to bind individuals and families together (Service 1962; Sahlins 1961, 1968). The challenge lies in

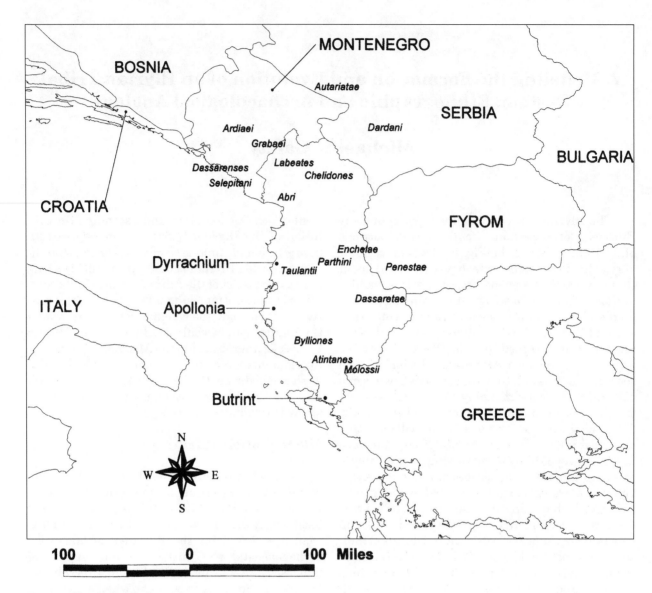

Fig. 1. Illyrian tribal territories.

finding evidence in the archaeological record for such societies, and for processes of segmentation and integration, as are generally attested in the ethnographic and ethno-historic records. In fact, because 'tribal' societies are characterized by a high degree of social and political elasticity and possess the ability to adapt to a wide range of ecological and economic conditions, we might expect them to appear in the archaeological record in all areas and time periods, though the characteristics that define tribes also render them difficult to spot. Their social and political structures are often in flux and their settlement and economic systems are usually non-specialized and decentralized, causing their archaeological footprints to be small and light and easily swept away, especially by larger, more com-

plex societies, particularly states. As a result, Fowles' call for diachronic approaches to the study of tribes, operating at various chronological scales (or 'trajectories'), may help to alleviate problems of recognizing 'tribal' societies in general and in the many cases where tribes actively engaged state-level systems, as in ancient Illyris. To paraphrase, we need to know what tribes *do* to understand what they *are*, and ideally, to apply tribal models archaeologically we need to know what tribes do over time and in response to threats, such as from colonization.

Fowles describes three different tribal 'trajectories', characterized by intra-generational, multi-generational, and long-term processes. These trajectories can be identified for North Albania (for

110

which the evidence is both ethnographic and ethnohistoric), for Colonial Virginia (for which the evidence is both ethnohistoric and archaeological), and—using the previous two to help frame archaeological questions—for Illyris. According to Fowles, humans make sense of time and the unfolding of events at varying scales. At one end of the continuum, history is understood at the level of the individual, while at the other end, it is appreciated in mythic terms by an entire society. For the individual, memory spans no more than a few decades and identity formation is driven by a personal experience of history, and the events—most mundane, others more meaningful—of which history is composed. For the tribe, memory and group identity are typically explained in oral tradition and are frequently inscribed onto a given landscape, a tribal territory. These two historical 'trajectories'— short- versus long-term, individual- versus group-directed—are clearly cybernetic in operation, and are necessarily integrated across time by a variety of multi- or inter-generational feedback loops, which act as bridges linking personal to social histories, and vice versa.

Intra-generational processes.

Within Fowles' framework, intra-generational processes structure an individual's experience of history and include such events as seasonal rounds, the rise and fall of tribal leaders, and episodes of conflict or alliance building. Such processes can be identified in ethnohistoric accounts of North Albanian tribes, and a particular event, such as a drought, revenge killing, or important tribal assembly, might have a direct and dramatic effect on an individual's life (cf. Kadare 1990). Similar events can be inferred for ancient Illyris and must have similarly affected Illyrian individuals, as when, for example, patterns of transhumance, which likely structured the average Illyrian's day-to-day existence, were disrupted by inter-tribal conflict. Colonization can seriously disturb intra-generational processes, particularly when patterns of daily tribal life are ruptured due to colonial expansion, as attested for Virginia in the writings of John Smith. Similar ruptures in intra-generational trajectories are evident in the archaeological record of tribal Illyris, caused by the coming of the Greeks, and alluded to by Greek historians. For example, the Greek slave trade, supplied in part from Illyrian sources, must have had a direct, probably negative, impact on the average Illyrian.

Long-term processes

Long-term processes allow a given tribe to record and interpret (often in myths) tribal history over hundreds, even thousands, of years (see Fowles, this volume, Chapter 2). Long-term tribal trajectories lead to the development of systems of subsistence, social and political inequality, and ritual, for example. In northern Albania, myths, supported by various ritual and superstitious practices, allowed tribes to explain a group's origins and idiosyncratic behaviors (Elsie 2001). Albanian origin myths typically traced the source of various tribes to a shared, legendary ancestor, as is common for tribal societies, thereby legitimizing tribal and lineage-based relationships. In addition, oral histories, passed down from generation to generation, often explained ways of being, knowing, or living, thereby limiting an individual's scope of action by situating one's personal behavior within a wider and deeper social context. Whereas Illyrian beliefs are largely lost to us, their ritual systems, in particular those related to burial, are quite open to investigation. Following Greek colonization and over the long term, Illyrian burial practices changed, likely signaling a shift in deeply held beliefs, as individual Illyrians became accustomed to new social realities. The Virginian tribes made similar accommodations, over several hundred years, as Indian practices and beliefs were overwhelmed by those of the Europeans. For example, as colonization took its toll on Indian societies, some Indians converted to Christianity (Gleach 1997:4), a long-term process perhaps analogous to processes of religious syncretism evident in later Illyrian burials.

Multi-generational processes

Multi-generational trajectories bridge the gap between intra-generational and long-term trajectories, usually extending over periods exceeding a century, or more (see Fowles, this volume, Chapter 2). Such historical processes help explain, for example, changes in settlement, such as the shifting location of villages, and can help make sense of new ideas and behaviors, especially those relating to the diffusion of technology. In northern Albania, systems of oral law, such as the 'Code of Lek', served to connect short- and long-term historical trajectories. These law codes were changed only with great difficulty and made manifest the vast array of rules and regulations—all related to personal and tribal 'honor'—responsible for reproducing tribal life over decades and centuries (Fox 1989; Hasluck 1954).

What is more, law codes could not function without some means for preserving, in the absence of written records, a tribe's particular history, which strung together events both recent and dimly remembered. For example, tribal leaders could not adjudicate a boundary dispute unless some practical means existed for remembering the location of a boundary marker. They could not end a blood feud that had lasted generations without knowledge of who killed whom and when. The law codes therefore provided very specific instructions with regard to preserving tribal memories, over various expanses of time. In the short term, individuals who had lived through the events in question were entrusted with their memory. Over the long term, important events were recorded in the landscape itself. (These processes are described in more detail below.) Thus, for the northern Albanian tribes, the 'law' is the key to explaining the structure of Albanian tribal society, and it can be argued that similar law codes were employed by Illyrian tribes. As with intra-generational and long-term tribal trajectories, multi-generational processes do indeed shift in response to colonial contact, often out of necessity. Such changes can cause great upheaval, and as a result, tribal elders often recall when and why they were made, as with the Chickahominy tribe's decision to join the Powhatan—for fear of the English—and with the introduction of *bajraktars* in northern Albania, as a response to Ottoman and Serbian aggression.

The Illyrians and the Illyrian Question

Albania is thought to encompass the heartland of territories once controlled by the so-called 'Illyrian' peoples. In fact, according to some archaeologists, much of Southeast Europe was at one time or another occupied by Illyrians (see discussion in Wilkes 1992), though it is clear that several different ethnic groups, broadly defined, shared the Balkan peninsula with them, including Thracians, Macedonians, and Greeks. As a result, the Balkan peninsula was divided, at least by Classical times, and almost certainly much earlier, into several ethnic spheres, separated by poorly-defined frontier zones. One of these frontier zones ran along what is now the border between Albania and Greece, and in the past, as is true today, this boundary did not clearly demarcate two different, mutually exclusive, ethnically defined territories, one Illyrian and the other Greek. In fact, in past times the situation was yet more complex than that. Both the Illyrian and the Greek 'nations', for lack of a

better term, were further subdivided into smaller tribal units, each possessing a different name (the Chaonians, Mollosians, Bylliones, etc.); and it is not at all clear how each of these different tribal groups was distinguished one from the other, whether by custom, such as dress, ancestry, or language. What made one group Greek and another Illyrian, and was this even a meaningful distinction in the past?

By the Early Iron Age so-called 'hill forts' were established throughout the frontier region between Illyris and Greece. These communities eventually evolved into Greek-style *poleis*, possessing theatres, stadiums, stoas, etc. It is often the case that these hill forts are considered Illyrian, but some of them, and not others, clearly identified more with the Greek world to the south, making dedications in Greek at the oracle of Dodona and sending participants to Greek athletic festivals (Wilkes 1992:104). There was indeed a distinction made between those individuals who were Greek and those who were not (i.e. barbarians), and the determining factor was in most cases language. However, just as the line dividing Greek from Illyrian ethnic territory is poorly defined, so are the political territories that once existed very poorly understood. As might be expected, one of the major research questions for Albanian archaeologists concerns the extent of Illyrian political control: Provided that the Illyrians are the ancestors of modern-day Albanians, is it possible to identify purely Illyrian settlements, thereby establishing, in recidivist fashion, which regions should belong to Albania, but do not? For example, was/is Epirus Greek, or was it Illyrian, and therefore by extension Albanian? Might it be, though, that groups living in the frontier regions were not purely Greek, nor were they purely Illyrian? Might it be that this dialectic—Greek versus Illyrian—marks a gross over-simplification of what must have been, in antiquity, a very complex, ever-changing web of ethnic, social, economic, and, most importantly for this paper, tribal relationships (for general discussion of these and similar issues, see Taylor 1994, Wells 1998)?

Finally, to further complicate things, Greek colonies were established in Albania, during Archaic times, along the eastern shore of the Adriatic, at Epidamnus-Dyrrachium, Apollonia, and Butrint, in regions ostensibly under Illyrian control. It seems likely that, especially in the case of Epidamnus, and perhaps Apollonia, Greek colonization occurred at the invitation, or with the grudging approval, of local Illyrians (Wilkes 1992:112). However, once the colonies had become established, to what extent did Greeks and Illyrians interact? Did they co-exist, fight, or ignore one another? Did they intermarry and trade? Were Illyrians slaves of the Greeks, as Aristotle might have us believe (Wilkes 1992:113)?

In order to address such questions, it is necessary to collect the relevant archaeological data. Such data are beginning to appear. For example, it is thought that Apollonia was established in 588 BC at a previously existing Greek-Illyrian trading post (*emporium*), perhaps at the invitation of the local Illyrian group (Wilkes 1992:112). That being the case, why is it that the Mallakastra Regional Archaeological Project has found almost no evidence for an Illyrian presence in the vicinity of Apollonia prior to Greek colonization (Davis et al. 2002)? Why is it that 'Illyrian' pottery (i.e. Early Iron Age pottery) has not been recovered from what was reputedly first an 'Illyrian' site? Have the historical documents that refer to Apollonia's foundation misled us? Actually, such negative archaeological evidence does make rather good sense given a tribal model of Illyrian social organization, especially if that model is wrapped around a Bronze/Iron Age model of pastoral economy (Hammond 2000:346-7). Prior to the later portions of the Iron Age, the Illyrian peoples lived a largely transhumant existence (Hammond 1992), spending their summers in the mountains of the interior and in the winter moving down towards the coastal plains, to places like Apollonia (one of the colony's primary exports was reportedly hides), in so doing making only a very light impression on the regional archaeological record. Such pastoral economies typically support tribal political systems, which are flexible enough to accommodate seasonal disaggregation. By the time hill forts had developed on the interior, the Illyrians were actively engaged in trade with the Greek city-states. In fact, the construction of settlements by the Illyrians in defensible locations mirrors the response of tribal, pastoral peoples, in various time periods and places, to competition with each other for access to trade with outside powers. In this case, a tribal model helps us to better understand particular archaeological results and additional research will allow us to further refine the model.

In constructing a tribal model of Illyrian sociopolitical organization, it would be useful to identify suitable analogs for tribal behavior as it might have evolved in a Greco-Albanian world. I will suggest two such possible analogs. First, a tribal socio-political system has functioned in northern Albania into the present day. This system, though poorly studied by modern anthropologists (for obvious reasons, but see Ulqini [1991] and Young [2000]), was described in some detail by early 20th-century travelers to the region. Their descriptions can, I will argue, serve to enlighten and inform our study of the Illyrians, if we are willing to allow some degree of historical connection between modern and ancient tribal systems. Second, relatively detailed ethno-historic accounts of the colonization by the English of what is now Virginia may provide examples of tribal response to an intruding culture, analogous to the Greek colonization of Illyria. In both cases, colonies were established in the midst of competing tribal entities, and in both cases, the responses of local leaders to colonization were broadly similar. This may indicate, therefore, that Illyrian and Algonquian societies, while operating in very different times and places, were nevertheless quite similar in their political organization.

Northern Albanian Tribes

Perhaps our best descriptions of the northern Albanian tribes, of which there were many dozens, come from early 20th-century travelers to the region, almost exclusively female, who often produced quite detailed analyses of tribal customs and relationships, which they feared would disappear under the new government of King Zog (e.g., Edith Durham 1909, 1928; Margaret Hasluck 1954; Rose Wilder Lane 1923). One of the most striking elements of the Albanian tribal system was (and still is) its dependence on the *Kanun* of Lekë Dukagjini, a system of oral law compiled by a 15th-century tribal 'chieftain' named Dukagjini (Durham 1909:25-27; Fox 1989:xvi). The Code of Lek, one code among many that operated in North Albania, was first written down in 1913 by a Franciscan friar (Fox 1989:xvii-xviii). It was extensively studied by Margaret Hasluck in the 1930s, as reported in *The Unwritten Law in Albania*, published posthumously in 1954. Importantly, it is thought that the origins of the *kanun*, being an oral code, can be traced to much earlier periods, perhaps back to the Illyrians themselves (Fox 1989:xvi). For example, many of the behaviors prescribed in the modern *kanun* have pre-Ottoman, ancient origins, and are described by Classical authors, especially Herodotus, as being purely 'barbarian' in practice (cf. Taylor 1994).

Traditionally, the *kanun* was interpreted by a council of elders from each tribe or *fis*, though there were traveling specialists who could consult on especially tricky cases. Each tribe was represented by a 'banner' (*bajrak*), thus the tribal headman was called *bajraktar*, or 'standard-bearer' (Ulqimi 1991). Cases typically revolved around: marriage and family relations; the theft or loss of livestock; territorial disputes; or, murder. Should a murder be committed, two houses (*shpi*) would then be 'in blood' and a cycle of revenge killings—the so-called 'blood feud'—would ensue. This cycle might only be ended when one family had been destroyed or blood had been paid, usually a cash payment from one family to the other (Durham 1909:30). As might be expected, the blood feud affected all aspects of daily life in northern Albania. A man marked for death (a black ribbon was worn around the right arm) could not leave his family's fortress-like house, or *kula*, unless a *besa*, an oath of peace, had been sworn. Interestingly, because women were not subject to the blood feud, they often were responsible for the family's economic well-being. Thus, for example, if her husband were marked for death, a woman might make trips to Skhodra, the regional capital, in his stead, to trade and do business (Durham 1909:16). The blood feud caused tribal alliances to constantly shift, and so tribal boundaries, often quite complex, were marked by the rock-piled graves (*muranë*) of those killed in feuds (Hasluck 1954:102; Kadare 1982). As a result, tribal groups could lay claim to land, marking that claim with graves, and this claim was recalled through a tribe's understanding of its own ancestry. And, as in most tribal societies the world over, clan lineage helped to determine tribal relationships:

> The largest of the Catholic tribes was the Mirdite, which was actually composed of three smaller clans. A legend explains the origin of the name Mirdite. Once there lived three brothers whose father left nothing when he died but a saddle and a winnowing sieve. The eldest son took the saddle (*shale*, in Albanian), the next the sieve (*shoshe*) and the youngest went his way empty handed, wishing his brothers good day (*mir dite*). This legend gives the three clans Shala, Shoshi and Mirdite a common ancestor. (Vickers 1995:103)

The marking of territory was of paramount importance in High Albania, as there was very limited pasturage. Much of the land in North Albania is arid and unproductive, so access to pasture could mean life or death for a family or clan. Individual members of clans marked tribal membership through clothing styles, such as in the patterns of black braids sewn onto a man's white wool pants, or hair styles, different patterns of head shaving (*perchin*) marking different tribes (Durham 1909:23, 50, 79). The native inhabitants of Virgin-

ia apparently did likewise, employing styles of dress to signal tribal affiliation (Hranicky 1996:87).

So, it is clear what factors led to the segmentation of Albanian tribal groups and what might lead to competition or antagonism between segments—boundary disputes, blood feud, the (sometimes amicable) separation of families, villages, or clans—but what drew non-related individuals and clans together, in times of war, for example?

As already mentioned, the primary means of bringing clans together, especially those in blood, was the swearing of a *besa*, an oath of peace. If a *besa* was to be permanent, however, it either had to be marked by an oath of blood brotherhood, a pact sealed by the sharing of blood—three drops in a glass of *raki*—between the two feuding parties, or by a marriage exchange (Durham 1909:24; Pettifer 1996:84). (Interestingly, this practice is described by Herodotus; see discussion in Taylor [1994:391]). On occasion, the leaders of various tribes might swear allegiance to a single *bajraktar*, though this was very rare. For example, the northern tribes gathered in Lezhe in 1444 to elect Skanderbeg their commander in the fight against the Ottomans. After his death, this tribal alliance dissolved and the Ottomans overran Albania. Likewise, in 1922, Zogu, from the region of Mati, was recognized by the northern tribes as primary chief, but, as might be expected, they refused to swear an oath of loyalty to the state, a concept they did not understand or appreciate, and demanded that they be allowed to gather to swear allegiance to Zogu personally (Vickers 1995: 106). As with Skanderbeg, Zogu was primary chief of the tribes in name only. The oath of allegiance did not involve a loss of political independence on the part of individual *bajraktars*, and when Zog fled Albania, the tribal system remained intact.

Apparent in this very brief sketch of the northern Albanian tribal system are examples of Fowles' various historical trajectories. The structure of the Albanian socio-political system (as described in detail by Hasluck [1954]) is purely tribal in nature and organization, and the law code is specifically designed to protect and foster tribal identity and independence. In fact, the *kanun* makes it almost impossible for one particular individual to usurp another's freedom, and in some ways, the checks and balances inherent in the Code of Lek are similar to those found in the Iroquois 'Great Law of Peace'. Decisions relating to the law were made in council, a so-called 'general assembly', and had to be unanimous, and the size of an assembly related to the importance of the deliberation (Hasluck 1954:148-153).

The 'Separation of Brothers'

Social and political leadership was defined first in the home(*shpi*), the oldest male of each household being the family leader, or 'Master of the House' (Hasluck 1954:34-50). The master of the house led family meetings and represented his household at clan and village assemblies. When the leader of an extended family died, his hand-picked successor took over (usually, but not always, the eldest son); however, if brothers no longer wanted to live together following their father's death, they could formally separate (Hasluck 1954:51-72). In fact, a large portion of the *kanun* is devoted to the 'Separation of Brothers', which probably reflects the danger of a new feud beginning during the delicate process of dividing a household's belongings (including the house itself) between two, and very often many more, brothers. Often, an equitable division was impossible, and so a wall (or walls) would be built within the house itself to physically separate one new family group from the other(s) (Hasluck 1954:57). (The 'Separation of Brothers' is remarkable, in that a similar organic process may have been responsible for producing the large pueblo structures of the American Southwest.)

Because the growth and separation of extended families was accorded such importance and was formally enshrined in oral law, every Albanian knew and remembered exactly how his household related to others in the larger clan (*fis*). Separation provides an excellent example of an event that would have had a strong impact on intra-generational trajectories, making a lasting impression on each individual involved. The separation itself was marked by a ritualized distribution of goods and belongings (which then became heirlooms), thus 'materializing' the event, helping to preserve its memory across generations: "Son, that is your great-grandfather's rifle, given to me by my father after his separation from your great uncle back in 1608..." The law code systematized separation, and thereby helped to reproduce tribal structures through time and across space. And, finally, famous (or infamous) separations might be raised to the status of myth (as in the Mirditë example above), and therefore help explain over the long term how certain villages and tribes came to be.

The marking of territory

The marking of territory also reinforced intra- and multi-generational, as well as long-term, historical processes. Large portions of the *kanun* are devoted to the establishment and preservation of territorial boundaries, between households, villages, and tribes, and to the means whereby lost boundaries were re-established (Hasluck 1954:95-109). The marking of territory was of absolute importance in North Albania, as good land, especially pasturage, was rare and of extremely high value. Traditionally, a tribe's territory could be expanded at the expense of another's during blood feuds. If, for example, a man was shot at the edge of his tribal territory, he could extend his tribe's boundary into the other's as far as he could crawl before dying, where his grave cairn (*muranë*) was constructed (Hasluck 1954:102-103). Presumably, this law was designed to discourage one man from maiming another; rather, one should not shoot unless a fatal blow could be dealt, thereby saving a family the expense of caring for an invalid and preserving the victim's honor. Obviously, boundaries marked in this fashion would be readily remembered by all parties, at least over the course of several generations. In cases where a boundary stone had been lost, elders might allow representatives of the quarreling tribes to "carry or throw stones" (Hasluck 1954:103). The two representatives either threw large stones or carried them on their backs, the winning toss or carry determining where the new boundary would be positioned. Again, such an event would have dramatically emphasized the culmination of an important tribal decision, one which needed to be remembered.

Upon the placing of a boundary stone, particular tribal elders were chosen to swear oaths of memory, laying their hands on the marker and vowing to recall where the boundary line had been established, or risk "carrying the stone and the whole wide world" on their shoulders for eternity (Hasluck 1954:100). If a dispute arose over a boundary marker's position, these elders could be called in to testify with regard to its location and historical significance. If all the elders involved in placing the stone had died, then individuals who were alive and present at the original marking, even as children, might be called upon to testify, swearing a similar oath of memory. Finally, if no one was alive who remembered the proper location of the boundary, a competition was held, or a feud might ensue. Again, as with the 'Separation of Brothers', tribal understanding of territory was 'materialized', in this case by marking (or 'inscribing') the landscape itself. Provisions were made for short- and long-term memory of boundary location, and particularly meaningful events (such as the violent death of an individual) were employed to brand the marking of territory with heavy symbolic importance.

The origin of the bajraktar

As mentioned above, a *bajraktar*, or 'standard-bearer', led each tribe. However, the Canon of Lek clearly recognizes that the bariak system was introduced by the Ottomans and was not an indigenous institution (Hasluck 1954:115; Ulqimi 1991). The Ottomans never fully conquered northern Albania, though Albanian men were encouraged to fight with Ottomans against Montenegrins and Serbs, which they were usually willing and eager to do. The man, usually a clan head, who was chosen to raise the levy was given a 'standard', which he carried as a mark of his rank and responsibility. The power of *bajraktars* was not formally enshrined by tribal law, but invariably, they were the leaders of the most powerful *fis*, or lineage. Thus, bearing a standard granted a tribal 'big man' a means to accrue even more prestige, especially in war. He probably also had easier access to Ottoman trade goods, access other big men lacked.

The evolution of the *bajraktars* seems to represent a particular response on the part of the late Medieval northern Albanians to the challenges of colonization and conquest, represented by the Ottomans. Their tribal system and oral law code were designed to allow segmentation and discourage processes of integration, especially if a tribe's independence was at stake. Thus, the system was in some ways extremely flexible, except when a particular situation called for cooperation, as when a coordinated defense became necessary. (This is why Skanderbeg had so much trouble uniting the tribes against the Ottomans in the 15th century, as did Zogu much later.) However, the need for integration also might allow certain individuals the opportunity to extend their power beyond that which was allowed by tribal law and tradition. In this sense, long-term historical trajectories that encouraged egalitarianism could be derailed by particular events, such as an external military threat. Similar challenges were surely faced by tribal Illyrians as they negotiated the risks and opportunities born of Greek colonization.

Modeling an Illyrian Tribal System

How does the northern Albanian tribal system compare to our archaeological and historical understanding of the Illyrians? Does it provide an appropriate analog and might there exist an his-torical connection? First of all, the scale of tribal territories, as described by ancient writers, seems to accord well with that of the northern highlanders (see map in Hasluck 1954). We might imagine an Illyrian system of competing tribal entities, perhaps employing systems of oral law similar to the Code of Lek. Tribes might have been led by a council of elders, similar to the Mycenaean *damos*, but generally, political power would have been shared between various tribal leaders, of varying degrees of social standing. These leaders (equivalent to 'big men') probably gained prestige and access to power based upon their performance in war, as attested by richly-appointed Illyrian-period warrior graves. The Illyrian council of elders would have interpreted tribal laws, and their decisions would have been enforced by tribal members (as when in modern Albania, the house of an offender is burned down by his fellow villagers). Such a socio-political system would have eventually produced, through cycles of competition, a two-tiered settlement hierarchy, including hill forts, central places associated with prominent tribes, and autonomous villages. Theoretically, evidence for settlement hierarchy can be collected through regional survey; in fact, during the summer of 2002, MRAP surveyed the hinterland of an Illyrian hillfort, the results of which are undergoing analysis (see Davis et al. 2002). Furthermore, a careful study of artifact styles across the wide expanse of Albania would allow identification of regional patterns, which might indicate tribal groupings.

In addition, it may be that patterns of segmentation, territoriality, and increasing social and political hierarchy similar to those of northern Albania can be identified for Illyria. For example, if Illyrian tribes were territorial (as the ancient writers seem to indicate), it may be that they marked boundaries with burial monuments, such as tumuli, in a fashion analogous to that of modern northern Albanians. Regional settlement systems should each include a hill fort community and a cluster of associated villages, surrounded by a substantial buffer zone, reserved for pasture, but also intended to separate one tribal entity from another. These zones, or 'frontiers', between tribes should be marked in some fashion, with burial mounds or stone markers. As this system evolved, and as it came into more sustained contact with the Greek city-states, particularly in the south, competition for access to trade would have ensued. Some tribal leaders may have garnered increased prestige through manipulation of this trade and in battle with other tribes as competition intensified. Eventually, hill forts came to dominate the landscape as individual big men were transformed into chiefs. In fact, as the Greeks intensified colonization of the coast, some big men may have allied themselves with the colonists in a system similar to that of the Ottoman *bajraktars*. Greek goods, such as weapons and drinking paraphernalia, would have been employed by Illyrian chiefs to mark their rank and position, in life and in death. It has also been suggested that in some regions Illyrian tribal federations formed in response to Greek encroachment (see various articles in Cabanes 1993). As Hellenism developed and spread (beginning with the death of Alexander in 323 BC), the southern Illyrian political system became less tribal and more 'Greek', and by the time of the Roman conquest (167 BC), southern Illyria, at least, had become firmly and irreversibly integrated into the Greco-Roman world. In the mountains of the north, though, Illyrian traditions lived on.

Virginia's Algonquian Tribes

Processes of competitive cycling, including segmentation and alliance building, are attested for numerous places and periods, perhaps the best example being North American pre- and proto-historic tribes and chiefdoms. I would like to suggest another analog for the proposed Illyrian tribal system, that of the Algonquian tribes of what is now Virginia in the eastern United States. At the time of European contact, the eastern seaboard of North America was home to hundreds of small tribal groups. These different tribes can be classified based on language into roughly three groups: Siouxan, Iroquoian, Muskhogean, and Algonquian speakers. (This, of course, is similar to the Balkan peninsula, where large ethnic groups spoke Illyrian, Greek, Thracian, or Macedonian languages.)

Most of our information about Virginia's Indians comes from the reports of English colonists who settled Jamestown in 1607, primarily the writings of John Smith. Between 1608 and 1624, Smith published remarkable descriptions of Virginia's tribes, especially the Algonquian-speaking groups found in the vicinity of Jamestown. He also compiled a map of tribal territories including village names. What is striking about this map is its similarity to the maps of tribal territories for northern Albania (e.g., Hasluck 1954) or those produced for tribal Illyria based on the work of Classical and Roman historians (examples in Wilkes 1992). The sizes of tribal territories in all three locations are

closely similar. What is more, Smith made a distinction on his map between those villages that possessed a *werowance*, a tribal 'chief' or 'big man', which he marked with a longhouse, and those that did not, marked by a circle (Potter 1993:15). In this way, tribal chieftains lent their name to their village (at least, according to Smith), and vice versa, and to the wider tribe itself, and a two-tiered settlement hierarchy was established. (As argued above, a similar system might have functioned in tribal Illyria, and such an hypothesis is archaeologically testable through site survey in the vicinity of hillforts and subsequent settlement pattern analysis; for an example of this approach in Virginia, see Potter 1993.)

Even more interesting, at the time of Jamestown's foundation, Virginia's tribal political system was in a state of flux (Barbour 1986). First of all, there is evidence that a shift had occurred at some point in the past away from communal styles of leadership towards individualized forms. For example, Smith notes that the Chickahominies were ruled by a council of eight great men, or *munguys*, as they are to this day. However, by the time of Smith's arrival, in all other tribes power had been vested in the person of a chief, usually a great warrior. Smith's nemesis Powhatan was just such a man. Second, by 1607 Powhatan had managed to become *mamanatowick*, or 'great king', paramount chieftain of the Virginian Algonquians. The subordination of other tribes to Powhatan was marked by a tributary relationship: Subordinated tribes were expected to send Powhatan annual tribute, especially maize, and his family was often inter-married with that of the subordinate *werowance*. Powhatan also controlled trade in the region, its transportation system, based on river travel, and access to communal hunting territories (Gleach 1997:28-31). Tribes that ignored Powhatan's decrees might be obliterated, as were the Chesapeakes, probably in the years just prior to 1607 (Rountree 1990:21). Third, apparently Powhatan was actively seeking to extend his control to include those tribes located at the 'ethnic fringe' of his territory, primarily those tribes found in the Potomac river valley and farther north in Maryland (Rountree 1990:13-14). And fourth, the Algonquians appear to have been under increased pressure from other, more distant groups, especially the expanding Iroquois Confederacy and the Eastern Sioux, specifically the Monacans, found west of the Blue Ridge.

The English colonists who settled at Jamestown faced numerous challenges, the foremost being an acute shortage of food. Smith's voyages around the Chesapeake were as much exploration as desperate searches for supplemental foodstuffs, which he most often obtained from werowances, sometimes through trade, but more often as a result of military action. What is more, he made clear to his new 'friends', as he often described them, that if need arose, he would return. Imagine the consternation these chiefs and their followers must have felt! They could hardly afford to pay tribute to two paramount chieftains, Powhatan and Smith; they had to choose, and choosing one meant having to fight the other. However, in paying 'tribute' to Smith, some tribes may have felt as though they gained a new ally in their struggle against Powhatan. This was especially true of tribes along Powhatan's ethnic fringe, which were more willing to subordinate themselves to Smith, perhaps because he offered more protection from the dreaded Iroquois than did Powhatan.

We might also imagine Powhatan's consternation when he learned that a new 'chief' was sailing around his territory demanding tribute from his subjects. In fact, Powhatan responded by kidnapping Smith and trying to force him to become his adopted 'son' (Gleach 1997:35; Rountree 1990:39). (Ironically, the colonists later sought to trick Powhatan into swearing fealty to the King of England, something he refused to do [Rountree 1990:47].) When that failed, Powhatan sent his daughter, Pocahontas (she of Walt Disney fame), who was probably thirteen at the time, to 'negotiate'. In truth, Powhatan probably hoped Smith would take his daughter as a wife, thereby directly subordinating him to the great chief, making him a sub-chief and member of the 'royal' family. Pocahontas eventually did marry a colonist, John Rolfe, in April of 1614, and while they were married (Pocahontas died in England on March 21, 1617), Powhatan-Colonial relations experienced a 'golden age' of relative peace (Gleach 1997:3; Rountree 1990:64). The peace did not last long, though, primarily because, as more colonists arrived, more land was appropriated, and a developing land rush was fueled by the growing European appetite for Indian tobacco (Gleach 1997:67; Rountree 1990:68).

During this time, Powhatan did not take military action against the English. On numerous occasions, his warriors could have crushed the colony (for instance, the colonists suffered several epidemics, during which time they were vulnerable to attack) and driven the English out of Virginia, but he never took action. Certainly, the Jamestown fort itself was an obstacle, but it may also be that Powhatan feared the English and their guns (Fausz 1979; contra Gleach 1997:45). However, this is quite hard to believe; by all indications, the Algonquians thought the colonists were entirely inept (Gleach 1997:55). It is more likely that Powhatan thought the colony would eventually fail (as other colonies, like Roanoke, had), and that, in the meantime, he could use Jamestown as a source of valuable trade goods, especially metal, which was very difficult to get (Gleach 1997:3). The Powhatans eventually did take military action against the colonists, but by the time of the First Powhatan War (1622) , the colony had been reinforced, Powhatan had died, and the former chief's cousin, Opecanchanough, failed to expel the English. Fear of the English caused the Chickahominies to suspend their council of *munguys* and they became a tributary tribe of the Powhatans; and forced the Powhatans to make peace with their traditional enemies, the Monocans (i.e. the Eastern Sioux). Finally, the Powhatans were defeated. In 1646, Opecanchanough was captured and executed, reportedly at the age of 100+. In a fascinating twist, Virginia's Indian tribes signed treaties with the colonial government explicitly switching allegiance away from the paramount chief to the King of England. As such, they were expected to present themselves to the governor annually, bearing tribute, just as they had once presented themselves to Powhatan. A tributary relationship between the state of Virginia and its Indian tribes is still, to this day, maintained.

The Illyrian Response to Colonialism

In Albania, beginning in the Archaic period, a colonial relationship was established between Greeks and Illyrians, one not dissimilar to that just described for the English and the Powhatans. I would argue that understanding the tribal political system of Virginia's Algonquian people and studying their response to an intrusive foreign power can help us to envision interactions between Greek colonists and tribal Illyrians, interactions that are reflected in Albania's archaeological record.

If the model already constructed for tribal Illyria, based in part on comparison to northern Albanian tribes, is accurate, then the Greeks probably entered a situation not unlike that described by John Smith for Colonial Virginia. It is not clear which Illyrian tribe first invited Greek colonization, but it may have been the Taulantii, who had been expelled—by invading Liburnians—from the city of Epidamnus, later Dyrrachium, now the modern port city of Durrës. Greeks from Corcyra, sponsored by Corinth, apparently helped the Taulantii re-take Epidamnus, which then became a Greek colony, one where Illyrian and Greek communities were, to some extent, ethnically integrated (Wilkes 1992:110-112). Thus, at least one Illyrian tribe, the Taulantii, had political and military motives for forging an alliance with Greeks, and, likewise, the same may have been true to the south, at Apollonia. However, although several tribal territories did apparently intersect near Apollonia's hinterland, it is not clear which tribe, if any, invited Greek settlement. Nevertheless, there does seem to be evidence for regular and sustained interaction at Apollonia between Illyrians and Greeks beginning with the foundation of the colony, in 588 BC. As did the English in Virginia, the Apollonian Greeks had no choice but to forge economic and political alliances with the various tribes in the region. Illyrian chiefs must have sought to trade with the Apollonians, as did Indian chiefs seek out John Smith and Jamestown. Illyrians gained access to valuable, foreign-made prestige goods, and Greeks reportedly received and exported a variety of Illyrian products, including hides, bitumen, and slaves (Pettifer 1996:170). In addition, there may have been conflict between the Apollonian Greeks and local Illyrians; there is at least one inscription (from Olympia) that describes Apollonia's annexation of a neighboring tribe's territory, that of the Abantes (Pettifer 1996:16).

In fact, contact with Europeans may have allowed, even necessitated, Powhatan's rise to power (Gleach 1997; Rountree 1993), just as the Ottoman presence in various ways encouraged the Albanian bariak system. The tributary chiefdom headed by Powhatan was young, poorly integrated, and therefore, unstable. The Algonquian 'ethnic fringe' (tribes such as those located on the Delmarva peninsula and to the north, along the Potomac, for example) continued to assert its independence, distracting Powhatan from securing his western boundary with the Monacans, a boon for John Smith and the colonists. The Indians of the eastern United States, including Powhatan, had met Europeans before the coming of the English in 1607—at Roanoke, for example. The Spanish also had explored the eastern seaboard in the century prior to the founding of Jamestown, establishing a series of short-lived missions, in Virginia (in 1570) and to the south, in what is now North and South Carolina, Georgia, and Florida (Gleach 1997:2). As a result, it is likely that the socio-political system of the Virginian tribes was in flux because of and in response to a perceived European threat, for fear of an invasion by the likes of the Spaniards. When the English arrived, Powhatan and his chiefs were ready; however, the English behaved very differently from the Spanish (Gleach 1997:3), and a colonial relationship evolved. Powhatan found he could perhaps use the English to his advantage, as they did not appear to present much of a threat. Little did he know.

As with Powhatan and the English, the Illyrians also knew of the Greeks well before colonization commenced. Beginning in the Bronze Age (if not earlier), Illyrian tribes traded with the Greeks. Even so, colonization must have come as a shock to most Illyrians, despite the possibility that it was invited by a particular tribe. Such an event— the founding of a colony—must have caused serious perturbations in Illyrian historical 'trajectories', as defined by Fowles (this volume, Chapter 2). For instance, the appearance of a city, such as Apollonia, in the midst of prime winter grazing land, along the shore of a large river (the Vjosë), must have disrupted regional patterns of transhumance and transportation. Furthermore, the slave trade must have produced ripple effects on the interior. As average Illyrians adjusted to a variety of new threats to their livelihood and well-being, they also witnessed the tribal system as a whole evolving, perhaps in directions they could not predict. The multi-generational processes that structured tribal life and behavior, such as were perhaps generated by oral law codes, were not designed to accommodate massive changes in the social and political order, such as those engendered by colonization. Thus, with the coming of the Greeks, the Illyrians were plunged into a period of intense turmoil, during which long-term trajectories, including world view, would have also been altered. Belief systems would have come into question, causing the mythic and spiritual underpinnings of Illyrian culture to crumble (as appears to have happened among the Powhatan; see Gleach 1997:42, though for the most part he downplays the impact of proselytizing by the English, see especially pp. 65-73). These changes are reflected in the religious syncretism evident in burials at Apollonia.

According to Aristotle, Apollonia functioned as an oligarchy, descendants of colonists ruling over an Illyrian serf population (Wilkes 1992:113). However, there is archaeological evidence that, as time went by, the two different groups—colonized and colonizer—began to merge. For example,

Greeks and Illyrians possessed very different burial customs. At the time of colonization, Greeks practiced individual inhumation, sometimes in *pithoi* (large storage jars), the body being accompanied by various types of grave goods, most often painted pottery. Illyrians, however, placed their dead in tumuli (earthen burial mounds), a practice that began in the Bronze Age. During the Bronze Age, wealthy graves, those of big men, sometimes those of so-called 'warrior' chieftains who were buried with arms and armor, might be placed near the center of the tumulus, with additional graves added to different portions of the tumulus as time went by. Presumably, those buried in the same tumulus were members of the same clan or lineage. Sometime during the Archaic period, however, Apollonians began burying their dead in tumuli in a large necropolis (composed of c. 100 mounds) located to the east of and outside the city's walls. Individuals placed in Illyrian-style tumuli were, however, provided Greek-style burial furnishings. By Hellenistic times, obviously wealthy Apollonians were being interred in tumuli in large marble sarcophagi, replete with fine imported pottery and gold jewelry. Moreover, individual burials were sometimes marked by stelae, carved with an image of the deceased, inscribed with his or her name. Interestingly, names carved on stelae are of both Greek and Illyrian origin (Cabanes 1993).

Given the foregoing, how might we explain the interactions between Illyrians and Greeks at Apollonia, especially in light of the (sometimes contradictory) documentary and archaeological evidence? Can we account for the process of cultural syncretism that appears to have taken place at the colony, as represented by changes in burial customs?

If, indeed, the Illyrians were a tribal people, many of whom were pastoral nomads, moving from the interior to the coast seasonally, then the Greeks at Apollonia probably colonized what appeared to be a very lightly settled landscape. However, Apollonia's hinterland did in fact belong to someone —to a particular tribe—and was used, most likely as winter pasture. If modern Albanian tribes are any guide, Illyrians probably possessed an intimate understanding of the tribal territorial landscape of Illyris, and carefully guarded territories from incursions by members of other tribes. Their response to the Apollonian Greeks may have at first been hostile (unless, of course, they really were invited to found a colony), but as tribal chiefs realized the potential for trade and political alliance with the colonists, their presence would have at

least been tolerated. If indeed armed conflict did occur between colonists and local Illyrians, the Illyrian style of fighting probably clashed with that of the Greeks, as did Algonquian battle styles offend the English (Gleach 1997:4-5). In time, though, certain tribes (or individuals) may have actually moved closer to Apollonia, to take advantage of new opportunities made available by the colony. A similar pattern was followed by the Algonquians with regard to Jamestown. There was at first, of course, some hostility on the part of the Indians, followed by a grudging tolerance of the presence of the English. Eventually, there was competition between tribes for access to the colony, with some tribes actually moving to be nearer to English settlement, such as the 'Richahecrians', who settled at the falls of the James river in 1656, having reportedly originated west of the Blue Ridge (MacCord 1993).

At Apollonia, colonists and natives would have, through time, interacted with one another more easily and intimately. For example, they would have learned each other's language, allowing trade to take place more easily and efficiently. As Aristotle insists, it may in fact be the case that Illyrians did, in some instances, become the serfs, servants, or employees of Greeks. Eventually, Greeks and Illyrians would have inter-married. Similar processes transformed the relationship of Virginia's Indians to the English. I have already mentioned the marriage of John Rolfe to Pocahontas, which may have been largely strategic, but in actuality marriages between English men and native women became a quite common feature of life in Colonial Virginia. For example, the Nansemond record in their tribal documents the marriage, in 1638, of Jon Basse, an Englishman, to a Nansemond woman given the Christian name Elizabeth (Breen 1998:41). For the Algonquians, as was true for modern-day Albanian tribes, a marriage marked an alliance between two families, and the binding together of two different lineage segments (the Albanian *fis*). In a colonial situation, as the numbers of marriages between colonized and colonizer increase, war becomes a less savory, though not always unavoidable, option. Greek and Illyrian marriages likely bound Greek to Illyrian lineages, and processes of cultural syncretism were set in motion. As an alternative to war, both native and non-native individuals may find themselves compromising to avoid conflict and, depending on the situation, gain political, social, and/or economic advantages. For example, Algonquians in Virginia traded land for peace, especially with bi-cultural consanguines. At first, losses of land to English farmers did not impinge upon native settlement and access to resources, but as the stream of colonists turned into a torrent, 'full-blooded' Indians increasingly found themselves to be minorities in their ancestral territories, often disenfranchised and impoverished (cf. Rountree 1989).

These processes of interaction, inter-marriage, and acculturation are reflected, I would argue, in the archaeology of Apollonia's hinterland. The Mallakastra Regional Archaeological Project has demonstrated that settlement of the city's hinterland occurred during the Hellenistic period, but not before (Davis et al. 2002). Whereas MRAP has thus far identified numerous small Hellenistic sites within a day's walk of the city, the majority of which were most probably single-family farmsteads, no Archaic or Classical settlement sites have yet been located. For several hundred years after the colony's foundation, Greeks (and perhaps acculturated Illyrians) lived within the bounds of the city's walls, but with the advent of the Hellenistic period, settlement dispersed. It is not yet clear whether this pattern was mirrored on the interior, in the areas surrounding Illyrian hill forts, but in the vicinity of Apollonia, at least, colonial interactions (such as trade) and processes of acculturation (such as intermarriage) eventually allowed what appears to have been an expansion of Greek settlement. It may be that this expansion was caused by changes in the economic relationship between Illyrians and Greeks. For example, if the Illyrians were providing hides and slaves to the Greeks, then extensive tracts of land were not necessarily needed by the colony, at least at first. However, as the population and function of the colony shifted away from the slave trade and towards agriculture, farm land was needed, requiring an expansion of settlement. A similar pattern is attested in the archaeological and historical records of Virginia: colonization, interaction and acculturation, and, finally, expansion of the colonial power at the expense of the native population. In Virginia, unlike Illyris, settlement expansion occurred very quickly, because land was required for the growing of tobacco. By the 18th century, native peoples and cultures had largely ceased to exist east of the Appalachians. Of the literally hundreds of tribes that once populated the Atlantic seaboard, only a handful remain today. Similarly, Illyrian tribal peoples in southern Albania were subsumed by successive waves of invaders and settlers, first Greeks, then Romans, later Ottomans, but in northern Albania, isolated in the 'accursed' mountains,

the heirs of the Illyrians managed to maintain a tribal ethos. Communism nearly destroyed that ethos, and western capitalism will likely finish the job.

Acknowledgements

I would like to thank Bill Parkinson for encouraging me to contribute to this volume. Wayne Lee provided very constructive comments on an early draft, especially as regards the Powhatan. Of course, mistakes and omissions are entirely my own. Research in Albania has been conducted under the auspices of the Albanian Institute of Archaeology, Tirana, and in Virginia with the assistance of the Blue Ridge Center for Environmental Stewardship.

References Cited

Barbour, P., ed.
1986   *The Complete Works of Captain John Smith (1580-1631) in Three Volumes.* The University of North Carolina Press, Chapel Hill.

Breen, Eleanor
1998   Basse's Choice: An Archaeological and Historical Analysis of Indian-English Interactions during the Contact Period. *Quarterly Bulletin of the Archaeological Society of Virginia* 53(2):34-43.

Cabanes, P., ed.
1993   *L'Illyrie méridionale et l'Epire dans l'Antiquité-II: actes du IIe Colloque internationale de Clermont-Ferrand, 25-27 octobre 1990.* De Boccard, Paris.

Davis, J., Muzafer Korkuti, Lorenc Bejko, M. Galaty, Skender Muçaj, and Sharon Stocker
2001   The Homepage of the Mallakastra Regional Archaeological Project. http://river.blg.uc.edu/mrap/MRAP.html.

Durham, Edith
1909[2000]   *High Albania: A Victorian Traveller's Balkan Odyssey.* Phoenix Press, London.

Durham, Edith
1976[1928]   *Some Tribal Origins, Laws and Customs of the Balkans.* AMS Press, New York.

Elsie, Robert
2001   *A Dictionary of Albanian Religion, Mythology, and Folk Culture.* Hurst and Company, London.

Fausz, J. Frederick
1979 Fighting 'Fire' with Firearms: The Anglo-Powhatan Arms Race in Early Virginia. *American Indian Culture and Research and Journal* 3(4):33-50.

Feinman, Gary, and Jill Neitzel
1984 Too Many Types: An Overview of Sedentary Prestate Societies in the Americas. *Advances in Archaeological Method and Theory* 7:39-102.

Fox, Leonard
1989 *The Code of Lekë Dukagjini*. Gjonlekaj Publishing Company, New York.

Gleach, Frederic
1997 *Powhatan's World and Colonial Virginia: A Conflict of Cultures*. Studies in the Anthropology of North American Indians Series. University of Nebraska Press, Lincoln.

Hammond, N. G. L.
1992 The Relations of Illyrian Albania with the Greeks and Romans. In *Perspectives on Albania*, edited by T. Winnifrith, pp. 29-39. Macmillan, New York.
2000 The Ethne in Epirus and Upper Macedonia. *Annual of the British School at Athens* 95:345-352.

Hranicky, Wm Jack
1996 A Briefe and True Report of the New Found Land of Virginia, Part XVIII—High Feasts, or Possible Ethnographic Description of a Solar Observatory. *Quarterly Bulletin of the Archaeological Society of Virginia* 51(2):86-92.

Hasluck, Margaret
1954 *The Unwritten Law in Albania*. Cambridge University Press, Cambridge.

Kadare, Ismail
1990 *Broken April*. New Amsterdam Books, Lanham, MD.

Lane, Rose Wilder
1923 *Peaks of Shala*. Harper-Collins, London and New York.

MacCord, Howard
1993 Commentary. Richahecrian Identity: One of Virginia's Many Archaeological Challenges. *Quarterly Bulletin of the Archaeological Society of Virginia* 48(4):187-188.

Pettifer, James
1996 *Blue Guide: Albania*. W.W. Norton, New York.

Potter, Stephen
1993 *Commoners, Tribute, and Chiefs: The Development of Algonquian Culture in the Potomac Valley*. The University Press of Virginia, Charlottesville.

Rountree, Helen
1989 *Pocahontas's People: The Powhatan Indians of Virginia Through Four Centuries*. University of Oklahoma Press, Norman, OK.

Rountree, Helen (editor)
1993 *Powhatan: Foreign Relations 1500-1722*. University Press of Virginia, Charlottesville.

Sahlins, Marshall
1961 The Segmentary Lineage: An Organization of Predatory Expansion. *American Anthropologist* 63:332-345.
1968 *Tribesmen*. Prentice Hall, Englewood Cliffs, NJ.

Service, Elman
1962 *Primitive Social Organization*. Random House, New York.

Taylor, Timothy
1994 Thracians, Scythians, and Dacians, 800 BC-AD 300. In *The Oxford Illustrated History of Prehistoric Europe*, edited by Barry Cunliffe, pp. 373-410. Oxford University Press, Oxford.

Ulqini, K.
1991 *The Bayrak in the Old Organization: The End of the 12th Century Up to 1912* (in Albanian). Akademia e Shkencave e RPS e Shqipërisë. Instituti i Kulturës Popullore, Tiranë.

Vickers, Miranda
1995 *The Albanians*. I.B. Tauris, London.

Wells, Peter
1998 Identity and Material Culture in the Later Prehistory of Central Europe. *Journal of Archaeological Research* 6(3):239-298.

Wilkes, John
1992 *The Illyrians*. Blackwell, Oxford.

Young, A.
2000 *Women Who Become Men: Albanian Sworn Virgins*. Berg, New York.

8. Mobility and the Organization of Prehispanic Southwest Communities

Sarah A. Herr and Jeffery J. Clark

The challenge facing the anthropologist is one of reconciling the problem of order with the problem of change (Gosden 1999:167). In this chapter we examine the ways in which individual, household, and supra-household mobility both forms and transforms communities of small scale agriculturalists. The importance of mobility in agricultural societies has not been addressed adequately in many models of social organization, including the 'tribal model'. In evolutionary constructs, agriculturalists are differentiated from foraging groups *because* of their reduced mobility. However, in the farming communities of the prehispanic American Southwest (see Fig. 1), mobility was an essential aspect of social organization and local and long-distance movements of individuals and households were commonplace. Mobility does not have to be a traumatic society-rending axis of change to have an effect on social structure (Bogucki 1996:308). Exploring the relationships between different forms of mobility and social organization among these groups requires an approach that can address both order and change.

In the following sections we define three different types of mobility in small scale agricultural societies and their archaeological signatures. These types include circulation, residential mobility and migration. The relationships between each form of mobility and social organization are illustrated with examples from the American Southwest. We argue that circulation and residential mobility are fundamental aspects of existing economic and social structures while migration can transform these structures. Two types of post-migration contexts also are recognized: 1) those where immigrants move into sparsely occupied frontier regions; and 2) those where immigrants move into existing settlements and coreside with the indigenous inhabitants. Cross-cultural regularities permit general models of migration and subsequent community formation, but historical contingency makes each situation unique, requiring an inductive approach to the data collected in each region.

Small Scale Agricultural Societies

As an evolutionary stage, the tribe has not been a particularly useful category. In the neo-evolutionary ladder the tribe is an ambiguous and ill-defined moniker for the diverse array of social organizations between mobile bands, on the one hand, and more sedentary chiefdoms and states, on the other. The term is further burdened with a heavy load of colonial and post-colonial period baggage with 'primitive' connotations of native societies in Africa and the Americas. In the Southwest, what are perceived to be less controversial and more descriptive terms include 'middle-range society' and 'small-scale agriculturalists'. 'Middle-range society', for example, includes what neoevolutionists term 'tribal' and 'chiefdoms'. 'Small-scale agricultural society' is a more literal term to describe sedentary or semi-sedentary farmers in communities of less than about 2500 people (Lekson 1989). These communities often are organized by kinship with minimal social stratification and limited ranking, and economic institutions are based on reciprocity and informal redistribution. Centralized authority is weakly developed, and may not outlast the lifetime of the leader. Power often derives from consensus rather than coercion.

Instead of offering an alternative to the tribal model this chapter focuses on the relationship between structure and agency to understand how small-scale agricultural societies are constituted. An emphasis on structure alone yields modal and static explanations and studies of agency alone obscure the relationship between individual choices and societal change. By examining the interaction of structure and agency dynamic social processes are elucidated.

The stronger the institutions that guided behavior, the stronger the modal or normative archaeological pattern will be. Variability in archaeological patterns is the result of many individual and corporate decisions to follow or reject societal norms. Mobility, the result of decisions enacted,

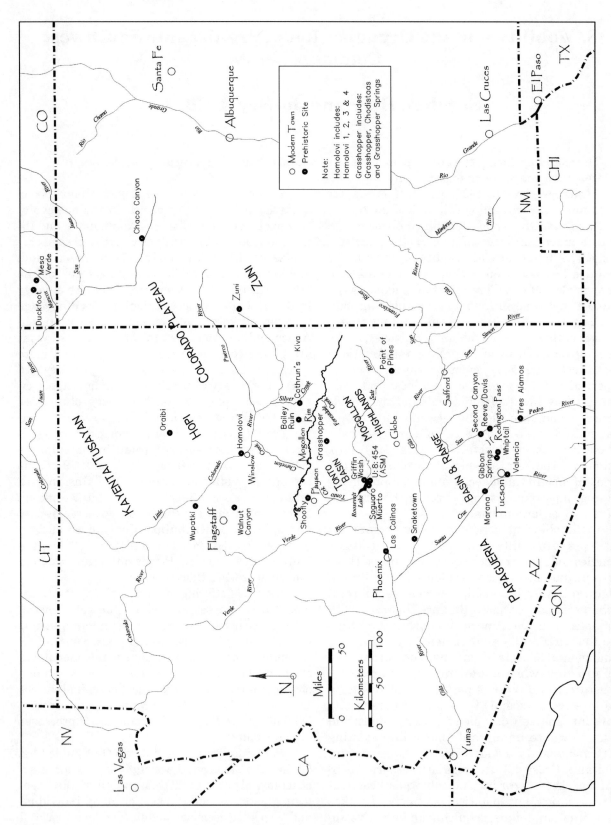

Fig. 1. The American Southwest and prehispanic sites noted in the text.

has the potential to leave material patterns that can be identified and quantified. Mobility factors into considerations of integration and interaction, cooperation, communication, and conflict in small-scale agricultural societies (Braun and Plog 1983; Haas 1993; Habicht-Mauche 1993). Furthermore, attention to the interplay of structure and agency can help us understand the organizational 'cycles' that characterize small-scale societies, as they exercise strategies of expediency or resilience (Adams 1978), power or efficiency (Stuart and Gauthier 1981), causing visible changes in the aggregation or dispersion of settlement.

The pattern of settlement on the landscape is inherently linked to patterns of mobility, one is the by-product of the other. Mobility plays a particularly strong role in organizations, such as many small scale agricultural societies, where private property and community territoriality are not rigidly demarcated. Use of land is more flexible in areas with relatively low population density and weakly developed institutional identification with place.

Definitions of Mobility

Mobility is one of the best avenues for investigating the relationship between structure and agency. Mobility can support the status quo or it can be an agent of change. The scale and frequency of mobility affect the character and stability of social institutions. In its most extreme forms it results in the interactions of societal structures through the face-to-face contact of people from different cultural backgrounds (Sahlins 1981). In such situations new means of integration and communication may develop.

Several different terms have been used to describe the movement of people. Ambiguity in the usage of these terms can create confusion about the processes being described. In particular, 'migration' and 'mobility' often are treated as synonymous processes. Here, we treat migration as one type of movement within a much broader range of mobility.

Mobility was first and best studied as a means of understanding foraging societies (Perlman 1985; Preucel 1990:9; Varien 1999). Societies with agricultural economies generally were assumed to be sedentary. Movements of agriculturalists were explained in terms of environmental changes that precipitated movements to better lands. (Dean 1988b; Orcutt 1991). This certainly was how researchers perceived the prehispanic pueblos of the

northern Southwest. However, since the 1980s we have been unpacking the definitions of terms such as 'sedentary' and 'complexity'. Research in the 1990s focused on "mobility, ethnicity, and culturally constructed landscapes" (Reid 1997:629). Better understanding of the small-scale agricultural societies comes from recognizing that there are different degrees of sedentism and certain types of mobility that facilitate it.

Generally, small-scale agricultural societies are composed of households that supply their own subsistence needs. The interdependence of households within communities varies, but households largely are responsible for their own production and reproduction, and mobility is a critical aspect of their daily life. It "...arises because of the spatial separation of obligations, activities, and resources that exist for all cultures" (Preucel 1990:17). Mobility is ubiquitous in the prehispanic American Southwest, the area from which we draw our examples. In many archaeological reports, the landscape is represented imprecisely by series of static maps of site locations at 100-year resolution. Yet, people walked daily from their homes to their fields, and seasonally to harvest wild plants and hunt animals from other ecozones. In the puebloan Southwest farmers moved their homes at least once a generation, their communities every several generations, and when the conditions warranted, they took the longer journeys we define as migrations (Clark 2001, Herr 2001; Mills 1994).

Forms of mobility are differentiated by the frequency of travel: daily, seasonally, every few years, more than once per generation, or once every few generations. The social consequences of mobility vary with the scale and structure of the group, the distance of travel, the frequency of movement, and the motivation for movement (see Table 1). The latter are often described as a balance between economic and social 'pushes' and 'pulls' in both the home and the destination regions (Anthony 1990).

In the prehispanic Southwest, most of the movements were by choice, rather than by the coercion of a central authority, and an individual or household's choice of destination was based upon information acquired through personal or second hand knowledge of the destination area. Table 2 lists possible motives for moving out of a home community and into a destination community. In addition to the perceived allure of a destination area, the migrant must also consider whether he or she is revoking access to land and social rights in the home community, the cost of the journey, and the possibility of imperfect knowledge about the destination area. Generally, the longer the distance move and the larger the number of migrants, the more likely that the movement will have significant social consequences in the home and destination communities. Long distance movements often followed known trade routes and trails (Herr and Clark 1997).

Circulation

Preucel (1990) borrowed the term 'circulation' from urban geographers and economists to describe a type of tethered mobility. Circulation is the repetitive and cyclic movement of individuals, families, and groups across the landscape from a single, permanent, residential location. Because a return

Table 1. Typical mobility patterns of small scale agriculturalists in the Southwest United States.

	Short-term Circulation	**Seasonal Circulation**	**Residential Mobility**	**Migration**
Description	Daily and overnight mobility away from home base	Seasonal pattern of mobility away and return to home base	Household relocation within community	Household relocation outside community/ settlement system
Frequency	Daily, weekly	Seasonal	1-2 times per generation	Variable, but less common
Distance	A days walk	Defined on an economic landscape, beyond the boundaries of the home resource area. Tens of miles	Defined on social landscape, within community boundaries	Defined on social landscape: beyond the boundaries of the community/ society
Prospects of return	Return expected	Return expected	Return unexpected	Return unexpected
Social scale	Individual/ household	Household	Household, groups of households	Individual, household, multi-household groups
Likely motivations	Primarily economic	Economic	Economic/ social	Economic/social pushes and pulls

Table 2. Example of a migration decision matrix.

	Push (away from home)	**Pull (toward destination)**
Economic	Climatic deterioration Resource depletion/ overexploitation Poor crop yields Increasing population	Good precipitation, warm weather Abundant resources Available land Low population density
Social	Factionalism/ political discord Raiding/ violence Immigration of others into home community Ideological failures	Kin ties Trading partners present Marriage opportunities More political stability Ideological benefits

is expected, movement away from the home community causes no loss of rights or interests. The frequency of this type of movement can vary from daily, periodic, and seasonal, to long term (Preucel 1990:18). Preucel describes daily circulation as that for which no overnight stay is necessary; periodic circulation is a movement of short duration; seasonal circulation is tied to the calendar; and long-term circulation can last over a year. The motivation for circulation is often economic, but social factors can play a role, particularly in the more distant movements. Examples of circulation for economic purposes include: farming, fuel collecting, foraging, hunting, and trade. These kinds of circulation play an essential role in the economic organization of the society. Social reasons for circulation include: marriage, visits to friends and family, ceremonies, festivals, recreation, and pilgrimages (Preucel 1990:19). Long-term circulation is a type of mobility most often associated with market economies and opportunities for wage labor. Daily and periodic circulation are collapsed here into a category called 'short term circulation'. This type of movement and seasonal circulation are the most common types of mobility for the small-scale agriculturalists of the prehispanic Southwest.

The best examples of short-term and seasonal circulation come from the farming schedules of modern Southwest Pueblos. The time spent away from home and the number of trips taken to the field is directly related to the amount of attention given to the field and the distance of the field (Preucel 1990; Young 1996). Two circulation patterns are known from historic Southwest Pueblos. Both have architectural correlates that offer potential for modeling past circulation patterns. Rio Grande area farmers at San Ildefonso, Santa Clara, San Juan, Tesuque, Nambé, Santo Domingo, and Sandia practice a pattern of short-term circulation in which they build insubstantial structures near their fields, such as field houses, ramadas, lean-tos, shades, etc. as temporary shelters, storage facilities, and land claims markers. Such structures are used by farmers who stay in their fields only for the day or overnight on any given trip. Farmers at Acoma, Zuni, Laguna, Santa Ana, Cochiti, and Isleta construct entire farm communities of multiple households near their fields, kilometers away from their primary habitation villages (Preucel 1990:43; Rothschild et al. 1993; Spicer 1962:182). Architecture at farming communities is more substantial than the previous example, because farmers are likely to live in these communities for much of the agricultural season.

In the *ranchitos* at Cochiti, women constructed bins and used metates in their single-room field homes. A late 19th century ethnographer (Poore 1894 as cited in Lange 1990:42) noted that special subterranean roasting ovens for green corn were found exclusively at *ranchitos* and were not found in the main pueblo. By the mid-twentieth century the Cochiti *ranchitos* were seldom used, but "in the old days ... most families left the pueblo either in early spring or just after the July 14th Saint's Day celebration. They remained at their ranches until after harvest time except for occasional trips home for additional supplies or for the celebration of various feast days. ... the village was virtually depopulated in the summer, nearly everyone going to the ranchos where they lived until September and October" (Lange 1990:42).

Artifact assemblages at field houses are notoriously small (Preucel 1990; Sullivan 1994:199), and assemblages at both field houses and farming communities lack the diversity of assemblages from the 'year round' home base sites. Often these short-term and seasonal residences lack evidence of whole classes of activities, particularly burial and ritual activities (Most 1987; Reid 1982:151-199; Schlanger and Orcutt 1986). The home community is the ritual center, and farmers travel back to their villages for important agricultural ceremonies. The smallest field structures may not have been occupied for more than a few days at a time, but were used multiple times over the course of a season and over a number of years.

In the late 14th and early 15th century, groups in the northern Rio Grande valley lived in large villages with hundreds of rooms. In this situation, families do not necessarily live near their fields. Instead, following patterns of short-term circulation, farmers walked between one and six km to their fields. Large aggregated villages and field houses have also been found in the Phoenix Basin between A.D. 750 and 950 (Mitchell 1989), the Mimbres region in the twelfth century (Nelson 1999:140), and the Flagstaff area between approximately A.D. 1065 and 1225 (Sullivan 1994), providing possible evidence for similar patterns of daily movement in these regions. Although difficult to demonstrate archaeologically, the use of field houses in dry farming strategies is consistent with the use of multiple fields by farmers—a behavior similar to that of the modern Hopi (Hack 1942). Short term tending of fields is indicated by limited labor expended to build shelters and the reduced number of activities indicated by artifacts and features. Such a strategy would be risky if it was only applied to a single field. However, apportioning time and effort among multiple fields is a means of minimizing agricultural risk by exploiting a number of microenvironments.

Short-term circulation includes the acquisition of wild, cultivated, and domestic foods. Archaeologists find evidence for exploitation of wild and cultivated resources from a number of ecological zones in both Ancestral Pueblo and Hohokam settlements across the Southwest (Fish and Fish 1994). In the Hohokam area of southern Arizona, rock piles situated above the Marana community, indicated that the residents exploited the resources (particularly agave) of areas above the floodplain and lower alluvial deposits where their settlements were located. The topographic setting of the Marana community makes it possible to exploit a wide variety of resources within a days walk. Northern Puebloan groups also took advantage of diverse environments. Residents of Chacoan outlier communities in the San Juan Basin had most of their fields within 4 km of their homes, but made use of a wide variety of environmental zones in the unoccupied areas between communities (Powers et al. 1983:289). Similar patterns have been observed in the upper Little Colorado region (Kintigh et al. 1996:139). In the northern Rio Grande between A.D. 1150 and A.D. 1450, fields were often located one to two km from habitations, and between A.D. 1450 and A.D. 1550 field distance increased to an average of 2 to 3 km, but fields could also be found more than 6 km away from the village. Throughout this occupation, these farmers exploited a variety of environments, a trend that only seems to have increased through time (Orcutt 1991:327; Preucel 1990:172).

Seasonal patterns of resource procurement have also been recognized in other areas of the Southwest in a number of time periods. For example, based on examination of architecture, lithic technology, and subsistence resources, Young (1996) posits that between A.D. 600 and 900, the residents of pithouse villages in the Homol'ovi area may have left their homes during the late summer and early fall to gather resources from Mogollon Rim or Flagstaff area uplands. Residents of Chodistaas Pueblo (A.D. 1263-1300), on the Grasshopper Plateau in the Mogollon Rim region, may have had their winter residences on the Colorado Plateau (Reid and Whittlesey 1999:38-39).

Residential mobility

The term 'residential mobility' was first applied to settlement relocations by foragers to sites near critical resources. This type of movement was contrasted with logistical mobility, in which small task groups would acquire resources without changing the location of their home base (Binford 1980; Young 1996). Binford (1980) points out that these two strategies are not mutually exclusive; both are used by a single society as circumstances warrant.

This framework can also be applied to small-scale agricultural societies. In the Southwest, residential mobility describes the movement of households within community territories. It can be differentiated from patterns of circulation (such as Binford's logistical mobility) by the lack of intention to return and, often, the forfeiture of rights to land in the home community. The frequency and distance of residential mobility in any given region or time period depends upon whether the primary residential pattern is one of dispersal or aggregation and whether families live near or away from their fields. The definition of residential mobility can also encompass the classic structuralist examples of village formation by 'budding' off from a parent settlement, for whatever reasons. Although 'daughter' settlements are initially dependent upon the parent, through time the full range of sustainable organizations are recreated, more households are attracted, and ultimately the daughter becomes an independent village, no longer dependant upon the parent. The expansion of Hohokam settlement in the Phoenix Basin between A.D. 750 and 950 has been described as a budding process. As main canals in the region were lengthened and lateral canals added, field houses were built to maintain these canals and associated fields on a temporary basis (Mitchell 1989). Permanent habitations were subsequently established as new tracts of land became available.

Varien (1999) identifies stable communities, as defined by centralized public architecture, in the Mesa Verde region between A.D. 950 and 1300, but is able to trace changing patterns of household aggregation and dispersion within these communities across generations. In northeast Arizona, around A.D. 1300 residents of small roomblocks at Homol'ovi III and IV probably moved a short distance to the larger roomblocks at Homol'ovi I and II (Lange 1994:43). Similarly, the late 13th century to early 14th century change from dispersed to aggregated habitation is in part the result of residential mobility as the residents of small roomblocks, such as Chodistaas and Grasshopper Springs, moved to the nearby Grasshopper Pueblo (Reid and Whittlesey 1999).

Varien's (1999) study of residential mobility and persistent communities in the Mesa Verde region not only identifies patterns of mobility on the landscape, but examines the social consequences of these movements. He proposes that individual decisions about household mobility have an effect on the structure of Mesa Verde society between A.D. 950 and 1290. As mobility patterns change, land ownership changes from the *usufruct* strategy of land use to more formally tenured systems, where farmers own land that is not actively used, as well as their current fields. Communities play a role in regulating land use, and changing land ownership has consequences for marriage and inheritance laws.

Migration

The least frequent movements that cover the greatest distance are migrations. Migration "is a long-term residential relocation" by individuals, households, or other social units, "across community boundaries as the result of a perceived decrease in the benefits of remaining residentially stable and/or a perceived increase in the benefits of relocating to the prospective destination" (Clark 1997:44). Points highlighted by this definition include the fact that 1) migration is a movement beyond, not within, social and territorial boundaries; 2) migration is a choice made and enacted by individuals or households—the movement of large social groups and entire communities is rare, 3) the choice to migrate is contingent upon changing perceptions of the economic and social environment in the home and destination communities—these perceptions are often termed 'pushes' and 'pulls' (Anthony 1990). Like residential mobility, part of the definition of migration is that there is no intention of prolonged return. In reality, return migrations are not uncommon (Anthony 1990). Unlike circulation, there is no predictable periodicity to migrations.

In popular perception, migrations are epic and historic in proportion, recalling images of people gathering for the western land-rushes in Oklahoma, Missouri, or Idaho (e.g., Limerick 1987:57). In the prehispanic Puebloan Southwest movement in such large groups was rare and individuals, households or small groups of households moved across the landscape, often in discrete movements. Migration is best studied as a process at a regional scale that includes both the home and destination areas, that can then be related to differences in the economic and social situation of the two areas.

When archaeological perspective is focused on a single site or cluster of sites, the appearance of migrants appears as an abrupt 'event' with the potential to dramatically change the course of local history.

Within the temporal scopes discussed in this volume, migration is both an intra- and multigenerational process. As an intragenerational process, migration is the result of decisions made by individuals and households that have a significant impact on community structure. Local social organizations are transformed as migrants leave old communities. In destination areas, there is often an economic, as well as a social priority accorded to those who come first (Kopytoff 1987; Levy 1992; Schlegel 1992; Stinson 1996; Mills 2000). When immigration is to an area with an existing population, immigrants must cooperate or compete with indigenous groups. When they settle in sparsely populated areas beyond the boundaries of extant political organization or 'frontiers', migrants create new communities (Herr 1999). The migration process can cause structural changes in the social organization of home and destination communities that have ramifications for subsequent generations.

Migration, as an event, appears in the histories of a number of regions across the Southwest. The degree of attention researchers have paid to migration varies from simple detection to more indepth studies about the significance of the migration in community and regional histories. Four methods for detecting migration have been used: trait lists, historical linguistics, and demographic and stylistic analyses. The trait list is the earliest means by which anthropologists identified migrants. This method generates a list artifacts or attributes that are intrusive in one area and connected historically with another in order to identify a migration event, with little regard to the behaviors reflected by these artifacts and attributes (which can include trade, imitation, and emulation) (Haury 1958; Kroeber and Driver 1932; Reed 1950; Wissler 1926). Historical linguistics also has a long history within anthropology. It has been used to track population movements through linguistic connections and discontinuities, both with and without attempts to correlate these patterns with archaeological signatures (Ford et al. 1972; Mera 1935, 1940; Shaul and Hill 1998). Demographic and stylistic approaches are more recent additions to the archaeological detection of migrants.

Demographic analyses are particularly effective in unpopulated or sparsely populated areas where migrations may be identified by significant increases in population size (Doelle 1995; Longacre 1970, 1976; Newcomb 1999; Schlanger 1987, 1988). The calculation of momentary population estimates from contemporaneous habitation room counts for a series of time intervals (e.g., 25, 50, or 100 years) can be used to create regional population curves for which rates of population increase or decrease can be estimated. These rates can then be compared to natural birth rates or mortality rates to assess whether immigration or emigration has occurred (Jackson 1994; Longacre 1976). The effectiveness of this demographic technique relies upon fine chronological control. Interpretation becomes more convincing when contemporaneous source and destination areas can be identified by notably declining populations in the former and rising populations in the latter (Longacre 1976). Population measurements also hinge upon discerning the number of habitation rooms (versus rooms used for manufacture, storage, or ritual), habitation room life span, rebuilding frequency, and the number of people estimated per room (Schlanger 1987).

Using similar classes of data, population distribution across the Southwest can be documented. Examination of changes in population size (Dean et al. 1994) and population density (Duff 1998) through time show the spatial expansion and contraction of settlement, patterns of population aggregation and dispersion, and broad scale changes in geographic preferences, such as the late thirteenth and fourteenth century shift from occupation of the Colorado Plateau to settlement in perennially watered or riverine areas. After migrations or abandonments have been detected at the local scale, general trends identified by macroregional syntheses can be used to reconstruct home and destination regions.

The detection of migration to areas with pre-existing populations hinges upon developments in stylistic theory. Generally, there are two types of styles, to which a number of terms have been applied (Larick 1987; Sackett 1977, 1982, 1985; Wiessner 1983, 1984, 1985; Wobst 1977). One type of style is highly visible, and exhibits 'signaling' behavior (Wobst 1977). This type of style has been called 'active' because it can be manipulated to convey certain social messages and can change rapidly. The other type of style has been called technological style (Childs 1991; Hegmon et al. 2000:219; Lechtman 1977; Lemonnier 1992; Stark et al. 1998). In small-scale agricultural societies, when more than one equally functional choice is possible for the manufacture of an item the method chosen is the one learned through close interaction or through hands-on instruction from family and neighbors. Because the message content of technological styles is low, these styles change slowly and reflect cultural backgrounds rather than conscious choices about identity.

Understanding the significance of style in past societies depends upon understanding the context of the artifact or feature exhibiting the style. Both the trait list approach and the stylistic approach use artifacts and architecture to make arguments about social differences. What distinguishes these methods is that the stylistic approach pays close attention to the social context of production, consumption, and distribution of material culture. Trait list approaches often fail to consider the behaviors that gave rise to the archaeological patterns.

Examples of technological styles that are relevant to the case studies presented below can be found in domestic architecture, ceramic manufacture, and foodways. For example, in the Southwest the two most common techniques for forming vessels are paddle and anvil construction and coil and scrape construction. Generally, the vessels produced are functionally equivalent, although they may look different. So when coil and scrape vessels are constructed of local materials in a region otherwise known to use the paddle and anvil method, it can be assumed that a non-local potter is present in the settlement. Recipes and food processing methods are among the most conservative technologies encountered world wide (Adams 1998; 1999; Baker 1980; Diehl et al. 1998; Ferguson 1992). Similarly, wall construction techniques, hearth construction, and even the organization of domestic space are strongly correlated to cultural learning (Cameron 1998; Clark 2001; Deetz 1977; Wyckoff 1990). The more types of artifacts produced by non-local technological styles in a given context, the stronger the argument for immigrant presence. Because technological styles can often be tied to certain regions, they not only help detect the presence of migrants, they help identify their homelands.

Because of the economic and social disjunctures created by long-distance movements, migrations can give rise to complex social interactions that change the course of local histories. Other types of mobility, such as circulation and residential mobility reinforce the existing economic and social structure of small-scale agricultural societies. In the remainder of this paper we describe both those generalized patterns of settlement and mobility that are an essential part of the daily lives of southwest residents, and some of the best cases for migrations. Both the mundane and more dramatic forms of mobility are essential aspects of small-scale agriculturalists in the Southwest.

Settlement and Mobility in the American Southwest

Patterns of circulation and residential mobility were an inherent part of Southwest society for hundreds of years. The importance of any particular type of mobility changed in relation to the environment and settlement decisions, but mobility was always an important means of implementing the daily economic and social choices of small scale agriculturalists.

The geographic terms used in the following discussion are defined as such: the northern Southwest includes the Colorado Plateau and the Mogollon Rim transition zone. The southern Southwest includes the basin and range environment south and west of the Mogollon Rim and the Papagueria of southwest Arizona. Central Arizona, a part of southern southwest by the above definition, is called out as a separate area. The Mogollon Rim is a geologic uplift that forms the southern boundary of the Colorado Plateau and crosses central and east-central Arizona. It is an area of rugged topography, and geographic transitions between the plateau to the north and the basin and range environment to the south. It is also an area of climatological transitions between the winter dominant rainfall pattern of the northern plateau, and the bimodal winter/summer rainfall pattern of the southern basin and range environment (Dean 1988a, 1996). In the past and present, groups who inhabit pueblos (Puebloans) live in the northern Southwest. In the past, the Hohokam lived in the basin and range environment of the southern Southwest—an area inhabited today by O'odham groups, the possible descendants of the Hohokam.

The relatively high degree of temporal resolution in much of the Southwest allows discussions of social change in periods ranging from one to three generations. Tree-ring dating and ceramic cross-dating allows sites and features to be assigned to intervals of 25 to 50 years in many cases, and sometime to within a few years. Accelerated mass spectrometer (AMS) radiocarbon and archaeomagnetic dating are commonly used to date sites in southern Arizona, providing statistical date ranges between 75 and 200 years. The effects of

any one migration last approximately two to three generations, as demonstrated in the following case studies. The number of individual movements to a particular destination, and their exact dates, remain beyond our resolution.

Mobility played different roles in the lives of Ancestral Pueblo and Hohokam groups we will be discussing. Generally speaking, the Puebloans lived in the low diversity pinyon-juniper biome of the Colorado Plateau, practiced dry farming, flood water farming, occasionally spring farming, and later irrigation, with varying degrees of reliance upon water control features such as check dams, terraces, and grid gardens. Direct ethnographic analogy (Hack 1942; Preucel 1990) to modern Pueblo groups suggests that tending multiple fields may have helped families alleviate the risks of the localized climatic variations that characterize this portion of the Southwest. Patterns of mobility include the daily and short-term circulation to the fields. Field houses, the best architectural indication of such patterns, are documented in the 11th century Black Range region of the Mimbres (Nelson 1999), the 12th century Flagstaff area (Pilles and Wilcox 1978), the 14th through 16th century Rio Grande (Orcutt 1991; Powers and Van Zandt 1999) and Zuni areas (Kintigh 1996). Field house use is part of a seasonal pattern. They are used primarily during the summers. After the harvest, farmers and their families return to the village for the winter. Before the historic period (before the arrival of Coronado in A.D. 1540), pueblos were occupied for relatively short periods of time.

Until approximately A.D. 750, residents of the Colorado Plateau and Mogollon Highlands lived in subterranean pithouses or rockshelters. Storage was in large pits located outside the houses (Young 1996). Pithouses were isolated or clustered, but the organization of these settlements is not well understood. After approximately A.D. 300, some pithouse settlements were organized around large circular integrative structures called great kivas, but other types of communal spaces, such as plazas and courtyards are extremely rare (Dohm 1994). Because of problems identifying pithouse structures based solely on surface manifestations what is known of this period is drawn mainly from excavated sites. Thus the pithouse period is underrepresented in theories of regional patterns of social organization. Based on studies of architecture, storage patterns, and lithic technology at excavated sites it is likely that seasonal circulation played an important role in the economic and social organization of these early agriculturalists (Buck and

Perry 1999; Young 1996).

Between A.D. 750 and 1100 most of the northern Southwest's farmers moved into above ground masonry, or masonry and jacal, structures, arranged into roomblocks. Rooms in these structures were initially used for habitation, storage, or manufacturing. Sometimes these activities warranted specialized rooms, other times all activities took place in a single room. After approximately A.D. 1200, ceremonial rooms were also constructed within roomblocks. With the change to above ground architecture there was increasing differentiation of ritual architecture. Subterranean, house-sized structures called kivas are thought to have been settings for secular or ritual gatherings. The use of circular and rectangular great kivas increased and circular great kivas became more formalized (Herr 1994). Plazas were enclosed by roomblocks in the late thirteenth century, and were probably the focus of community activities, as the use of great kivas decreased (Haury 1985b).

From the ninth through early eleventh centuries, Chaco Canyon, situated in northwest New Mexico, was the largest social and political entity on the landscape. The nature of its organization as a political or ritual center is a subject of debate, as data continues to be gathered from the canyon itself and from outlying areas. Evidence suggests that the majority of households within the Chacoan organization were like most households across the northern Southwest. They were economically autonomous and engaged in production and distribution activities that mainly benefitted themselves. What distinguishes the Chacoan organization from others is the evidence for corporate power at the community and regional levels. At the center of the phenomenon, in Chaco Canyon itself, there is clear evidence that acquisition of exotics had an importance that is absent in much of the rest of the region (Lekson 2000). There is also a high degree formalization of public architecture in the 9th through mid-12th centuries in the San Juan Basin (Judge 1991; Lekson 1991). Chaco and its outliers form the strongest archaeological pattern on the landscape implying close social interaction created through widespread membership in or emulation of Chacoan society. The early to mid-eleventh century is described as the period of greatest expansion (Dean et al. 1994) with new Chacoan settlements extending into the southern San Juan Basin and into the Puerco Valley (Hartesveldt et al. 1998:41) through a combination of short and long-distance movements within the Chacoan region and migration beyond.

Across the northern Southwest populations periodically aggregated and dispersed, moving homes and villages relatively frequently. The Chacoan expansion just described, is part of a pattern of settlement dispersion. Dispersed communities were composed of habitation sites, thought to be situated close to arable lands and clustered around communal facilities at larger 'central' sites (Herr 2001; Varien 1999). This type of settlement patterning is conducive to daily circulation patterns to more distant fields and periodic circulation to public facilities for socializing and ceremonies. The deterioration of fields or structures provided incentives for residential mobility. The community often had a durability that the frequently moving households did not, making this one of the stronger institutions on the puebloan social landscape. Residential mobility was a common practice of the Puebloans. In the Mesa Verde region, pit structures lasted no more than ten years without remodeling (Schlanger and Wilshusen 1993). Based on artifact accumulation rates, Varien (1999:195-6) estimates that earthen structures such as pithouses were used between 16 and 26 year in the years between A.D. 900 and 1100 and that between A.D. 1100 and 1300, masonry and earth surface structures were used, on average, for 44 years, although occupation of these structures ranges between 19 and 80 years (also Lightfoot 1993, 1994). Larger aggregated pueblos were occupied longer, but rooms within the pueblos were often remodeled, and studies of formation processes indicate that few were inhabited for the entire duration of occupation. Households within the pueblo moved elsewhere, and abandoned rooms might be remodeled, change functions, or be dismantled or used as a trash dump. Short-term seasonal mobility and residential mobility were common among the Puebloan groups.

By contrast to the mobility that characterizes the puebloan groups of the northern Southwest, the term 'deep sedentism' has been used to describe the Hohokam (Lekson 1990) of the Phoenix, Tucson, and Tonto basins, and the middle Gila river valley, in south and central Arizona. These agriculturalists were tethered to their lands by extensive irrigation systems and the limited availability of arable land apart from river floodplains. Daily and periodic circulation were part of the regular economic structure. Seasonal circulation was certainly practiced, but probably played a lesser part than in the northern Southwest, and residential mobility was not as important to the Hohokam as to their Puebloan neighbors. The Hohokam had a greater residential stability than other parts of the Southwest and settlements were often occupied centuries longer than similarly populated settlements in the northern Southwest. When houses and public facilities fell into disuse, only minor settlement shifts occurred (Dean et al. 1994:70). At many sites new pithouses are built in or near the abandoned pits of previous houses. At the Valencia site in Tucson, Arizona the location of plazas and houses shifts only several hundred meters south over the course of nearly six centuries (Doelle 1985; Henry Wallace, personal communication). However, the Hohokam expansion into new regions, such as the Tonto Basin in the eighth century A.D., probably occurred through migrations (Gregory 1995; Stark et al. 1995). This movement was characterized by early researchers as 'colonization', accounting for the designation of the "Hohokam Colonial period" (Haury 1932). Migration was certainly a type of mobility periodically used by even these more sedentary farmers.

Southern and central Arizona were occupied by farmers who constructed their villages alongside canal systems and around public architecture, first ballcourts and later platform mounds. The social organization of the Hohokam is apparent in the distinctive layout of their settlements. Before approximately A.D. 1100, the Hohokam lived in subterranean or semi-subterranean pithouses arranged in 'courtyard groups' oriented to face common extramural spaces (Wilcox et al. 1981). It is often assumed that the groups sharing these spaces were socially and genetically related. Courtyard groups also shared cemeteries and trash disposal areas. Courtyard groups formed segments of larger settlement, which were often organized around public architecture and plazas. Roasting pits, borrow pits, and cemeteries were often on village margins (Doelle et al. 1987; Gregory 1991; Sires 1987). After A.D. 1100 the organization of domestic space around courtyards continues, but adobe or post-reinforced adobe walls were constructed to enclose these spaces and associated surface rooms within compounds (Sires 1987; Clark 1995).

As in the northern Southwest, changes in public architecture coincided with changes in domestic architecture. Between A.D. 700 and 1200 Hohokam villages were organized around ballcourts and plazas (Fish 1989:37; Wilcox 1991), although the construction and use of ballcourts declined after about A.D. 1050. Ballcourts were built at both large and small sites, but not at all villages. Between A.D. 1150 and 1350 platform mounds served as community centers (Elson 1998). Often,

although not always, communities were regularly spaced along canal systems (Doelle et al. 1987; Gregory and Nials 1985).

Duration of occupation in Hohokam settlements is often counted in the hundreds of years (Dean et al. 1994), rather than the tens of years of the Puebloan occupations (Mills 1994). Wild plants collected from the lush Sonoran Desert habitats supplemented the food of the irrigation farmers and were even more critical for those in non-riverine environments. Settlements outside the Phoenix and Tucson irrigation systems probably relied more frequently upon mobility to meet their subsistence needs (e.g., Gasser 1979). Short-term circulation and seasonal rounds were the most common types of Hohokam mobility patterns. Residential mobility was far less common than it was among Puebloan groups.

Migration was not commonplace in either area, but was also not a rare occurrence. In the following examples it is associated with dramatic social upheavals in two periods of Southwest prehistory: the restructuring of Puebloan communities in the mid to late eleventh century, coincident with the emigrations of some groups from the Chacoan region; and the 'Great Drought' (A.D. 1276-1299) and residential abandonment of the Four Corners regions. Incidences in less uncertain periods are also known (Wilshusen and Ortman 1999).

The examples we provide are not unique. Numerous examples of migrations dating to the mid-eleventh and to the late thirteenth century can be demonstrated. As noted above, the mid-eleventh century was a period of population expansion in the northern Southwest, as people moved into regions previously only sparsely settled (Dean et al. 1994). Just over two hundred years later, the settlement patterns of the northern Southwest were transformed during and after the Great Drought. Twenty-three years of dry weather and warm temperatures (Salzer 2000) adversely affected the productivity and thus the value of land and crops in dry-farming communities, disrupting the economic and social structure. Although the demographic collapse of the Four Corners region occurred rapidly on an archaeological time scale, available evidence suggests multiple migrations to a variety of destinations and planned abandonment (Lyons 2001). Migrations during the Great Drought include journeys from Mesa Verde to the Rio Grande, and from Kayenta and Tusayan region of Northern Arizona to the Mogollon Rim, Point of Pines, Verde River Valley, Safford Basin, and San Pedro River Valley in the south and central mountains of

Arizona. The Grasshopper region, below the Mogollon Rim was also substantially settled at this time. Sites such as Chodistaas, Grasshopper Springs, and Grasshopper Pueblo were likely inhabited by migrants from both the Colorado Plateau and the Mogollon Highlands regions, and possibly also by Hohokam households from the South (Reid and Whittlesey 1999:31). The process of serial displacement—by which immigrants entering a community cause further migrations—is also responsible for some of the movements at this time, as groups in intervening regions along migrations routes were driven further south.

Migration and Community Organization

As the most dramatic form of mobility, migration also has the greatest potential to change community organization and the basic structure of society. Just as migration is often understood as a series of individual choices, so too is the process of community formation or reconstitution afterwards. It is in the interval immediately after migration when the relationship between agency and structure is most apparent. To illustrate the migration process and its effects on social organization we draw examples from the period between A.D. 1000 and 1400 in the Mogollon Rim region of east-central Arizona, the Tonto Basin of central Arizona, and the San Pedro River Valley in southeast Arizona. In the following examples, we provide evidence for the identification of the migration, and describe the effects of immigration on destination communities in frontiers and coresidence contexts.

Frontier communities

Frontier communities result from migration into sparsely populated areas. Frontier communities share characteristics with the migrants' homeland, but they are not cookie-cutter replications. Early frontiers are characterized as land-rich and labor-poor, a situation that is not commonly considered by anthropologists, who use models more relevant to modern contexts where labor is readily available and land is contested. Frontiers are short term social formations that last only a few generations. They may then be depopulated or increasingly populated to the point where they cease to be frontiers. When populations increase later in the history of the frontier, households may either be accepted into the larger social and political enti-

ties to which they used to be marginal, or they may form their own political entities.

The following example is derived from recent research in the Silver Creek drainage by the Silver Creek Archaeological Research Project (Mills et al. 1999). The project excavated six sites dating between A.D. 1025 and 1330 and compiled settlement information from the eleven percent of the drainage that has been surveyed.

From approximately 6000 B.C.E. on, the Mogollon Rim region was exploited sporadically for its wild plant and animal resources. The earliest evidence of seasonal or year round habitation structures in the region are sites dating to approximately A.D. 300 (Haury and Sayles 1985; Newcomb 1999). Many models of mobility consider the Mogollon Rim region a zone for seasonal resource exploitation (Redman 1993:158), often based on analogies with the historic Apache use of the area (Rice and Henderson 1990; Welch 1996; Young 1996). Lacking evidence for extensive habitation, the area is described as a 'population trough' between areas of higher population density (Dean et al. 1994). However between approximately A.D. 1000 and 1050, after centuries of seasonal exploitation and minimal occupation, population increased dramatically, at a rate of between 1.8 and 2 percent per year in the Silver Creek drainage (Newcomb 1999). This rate is four times the estimated natural birth rate of small-scale agriculturalists (Hassan 1981). The evidence for migration into the region is convincing, and is complemented by the fact that around A.D. 1050 the population of the northern Southwest reached its greatest spatial extent as groups moved out of the San Juan Basin (Dean et al. 1994). Although many of the migrants came from this area and other portions of the Colorado Plateau, it is also likely that population movements were occurring in regions less visible to the archaeological eye, and that households from other areas were moving into the Mogollon Rim region. In particular, designs on pottery produced in the Forestdale Valley are reminiscent of Mimbres designs. The indigenous population also played a role in these communities, but so little excavation has occurred at sites dating prior to A.D. 1000, that we know little about the pre-migration inhabitants. Those migrants who moved into this region between A.D. 1000 and 1150 lived on the edge of the Pueblo world (Herr 2001).

After A.D. 1000 site frequency and diversity in the Mogollon Rim region increased dramatically. Limited activity, field house, and habitation sites were built on a variety of land forms in the areas beyond community boundaries. Houses were constructed and abandoned with only limited remodeling. Residential mobility in the region was high and land use was extensive. Little effort was invested in the construction of water and soil control features. Instead, when land was expended, farmer moved to new, and readily available, plots. Craft production was at the household level, and households engaged in independent trade relations. Nonetheless, trade relations spanned relatively large geographic scales. At Cothrun's Kiva site, non-local ceramics were varied and indicate ties to households across Arizona. However ties to nearby households were relatively weak. There was some sense of community, as evidenced by the construction of circular great kivas, but other indicators of social integration were apparently absent. In contrast to the Chacoan area, no household kivas (the structures that are thought to house clans, lineages, or sodality organizations) have been found at sites in the Mogollon region at this time.

The Mogollon Rim immigrants constructed circular great kivas and settled around these community centers (Fig. 2). Circular great kivas had a great deal of meaning on the 11th century ritual landscape (Fowler et al. 1987). Although these ceremonial structures were constructed throughout the puebloan Southwest after A.D. 300, by approximately A.D. 900 they were almost exclusively associated with Chacoan organization, the dominant sociopolitical organization in the region. In the 11th century and thereafter the use of these structures indicates either direct social ties to the Chacoan sphere or the desire for such ties (Kintigh et al. 1996).

Although production was largely a household affair in this region, social reproduction was a concern of the community. Considering the limited size of the population, between 774 and 1670 (Newcomb 1997) people in the 883 sq km of the Silver Creek drainage, a great deal of floor space was devoted to community level integrative architecture. Large semi-subterranean great kivas were constructed by some of the earliest migrants (e.g., Cothrun's Kiva) in the region and were intended to attract outside households into their community. In so doing 'firstcomers' gained social prestige. In frontier regions such as this, where land is plentiful, and people few, 'wealth-in-people' is more important than material wealth—a situation that has important repercussions for understanding leadership in frontier situations (Mills 2000). Labor was valued more highly than land, and those pioneers with multiple skills and creativity fared best.

By attracting more people to serve as labor and as mates, communities ensured continuity into successive generations. The liminal placement on the political landscape and shift in values on frontiers shaped aspects of social organization, as transient households attempted to form sustainable communities.

The dispersed pattern of great kiva-centered communities of the Mogollon Rim region changed in the mid- to late 12th century, when residents of the region constructed more aggregated roomblocks of 40 to 75 rooms. Reasons for changing habitation and land use patterns are unclear as work on the subsequent period is only just beginning. By the beginning of the 14th century economic patterns and division of labor had changed as pueblo communities across the Southwest reorganized. Hunting was practiced in larger groups, craft production was increasingly specialized, trade was almost exclusively with partners to the northeast. Rituals and community life centered around roomblock kivas and plazas. Further migrations to, and through, the Mogollon Rim region to areas further south and west marked the end of the frontier era.

Coresidential communities

Some of the first coresidential situations were identified using the trait list approach. In the Forestdale Valley of east-central Arizona, Haury (1985a) differentiated the pithouses of people from the Colorado Plateau from those of the Mogollon Highlands at the 7th to 9th century site of Bear Ruin. The diversity of architecture in the sub-Mogollon Rim region has led to suppositions of coresidence at Shoofly Ruin in the 13th century (Redman 1993). Distinctive wall construction style and decorated ceramics were used to identify people from Mesa Verde, who resided in Chaco Canyon and the San Juan Basin between A.D. 1240 and 1300 (Judge 1991:26). At Snaketown and Las Colinas in southern Arizona, the spatial distribution of plain ware ceramics was used to identify Yuman barrios (Beckwith 1988). At a larger scale, inventory surveys of two different National Monuments in the Flagstaff Area, Walnut Canyon and Wupatki, demonstrate very different distributions of utilitarian ceramics. While settlement in Walnut Canyon area appears typical of the Flagstaff area, the Wupatki area may have been settled by Kayenta Anasazi populations sometime around A.D. 1130. A concurrent Kayenta depopulation of the homeland area adds support to the argument (Sullivan 1994:193). The following three examples examine the relations between immigrant groups who move into existing communities and the indigenous inhabitants of those communities. Both cooperation and conflict are expected in such situations. Neither is simple to measure, as immigrants and indigenous residents interact in economic, social, and ritual activities, as well as in private and public contexts. At a most basic level, groups must coordinate sub-sistence and other production activities within their shared environment, in order to ensure their own survival (Fish and Fish 1993:101). The groups must also negotiate their social and ritual roles within the coresidential community. The expressions of identity differ in private (domestic) and public contexts. For example, the identity assumed within the home may be different from that assumed

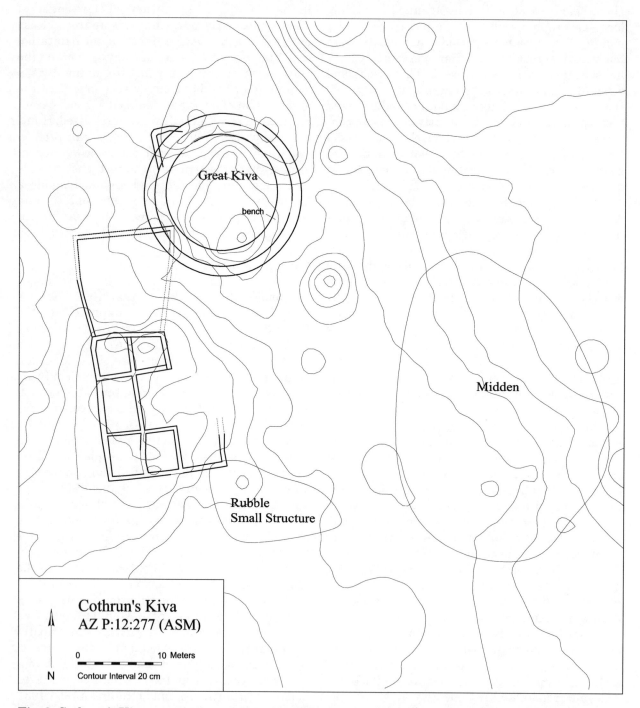

Fig. 2. Cothrun's Kiva, a typical great kiva site of the Mogollon Rim region in the eleventh century A.D.

publically. Certain kinds of artifacts and architecture may be associated with private or public expressions of affiliation.

Coresidential situations are good places to example the relationship between migration, production, and organizational structures within societies, and the potential for both cooperation and conflict between immigrant and indigenous groups. Hopi history describes the relationship between the arrival of immigrants at the modern Hopi villages and social organization. Levy (1992:33) summarizes the history of the settlement of the village of Orayvi (also known as Oraibi), "The earliest arrivals received some of the best lands and also 'owned' the most important ceremonies. The last arrivals received no land at all nor were their contributions to the ceremonial cycle very great." Some of those with the least access to food worked as 'slaves' and survived by working the land of others (Brandt 1954:23-24; Levy 1992:32). Perhaps the best known evidence for conflict between local and immigrant groups in the prehispanic Southwest is at Point of Pines in the rugged mountains of east-central Arizona. The earliest migrants to the community resided in pithouses on the edge of the settlement, before moving into more permanent rooms. However, a violent outcome of immigrants and locals interactions is posited. The later rooms of the immigrants were burned catastrophically and their occupants were forced out of the community, possibly settling in regions farther south (Haury 1958; Lindsay 1987). Social tension between immigrants and local residents are expected, but overt conflict has not been identified in the archaeological examples that follow.

Puebloan coresidence on the
Grasshopper Plateau

After more than 30 years of investigation by the University of Arizona Grasshopper Project, Grasshopper Pueblo provides a good case for migration (Reid 1997). The evidence for migration derives its strength from correlations between specialized studies of architecture, human remains, demography, and a number of material classes. A demographic simulation, based in part on the analysis of nearly 575 burials from the site, revealed that the period between A.D. 1300 and 1330 was one of population growth beyond what could be expected from natural birth rates alone (Longacre 1976). The pueblo drew some of its population from residential mobility, as evidenced by the contemporaneous abandonment of nearby roomblocks.

Differences in room size and shape, and domestic features suggest that some village residents migrated to the area from puebloan homelands on the Colorado Plateau and other parts of the Mogollon Highlands (Riggs 1999). These indications of migration are supported by observed differences in: head shape caused by different cradleboard constructions, grave construction (Reid and Whittlesey 1999), bone and tooth chemistry (Ezzo 1993), ceramic vessel manufacture (Triadan 1997; Zedeño 1994), and ceramic design execution (Van Keuren 1999). Migration into the Grasshopper pueblo is attributed to two processes: women entering the pueblo as brides and the migration of entire households (Longacre 1976; Reid and Whittlesey 1999).

Examination of burial data shows strong patterns in the distribution of funerary offerings in the grave. Four all-male sodalities have been identified, each of which is defined by the presence of a particular artifact type: bone hairpins, *Glycymeris* shell pendants, *Conus* shell tinklers, or arrows. Men from the Colorado Plateau were allowed to participate in both the bone hairpin and shell pendant societies, but were excluded from other groups. Men from the Mogollon Rim region, on the other hand, could participate in all four societies (Reid and Whittlesey 1999; Whittlesey 1978). Such patterns suggest that migrant men were included in some ceremonial activities, but were excluded from others. The relationship between locals and migrants does not appear to have been one of overt conflict; there is little evidence for violence. However, it appears that migrants maintained an identity distinct from that of the indigenous inhabitants and did not completely assimilate into the Grasshopper society. They may have occupied a place of less status than the indigenous residents, based on their restricted access to presumably prominent social roles in the community.

Puebloan migrations into the Tonto
Basin, Central Arizona

Another well documented archaeological example of migration and subsequent integration of migrants is found in 13th and early 14th century communities in the eastern Tonto Basin of central Arizona. The Tonto Basin is centered on the junction of Tonto Creek and the Salt River. Today, the largest landmark in the region is the artificially constructed Roosevelt Lake. Raising the level of the lake, and improvements to the highways of central Arizona, have led to a great deal of research in the Tonto Basin in the past fifteen years, particularly in the eastern portion of the basin along the Salt River (Ciolek-Torello and Welch 1994; Elson et al. 1994; Elson, Gregory, and Stark 1995; Jacobs 1994; Lindauer 1995, 1996, 1997; Rice 1998).

The Tonto Basin was on the northeast periphery of the Hohokam core area in the Phoenix period. The floodplain is wide along the southern half of the basin and was inhabited throughout much of the prehistory of the Southwest. Tonto Basin Hohokam settlements were similar to occupations elsewhere in the southern Southwest at this time. People lived in rooms constructed of post-and-cobble-reinforced adobe and masonry, arranged around courtyards and enclosed by compound walls. The compounds formed villages, and villages formed communities, organized around platform mounds along Tonto Creek and the Salt River (Elson, Gregory, and Stark 1995). Fields were probably irrigated by networks of canals.

Migration is not a new topic among archaeologists working in the Tonto Basin. A number of early Southwest researchers invoked migration and the arrival of a new cultural groups as an explanation for discontinuities in architecture and artifact assemblages (Gladwin and Gladwin 1935, Haury 1945). Trait-based approaches to migration described intrusive patterns of decorated pottery types, utilitarian ceramic wares, multi-storied masonry architecture, wall construction, manos, metates, axes, projectile points, arrow shaft-straighteners, burial practices, cranial deformation, domesticated animals, and ornaments (turquoise, shell, and bone jewelry), among others (Gladwin and Gladwin 1935:27; Haury 1945:207). These early arguments for migration did not convince all, leading to debates about the cultural development in the Tonto Basin (Doyel 1976; Steen 1962; Wood and McAllister 1982).

Recent work in the area has presented the most convincing evidence for both identifying migrant households and understanding their place in transforming local social structure (Clark 2001; Stark et al. 1995). What distinguishes these more recent arguments from the earlier work, is a greater number of well-dated excavated sites, an increased sophistication in modeling archaeological migration, more attention to the temporal and spatial patterns of architecture and artifacts, and consideration of the consequences of population movement on social organization after the migration. The example described below comes from the intensively studied eastern Tonto Basin along the

Salt River, immediately east of Roosevelt Lake.

Evidence for migration into the eastern Tonto Basin comes from demographic, architectural and artifactual data. Conservative estimates place the migrations within a 75-year period between A.D. 1250 to 1325; more conjectural estimates restrict the dates to 30 years between A.D. 1270 and 1300 (Elson 1996; McCartney et al. 1994).

Like the Hohokam elsewhere in southern Arizona, Tonto Basin potters formed brown utilitarian vessels with the paddle-and-anvil technique. However, in the 12th and 13th centuries, the usual cooking and storage vessel repertoire was augmented by coil-and-scrape, corrugated ceramics manufactured with local materials. The brown corrugated vessels were for local utilitarian use and were not widely distributed. However, they were made using a non-local technological style. Corrugation is also found on locally produced red-slipped bowls in the 13th century. The red-slipped bowls were manufactured in the same non-local technological style, but they were probably produced to be traded. They are found in higher proportions in ceramic assemblages across much of the basin. Because they were widely exchanged, their distribution can not be used as a marker of migrant households. Provenance studies used to link ceramic sand tempers to the drainages from which the sands were collected by potters, are used to differentiate locally and non-locally produced vessels (Miksa and Heidke 1995, 2001). These studies conclude that corrugated brown ware ceramics were made with local materials across the eastern Tonto Basin, but that red-slipped corrugated ceramics were made within only the limited portion of the eastern Tonto Basin that includes Griffin Wash, a site suspected to be occupied by migrants, as described below (Clark 2001).

Habitation structures at three sites in the eastern Tonto Basin were constructed with non-local technologies. Tonto Basin inhabitants at this time lived in compound structures, similar to Hohokam compounds described above, and the earliest compounds were constructed primarily of post-reinforced adobe with cobble footers. However, at Saguaro Muerto, Griffin Wash (Fig. 3), and AZ U:8:454 (ASM), walls were constructed largely of coursed masonry. Rooms at these sites were not arranged in dispersed compounds, as at neighboring sites. Instead, they formed roomblocks. The occupants of Saguaro Muerto and U:8:454 (ASM) used local materials to roof their rooms, such as mesquite, juniper, palo verde, cottonwood, and creosote. The residents of Griffin Wash imported

Fig. 3. Griffin Wash, Locus A, a puebloan enclave in the Tonto Basin.

beams from at least 25 km away to construct their roofs. Ponderosa pine, Douglas fir, and white fir—common roofing materials among the pueblos—were used for roofs of many of the Griffin Wash rooms (Elson et al. 1995; Stark et al. 1995).

The intrusive technological styles provide a good indication of the possible homeland of the migrants to the Tonto Basin, as corrugated ceramics, coursed masonry architecture, and roomblock organization, are technologies characteristic of the Puebloan areas of the Colorado Plateau and along the Mogollon Rim. A changing pattern of trade relations supports this conclusion. Before approximately A.D. 1100 decorated ceramics used by Tonto Basin residents were produced in the Phoenix Basin or Middle Gila River Valley to the south and west. Thereafter, residents participated in exchange relations with potters from the Colorado Plateau or Mogollon Highlands to the north and east. The line of communication opened by this trade may have facilitated the subsequent development of migration routes in the 13th century.

Finally, the detection of migration is augmented by demographic evidence of a 25 percent increase above the projected natural birth rate in Tonto Basin population between A.D. 1200 and 1325 (Doelle 1995; Stark et al. 1995). The northeast portion of Arizona was abandoned in the latter half of this same time period. These migrants likely moved into and through the Mogollon Rim region and Mogollon Highlands where they displaced and mingled with local populations. Hence the migrants entering the Tonto Basin were likely to be a mixed group from both the Colorado Plateau and the mountainous highlands. This is supported by an analysis of genetic-based dental traits from 13th century burial populations recovered from the eastern Tonto Basin (Turner 1998).

The Puebloan migration into the eastern Tonto Basin did not result in a replacement of the indigenous population. The spatial distribution of coursed masonry architecture, roomblocks, and brown corrugated ceramics indicate that Puebloans settled on the margins of the eastern basin community. Botanical evidences shows that they had access to local agricultural products, such as corn and cotton, but that wild or cultivated foods (such as agave) formed an important part of their diet as well. Whether or not they were immediately allowed access to the fields on the floodplains is unknown. One explanation for the wide distribution of the red-slipped corrugated ceramics is that they were produced by migrants who did not have sufficient access to fields and exchanged these

vessels for agricultural products (Stark et al. 1995). Similar instances of craft production in exchange for agricultural products have been documented archaeologically and ethnographically.

Tonto Basin communities reorganized in the early 14th century and the cultural differentiation among subsequent population is no longer so apparent. A significant portion of the thirteenth century settlements were abandoned by A.D. 1325 and in the eastern Tonto Basin the only settlement of any appreciable size was a large aggregated village at Schoolhouse Point. It may have been inhabited by indigenous groups (Lindauer 1996), Puebloan immigrants (Ciolek-Torello 1997) (whose numbers may have been reinforced by additional migrations), or some combination of the two (Rice et al. 1998).

Puebloan migrations into Southeast Arizona

Regional scale populations movements in the northern Southwest are often attributed to the Great Drought of the late 13th century. During this period groups from the Colorado Plateau moved into areas that had previously been used for a limited range of activities. These population movements had ramifications for communities in central and southern Arizona, where the climatic change had less of an impact. Settlement in the northern Southwest was transformed in this period. Through initial migrations and serial displacements, people from the northern Southwest moved south toward perennial sources of water such as rivers and springs, causing social changes in settlements along the migration routes, if smaller in effect.

Research in the San Pedro River Valley by the Center for Desert Archaeology is ongoing (Clark et al. n.d.). To date, much of the work has focused on the identification of migration in this and other related areas of Southern Arizona, but tentative conclusions about the consequences of Pueblo migrations into southern Arizona communities can be drawn.

The San Pedro River Valley extends from headwaters near the Mexican border until it joins the Gila River just north of modern Winkleman, Arizona. A multi-year survey of 75 miles of the northern San Pedro River Valley identified 442 sites and relocated 46 others.

Settlement information shows that Hohokam settlements, dating between A.D. 700 and 1400, were situated along the northern portion of the river. Household groups formed communities around ballcourts between approximately A.D. 700 and 1100 (the pre-Classic period), and constructed houses and compounds around and on platform mounds between A.D. 1100 and 1400 (the Classic period). Between A.D. 1000 and 1100 (the late pre-Classic) the use of ballcourts declines and the settlement pattern becomes more dispersed, although late pre-Classic occupations may be partially masked by overlying Classic Period constructions. The timing of the abandonment of ballcourts and the construction of platform mound accords well with patterns in other portions of the Hohokam region. Changes in domestic architecture, from pithouses in the pre-Classic period to cobble and post or rock-reinforced adobe constructions arranged in compounds in the Classic Period, also parallel patterns known across southern Arizona.

The intrusion of Puebloan households can be viewed in relation to the changing San Pedro social landscape. In the pre-Classic period two types of plain ware ceramics dominated ceramic assemblages: San Simon Brown Ware was most common in the south and Aravaipa Buff Ware and Aravaipa Brown Ware were most common in the northern portion of the San Pedro River Valley. The boundary between the two areas is at an important geographic transition point midway up the valley and about 15 km west of Redington Pass, a likely route from the San Pedro Valley into the Tucson Basin. An extremely large ballcourt at the site of Redington, near this transition zone, may have been a locus for rituals that symbolically integrated the two areas. In the Classic period, platform mound communities in the San Pedro are found *only* north of this inferred social boundary.

Overlain upon this background of Hohokam settlement, are instances of ceramic and architectural technologies that are common in northern Arizona, but not in southern Arizona. As in the Tonto Basin, the critical indicators of the transplanted households are those conservative domestic technologies that are not subject to social manipulation—in this case ceramic production and architectural construction (including wall construction and domestic installations). Technologies used by local residents of the San Pedro River Valley include the construction of ceramic vessels using the paddle and anvil technique, the arrangement of rooms in courtyards or compounds, and the use of cobbles and coursed adobe to construct walls in surface structures. Intrusive technologies include coil-and-scrape forming techniques, corrugated

surfaces on cooking and storage vessels, roomblocks, and shaped coursed and shaped masonry. In a couple instances, immigrants built ritual structures in their new communities that were unlike those used by Hohokam groups.

Two discrete migrations have been identified in the San Pedro River Valley. In the early thirteenth century, migrants from the Mogollon Highlands settled on the margins of local populations in the area immediately south of the platform mounds communities—an area that was also a pre-Classic social boundary zone. As seen at Point of Pines and sites in the Tonto Basin, when migrants settle in an existing community it is often on the margins. At Second Canyon Ruin, corrugated ceramic distributions suggest that the first immigrants settled on the south edge of a pithouse hamlet occupied by local groups. The continued presence of immigrants in this part of the site in the subsequent compound is signaled by concentrations of corrugated ceramics and slab mealing bins—a type of domestic installation common among contemporaneous Pueblo groups to the north. Other sites in the San Pedro River Valley with potential immigrant enclaves include Tres Alamos and HC-35. Tres Alamos has extremely high proportions of corrugated ceramics produced from local materials. Rooms at HC-35, in the bajada zone above the river valley, are found in a contiguous arrangement that is more characteristic of Puebloan spatial organization.

That these groups ultimately entered the northeast Tucson Basin is evident from excavations at Gibbon Springs and Whiptail Ruin. These two communities may have been the destination of several Puebloan households. On the margins of the Gibbon Springs site a dense area of locally produced corrugated ceramics called the 'Northeastern village' is located outside the compound wall that defines the central portion of the Gibbon Springs settlement. Analysis of Whiptail Ruin is ongoing, but the site has the contiguous architecture characteristic of Puebloan groups and the high proportions of corrugated pottery was probably locally produced (Clark et al. n.d.; Slaughter 1996a, 1996b; Slaughter and Roberts 1996).

A second migration into southeast Arizona occurred in the late thirteenth to early fourteenth century. Migrants from the Kayenta and Tusayan areas of northeast Arizona settled in the Mogollon Rim region, Point of Pines region, the Safford Basin, and the San Pedro River Valley (Clark et al. n.d., Woodson 1998). The two San Pedro sites associated with the Kayenta/Tusayan migrants are

Reeve Ruin (DiPeso 1958) and Davis Ranch Ruin (Gerald 1975). Reeve Ruin (Fig. 4) was constructed in a previously unoccupied, highly defensive location on an inaccessible ridge overlooking the river. Davis Ruin is also situated above the San Pedro, in a site that was previously occupied, as indicated by the presence of pithouses below the late thirteenth and fourteenth century settlement. These sites are on opposite sides of the river just south of the Redington Pass boundary zone that attracted set-

tlers from the Mogollon Highlands a half century or so earlier.

In both settlements, the construction of contiguous-room structures provides evidence of Puebloan immigrants. The fact that the walls of Reeve Ruin were constructed of coursed and shaped masonry reinforces the argument for migration to that site. Domestic installations in the roomblocks, including slab-lined hearths and entry boxes, are also reminiscent of northern Southwest construc-

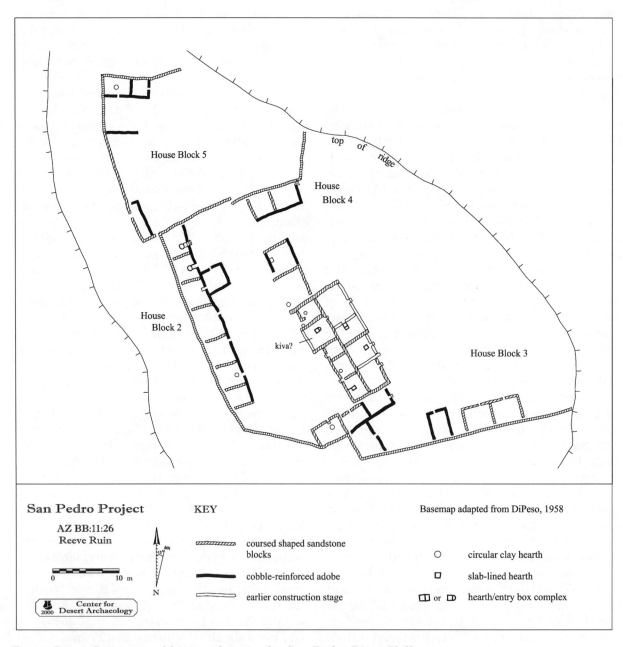

Fig. 4. Reeve Ruin, a puebloan enclave in the San Pedro River Valley.

tions. The majority of ceramics from these sites are produced with local manufacturing methods, but locally made perforated ceramic plates, (a form that seems to be an index marker of Tusayan/Kayenta immigrants [Christensen 1994; Mills 1998]) have been found at the sites. Ceremonial architecture is not always a reliable indicator of migration, but the kivas found in conjunction with the Puebloan roomblocks add strength to the identification of these Kayenta/Tusayan enclaves. Kayenta/ Tusayan area ceramic design styles spread rapidly across the Southwest at this time, too, although designs are an 'active' style that can be easily copied, and thus are not necessarily indicative of the movement of potters. The kiva at Davis Ruin was abandoned before the end of occupation at the site and later architectural constructions are of local styles, suggesting that immigrants were quick to learn local traditions and integrate with the indigenous residents.

Although we cannot reconstruct the significance of immigration to specific households, it is possible to make more generalized settlement-based claims about the relationship between Puebloan migration and social organization in southeast Arizona. In all cases described above (with the possible exception of Davis Ranch Ruin) migrants settled on the margins of existing communities or in previously unsettled areas. The marginal location of migrant houses suggests that newcomers were identified or self-identified as a distinct group, and were not given the same access to territory within the community or settlement. The claims of local groups to agricultural land as tenant or owner are unknown. There is no direct evidence that the defensive position of Reeve Ruin indicates overt conflict between local and immigrant groups, although it certainly indicates that occupants perceived a threat.

The early migrants from the Mogollon Highlands lived in pithouses that are not easily identified as 'local' or 'nonlocal' constructions but used Puebloan technology to produce corrugated ceramics. The later Kayenta/ Tusayan migrants lived in structures built in non-local styles. The differences in technologies at the earlier and later sites suggest that the impact of immigrants within local communities was different with each migration, although the specifics are, as yet, unknown.

Conclusions

The ultimate goal of an integrated approach to agency and structure is, as Netting (1990) said, to unpack the evolutionary portmanteau—to get away from typologies and their predetermined relationships between defined 'subsystems' of societies (economic, subsistence, ritual, etc.) and instead examine historical processes at the highest spatial and temporal resolution (Yoffee 1993). Rather than focusing on structures and institutions, a dynamic approach emphasizes the decisions and underlying motivations of individuals and small groups with respect to their specific economic and social environments. The objective is to examine changes in social structure that result both from specific local events and regional processes with cross-cultural applicability.

Just as the tribal model has been criticized for being too static for archaeological studies of long term change, and its emphasis on structure at the expense of process (Parkinson, this volume, Chapter 1; Fowles, this volume, Chapter 2), discussions of small-scale agricultural societies, even outside the tribal model, often do not pay enough attention to the role of mobility in social organization. As part of a society's economic and social structure, circulation and residential mobility create strong archaeological patterns but often do not leave the distinct material signatures that facilitate archaeological detection. Migration, the most archaeologically visible form of mobility, has attracted more attention, particularly over the past decade.

The examples in this paper show that mobility is an essential element of structure and the transformation of structure in small-scale agricultural societies. Mobility affects the lives of residents of the destination community, and it also affects the lives of the migrants and the residents of home communities. Short-term and seasonal circulation are intrinsic aspects of the economies of sedentary agricultural societies, and these types of movements do not affect the farmer's rights and duties in the homeland. Residential mobility also plays a significant role in the land use patterns of the prehispanic period pueblos, and changes in patterns of residential mobility affected the distribution and ownership of land in these communities (Varien 1999). Migration, the least predictable type of mobility, is often the most costly in social and economic terms. Migrants abandon structures, land, and rights in the homeland, and travel long distance to create new lives in the destination area.

Migrations both to sparsely populated frontiers and to occupied regions can affect structural transformations—economic, social, and ritual – both in the home and in destination communities.

Frontier communities are the combined products of the history the migrants bring with them from the homeland, interactions with other immigrants, and the socioeconomic consequences of living beyond the edge of more defined and better populated social entities. The basic values of the homeland changed in the new environment as people moved from areas with abundant labor and scarce land, to those that were land-rich and labor-poor. When people are more highly valued than possessions, their relations to the material world are transformed. In the Mogollon Rim case described above, this was expressed by the relatively great effort made to attract people to communities with great kiva constructions. On frontiers, individuals demonstrate creative solutions for adapting to new situations, individual households have a great deal of freedom, and communities exhibit structural flexibility.

Coresidential communities are created by the movement of migrants into pre-existing communities in the destination area. The relations between the groups can be cooperative or competitive, as migrants attempt to create an economic or social place for themselves. The examples presented in this paper show variation in the way migrants and indigenous households mediate this situation through the creation of specialized economies and distribution networks, the continuation of homeland ritual practices in the destination areas or the adoption of the rituals of new neighbors, and the development of sodalities and other organizations that crosscut differences in kinship and cultural background. Mediation may ultimately be unsuccessful and lead to inequality between various migrant and local groups. In extreme cases, violence and conflict may also result. Social and economic stresses can lead to further movement by one or more of the constituent groups and represent a dynamic force in the continuation of migration processes and community organization. Coresidential communities are not merely the acculturative blends of various migrants and local groups. As these groups negotiate their new social environment, existing economic and social institutions are transformed and new organizations are created.

In the small-scale agricultural societies of the American Southwest, mobility affects social institutions at all levels. It is one avenue through which individual choices about economic and social landscape are enacted. Repetitive forms of mobility within communities and regions are part of the normative foundations of some small scale agri-

cultural societies. Less common types of mobility, such as migration, places people in situations where the values of the homeland are reevaluted and changed, and where they must carefully negotiate their private and public identities. These actions may cause significant changes in social structure. Such examinations of the interaction of agency and structure make it possible to understand the variability expressed in small-scale societies.

Acknowledgements

We would like to thank Barbara Mills and Mark Elson for comments on an early draft of the paper. Henry Wallace provided insightful comments on Hohokam settlement. Doug Gann, Catherine Gilman, Susan Hall, and Geo-Map, Inc. produced the graphics. Thanks also to the Silver Creek Archaeological Research Project of the University of Arizona, Desert Archaeology, Inc. and the Center for Desert Archaeology for their creative research environments and institutional support.

References Cited

Adams, Jenny L.
  1998 The Ethnicity of Ground Stone Technological Traditions. Paper presented at the 63rd Annual Meeting of the Society for American Archaeology, Seattle.
  1999 Refocusing the Role of Food-Grinding Tools as Correlates for Subsistence Strategies in the U.S. Southwest. *American Antiquity*, 64(3): 475-498.
Adams, Robert McC.
  1978 Strategies of Maximization, Stability, and Resilience in Mesopotamian Society, Settlement, and Agriculture. *Proceedings of the American Philosophical Society* 1212:329-35.
Anthony, David
  1990 Migration in Archeology: The Baby and the Bathwater. *American Anthropologist* 92:895-914.
Baker, Vernon G.
  1980 Archaeological Visibility of Afro-American Culture: An Example from Black Lucy's Garden, Andover. In *Archaeological Perspectives on Ethnicity in America: Afro-American and Asian American Culture History*, edited by R.L. Schuyler, pp. 29-37. Baywood Publishing Co., New York.

Beckwith, Kim
1988   Intrusive Ceramic Wares and Types. In *The 1982-1984 Excavations at Las Colinas: Material Culture*, edited by D. R. Abbott, K. E. Beckwith, P. L. Crown, R. T. Euler, D. A. Gregory, J. R. London, M. B. Saul, L. A. Schwalbe, M. Bernard-Shaw, C. R. Szuter, and A. W. Vokes, pp. 199-256. Archaeological Series No. 162, Volume 4. Arizona State Museum, University of Arizona, Tucson.

Binford, Lewis R.
1980   Willow Smoke and Dogs' Tails: Hunter-Gatherer Settlement Systems and Archaeological Site Formation. *American Antiquity* 45(1):4-20.

Bogucki, Peter
1996   Sustainable and Unsustainable Adaptations by Early Farming Communities of Northern Poland. *Journal of Anthropological Archaeology* 15: 289-311.

Brandt, Richard B.
1954   *Hopi Ethics: A Theoretical Analysis.* University of Chicago Press, Chicago.

Buck, Paul E. and Laureen Perry
1999   A Late Basketmaker III Storage and Habitation Site near Hurricane, Utah. *Kiva* 64(4): 471-494.

Cameron, Catherine M.
1998   Coursed Adobe Architecture, Style, and Social Boundaries in the American Southwest. In *The Archaeology of Social Boundaries*, edited by Miriam T. Stark, pp. 183-207. Smithsonian Institution Press, Washington.

Childs, Terri
1991   Style, Technology, and Iron Smelting Furnaces in Bantu-Speaking Africa. *Journal of Anthropological Archaeology* 10:332-359.

Christensen, Andrew
1994   Perforated and Unperforated Plates as Tools for Pottery Manufacture. In *Function and Technology of Anasazi Ceramics from Black Mesa, Arizona*, edited by M.F. Smith, Jr., pp. 55-65. Center for Archaeological Investigations Occasional Paper 15. Southern Illinois University, Carbondale.

Ciolek-Torrello, Richard S.
1997   Prehistoric Settlement and Demography in the Lower Verde Region. In *Vanishing River: Landscapes and Lives of the Lower Verde Valley*, edited by Stephanie M. Whittlesey, Richard Ciolek-Torrello, and Jeffery H. Altschul, pp. 531-595. SRI Press, Tucson.

Ciolek-Torrello, Richard S. and John Welch (eds.)
1994   *The Roosevelt Rural Sites Study: Vol. 3. Changing Land Use in the Tonto Basin.* Technical Series No. 28. Statistical Research, Inc., Tucson.

Clark, Jeffery J.
1995   Domestic Architecture in the Early Classic Period. In *The Roosevelt Community Development Study: New Perspectives on Tonto Basin Prehistory,* edited by M. D. Elson, M. T. Stark, and D. A. Gregory, pp. 251-305. Anthropological Papers No. 15. Center for Desert Archaeology, Tucson.

2001   *Tracking Prehistoric Migrations: Pueblo Settlers among the Tonto Basin Hohokam.* Anthropological Papers of the University of Arizona 65. The University of Arizona Press, Tucson.

Clark, Jeffery J., M. Kyle Woodson, and Mark C. Slaughter
n.d.   Those who Went to the Land of the Sun: Puebloan Migrations into Southeastern Arizona. In *Between Mimbres and Hohokam: Exploring the Archaeology and History of Southeast Arizona and Southwest New Mexico*, edited by Henry D. Wallace. in prep.

Dean, Jeffrey S.
1988a   Dendrochronology and Paleoenvironmental Reconstruction on the Colorado Plateaus. In *The Anasazi in a Changing Environment*, edited by George J. Gumerman, pp. 119-167. Cambridge University Press, Cambridge.

1988b   The View from the North: An Anasazi Perspective on the Mogollon. *The Kiva* 53(2):197-199.

1996   Demography, Environment, and Subsistence Stress. In *Evolving Complexity and Environmental Risk in the Prehistoric Southwest: Proceedings of the Workshop "Resource Stress, Economic Uncertainty, and Human Response in the Prehistoric Southwest," Held February 25-29, 1992 in Santa Fe, New Mexico*, edited by Joseph A. Tainter and Bonnie Bagley Tainter, pp. 25-56. Santa Fe Institute Studies in the Sciences of Complexity, vol. XXIV. Addison-Wesley Publishing Company, Reading, Massachusetts.

Braun, David P. and Stephen Plog
1982 Evolution of "Tribal" Social Networks: Theory and Prehistoric North American Evidence. *American Antiquity* 47(3): 504-527.

Dean, Jeffrey S., William H. Doelle, and Janet D. Orcutt
1994 Adaptive Stress: Environment and Demography. In *Themes in Southwest Prehistory*, edited by George J. Gumerman, pp. 53-86. School of American Research Advanced Seminar Series, School of American Research Press, Santa Fe.

Deetz. James
1977 *In Small Things Forgotten: The Archaeology of Early American Life*. Anchor Books, New York.

Diehl, Michael W., Jennifer A. Waters, and J. Homer Thiel
1998 Acculturation and the Composition of the Diet of Tucson's Overseas Chinese Gardeners at the Turn of the Century. *Historical Archaeology* 32(4):19-33.

DiPeso, Charles
1958 *The Reeve Ruin of Southeastern Arizona: A Study of Prehistoric Western Pueblo Migration into the Middle San Pedro Valley*. Publication No. 8. Amerind Foundation, Dragoon, Arizona.

Doelle, William H.
1985 *Excavations at the Valencia Site: A Preclassic Hohokam Village in the Southern Tucson Basin*. Institute for American Research Anthropological Papers 3, Tucson.

1995 Tonto Basin Demography in a Regional Perspective. In *The Roosevelt Community Development Study: New Perspectives on Tonto Basin Prehistory*, edited by M.D. Elson, M.T. Stark, and D.A. Gregory. Anthropological Papers 15. Center for Desert Archaeology, Tucson.

Doelle, William H., Frederick W. Huntington, and Henry D. Wallace
1987 Rincon Phase Reorganization in the Tucson Basin. In *The Hohokam Village: Site Structure and Organization*, edited by David E. Doyel, pp. 71-96. Southwestern and Rocky Mountain Division of the American Association for the Advancement of Science, Glenwood Springs, Colorado.

Dohm, Karen
1994 The Search for Anasazi Village Origins: Basketmaker II Dwelling Aggregation on Cedar Mesa. *Kiva* 60(2): pp. 257-276.

Doyel, David E.
1976 Salado Cultural Developments in the Tonto Basin and Globe-Miami Areas, Central Arizona. *Kiva* 42:5-16.

Duff, Andrew I.
1998 The Processes of Migration in the late Prehistoric Southwest. In *Migration and Reorganization: The Pueblo IV Period in the American Southwest*, edited by Katherine A. Spielmann, pp. 31-52. Anthropological Research Papers No. 51. Arizona State University, Tempe.

Elson, Mark D.
1996 A Revised Chronology and Phase Sequence for the Lower Tonto Basin of Central Arizona. *Kiva* 62(2):117-147.

1998 *Expanding the View of Hohokam Platform Mounds: An Ethnographic Perspective*. Anthropological Papers of the University of Arizona No. 63. The University of Arizona Press, Tucson.

Elson, Mark D., Suzanne K. Fish, Steven R. James, Charles H. Miksicek
1995 Prehistoric Subsistence in the Roosevelt Community Development Study Area. In *The Roosevelt Community Development Study: Vol. 3. Paleobotanical and Osteological Analyses,* edited by M.D. Elson and J.J. Clark, pp. 217-260. Anthropological Papers No. 14. Center for Desert Archaeology, Tucson.

Elson, Mark D., David A. Gregory, and Miriam T. Stark
1995 New Perspective on Tonto Basin Prehistory. In *The Roosevelt Community Development Study: New Perspectives on Tonto Basin Prehistory*, edited by M.D. Elson, M.T. Stark, and D.A. Gregory, pp. 441-479. Anthropological Papers No. 15. Center for Desert Archaeology, Tucson.

Elson, Mark D., Deborah L. Swartz, and Douglas B. Craig, and Jeffery J. Clark
1994 *The Roosevelt Community Development Study: Vol. 2. Meddler Point, Pyramid Point, and Griffin Wash Sites*. Anthropological Papers No. 13. Center for Desert Archaeology, Tucson.

Ezzo, Joseph A.
1993 *Human Adaptation at Grasshopper Pueblo, Arizona: Social and Ecological Perspectives*. International Monographs in Prehistory, Archaeological Series 4, Ann Arbor.

Ferguson, Leland
  1992 *Uncommon Ground: Archaeology and Early African America, 1650-1800.* Smithsonian Institution Press, Washington, D.C.
Fish, Paul R.
  1989 The Hohokam: 1,000 Years of Prehistory in the Sonoran Desert. In *Dynamics of Southwest Prehistory*, edited by Linda S. Cordell and George J. Gumerman, pp. 19-63. A School of American Research Advanced Seminar Book. Smithsonian Institution Press, Santa Fe.
Fish, Paul and Suzanne Fish
  1984 Agricultural Maximization in the Sacred Mountain Basin. In *Prehistoric Agricultural Societies in the Southwest*, edited by S. Fish and P. Fish, pp. 147-160. Anthropological Research Papers 33. Arizona State University, Tempe.
Fish, Suzanne K. and Paul R. Fish
  1993 An Assessment of Abandonment Processes in the Hohokam Classic Period of the Tucson Basin. In *Abandonment of Settlements and Regions: Ethnoarchaeological and Archaeological Approaches*, edited by Catherine M. Cameron and Steve A. Tomka , pp. 99-110. New Directions in Archaeology. Cambridge University Press, Cambridge.
Ford, Richard I., Albert H. Schroeder, and Stewart L. Peckham
  1972 Three Perspectives on Puebloan Prehistory. In *New Perspectives on the Pueblos*, edited by Alfonso Ortiz, pp. 19-39. A School of American Research Book. University of New Mexico Press, Albuquerque.
Fowler, Andrew P., John R. Stein, and Roger Anyon
  1987 *An Archaeological Reconnaissance of West-Central New Mexico: The Anasazi Monuments Project.* Ms. on file at New Mexico State Historic Preservation Office, Santa Fe.
Gasser, Robert E.
  1979 Seeds, Seasons, and Ecosystems: Sedentary Hohokam Groups in the Papagueria. *The Kiva* Vol. 44 (2-3): 101-112.
Gerald, Rex E.
  1975 *Drought-correlated Changes in Two Prehistoric Pueblo Communities in Southeastern Arizona.* Unpublished Ph.D. dissertation, University of Chicago, Chicago.

Gladwin, Winifred, and Harold S. Gladwin
  1935 *The Eastern Range of the Red-on-Buff Culture.* Medallion Papers No. 16. Gila Pueblo Foundation, Globe, Arizona.
Gosden, Chris
  1999 *Anthropology and Archaeology: A Changing Relationship.* Routledge Press, London.
Gregory, David A.
  1991 Form and Variation in Hohokam Settlement Pattern. In *Chaco and Hohokam: Prehistoric Regional Systems in the American Southwest*, edited by Patricia L. Crown and W. James Judge, pp. 159-194. School of American Research Advanced Seminar Series. School of American Research Press, Santa Fe.
  1995 Prehistoric Settlement Patterns in the Eastern Tonto Basin. In *The Roosevelt Community Development Study: New Perspectives on Tonto Basin Prehistory*, edited by Mark D. Elson, Miriam T. Stark, and David A. Gregory. Anthropological Papers 15: 127-184. Center for Desert Archaeology, Tucson.
Gregory, David A. and Fred Nials
  1985 Observations Concerning the Distribution of Classic Period Hohokam Platform Mounds. In *Proceedings of the 1983 Hohokam Symposium*, edited by Alfred E. Dittert, Jr. and David E. Doyel, pp. 373-388. Arizona Archaeological Society Occasional Paper 2, Phoenix.
Haas, Jonathan and Winifred Creamer
  1993 Stress and Warfare Among the Kayenta Anasazi of the Thirteenth Century A.D. *Fieldiana Anthropology, New Series, No. 21.* Field Museum of Natural History, Chicago.
Habicht-Mauche, Judith A.
  1993 *The Pottery from Arroyo Hondo Pueblo, New Mexico: Tribalization and Trade in the Northern Rio Grande.* School of American Research Press, Santa Fe.
Hack, John T.
  1942 *The Changing Physical Environment of the Hopi Indians.* Papers of the Peabody Museum of American Archaeology and Ethnology, Harvard University 35(1). Harvard University, Cambridge.
Hartesveldt, Eric van, Kelley Hays-Gilpin, and Dennis Gilpin
  1998 Prehistoric Ceramics of the Middle Rio Puerco Valley: An Overview. In *Prehis-*

toric Ceramics of the Puerco Valley: The 1995 Chambers-Sanders Trust Lands Ceramic Conference, edited by Kelley Hays-Gilpin and Eric van Hartesveldt, pp. 33-51. Museum of Northern Arizona Ceramic Series Number 7, Museum of Northern Arizona.

Hassan, Fekri
1981 *Demographic Archaeology*. Academic Press, New York.

Haury, Emil W.
1932 Roosevelt:9:6: A Hohokam site of the Colonial Period. *Medallion Papers* 11. Gila Pueblo, Globe, Arizona.

1945 *The Excavation of Los Muertos and Neighboring Ruins in the Salt River Valley, Southern Arizona*. Papers of the Peabody Museum of American Archaeology and Ethnology No. 24(1). Harvard University, Cambridge.

1958 Evidence at Point of Pines for a Prehistoric Migration from Northern Arizona. In *Migrations in New World Culture History*, edited by Raymond H. Thompson, pp. 1-6. The University of Arizona Press, Tucson.

1985a Excavations in the Forestdale Valley, East-central Arizona. In *Mogollon Culture in the Forestdale Valley, East-Central Arizona*, edited by Emil W. Haury, pp. 135-279. The University of Arizona Press, Tucson.

1985b A Sequence of Great Kivas in the Forestdale Valley, Arizona. In *Mogollon Culture in the Forestdale Valley, East-Central Arizona*, edited by Emil W. Haury, pp. 415-422. The University of Arizona Press, Tucson.

Haury, Emil W., and E. B. Sayles
1985 An Early Pit House Village of the Mogollon Culture, Forestdale Valley, Arizona. In *Mogollon Culture in the Forestdale Valley*, edited by Emil W. Haury, pp. 281-371. The University of Arizona Press, Tucson.

Hegmon, Michelle, Margaret C. Nelson, and Mark J. Ennes
2000 Corrugated Pottery, Technological Style, and Population Movement in the Mimbres Region of the American Southwest. *Journal of Anthropological Research* 56: 217-240.

Herr, Sarah A.
1994 *Great Kivas as Integrative Architecture in the Silver Creek Community*. Unpublished M.A. thesis, University of Arizona, Tucson.

2001 *Beyond Chaco: The Great Kiva Communities of the Mogollon Rim Frontier*. Anthropological Papers of the University of Arizona 66. The University of Arizona Press, Tucson.

Herr, Sarah A. and Jeffery J. Clark
1997 Patterns in the Pathways. *Kiva* 62(3).

Jacobs, David
1994 *Archaeology of the Salado in the Livingston Area of Tonto Basin, Roosevelt Platform Mound Study*. Roosevelt Monograph Series 3. Anthropological Field Studies No. 32. Office of Cultural Resource Management, Arizona State University, Tempe.

Jackson, Robert H.
1994 *Indian Population Decline: The Missions of Northwestern New Spain, 1687-1840*. The University of New Mexico, Albuquerque.

Judge, W. James
1991 Chaco: Current Views of Prehistory and the Regional System. In *Chaco and Hohokam: Prehistoric Regional Systems in the American Southwest*, edited by Patricia L. Crown and W. James Judge, pp. 11-30. School of American Research Advanced Seminar Series. School of American Research Press, Santa Fe.

Kintigh, Keith W.
1996 The Cibola Region in the Post-Chacoan Era. In *The Prehistoric Pueblo World, A.D. 1150-1350*, edited by Michael Adler, pp. 131-144. The University of Arizona Press, Tucson.

Kintigh, Keith W., Todd L. Howell, and Andrew I. Duff
1996 Post-Chacoan Social Integration at the Hinkson Site, New Mexico. *Kiva* 61(3): 257-274.

Kopytoff, Igor
1987 The Internal African Frontier: The Making of African Political Culture. In *The African Frontier: The Reproduction of Traditional African Societies*, edited by Igor Kopytoff, pp. 2-84. Indiana University Press, Bloomington.

Kroeber, Alfred, and H. Driver
1932 *Quantitative Expressions of Cultural Relationships*. University of California Publication in American Archaeology and Ethnology No. 29, pp. 354-423.

Lange, Charles H.
1990 *Cochiti: A New Mexico Pueblo, Past and Present*. University of New Mexico Press, Albuquerque.

Lange, Richard C.
1994 People and the Prehistory of the Homol'ovi Ruins State Park, Winslow, Arizona. In *Middle Little Colorado River Archaeology: From the Parks to the People*, edited by Anne Trinkle Jones and Martyn D. Tagg, pp. 33-46. The Arizona Archaeologist No. 27. Arizona Archaeological Society, Phoenix.

Larick, Roy
1987 Men of Iron and Social Boundaries in Northern Kenya. In *Ethnicity and Culture*, edited by R. Auger, M. Glass, S. MacEachern, and P. McCartney, pp. 67-76. University of Calgary Press, Calgary.

Lechtman, Heather
1977 Style in Technology – Some Early Thoughts. In *Material Culture: Styles, Organization, an d Dynamics of Technology*, edited by Heather Lechtman and Robert S. Merrill, pp. 3-20. West Publishing, New York.

Lekson, Stephen
1989 The Community in Anasazi Archaeology. In *Households and Communities*, edited by Scott MacEachern, David J. W. Archer and Richard D. Garvin, pp. 181-183. Chacmool: proceedings of the 21st Annual Chacmool Conference, University of Calgary, Calgary.
1990 *Sedentism and Aggregation in Anasazi Archaeology*. In Perspectives on Southwest Prehistory, edited by Paul E. Minnis, and Charles L. Redman, pp. 333-340. Westview Press, Boulder.
1991 Settlement Patterns and the Chaco Region. In *Chaco and Hohokam: Prehistoric Regional Systems in the American Southwest*, edited by Patricia L. Crown and W. James Judge, pp. 31-55. School of American Research Advanced Seminar Series. School of American Research Press, Santa Fe.

2000 Great! In *Great House Communities Across the Chacoan Landscape*, edited by John Kantner and Nancy M. Mahoney, pp. 157-163. Anthropological Papers of the University of Arizona Number 64. The University of Arizona Press, Tucson.

Lemonnier, Pierre
1992 *Elements for an Anthropology of Technology*. Anthropological Papers. Museum of Anthropology 88. University of Michigan, Ann Arbor.

Levy, Jerrold
1992 *Orayvi Revisited: Social Stratification in an "Egalitarian" Society*. School of American Research Press, Santa Fe.

Lightfoot, Ricky R.
1993 Abandonment Processes in Prehistoric pueblos. In *Abandonment of Settlements and Regions: Ethnoarchaeological and Archaeological Approaches*, edited by Catherine M. Cameron and Steve A. Tomka , pp. 165-177. New Directions in Archaeology. Cambridge University Press, Cambridge.
1994 *The Duckfoot Site: Archaeology of the House and Household*. Occasional Paper No. 4. Crow Canyon Archaeological Center, Cortez.

Limerick, Patricia Nelson
1987 *The Legacy of Conquest: The Unbroken Past of the American West*. W.W. Norton and Company, New York.

Lindauer, Owen
1995 *Where the Rivers Converge, Roosevelt Platform Mound Study: Report on the Rock Island Complex*. Roosevelt Monograph Series 4. Anthropological Field Studies No. 33. Office of Cultural Resource Management, Arizona State University, Tempe.
1996 *The Place of Storehouses, Roosevelt Platform Mound Study: Report on Schoolhouse Point Mound, Pinto Creek Complex* Pts. 1 and 2. Roosevelt Monograph Series 6. Anthropological Field Studies No. 35. Office of Cultural Resource Management, Arizona State University, Tempe.
1997 *The Archaeology of Schoolhouse Point Mesa, Roosevelt Platform Mound Study: Report on the School House Point Sites, Schoolhouse Management Group, Pinto*

Creek Complex. Roosevelt Monograph Series 8. Anthropological Field Studies No. 37. Office of Cultural Resource Management, Arizona State University, Tempe.

Lindsay, Alexander J., Jr.
1987 Anasazi Population Movements to Southern Arizona. *American Archaeology* 6: 190-198.

Longacre, William
1970 *Archaeology as Anthropology.* Anthropological Papers of The University of Arizona 17. University of Arizona Press, Tucson.
1976 Population Dynamics at the Grasshopper Pueblo, Arizona. In *Demographic Anthropology: Quantitative Approaches*, edited by Ezra B.W. Zubrow, pp. 169-184. A School of American Research Book, University of New Mexico Press, Albuquerque.

Lyons, Patrick C.
2001 *Winslow Orange Ware and the Ancestral Hopi Migration Horizon.* Unpublished doctoral dissertation. The Department of Anthropology, University of Arizona, Tucson.

McCartney, Peter H., Owen Lindauer, Glen E. Rice, and John C. Ravesloot
1994 Chronological Methods. In *Archaeology of the Salado in the Livingston Area of Tonto Basin, Roosevelt Platform Mound Study*, by David Jacobs, pp. 21-50. Roosevelt Monograph Series No. 3. Office of Cultural Resource Management Anthropological Field Studies No. 32. Arizona State University, Tempe.

Mera, Harry P.
1935 *Ceramic Clues to the Prehistory of North Central New Mexico.* Laboratory of Anthropology Technical Series, Bulletin No. 8. Laboratory of Anthropology, Santa Fe.
1940 *Population Change in the Rio Grande Glaze-Paint Area.* Laboratory of Anthropology Technical Series, Bulletin No. 9. Laboratory of Anthropology, Santa Fe.

Miksa, Elizabeth and James M. Heidke
1995 Drawing a Line in the Sands: Models of Ceramic Temper Provenance. In *The Roosevelt Community Development Study: Volume 2: Ceramic Chronology, Technology, and Economics*, edited by James M. Heidke and Miriam T. Stark, pp. 133-206. Anthropological Papers 14,

Number 2. Center for Desert Archaeology, Tucson.
2001 It All Comes Out in the Wash: Actualistic Petrofacies Modeling of Temper Provenance, Tonto Basin, Arizona, USA. *Geoarchaeology: An International Journal* Vol 16(2), 177-222.

Mills, Barbara J.
1994 Community Dynamics and Archaeological Dynamics: Some Considerations of Middle-Range Theory. In *The Ancient Southwestern Community: Models and Methods for the Study of Prehistoric Social Organization*, edited by W.H. Wills and Robert D. Leonard, pp. 55-65. The University of New Press, Albuquerque.
1998 Migration and Pueblo IV Community Reorganization in the Silver Creek Area, East-Central Arizona. In *Migration and Reorganization: The Pueblo IV Period in the American Southwest*, edited by Katherine A. Spielmann, pp. 65-80. Anthropological Research Papers No. 51. Arizona State University, Tempe.
2000 Alternative Models, Alternative Strategies: Looking at Leadership in the Greater Southwest. In *Alternative Leadership Strategies in the Prehispanic Southwest*, edited by Barbara J. Mills, pp. 3-18. The University of Arizona Press, Tucson.

Mills, Barbara J., Sarah A. Herr, and Scott Van Keuren (editors)
1999 *Living on the Edge of the Rim: Excavations and Analysis of the Silver Creek Archaeological Research Project, 1993-1998.* Arizona State Museum Archaeological Series 192. Arizona State Museum, Tucson.

Mitchell, Douglas R.
1989 Settlement Patterns and Social Organization for the Phoenix Area Classic Period. In *Archaeological investigations at the Grand Canal Ruins: A Classic Period Site in Phoenix, Arizona*, edited by Douglas R. Mitchell, pp. 859-878. Soil Systems Publicaitons in Archaeology Number 12, Phoenix.

Most, Rachel
1987 *Reconstructing Prehistoric Subsistence Strategies: An Example from East-Central Arizona.* Unpublished Doctoral dissertation, Department of Anthropology, Arizona State University, Tempe.

Nelson, Margaret C.
1999 *Mimbres during the Twelfth Century: Abandonment, Continuity, and Reorganization.* The University of Arizona Press, Tucson.

Netting, Robert Mc.
1990 Population, Permanent Agriculture, and Polities: Unpacking the Evolutionary Portmanteau. In *The Evolution of Political Systems: Sociopolitics in Small-Scale, Sedentary Societies*, edited by S. Upham, pp. 21-61. Cambridge University Press, Cambridge, England.

Newcomb, Joanne
1997 *Prehistoric Population Dynamics in the Silver Creek Area, East_Central Arizona.* Unpublished Masters thesis, Department of Anthropology, The University of Arizona, Tucson.
1999 Silver Creek Settlement Patterns and Paleodemography. In *Living on the Edge of the Rim: Excavations and Analysis of the Silver Creek Archaeological Research Project, 1993-1998*, edited by Barbara J. Mills, Sarah A. Herr, and Scott Van Keuren, pp. 31-52, Arizona State Museum Archaeological Series, University of Arizona, Tucson.

Orcutt, Janet D.
1991 Environmental Variability and Settlement Changes on the Pajarito Plateau, New Mexico. *American Antiquity* 56(2): 315-332.

Perlman, Stephen M.
1985 Group Size and Mobility Costs. In *The Archaeology of Frontiers and Boundaries*, edited by Stanton W. Green and Stephen M. Perlman, pp. 33-50. Academic Press, Orlando.

Pilles, Peter J., Jr., and David R. Wilcox
1978 The Small Sites Conference: An Introduction. In *Limited Activity and Occupation Sites: A Collection of Conference Papers*, edited by Albert E. Ward, pp. 1-5. vol. 1. Contributions to Anthropological Studies, Albuquerque.

Poore, Henry R.
1894 Condition of 16 New Mexico Indian Pueblos, 1890. Report on Indians Taxed and Indians Not Taxed in the United States (except Alaska) at the Eleventh Census: 1890. Department of the Interior, Census Office, 52nd Congress., 1st session, H. Misc. Doc. No. 340, Part 15, pp. 424-440.

Powers, Robert P., William B. Gillespie, and Stephen H. Lekson
1983 The Outlier Survey: A Regional View of Settlement in the San Juan Basin. *Reports of the Chaco Center 3*. National Park Service, Albuquerque.

Powers, Robert P. and Tineke Van Zandt
1999 An Introduction to Bandelier. In *The Bandelier Archaeological Survey: Volume I*, edited by Powers, Robert P. and Janet D. Orcutt. Intermountain Cultural Resources Management Professional Paper No. 57. National Park Service, Santa Fe.

Preucel, Robert W., Jr.
1990 Seasonal Circulation and Dual Residence in the *Pueblo Southwest: A Prehistoric Example from the Pajarito Plateau, New Mexico.* Garland Publishing, Inc., New York.

Redman, Charles L.
1993 *People of the Tonto Rim: Archaeological Discovery in Prehistoric Arizona.* Smithsonian Institution Press, Washington.

Reed, Erik K.
1950 East-central Arizona Archaeology in Relation to the Western Pueblos. *Southwestern Journal of Anthropology* 6(2): 120-138.

Reid, J. Jefferson (editor)
1982 *Cholla Project Archaeology Volume 2: The Chevelon Region.* Arizona State Museum Archaeological Series No. 161. Arizona State Museum, Tucson.

Reid, J. Jefferson
1997 Return to Migration, Population Movement, and Ethnic Identity in the American Southwest: A Peer Reviewer's Thoughts on Archaeological Inference. In *Vanishing River: Landscapes and Lives of the Lower Verde Valley*, edited by Stephanie M. Whittlesey, Richard Ciolek-Torrello, and Jeffery H. Altschul, pp. 629-638. SRI Press, Tucson.

Reid, Jefferson and Stephanie Whittlesey
1999 *Grasshopper Pueblo: A Story of Archaeology and Ancient Life.* The University of Arizona Press, Tucson.

Renfrew, Colin and John F. Cherry (editors)
1986 *Peer Polity Interaction and Socio-political Change.* Cambridge University Press, Cambridge.

Rice, Glen E.
1998 *A Synthesis of Tonto Basin Prehistory: The Roosevelt Archaeology Studies, 1989 to 1998.* Roosevelt Monograph Series 12.

Anthropological Field Studies No. 41. Office of Cultural Resource Management, Arizona State University, Tempe.

Rice, Glen E. and Katherine Henderson
1990 *A Study of Archaeological Sites Along the Payson to Preacher Canyon 69V Transmission Line. Office of Cultural Resource Management Report #74.* Department of Anthropology, Arizona State University, Tempe.

Rice, Glen E., Charles L. Redman, and David Jacobs, and Owen Lindauer
1998 Architecture, Settlement Types, and Settlement Complexes. In *Roosevelt Platform Mound Study: A Synthesis of Tonto Basin Prehistory: The Roosevelt Archaeological Studies, 1989-1998*, edited by Glen E. Rice, pp. 55-83. Roosevelt Monograph Series 12. Anthropological Field Studies No. 41. Office of Cultural Resource Management, Arizona State University, Tempe.

Riggs, Charles R., Jr.
1999 *The Architecture of Grasshopper Pueblo: Dynamics of Form, Function, and Use of Space in a Prehistoric Community.* Ph.D. dissertation, Department of Anthropology, The University of Arizona, Tucson.

Rothschild, Nan A., Barbara J. Mills, T.J. Ferguson, and Susan Dublin
1993 Abandonment at Zuni farming villages. In *Abandonment of Settlements and Regions: Ethnoarchaeological and archaeological approaches*, edited by Catherine M. Cameron and Steve A. Tomka, pp. 123-137. Cambridge University Press, Cambridge.

Sackett, James R.
1977 The Meaning of Style in Archaeology: A General Model. *American Antiquity* 42:369-380.
1982 Approaches to Style in Lithic Archaeology. *Journal of Anthropological Archaeology* 1:59-112
1985 Style and Ethnicity in the Kalahari: A Reply to Weissner. *American Antiquity* 50:154-159.

Sahlins, Marshall
1981 *Historical Metaphors and Mythical Realities: Structure in the Early History of the Sandwich Islands Kingdom.* Association for Social Anthropology in Oceania Special Publications 1. The University of Michigan Press, Ann Arbor.

Salzer, Mattew W.
2000 Temperature Variability and the Northern Anasazi: Possible Implications for Regional Abandonment. *Kiva* 65(2):295-318.

Schlanger, Sarah H.
1987 Population Measurement, Size, and Change, A.D. 600-1175. In *Dolores Archaeological Program Supporting Studies: Setting and Environment.* Compiled by K. Petersen and Janet D. Orcutt. U.S. Department of the Interior, Bureau of Reclamation, Engineering and Research Center, Denver.
1988 Patterns of Population Movement and Long-Term Population Growth in Southwestern Colorado. *American Antiquity* 53:733-793.

Schlanger, Sarah H. and Janet D. Orcutt
1986 Site Surface Characteristics and Functional Inferences. *American Antiquity* 51(2): 296-312.

Schlanger, Sarah H. and Richard H. Wilshusen
1993 Local abandonments and regional conditions in the North American Southwest. In *Abandonment of Settlements and Regions: Ethnoarchaeological and Archaeological Approaches*, edited by Catherine M. Cameron and Steve A. Tomka , pp. 85-98. New Directions in Archaeology. Cambridge University Press, Cambridge.

Schlegel, Alice
1992 African Political Models in the American Southwest: Hopi as an Internal Frontier Society. *American Anthropologist* 94:376-397.

Shaul, David Leedom and Jane H. Hill
1998 Tepimans, Yumans, and Other Hohokam. *American Antiquity* 63(3): 375-396.

Sires, Earl W., Jr.
1987 Hohokam Architectural Variability and Site Structure during the Sedentary-Classic Transition. In *The Hohokam Village: Site Structure and Organization*, edited by David E. Doyel, pp. 171-182. Southwestern and Rocky Mountain Division of the American Association for the Advancement of Science, Glenwood Springs, Colorado.

Slaughter, Mark C.
1996a Architectural Features. In *Excavation of Gibbon Springs Site: A Classic Period Village in the Northeastern Tucson Ba-*

sin, edited by Mark. C. Slaughter and Heidi Robert, pp. 69-140. Report No. 94-87. SWCA, Tucson.

1996b Summary and Concluding Thoughts. In *Excavation of Gibbon Springs Site: A Classic Period Village in the Northeastern Tucson Basin*, edited by Mark. C. Slaughter and Heidi Robert, pp. 523-534. Report No. 94-87. SWCA, Tucson.

Slaughter, Mark C. and Heidi Roberts (editors)

1996 *Excavation of the Gibbon Springs Site: A Classic Period Village in the Northeastern Tucson Basin*. Report No. 94-87. SWCA, Tucson.

Spicer, Edward H.

1962 *Cycles of Conquest: The Impact of Spain, Mexico, and the United States on the Indians of the Southwest, 1533-1960*. The University of Arizona Press, Tucson.

Stark, Miriam T., Jeffery J. Clark, and Mark D. Elson

1995 Causes and Consequences of Migration in the 13th Century Tonto Basin. *Journal of Anthropological Archaeology* 14, pp. 212-246.

Stark, Miriam T., Mark D. Elson, and Jeffery J. Clark

1998 Social Boundaries and Technical Choices in Tonto Basin Prehistory. In *The Archaeology of Social Boundaries*, edited by Miriam T. Stark, pp. 208-231. Smithsonian Institution Press, Washington.

Steen, Charlie R.

1962 Excavations at the Upper Ruin, Tonto National Monument. In *Archaeological Studies at Tonto National Monument*, edited by L.R. Caywood, pp. 1-30. Southwestern Monuments Association Technical Series 2. Globe, Arizona.

Stinson, Susan L.

1996 *Roosevelt Red Ware and the Organization of Ceramic Production in the Silver Creek Drainage*. Unpublished M.A. thesis, Department of Anthropology, The University of Tucson, Arizona.

Stuart, David E. and Rory P. Gauthier (with contributions by Thomas W. Merlan).

1984 *Prehistoric New Mexico: Background for Survey*. University of New Mexico Press, Albuquerque.

Sullivan, Alan P., III

1994 Frontiers, Barriers, and Crises Today: Colton's Methods and the Wupatki Survey Data. In *The Ancient Southwestern Community: Models and Methods for the Study of Prehistoric Social Organization*, edited by W.H. Wills and Robert D. Leonard, pp 191-207. University of New Mexico Press, Albuquerque.

Triadan, Daniella

1997 *Ceramic Commodities and Common Containers: Production and Distribution of White Mountain Red Ware in the Grasshopper Region, Arizona*. Anthropological Papers of the University of Arizona No. 61. The University of Arizona Press, Tucson.

Turner, Christie

1998 Physical Anthropology Synthesis of the Roosevelt Platform Mound Study. In *Roosevelt Platform Mound Study: A Synthesis of Tonto Basin Prehistory: The Roosevelt Archaeological Studies, 1989-1998*, edited by Glen E. Rice, pp. 181-191. Roosevelt Monograph Series 12. Anthropological Field Studies No. 41. Office of Cultural Resource Management, Arizona State University, Tempe.

Van Keuren, Scott

1999 *Ceramic Design Structure and the Organization of Cibola White Ware Production in the Grasshopper Region, Arizona*. Arizona State Museum Archaeological Series 190. Arizona State Museum, The University of Arizona, Tucson.

Varien, Mark D.

1999 *Sedentism and Mobility in a Social Landscape: Mesa Verde and Beyond*. The University of Arizona Press, Tucson.

Weissner, Polly

1983 Style and Social Information in Kalahari San Projectile Points. *American Antiquity* 48:253-276.

1984 Reconsidering the Behavioral Basis for Style: A Case Study among the Kalahari San. *Journal of Anthropological Archaeology* 3:190-234.

1985 Style or Isochrestic Variation? A Reply to Sackett. *American Antiquity* 50:160-166.

Welch, John R.

1996 *Archaeological Measures and Social Implications of Agricultural Commitment*. Unpublished doctoral dissertation. Department of Anthropology, University of Arizona, Tucson.

Whittlesey, Stephanie M.
  1978 *Status and Death at Grasshopper Pueblo: Experiments toward an Archaeological Theory of Correlates.* Ph.D. dissertation, University of Arizona, Tucson. University Microfilms, Ann Arbor.

Wilcox, David R.
  1991 Hohokam Social Complexity. In *Chaco and Hohokam: Prehistoric Regional Systems in the American Southwest*, edited by Patricia L. Crown and W. James Judge, pp. 253-275. School of American Research Advanced Seminar Series. School of American Research Press, Santa Fe.

Wilcox, David R., Thomas R. McGuire, and Charles Sternberg
  1981 *Snaketown Revisited.* Arizona State Museum Archaeological Series 155. University of Arizona, Tucson.

Wilshusen, Richard H. and Scott G. Ortman
  1999 Rethinking the Pueblo I Period in the San Juan Drainage: Aggregation, Migration, and Cultural Diversity. *Kiva* 64(3):369-399.

Wissler, Clark
  1926 *The Relation of Nature to Man in Aboriginal America.* Oxford University Press, New York.

Wobst, H. Martin
  1977 Stylistic Behavior and Information Exchange. *Michigan Anthropological Papers* 61:317-342.

Wood, Scott J. and Martin McAllister
  1992 The Salado Tradition. An Alternative View. In *Cholla Project Archaeology: Vol. 1. Introduction and Special Studies*, edited by J. J. Reid, pp. 81-94. Archaeological Series No. 161. Arizona State Museum, University of Arizona, Tucson.

Woodson, M. Kyle
  1998 Migrations in Late Anasazi Prehistory: The Evidence from the Goat Hill Site. *Kiva* 64(2).

Wyckoff, Lydia L.
  1990 *Designs and Factions: Politics, Religion, and Ceramics on the Hopi Mesas.* University of New Mexico Press, Albuquerque.

Yoffee, Norman
  1993 Too Many Chiefs? (or, Safe Texts for the '90s). In *Archaeological Theory: Who Sets the Agenda?,* edited by Norman Yoffee and Andrew Sherratt, pp. 60-78. Cambridge University Press, Cambridge.

Young, Lisa C.
  1996 *Mobility and Farmers: The Pithouse-to-Pueblo Transition in Northeastern Arizona.* Unpublished PhD. dissertation. Department of Anthropology, The University of Arizona, Tucson.

Zedeño, María Nieves
  1994 *Sourcing Prehistoric Ceramics at Chodistaas Pueblo, Arizona: The Circulation of People and Pots in the Grasshopper Region.* Anthropological Papers no. 58. The University of Arizona Press, Tucson.

9. Building Consensus:
Tribes, Architecture, and Typology in the American Southwest

Michael Adler

Introduction

As the subdisciplines of anthropology continue to diversify and specialize, a precious few 'big questions' still animate research throughout the discipline. One such question is the development and social reproduction of power and inequality in human groups. Any broad understanding of sociopolitical hierarchy and power structures requires a definition of organizational strategies that allow us to compare, in an appropriate manner, social groups from New Guinea to New Grange. From a particularist perspective, human participation in societies can be shown to have generated markedly variable systems of belief and social reproduction as new webs of relationships are spun and respun at a dizzying rate. But despite this potential for organizational diversity, anthropological research continues to illuminate distinct higher order regularities and co-occurrences of certain behaviors, institutions, and social strategies throughout the ethnographic and archaeological records. The grand questions of how and why human societies develop and recapitulate these regularities through time and space integrates the increasingly divergent interests of ethnology and archaeology. Archaeologists benefit from the extensive ethnographic literature that documents the synchronic functioning of social groups. In turn, ethnographic studies of contemporaneous social systems profit from the temporally deep record of diversity in human behavioral strategies that archaeological research generates.

This chapter utilizes archaeological and ethnographic information to assess how 'tribal' communities work, with a particular focus on ancestral and historic Pueblo communities in the American Southwest. Most specifically my interest is in how we might best use our anthropological perspectives on the creation, use, and abandonment of public (ritual) architectural space within Pueblo communities. To date, our understanding of tribal social organization has, in large part, relied on neoevolutionary typologies of social organizational variability. This chapter presents a short discussion of typological approaches to social organization, and focuses on recent revisions to social organizational models, namely the heterarchy and dual processual models. In particular, I explore the utility of the dual processual model as it applies to archaeological data from ancestral Pueblo communities in northern New Mexico, communities that have left architectural 'footprints' approximating some of the expectations for the 'corporate organizational strategy' as outlined in the model. At the same time, however, I argue that the dual processual model still suffers from the tyranny of the typological approach. Our analytical approaches need to go beyond identification of modal 'strategy classes' to provide more dynamic explanations of how social power is created and reproduced in these and other tribal communities.

Tribes and Tribulation: Going Beyond Stage-Based Social Typologies

The construction of models of long-term change in social organizational strategies remains one of the holy crusades of modern anthropological archaeology. The optimism generated by the New Archaeology of the second half of the 20th century has been tempered by the subsequent realities of fitting complex models to the often ambiguous and incomplete patterning in the archaeological record. Archaeologists are fortunate to recover evidence of even the scantiest portion of the dynamics of past social systems, but I think that we are making progress. One realm of research promise is the ongoing revisions to our intellectual legacy of social evolutionary typologies, the stage-based explanatory approaches of Sahlins (1963, 1968; Sahlins and Service 1960), Service (1971), and Fried (1967).

This is not another neoevolutionary stage-bashing party. As many of the authors in this volume argue, earlier stage-based approaches to organizational variability continue to provide us with a common terminology, but have fallen short of providing us with truly processual explanations of what generates and selects for various aspects of leadership strategies across different social, economic, and demographic contexts. But at the same time, we have to realize that the heuristic typologies we know as 'band-tribe-chiefdom-state' and 'egalitarian-ranked-stratified' have provided a common ground for the discussion of past and present cultural variability, a set of mutually understood terms. The way a defined group of individuals behaves requires terms and classifications, necessarily collapsing much of the inherent organizational variability into a limited set of classificatory terms and coincidental cultural traits.

The tallying and comparison of organizational, economic, political, demographic, and other traits has occupied a great deal of anthropological analysis over the past fifty years. This is particularly true for that entity that has come to be called the 'tribe'. Spanning that tumultuous organizational terrain between relatively small-scale, mobile foragers and the entrenched hierarchical polities associated with stratified sociopolitical organization, the tribe has generally been defined on what is *not* present as much as it is by organizational strategies that can be isolated through ethnographic or archaeological research. Tribes are often characterized as organizationally 'middle-range' societies for good reason. They comprise those societal bundles that simultaneously manifest aspects of organizational hierarchy and redundancy, leadership positions that may or may not be generationally heritable, and other political strategies that today seem relatively egalitarian and tomorrow appear to be centralized and hierarchical.

After decades of debating the traits of the tribe and the rest of the classificatory pigeonholes, we do have to admit to the pitfalls of these neoevolutionary typologies. The problem is not that we lack organizational traits with which to define the 'tribe', but rather that our trait lists are still *descriptions, not explanations*. Classifications are descriptive heuristic devices that are meant to control observations of variability, not explain the variability. While we will always require some level of classification to provide the common terminological grounds (Dunnell 1982), descriptive taxonomy alone lacks the content that is required for expla-

nation. Tribes are a very complex interplay of varying social and economic strategies that simultaneously play out on many different organizational levels within the household, suprahousehold, community, and intercommunity levels, and I would argue that we can document the material remains of some of these strategies. Our archaeological investigations too often end with checklists indicating the presence or absence of social organizational features that we have inferred from the archaeological record. When evidence of egalitarian burials, household production, and politically autonomous communities line up like triple cherries on a slot machine we call 'jackpot', collect our winnings, and go on to explore for these same traits in other archaeological contexts. Typologies tell us more about how tribal social formations are structured, but as static structures the descriptions don't provide models of 'how tribes act' through time and space (see Fowles, this volume, Chapter 2).

Recent Models of Political Organization and Action

One of the outgrowths to archaeology's dissatisfaction with stage-based models of sociopolitical organization is the current desire to emphasize the simultaneity of competing and even contradictory organizational strategies within single social systems. Recent discussions of heterarchy and dual processual theory, for example, may be viewed as direct manifestations of this desire. Heterarchy theory has been championed by Carole Crumley and others (Crumley 1979, 1995; Crumley and Marquardt 1987) as a way of breaking down the earlier unilineal models of hierarchy and leadership. Heterarchical systems are those in which several different sources of social power can coexist within a social system. Each source of power can be operative depending on the scale of social action that is under scrutiny at any given time or place.

Alison Rautman (1998) and Keith Kintigh (2000) have applied heterarchy theory to Southwestern societies based on the observation that egalitarian and nonegalitarian leadership and decision-making roles were simultaneously present, at least among historic Pueblo groups. This purposefully contrasts with earlier schemes, such as that of Service (1971), that were heavily invested in the idea that social contexts might be characterized as singularly egalitarian or hierarchical, in other words, either tribal or chiefly. Heterarchy theory, however, outlines systems in which component elements may be unranked with respect to other elements and/or ranked relative to other components depending on the state of the system (Crumley 1979:144). In other words, there is an inherent flexibility in how component elements relate to other components. While heterarchies certainly may have ranked relationships that stabilize over time, it is not expected that particular sources of power will replace other source of power in a logical and unilineal progression. Heterarchy theory allows for and indeed expects alternative leadership options within any range of societal contexts, creating the potential for both shared and exclusive power structures. I agree that we do need to recognize the simultaneity of seemingly contradictory avenues to leadership. Heterarchy theory widens the playing field within which power and influence are negotiated, but currently lacks specific expectations regarding how leadership and organizational contradictions play out over time.

The dual-processual model is a more explicit attempt to map out the social structural variability that accompanies contradictory and complementary leadership dynamics in social groups. In a similar vein to heterarchy theorists, Blanton (1998) and others (Blanton et al. 1996; Feinman 1995, 2000) proposed the dual processual model of leadership strategies to avoid the weaknesses of earlier stage-based approaches to leadership and social hierarchy. The dual-processual model shares the heterarchy model's appreciation of the multivalent nature of social power. Both take as their basic assumption that power and leadership may develop simultaneously along different, and at times, contradictory social avenues. The two models do part ways in at least one important respect, namely that the dual processual model expects the 'clustering' of certain types of leadership strategies within particular socioeconomic contexts. Heterarchy theory does not appear as willing to grant as strong an expectation for modalities in political and economic systems. Given the more explicit structural expectations of the dual processual model, I turn my focus to the modalities that the model predicts for tribal contexts.

Expectations of the Dual Processual Model for Tribal Contexts

Though numerous sources of power, economic control, and leadership can co-exist, the dual processual model expects certain suites of social and economic strategies will be found in association with one another. The dual-processual model dif-

ferentiates between suites of strategies associated with the 'corporate' and 'network' modes. The corporate mode emphasizes "staple food production, communal ritual, public construction, shared power, large cooperative labor task, social segments woven together through broad integrative ritual and ideological means, and suppressed economic differentiation" (Feinman 2000:214).

The more exclusionary network mode or strategy often, but not always, is manifested by "greater significance on personal prestige, wealth exchange, individualized power accumulation, elite aggrandizement, lineal patterns of inheritance and descent (e.g., patriarchy), particularizing ideologies, personal networks, princely burials, and the specialized (frequently attached) manufacture of status-related craft goods" (Feinman 2000:214). These are not necessarily all present all of the time, but are modal patterns.

One primary factor differentiating the network and corporate strategies is the degree to which network leadership excludes the involvement of local community members and includes leaders from outside one's descent group. In contrast, the corporate strategy is one in which leaders derive power primarily from one's own local group, and there is less dependence on individual prestige generated by relationships with non-local leaders from other communities. Blanton and others expect there to be a greater reliance on communal architecture in corporate systems. The corporate strategy includes leadership positions in which public architecture is used to organize community labor and resources more commonly than do those individuals in leadership positions in network-based systems. Individualization of power and decision-making roles is less prevalent in corporate systems relative to network systems, largely because descent groups provide the most important sources of labor, authority legitimization, and esoteric knowledge.

In contrast to the corporate system where power comes largely from the collective, network strategies generate leadership and social power through individual-to-individual connections between leaders in other communities or polities. The reproduction of leadership power in network systems relies increasingly on the use of portable wealth and prestige items and there is a decreased emphasis on communal architecture relative to corporate systems of leadership. One key to applying the corporate-network approach is to understand how individuals and groups operate on both the local and regional levels. The corporate strategy stresses interaction and integration of the local community, with group predominance in decision-making. In contrast, network systems focus on production at the local level, but leaders practice expenditure on the regional level. This is 'chief-building' on the regional scale, involving a substantial amount of gifting, visiting, and validation of authority. The network strategy relies on the ability to move high status goods and deposit them in a politic manner with other leaders inside and outside one's own community.

Feinman (2000) has discussed this model with respect to social formations in the American Southwest, emphasizing that the gradient between corporate and network strategies is not meant to replace the focus on hierarchical complexity that forms the basis for Service's distinction between tribe and chiefdom. Instead, the dual processual model emphasizes the degree to which leadership is more or less socially exclusive within the social context. The dimension of exclusivity varies across institutions, as does hierarchy, and the dual processual model attempts to differentiate these two aspects of leadership systems rather than assuming that exclusivity is a direct result of hierarchical complexity.

In the next section I outline one aspect of the dual-processual model that has been used to differentiate corporate and network systems, namely the presence and function of public architectural features. As mentioned above, corporate leadership systems emphasize the construction and use of ritual architecture, particularly for community integrative activities. These integrative spaces tend to be utilized less frequently in network systems, or if they are utilized, the layout and uses of the structures are more socially exclusive relative to the same spaces in corporate systems. The archaeological and ethnographic data on the uses of public architecture within northern Rio Grande puebloan communities has a strong fit with the corporate hierarchy mode of the dual processual model. Possible reasons for the long-term dependence on this strategy are discussed, including the inclusiveness of kin and sodality groups in puebloan societies and abandonment strategies utilized by these same communities through time.

Architecture, Social Strategies and Ancestral Pueblos: A Northern Rio Grande Perspective

Situated in the northeastern reaches of the geographic distribution of Anasazi, or ancestral

Pueblo, settlements, the northern Rio Grande region has attracted many decades of archaeological interest (Bandelier 1890-1892; Jeançon 1929; Wetherington 1968; Crown 1990). As with the rest of the ancestral Pueblo world, changes in the size and composition of prehistoric communities are evident during the later precontact period, roughly A.D. 1200-1600. Major alterations include the adoption of aggregated site layouts, the use of both small and large-scale social integrative public architecture, and an increasing dependence on agricultural strategies that modified the natural landscape.

Of all of the changes experienced by puebloan peoples across the American Southwest, population aggregation had one of the most important impacts on today's archaeological record. The transition from small, dispersed pit houses and scattered surface structures (unit pueblos) to large aggregated villages occurs throughout the ancestral Pueblo world between A.D. 800-1300. The products of the aggregation process are my primary focus here, particularly the manifestation of village aggregation in the vicinity of the modern community of Taos, New Mexico (Fig. 1).

The initial occupation of the Taos area by agrarian populations occurred during the 11th and 12th centuries A.D. Though chronological ambiguities still exist (Cordell 1979; Crown 1990), it appears that nearly all of the settlements occupied prior to A.D. 1200 contain four or fewer pit houses.[1] The little we know about the unit pueblo occupation of the area between about A.D. 1200-1260 indicates these sites contained a single pit structure and a dozen or fewer adobe surface rooms (Jeançon 1929; Morenon 1976). Many of these early pit house and unit pueblo settlements contained subterranean structures that appear to have served as socially integrative, ritual structures, though I have argued that these early forms of public architecture served multiple functions, including residential and ritual uses (Adler 1994).

Prior to the mid-13th century, these early dispersed settlements of the Taos District probably housed at least one nuclear family and as many as several extended families. Each settlement was part of a larger community of many such dispersed settlements. At least two such communities are posited to have existed in the Taos area, one in the northern reaches of the Taos area and a second community to the south of the modern town of Taos (Boyer et al. 1994). It is in this southern community of pit houses and small unit pueblos that we see the founding of Pot Creek Pueblo (LA260), one of the largest aggregated pueblo settlements in the

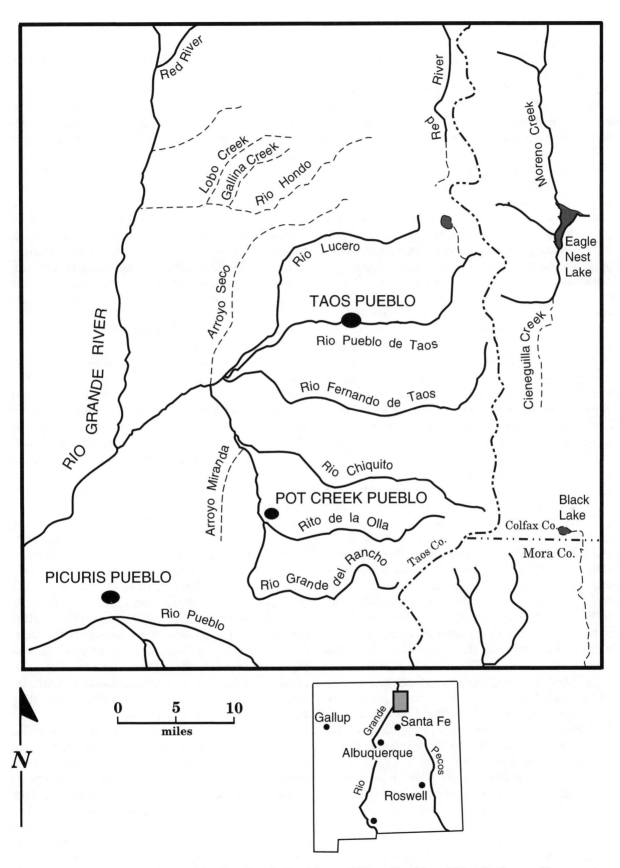

Fig. 1. Location of Picuris Pueblo, Pot Creek Pueblo, and Taos Pueblo within the larger Taos region.

northern Rio Grande region. Archaeological excavations, tree-ring dates, and surface clearing have provided a wealth of information on the growth and subsequent abandonment of this large settlement, and it is to these data that I now turn.

The founding settlement at Pot Creek Pueblo is largely overlain by the later village, but it is likely that agrarian households occupied pit houses on this site as early as the 12th century A.D. The first roomblocks of coursed adobe construction may have been built at the site as early as 1230 A.D., but the first rooms of the latest occupation were constructed between 1260-1270 A.D. Six or more spatially separate roomblocks were built, each with its own small plaza area and subterranean kiva. Construction of surface rooms continued, but significantly fewer building beams were cut and used for construction between about 1285-1300. This late 13th century lull in construction may indicate the stabilization of population levels at the settlement, or possibly even a short-term drop in population (Adler 1997). Recent analyses indicate the construction of 60-70 rooms and 4 kivas can be securely dated to the A.D. 1270-1300 occupation period at the site (Diemond-Arbolino 2001). Given that half of the site remains unexcavated, it is likely that at least double this number of rooms were built in the first half of the site occupation.

A significant period of new construction begins at Pot Creek Pueblo in 1300, continuing through about 1315, when the number of tree-ring dates again drops severely. The resurgence of construction included major changes to the layout of the settlement, most notably the construction of rooms to conjoin previously separate roomblocks. The settlement layout was transformed from a relatively open cluster of roomblocks to an architecturally bounded, less accessible village. The early 14th-century building phase added at least fifty new rooms and two kivas to the pueblo. Doubling this figure brings another 100 hundred rooms to the post-1300 A.D. occupation of the settlement. To date a total of 288 ground-floor rooms have been excavated or exposed. Estimating multiple story architecture of 2-3 stories for at least half the site brings a room total prior to abandonment of approximately 350-400 rooms.

The latest cutting date of 1319 at Pot Creek Pueblo comes from the excavated great kiva. Though we do not have dated materials from approximately half of the site, the large sample of dates from across the site can be more or less taken as representative of the site as a whole. Assuming that some reconstruction and repair is required for the upkeep of multiple-story adobe structure at Pot Creek Pueblo, the lack of cutting dates after this time and absence of ceramics post-dating A.D. 1350 indicate that occupation at the settlement ceased some time between A.D. 1320-1350. A relatively conservative abandonment date of 1330 would place the entire cycle of aggregation, occupation and abandonment at Pot Creek Pueblo within a span of seventy years.

If we are to better understand how tribes act through time and across space, these are the sort of data that can be used to specify the social scale and potential organizational roles of the social 'agents' within ancestral communities. In the following sections I discuss three idealized organizational levels at Pot Creek Pueblo – the household, suprahousehold group, and community – in light of the expectations of the dual-processual model.

Pueblo Household Organization

To deal effectively with the sociopolitical dynamics of tribal communities we need to be sensitive to the scales at which those dynamics are played out. As the minimal social unit within a society, the household is a good place to begin. Wilk and Netting (1984) have argued that because the household does not necessarily correspond cross-culturally with a single definable architectural space, households are best understood as a basic unit of production and reproduction. Fortunately the aggregated nature of ancestral Pueblo settlement makes it likely that households utilized contiguous architectural space for residential and storage space. Ancestral Pueblo household space has been interpreted in various ways at Pot Creek Pueblo (Holschlag 1975; Crown and Kohler 1994; Adler 1997; Diemond-Arbolino 2001). I use several criteria for identifying households, including the location of internal doorways and hatchways connecting rooms within suites of two or more rooms, the presence of hearths and food processing features, and the presence of shared walls that are built in a single construction episode.

Throughout the sample of architectural units for which we have excavated data there is little evidence for differentiation between households based on the size of residential units, effort expenditure on residential features, access to wealth or prestige items, spatial separation of higher-effort architectural units, or any of the other criteria expected within a network leadership strategy. Rather, the patterns are very much in keeping with the low diversity, highly redundant architectural patterns expected of households organized in the corporate leadership mode. Taking individual rooms as a sample, room size averages 9.9 m^2 (s.d. =2.5 m^2) for the entire span of the site occupation. Crown and Kohler (1994:117) document a slight increase in average room size at the site through time (from 9.3 to 11.3 m^2), a trend they attribute to an increased reliance on extended family organization. They also document an increase in the average number of rooms per household (2.6 to 4.7 rooms per household), but this may also be a result of different uses for internal architectural space at the site through time. Dohm (1990) finds a similar trend in average household size in historical pueblos, but attributes this to the need for more privacy and storage space in increasingly crowded village settings. The increase in household size, as measured by room count, may also be a result of changes in the size of groups moving into Pot Creek Pueblo. Crown (1991) argues for a substantial increase in site population after A.D. 1300, coincidentally a time of great population relocation and migration following the abandonment of the Four Corners region.

Though there are changes in the overall layout of household residential space through time, the amount of variability between households remained minimal. In other words, if differential prestige and wealth can be tied to the size, layout, and effort expended on residential architecture (see Netting 1982 for cross-cultural support for these relationships), the housing at Pot Creek Pueblo does not indicate the privileging of one household over others during the occupation span. From these data, the community at Pot Creek Pueblo very clearly followed a corporate strategy, or what Renfrew (1974) earlier identified as a group-oriented political form, in which economic differentiation is suppressed.

Suprahousehold Organization

Compared to households, the suprahousehold scale of organization tends to be much more elusive with respect to the archaeological record. Kin groups, sodalities, and other groupings comprising members from multiple households generally do not occupy a single bounded cluster of structures. Given this caution, it is nonetheless possible to observe at Pot Creek Pueblo, as well as at many other ancestral Pueblo settlements across the Southwest, architectural layouts that purposefully segregated multihousehold residential groups (Adler 1990). At Pot Creek Pueblo there are at least ten roomblocks that are defined by a core set of household units, a relatively well-enclosed plaza space, and a single subterranean kiva (Fig. 2). These roomblocks contain as few as ten rooms and as many as 54 ground-floor rooms, with an average of about 29 rooms per roomblock. As would be expected given site growth data, the roomblocks with the largest number of rooms also have among the longest occupation histories, meaning that architectural accretion has a great deal to do with the variability in the size of the roomblocks.

If we assume that separate roomblocks were founded by groups that may have had some sort of lineal or kin-based corporate identity, it is likely that the sequence of occupation at Pot Creek Pueblo did play into the dynamics of leadership and power within this community. Arrival sequence of clans and other kin groups is a well-established avenue to leadership in the ritual realm among the historic Hopi (Whiteley 1988; Levy 1992), and is also quite common in cross-cultural studies of agrarian communities outside of the American Southwest (Adler 1996).

Despite the potential for economic differentiation between the residents of earlier established roomblocks and those in the later roomblocks, again there is a lack of any significant differences in room size, distribution of extralocal ceramics or other special economic goods between roomblock units at Pot Creek Pueblo. Any significant differences would provide support for the presence of a network-based leadership strategy that might have been utilized at Pot Creek Pueblo. But as with the household data, the suprahousehold residential units also appear to more closely fit the expectations of the corporate hierarchy strategy.

The importance of the corporate strategy for organizing suprahousehold hierarchies is all the more interesting in light of the one possible pattern that distinguishes roomblock architectural layout at Pot Creek Pueblo, namely the association of subterranean kivas with those roomblocks established early in the site occupation. Of the six roomblocks with well-dated contexts, two roomblocks (1 and 4) were built largely after A.D. 1300, and each lacks an architecturally enclosed plaza and kiva. The three roomblocks with the longest occupation history (2, 3, 6) all have enclosed plazas and kivas. There are very few cutting dates from roomblock 5, but samples from both the kiva and one surface room date between A.D. 1280-1300, fitting the pattern set by the other three well-dated roomblocks that also have enclosed plazas and a kiva.

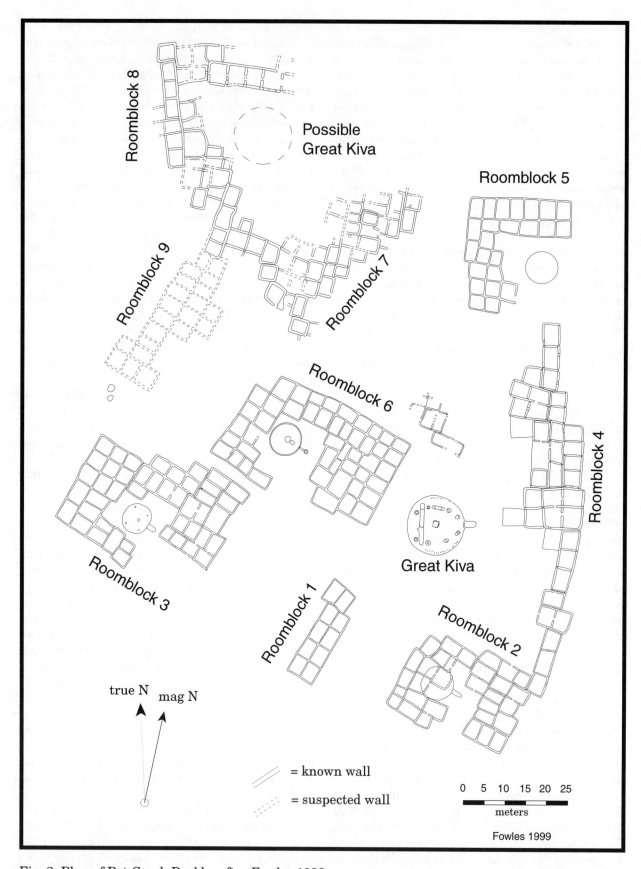

Fig. 2. Plan of Pot Creek Pueblo, after Fowles 1999.

Corporate Architecture and Social Integration

This patterning approximates Feinman's (2000:216) expectations regarding corporate hierarchies among historic and pre-contact period puebloan social contexts. These findings also match up well with recent applications of the dual-processual model and other newer models of leadership strategies to archaeological data from the American Southwest (Mills 2000). Corporate hierarchies tend to emphasize public architecture and monumental ritual spaces, places where power can be embedded in social contexts through group association and affiliation. Kivas serve this function throughout ethnographically recorded Pueblo societies, and I have argued that this was much the same with precontact kivas (Adler 1994). Ritual and socially integrative architecture such as kivas are those parts of the built environment that serve as the context for group-oriented integrative performance, storage of ritual items, and meetings, to name a few important functions. In the ethnographic record, such architecture is relatively abundant throughout politically nonstratified societies. Fortunately for the archaeologist, there is cross-cultural variability in the scale of ritual integrative facility size, use, and clientele (Adler 1989). I use the term 'low-level' to refer to those facilities that serve to integrate only a portion of a community. I would include the smaller kivas at Pot Creek Pueblo and structures of similar scale at other ancestral Pueblos across the northern Southwest in this class of integrative facility. 'High-level' facilities are utilized for social activities involving larger groups from multiple low-level facilities. Often the high-level facilities integrate an entire community. Cross-cultural data support a strong correlation between the population size of the group using the integrative facility and the floor area of the facility. This relationship is the strongest for the low-level integrative facilities in my cross-cultural sample, which vary in floor area between 20 and 60 square meters. The use group associated with these facilities range between 25 and 75 people, close to the estimated average population for a single roomblock at Pot Creek Pueblo. The small roomblock kivas at Pot Creek Pueblo fall right into the middle of the cross-cultural scattergram with 30-40 m^2 of floor space (Adler 1994). Relatedly, I would expect such facilities to be the integrative focus of smaller subsets of the community population. I am not proposing that each small kiva at Pot Creek Pueblo served only the inhabitants of the roomblock surrounding each kiva since kin and sodality group membership are not necessarily correlated with single architectural units in tribal or other societies. As proposed below, sponsorship of kivas may well be through an individual or household associated with that roomblock, but group membership is not necessarily coincident with proximity to each of these structures.

Going Up: The Scale of the Tribal Community

The highest level of social integration I consider here is the community. While this does not obviate the possibility of multi-community levels of organizational complexity in tribal societies (see Spielmann 1994 for a consideration of this topic), the community is consistently the highest level of social and political integration within tribal societies (Adler 1990). By community I refer to a spatially localized group of people who share a common identity and set of rules for determining and defending their rights and identities vis-à-vis other localized groups. Among tribal groups the community often occupies a single, large village, as with Pot Creek Pueblo, but there are many examples of locally disaggregated communities comprising many dispersed households. Given the potential for corporate and network hierarchies within and between Pueblo communities, we need to assess the degree to which leadership strategies may have shaped the local and regional political realms across this small corner of the ancestral Pueblo world.

Criteria for identifying community hierarchies include significant differences in settlement size within contemporaneous clusters of aggregated settlements, the unequal distribution of community-level ritual integrative architecture, and the differential distribution of prestige goods between communities (Blanton et al. 1996). Any consideration of site size hierarchies is not presently possible for the Taos region given that there were only two aggregated pueblos besides Pot Creek Pueblo with occupations dating to the 13th and 14th centuries, namely Picuris Pueblo and Cornfield Taos (located near modern Taos Pueblo). Excavations at Picuris Pueblo focused primarily on post-14th century architectural contexts (Adler and Dick 1999), and no excavations have been allowed in architectural contexts at Taos Pueblo or its earlier component at Cornfield Taos. Differential access to prestige goods is similarly impossible to assess. The only avenue to understanding community organizational dynamics rests again with public architecture. Large kivas with several times the floor area of small plaza kivas were uncovered at both Picuris Pueblo and Pot Creek Pueblo. The single large kiva (Kiva 1) at Pot Creek Pueblo (Fig. 2) contained floor features that set it apart from the smaller kivas, including floor vaults and possible internal wall alignments (Wetherington 1968). Floor vaults were found in the partially excavated large kiva at Picuris (Dick et al. 1999). Interestingly, both Pot Creek Pueblo and Picuris Pueblo show evidence of a second large kiva (Figs. 2 and 3), indicating that paired community-level public architectural features may have been present in these Pueblo communities.

Ethnographically recorded tribal communities commonly, but certainly not always, build or set aside space for community-level integrative ritual structures, and these spaces pattern with use group size. Floor areas of high-level integrative facilities generally range between 100–300 m², similar to the large kivas at Pot Creek Pueblo (105 m²) and Picuris (135 m²). Cross-cultural surveys indicate that community-level integrative facilities are generally utilized by groups ranging from 250 to 600 people, well within the size range of both of these Pueblo settlements. Moiety organization is one possible explanation for these large structures, another expectation of the corporate hierarchy strategy as outlined in the dual-processual model of organizational complexity.

Kivas and Clout: Explaining Corporate Strategies in the northern Rio Grande

There is abundant evidence that the organization of leadership and power at Pot Creek Pueblo, the best-recorded ancestral Pueblo community in the Taos region, appears to approximate the 'corporate hierarchy' mode as defined by Blanton, Feinman and others. Network hierarchical systems integrate leadership from outside one's own community. Leaders look to power partnerships that move prestige between increasingly smaller numbers of individuals situated in more distinct localities. Whether one considers artifacts, settlement layout, domestic or public architecture, there is no evidence of network hierarchical system dynamics in the archaeological remains at Pot Creek Pueblo. Corporate strategies situate power in segmentally organized corporate groups. In all the contexts available for analysis at Pot Creek Pueblo, including the organization of social groupings, spatial size and association of public architecture, redun-

dancy in household size and architectural features, and minimal variability in other indicators of economic differentiation, the primacy of the group over the individual is consistent throughout.

This, I would argue, is a very promising *beginning* for our improved understanding of leadership and power relations within prehistoric contexts such as those discussed above. Yet after all is said and done, we are still left with the *classification* of Pot Creek Pueblo as another fine example of a corporate hierarchy. Many questions still remain. How did group interests continue above that of potentially self-interested leadership? What short- and long-term dynamics within these communities accord privilege to some groups over the interests of other groups and individuals?

Approaches to these questions can be sought in the archaeological contexts, those same data sets that supply us with the patterning to discriminate between corporate and network hierarchies. As archaeologists we rely on the durability of architecture to indicate how and when people built these bounded features. At the same time, the longevity of these same contexts can inform on the dynamics of leadership and control within past social systems. Architectural features commonly require labor coordination above the individual and household level, again requiring social negotiation and interdependence. The construction of durable walls and roofs also supports and reproduces concepts of ownership and control, often on an intergenerational time scale. In other words, the physical creations we call architecture are both profoundly physical and socially active aspects of the community landscape.

Let's go back to our consideration of kivas and public architecture at Pot Creek Pueblo. As mentioned above, it is possible that the association of the small kivas with surface residential architecture may be indicative of differential control over ritual architecture by those corporate groups with the deepest history of occupation at Pot Creek Pueblo. At the same time, however, kivas are anything but static ritual integrative facilities. In fact, there are intriguing patterns related to the construction, repair, and subsequent disuse of kivas at Pot Creek Pueblo, some of which may point to generational changes in kiva use and identity at the site. These patterns are informed by ethnographic observations of kiva construction, sponsorship, and corporate group identity at Picuris Pueblo. Taken as a whole these archaeological and ethnographic data point to a corporate hierarchy strategy that incorporates community-level con-

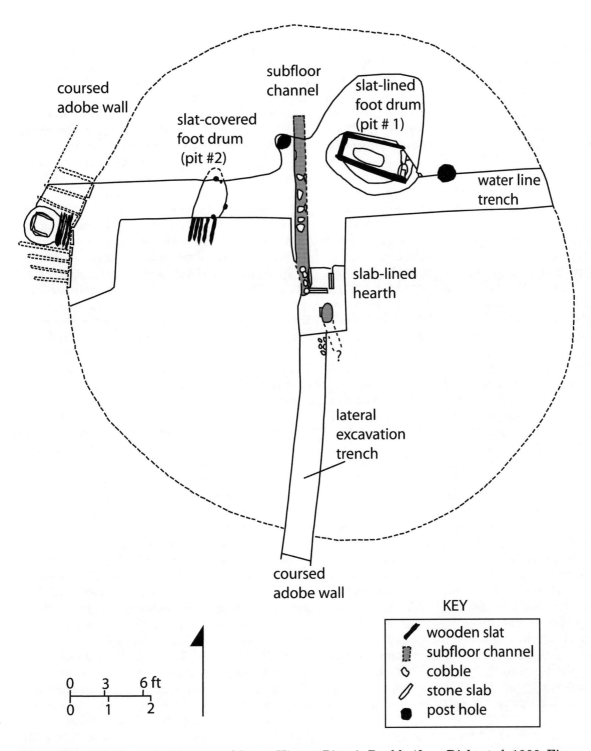

Fig. 3. Kiva M, a Partially Excavated Large Kiva at Picuris Pueblo (from Dick, et al. 1999: Figure 4.11). Used with permission of Michael Adler and the Clements Center for Southwest Studies.

trol over important ritual spaces to the extent that individual or household control of these contexts is effectively leveled out on the intergenerational temporal scale.

First, a consideration of temporal trends in kiva construction and abandonment at Pot Creek Pueblo. Not all small kivas remained in use throughout the occupation of the settlement. From tree-ring data, we find that the kiva in roomblock 2 was constructed between A.D. 1260-1280, but was filled in and built over approximately 20 years later. Once the kiva was filled in, additional rooms were built over the remains of the structure, and the surrounding surface rooms of roomblock 2 continued to be occupied. The kivas in roomblocks 3 and 6 were also constructed early in the site occupation, prior to 1280. The roomblock 6 kiva was completely refurbished in about 1306 A.D. through the construction of a new floor, replacement of the roof support beams, and a repaired roof. The kiva on roomblock 3 was remodeled during the 1280s and again after about 1300. There is insufficient data to discuss the kiva on roomblock 5.

Remodeling episodes approximately every two decades have already been proposed for surface architectural units at the site. In her consideration of the surface architecture at Pot Creek Pueblo, Patricia Crown argues for episodes of repair and upkeep of the adobe surface architecture about every 19 years. Crown points out that this periodicity in rebuilding might be related to the inherent instability of earthen architecture. Crown goes on to propose that this periodicity might also be conditioned by generational changes at the household level within this settlement. Archaeological evidence from other 14th century pueblos outside of the Taos area indicates a life expectancy of 30-40 years. Over the course of an average lifespan, then, individuals who survive to marriageable age (17 years old) might presumably build a new household. Life expectancy beyond that point would be an additional 13 to 23 years (Crown 1991:305). In other words, construction and repair may be associated with what Goody (1958) and others described as the household 'domestic cycle'. There is no method to differentiate between the relative influence of architectural instability and domestic cycles since these are not mutually exclusive processes. For the sake of argument here I assume that domestic cycles do play at least some role in the periodicity of repair episodes at Pot Creek Pueblo.

Repair cycles of 19 years are based on the sample of surface architecture at Pot Creek, spaces most often associated with household domestic space. Yet my analysis of kiva architecture at the site indicates a similar temporal span of about 20 years separates events of kiva construction, repair, and abandonment. The question then, is why a 'domestic cycle' of modifications should also characterize those facilities that we characterize as 'suprahousehold' in identity, function, and control?

One possibility is that while public integrative facilities such as the kiva are identified with group activity and public functions, the actual construction and upkeep may be 'sponsored' at the individual or household level. This is the sort of potential contradiction expected in both the heterarchy and dual processual models, and so deserves specific attention to dynamics and detail.

In the next section I present ethnographic information from Picuris Pueblo that provides support for this assertion, elaborating our understanding of the social dynamics associated with generational sponsorship of kivas and public architecture that is germane to our discussion of leadership and hierarchy. The following example is presented more as an illustration of how social control of important ritual contexts is manifested in corporate hierarchies, of which Picuris is a good example, rather than as a direct historical analogy for how public architecture was utilized in Pot Creek Pueblo.

Leadership, Historical Contingency, and Ritual Space: The Lesson of Picuris

Nearly forty years ago Donald Brown conducted ethnographic research as part of an archaeological project at Picuris Pueblo directed by Herbert Dick (Brown 1972; 1999). Brown's elderly informants identified five major ritual structures at Picuris that were in use at the beginning of the 20th century. These included one circular surface structure (the Round House) and four subterranean kivas (Fig. 4), each of which had a unique history and individual custodian. For example, until 1940 the Round House was used for a series of three summer rain dances conducted by different ceremonial organizations. During the use life of the structure, the Round House was 'owned' by the head of the Summer People, a ceremonial organization. Ownership, in this sense, is better understood as 'sponsorship'. In other words, Round House use, maintenance, and access rights were all dictated by the eldest member of the Summer People. At the same time, sponsorship of these special facilities was anything but static within Picuris society. In the case of the Round House, sponsorship was active as long as Round House ceremonies remained part of the Summer People's ritual responsibilities. When the summer rain ceremonials were discontinued in the 1940s, the control and sponsorship of the Round House reverted to the entire community of Picuris. Based on the community consensus at that time, the Round House was

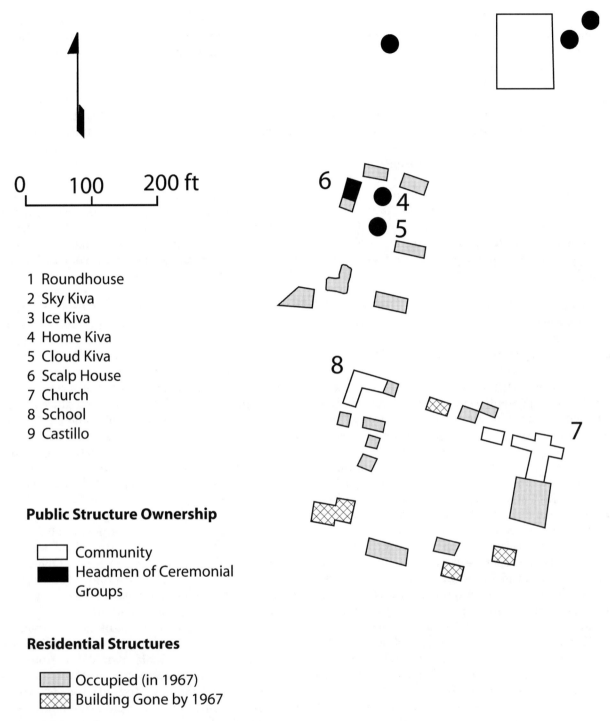

1 Roundhouse
2 Sky Kiva
3 Ice Kiva
4 Home Kiva
5 Cloud Kiva
6 Scalp House
7 Church
8 School
9 Castillo

Public Structure Ownership

☐ Community
■ Headmen of Ceremonial
Groups

Residential Structures

▦ Occupied (in 1967)
▧ Building Gone by 1967

Fig. 4. Public Architecture at Picuris Pueblo (from Brown 1999:figure 3.2). Used with permission of Michael Adler and Clements Center for Southwest Studies.

subsequently removed from use and ceased to play an active part of the community's ritual architectural realm.

Other ritual architectural features at Picuris were subject to much the same system of sponsor-ship and corporate group control during the use life of each structure. For instance, Sky Place and Cloud Place kivas functioned as moiety kivas. Sky Place kiva was controlled by the headman of the South-side Moiety, but was no longer in use by 1964-5 when Brown was conducting his field research. Cloud Place kiva was controlled by the son of the last leader of the Northside Moiety. After the abandonment of the Sky Place kiva, the Cloud Place kiva was used by both moieties for any large-scale rituals. At the end of its use life, control of the Sky Place kiva reverted from the Southside moiety to the entire Picuris community. The third kiva, Ice Place, was controlled by the headman of the Winter People, a ceremonial organization that ceased using the kiva after the 1950's. The fourth kiva, Home Place, was owned by the cacique, or ceremonial leader, of Picuris, and was used for the meetings of the elder council of Picuris. Upon the death of the cacique in 1967, Home Place kiva, along with the Sky Place and Ice Place kivas, reverted to community property.

There is no information on actual repair episodes associated with the kivas, but these anecdotal cases clearly indicate that the disuse of these ritual structures often coincided with the life histories of corporate group leaders. During the leader's life the control and upkeep of the facilities was identified with the leader, but only as long as the leader represented the interests of the moiety, medicine society, or other corporate group. Most anthropologists studying tribal societies observe that, as at Picuris Pueblo, leadership and control are often situationally contingent, depending on context and constituency. At Picuris, as important sponsorships of sodality and moiety kivas lapsed, or ceremonies stopped being performed, these important ritual contexts reverted to community property. Control was not immediately co-opted by another tribal corporate group. Instead, control of the structure and space was renegotiated at the community level. The unique nature of these social segments dampens processes of political consolidation and bureaucratic specialization.

Notice also that the Picuris system explicitly decouples ritual space and individual personage. Though sponsorship of ritual space construction and use rested with individuals, each of these leaders drew their influence from their leadership roles in various social groups. These leaders could pass their mantle of power on to others within their corporate group, but at the most basic level the ritual facilities were under the sponsorship of that structural segment of the larger community. Significant changes in the control of ritual facilities generally resulted in those facilities reverting to the control of the entire community. At Picuris, an ambiguity in terms of ritual structure use results in the control of that space flowing up the organizational scale to the community, not down to individuals. Under these circumstances there is little opportunity for an individual to pass on the control of these facilities to other individuals since control always defaults to the more inclusive social level. Feinman and others note the importance of social inclusivity within systems of corporate hierarchy. In contrast, network hierarchy relies upon the ability of leaders to exclude others from important ritual and residential contexts (Feinman 2000). Ancestral Pueblo societies invested significant time and effort in the creation of ritual architecture and significant places. At the same time, though, the importance of these spaces appears to have been situational and their duration relatively short-lived, both organizational characteristics of tribal societies as defined by others.

A final anecdote from Picuris emphasizes the contingent nature of leadership, architecture, and change in a tribal community. In 1963, excavations at Picuris by Herbert Dick exposed a kiva (Kiva D) that, based on ceramic seriation, had been abandoned during the early 18th century (Dick, et al 1999:68). Rather than being transferred to community property, which would have allowed the structure to be reassigned or abandoned and allowed to decompose, Kiva D was 'erased' from the community ritual realm. First, all of the important ceremonial wall niches, into and out of which prayers and powers flow, were filled with plaster. The central hearth was filled, and the ventilator shaft was plugged. The structure was then purposefully burned. Herbert Dick never got the full story for the abandonment of this place, still referred to as the "Cochiti Witch Kiva." One elder mentioned that the structure had to be "killed" because of its association with a non-Picuris person who was accused of witchcraft.

Anecdotal, yes, but this also illustrates another dynamic in corporate hierarchies that diminishes the capacity for individuals or small kin groups to control ritual space to the exclusion of other groups. Corporate ritual space, vested with the identity of multi-household groups, may have commonly been destroyed by those same groups to prevent unauthorized access by potentially dangerous outsiders (Adler 1994). Such a practice would diminish the long-term control of ritual spaces by individuals or kin groups simply because of the built-in obsolescence in the structure itself.

These strategies of power-sharing and power-limitation among tribal segments still allow hierarchy because not all groups share the same history of immigration and land use in a settlement or region. At Pot Creek Pueblo and other communities these differing group histories may have influenced the differential distribution of ritual space across the settlement. While unequal access to ritual space may have supported ritual imbalances between corporate groups during the occupation of the settlement, opposing dynamics may also have served to redistribute and mute long-term control and exclusivity of important spaces and leadership contexts. The power of corporate groups may have been kept in check by other competing groups through a number of structural dynamics. For instance, the architectural layout of the settlement appears to be the product of institutional redundancy, so there were probably multiple corporate groups vying for influence within the community. In addition, as exemplified by the case of the Picuris kivas, ritual spaces and leadership roles at Pot Creek Pueblo have reverted to the community level with each transition in the use of ritual space or the roles associated with those spaces. At least in the case of Picuris this dynamic forces the constant renegotiation of roles and power within the community. Such a dynamic is less dominant in network systems wherein heritability and passage of power is manifested at the community and intercommunity levels, but the actual lines of heritability are already determined. In other words, spaces and power are vested in families or other more exclusive groupings. Negotiation is not on the community level, but is already decided.

The modal patterns of corporate organizational and hierarchy do show up in the archaeological record of architectural contexts. At Pot Creek Pueblo there is a strong pattern of redundancy in the location and size of ritual spaces, a good indicator that power is not yet restricted to one or a few lines of social transmission. Ritual spaces in corporate systems, because of the redundancy, tend not to be temporally long-lived. At Picuris, Pot Creek Pueblo, and other puebloan settlements, ritual architecture is used and abandoned, replaced by other spaces as the negotiation between and within corporate groups continues through the history of each community. In contrast, ritual spaces associated with network systems are often long-lived, increasingly separated from the residential sectors of the community, and are often associated with the residences of the increasingly socially differentiated leaders of the community.

Analysis of architectural space does hold out promise for better understanding the dynamics of how corporate hierarchies may, over time, become more network-oriented. At Pot Creek Pueblo and

Picuris we see temporal and spatial limitations in the use of public architecture. Kivas do not appear to have been constructed in association with all residential roomblocks, and it may have been those residential groupings with the longest tenure at the site that controlled these smaller integrative facilities. At the same time, the relatively short duration of individual and corporate control of these spaces, basically at the generational scale, may well be one dynamic that generates the variability that we perceive over the 'longue durée' as flexibility. What this comes down to is a renewed consideration of the wonderful strategic role played by 'leveling devices' within tribal societies. Sahlins (1968) and others focused on leveling devices because, as they rightly pointed out, there is nothing inherent in human societies that drives humans to hierarchical organization. Equality, like inequality, is manufactured through the dependence on various strategies that operate on daily, annual, and intergenerational time scales.

Conclusions

Archaeological explanations of past social organizational strategies always rest in part on classificatory categories. The social organizational strategies that we crystallize in our theories and terminologies are necessarily simplified caricatures of ever dynamic social contexts. These 'shorthand' descriptions of dynamic contexts should, in the best of all worlds, be equally applicable to the archaeological records of the Anasazi, the Hopewell, and the Natufian. Any understanding of the common co-occurrence of social structures, relationships, and political roles should begin with some sort of classification and subdivision of cross-cultural and archaeological examples, but should certainly not end there. Typologies are generally good to 'think with', but variability has to be explained according to dynamics that rest outside the statics of the typology. The crux of the problem with typologies of social complexity derives from the confounding of description and explanation.

But we know that archaeological explanation does not exist in the best of all worlds, it creates scenarios of past worlds based upon limited data and derived interpretations. The conundrum that faces those studying 'middle range' or 'tribal' societies derives from the realization that we're trying to define an enigma that is understood not only by what it has contributed to the archaeological record, but also by what is absent in its material remains. Like Alice's Cheshire cat, the archaeological remains

169

of a 'tribal society' sometimes contains the corporeal outline of an entirely coherent societal body. Sometimes those remains tease us with only a small component of that body.

We have archaeological and ethnographic data that are relevant to our search for the foundations of social, political, and economic inequality, those processes of change that transform 'middle range' societies into increasingly complex and hierarchical social formations. I have focused on the role of public, ritually integrative architecture, arguing that the use-lives, distribution, number, and abandonment modes of these spaces do inform on how the processes through which power and leadership are reproduced, elaborated, and muted within the various organizational contexts of puebloan communities.

At first blush, the differentiation of leadership strategies into 'corporate' and 'network' organizations appears to be simply another typology, dichotomizing ethnographic and archaeological case studies into two types of leadership systems rather than Service's four types or Fried's tripartite typology. Dual-processual theorists steadfastly argue that they are not providing yet another societal typology (see Feinman 2000:213), nor do they want to diminish the importance of understanding the role of hierarchical complexity in social systems. The dimensions described above for the corporate and network strategies are best understood, they argue, as continuous, and various aspects of each dimension may coexist within any particular social context depending on the scale of the social field under scrutiny. The focus is on defining various avenues along which power can be manipulated and created, with an explicit move away from unilineal or unidimensional frameworks for explaining social organizational systems. In other words, Blanton and others recognize co-occurrence of various modes of social, economic, and leadership strategies, but neither the corporate nor network strategy requires each of these strategic modes for its use as a heuristic classification of a leadership system.

I do agree that the dual-processual model and similar approaches contained within the heterarchy model leave open the possibility that tribal social contexts can manifest aspects of both inclusive and exclusive (corporate and network) leadership systems. The dual processual and heterarchy models seek to avoid the pitfalls of assigning labels of 'egalitarian' or 'hierarchical' to prehistoric social organizational systems. But like their intellectual forebearers, each of these models still re-mains a descriptive framework that is susceptible to the same criticisms levied against the stage-based typologies. Models only reach explanatory goals when we can propose causal links between the criteria that define whether, for example, we are looking at a network or corporate leadership system. Proposing these links, then, remains the real challenge for those seeking to explain the modalities in the organizational strategies of both past and present societies.

Notes

[1] One possible exception is the El Pueblito site near Arroyo Seco (Boyer and Mick-O'Hara 1991).

References Cited

Adler, Michael
1989 Ritual Facilities and Social Integration in Nonranked Societies, in *The Archaeology of Social Integration in the Prehistoric Pueblos*, edited by William Lipe and Michelle Hegmon, pp. 35-52. Crow Canyon Publications in Archaeology, no. 1. Cortez, CO
1990 Communities of Soil and Stone: An Archaeological Investigation of Population Aggregation among the Mesa Verde Anasazi, A.D. 900-1300. Unpublished Ph.D. dissertation, University of Michigan, Ann Arbor.
1994 Why is a Kiva? New Interpretations of Prehistoric Social Integrative Architecture in the Northern Rio Grande Region of New Mexico. *Journal of Anthropological Research* 49(4):18-27.
1996 Fathoming the Scale of Mesa Verde Region Communities. In *Interpreting Southwest Diversity: Underlying Principles and Overarching Patterns*, edited by Paul Fish and J. Jefferson Reid, pp. 22-40. Arizona State University Anthropological Papers, Tempe.
1997 Report of Excavations at Pot Creek Pueblo, 1996 Field Season. Report on file, Fort Burgwin Research Center, Ranchos de Taos, NM.
Adler, Michael A., and Herbert W. Dick (editors)
1999 *Picuris Pueblo Through Time: Eight Centuries of Change at a Northern Rio Grande Pueblo.* Clements Center for

Southwest Studies, Southern Methodist University, Dallas.

Bandelier, Adolph F.
1890-2 Final Report of Investigations Among the Indians of the Southwestern United States. Pts. 1&2. Papers of the Archaeological Institute of America, American Series, Cambridge.

Blanton, Richard
1998 Beyond Centralization: Steps Toward a Theory of Egalitarian Behavior in Archaic States. In *Archaic States*, edited by Gary Feinman and Joyce Marcus, pp. 135-72. School of American Research Press, Santa Fe, NM.

Blanton, Richard E., Gary M. Feinman, Stephen A. Kowalewski, and Peter N. Peregrine
1996 A Dual-Processual Model for the Evolution of Mesoamerican Civilization. *Current Anthropology* 37:1-14.

Blumenschien, Helen
1956 Excavations in the Taos Area, 1953-1955. *El Palacio* 65(3):107-111.

Boyer, Jeffrey, and Linda Mick-O'Hara
1991 Excavation of a Human Burial at the El Pueblito site, LA 12741, Taos County, New Mexico. *Archaeology Notes* 29, Office of Archaeological Studies, Museum of New Mexico, Santa Fe.

Boyer, Jeffrey L., James L. Moore, Daisy F. Levine, Linda Mick-O'Hara, and Mollie S. Toll
1994 Studying the Taos Frontier: The Pot Creek Data Recovery Project (2 vols.). *Archaeology Notes* 68, Museum of New Mexico, Office of Archaeological Studies, Santa Fe.

Cordell, Linda
1979 *A Cultural Resources Overview of the Middle Rio Grande Valley*. USDA Forest Service, Southwestern Region, Albuquerque.

Crown, Patricia
1990 The Chronology of the Taos Area Anasazi. In *Clues to the Past: Papers in Honor of William M. Sundt*, edited by Meliha Duran and David Kirkpatrick. *Papers of the Archaeological Society of New Mexico*, no. 16, Albuquerque.
1991 Evaluating the Construction Sequence and Population of Pot Creek Pueblo, Northern New Mexico. *American Antiquity* 56(2):291-314.

Crown, Patricia L., and Timothy A. Kohler
1994 Community Dynamics, Site Structure, and Aggregation in the Northern Rio Grande. In *The Ancient Southwestern Community: Models and Methods for the Study of Prehistoric Social Organization*, edited by W. H. Wills and Robert D. Leonard, pp. 103-117. University of New Mexico Press, Albuquerque.

Crumley, Carole
1979 Three Locational Models: An Epistemological Assessment for Anthropology and Archaeology. In *Advances in Archaeological Method and Theory*, vol. 2, edited by Michael B. Schiffer, pp. 141-73. Academic Press, New York.
1995 Heterarchy and the Analysis of Complex Societies. In *Heterarchy and the Analysis of Complex Societies*, edited by Robert M. Ehrenreich, Carole L. Crumley, and Janet E. Levy, pp. 1-5. Archaeological Papers of the American Anthropological Association no. 6. Washington, D.C.

Crumley, Carole L., and William H. Marquardt
1987 Regional Dynamics in Burgundy. In *Regional Dynamics: Burgundian Landscapes*, edited by Carole L. Crumley and William H. Marquardt, pp. 609-23. Academic Press, New York.

Dick, Herbert W., Daniel Wolfman, Curtis Schaafsma, and Michael Adler
1999 Prehistoric and Early Historic Architecture and Ceramics at Picuris. In *Picuris Pueblo Through Time: Eight Centuries of Change at a Northern Rio Grande Pueblo*, pp. 42-100. Clements Center for Southwest Studies, Southern Methodist University, Dallas.

Diemond-Arbolino, Risa
2001 Agricultural Strategies and Labor Organization: An Ethnohistoric Approach to the Study of Prehistoric Farming Systems in the Taos Area of Northern New Mexico. Unpublished Ph.D. dissertation, Department of Anthropology, Southern Methodist University.

Dohm, Karen
1990 Effects of Population Nucleation on House Size of Pueblos in the American Southwest. *Journal of Anthropological Archaeology* 9:201-239.

Dunnell, Robert
1982 Science, Social Science and Common Sense: The Agonizing Dilemma of Modern Archaeology. *Journal of Anthropological Research* 38:1-25.

Feinman, Gary
  1995 The Emergence of Inequality: A Focus on Strategies and Processes. In *Foundations of Inequality*, edited by T. Douglas Price and Gary M. Feinman, pp. 255-79. Plenum Press, New York.
  2000 Dual-Processual Theory and Social Formations in the Southwest. In *Alternative Leadership Strategies in the Prehispanic Southwest*, edited by Barbara J. Mills, pp. 207-224. University of Arizona Press, Tucson.
Fried, Morton H.
  1967 *The Evolution of Political Society: An Essay in Political Anthropology*. Random House, New York.
Goody, J. (editor)
  1958 *The Developmental Cycle in Domestic Groups*. Cambridge University Press, Cambridge.
Holschlag, Stephanie
  1975 Pot Creek Pueblo and the Question of Prehistoric Northern Tiwa Household Configuration. Unpublished Ph.D. dissertation, Dept. of Anthropology, Washington State University, Pullman.
Jeançon, J. A.
  1929 Excavations in the Taos Valley, New Mexico during 1920. *Smithsonian Miscellaneous Collections* 81:12.
Kintigh, Keith
  2000 Leadership Strategies in Protohistoric Zuni Towns. In *Alternative Leadership Strategies in the Prehispanic Southwest*, edited by Barbara J. Mills, pp. 95-116. University of Arizona Press, Tucson.
Levy, Jerrold E.
  1992 *Orayvi Revisited: Social Stratification in an "Egalitarian" Society*. School of American Research Press, Santa Fe.
Mills, Barbara J. (editor)
  2000 *Alternative Leadership Strategies in the Prehispanic Southwest*. University of Arizona Press, Tucson.
Morenon, Pierre
  1976 The Evaluation of Predictive Models and Inferences about Human Behavior. Manuscript on file, Fort Burgwin Research Center, Ranchos de Taos, NM.
Netting, Robert
  1982 Some Home Truths on Household Size and Wealth. *American Behavioral Scientist* 25:641-62.

Rautman, Alison
  1998 Hierarchy and Heterarchy in the American Southwest: A Comment on McGuire and Saitta. *American Antiquity* 63:325-33.
Renfrew, Colin
  1974 Beyond a Subsistence Economy: The Evolution of Social Organization in Prehistoric Europe. In *Reconstructing Complex Societies: An Archaeological Colloquium*, edited by Charlotte B. Moore, pp. 69-95. Supplement to the American School of Oriental Research, no. 20, Cambridge.
Sahlins, Marshall
  1963 Poor Man, Rich Man, Big-Man, Chief: Political Types in Melanesia and Polynesia. *Comparative Studies in Sociology and History* 5:285-303.
  1968 *Tribesmen*. Prentice-Hall, New York.
Sahlins, Marshall, and E. Service (editors)
  1960 *Evolution and Culture*. University of Michigan Press, Ann Arbor.
Service, Elman
  1971 *Primitive Social Organization: An Evolutionary Perspective, 2nd ed.* Random House, New York.
Spielmann, Katherine
  1994 Clustered Confederacies: Sociopolitical Organization in the Protohistoric Rio Grande. In *The Ancient Southwestern Community: Models and Methods for the Study of Prehistoric Social Organization*, edited by W. H. Wills and Robert D. Leonard, pp. 45-54. University of New Mexico Press, Albuquerque.
Wetherington, Ronald K.
  1968 Excavations at Pot Creek Pueblo. Fort Burgwin Research Center Report No. 6. Fort Burgwin Research Center, Ranchos de Taos, N.M.
Whiteley, Peter
  1988 *Deliberate Acts: Changing Hopi Culture Through the Oraibi Split*. University of Arizona Press, Tucson.
Wilk, Richard and Robert Netting
  1984 Households: Changing Forms and Functions. In *Households: Comparative and Historical Studies of the Domestic Group*, edited by R. McC. Netting, R. R. Wilk, and E. J. Arnould, pp. 1-28. University of California Press, Berkeley.
Woosley, Anne I.
  1986 Puebloan Prehistory of the Northern Rio Grande: Settlement, Population, Subsistence. *Kiva* 51(3):143-164.

10. Fractal Archaeology: Intra-Generational Cycles and the Matter of Scale, an Example from the Central Plains

Donald J. Blakeslee

Abstract

In this paper, I examine culturally specific cycles including the annual round, the swidden cycle and household fissioning to illuminate a portion of the archaeological record from the Central Plains of North America. My examples are drawn from the Central Plains Mosaic, a set of archaeological phases that date between A.D. 1000 and 1400. The patterning in this archaeological record reflects the intersection of cultural cycles and natural processes at a variety of scales, from intra-site to regional. The record of intra-generational cycles is read quite easily; records of the structural organization of these societies is far more difficult. Analysis of the record in terms of cycles is new, and new avenues for research are illuminated.

Introduction

Imagine that you are viewing a giant mural. At a distance, you see a cohesive image, but as you draw closer, the individual tiles that comprise that image become noticeable. As you draw still nearer you notice that the individual tiles of this particular mural are not uniform, but that some of them are patterned. So you draw even closer, where you discover that the patterned tiles are themselves images. Intrigued, you advance still further, only to discover that the patterned tiles are themselves murals, made up of smaller tesserae. Do you dare draw closer still, to discover that this next level of tiles are patterned, too, and that they are composed of still smaller images? And what if you back away from the original image to find that it comprises a single tile in a larger pattern? And so on ad infinitum.

Fractal images "are characterized by the coexistence of distinctive features of every conceivable linear size . . . ." (Mandelbrot 1982:C16). Such images are generated by recursive mathematical functions. Parts of a fractal image are independent of scale, a phenomenon called scale invariance. That is, a magnified piece of the image looks like the whole image. But this is not always the case, either in the realm of images generated on a computer by a mathematical function or in nature. A fractal image is not absolutely uniform, so that different parts of the larger pattern look quite different from one another (cf. the images in Pielgen and Richter 1986). There are also limits to the fractal nature of natural objects, as "no real structure can be magnified repeatedly an infinite number of times and still look the same" (Pielgen and Richter 1986:5).

In this paper, I argue that the archaeological record is fractal in nature and that analysis reveals different patterns at different scales. The patterns within patterns are, like fractals, the products of recursive phenomena. These phenomena are the subject of this volume—the cycles that exist at various temporal scales in tribal societies. Viewing the archaeological record in terms of the cycles that exist at various temporal scales is a new approach, and one measure of its productivity consists of the new research questions it generates. I highlight some new questions in the pages that follow.

One of the properties of the archaeological record that makes it so difficult to read is that it is the product of not just one recursive function but of many cycles operating at the same time and at different spatio-temporal scales. Understanding of the cycles visible to ethnographers, however, provides the archaeologist with keys to understanding the palimpsest of images that excavation uncovers. Some cycles produce quite different patterns when viewed at different spatial scales, while others, as the fractal metaphor implies, exhibit scale invariance.

My examples are drawn from the Central Plains Mosaic. This complex formerly was called the Central Plains Tradition, but a recent re-analysis (Blakeslee 1999:36-38) showed that it consists of a set of more or less contemporaneous phases, which is not what Willey and Phillips (1958) had in mind when they coined the term, tradition. Furthermore, this tradition was classified as one of a set of units within another (Plains Village) tradition. For reasons that will become clear below, I renamed the larger taxon the Plains Horticultural Tradition and I suggested using Central Plains Mosaic as a substitute for the Central Plains Tradition. One of the advantages I saw in the word, mosaic, is that has no connotations with respect to structural units such as biological populations, language communities, ethnic groups or tribes.

The cultural system that produced the Central Plains Mosaic (hereafter CPM) appears in the Central Plains at about A.D. 1000 and lasts to around A.D. 1300 in Kansas and to at least A.D. 1400 in Nebraska. The first appearance the CPM seems to have been rather abrupt, and the transition from Late Woodland complexes into CPM has not been traced adequately. We do know, however, that it involved a shift away from a subsistence pattern that relied very little on cultigens and that generated a settlement pattern consisting of base camps and special purpose camps.

CPM sites were occupied year round, and utilized a generalized subsistence economy. Crops grown include maize, squash, marshelder, sunflower, beans, little barley, goosefoot and tobacco (Adair 1988). Gathered vegetable foods that have been preserved in CPM sites include wild sunflower, grapes, plums, cherries, hackberries, elderberries, walnuts, hickory nuts, hazelnuts, butternuts and prairie turnips. Faunal remains include nearly every mammalian species known to have inhabited the region, along with numerous species of birds and fish and some amphibians and reptiles. Sites consist of from one to twenty or more house remains usually located along creeks as opposed to major rivers. Isolated homesteads seem to have been the preferred settlement type.

The disappearance of the CPM is tied, at least in part, to a migration of some populations from the Central Plains into South Dakota where they gave rise to the Initial Coalescent variant. The debate over the reasons for the migration is elaborated in a later section. When the Central Plains were re-occupied, it was by people who lived in village units and who relied primarily on bison and corn. The seasonal round included two long-distance bison hunts per year that were organized at the village level. Cache pits in the protohistoric villages, from 6 to 12 feet deep, reveal an impressive increase in storage capacity over the CPM settlements.

The CPM is divided into a series of constituent phases (Fig. 1). Differences between the phases lie primarily in house form and ceramics, with differences in chipped and ground stone tool assemblages attributable mainly to the availability of raw materials. This is not to say that no significant variance in assemblages exists at a regional scale, but the lack of consistent artifact typologies and descriptions precludes accurate comparisons using the available literature.

The eastern phases (Nebraska, Smoky Hill and St Helena) share a house form that is basically square with rounded corners, four (or four sets of) central roof supports, a central hearth, and an extended entryway. Houses in the western phases are frequently rectangular and more rarely circular or trapezoidal. They often lack a clear pattern of central support posts, and the hearth is sometimes offset from the center toward the entryway.

Ceramic differences between phases include kinds of temper, the extent to which originally cord-roughened surfaces have been smoothed, differing frequencies of direct and collared rim jars, and the frequencies, placements and motifs of rim decoration. Shoulder decoration is restricted primarily to sites of the Nebraska and Smoky Hill phases in the southeastern part of the Central Plains, while the frequency of rim decoration increases from south to north between phases and within (at least) the Nebraska phase (Blakeslee and Caldwell 1979).

The annual subsistence round is an obvious place to start a discussion of cycles in tribal life. I have chosen three data sets from my recent reanalysis of some large collections from the Glen Elder locality in north-central Kansas (Blakeslee 1999) to illuminate the seasonal rounds that generated the sites. They are: lithic source patterns, chipped stone artifact categories and functional categories of artifacts regardless of the material from which they are made.

The people who created CPM sites in this locality relied heavily on chipped stone tools, and they acquired the bulk of their lithic raw materials from outside the locality. Some local gravels (including pieces of Smoky Hill jasper, petrified wood and quartzites) were used, but the bulk of the lithics in the sites in the Glen Elder locality came either from bedrock sources of Smoky Hill jasper about 50 km northwest of the locality or Permian age chert from the Flint Hills about 150 km to the east. Much smaller amounts of Alibates chert from Texas and Flattop chalcedony from northern Colorado are also present.

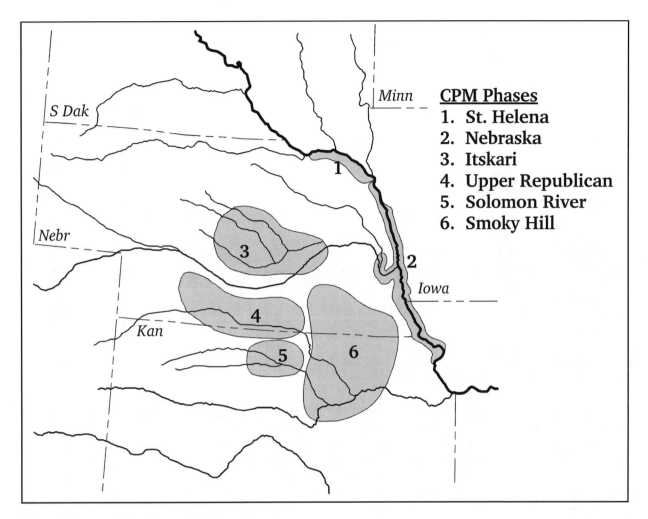

Fig. 1. Phases of the Central Plains Mosaic.

To maintain a viable tool kit and blanks or preforms ready for use, the inhabitants of the locality would have had to obtain their raw materials on a regular basis. The pattern of distribution of lithic materials (Blakeslee 1999:Table 44) suggests that they obtained both the Permian chert and the Smoky Hill jasper directly from the quarries; cores of these materials constitute over 96 percent of the cores in the Waconda Lake assemblages. Since reliance on a chipped stone tool technology creates a more or less constant need for raw material (because stone tools dull relatively quickly and get used up rapidly as they are resharpened), we can be fairly sure that lithic procurement occurred at least once a year and probably more frequently than that.

The kinds of tools and debitage that make up a chipped stone assemblage are another reflection of the annual round. Frequently used items, because they wear out or break and are discarded, will be more heavily represented in the archaeological assemblages than tools that are used (and used up) less frequently. The same argument can be made for tools made from other kinds of material as well. Most of the archaeological assemblage from any year-round habitation site will be dominated by trash, broken and used-up items and the debitage from their manufacture.

Tables 1 through 3 present the frequencies by site of lithic sources, chipped stone tool and debitage categories, and functional categories of tools for the available sample of sites from the Glen Elder locality. The number of sites included in each table varies somewhat depending on adequate sample sizes and other factors. For instance, I have used Lippincott's (1976) analysis of the chipped stone categories, and site 14OB27 was not in his sample of sites. Site 14OB26 is not included in either Table 1 or Table 2 because the sample of chipped stone tools from it is too small for reliable results.

Donald J. Blakeslee

Table 1. Lithic source variance in the Glen Elder locality.

Lithic Percentages

Site	Smoky Hill Jasper	Permian	Flattop	Alibates	Oglalla Quartzite	Petrified Wood	Total Amount
14ML310	67.7	31.7	0.0	0.0	0.6	0.0	161
14ML17	68.5	22.4	2.1	0.0	7.0	0.0	143
14ML15	74.4	20.5	0.3	2.7	1.9	0.3	2383
14ML5	73.0	24.3	0.0	0.2	2.6	0.0	976
14ML8	74.5	17.4	1.9	2.5	3.7	0.0	161
14ML371	77.4	17.5	0.0	0.7	4.4	0.0	274
14ML16	79.1	18.8	0.0	0.9	1.2	0.0	335
14ML307	80.5	14.4	0.0	4.2	0.9	0.0	118
14ML376	81.4	10.6	0.8	1.8	3.4	2.1	388
14ML11	87.3	11.1	0.0	1.6	0.0	0.0	640
14ML306	88.7	7.6	0.0	1.1	2.7	0.0	185
14ML311	90.8	2.6	0.0	0.8	0.8	5.0	120
14OB27	96.4	3.6	0.0	0.0	0.0	0.0	1082
14OB28	82.8	2.8	16.7	0.0	0.0	0.0	70

Average coefficient of difference = 18.8 ± 3.24

What is of particular interest here is the scale and the nature of the variance between sites for each kind of data. Since the habitation sites were occupied for at least several annual rounds, the year-to-year variations in the annual round should tend to become averaged out, so that the differences between sites are small. Indeed, the average coefficients of difference (on a 100 point scale[1]) are all small, 18.8 ± 3.24, 17.8 ± 3.35, and 6.25 ± 3.25 for the lithic sources, chipped stone categories and artifact function categories respectively.

The differences in lithic source frequencies are more or less evenly distributed, which can be seen by inspection of Table 1, in which the sites are arranged by the frequencies of the common lithic types. The sites do not fall into clusters; instead they are on a continuum with a limited range. At the ends of the distribution are sites with relatively small sample sizes, which probably reflects sampling error. The lithic frequencies do not correlate with site location within the locality, except for a tendency for the westernmost sites (from Osborne County) to have high proportions of Smoky Hill jasper, which derives from the west and north of the locality and (in 14OB28 only) Flattop chalcedony, also a western source. The frequencies also do not correlate with house form or ceramic assemblages (topics which are discussed below).

I also calculated the contribution of each cell to the chi-square value to determine which cells re-flect the most significant elements of the variance in the table. The only large values were for 12 pieces of Flattop chalcedony from 14OB28 and six and eight pieces of petrified wood from sites 14ML311 and 14ML376 respectively. Thus, the significant variance occurs in the form of relatively small amounts of the lithic raw materials that occur only rarely in this set of sites.

Since it is likely that the sites in the sample were occupied at different times, the data suggest that same lithic procurement system was maintained throughout the occupation of the locality. It may well have been an invariant part of the seasonal round. In the future, feature by feature analysis of lithic sources might help to show when acquisition of stone occurred by association with seasonal indicators such as mussel shells, deer mandibles and the like. For the present, one can only say that since the two main sources of chippable stone lay in opposite directions from the locality, possibly the stone was acquired during at least two different seasons. Some of the uniformity in the assemblages also might be the result of lithic acquisition expeditions by social units larger than a single household, although regular exchanges of raw materials among neighbors could also explain the pattern.

When equivalent data are assembled for other localities, I would expect to see profound differences in the lithic frequencies from one locality

Table 2. Chipped stone categories in the Glen Elder locality.

	ML 17	ML 371	ML 16	ML 15	ML 8	ML 310	OB 28	ML 307	ML 376	ML 5	ML 11	ML 306	ML 311
Notched Points	1.9	1.1	2.2	1.9	3.0	2.3	2.4	0.7	0.7	1.6	0.6	1.0	0.0
Unnotched Points	1.9	1.8	2.2	2.8	3.5	1.7	2.4	1.5	0.9	0.8	0.0	0.5	0.8
Small Thin Bifaces	4.3	2.9	4.7	2.7	2.0	2.9	3.7	3.0.	2.5	1.3	1.9	0.0	4.2
Large Thin Bifaces	0.6	3.6	3.6	0.0	0.0	1.7	0.0	0.0	2.2	1.1	2.7	2.5	0.8
Small Thick Bifaces	0.0	2.1	1.4	0.0	0.0	2.3	2.4	0.0	0.0	0.9	0.0	1.0	0.0
Large Thick Bifaces	8.0	0.4	1.1	1.7	5.0	0.0	0.0	0.0	2.9	1.6	0.3	0.5	0.0
Beveled Knives	0.6	0.0	0.6	0.6	0.0	0.6	0.0	0.0	0.0	0.1	0.3	0.0	0.0
End Scrapers	3.7	5.0	4.4	2.8	4.0	4.1	4.9	3.0	2.9	3.7	2.1	1.5	0.0
Gravers	0.0	0.4	0.3	0.3	0.0	0.0	0.0	0.0	0.0	0.2	0.0	0.0	0.0
Retouched Flakes	19.1	26.4	19.0	19.7	13.4	11.0	11.0	11.9	9.6	8.4	8.4	11.0	5.0
Utilized Flakes	11.1	6.4	7.4	11.6	12.4	2.9	7.3	6.7	11.4	6.5	5.8	6.5	2.5
Debitage	47.5	50.0	53.3	55.9	60.9	69.4	64.6	71.9	65.7	70.6	73.7	75.6	86.7
Cores	1.2	0.0	0.0	0.0	0.5	1.2	1.2	1.5	1.3	3.3	4.3	0.0	0.0
Raw Totals	162	280	364	2646	202	173	82	135	449	1020	676	201	120

Table 3. Artifact function classes in the Glen Elder locality.

Category	ML 311	ML 310	ML 307	ML 306	ML 377	ML 376	ML 11	ML 15	ML 5	OB 27	OB 28	ML 371	ML 8	ML 17	OB 26	ML 16
1	2.9	6.2	3.8	0.0	3.5	4.4	4.1	5.8	8.3	8.0	7.8	6.8	6.2	5.3	3.5	3.1
2	2.2	4.3	3.1	1.9	3.5	4.7	5.4	6.7	6.6	4.6	7.8	6.2	6.6	8.1	2.4	2.9
3	0.7	1.4	0.0	0.9	0.9	0.9	3.5	3.7	2.2	4.6	2.6	3.3	4.3	4.0	2.4	1.7
4	0.7	1.9	0.0	0.5	1.8	1.3	1.8	2.6	2.2	2.1	0.9	4.6	3.6	1.6	4.7	1.2
5	0.0	0.0	1.3	0.5	0.9	1.0	0.3	1.1	1.5	0.8	0.9	4.4	1.6	0.4	1.2	0.0
6	15.8	22.5	28.3	34.9	31.0	28.8	25.9	26.4	18.4	24.5	30.4	37.8	38.4	41.3	44.5	41.2
7	77.7	63.2	62.9	61.3	57.5	57.4	57.9	51.5	57.5	52.1	48.7	34.7	36.4	37.7	38.8	44.6
8	0.0	0.0	0.0	0.0	0.0	0.0	0.5	0.3	0.9	0.2	0.9	1.3	0.0	0.4	1.2	3.9
9	0.0	0.5	0.6	0.0	0.9	1.3	0.5	2.0	2.6	0.6	0	1.1	3.0	1.2	1.2	1.5
Raw Totals	139	209	159	212	113	676	734	3702	1556	1571	115	453	305	247	85	413

to another, as lithic sources definitely reflect differential access to resources and the extent of hunting territories (cf. Holen 1991; Zehnder 1998).

The chipped stone categories in Table 2, taken from Lippincott (1976) are also remarkably uniform, with a coefficient of difference of 17.8 ± 3.35. A seriation of the sort developed by Renfrew and Sterud (1969) generates no clusters of sites, only a continuum determined primarily buy the amount of debitage found during the excavations. The sites at the extremes of the distribution, 14ML17 and 14ML311, both have relatively small assemblages. Thus sampling error resulting from both raw sample size and from the portion of the site excavated (i.e., the extent to which the excavations uncovered chipping stations) have generated some of the variance, which is relatively small to begin with. Deleting the debitage from consideration does not change the general pattern; there are no patterned differences between the sites generated by the formal tool categories. Thus, as with the lithic source frequencies, these data imply site-to-site similarities in the seasonal round.

When similar data become available from other localities, I would expect to see a degree of scale invariance, with much more similarity across localities in the chipped stone tool categories than in the lithic sources used. Different environments should generate some differences in the types of tools used, but these are apt to be moderate if, as discussed below, the people who created the sites were swidden foragers.

Table 3 shows the frequencies generated when all artifacts are allocated among a set of functional categories regardless of the material from which they were made (Blakeslee 1999:132-133). The categories are:

1. **Large game hunting and hide processing:** points, end scrapers, choppers, beveled knives, perforators, fleshers, hide grainers;
2. **General hunting/fishing:** points, knives, fishhooks, fish gorges
3. **General hide working:** perforators, flake scrapers, awls, needles, beamers;
4. **Swiddening:** axes, celts, adzes, hoes, digging stick tips, ulna picks, antler rakes, squash knives, deer mandibles;
5. **Gathering:** nutting stones, digging stick tips;
6. **Food preparation and storage:** ceramic vessels, knives, milling stones, manos, mortars, spoons, shell scrapers;
7. **General Manufacturing:** gravers, drills, abraders, shaft smoothers, hammerstones, lithic debitage, shaft wrenches, paintbrushes, flaking tools;
8. **Clothing and adornment:** beads, pendants, earspools, tinklers, gorgets, pins; and
9. **Ceremonial:** pipes, crystals, human calvaria, eagle bone whistles, rattles, exotic shell objects.

The coefficient of difference for the frequencies of artifacts in the functional categories is a miniscule 6.25 ± 3.25, which probably reflects in part the large sample sizes generated by lumping all of the artifacts from the excavations into only nine broad categories. It also reflect the fact that some objects, such as points, are counted in more than one category. Once again, the sites do not form clusters, and the differences between them are not only minor but apparently random. Analysis of the contributions to Chi square shows that the most significant differences are actually minor. Site 14ML15 has fewer than expected food preparation items, while site 14Ml16 has more items of adornment than expected and fewer of general manufacturing. Since this site contained an ossuary in addition to a habitation site, this result is not surprising.

To the extent that the residents of different localities made their living using somewhat different resources, we might expect to find some differences at the regional scale in the functional categories once similar data are made available. Given the general similarities already reported in the literature, however, such differences are likely to be moderate.

In all three sets of data, then, we find relative uniformity among the sites. Neither lithic sources used, categories of chipped stone nor functional categories of all artifacts vary much from one habitation site to another within this locality. This is exactly what one would expect from the repetition of the annual cycle over a period of years, as year-to-year variations are averaged out in the total site assemblage. With the products and byproducts of longer cycles or episodic events, however, one might find larger inter-site variance, as we shall see below.

If the same sorts of data as reported in Tables 1-3 were available from other localities, we would expect to find large differences between localities in lithic sources used, because the distance to quarries is such an important consideration. On the other hand, one would predict only moderate differences in functional classes of tools and chipped stone tool categories, as these reflect the general way of life of the people who created the CPM.

Indeed, the scale of the differences in general adaptation between localities is an important research question that has not yet been addressed adequately.

Neither have the details of the seasonal round. A debate over whether CPM sites were occupied year-round (Lippincott 1976; Dorsey 1998; Wedel 1970) or whether they were abandoned for seasonal long distance hunts (Falk 1969; Morey 1982) has only recently been resolved in terms of the former option (Blakeslee 1999:43-44). The year-round model helps to explain differences between CPM faunal assemblages and those of protohistoric villages in that bones of large mammals (other than bone tools) are relatively rare in CPM sites. The long list of crops grown, especially the Little Barley, suggests the existence of more than one harvest season and at least an extended planting season. Blakeslee (1999:Table X) provides a list of the gathered wild foods that includes the seasons in which they were available, but much remains to be done. Analysis of individual cache pit assemblages, which are composed of trash that accumulated over relatively short periods, might help to resolve elements of the annual round.

Swidden Cycles, Foraging and the Faunal Record

Subsistence in the CPM was based on a combination of swidden horticulture and foraging (Anderson and Zimmerman 1976:149; Blakeslee 1990, 1993, 1999; Krause 1969, 1970; Wood 1969:104). In the Central Plains, swiddening involved two interlinked cycles. The shorter-term cycle consisted of clearing and using a garden until the soil fertility was depleted, followed by repetitions of the cycle in neighboring plots until the resources of the general vicinity were depleted. This led to the initiation of the longer-term cycle, in which a new location was settled and new gardens cleared. The length of occupation of any one spot was dependent on the amount and nature of the critical resources available, which varied considerably from region to region and from locality to locality.

In slash and burn horticulture, a garden is created by chopping down or merely killing trees, then clearing, drying and burning the undergrowth. In the Plains area, swidden gardeners preferred mature stands of hardwood forest. Hardwood trees can be killed merely by girdling them—chopping through the bark around the circumference of the tree. Softwoods have to be chopped down, and even then they will send up numerous shoots that the

gardener must fight. Mature forest may contain as few as ten to twelve trees per acre, with a minimum of undergrowth as a result of the shade cast by the large trees. The extent of mature hardwood forest, then, was a critical factor in determining how long the occupation of any spot could continue before the pioneering cycle repeated.

Soil fertility and replenishment were similarly critical to the length of the garden cycle. In temperate zones, vegetal growth and hence soil replenishment in fallow fields is slow because growth ceases in winter. In the Plains, a long dry season also inhibited soil replenishment. Without a plow to turn soil over and bring new nutrients to shallow-rooted crops such as maize, gardens could be used for only a few years before crop production waned.

Figure 2 is a model of what the swidden cycles may have been like in the Central Plains. It shows the availability of various resources through one pioneering cycle that encompasses two garden cycles. At the beginning of the pioneering cycle, the gardens are productive, local large game has not yet been hunted out, and firewood is readily available. As time goes on, the productivity of the first gardens begins to decline, large game is less plentiful near the habitation site, pest populations invade the gardens, but edge species become more common. Eventually, garden productivity fails to provide adequate food for the winter, and lower quality resources such as mussels and small rodents have to be harvested in quantity. At that point, new gardens are cleared, and the garden cycle repeats, but large game and firewood continue to become increasingly scarce, and eventually the population moves on to a new spot to repeat the pioneering cycle.

At the Schmidt site in central Nebraska, the microfaunal assemblages appear to reflect the crises in the garden cycle. Satorius-Fox (1982) reports the microfauna from the Schmidt site, giving MNIs for each feature. I have extracted the data in Table 4 from her report, eliminating those features with very small total MNIs (<10) and the species that are poorly represented at the site (MNI for all features < 6) in order to make clear the pattern of variance among the richer pits and the better represented species. The five trash-filled pits with MNIs greater than 10 yielded from 8 to 47 of the well-represented microfaunal species. The average coefficient of difference between all of the pits is 52.8 ± 13.9. No two pits are very much alike in their microfaunal contents, the bulk of which are food remains. (Lengthy justifications for this

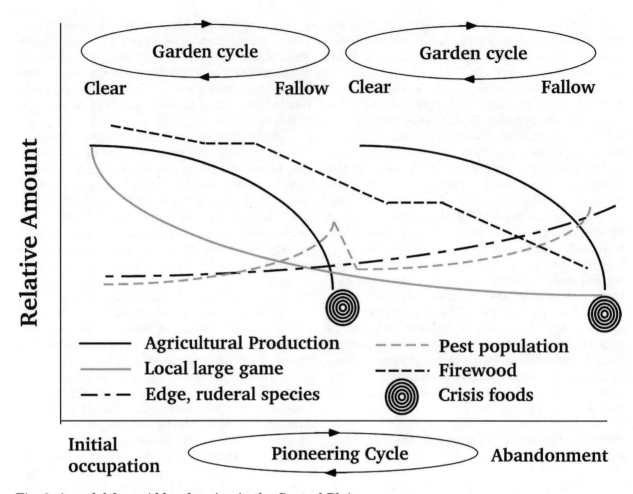

Fig. 2. A model for swidden foraging in the Central Plains.

Table 4. MNIs of common microfauna from selected features at the Schmidt site.

Species	F78	F3	F135	F76	F221
Blarina brevicauda	4.6	0.0	2.1	11.1	8.9
Spermophilus tridecemlineatus	0.0	7.1	6.4	11.1	1.8
Geomys bursarius	4.6	7.1	2.1	11.1	5.4
Perognathus hispidus	45.5	7.1	4.3	22.2	1.8
Peromyscus maniculatus	27.3	42.9	34.0	0.0	1.8
Onychomys leucogaster	0.0	7.1	17.0	0.0	0.0
Oryzomys palustris	4.6	14.3	29.8	33.3	25.0
Microtus pennsylvanicus	4.6	7.1	0.0	0.0	42.9
Pedomys ochrogaster	9.1	7.1	4.3	11.1	12.5
Feature Totals	22	14	47	9	56

assertion can be found in Satorius-Fox (1982) and Blakeslee (1999:77-85)).

Some of the diversity across pits might be attributed to small sample sizes, but the average coefficient of difference (52.8) is much greater than the standard deviation of 13.95. The variability might also reflect both the nature and the timing of the trash pit fill. Cache pits eventually were invaded by mold, insects, and rodents, and so had to be replaced, generating another cycle that affected the archaeological record. When a storage pit was abandoned, it usually was filled immediately in order to prevent accidents (Weltfish 1965:297). Usually, it was filled with trash that happened to be readily available. Most of the items in a trash-filled pit, therefore, derive from a fairly short (but not precisely definable) interval. The relatively brief period of accumulation means that the trash has the potential to reveal something about both seasonal and longer term cycles. That is, independent of the effect of small sample size, trash-filled cache pit assemblages can be expected to have high variance, precisely what is seen in the Schmidt site faunal assemblages.

Figure 2 depicts my explanation for the tendency for one or two small mammal species to dominate the fill of those pits that have any significant number of small rodents. I believe that these faunas are the results of intensive small mammal hunts that took place at that point in the garden cycle when the harvest of domesticated crops fell off. The population of small mammal pests, especially those that raid the gardens would have grown over the years, making such a hunt productive, especially when it involved those animals that store vegetable foods for the winter.

A similar pattern exists in the distribution of large assemblages of freshwater mussel shells. Mussels are low quality resources. They have relatively low nutritional value, are essentially tasteless, and have the chewing consistence of a rubber eraser. Yet both large and small assemblages of mussel shells occur regularly in CPM sites. At Waconda Lake, Dorsey (1998) found 153 assemblages from 15 sites, of which 20 were large (MNI > 100). The large assemblages reflect on the order of 476-8193g (1-18 lb) of meat.

A large clambake will deplete the mussel population in the vicinity of a site (Wedel 1986:127). By determining age at death of the individuals in the assemblages, Dorsey was able to estimate the periodicity of the large clambakes in the sites from the Glen Elder locality. He found that the assemblages were missing individuals below the age of

two (which are small and bury themselves deeply in the stream beds) and those above the ages of five to eight. From these data he was able to deduce that the interval between large clambakes ranged from four to seven years, with most of the intervals being five years. Furthermore, he was able to determine that all of the large clambakes occurred in the late fall to early winter. The small assemblages, on the other hand, appear to have occurred between the large clambakes, resulting in lower ages at death for the specimens in them, and the small events occurred throughout the year.

The regularity of the large clambakes—once every five years on average—and the season in which they occurred make it appear likely that mussels were one of the crisis foods that CPM populations depended on. When the relative failure of the garden harvest became clear in the early fall, the people would have known that they would not have enough food for the winter. Freshwater mussels would have been available if no large clambake had occurred since the last crisis some five years previous. The best time to collect them would be before the really cold weather set in, as collecting them involved wading in waist-deep water. The beginning of winter would have been the best time for hunting small rodents as well. Some species store foods for the winter, and at the beginning of that season, their caches would have been at their largest. Also, with the onset of cold weather, some rodent species create communal nests so that their body heat will help to ward off the cold. Such communal nests would produce the most meat for human hunters.

In contrast to the features listed in Table 4, fourteen trash-filled pits at the Schmidt site (Satorius-Fox 1982:Table 4) reflect a different pattern. They contain only a few small rodents each: from one to nine individuals from 15 different species. In none of these pits are more than two individuals from a single species. Satorius-Fox's data show that most of them were eaten, even though they would have constituted little more than a snack. They are comparable to the many small mussel shell assemblages in the Glen Elder locality that reflect an occasional meal, food collected when foraging failed to yield anything else (Dorsey 2000:17). Casual garden hunting using snares may have produced the occasional small rodent from a wide variety of species that are found in the bulk of the cache pits.

The similarities between the patterns of occurrence of micromammals and freshwater mussels are the result of foraging as the means of providing meat in the diet. Foraging, as opposed to scheduled, organized long-distance hunts seems to have been the mode in all CPM sites with the possible exception of the far western sites called High Plains Upper Republican. Those sites aside, no CPM bison kill or other communal hunting sites have been found. It may be that foraging was conducted by household groups rather than by larger community groups.

This might help to explain the extraordinary diversity in the faunal remains from CPM sites. Bozell (1991) documented this, using examples drawn from six sites, the only CPM sites which had been fine-screened, ensuring adequate recovery rates for small species. I was able to add two sites to his set from work published later by others (Koch 1995; Scott 1993). The results are shown in Table 5.

At this larger scale of analysis—across sites and phases—total CPM faunas show the same level of diversity as the microfaunas from the Schmidt site features, a clear example of scale invariance. What makes the diversity in the inter-site data so striking is 1) the breadth of the faunal categories, and 2) that the sites appear to have been occupied year-round. Since faunal remains reflect the seasonal round, one might expect to find the low level of diversity found in the lithic sources, chipped stone categories and functional classes seen in the Glen Elder locality. This is clearly not the case.

The largest game, bison and elk, range from 0.4 to 22.1 percent of the site assemblages, while fish and reptiles range from 8 to 77.3 percent. Only birds (3.3 to 17.8) have a somewhat restricted range of variation across sites. Some of the differences might be attributed to the fact that the sites are drawn from three different phases, but there is little similarity among the sites from a single phase. For instance, the Schmidt site is only 24 miles from the Hulme site, yet the coefficient of difference between them is 46.4 compared to the average coefficient of difference among all of the sites of 43.8. That is, these two sites are no more similar to one another than any pair chosen randomly from the full set.

One factor that may have helped to generate this high level of diversity is the use of the NISP statistic—the number of identified specimens in each taxon. NISP is sensitive to butchering and disposal patterns, as a single individual can generate over 200 bones. Bozell (personal communication), however, attempted to alleviate this problem in extreme cases, by lumping some fragmentary bones when it was obvious that they came from a single individual. Nevertheless, MNIs (minimum number of individuals) would be likely to have somewhat lower variance.

Another factor may be the nature of the CPM adaptation, in which foraging by household groups seems to have been the norm. This contrasts with

Table 5. Site to site variation in Central Plains faunas.

% of NISP	Marvin Coulson	Hulme	25HN36	Palmer Johnson	Witt	Mowry Bluff	Schmidt	McIntosh
Bison/ Elk	15.8	1.8	1.1	0.4	0.8	13.2	22.1	15.6
Deer/ Pronghorn	50.8	50.0	32.1	1.9	17.6	9.6	10.6	1.3
Small Mammals	19.5	21.9	39.2	37.2	44.1	39.8	7.7	2.9
Birds	5.9	14.3	4.7	3.3	10.8	17.8	15.0	2.9
Fish/ Reptiles	8.0	12.0	22.9	57.2	26.8	19.6	44.6	77.3
Totals	917	1720	769	786	1189	451	3332	3791

the protohistoric pattern of long-distance bison-hunting expeditions mounted by village-sized groups (cf. Blakeslee et al. 2001). Utilizing dog traction and later horse traction, the protohistoric hunters returned from their highly focused expeditions with massive amounts of meat and enough bones to make bison the dominant species in all village assemblages. It may be that CPM foragers returned fewer bones from any significant distance to their habitation sites than later peoples did, with the result that the sporadic taking of animals close to home (i.e., foraging) looms large in the habitation site faunas.

A third potential factor is the temporal scale. Most of the sites in Table 5 consist of a single excavated house, and CPM houses appear to have been occupied for fairly brief intervals of time. Estimates of the life spans of the prehistoric houses range from five (Wedel 1986:105; Wood 1969:105) to ten or twenty years (Billeck 1993:22). In the Central Plains, year to year variations in weather are often extreme, and the average precipitation has little meaning. The faunal record could well reflect small time slices of short-distance foraging in a fluctuating environment (cf. Blakeslee 1999:figure 24). What the data clearly show, however, is a discordance between the highly variable faunal assemblages on the one hand and the relatively uniform artifact assemblages.

Swidden Cycles and Settlement Patterns in the Plains Area

The distinguishing characteristic of the Plains Horticultural Tradition is the consistent presence of evidence for swidden horticulture. The tools of swidden gardeners are found, not only in CPM sites, but in contemporaneous archaeological complexes across most of the Great Plains. The other units include the Middle Missouri Tradition in the Dakotas and Iowa, the Pomona Variant of Kansas and Missouri, and the Canark Variant of Colorado, Oklahoma and Texas, among others. Assemblages from these complexes often include chipped or ground stone celts; hoe blades made most frequently from bison scapulae but also from bison frontal bones, stone or mussel shells; bison tibia digging stick tips; and deer mandible sickles.

At the scale of the Great Plains area, the swidden cycles produced very different settlement patterns in different environmental zones. Three examples drawn from different regions will suffice to show that the single basic adaptation marking the Plains Horticultural Tradition generated

widely different archaeological records. In the Middle Missouri region, swidden cycles produced mostly compact village sites, in the Central Plains they generated loose clusters of houses, while in the Osage Cuestas, they created long strings of rather isolated houses.

In the Middle Missouri region (the trench of the Missouri River in the Dakotas), forest is restricted to the river floodplain, and mature forest is limited to groves located near the bases of meander loops of the river. Mature groves are the product of a vegetational succession that begins with newly deposited river sediments and ends with large, widely spaced examples of bur oak, green ash, box elder, and American elm (Griffin 1977). A stand of mature forest may have only ten or twelve trees to the acre with sparse undergrowth, making the creation of gardens relatively easy.

The fallow period in this environment was only two years because the soils were replenished by new sediments derived from annual floods (Wilson 1917:113-114). The flooding also ensured plentiful soil moisture to start the growing season. Long term use of a single location seems to have been limited primarily by the meandering of the river channel, which could erode away the groves of trees, starting the vegetational cycle over again.

In this environment, the swidden cycle generated a pattern of archaeological sites that consist of compact villages of pithouses, often with deep midden deposits. Middle Missouri Tradition sites usually are found at the edge of a terrace overlooking the arable ground. Many villages are located at the mouths of tributary streams, where a cove in the side of the main valley protected the forest from erosion by the main channel. Dwellings in these villages were usually set into pits, which could be excavated with only digging sticks and scapula hoes because the villages were on prairie rather than on root-infested forest land. Sites are usually compact and are often fortified because critically important farmland had to be defended (Fig. 3a).

Finally, compared with most contemporary sites in other parts of the Plains, Middle Missouri Tradition sites appear to have been occupied for long periods of time. As a result rich midden deposits accumulated. The stability of occupation can be seen as a gift of the river, an environment in which only a couple of garden plots, one active and one fallow, were needed to support each household until the river eroded away the land.

The faunal assemblages in the site middens lack the variability seen in the CPM. All habitation site faunas are dominated by bison (Bozell

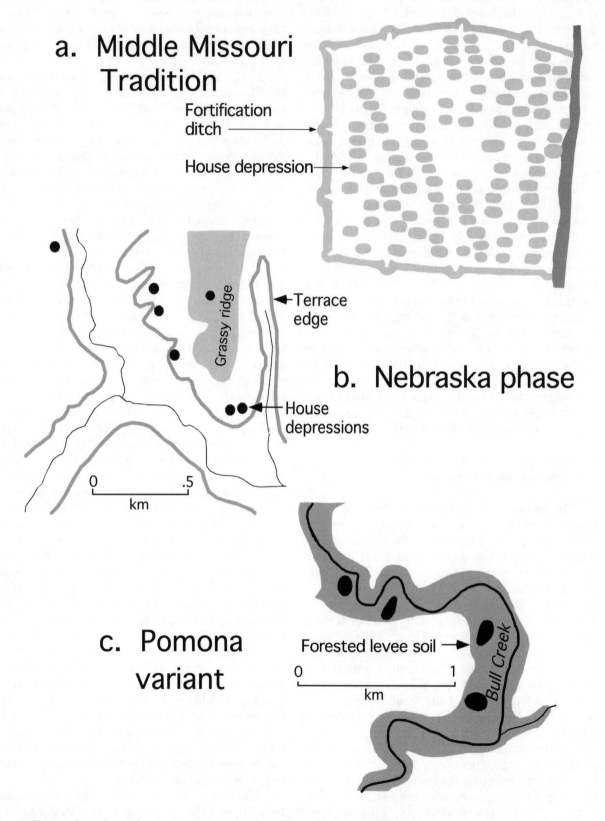

Fig. 3. Examples of settlement patterns in the Plains Horticultural Tradition (a. after Wood 1967).

1995:151; Falk 1977:154-155). The relatively long life spans of the villages would tend to eliminate the effects of the short term weather variations that appear to affect the CPM record. Furthermore, the village level of organization may have allowed village-level collective bison hunts. Finally, there may have been larger herds of bison in the Dakotas than in the Central Plains during the period in question.

The existence of stable village-sized populations must have affected the social structure: Face-to face contact among several hundred people on a daily basis must have called for a relatively complex social organization. Village chiefs, warrior societies and unilineal descent groups were features of the organization of the Mandan and Hidatsa tribes, the likely historical descendants of the Middle Missouri Tradition. Village size meant that some tasks could be carried out by groups larger than the household. In addition to policing collective bison hunts, members of associations may have carried out some harvest-related tasks, as was the case among the historic Hidatsa (Wilson 1917:43). Village level rituals and village origin myths are likely to have existed.

A contrasting pattern is found in the Central Plains Mosaic in the period A.D. 1000-1450. Here, very few compact sites occur, and it is not clear whether the exceptions are, in fact, the products of villages as opposed to long-term occupation of well-endowed sites by small populations. There is variation in the Central Plains environment, especially from east to west, with some resulting variation in the settlement pattern. For our present purposes, however, a single example will suffice.

The Nebraska Phase is found in the Eastern Glaciated region of eastern Nebraska, westernmost Iowa, northeastern Kansas, and northwestern Missouri. This is a region of steep loess bluffs dissected by creek valleys of varying size. The Missouri River floods occur later here than in the Dakotas, shortening the growing season. Perhaps as a result Nebraska Phase sites tend to be oriented to the valleys of the tributary streams.

Hardwood forests are widespread in these valleys (Johnson 1972:8-10), but trees usually do not extend to the ridge tops, which support prairie grasses. While the soils of the tributary valleys are quite rich, they are not replenished by regular floods. The relative lack of soil replenishment prevented the prehistoric gardeners from using a garden for as long a period as was possible in the Middle Missouri region. As a result, the sites are not as rich in midden deposits as those farther north.

The settlement pattern consists of diffuse random scatters of house depressions (Fig. 3b) and occasionally a line of house depressions, especially on ridge tops. Houses are usually widely spaced, and in some cases it is difficult to determine where one site leaves off and the next one begins. There is also a tendency for large houses to be on ridge tops, and another for large houses to be found in sites that contain very few houses (Blakeslee and Caldwell 1979:30-33; Hotopp 1982:183).

I recently (Blakeslee 1990) proposed a model that accounts for this settlement pattern. It posits that the initial settlement in most spots was on a grassy ridge top. By building on the ridge top, the people avoided having to deal with tree roots while excavating a house pit. Construction of a succession of houses over time on a ridge top would produce one of the lines of houses seen in the settlement pattern of this phase. An alternative to continuing to build successive houses on the ridge top was to build later houses in fallow fields from which the tree roots had rotted. Such a decision would provide easier access to both water and garden plots. A final element in this model has the first houses at a spot being multi-family structures which were later replaced with individual family houses once the heavy work of pioneering a new location had been accomplished. Construction of a single dwelling for more than one family would have reduced labor costs at a time when the first gardens had to be established. Thus there is more than just the swidden cycle at work in generating this pattern. In addition, we have to pay attention to a household cycle that includes both multi-family and single (extended) family dwellings and a cycle of house construction, decay and replacement. We will return to these topics below.

The slow rate of soil replenishment in this environment necessitated the abandonment of gardens plots after a period of several years. On the other hand, a single valley with widespread forest could have been occupied for a lengthy period, resulting in the gradual accumulation of house ruins. Each individual house, however, would have been occupied for a shorter time than a typical Middle Missouri village, resulting in less midden accumulation.

Nebraska Phase sites are not fortified, but there is abundant evidence that warfare was present in the CPM in general and in the Nebraska phase in particular (cf. Blakeslee 1999:151-152 for an a review of the data). The lack of fortifications appears to reflect a different response to raids than was possible in the Middle Missouri region. In the Central Plains, there was no scarce resource that had to be defended. Rather than investing in elaborate fortifications that could be manned by the populations of the compact villages of the Dakotas, people in the dispersed settlements of the Central Plains probably ran away from raids (cf. Robarchek and Robarchek 1998 for an ethnographic example of this sort of adaptation to raids).

One might expect a far different form of social organization than in the Middle Missouri region. Given the dispersed settlement patter, there would have been far less face-to-face contact on a daily basis; and it would have been harder to organize large cooperative work groups. Local communities could have come into existence, grown and declined in less than an individual person's lifetime. A more flexible social organization therefore seems likely than in the Dakotas, and headmen rather than formal leadership might have been the rule.

A third contrasting settlement pattern is found in the Pomona variant of the Osage Cuestas region of eastern Kansas and western Missouri (Brown 1984). The Osage Cuestas are a land of rolling plains and east-facing escarpments. Both uplands and much of the lowlands are covered with tall-grass prairies. Narrow gallery forests line the streams, while slough grass filled much of the rest of the lower ground. Much of the lowlands consist of heavy clay soils not suited for working with digging sticks and scapula hoes. Land appropriate for swidden is restricted to natural levees on which the rate of soil accumulation is extremely slow. Because all but the very largest streams are entrenched, natural levee soils do accumulate and the forest that grows on them has the chance to develop climax communities.

The Pomona settlement pattern consists of widely-spaced sites within the gallery forest zone on the levee soils (Fig. 3c). Houses in them were lightly-built and lacked house pits. The lack of a house pit and the slow rate of soil accumulation have made the archaeology of this region difficult; most Pomona deposits lie within the modern plow zone, and usually only the centers of well-trampled house floors remain intact.

The narrow, linear gallery forests generated the linear Pomona settlement pattern of houses constructed on the ground surface. Only the natural levees had soils that drained quickly enough for comfortable living, but the roots of the levee forest made digging house pits impossible with tools of wood and bone . The only suitable places for gardens were also in the levee soils, and it would have been cost effective to reserve garden spaces

on both sides of a house. As a result, houses are widely spaced in a linear pattern. Finally, the very slow rate of soil replenishment meant that gardens would have to be abandoned after only a few years and that re-settlement in the same spot or nearby was precluded. As a result, houses are lightly built surface structures that were probably inhabited for only one garden cycle, after which the household moved to another spot. At any rate, the contents of Pomona sites are far more sparse than those of the CPM, which in turn are scantier than those of the Middle Missouri Tradition.

The communities that produced the Pomona variant thus were even more dispersed and even more ephemeral than those that generated the Nebraska phase. The social organization may have been more like that of bands than tribes. It is likely that boundaries between local groups were diffuse. Indeed, although Brown (1984) defined several phases within the distribution of the Pomona variant, the differences between them are minimal, and most archaeologists working in the region do not use the phase names. In such a society, there is little reason to imagine that formalized leadership roles existed, and large work groups are also apt to have been absent.

To sum up, at the scale of the archaeological area, we find that the swidden cycle is responsible for different settlement patterns and social systems in different regional environments. The three subdivisions of the Plains Horticultural Tradition considered here shared a basic lifeway that demanded adaptation to local environments which in turn generated much of the diversity in the archaeological record. In only one unit, the Middle Missouri Tradition, is there a reasonable correspondence between archaeological sites and the social units that created them. In the CPM and in the Pomona Variant, with their dispersed settlement patterns, it is extremely difficult to discern communities in the archaeological record.

Household Cycles, Houses and Sites within a Phase

CPM houses, especially those of the Nebraska phase, come in a wide range of sizes, from 3.3 to 15.9 meters on a side. The very smallest houses appear to be special purpose structures, but even so, the range of normal houses is from 4.9 to 15.9 meters on a side, which is more than a tenfold variation in floor area. Such high variance could have several causes, including differences between summer and winter dwellings, variations in wealth and social status, the presence of large ceremonial structures among smaller dwellings. changes in household size over time, differences between local societies, and the space requirements of specialization of labor.

I tested these possibilities by comparing the contents of a sample of large and small houses (Blakeslee 1990:33-37). The test implications were straightforward: warm weather dwellings should have horticultural tools in them, ceremonial structures should contain ritual items and features, the homes of the wealthy should contain items of value, those of craft specialists should contain specialized tool kits, there should be a difference in location if different groups were responsible for the variance in house size, and houses of different ages should have both different radiocarbon dates and different ceramic assemblages. None of these hypotheses were supported by the archaeological data, and I was led to conclude that most of the differences in house size reflected variations in household population that occurred within the lifetime of individual sites.

How much variation in household population would account for the range of house sizes? The well-known approaches of Naroll (1962) and Cook and Heizer (1968) do not apply, not only in this instance but everywhere else as well (Blakeslee 1989:4-8). Naroll took variance *across* societies and implied that his regression (one person per 10 square meters) could be applied to variance *within* single societies, an assertion that the mathematical model does not support. Further, he looked only at the space used in the capitals of various societies, not at living space in ordinary settlements. And finally, if one uses his formula to predict populations for the sites in his original sample, one finds that it is a very poor predictor of actual population sizes (Asch 1976:15-17).

Cook and Heizer's (1968) formula (20 square feet per person until a house size of 120 square feet is reached; ten square feet per person thereafter) has an even weaker basis. To derive their formula, they did not employ actual household populations; instead they used estimates calculated by multiplying the *mean* number of people per nuclear family times the *average* number of families per house in each of 27 societies (Blakeslee 1989:6). The resulting number was compared to the *mean* house size in the same societies in order to calculate their regression formula. Obviously, such a regression cannot reveal the relationship between *variance* in house size in a single society and the *variations* of household populations within sites. Finally, the

first part of their formula resulted from drawing a straight line from the origin point of their graph (no population; zero floor area) to the first household size for which they had data. That is to say, it is based on no data at all.

Wedel (1979) noted that neither Naroll nor Cook and Heizer included any Plains settlements in the data sets used to calculate their regressions. He remedied this by assembling data for early historic households and house sizes among the Pawnees and Wichitas. His estimator — one person for every five square meters — if applied to the prehistoric Nebraska phase houses (over a gap of several centuries), yields populations of 5 for the smaller houses and 50 for the largest. My own estimates, based on calculating how many beds each house could hold, range from 6-8 people for the smallest houses to 32-44 people for the very largest (Blakeslee 1989:12).

If household population is the primary cause of the variation in house size, there is still some explaining to do. A range of household population from 5 to 50 (or from 6 to 32) in the same society seems a bit extreme, given the lack of archaeological evidence for differences in wealth and class. What is more, the variation in house size is related inversely to the variation in size of sites. The sites that contain only one house tend to contain large ones, while sites that have more than one house contain mostly small houses (Blakeslee and Caldwell 1979:30-33). Hotopp (1982:183) also noted that in the Glenwood locality, at least, the larger houses occur on the ridge tops, while smaller houses are found on the lower slopes and stream terraces.

Here are three kinds of variation to be explained: house size, site size and house location. I believe that all of them can be understood in terms of the various cycles that operated within the tribal society that generated the Nebraska phase. In addition to the swidden cycles, there is another involving the decay and replacement of the houses themselves. As mentioned above, estimates of the life spans of the prehistoric houses range all the way from five to twenty years. The earthlodges of the historic village tribes were, on average, of more substantial construction than the CPM houses, and they appear to have lasted from seven to fifteen years (Weltfish 1965:86; Wilson 1934:356, 372). Recent evidence from a modern earthlodge replica constructed by Les and Jan Hosick of Wellfleet, Nebraska, and disassembled by students from Kansas State and Wichita State universities, showed that the timbers used can last 10 years or more. Since the replica was built far more substantially than most of the prehistoric structures, a span of ten years or less for the latter seems a reasonable estimate, but one that needs to be tested through experimental archaeology. The critical factor appears to be rotting of the buried ends of support posts (Roper n.d.), and Wichita State University has just initiated a long-term experiment to determine how long posts of commonly used woods last in different plains environments.

Another cycle is that of the household population. Part of the variance in house sizes could reflect the cycle of growth and fission inherent in extended family households. A two-generation family requires a relatively small house, but as children mature and some remain at home after marriage and then have children of their own, a larger house will be needed. Conversely, when grandparents die or other events trigger division of a large household, new and smaller units are created. Since the life spans of CPM houses appears to have been shorter than the generational cycle, it was possible to adjust the size of the house to the size of the family every time a new structure was built. Then with the death of the grandparents, the household might fission, beginning the cycle once more.

House construction was probably synchronized with the pioneering swidden cycle. When people moved to a new location cleared a garden or gardens they may well have used some of the timbers to build a house. So long as the immediate vicinity would support continued occupation, the cycle of house construction, decay and replacement would generate more and more house remains. Lengthy occupations in environmentally favorable spots would produce the largest sites. Less favored spots might support only a single house cycle. As will become clear below, it is likely that more than one house was occupied at a time in the largest accumulations, but no one has yet developed a way to sort out which ones were contemporaneous and which ones were sequential. Since site size may reflect length of occupation as well as the size of the local community, because since houses are widely and irregularly spaced, the size and organization of the communities cannot be estimated directly from the site records.

I have argued above that the largest houses in the Nebraska phase are multi-family dwellings that were the first houses constructed when people moved to a new location. If the occupation of a spot did not last past the lifetime of a single house, the result would be a large house in a single house site. If the site allowed a longer occupation, individual families could move into separate dwellings when it came time to replace the original structure. As a result, the sites with more than one house tend to have a smaller average house size. In the large sites which have seen extensive excavation, one or two large houses are found along with the smaller dwellings (Blakeslee and Caldwell 1979:32).

Since Nebraska phase houses were constructed in pits, the first house at a site usually was built on a grassy ridge top rather than on a forested lower slope or stream terrace. The latter locations were where the gardens were cleared. Later, when the posts of the original house had rotted, so had the tree roots in the first gardens cleared, and the residents could erect new houses closer to water and to their gardens.

This set of cycles is summarized in Figure 4. The model presented there accounts for the locations of the largest houses (on ridge tops), for the inverse relationship between house size and the number of houses in a site, and for the variation in site size within the phase. An accurate model can also predict new data. During the excavation of a Nebraska phase site that held several houses Bozell and Ludwickson (1999:figure 5) noted that the details of construction of the two sides of the largest house differed, as though two construction crews using two slightly different models had erected the house. They suggested that the house was built by and for two extended families.

The model implies that the size of Nebraska Phase sites does not correspond to the size of the communities of the people who left the remains. I do not doubt that there were some sort of social units larger than single households, but in the archaeological record, they are hard to discern. We do not have the chronological control necessary to determine which households were occupied contemporaneously and hence cannot delimit communities within the overall scatter of house remains.

Some sort of larger community may have provided support for households during the food crises inherent in swidden horticulture. So long as gardens were started in different years, some neighbors may have had relatively plentiful food supplies, and some form of reciprocity would have been useful. In addition to the recurrent garden failures, another form of variance required an adaptive response. In the Central Plains, most precipitation during the growing season comes from convective storms that cover very limited areas. While one spot may receive adequate precipitation, another only a few miles away may be having a drought. A dispersed community that practiced

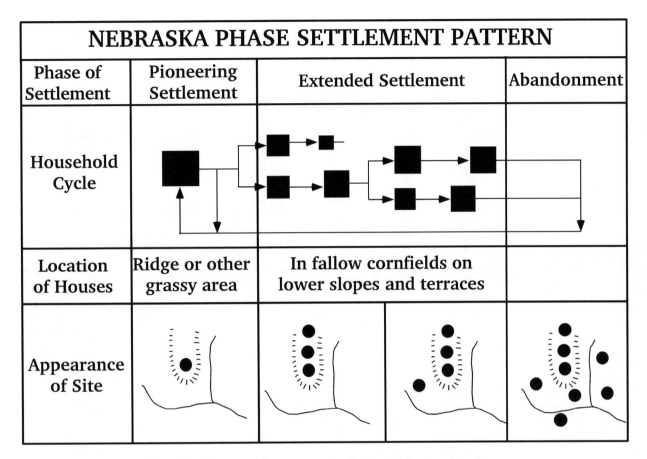

Fig. 4. A model for Nebraska Phase settlement cycles (after Blakeslee 1990).

reciprocity may have been one adaptation to the resulting local-scale variance in productivity.

In the Solomon River phase, however, I was able to demonstrate that an ossuary site adjacent to a habitation site held more bodies than that single site could possibly have generated and at the same time that the ceramics in it did not come from all of the occupied spots in the Glen Elder locality (Blakeslee 1999:121-122, 145-147). This appears to suggest the presence of a form of community organization above the level of the site but below the level of the population of a whole locality. Ossuaries have been excavated in a few other localities, but to date no one has performed a comparative analysis of them.

Household Cycles, Architecture and Ceramics in Three Localities

The three most closely studied localities in CPM archaeology are the Glenwood locality of southwestern Iowa, the Medicine Creek locality of southwestern Nebraska, and the Glen Elder locality of north-central Kansas. All three have generated large data sets which have seen extensive analysis. In all three there are variations in houses and ceramics explicable in terms of the swidden and household cycles.

The nature of the ceramic variance in the Glenwood locality was first reported by Anderson (1961) who reported sites that yielded up to 85 percent collared rims. The sites with the high proportions of collared rims were long considered anomalous because 1) the CPM sites in the locality were assigned to the Nebraska phase, and 2) the Nebraska phase was originally defined, in contrast to the Upper Republican phase, as having low percentages of collared vessels (Strong 1935:245-254). Billeck (1993:32), however, not only documented the importance of collared rims in some Glenwood assemblages but also demonstrated the presence of a strong cline in the distribution of collaring within the locality (Fig. 5). At the eastern end, sites yield up to 85 percent collared vessels, while at the western end, only 12 km away, sites contain from four to twelve percent collared rims. The scale of

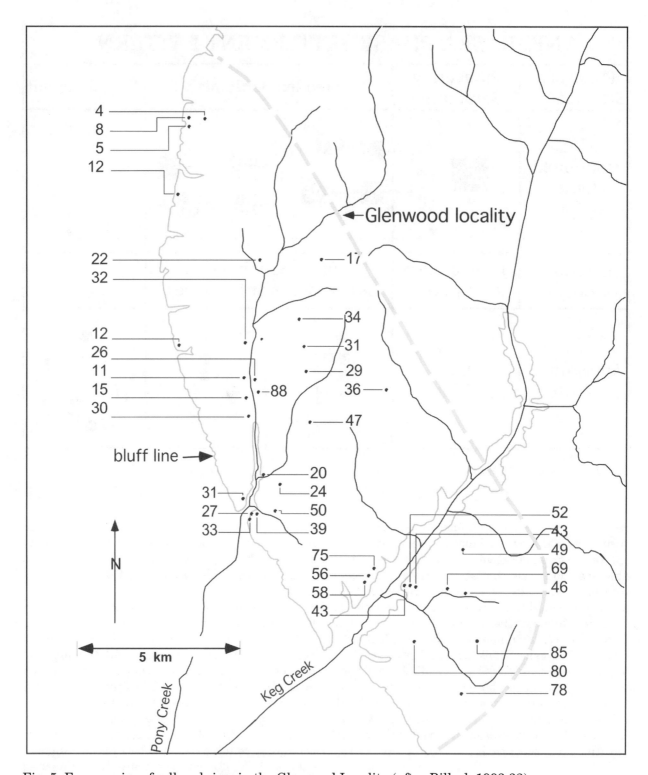

Fig. 5. Frequencies of collared rims in the Glenwood Locality (after Billeck 1993:32).

the differences within the locality are similar to those supposed to exist between the Nebraska and Upper Republican phases, another example of phase invariance.

Details of houses construction also differ within the locality, although this variance has been given little recognition. Houses near the mouth of Keg Creek (14ML128, 14ML129, 14ML130) are approximately square, with rounded corners (Billeck 1983:80,89, 96). They have many wall posts, and cache pits are lined up neatly along the walls. Each has a set of four center posts. In the eastern portion of the Keg Creek drainage three other houses (14ML132, 14ML134, 14ML135) form part of a cluster (Billeck 1983:105, 111, 115). Unfortunately parts of the floors of two of them were destroyed prior to excavation. Enough remains of the partial floors to indicate that, like the complete one, they are far from square. Near the mouth of Pony Creek is another cluster of houses (14ML126, 14ML136 and 14ML139). One had been disturbed by historic construction resulting in only a partial floor plan, and another had intrusive historic graves in it. All three have numerous internal postmolds, and in none of them is there a clear center post pattern that is centered within the house walls. Cache pits are not restricted to areas along the walls but also occur toward the centers of the houses (Billeck 1983:66, 102, 136).

In the Glen Elder locality, similar spatial patterning in the domestic architecture is evident. Several distinct styles of houses are present in and near the locality (Blakeslee 1999:60-72). Within the federal property around Waconda Lake, three styles of houses occur. One style is square, with four substantial center posts and relatively few wall posts (Fig. 6a). The two examples of this style are found in adjacent sites. Another style lacks a pattern of four center posts; instead there are many small posts that appear to have supported the roof. This style of house lacks many internal caches but has large numbers of wall posts crowded together (Fig. 6b). One of these houses came from a site that contained a second house of a different style; the second came from a site farther up the same stream. Finally, along the South Solomon River are three sites containing five houses of a third style. These are rectangular, with numerous wall posts, especially along the front wall, and numerous internal caches, fireplaces slightly offset toward the front of the house, and no clear pattern of central support posts (Fig. 6c).

Just northeast from the lake, site 14ML417 contained a house that did not look like any at the lake, and site 14OB27 to the west of the lake has yielded a series of trapezoidal houses. Thus at least five styles of houses have been found in the part of the Glen Elder locality adjacent to the Solomon River. Other styles may well occur in the sites known to exist high up the tributary streams.

These various styles of houses do not appear to differ in age. Radiocarbon dates are available for all five styles of house, and the radiocarbon ages of four of them overlap. One style, however, is restricted to the earliest site in the local sequence, 14OB27. Still, most of the variation (four styles out of five) does not appear to have chronological significance.

The ceramics from the Glen Elder locality also exhibit clear spatial patterning, although the differences from spot to spot are not as distinct as in the Glenwood locality (Blakeslee 1999:115-121). Four ceramic 'dialects' can be identified among the 17 excavated sites in and near the Glen Elder locality. They differ in attributes that, for the most part, are not reflected in traditional ceramic classifications. For instance, rim height, angle of rim flare and precise location of decorative elements (lip edge versus top of lip, collar face versus collar base) are important. These spatially patterned differences do not appear to reflect change through time; that is, here are no discernable differences in the radiocarbon dates from the four sets of sites.

In the Medicine Creek locality, similar variations in house style exist. Close examination of the house plans in Kivett and Metcalf's (1997) monograph on Medicine Creek archaeology, shows that the houses that are most similar to one another come from the individual sites or from immediately adjacent sites. Not only are there differences in architectural details, but as is true in the other localities, the different styles of houses are not randomly distributed within the locality; instead, the examples of each style are clustered. I suspect that there are spatially patterned ceramic variations as well, but the collections from Medicine Creek are now scattered, and the tabular data in Kivett and Metcalf's (1997) report are not sufficient to analyze them.

To sum up, in all three closely studied localities within the Central Plains, house styles vary from spot to spot within localities, and ceramics in at least two localities vary in the same fashion. In the historic period, both architecture and ceramic production were handled by part-time specialists (e.g., Bowers 1965:165; Wilson 1934:356), and there is some scanty evidence to suggest that CPM ceramics were made by specialists (e.g., Rounds 1988:50-52). Even in the absence of part-time specialists, knowledge of house design must have been handed down within local communities, and the same is true for ceramic technology, and in combination with the household and swidden cycles may explain the spatial patterns. A family's way of constructing a house, in conjunction with the effects of the swidden cycle on CPM settlement patterns,

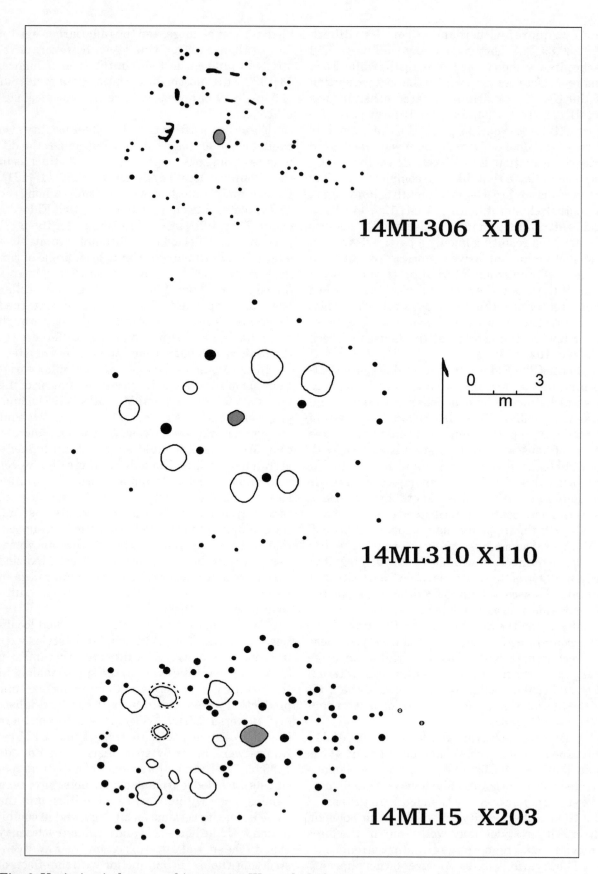

Fig. 6. Variation in house architecture at Waconda Lake.

would generate clusters of sites with similar houses. In the same way, a single potter would, over an adult lifetime, create pots that would show up in four or five houses even if that person only made vessels for his or her own family. If ceramics and architecture were part-time specialties, a single person's creations would end up in a much larger number of sites, most of which would be concentrated in one spot in each locality.

Longer Term Cycles and the CPM Mosaic

One has to turn to longer term cycles to explain the origin and demise of the CPM. To date, approaches to both questions, but especially to the origin of the pattern, have been piecemeal. Both Roper (1995) and I (Blakeslee 1997) have addressed the timing of the origin of the CPM, with different results. Roper examined the published radiocarbon dates, and by mapping the localities that yielded dates from different centuries, suggested that the CPM appeared first in the Glenwood locality and spread from there. This analysis superceded an earlier study (Roper 1976) in which she had used trend-surface analysis of the dates, but that she later had come to reject (Roper 1985).

I have attempted to distinguish (Blakeslee 1997) between beginning dates (when a phase actually began) and initial dates (the earliest well-dated sited from the sample of dated sites). I also excluded potentially misleading radiocarbon outliers before determining the initial dates for each phase. My results differ somewhat from Roper's, indicating a south to north trend in initial dates, but the samples of dated sites from the two most northerly phases are far too small to be reliable. Whichever analysis is more precise, the spread of the CPM across the Central Plains appears to have been far too rapid to explain in terms of population growth. Either several (presumably Late Woodland) populations made the transition from their earlier adaptation to the one that generated the CPM (cf. Adair and Brown 1981; Benn 1981; Steinacher 1976) or the CPM had its origin in a massive migration from elsewhere (Wedel 1959, 1961), or perhaps a combination of migration and transition in place is needed to explain the whole record.

Calabrese (1969) saw the Steed-Kisker phase as a possible ancestor of the Nebraska phase. Steed-Kisker is a complex in the Kansas City area (Wedel 1943; O'Brien 1978a, 1978b) that exhibits a combination of Mississippian traits and elements of the CPM. Ceramics, burial mounds and some house types are clearly Mississippian in origin. Other houses and the bulk of the non-ceramic artifacts, on the other hand, would be lost in most CPM assemblages. In addition, such Mississippian traits as fortifications, towns and platform mounds are missing from both Steed-Kisker and the CPM.

Wedel (1943) initially suggested that Steed-Kisker may have originated in a migration from the Mississippian homeland, and in combination with Calabrese's idea would suggest a Mississippian to Steed-Kisker to Nebraska phase sequence. While Steed-Kisker clearly begins earlier than the Nebraska phase (Blakeslee 1997:319), there are reasons for doubting the sequence. Adair (1988:92-93) notes that while Steed-Kisker may have begun with a migration (she has some reservations) and while Steed-Kisker cultigens are most similar to those in contemporary Mississippian sites, the Steed-Kisker horticultural complex is not identical to that of the CPM, including the Nebraska phase. Similarly, O'Brien (1978b) argues that there is no continuity in ceramic decoration between Steed-Kisker and the Nebraska phase. The decorative motifs on the shoulders of Steed-Kisker vessels do not occur on Nebraska phase jars, and the single motif typical of the Nebraska phase (hachured triangles set in an alternating pattern) does not occur in Steed-Kisker.

Steed-Kisker aside, however, there are no realistic candidates for a complex that is likely to be ancestral to the CPM. Wedel (1959:570) once suggested that among the CPM units then defined, the Smoky Hill phase might be ancestral to the Upper Republican phase, an idea elaborated by Steinacher (1976). The radiocarbon dates now available, however, show that Smoky Hill is contemporaneous with both Steed-Kisker and the Solomon River phases. The earliest well-dated sites (ca. A.D. 1000) that have been identified include the Two Deer site in southern Kansas (Adair 1988) and 14OB27 in north-central Kansas (Blakeslee 1999; Krause, personal communication).

The transition from Late Woodland to CPM certainly generated a dramatic change in the archaeological record. The settlement pattern changed, and year-round habitations appear to have replaced base camps and special-purpose resource extraction camps. Sites became larger, with dramatically richer middens. Houses also became larger and more substantially built. Storage capacity, as reflected in cache pit numbers and sizes, appears to have increased. Ceramic vessels became globular, and collared rims appeared. Side-notched arrow points replaced corner-notched forms, end scrapers became both more common and more elongated, and there were changes in both the frequency of occurrence and formal attributes of other artifacts as well.

This trait list is a recitation of the classical material culture approach, and it ignores the social and ideological requirements of the very profound transformation that took place. Adair (1988:96) suggests what factors may lie behind the material changes:

> The decision to increase the availability of cultigens was primarily cultural and was related to existing parameters of social organization, division of labor, and technological skills. Changes in these institutions are relatively gradual processes in their own right and if related to subsistence strategies, they developed along with agricultural systems.

One could add to Adair's list; it seems reasonable to assume that fundamental religious changes accompanied the thorough re-working of the rest of social life. Still, we are left with some difficult evidentiary questions. If we are dealing with a transition among populations already in place, and if the changes were gradual, where are the sites with CPM houses and Late Woodland ceramics or vice versa? If 14OB27 and the Two Deer site are transitional, what is it about them other than the radiocarbon dates that appears to be transitional?

Of course, the place to look for the reasons for the transition is not in CPM sites but in the preceding Late Woodland adaptations and in the larger patterns of change in the midcontinent Adair (1988:93-97) suggests that in addition to internal pressures generated in the Late Woodland adaptations, new varieties of maize and climate change may also have played a part. To follow up on her suggestions, however, will require a great deal of intensive effort.

The demise of the CPM is, at best, only a little better understood that its origins. Analysis of the radiocarbon dates suggest that the southern phases of the CPM and the Steed-Kisker phase ended by A.D. 1300. The more northerly phases appear to have ended somewhat later, but radiocarbon samples from the Itskari and St. Helena phases are woefully inadequate. Following the demise of CPM, much of the central Great Plains was unoccupied for centuries, except for an intrusion of western Oneota called the White Rock phase (Logan 1995; Blakeslee et al. 2001). This episode seems to have been short, and following it, the central plains were empty until the protohistoric period,

when full-scale villages appear in the Lower Loup phase.

Two competing models for the abandonment have been offered, one climatic and one cultural. The climatic explanation is the earlier of the two, coeval with the recognition that the Coalescent Tradition of the Dakotas had its roots in the central plains (Lehmer 1954). The basic idea is that a drought caused abandonment of the region by horticulturalists, with the population migrating to the northern plains to form the Initial Coalescent variant and/or to the southern plains to form the Panhandle Aspect. The hypothesis that western CPM groups moved to Oklahoma and Texas to settle in the Canadian River valley is no longer tenable (Lintz 1986:218-222), but most scholars still find the CPM-Initial Coalescent argument cogent.

Today, the moot question is not the migration to the north but the causes that lay behind it. If a climate change were the cause, one would expect that the areas of abandonment and new settlement would fit both the time and the pattern of the climate change. I have tested these implications (Blakeslee 1993), using Bryson's model of the onset of the Pacific I climatic episode. Neither the timing nor the pattern of movement seem to fit, and a compilation of all of the microfaunal data for the northern half of the Plains (Blakeslee 1999:Table 5) fails to provide convincing evidence for a significant climate change at the time that Bryson's model predicts..

The abandonment may instead be the product of an imbalance in the CPM horticultural adaptation. For the most part, there appears to be very little evidence for CPM abandonment and re-occupation of sites. Such a pattern would be expected if the swidden cycle involved temporary abandonment followed by re-occupation when the fields had lain fallow long enough to restore soil fertility. So far, only one Nebraska phase house has been offered as evidence of re-occupation os a site (Bozell and Ludwickson 1999), in spite of the fact that over 100 Nebraska Phase houses alone have been excavated.

The general lack of evidence for re-occupation suggests that the CPM swidden system was one that constantly, or at least episodically, generated the need for new land. Rather than being a stable adaptation to one territory, it may have forced its practitioners to move on after a number of generations. If so, one would expect that the regions occupied first would also be the first to be abandoned, and the radiocarbon dates seem to bear this out (Blakeslee 1993:202). If this model is correct, the next step in the research program is to identify what factor(s) led to abandonment of localities and regions. One possible factor is the local extinction of hardwood groves as the result of swidden gardening. The distribution of hardwoods is limited in the Central Plains, and (as mentioned above) it is far easier to create garden spaces in stands of hardwood than in softwood groves. Recent excavations in southwestern Kansas (Bevitt 1999) uncovered evidence for black walnut trees in a region that contained no hardwoods at the beginning of the historic period.

One could argue just as convincingly that the black walnuts in southwestern Kansas became extinct as a result of climate change, so the next logical step in the research should involve a method that can distinguish between the effects of climate change and human-induced local extinctions. One possibility is implicit in the work of a Canadian research team (Laird et al. 1996). They use the relative frequency of diatom species in lakes in closed basins as a measure of salinity, and the salinity in turn is the product of both precipitation and temperature, i.e. of climate. If swidden horticulture caused local extinctions of hardwoods without independently of any climate changes, then the diatom and pollen records from a closed lake basin in the Central Plains might show a decrease in hardwood pollen without a simultaneous change in diatom frequencies. Furthermore, the pollen and charcoal profiles should reflect both the occupation and abandonment of the locality by its CPM population. One lake that might generate appropriate data is Medicine Lake, in the heavily occupied (in CPM times) Medicine Creek valley of southwestern Nebraska.

Discussion and Conclusions

I have used the metaphor of fractal imagery to draw attention to certain patterns in the record. Fractal images are generated by recursive functions, while the archaeological record can be viewed as being produced by cycles that operate at different temporal frequencies (see Fowles, this volume, Chapter 2). In the CPM, such cycles include the manufacture, use and discard of tools; excavation, use and abandonment of cache pits; the annual round of planting, harvesting gathering and hunting; a garden cycle that (at least in the Glen Elder locality) took five years on average; the erection, use and abandonment of houses; a household cycle that involved the growth and eventual fissioning of extended families; and a pioneering cycle of ini-

tial use and final abandonment of habitable spots.

The archaeological record so created may be analyzed at a variety of spatial scales—individual features, houses, sites, spots within a locality, localities, regions and area. At each of these different scales, the effects of only some of the cycles will be evident. At the scale of individual pits within a site, each filled with trash that had accumulated over a relatively short period of time, one can see the occasional use of crisis foods, a reflection of the garden cycle.

At the scale of sites within a locality, the annual round generates uniformity in lithic resource acquisition and frequencies of tools and chipped stone debitage. At the scale of spots within a locality, we find clusters of similar houses and ceramic dialects. At the scale of different site assemblages within a region, local foraging and fluctuations in the weather create remarkable differences in faunal assemblages. Some of the archaeological data are equally variable when viewed at several spatial scales, just as fractal images are. But sometimes, distinct patterns emerge at yet another spatial scale. This is certainly the case when the settlement patterns from different regions are compared; an underlying similarity (the swidden adaptation) produces very different pictures in different environments.

I hope to have shown the productivity of recasting research questions in terms of cycles rather than in terms of the structural units that composed the CPM. Structural analysis is bound to fail when the archaeologist cannot say which sites belonged to a single dispersed community, and worse yet, cannot say where one site leaves off and the next one begins. Indeed, the variations between groups of sites within the three intensively-studied localities in the Central Plains—differences in both house form and ceramics—suggest that the archaeological units at a larger spatial scale may also bear no necessary relationship to prehistoric social units. If we find levels of variation in houses and in ceramics within localities that are similar in magnitude to those used to define phases, it is logical to question the reality of the phases themselves. At a minimum one must question whether the phases reflect any prehistoric social units as opposed to being heuristic devices invented by archaeologists.

Another kind of productivity is the generation of new research questions. Paying attention to the various cycles that existed in the past calls attention to our lack of control over important parameters. Experimental archaeology could tell us how long the soils of various localities remain productive when the appropriate crops are grown in them, and it could also give us far more precise estimate of how long houses made with various species of wood lasted in the various local environments. Other information can probably be squeezed from existing collections. As mentioned above, analysis of the contents of individual trash-filled pits may yield information on both the seasonal round and on the swidden cycles. And to the extent that the products of individual flintknappers and potters can be defined (Blakeslee 1999:128-132; Rounds 1988:52-55) it might be possible to trace the products of individuals through the houses that they occupied as productive adults.

[1] I have chosen to use a variant of the Robinson (1951) Coefficient of Similarity as a means to quantify the scale of the variance in these data sets. The Coefficient of Difference is calculated for each pair of assemblages by adding the difference in frequency for each of the taxa (such as lithic types) being considered. This gives a total difference which is divided by two to obtain a coefficient that has a 100 point scale, from zero (no difference) to 100 (no similarity). I also calculate an uncertainty estimate (based on the standard error of the proportion) for each coefficient. This allows one to determine the likelihood that sampling error has affected the results.

References Cited

Adair, Mary J.
　1988　*Prehistoric Agriculture in the Central Plains*. Publications in Anthropology 16. University of Kansas, Lawrence.

Adair, Mary J. and Marie E. Brown
　1981　The Two Deer Site (14BU55): A Plains Woodland-Plains Village Transition. In *Prehistory and History of the El Dorado Lake Area, Kansas (Phase II)*, edited by Mary J. Adair, 237-351. Museum of Anthropology, University of Kansas, Project Report Series, 47. Lawrence.

Anderson, Adrian D.
　1961　The Glenwood Sequence. *Journal of the Iowa Archaeological Society* 10(3):1-101.

Anderson, Adrian D. and Larry J. Zimmerman
　1976　Settlement-Subsistence Variability in the Glenwood Locality. *Plains Anthropologist* 21:141-154.

Asch, David
　1976　*The Middle Woodland Population of the Lower Illinois Valley: A Study in Paleodemographic Methods*. Northwestern Archaeological Program Scientific Papers 1. Evanston.

Benn, David W.
　1981　Archaeological Investigations at the Rainbow Site, Plymouth County, Iowa. Report submitted to Interagency Archaeological Services, Denver.

Bevitt, Christopher Tod
　1999　Life on the High Plains Border: Archaeological Investigations of Three Prehistoric Habitation Sites in Southwestern Kansas. M.A. thesis, Department of Anthropology, Wichita State University.

Billeck, William T.
　1993　Time and Space in the Glenwood Locality: The Nebraska Phase in Western Iowa. Ph.D. dissertation, Department of Anthropology, University of Missouri, Columbia.

Blakeslee, Donald J.
　1989　On Estimating Household Populations in Archaeological Sites, with an Example from the Nebraska Phase. *Plains Anthropologist* 34(124, Pt. 2):3-16.
　1990　A Model for the Nebraska Phase. *Central Plains Archaeology* 2(1):29-56.
　1993　Modeling the Abandonment of the Central Plains: Radiocarbon Dates and the Origin of the Initial Coalescent. *Plains Anthropologist* 38(145):199-214.
　1997　Assessing Sets of Radiocarbon Dates: An Example from the Central Plains. *North American Archaeologist* 18(4):303-326.
　1999　Waconda Lake: Prehistoric Swidden-Foragers in the Central Plains. *Central Plains Archaeology* 7(1).

Blakeslee, Donald J. and Warren W. Caldwell
　1979　*The Nebraska Phase: An Appraisal*. J&L Publishing, Lincoln, NE.

Blakeslee, Donald J., Michelle Peck and Ronald A. Dorsey
　2001　Glen Elder: A Western Oneota Bison Hunting Camp. *Midcontinental Journal of Archaeology* 20(1):79-104.

Bowers, Alfred E.
　1965　Hidatsa Social and Ceremonial Organization. *Bureau of American Ethnology Bulletin* 194. Washington, D.C.

Bozell, John R.
  1991 Fauna from the Hulme Site and Comments on Central Plains Tradition Subsistence Variability. *Plains Anthropologist* 36(136):229-253.
  1995 Culture, Environment and Bison Populations on the Late Prehistoric and Early Historic Central Plains. *Plains Anthropologist* 40(152):145-163.

Bozell, John R. and John Ludwickson
  1999 *Archeology of the Patterson Site: Native American Life in the Lower Platte Valley*. Report prepared for the Nebraska Department of Roads. Nebraska State Historical Society, Lincoln.

Brown, Kenneth
  1984 Pomona: A Plains Village Variant in Eastern Kansas and Western Missouri. Ph.D. dissertation, Department of Anthropology, University of Kansas.

Calabrese, F. A.
  1969 Doniphan Phase Origins: An Hypothesis Resulting from Archaeological Investigations in the Smithville Reservoir Area, Missouri. M.A. thesis, Department of Anthropology, University of Missouri, Columbia.

Cook, Sherburne F. and Robert F. Heizer
  1968 Relationships among Houses, Settlement Areas, and Population in Aboriginal California. In *Settlement Archaeology*, edited by K. C. Chang, pp. 79-116. National Press Books, Palo Alto.

Dorsey, Ronald D.
  1998 Freshwater Mussels and Archaeological Sites on the Solomon River. M.A. thesis, Department of Anthropology, Wichita State University.
  2000 Archaeological Interpretation of Freshwater Mussel Assemblages on the Solomon River. *Central Plains Archaeology* 8(1):13-24.

Falk, Carl R.
  1969 Faunal Remains. In Two House Sites in the Central Plains: An Experiment in Archaeology. Edited by W. R. Wood. *Plains Anthropologist* 14-44 (Part 2): 102.
  1977 Analysis of Unmodified Fauna from Sites in the Middle Missouri Subarea: A Review. *Plains Anthropologist* 22(78 Pt. 2):151-161.

Griffin, David
  1977 Timber Procurement and Village Location in the Middle Missouri Subarea. *Plains Anthropologist* 22(78 Pt 2):177-185.

Holen, Stephen R.
  1991 Bison Hunting Territories and Lithic Acquisition Among the Pawnee: An Ethnohistoric and Archaeological Study. In *Raw Material Economics among Prehistoric Hunter-Gatherers*, edited by Anta Montet-White and Steven R. Holen. University of Kansas Publications in Anthropology 19.

Hotopp, John A.
  1982 Some Observations on the Central Plains Tradition in Iowa. In *Plains Indian Studies: A Collection of Essays in Honor of John C. Ewers and Waldo R. Wedel*, edited by Douglas H. Ubelaker and Herman J. Viola, pp. 173-192.. Smithsonian Contributions to Anthropology 30

Johnson, P. C.
  1972 Mammalian Remains Associated with Nebraska Phase Earth Lodges in Mills County, Iowa. M.A. thesis, Department of Geology, University of Iowa.

Kivett, Marvin F. and George S. Metcalf
  1997 The Prehistoric People of the Medicine Creek Reservoir, Frontier County, Nebraska: An Experiment in Mechanized Archaeology (1946-1948). *Plains Anthropologist* 42(162).

Koch, Amy
  1995 The McIntosh Fauna: Late Prehistoric Exploitation of Lake and Prairie Habitats in the Nebraska Sand Hills. *Plains Anthropologist* 40(151):39-60.

Krause, Richard
  1969 Correlation of Phases in Central Plains Prehistory. In Two House Sites in the Central Plains: An Experiment in Archaeology. Edited by W. R. Wood. *Plains Anthropologist* 14(44 Pt. 2):82-96.
  1970 Aspects of Adaptation Among Upper Republican Subsistence Cultivators. In *Pleistocene and Recent Environments of the Great Plains*, edited by W. Dort and J. K. Jones, pp. 103-115. University of Kansas Press: Lawrence.

Laird, K. R., S. C. Fritz, K. A. Maasch, and B. F. Cumming
  1996 Greater Drought Intensity and Frequency Before A.D. 1200 in the Northern Great Plains, USA. *Nature* 384:552-554.

Lehmer, Donald J.
  1954 Archaeological Investigations in the Oahe Dam Area, South Dakota, 1950-51. *Bureau of American Ethnology Bulletin* 158. Washington, D.C.

Lintz, Christoper R.
  1986 *Architectural and Community Variability with the Antelope Creek Phase of the Texas Panhandle.* Studies in Oklahoma's Past 14. Norman: Oklahoma Archaeological Survey.

Lippincott, Kerry
  1976 Settlement Ecology of Solomon River Upper Republican Sites in North Central Kansas. Ph. D. dissertation, Department of Anthropology, University of Missouri.

Logan, Brad
  1995 Phasing in White Rock: Archaeological Investigation of the White Rock and Warne Sites, Lovewell Reservoir, Jewell County, Kansas, 1994-115. *University of Kansas Museum of Anthropology Project Series* 90.

Lyman, R. Lee, Michael J. O'Brien and Robert C. Dunnell
  1997 *The Rise and Fall of Culture History.* Plenum Press, New York.

Mandelbrot, Benoit B.
  1982 *The Fractal Geometry of Nature.* W. H. Freeman, San Francisco.

Morey, Darcy
  1982 *A Study of Subsistence and Seasonality in the Central Plains.* Technical Report No. 82-12. University of Nebraska, Lincoln.

Naroll, Raoul
  1962 Floor Area and Settlement Pattern. *American Antiquity* 27(4):587-589.

O'Brien, Patricia J.
  1978a Steed-Kisker and Mississippian Influences on the Central Plains. In *The Central Plains Tradition: Internal Development and External Relationships*, ed. by Donald J. Blakeslee, pp. 67-80. Office of the State Archaeologist, Report 11. Iowa City.
  1978b Steed-Kisker: A Western Mississippian Settlement System. In *Mississippian Settlement Patterns*, ed. by Bruce D. Smith, pp. 1-18. New York: Academic Press.

Pielgen, H-O. and P. H. Richter
  1986 *The Beauty of Fractals: Images of Complex Dynamical Systems.* Springer-Verlag, Berlin.

Renfrew, Colin and Gene Sterud
  1969 Close-Proximity Analysis: A Rapid Method for the Ordering of Archaeological Materials. *American Antiquity* 34(3):265-277.

Robarchek, Clayton and Carole Robarchek
  1998 *Waorani: The Contexts of Violence and War.* Harcourt, Brace, Fort Worth.

Robinson, W. S.
  1951 A Method for Chronologically Ordering Archaeological Deposits. *American Antiquity* 16(4):293-301.

Roper, Donna C.
  1976 A Trend Surface Analysis of Central Plains Radiocarbon Dates. *American Antiquity* 41:181-188.
  1985 Some Comments on Kvamme's Reexamination of Roper's Trend-Surface Analysis. *Plains Anthropologist* 30(109):259-261.
  1995 Spatial Dynamics and Historical Process in the Central Plains Tradition. *Plains Anthropologist* 40-153:203-222.
  n.d. Lessons from an Earthlodge: An Observational Study of Deterioration in a Replica North American Plains Earthlodge. Manuscript in preparation.

Rounds, Leslie
  1988 Processual Analysis of the Ceramics from Annie's Site. In *The St. Helena Phase: New Data, Fresh Interpretations*, edited by Donald J. Blakeslee, pp. 47-62. J&L Reprint, Lincoln.

Satorius-Fox, Marsha R.
  1982 *Paleoecological Analysis of Micromammals from the Schmidt Site, Howard County, Nebraska.* Technical Report 82-13, Division of Archaeological Research, Department of Anthropology, University of Nebraska.

Scott, Susan L.
  1993 Faunal Remains. In Archaeological Investigations at the Marvin Coulson Site, 25FT158, ed. by Donna Roper. Report to the Bureau of Reclamation, Great Plains Region.

Steinacher, Terry L.
  1976 The Smoky Hill Phase and its Role in the Central Plains Tradition. Masters thesis, Department of Anthropology, University of Nebraska, Lincoln.

Strong, William D.
  1935 *An Introduction to Nebraska Archaeol-*

ogy. Smithsonian Miscellaneous Collections 93 (10). Washington, D.C.

Wedel, Waldo R.

1943 *Archaeological Investigations in Platte and Clay Counties, Missouri.* U. S. National Museum Bulletin 183. Washington, D.C.

1959 An Introduction to Kansas Archaeology. *Bureau of American Ethnology Bulletin 174.* Washington, D.C.

1961 *Prehistoric Man on the Great Plains.* University of Oklahoma Press.

1970 Some Observations on Two House Sites in the Central Plains: An Experiment in Archaeology. *Nebraska History* 51 (2):225-252.

1979 House Floors and Native Settlement Populations in the Central Plains. *Plains Anthropologist* 24(84 Pt. 1):85-98.

1986 *Central Plains Prehistory: Holocene Environments and Culture Change in the Republican River Basin.* University of Nebraska Press, Lincoln.

Weltfish, Gene

1965 *The Lost Universe.* Basic Books, New York.

Willey, Gordon R. and Philip Phillips

1958 *Method and Theory in American Archaeology.* University of Chicago Press, Chicago.

Wilson, Gilbert L.

1917 *Agriculture of the Hidatsa Indians: An Indian Interpretation.* University of Minnesota Studies in the Social Sciences, No. 9. Minneapolis.

1934 *The Hidatsa Earthlodge.* Anthropological papers 33(5):341-420. American Museum of Natural History, New York.

Wood, W. Raymond

1967 *An Interpretation of Mandan Culture History.* Bureau of American Ethnology Bulletin 198. Washington: U.S. Government Printing Office.

1969 Two House Sites in the Central Plains: An Experiment in Archaeology. *Plains Anthropologist* 14(44) Pt. 2.

Zehnder, Jon

1998 Relationships Between Two Little River Focus Sites in MacPherson and Rice Counties of Central Kansas Based on Excavated Lithic Debitage. M.A. thesis. Department of Anthropology, Wichita State University.

11. Material Indicators of Territory, Identity, and Interaction in a Prehistoric Tribal System

John M. O'Shea and Claire McHale Milner

Abstract

Tribes are flexible systems for organizing population within defined territories in the absence of hierarchical structures of social and political control. The ability of such organizational forms to accommodate very different structural poses over time while maintaining their overall coherence makes them adaptively robust and a potential springboard for evolutionary change. These changing spatial configurations generate archaeological signatures that can reveal a great deal about the organization and workings of the past society. The late prehistoric Juntunen Phase of the upper Great Lakes region provides an example of a tribal social formation in which population adopted markedly different patterns of aggregation or dispersal on both a regular (seasonal) and episodic basis. In this paper we examine some of the differing social and spatial scales that are represented in the regional archaeological record. We first describe the larger scales of social integration that were formally demarcated within the Juntunen tribal system and then consider how common classes of material culture are patterned by the differing spatial scales of interaction.

Introduction

At its most essential, tribal social organization is a means of predictably organizing people within a defined territory. In contrast to Earle's (1997) definition of chiefdoms (i.e., a centralized organization of population within a territory), tribal organization lacks the strong central organizing mechanisms of the chiefdom, and instead relies on a variety of 'lateral' mechanisms, (kinship, ideology, cosmology, language, etc.) to structure and coordinate the autonomous communities that constitute a tribe (Tooker 1971; Whiteley 1985). At the same time, tribes share with chiefdoms, as distinct from simpler bands, a greater absolute size and a firmer definition of territoriality and corporate ownership.

Tribal organization is inherently fluid and flexible. This fluidity is expressed in the degree to which individuals and communities may choose to affiliate with, or participate in, the tribal organization. It is also apparent in the varying ways that population can be distributed within the bounded territory over time. Societies organized as tribes, or as autonomous villages within a tribal confederacy, often exhibit changing patterns of spatial organization. This variation can take many forms. It is most commonly observed as a pattern of regular seasonal moves over the course of an annual cycle (see, for example, Blakeslee, this volume, Chapter 10). At the other extreme, change in spatial organization may occur over long spans of time, reflecting a major reorganization and relocation of population (see, for example, Parkinson, this volume, Chapter 18). Change of this type may, itself, be cyclical, as in periods of aggregation and dispersal of population, or directional, reflecting a permanent change in the relationship between population, society and geography (cf. Minc and Smith 1989). Tribal segments may also shift their spatial configuration episodically over shorter time scales. These changes are often responses to short-term fluctuations in local circumstances or resource availability. Change in spatial distribution is necessarily accompanied by social accommodation and restructuring, as population disperses or aggregates in targeted seasonal postures, or irregularly in response to unexpected stresses or opportunities. Perceived in this light, the flexibility inherent to tribal organization can be seen as both a major adaptive benefit and as a potential seedbed for evolutionary change.

Yet, organizational fluidity is only advantageous if the system also maintains predictability and coherence; i.e. integration. Individuals and communities must be able to reliably predict the actions of others within the tribe. A tribesman must know how he will be received when he visits another community, and the community must similarly be able to predict the likely course of events when they host or travel to another village in times of plenty or in times of famine. Without this predictability, the ecological and social advantages of tribal organization disappear.

How do you maintain predictability and coordination among autonomous communities? This is where the lateral integrative mechanisms of kinship and ideology come into play. Together they provide a cognized floor plan that describes the cosmological origin and interrelationships among the people and their lands, a shared knowledge base of experiences, and norms of proper situational behavior (cf. Ardener 1981; Rappaport 1979; Sobel and Bettles 2000). It is the existence of this plan, which circumscribes the social and spatial parameters of alternative tribal postures, that provides the essential integration and predictability to the social system. This plan, which is latent in the ideological structures of the communities, is maintained regardless of whether a particular alternative pose is actualized during the lifetime of any given individual. In time of need or opportunity, a shared and legitimized expectation for how the constituent groups should behave and interact is readily found in the ideological sphere.

In essence tribal systems must regularly solve two opposing problems: large-scale integration and local differentiation. To maintain the integrity and functioning of the larger tribal confederacy, it is necessary to maintain ideological and social mechanisms that will promote the tribal identity beyond the range of normal, face to face or familial connections. Common ancestry, language, kinship and cosmology contribute to the creation and maintenance of such an identity. Material culture is frequently used in this role as well, marking group and individual identities in a visible and tangible way (Wiessner 1983, 1984). At the local scale, autonomous communities existing within a tribal confederacy often demarcate their territory and assert their specific identities and resource claims, but without threatening the fabric of the whole.

Several aspects of tribal organization make it particularly amenable to archaeological study. First, since tribal organization is essentially a system for predictably organizing population within a landscape over time, there will inevitably be material representations of this patterned activity (Holl 1993). Secondly, since the archaeological record is *cumulative*, the distinct spatial and organizational poses adopted by the society will all be represented. In essence, where a living observer might only see one particular organizational mode, the archaeological record will contain traces of all of the poses that have been actualized by the society. While it remains the archaeologist's task to unravel the palimpsest of differing organizational patterns, the traces themselves are there to be recognized in the record.

A third advantage lays in the role that material culture plays in marking and maintaining social relations in tribal societies. Material objects, whether personal tools, houses, burials or monuments can all play an important role in establishing identity, asserting rights of ownership, and signaling membership in corporate units (cf. Stevenson 1989). To the degree that these important messages and relationships are encoded in material objects, they too may be represented in the archaeological record. Furthermore, since the importance of material objects in denoting personal and group identity increases at greater social distance, i.e., the less frequent the face to face contact (cf. Wobst 1977, 1999), material symbols may provide particular insight into the larger scales of tribal identity and membership (cf. Welsch and Terrell 1998). At the same time, material culture may also provide information relating to patterns of interaction and learning that may not have been intentionally encoded by the past communities (cf. Sackett 1982), or which may only have been recognized by a specialized subset of the population (Wiessner 1983). This aspect of the material record is also accessible to archaeological analysis.

In the balance of this paper, we describe several levels of spatial organization that were regularly signaled in the late prehistoric Juntunen system of the upper Great Lakes. The unique cultural and ecological context of the Juntunen populations provides a particularly useful case for examining the archaeological representation of a flexible tribal system. The late prehistoric period also represents a time frame within which a relatively stable territorial system can be viewed without the confounding influence of European contact or interaction with other socially complex polities. Following a brief overview of the Juntunen system, we will describe how significant scales within this system were given material expression by the Juntunen people, and then consider how these and other scales of social interaction and identity are manifested in other common classes of archaeological material.

The Juntunen Phase

The late prehistoric Juntunen Phase in the upper Great Lakes derives its name from the Juntunen site, (20MK1), a multi-component fishing camp and ossuary located on the western end of Bois Blanc Island in northern Lake Huron (McPherron 1967a). The Juntunen phase traditionally dates from the beginning of the 13th century and continues, at least in its material form, until the time of contact (Milner and O'Shea 1990). The main site occurrences stretch from the region around the northeast shore of Lake Superior and Sault Ste. Marie, through the Straits of Mackinac south along the lacustrine zone to roughly the Au Sable River in northeastern Lower Michigan, and eastward on the northern Lake Huron shore and islands as far as Manitoulin Island (Fig. 1). Although the sites of the Juntunen phase are relatively limited in their spatial distribution,

Juntunen type ceramics are found over a much wider area.

The unique coastal focus of the Juntunen distribution is a product of a complex subsistence system that coupled hunting, gathering and fishing, with the cultivation of maize. While hunting, gathering, and fishing were long practiced in the region, maize appears to be a relatively late addition to the diet (cf. Crawford et al. 1997). Nevertheless, during the Juntunen phase, isotopic evidence suggests maize contributed significantly to the diet (in the range of 14-18% of the total dietary intake, Brandt 1996). The viability of maize cultivation was, in turn, strongly influenced by the micro-climatic influence of the Great Lakes. This phenomenon, known as 'lake effect', produces an ameliorated climate and a significantly lengthened growing season in those land areas adjacent to the Great Lakes (cf. Albert et al. 1986; Phillips and McCulloch 1972). This climatic effect increases the effective

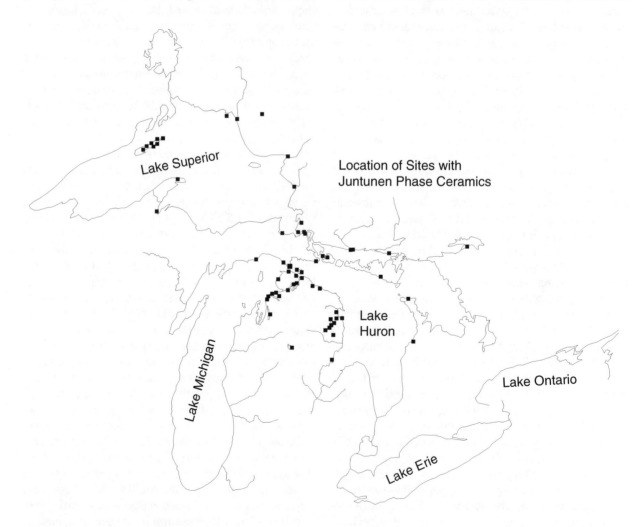

Fig. 1. Map of Juntunen territory and site distribution.

growing season to 120-140 days, (compared with an average regional growing season of 70 days inland) enabling acceptably reliable maize cultivation to take place (USDA 1911). The regional distribution of Juntunen Phase sites closely mirrors the area of significant lake effect around the margins of the upper lakes.

While maize could be grown successfully in the coastal areas, cultivation still entailed substantial risk. The intensively agricultural Hurons in northern Ontario experienced frequent failures (Heidenreich 1971; Trigger 1987). For example, during the period AD 1628-1650 when accounts are provided by Jesuit observers, the Hurons experienced severe crop failure one in every three to six years (O'Shea 1989:64). The character of this risk can be illustrated by considering historical data on crop yields during the earlier half of this century (prior to the introduction of high productivity hybrids) along the western Lake Huron shore area (Fig. 2). During the 34 years between 1909 and 1949 for which records are available, the average yield of corn from Alcona County farms was 28.9 bushels per acres, yet the actual yield values exhibit a series of sharp peaks and troughs, ranging from a maximum value of 48 bushels per acre to a minimum of 12 bushels per acre. This pattern of extreme interannual fluctuation in yield is a hallmark of agriculture when practiced in marginal settings. The potential yield does not significantly decrease, but variability in yield from year to year becomes more pronounced.

A second important aspect of upper Great Lakes agriculture, which has a major impact on the Juntunen system, is the pattern of *spatial variability* in productivity. While maize yields are similarly variable in adjacent areas, the timing of good and bad years is not strongly correlated (Table 1). For example, the correlation of annual maize yields between Alcona and Iosco County (the county immediately to the south of Alcona) was only 0.32 which, in terms of predictability, means one can only explain about 10 percent of the yield of one county by knowing the value of the other county. The correlation between Alcona and Alpena County (the next county to the north) is somewhat stronger at 0.68, but which still predicts less than 50 percent of the variation in values between the counties.

The significance of these weak correlations for a subsistence cultivator is that your 'bad year' often will not be a bad year for your neighbor. As such, social relations that interlink farmers throughout a region can level out shortages result-ing from poor local harvests. In regions exhibiting more homogeneous patterns of good and poor harvests, such a social strategy would have been of limited value (cf. Halstead and O'Shea 1982). In essence, the Juntunen communities were tied both to the lake effect zone of the major lakes and to a spatially extensive network of relatives and trade partners.

Since the Juntunen settlements were confined to the relatively narrow lake effect zone, the rudiments of their territories and exploitation zones can be approximated with some confidence. In northeastern lower Michigan, for example, exploitation areas would have been anchored on the Lake Huron shore and extend inland following the region's major waterways (Cleland 1992) to the edge of the lake effect zone (Fig. 3). An estimate of the size and likely population composition of band territories in the region are derived from the spatial extent of probable exploitation zones as well as from evidence for field size and storage capacity (Table 2) (O'Shea 1988). Since these territories are parallel to one another along the Lake Huron coast, each band would share the same configuration of neighbors and boundaries. Each would interact with adjacent Juntunen bands to both the north and south. Likewise, each territory would have shared an 'international' boundary at the Lake Huron shore along which interaction with Iroquois populations from the east occurred; and a less distinct inland boundary, which may have served as the zone of contact with inland hunter-gatherers. Given this configuration of spatial relationships, distinct kinds of expected interaction and social marking can be anticipated in each direction.

The Juntunen tribal system can be visualized as a nested series of progressively larger interaction zones (Table 2). At its base, the Juntunen system appears to be composed of very small residential units, in the range of 30 persons (possibly 4-6 families). The location of these settlements shifted regularly as differing wild and domesticated resources were sequentially exploited over the course of the year.

Three to four such residential groups occupied immediately adjacent, and possibly even overlapping, areas in what constituted a band territory. The band territories, as presently modeled, average about 1250 km^2 (compared with a total Juntunen system that is on the order of 17,000 km^2 in area), oriented perpendicular to the Lake Huron shore (Fig. 3). These territories, each containing on the order of 125 persons, probably equate with the areas of local exchange.

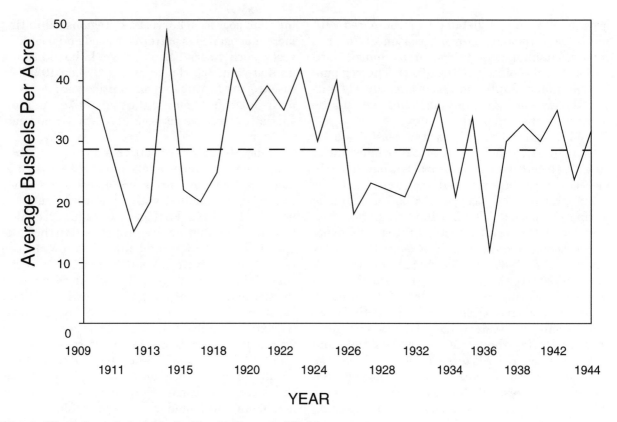

Fig. 2. Historic maize yields in Alcona County, Michigan.

Table 1. Correlation of annual maize yields by county, 1909-1949.

County	Correlation (r)	Explained Variance (r²)
Alcona–Alpena	.680	46%
Alcona–Iosco	.323	10%
Alpena–Iosco	.543	29%

This local level would be the most commonly utilized scale of interaction beyond the residential group, itself. Interaction between the small residential units would be common. Such groups may have seasonally aggregated for resource harvesting and would presumably be the first to be called upon in the event of local scarcity. In addition, they would have been an important source of both mates and manpower for cooperative undertakings. Such interactions were undoubtedly structured through ties of kinship and marriage, although as McClurken (1988) notes for the historic era Ottawas, such ties were extremely fluid and opportunistic in nature. Furthermore, they probably necessitated few formalities to legitimize and maintain the relationships.

Above the scale of the band territories, there is evidence to suggest interaction at the level of the macro-region and beyond. Within the Juntunen system, this higher level, termed here the tribal level, in fact may not truly have operated at the scale of the Juntunen system as a whole, but rather as northern and southern macro-regions (see discussion of ceramics below). Large numbers of people from these macro-regions aggregated periodically at particular localities for ritual activities, such as those surrounding secondary burial in large collective ossuaries. Since relatively large numbers of people would have to be provisioned, the range of potential locations for such aggregations was probably limited to areas with extremely abundant fish resources, such as the Straits of Mackinac

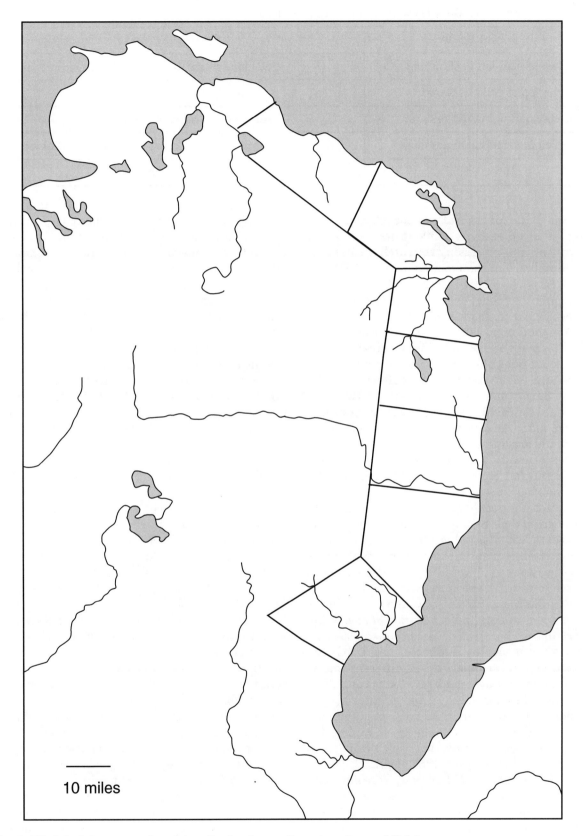

Fig. 3. Modeled Juntunen band territories in northeastern lower Michigan.

Table 2. Organizational scales within the Juntunen tribal system.

Social Scale	Spatial Scale
Residential Unit (30 persons)	Settlement Locality (280-420 km^2)
Band (125 persons)	Band Territory (1250 km^2)
Inter-Band (375 persons)	Adjacent Territories (3750 km^2)
Tribal (1500-2000 persons)	Major Aggregation Sites, Tribal Territory (17,000 km^2)
Inter-Tribal	A Large Area

and Sault Ste. Marie. At these localities, the limiting factor on resource exploitation is labor for harvesting and processing the catch, rather than the abundance of the resource itself (cf. Cleland 1982). As such, relatively large autumn and winter populations could be provisioned without serious ecological consequences.

A second important feature of these aggregation sites was their potential for leveling out more serious episodes of resource failure, which might overwhelm local and regional buffering mechanisms. Such a movement of people at the tribal level was more deliberate, entailing the movement of large numbers of people, perhaps whole bands, and would accordingly have been accompanied by greater formality. Although such locales provided a potential fall back in years of serious agricultural shortage, there were limits to the density of population that could remain in these places for any length of time. Similarly, a band that was forced to relocate would be vulnerable to loss of the permanent facilities and fields that existed in their home territory, and would have had a strong incentive to return as soon as possible.

Regular interaction also occurred at the intertribal scale during the Juntunen Phase. While intertribal exchange may, in some instances, have occurred over smaller distances than tribal contacts, they were set apart by the different character of the interaction and by its likely content. In the case of the historic era Huron of Ontario, trade outside of the confederacy had a strongly complementary character; exchange was employed to acquire goods or materials that were locally scarce or not available (Trigger 1985, 1987; G. Wright 1967). These exchanges, however, were not exclusively complementary and included a wide range of bulk foodstuffs. The exchange of complementary goods and durable items served to regularize and maintain these foreign linkages over time (cf. Ford 1972; O'Shea 1981).

Given the linear arrangement of Juntunen territories, the focus of intertribal trade would vary depending on placement within the Juntunen territory. In the southern portion of the Juntunen distribution, for example, exchange appears to have linked Juntunen populations with both more intensively agricultural peoples in the Saginaw Valley to the south, and with mobile hunting-gathering groups living in the colder interior of the Lower Peninsula of Michigan. Similar connections linking Juntunen settlements with other agricultural and forager systems would have existed throughout the Juntunen area, although the specific directions and areas articulated would have been unique for each locality.

The Juntunen tribal system can best be understood as a loose series of small social units that during normal years shifted from subsistence focus to subsistence focus within the limits of a defined home territory. During years of scarcity, these groups might move considerable distances and aggregate into large elaborate encampments, and then return again to their small settlements. Such a system would obviously imply different kinds of interactions at differing social scales. Within a band territory, or even between adjacent territories, we would expect there to be a fair degree of regular, face to face contact, as well as significant levels of intermarriage and immediate kin relationships. At larger social and spatial scales, relations would presumably be more formalized, relying less on direct prior contact and more on conventions and tribal ideology. Nevertheless, prolonged contact among individuals at these aggregation sites would no doubt also have repercussions in terms of friendships and future trade partnerships.

With this brief introduction, we can now turn to consider how natural features, built structures and portable material culture were used to denote and facilitate the operation of the regional system. In much of the discussion that follows, observations from northeastern Lower Michigan, and the Hubbard Lake region in particular, are used to represent the regional operation of the Juntunen tribal system. In the later discussion of material culture patterning, the entire Juntunen distribution is considered directly.

Marking Tribal and Local Identities within the Juntunen System

In a tribal system such as that described for the late prehistoric Juntunen system, material culture can represent differing levels of interaction and integration both overtly and passively. By overt, we mean the intentioned and conventionalized use of material markers to designate identity, boundaries and ownership. Such overt uses would be recognized by most members of the society, and possibly even by individuals outside the tribal system. By passive use, we mean identifiable distinctions that arise as a result of regularized patterns of interaction but which were not specifically created to communicate distinction or identity. Passive markers may, at a very fine scale such as the individual maker, have been designed to express ownership or maker, but such markers would have only been recognizable to a small segment of the total population, and as such could not have performed a meaningful role in asserting group identity or membership (Wiessner 1983).

In this distinction between overt and passive use of material culture, we are in one sense returning to the distinction between functional and isochrestic variation discussed by Sackett (1985) and Weissner (1985). Our focus, however, which is explicitly concerned with integrating differing social and spatial scales of interaction, renders moot some of the issues in that earlier controversy. For instance, a single category of material may simultaneously express overt meaning at one level of scale and passive variation at another. Our purpose here is not to further engage in that particular debate, but rather to illustrate how these different kinds of patterning in material culture are represented in the record of the Juntunen tribal system.

Overt patterns of identity and boundary marking in the Juntunen system occur at three levels: the level of the tribal confederacy as a whole, the level of the macro-region, and the level of band territories. At the apex of the hierarchy is the demarcation of the tribal system as a whole. Ceramics are particularly useful in this role since they provide a visible and highly malleable medium for

the creation of such messages. Since they also have a relatively short use life, the designs must be regularly reproduced as new vessels are made, reinforcing the immediacy of the identity.

The second scale at which intentional identity marking is observed is the level of the macro-region. Such marking behavior is actualized at aggregation localities where individuals without prior face-to-face contact must reside and cooperate under potentially stressful conditions. These sites are the locations on which the critical success or failure of the system rests. The extreme importance of these localities suggests that a broad range of cultural, ideological and material means to ensure acceptance and cooperation should be exploited (cf. Smith 1996:283). These are the locations where meeting rituals, including collective ossuaries, will occur and in which material symbolism of mutual identification is expected.

The third scale at which overt identity marking is observed is at the level of the band territories. Given the necessary orientation of these territories, each band would share a common boundary with two other Juntunen bands, an 'international' border with anyone traveling along the shore of the Great Lakes, and a less distinct interior boundary, potentially shared with non-agricultural forager groups. These boundaries were created via a combination of built structures and the ideological incorporation of major nature features. Together these produced a cultural landscape that was at once distinctive and recognizable.

Natural Features and Built Structures in the Demarcation of Tribal Boundaries

Over much of the Juntunen site distribution, and particularly in its southern extent along the western shore of Lake Huron, the region lacks the major outcrops or rock faces, which might be utilized for marking territories via rock art or representation (cf. Dewdney and Kidd 1962; Zurel 1999a). As such, other kinds of features were used to demarcate space. In character, these features would need to be analogous to rock art in the significance of their location, their visibility and their relative permanence. In northeast Lower Michigan, such marking was achieved via a combination of built structures and named natural features, which provided a cultural annotation to the natural landscape.

The most striking expression of the blended use of natural and built features is found along the

Lake Huron shore, itself. The shores of the Great Lakes provided for a level of population movement and goods transport that was simply not possible in most inland areas of North America. If early European accounts are any guide, native transport technology was well developed and extensively utilized (cf. Morse 1984). Travelers, however, seldom struck across open water; they usually opted for the comparative safety of coastal waters. In the absence of formal navigational charts or maps, the recognition of landmarks was of great importance.

The lakeshores provided many obvious landmarks; river mouths, spits, points and bays. The addition of constructed features, such as mounds, offering stones, marker rocks and built enclosures, transformed the coasts into a cultural landscape, signaling collective claims of identity and ownership (Hinsdale 1931). For example, the cultural annotation of the natural lakeshore features along the western shore of Lake Huron is striking (Fig. 4a). Mound groups are located on a number of these natural features. Along stretches of the lakeshore where prominent natural features are lacking, named 'sacred rocks' seem to perform a similar function. The lakeshore is also annotated by the presence of 'offering stones', which again tend to occur on prominent features. In effect, the important 'international' boundary represented by Lake Huron, was rendered meaningful by layering a cultural veneer over the top of highly visible natural features.

Many of these same elements, such as enclosures and mounds, were employed to mark other kinds of boundaries as well. For example, elaborate built stone enclosures were constructed at the northern and southern ends of Thunder Bay. Unlike the markers along the lakeshore, these features cannot be directly observed from the water. While their function and origin remain enigmatic, they may mark lateral boundaries between bands, rather than the 'international' boundary represented by Lake Huron. Earthwork enclosures and mounds also seem to have been used to denote boundaries between Juntunen bands and possibly also to establish resource claims vis-à-vis inland hunter-gatherer groups (see Fig. 4b). Each of these categories of markers is briefly described below.

While waterways and major shoreline features appear to have figured prominently in Juntunen territorial marking, they were not the only natural features utilized in this role. A series of large glacial erratics along the Lake Huron shore were accorded particular significance by local inhabitants as noted in early histories of the region (see Fig. 4a).

These include the 'White Rock' near Presque Isle and the 'Black Rock' near Greenbush. Both are large isolated boulders that stand on the beach near the water's edge. In the case of the White Rock, at least, the boulder was annotated with pecked images. The location of these two named boulders is interesting, since both occur on long featureless stretches of the lakeshore and are easily visible from the water. There were, no doubt, other isolated boulders along the lakeshore that were significant, but no record of their location and importance survives. Indeed, the existence of the White Rock is only known through photographs taken by Wilbert Hinsdale in the 1920's (on file UMMA). Hinsdale also reported seeing offerings placed on White Rock during this visit, suggesting that the stone retains an ongoing importance to at least some local inhabitants.

A related category of marker is offering stones (sometimes termed Manitou stones). McKenney, in his tour of the Great Lakes in 1826, provides a striking description of one such offering stone that was located on North Point on Thunder Bay:

> It is about one hundred yards from our encampment [on North Point], and forty steps from the beach, in a thicket of pine and spruce, and aspen. The place is cleared of all kinds of undergrowth, and is of an oval figure, about twenty feet by ten feet, in the longest and broadest parts. In the center of it are about twenty stones, four of which are larger than the rest; and each of these, I should judge, would measure three feet every way. The path leading to this sacred place is well trod by those who come to make their offerings to this pile of stones, *which is the manito!* Upon the four principal stones were the offerings of these benighted people, in tobacco, bits of iron, pieces of old kettles, pipes, and various other things. The four large stones the Indians said had been there always, and the little ones had gathered around them since.
> McKenney 1972:330 (emphasis in the original)

A portage camp was found in this vicinity during archaeological survey, although the shrine was not relocated. A similar offering stone is traditionally attributed to the top of Mount Maria at the south end of Hubbard Lake. Early historians claim this stone was hollow, covered by a stone lid, and possibly incised on one side with a face. According to local traditions, offerings were placed within the stone's hollow compartment. The existence of such shrines is relatively common among Algonquian peoples, and it is likely that many more once existed in the region. Unlike the prominent named

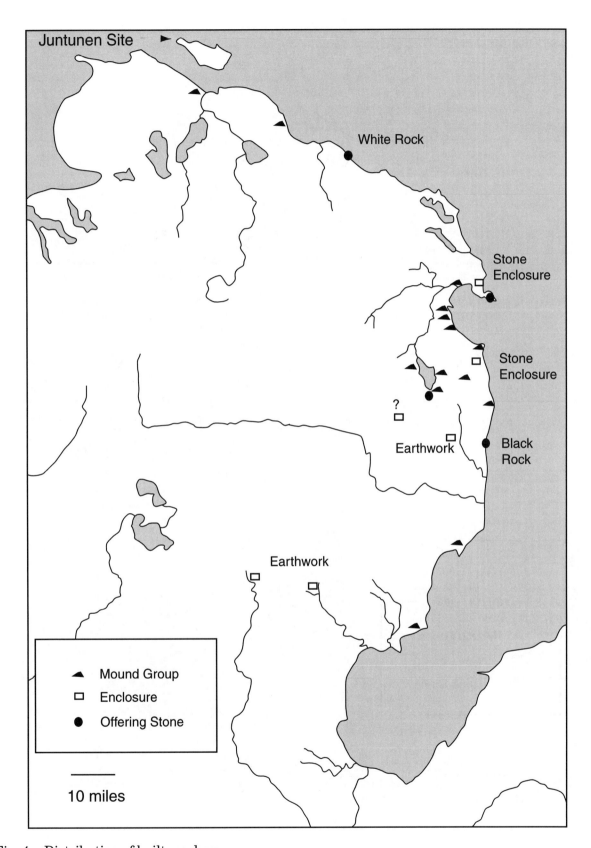

Fig. 4a. Distribution of built markers.

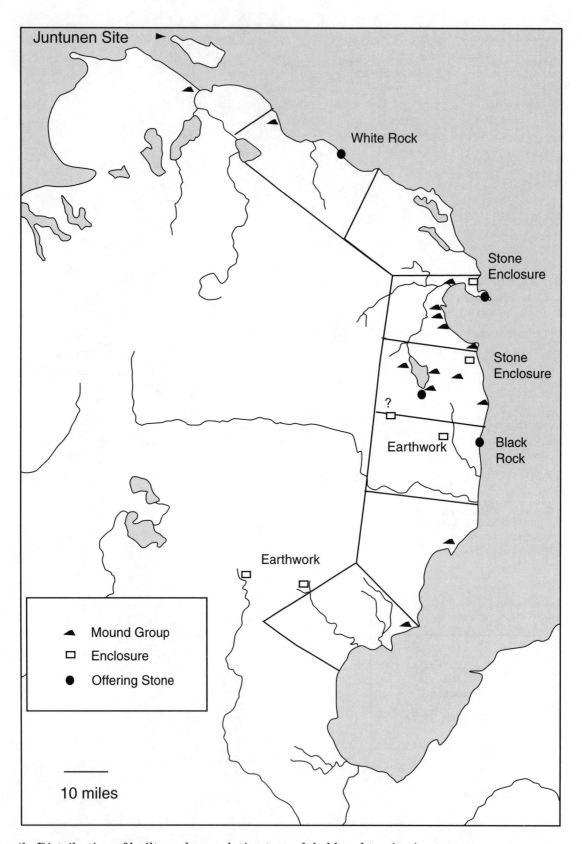

Fig. 4b. Distribution of built markers relative to modeled band territories.

rocks, these latter two offering stones both are sited in locations that would not be directly visible from the water, although by virtue of occurring on major topographical features, they would have been easy to locate.

Possibly related to the offering stones are hollow stone cairns, which are recorded in a number of locations in the coastal areas. Constructions of this kind are known from Drummond Island where they appear to have functioned in historic times as burial receptacles (Charles Cleland, pers. comm.). Yet cairns of this same form have been observed on the western Lake Huron shore and do not appear to have contained human remains. The hollow character of these structures raises the possibility that they may have functioned in a manner similar to the offering stones, or that they may have been used as temporary receptacles or caches. The cairns known from northeastern Michigan are associated with stone enclosures (see below).

Two classes of built structures—enclosures and mounds—may have demarcated Juntunen band territories. These built features appear to have had somewhat different functions. Enclosures—also called earthworks—tend to be roughly circular in shape with an encircling ditch. Earth was piled on the inward side to form an embankment. The northern Michigan enclosures that date to the later Woodland period range in size from 150 to 360 feet in diameter (Greenman 1927; Milner and O'Shea 1998).

There has been considerable debate about the function of these enclosures. By virtue of the ditch and bank, they were initially supposed to be defensive works. This interpretation continues to prevail for the enclosures in southern Michigan (cf. Zurel 1999b). The frequent gaps in the embankments, inconsistent occurrence of palisades, and the absence of other overt signs of violence have, however, made warfare a less likely explanation for the northern enclosures. Instead, their location, typically at the head of major watersheds, points to the possibility that they served as meeting places for ceremonies and trade (Milner and O'Shea 1998). One such enclosure that can be linked with certainty to the Juntunen system in northeast Michigan is the Mikado Earthwork (20AA5) (Carruthers 1969). Mikado is located well up the watershed of the Pine River near the point where the 'lake effect' would have had little effect on the growing season. However, the enclosure is in a position to facilitate exchange between Juntunen band territories, as well as with inland hunter-gatherers. While earthworks tend to occur in simi-

lar settings, e.g. on high ground near the head of branching river systems, they would not be visible at any distance within the prevailing forested environment.

A second variety of enclosure has become known only recently. These are stone enclosures, of which two are known from the western Lake Huron shore, one on North Point near Thunder Bay, and the other near South Point. These structures are represented by low linear walls of stacked stone, which enclose roughly rectangular areas. Neither stone enclosure appears to have had a ditch. Both enclosures do have hollow cairns located within and around them. During the historic period, local farmers have extensively modified the South Point structure, thus obscuring its original configuration. The North Point enclosure is more sheltered and is located in an area that has not been cultivated. As such, it provides a better idea of the overall plan of the structure. The stone enclosures are located in the vicinity of prominent landmarks, yet like the earthworks, their actual existence would not have been obvious without prior knowledge of their presence.

The final category of built structure employed in the Juntunen territorial system is mounds. The secondary function of funerary structures as territorial markers and resource claims is well documented cross-culturally (cf. Goldstein 1976). The Late Woodland mounds of the Juntunen region appear to have been used in this way. The mounds are not particularly large, rarely exceeding a meter in height, although they may occur in clusters. When such mounds have been excavated, they often reveal a sequence of single interments, which may suggest a periodic reuse or renewal of the feature and its associated cultural claims (cf. Hinsdale 1929).

Mounds are found in two settings. Along the Lake Huron shore, mounds (more typically mound groups) were a primary means of marking shoreline landmarks (see Fig. 4a). The mounds are not scattered continuously along the shore, but are clustered on key landmarks. They appear to assert both the cultural identity of the shoreline and presumably also the edges of individual band territories. The second context in which mounds occur is along inland lakes. Large lakes, such as Hubbard Lake, had at least three clusters of mounds at different places around the lake. Smaller lakes typically had only a single mound or mound cluster. These mounds do not delineate the edges of territories, but rather seem to represent specific resource claims within band territories.

A consideration of northern mounds as an element in the Juntunen territorial system raises issues of a purely chronological and cultural-historical nature. Mound burial becomes common in northern Michigan during the Middle Woodland period, and continues into the Late Woodland period. In later Late Woodland times, secondary interment in collective ossuaries becomes common, although mound burial continues to be used, at least in the upper Great Lakes. The long time period during which mound burial is practiced raises the question of the specific cultural origin of the mounds that are being attributed to the Juntunen territorial system. Unfortunately, this is an issue that cannot be directly assessed. Many of the mounds reported in the early part of the twentieth century have been destroyed or looted, and mounds that do survive to the present are rarely investigated, out of respect for Native American wishes. Among the small number of mounds that have been studied, most are of Late Woodland age. Some, such as the Devil's River mound group, can be definitively attributed to Juntunen times (Fitting 1970). This is interesting in and of itself since it implies that both ossuary and mound burial were practiced by the same cultural group. Yet, from the perspective of the territorial system, the chronological origin of a particular mound group may be less important than the geographic location it occupies.

Over time, built structures also become a part of an evolving cultural landscape. In this role, the prior constructions of earlier peoples are incorporated into new and unrelated systems of cultural meaning. This phenomenon is well known in the incorporation of Neolithic structures and Bronze Age barrows into the social landscape of late prehistoric Europe (cf. Bradley 1993). The same process of incorporation may have operated in the Juntunen territorial system. Preexisting mounds occurring in the proper location were incorporated into the Juntunen territorial system, complementing new mounds constructed by Juntunen peoples.

Two other features that modify the cultural landscape, in this case as a means of legitimizing and solidifying identification with the macro-region scale of the tribal system, are the ossuaries and long house at the Juntunen site. The large long house was constructed early in the Juntunen sequence and was repaired or rebuilt numerous times during the period of site occupation (McPherron 1967:233-236). The use of a long house is extremely interesting in this context since in

'normal' times, the Juntunen people do not appear to have dwelt in such structures (although they were presumably well known throughout the Great Lakes region). The implicit symbolism of bringing the many visitors to the site 'under one roof' in a long house must have been particularly potent. It may also have provided a living parallel to the collective symbolism represented by the adjacent ossuaries.

A second distinguishing, and no doubt highly significant, feature was the creation of a series of collective ossuaries. These ossuaries represented the secondary interment of the skeletal remains of numerous individuals. Clark (n.d.) has shown that the deposition of remains within the ossuaries was not haphazard, but rather that sets of remains were held within bark containers, which were then deposited into the ossuaries. The collection of the remains of deceased relatives, and the transport of these to the Juntunen ossuary would most assuredly have been an evocative act, as would the joining of these remains with those from the other Juntunen communities. In addition to the ossuaries, numerous ritual deposits were also encountered at the site, including the interment of a dog, an eagle and a snowshoe hare (McPherron 1967:193; for discussion on animal burials elsewhere in the upper Lakes, see Smith 1987). All of these features would have promoted an enduring and overarching identity as well as a permanent claim to place that would have persisted even in the absence of actual occupancy.

While both mound burial and ossuaries appear to have played a role in the demarcation of the Juntunen territorial system, the integration of these differing forms of funerary treatment does merit some additional comment. By the later Late Woodland period, mound burial was not the normative pattern for the disposal of the dead, this role having been assumed by the multistage collective burial system observed at the Juntunen site. Rather, mound burial appears to have been a specialized form of interment that was employed episodically (for a similar situation in southern Michigan, see Norder et al. 2002). Based on present evidence, it appears that collective ossuaries and mounds played complementary roles in the Juntunen social system. While the mounds emphasized boundaries and restricted claims, the Late Prehistoric ossuaries evoked the collective aspect of macro-regional, if not tribal, membership. For example, the Juntunen ossuary occurs at a regional aggregation site and consists of the commingled remains of individuals from throughout the

Juntunen region. These individuals were initially interned in their home territories and then, at a later point, their skeletal remains were transported to the Juntunen ossuary. The poignant symbolism of death appears to have played a role in both the long-term demarcation of local boundaries and in the assertion of tribal membership. The connection between individuals receiving mound burial and the territorial functions of the mounds raises interesting possibilities, although we cannot on present evidence specify the nature of this connection.

While the combination of built and natural features provides an interesting glimpse of the Late Prehistoric territorial system, there are obvious analytical issues. First, mounds, earthworks, and shrines are extremely vulnerable to destruction and vandalism. At best, the surviving sample of markers can only be taken as a chance remnant sample of the monuments that once existed in the landscape. Second, many of the built markers appear to have stood in lieu of distinctive natural features, such as points, river mouths, which may have been the more important and preferred markers. As such, to what extent can prominent natural features, by themselves, be assumed to have served as territorial markers or landmarks? This, of course, opens the door to tautology if a particular river or point was not redundantly marked by cultural constructions.

In the Juntunen case, we derive some assistance from the ecological constraints of the subsistence system, and from the orienting effect of Lake Huron. We also benefit from relatively recent archaeological data and the ability to draw upon historic and ethnographic sources. However, such aids will not always be available, particularly for studies of ancient tribal systems. It is useful, therefore, to consider how the dynamics of the tribal territorial system is imprinted and detectable in common categories of material remains such as ceramics and lithics.

Material Culture and Spatial Variability

To this point, we have considered natural and built features that were used intentionally and assertively to demarcate territories, resource claims, and to signify membership in the tribal confederacy. These features essentially represent the boundaries within which the elements of the tribal system predictably operated. They provide a plan for integrating and regularizing the shifting

adaptive posture of local communities. It is likely, of course, that other media of material culture performed similar roles, although probably with a less long lasting duration.

Material culture can also be expected to show the *results* of episodic patterns of aggregation and dispersal, representing the interactive side of the tribal dynamic. We term these patterns *passive*, in the sense that they were not intentionally designed to communicate meaning (and indeed may not have communicated anything beyond the identity of individual makers or procurers in the context of the Juntunen system). While not arising as a result of specific intent, various classes of material culture do show evidence for regular long-terms patterns of interaction. In our discussion here we briefly describe evidence for two classes of material culture that show the effects of tribal interaction during the Juntunen period.

Ceramics

A recent study of regional variability in Juntunen phase ceramics (Milner 1998) indicates that while pottery played an overt role in demarcating the Juntunen confederacy as a whole, it also varied at differing spatial scales within the Juntunen territory as a result of long-term patterns of interaction. The highly standardized style canon of Juntunen ceramics, despite the broad geographic distribution of Juntunen pots, has been commented upon for some time (McPherron 1967a, 1967b). In fact, the homogeneity of Juntunen pottery contrasts sharply with the stylistic profile of earlier phases during which ceramic variation is minimal and occurs in a pattern that largely reflects declines in interaction among relatively mobile pot producers with distance (cf. Brashler 1981).

Claims of stylistic patterning across space, however, have rested on impressionistic comparisons between a limited number of sites. Furthermore, it has only been recently demonstrated that the Juntunen phase lasted for 400 years rather than the previously held 200-year duration (Milner and O'Shea 1990; Milner 1998). Analysis of Juntunen phase style, unfortunately, remains constrained by an uneven distribution of known sites, small and extremely variable sample sizes, and poor temporal control. Despite these caveats, a systematic look at an expanded sample of 66 Juntunen phase sites reveals an overarching regional homogeneity as well as some intra-regional ceramic variability. Indeed, the fact that these patterns were identified despite sample limitations suggests that the data are inherently robust and can provide insight into Juntunen phase tribal organization.

During the Juntunen phase, ceramic vessels were directly involved in food preparation and consumption. The high percentage of vessels with food residues (57%; N=1063) and the wide range of vessel sizes, reaching diameters of at least 42 cm, indicate these functions. Vessels may have entered directly into feasting or food sharing activities among people who interacted daily as well as with socially more distant people. The functional data, therefore, indicate that Juntunen vessels had the potential to enter into overt communication of identity as well as carry other types of information about interaction at a variety of spatial scales within the tribal system.

The significance of tribal scale identification and interaction is reflected in the overarching homogeneity of style, the nature of clinal variation, and the persistence of the Juntunen style. Juntunen style homogeneity is evident in a wide range of stylistic variables. This homogeneity is defined by co-variation among attributes, redundancy between attributes from different levels of a design hierarchy, and strong constraints on diverse design choices including the shape and size of vessels, the number of decorative bands, and the types of design configurations placed in different design fields (Table 3). The overall simple layout of Juntunen design permits replication by socially distant members of the region, while some latitude in detail and technical attributes is retained. In fact, it is surprising that any patterned intra-regional variation was discovered considering the remarkable adherence to relatively rigid stylistic canons.

Some stylistic characteristics vary in a clinal pattern across the region for the entire phase. Clinal variation is evident in lip thickness, shape and surface treatment; decorative technique and design configuration on the rim; and the number of decorative bands below the rim. Although this patterning may be partly due to declining interaction from community to community and movement of people among them, there is no way to discriminate among possible sources of variation with the available data. However, the steady rather than random or heterogeneous patterning across the region in multiple traits does indicate a relatively stable spatial configuration of population at the regional scale.

Interestingly, the Juntunen region can be divided into northeast and southwest style macro-regions based on diverse traits ranging from decorative techniques to configuration choices (Fig. 5). For example, sites in the northwest Lower Peninsula of Michigan, the western Upper Peninsula, and the Straits of Mackinac are characterized by higher frequencies of exterior punctate and interior decoration, and multiple rows of decoration below the collar than sites along Lake Superior and the St. Marys River. This division could be an artifact of poor sample sizes and uneven site distribution, but the number and types of variables that reflect this boundary as well as its duration for 400 years is intriguing.

The existence of these intra-tribal macro-regions is further demonstrated by the stylistic profiles found in aggregation site assemblages. People

Table 3. Constrained stylistic attributes of Juntunen pottery.

Attribute	Proportion	Number
Presence of Interior decoration	65.0	927
Presence of Lip decoration	87.1	858
Below the collar decoration	86.0	700
Punctate lip decoration	83.7	739
Horizontal linear rows of collar exterior decoration	72.0	1083
Single band of interior decoration	87.6	601
Single row of elements below the collar	70.2	598
Collars	96.0	771
Regular collar type	75.4	740
Castellations	76.6	245
Square lips	76.1	937
Smooth exterior surfaces	82.8	1051

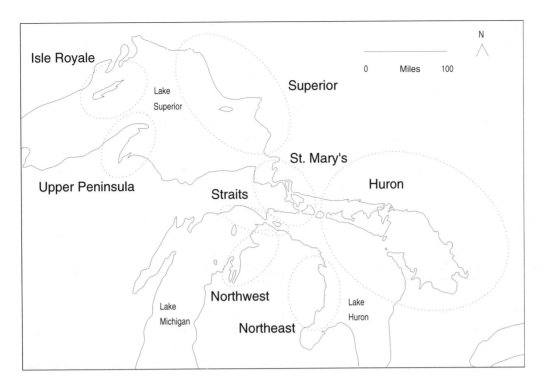

Fig. 5. Juntunen ceramic style regions.

from different local groups periodically gathered to affirm alliances that tied bands together into larger social spheres and, at the largest scale, the tribal region. The ceramic assemblage at the Juntunen site shares characteristics with assemblages from both macro-regions within the tribal region. For instance, the Juntunen site falls between the two macro-regions in percentages of round and paddled lips, and punctate exterior decoration. People from a large area with somewhat different stylistic practices were attracted to the site.

The stylistic profile of another aggregation site, Whitefish Island, suggests changes in the social use of the island (Conway 1977). Prior to A.D. 1400, the site was probably visited by small groups of people to exploit the rich fishery, many of whom came from the northeastern part of the Juntunen region. The assemblage of Juntunen pots shared most characteristics, including high percentages of square lips and thick high rims, with sites along the northeast shore of Lake Superior and sites located farther east. Numerous Iroquois vessels indicate contact with Iroquois visitors as well. Some time after A.D. 1400, however, visits by the Iroquois to Whitefish Island had a stylistic impact, seen in the increase of incised designs that are similar to those on the Iroquois type Lawson In-

cised (Wright 1973). Considering more Late Iroquois stage vessels were found at Whitefish Island than vessels from earlier Iroquois stages, it is probable that sustained intensive inter-regional contact did involve social comparison and related stylistic behavior to sustain inter-regional alliances.

Another stylistic indicator of differing spatial postures within the tribal region points to the existence of band territories. Highly visible and complex stylistic markers such as bands of obliquely oriented impressions and the presence of interior decoration that appear most often in assemblages from the northwest Lower Peninsula of Michigan distinguish one territory from all other territories in the Juntunen region. In a few cases, some relatively rare traits, such as short vertical cord impressions on short bulbous collars, occurred almost exclusively in particular areas, in this case in the northeast Lower Peninsula of Michigan, but they only occurred on a handful of vessels.

Variation between band territories is often quite subtle, occurring as differences in percentages rather than exclusive occurrences of traits. Differences in percentages of subtle, low-level traits are more consistent with passive sharing of traits due to intensive interaction within territories rather than intentional communication of band identity. Sharing of attributes reflects the existence of stable band territories comprising the region, but does not preclude the movement of small groups of people locally. Unfortunately, known archaeological sites are scattered so thinly across the region that possible variation in minor elements and technical attributes due to differential interaction among local communities is difficult, if not impossible, to isolate. Regardless, the same vessels may be decorated with subtle or minor traits resulting from intensive interaction within bands as well as more visible stylistic markers that may indicate assertion of band membership.

Several unexpected ceramic patterns have been identified that point to the role of inter-regional contacts in tribal organization. First, attributes varying at the scale of the band territory were often derived from contact with extra-regional populations that participated in different ceramic traditions. The results were not failed attempts to copy all stylistic attributes of other traditions, but particular elements or layouts were translated to fit into the overall Juntunen style grammar. For instance, oblique band motifs and horizontally oriented configurations with more than the usual number of rows, all made with cord impressions, characterize Juntunen phase pots found on sites in the western reaches of the Upper Peninsula of Michigan. These characteristics are typical of Wisconsin ceramic tradition pots (Hurley 1975; Salzer 1974). However, Juntunen potters on the Upper Peninsula of Michigan did not adopt the markedly different collar and castellation shapes of the foreign ceramic tradition.

Second, territories that lay along the Juntunen region's perimeter, such as the northwestern quadrant of Michigan's Lower Peninsula and the northeastern shore of Lake Superior, were stylistically more distinctive than other territories. Potters in these territories frequently adopted extra-regional traits that were different from or were minor occurrences in other Juntunen assemblages. In contrast, assemblages from sites along the Straits of Mackinac that lay near the geographic center of the region tended to split stylistic differences between neighboring territories and had far fewer unique characteristics. Obviously, the range of stylistic variation to which groups were exposed was different.

There was also considerable variation in the amount of stylistic sharing across inter-regional boundaries. Similarities between Juntunen and Iroquois vessels in the St. Marys territory were myriad, while Upper Mississippian and Juntunen vessels co-occur at the Sand Point (Dorothy 1980)

and Scott Point sites (Buckmaster 1980) with little if any stylistic interchange. These patterns indicate that contacts across the region's boundaries were commonplace, although some inter-regional boundaries were more permeable than others.

Inter-regional populations continued to employ fundamentally different design structures, often placed on morphologically distinctive vessel forms. Despite this emphasis on difference, these populations obviously had interacted for many years and shared some stylistic attributes. When these populations came together, they brought these different stylistic practices or the pots themselves with them, resulting in assemblages of vessels from different ceramic traditions. The frequent occurrence of assemblages with mixed ceramic traditions in the upper Great Lakes has been recognized for years (Dawson 1979; Pollock 1975; Wright 1963, 1965). Many Juntunen phase sites have yielded vessels from other ceramic traditions, particularly sites that are located along the region's borders such as Sand Point or along major waterways such as Scott Point and Whitefish Island.

At one level, potters operated within a relatively rigid style canon that enabled the fundamental Juntunen identify to be expressed and reaffirmed across a substantial expanse of both space and time. The scale of patterning can only be accounted for via the overt and intentioned use of the ceramics as a medium to express this overarching identity. Yet, in the finer detail of vessel design and decoration, subtle patterns of stylistic variation are detected, which arise as a result of the specific patterns of regular social interaction within the extensive Juntunen territory and with adjacent foreign groups. As such, the same ceramic vessels provide evidence of both overt and passive social marking.

Lithics

The distribution of lithics, and particularly the exploitation of specific raw material sources, is a common topic of investigation, and one that has been explored extensively in the Great Lakes region (cf. Ludtke 1976; Janusas 1984; Fox 1990a; 1990b; Lepper et al. 2001). It has been argued, for example, that the distribution of raw materials in lithics typically will be more informative of local territories, while stylistic elements in other materials, such as ceramics, may be expected to reflect more the movement and interaction of people (cf. Wright 1965). Given its large regional extent, differing portions of the Juntunen system have distinct local sources of preferred materials. As such, they should exhibit distinct patterns of preferred local cherts and also should exhibit different representation of 'exotic' cherts. This offers the potential for detecting not only the limits of regional provisioning areas, which should overlap local band territories, but will also have the potential to reveal interaction with other macro-regions via the distribution of exotic raw materials.

Before this patterning is presented, though, several caveats are in order. The total number of identified Late Prehistoric sites in the study region is limited, so any patterns observed must be viewed as suggestive, rather than conclusive. Similarly, there are very few single component sites of this age and, given the shallow and sandy character of site deposits within the region, the certainty with which debitage from individual components on a site can be separated is limited. Nevertheless, basic patterns of resource use and provisioning can be discerned.

Along the western Lake Huron shore, the commonly utilized local raw materials are a Devonian chert, known as Bois Blanc or colloquially as 'northern gray', glacially derived nodules of varying size and quality, and Bayport chert, an Upper Mississippian chert with exposures around Saginaw Bay.

More exotic cherts include Norwood, from outcrops in northwest Lower Michigan, cherts from the lower Lake Huron and Lake Erie basins, such as Flint Ridge, Kettle Point, and Upper Mercer, and Wyandotte (Hornstone) from the southern Lake Michigan basin (Luedtke 1976).

Other things being equal, the fall-off in the proportion of raw materials in the lithic assemblages typically reflects two axes, distance and quality. Said another way, we expect the proportion of a given raw material present in an assemblage to be inversely related to the distance from its source, and to be positively related to its quality. Deviations from these expectations may reflect unique properties of the raw material or of the technology involved in its acquisition and distribution. It may also reflect the presence of social boundaries that may impede or facilitate distribution.

The interplay of these factors can be seen in the relative proportions of Bayport chert that are found in Late Prehistoric assemblages as one moves north into the Juntunen territory and away from the Bayport source areas (Table 4; Fig. 6a). There is a clear fall-off in the proportion of Bayport chert as one moves progressively north away from the source area. There is also a coastal effect, in which

Table 4. Bayport chert as a proportion of the entire lithic assemblage and as a proportion of all flaked stone implements.

Site	Proportion Bayport	Proportion Implements Bayport	Period	Site Type
Hampsher	16.6	21.3	Late Prehistoric	Coastal, excavation
Gordon-McVeigh	28.2	35.3	Late Prehistoric	Inland, excavation
Mikado	71.6	66.7	Late Prehistoric	Inland, excavation
Scott	35.7	59.3	Late Prehistoric	Inland, excavation
Scott	42.7	42.4	Early Late Woodland	Inland, excavation
Gaging Station	5.2	16.0	Late Prehistoric	Inland, excavation
Gaging Station	18.9	33.3	Middle Woodland	Inland, excavation
Robb	18.4	44.0	Late Prehistoric	Inland, excavation
Churchill Point	41.1	40.0	Early Late Woodland	Inland, excavation
Allyn' s Camp	44.0	48.9	Archaic	Inland, excavation
Beaver Lake	42.9	33	Aceramic	Inland, surface
Calvary Cemetery	50.0	50.0	Archaic	Inland, surface
Goat Lady	26.7	42.9	Late Prehistoric	Inland, surface
Potter' s Spring	30.0	40.0	Late Woodland	Inland, surface
Taylor/North Point	42.5	40.0	Late Prehistoric	Coastal, surface
South Point	88.4	66.7	Aceramic	Coastal, surface

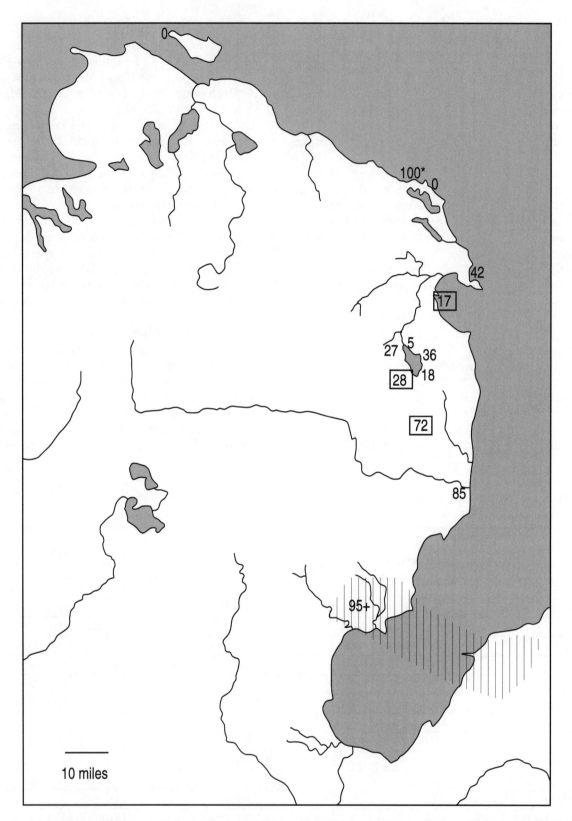

Fig. 6a. Proportions of Bayport chert in late prehistoric lithic assemblages. The values that have a box around them represent excavated single component Juntunen sites, and the hatching represents the source area for Bayport chert. The value marked with an asterisk represents the only lithic associated with a surface site.

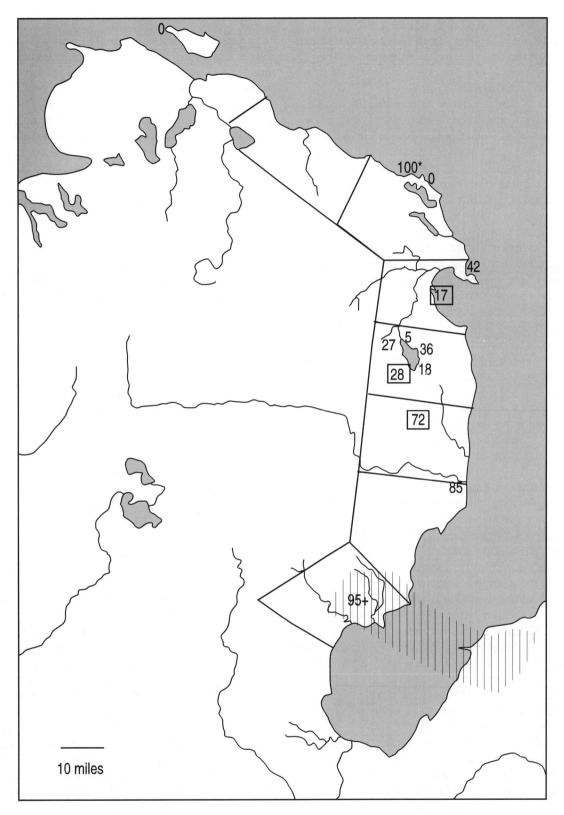

Fig. 6b. Proportions of Bayport chert relative to modeled band territories. The values that have a box around them represent excavated single component Juntunen sites, and the hatching represents the source area for Bayport chert. The value marked with an asterisk represents the only lithic associated with a surface site.

sites on or near Lake Huron tend to have a higher proportion of Bayport chert compared to inland sites at the same latitude. This presumably reflects an 'ease of transport' effect produced by canoe travel on the lake.

This general pattern was noted by Luedtke (1976), who observed a similar and complementary spatial fall-off of both Norwood and Bayport cherts when she compared a more limited sample of regional sites from all time periods. In the case of the Bayport chert during the Late Prehistoric Period, however, the fall-off to the north is not gradual, as would be expected for simple distance decay, but rather is stepped. Furthermore, these steps broadly correspond to the marked territories of Juntunen bands (Fig. 6b). This pattern suggests a third axis of variation, reflecting the influence of relatively stable territories on the distribution of chert. As a check on this conclusion, the spatial distribution of Bayport was considered for sites predating the Juntunen Phase in the same region (Fig. 7). These site assemblages also show a significant fall-off in a northerly direction, but the fall-off is both smoother and of lesser magnitude than is seen in the Late Prehistoric Period. This form of distribution makes good sense if the earlier hunting, gathering, and fishing societies were more wide ranging in their pattern of resource exploitation and were not participating in a tribal system with smaller and more stable social territories.

The regional distribution of cherts within the Juntunen system is consistent with the expectation for passive material marking. Juntunen sites along the western Lake Huron shore exhibit a 'stepped' fall-off in the quantities of Bayport chert in the assemblages, along with a progressive restriction of the use of Bayport chert for the manufacture of durable, curated tools. In northwestern Lower Michigan, a similar pattern of fall-off is observed, but with Norwood chert rather than Bayport as the preferred high quality local material (cf. Lovis 1973; Hambacher 1992). In addition, the more distant of these chert types, Bayport in the northwest and Norwood in the east, occur regularly in low quantities (in the range of 1 to 5 %) as exotic materials used for the manufacture of durable, curated implements.

While fall-off from a source area, or the wide ranging distribution of materials as exotics, are hardly earth shaking discoveries in the Great Lakes region, the more subtle effect that band territories produced on lithic distribution is much more interesting. The pattern, in all probability, is arising not as a result of any conscious effort to control

access to sources or to control the movement of quarried materials. Rather, the fall-off is likely the result of habitual patterns of population movement and provisioning within the Juntunen territories. In this sense, band territories are affecting the distribution of lithics only in so far as they are tending to shape and channel habitual movements and interactions of the individuals and communities within the region. And, since we are dealing with a combined and cumulative record of such interaction, the very discernability of the patterns in the material record indicates a high degree of stability to these patterns of interaction.

Discussion

This admittedly brief consideration of tribal boundaries and interaction within the Late Prehistoric Juntunen system clearly cannot do justice to the complexity or variability of the archaeological evidence, nor to the cultural variation inherent to the region during the Late Prehistoric period (cf. Bishop and Smith 1975). Yet, even this brief overview is sufficient to illustrate that the Juntunen system exhibited the same core features of tribal organization that are repeatedly described in the contributions to this volume. While the Juntunen system operated for some 400 years and was robust in the face of challenging environmental and subsistence conditions, it was not robust in the face of European contact, and was radically transformed even before the first European observer arrived to record his impressions of the upper Great Lakes. The rapid transformation of this formerly stable social system must give us pause, particularly when we attempt to utilize ethnographic descriptions of tribal organization as models for tribes in all times and all places.

From the perspective of territories and identities within a tribal social system, the levels at which overt marking is observed is in good agreement with theoretical expectations both for the marking of boundaries and specifically for the scales at which material culture is expected to play a formal role. For example, at the base of the spatial hierarchy, it would be unlikely that the members of the small co-residential group would require any material formalization of their identities, nor would we expect to see overt identity marking between the small co-residential groups that comprise the territorial band. Close kinship and frequent face-to-face interaction would render such marking unnecessary and redundant. This is not to say that differences in material culture would not arise among such

Fig. 7. Proportions of Bayport chert in lithic assemblages from earlier time periods.

groups, but rather that formalized social marking of identity between such groups would be unlikely. And even if such relations were marked in the material culture, the cumulative character of the archaeological record would, in all probability, render its recognition impossible. Overt material marking is deployed in those instances where there is less common face-to-face contact, and in those situations where bands do not maintain permanence of place and in which material markers must stand surrogate, asserting claims to use and ownership in the absence of the actual people. Passive marking, by contrast, was observed between areas at many scales, and was a sensitive indicator of regular contact, movement, and interaction.

Beyond the specifics of the Juntunen case, the study highlights a series of more general points relating to the archaeological study of tribal societies. One relates to the interplay between overt and passive social marking. The Juntunen case illustrates one way in which overt marking of social and territorial distinctions is achieved. The particular medium of expression, for example rock art or built structures, and the kinds of natural features that are annotated by such markings, will obviously vary from case to case, but the underlying relationship between long lasting cultural constructions and significant natural features of the landscape can be expected to play out again and again. In the same way, the subtle influence of regular, structured interaction on material cultural should also be encountered frequently. Ceramics, as in the Juntunen case, can actually exhibit both varieties of patterning at different (and again predictable) levels of detail. Yet, these subtleties of patterning only became recognizable when large assemblages from the entire region were compared in depth. Another interesting aspect of passive marking that is particularly relevant to tribal studies is that the patterns emerge without intent and without the influence of any centralized control. For example, the discontinuous distribution of Juntunen lithics is visible in the record even though no one overtly controlled access or distribution.

A feature that was crucial to our ability to recognize subtle patterns in the record is the cumulative nature of the archaeological record itself. The cumulative overlay or palimpsest of remains deriving from multiple overlapping uses of sites and localities is often seen as a major limitation for archaeological investigation. Yet in the present case, the emergence of coherent patterns from these palimpsests was a critical element in the detection

and explanation of their occurrence. The shaping influence of the territorial system affected not only the tendencies and habitual behavior of the people in the past, but also the material remains left by them in the archaeological record. Had there been less stability and more variation in the territorial system, the coherent patterns observed in the various classes of material culture would not have existed, and we would instead have witnessed an incoherent smear of variability. In effect, the persistence of patterning within such a cumulative deposit provides increased confidence that the observed patterns are real, and that they are indicative of long-term stability in behavior and interaction.

Finally, while the discussion in the paper was primarily concerned with symbolic marking and identity, our entrée into this system was provided by the unique ecological circumstances of the region and by the particular cultural adaptation to that unique ecology. This should remind us that regardless of our particular research focus, we ultimately are dealing with the products of whole communities and whole societies, and that the patterns we observe are the result of an elaborate and complex overlay of the interests, needs, and intents of the people whose remains we study. Like the cumulative archaeological record itself, we should view this complexity and interdependence as an asset, since it is through these mutual dependencies that we can use archaeology to investigate the workings of tribal societies in the past.

References Cited

Albert, D. A., S. R. Denton, and B. V. Barnes
1986 *Regional Landscape Ecosystems of Michigan*. The University of Michigan School of Natural Resources, Ann Arbor.

Ardener, S.
1981 Ground Rules and Social Maps for Women: An Introduction. In *Women and Space: Ground Rules and Social Maps*, edited by S. Ardener, pp. 11-34. Croon Helm, London.

Bishop, Charles and M. Estellie Smith
1975 Early Historic Populations of Northwest Ontario: Archaeological and Ethnohistorical Interpretations. *American Antiquity* 40(1):54-63.

Bradley, Richard
1993 *Altering the Earth: The Origins of Monuments in Britain and Continental Europe*.

Society of Antiquaries of Scotland Monography Series 8, Edinburgh.

Brandt, K. L.
1996   *The Effects of Early Agriculture on Native North American Populations: Evidence from the Teeth and Skeleton.* Unpublished Ph.D. dissertation, Department of Anthropology, The University of Michigan, Ann Arbor.

Brashler, Jane
1981   *Early Late Woodland Boundaries and Interaction: Indian Ceramics of Southern Lower Michigan.* Publications of the Museum, Michigan State University, Anthropological Series 3(3), Lansing.

Buckmaster, M.
1980   Scott Point: A Stratified Late Woodland Site on the North Shore of Lake Michigan. Paper presented at the Midwestern Archaeological Conference, Chicago.

Carruthers, Peter J.
1969   The Mikado Earthwork: 20Aa5. Master's thesis, Department of Archaeology, University of Calgary, Alberta, Canada.

Clark, J. E.
n.d.   Late Woodland Mortuary Practices at the Juntunen Site. Manuscript on file, University of Michigan Museum of Anthropology.

Cleland, Charles E.
1982   The Inland Shore Fishery of the Northern Great Lakes: Its Development and Importance in Prehistory. *American Antiquity* 47:761-784.

1992   From Ethnohistory to Archaeology: Ottawa and Ojibwa Band Territories of the Northern Great Lakes. In *Text-Aided Archaeology,* edited by B. Little, pp. 97-102. CRC Press, New York.

Conway, T.
1977   Whitefish Island—A Remarkable Archaeological Site at Sault Ste. Marie, Ontario. Research Manuscript Series, Data Box 310. Ministry of Culture and Recreation, Sault Ste. Marie, Ontario.

Crawford, G., D. Smith, and V. Bowyer
1997   Dating the Entry of Corn (*Zea mays*) into the Lower Great Lakes Region. *American Antiquity* 62(1):112-119.

Dawson, K. C. A.
1979   Algonkian Huron-Petun Ceramics in Northern Ontario. *Man in the Northeast* 18:14-31.

Dewdney, Selwyn and Kenneth E. Kidd
1962   *Indian Rock Paintings of the Great Lakes.* University of Toronto Press, Toronto.

Dorothy, L. G.
1980   The Ceramics of the Sand Point Site (20BG14), Baraga County, Michigan: a Preliminary Description. *The Michigan Archaeologist* 26(3-4):39-90.

Earle, Timothy
1997   *How Chiefs Come to Power: The Political Economy in Prehistory.* Stanford University Press, Stanford.

Fitting, James E.
1970   Rediscovering Michigan Archaeology: The Gillman Collections at Harvard. *The Michigan Archaeologist* 16(2):33-41.

Ford, Richard I.
1972   Barter, Gift or Violence: An analysis of Tewa Inter-tribal Exchange. *University of Michigan Museum of Anthropology, Anthropological Papers* 46:21-45.

Fox, William A.
1990a   The Odawa. In *The Archaeology of Southern Ontario to A.D. 1650,* edited by C. Ellis and N. Ferris, pp. 457-473. Occasional Publication of the London Chapter, OAS, Number 5. Ontario Archaeological Society, London, Ontario.

1990b   Odawa Lithic Procurement and Exchange: A History Carved in Stone. *Kewa, Newsletter of the London Chapter of the Ontario Archaeological Society*, 90(7):2-7.

Goldstein, Lynne G.
1976   Spatial Structure and Social Organization: Regional Manifestations of Mississippian Society. Unpublished PhD. dissertation, Northwestern University, Evanston.

Greenman, Emerson F.
1927   The Earthwork Enclosures of Michigan. Unpublished Ph.D. dissertation, University of Michigan, Ann Arbor.

Halstead, Paul and John O'Shea
1982   A Friend in Need is a Friend in Deed: Social Storage and the Origins of Social Ranking. In *Ranking, Resources and Exchange: Aspects of the Archaeology of Early European Society*, edited by C. Renfrew and S. Shennan, pp. 92-99. Cambridge University Press, Cambridge.

Hambacher, Michael J.
1992   The Skegemog Point Site: Continuing Studies in the Cultural Dynamics of the Carolinian-Canadian Transition Zone.

Unpublished Ph.D. dissertation, Michigan State University, East Lansing.

Heidenreich, Conrad E.
1971 *Huronia: A History and Geography of the Huron Indians, 1600-1650*. McClelland and Stewart, Toronto.

Hinsdale, Wilbert B.
1929 Indian Mounds, West Twin Lake, Montmorency County, Michigan. *Papers of the Michigan Academy of Science, Arts and Letters* X:91-102.
1931 *Archaeological Atlas of Michigan*, Michigan Handbook Series No. 4.

Holl, A.
1993 Late Neolithic Cultural Landscape in Southeastern Mauretania: An Essay in Spatiometrics. In *Spatial Boundaries and Social Dynamics*, edited by A. Holl and T. Levy, pp. 95-133. International Monographs in Prehistory, Ann Arbor.

Hurley, W. M.
1975 *An Analysis of Effigy Mound Complexes in Wisconsin*. Anthropological Papers No. 59. Museum of Anthropology, The University of Michigan, Ann Arbor.

Janusas, S.
1984 *A Petrological Analysis of Kettle Point Chert and Its Spatial and Temporal Distribution in Regional Prehistory*. National Museum of Man, Archaeological Survey of Canada, Mercury Series, Paper 128.

Lepper, Bradley, Richard Yerkes and W. Pickard
2001 Prehistoric Flint Procurement Strategies at Flint Ridge, Licking County, Ohio. *Midcontinental Journal of Archaeology* 26(1):53-78.

Lovis, William A.
1973 Late Woodland Cultural Dynamics in the Northern Lower Peninsula of Michigan. Unpublished Ph.D. dissertation, Michigan State University, East Lansing.

Luedtke, Barbara
1976 Lithic Material Distributions and Interaction Patterns During the Late Woodland Period in Michigan. Unpublished PhD. dissertation, University of Michigan, Ann Arbor.

McClurken, James M.
1988 We Wish to be Civilized: Ottawa-American Political Contests on the Michigan Frontier. Unpublished Ph.D. dissertation, Michigan State University, East Lansing.

McKenney, Thomas L.
1972 Sketches of a Tour to the Lakes, of the character and customs of the Chippeway Indians, and of incidents connected with the Treaty of Fon Du Lac. Barre, Massechusetts, Imprint Society.

McPherron, Alan
1967a *The Juntunen Site and the Late Woodland Prehistory of the Upper Great Lakes Area*. Museum of Anthropology, University of Michigan, Anthropological Papers 30, Ann Arbor.
1967b On the Sociology of Ceramics: Pottery Style Clustering, Marital Residence, and Cultural Adaptations on an Algonkian-Iroquoian Border. In *Iroquois Culture, History, and Prehistory*, edited by E. Tooker, pp. 101-107. Proceedings of the 1965 Conference on Iroquois Research, New York State Museum of Science Service, Albany.

Milner, Claire McHale
1998 Ceramic Style, Social Differentiation, and Resource Uncertainty in the Late Prehistoric Upper Great Lakes. Unpublished PhD. dissertation, University of Michigan, Ann Arbor.

Milner, Claire McHale and John O'Shea
1990 Life After the Juntunen Site? Late Prehistoric Occupation of the Upper Great Lakes. Paper presented at the Midwestern Archaeological Conference, Evanston, Illinois.
1998 The Socioeconomic Role of Late Woodland Enclosures. In *Ancient Earthen Enclosures*, edited by R. Mainfort and L. Sullivan, pp. 181-201. University Press of Florida, Gainsville.

Minc, Leah and K. Smith
1989 The Spirit of Survival: Cultural Responses to Resource Variability in Northern Alaska. In *Bad Year Economics: Cultural Responses to Risk and Uncertainty*, edited by P. Halstead and J. O'Shea, pp. 8-39. Cambridge University Press, Cambridge.

Morse, E. W.
1984 *Fur Trade Canoe Routes of Canada, Then and Now*. University of Toronto Press, Toronto.

Norder, John, Jane Baxter, Albert Nelson, and John O'Shea
2002 Stone Tombs and Ancient Ritual Status Marking and Social Roles in the Early

Late Woodland of Southeastern Michigan. *Midcontinental Journal of Archaeology* X-XX.

O'Shea, John M.

1881 Coping with Scarcity: Exchange and Social Storage. In *Economic Archaeology*, edited by A. Sheridan and G. Bailey, pp. 167-83. British Archaeological Reports, International Series 96, Oxford.

1986 Social Organization and Mortuary Behavior in the Late Woodland Period. In *Interpretations of Culture Change in the Eastern Woodlands during the Late Woodland Period*, edited by R. W. Yerkes, pp. 68-85. Occasional Papers in Anthropology No. 3. Department of Anthropology, The Ohio State University, Columbus.

1988 "Marginal Agriculture or Agriculture at the Margins: A Consideration of Native Agriculture in the Upper Great Lakes". Paper presented at the Society for American Archaeology Annual Meetings, Tempe, AZ.

1989 The Role of Wild Resources in Small-Scale Agricultural Systems: Tales from the Lakes and Plains. In *Bad Year Economics: Cultural Responses to Risk and Uncertainty*, edited by P. Halstead and J. O'Shea, pp. 57-67. Cambridge University Press, Cambridge.

Phillips, D. W., and J. A. W. McCulloch

1972 *The Climate of the Great Lakes Basin.* Environment Canada-Climatological Studies 20, Toronto.

Pollock, J. W.

1975 *Algonquian Culture Development and Archaeological Sequences in Northeastern Ontario.* Canadian Archaeological Association Bulletin No. 7.

Rappaport,, Roy A.

1979 *Ecology, Meaning and Religion.* North Atlantic Books, Richmond, CA.

Sackett, James R.

1982 Approaches to Style in Lithic Archaeology. *Journal of Anthropological Archaeology* 1:59-110.

1985 Style and Ethnicity in the Kalahari: a Reply to Wiessner. *American Antiquity* 50:154-159.

Salzer, R.

1974 The Wisconsin North Lakes Project: a Preliminary Report. In *Aspects of Upper Great Lakes Anthropology: Papers in*

Honor of Lloyd A. Wilford, edited by E. Johnson, pp. 40-54. Minnesota Prehistoric Archaeology Series No. 11. Minnesota Historical Society, St. Paul.

Smith, B. A.

1987 Dog Burials of Late Prehistoric Algonquian Sites in Northeastern Ontario. Paper presented at the Society for American Archaeology Annual Meetings, Toronto.

1996 Systems of Subsistence and Neworks of Exchange in the Terminal Woodland and Early Historic Periods in the Upper Great Lakes. Unpublished PhD. dissertation, Michigan State University, East Lansing.

Sobel, Elizabeth and Gordon Bettles

2000 Winter Hunger, Winter Myths: Subsistence Risks and Mythology among the Klamath and Modoc. *Journal of Anthropological Archaeology* 19(3):276-316.

Stevenson, M. G.

1989 Sourdoughs and Cheechakos: The Formation of Identity-signaling Social Groups. *Journal of Anthropological Archaeology* 8:270-312.

Tooker, Elisabeth

1971 Clans and Moieties in North America. *Current Anthropology* 12(3):357-376.

1964 *An Ethnography of the Huron Indians, 1615-1649.* Bureau of American Ethnology Bulletin 190, Washington D.C.

Trigger, Bruce G.

1985 Natives and Newcomers: Canada's "Heroic Age" Reconsidered. McGill-Queen's University Press, Montreal.

1987 *The Children of Aataentsic: A History of the Huron People to 1660.* 2 vols. McGill-Queen's University Press, Toronto.

United States Department of Agriculture (USDA)

1911 *Yearbook of Agriculture.* U.S. Government Printing Office, Washington, D.C.

Welsch, R. L. and J. E. Terrell

1998 Material Culture, Social Fields, and Social Boundaries on the Sepik Coast of New Guinea. In *The Archaeology of Social Boundaries*, edited by M. Stark, pp. 50-77. Smithsonian Institution Press, Washington.

Whiteley, P. M.

1985 Unpacking Hopi 'Clans': Another Vintage Model Out of Africa? *Journal of Anthropological Research* 41(4):359-374.

Wiessner, Polly

1983 Style and Social Information in Kalahari San Projectile Points. *American Antiquity* 49:253-276.

1984 Reconsidering the Behavioral Basis of Style. *Journal of Anthropological Archaeology* 3:190-234.

1985 Style or Isochrestic Variation? A Reply to Sackett. *American Antiquity* 50(1):160-165.

Wobst, H. Martin

1977 Stylistic Behavior and Information Exchange. In *For the Director: Research Essays in Honor of James B. Griffin,* edited by C. Cleland, pp. 317-344. University of Michigan Museum of Anthropology, Anthropological Papers 61, Ann Arbor.

1999 Style in Archaeology or Archaeologists in Style. In *Material Meanings,* edited by E. Chilton, pp. 118-132. The University of Utah Press, Salt Lake City.

Wright, G. A.

1967 Some Aspects of Early and Mid-Seventeenth Century Exchange Networks in the Western Great Lakes. *The Michigan Archaeologist* 13:181-197.

Wright, J. V.

1963 *An Archaeological Survey Along the North Shore of Lake Superior.* Anthropology Papers 3. National Museum of Canada, Ottawa.

1965 A Regional Examination of Ojibwa Culture History. *Anthropologica* 7(2):189-227.

1969 *The Michipicoten Site.* Anthropological Series 82, Contributions to Anthropology VI: Archaeology and Physical Anthropology Bulletin 224:1-85. National Museum of Canada, Ottawa.

1973 *The Ontario Iroquois Tradition.* Bulletin No. 210, National Museum of Canada, Ottawa.

1981 Prehistory of the Canadian Shield. In Subarctic, edited by J. Helm, pp. 86-96. *Handbook of North American Indians,* vol. 6, W. C. Sturtevant, general editor. Smithsonian Institution, Washington, D.C.

Zurel, Richard L.

1999a Michigan's Rock Art. In *Retrieving Michigan's Buried Past,* edited by J. Halsey, pp. 249-252. Cranbrook Institute of Science Bulletin 64, Bloomfield Hills.

1999b Earthwork Enclosure Sites in Michigan. In *Retrieving Michigan's Buried Past,* edited by J. Halsey, pp. 244-248. Cranbrook Institute of Science Bulletin 64, Bloomfield Hills.

12. Hopewell Tribes: A Study of Middle Woodland Social Organization in the Ohio Valley

Richard W. Yerkes

Abstract

It is difficult to reconstruct the social organization of the Ohio Valley Hopewell. Their artifacts, burials, mounds and earthworks are spectacular. They comprise the most elaborate built environment in the prehistoric United States (Clay 1998; Yerkes 2000). For many, the magnitude of Hopewell earthwork construction and the abundance of exotic artifacts is difficult to explain in the absence of a hierarchical social structure, well-developed agriculture, craft specialization, and centralized redistribution (Hall 1997:156), the very elements that define a chiefdom.

Several archaeologists believe that the Ohio Hopewell were sedentary swidden farmers occupying dispersed hamlets near large, vacant, ceremonial centers. In this model, the ancestors of the Hopewell were complex hunter-gatherers living in areas where wild food was abundant. Around 100 B.C., the Hopewell gradually domesticated several native weedy plants (Dancey and Pacheco 1997; Wymer 1993). The proposed shift to farming in the Ohio Valley follows the 'new perspectives' on how and why foragers became farmers. It is assumed that domesticates were added to a broad-spectrum of wild foods, but eventually they became the main food source of the Hopewell. These archaeologists believe that the transition to farming was also marked by changes in economic and social organization, with communal sharing giving way to household accumulation, followed by increased social differentiation, wealth, and craft specialization (Green 1994; Mainfort and Sullivan 1998; Price and Gebauer 1995; Scarry 1993). However, there is no empirical evidence for *any* of these features in Ohio Hopewell Societies.

A different view of Ohio Hopewell is more appropriate. For years, Hall (1980, 1997) and Griffin (1964, 1997) described Hopewell societies as egalitarian and decentralized. There were no Hopewell merchant princes sustained by agricultural surpluses. Like most American Indians, the Hopewell probably gained prestige not by accumulating wealth, but by giving gifts to others (Hall 1997:156). Consumption of domesticated plants does not transform the Ohio Hopewell into farmers, and the construction of elaborate ceremonial and mortuary features does not make them a chiefdom. They were complex without being sedentary. The few small domestic Hopewell sites that have been excavated have not produced any evidence that they were occupied for long periods of time. The social organization of the Ohio Hopewell allowed them to be mobile and dispersed, yet well integrated. The construction of monumental earthworks, the production and distribution of exotic goods, and the emergence of some status differentiation probably developed within a segmentary society or complex tribe. The flexibility of tribal models provides a more useful framework for understanding Hopewell social organization (see Fowles, this volume, Chapter 2).

The Hopewell do not reveal their secrets easily, and there are aspects of their behavior that we may never understand. However, their elaborate cultural landscape testifies to their ability to maintain local and individual autonomy within an extensive tribal network for several centuries. The Ohio Hopewell earthworks and the elaborate goods that are found within them were not products of emerging Middle Woodland chiefdoms that were competing with each other for political and social territories. In this regard they stand in stark contrast to the later Mississippian societies. An elaborate ceremonial complex may have been necessary to bind the small mobile populations that formed the Hopewell tribes (Hall 1997). The Hopewell show us the degree of cultural complexity that can be achieved with the organizational flexibility of tribal networks, even if the Hopewell lacked food surpluses, specialized production, and permanent residences.

Introduction

What we call *Hopewell* is one of the best known, but least understood prehistoric cultural complexes in the world. The type site on the M. C. Hopewell farm west of Chillicothe, Ohio (Fig. 1) was excavated by Warren K. Moorehead in 1892 to collect artifacts for display in Chicago at the World Columbian Exhibition (Hall 1997:155). It was not long before other Midwestern and Southeastern Hopewell complexes were identified. It was clear that Hopewell was widespread, but it was not clear how the different Hopewell groups were related. In fact, it was not clear exactly what this thing called Hopewell really *was*.

The idea that Hopewell was the culture of a lost race of Moundbuilders died hard, but it was laid to rest by the beginning of the 20th century. The idea that Hopewell culture spawned the Middle Mississippians persisted until radiocarbon dating showed that at least 400 years separated the two complexes (Carr and Haas 1996; Hall 1997:155). Some saw Hopewell as an 'overlay' of religious traits on local Middle Woodland societies (Prufer 1965) or as an example of a widespread religious diffusion like the *Ghost Dance* (Murphy 1989:215-219). However, Joseph R. Caldwell (1964) employed concepts coined by Robert Redfield to describe Hopewell as a *Great Tradition* that was shared by many *small traditions* such as Ohio (or Scioto) Hopewell, Illinois (or Havana) Hopewell, Kansas City Hopewell, and Marksville. Caldwell recognized that each manifestation of Hopewell is different because each is based on a different regional tradition (Brose and Greber 1979; Brown 1964a; Caldwell and Hall 1964; Deuel 1952; Griffin et al. 1970; Hall 1997:156; Prufer 1965; Seeman 1979a). He used the term *Hopewell Interaction Sphere* to describe the way that materials and ideas spread or diffused among the far-flung regions. Robert L. Hall (1979, 1997) showed how the ideology of the Hopewell great tradition provided the shared symbols and ideas that were expressed in the artifacts and features found in the different small traditions. The scale of this interaction was vast, with Hopewell complexes spread over much of the Midwestern and Southwestern USA, and Canada, but there were many contemporary Middle Woodland societies in North America that were not involved in the Hopewell Interaction Sphere (Muller 1986:95-126). Berle Clay and Charles Niquette (1989) remind us that between 100 BC and AD 400, when the Ohio Valley Hopewell reached a cultural climax marked by elaborate earthworks, exotic goods, and complex mortuary ceremonies, nearby areas followed a different social trajectory and did not invest time and labor in such elaborate cultural features.

The interaction sphere concept has been used to examine the spread of religious symbols among emerging prehistoric states in Latin America, and to describe the connections between Mississippian chiefdoms (Hall 1997:155-156). The Hopewell Interaction Sphere operated in a different way. It was a network of Middle Woodland tribal societies (Braun and Plog 1982; Fortier 1998). As Hall (1997:156) observed, this interaction allowed ideas and materials to move, "without great hindrance over great stretches of the North American Continent." The valued artifacts that moved through the interaction sphere were not tribute, status symbols, or wealth accumulated by elite classes. Robert L. Hall reminds us that Hopewell leaders were not powerful chiefs or merchant princes. Like most North American Indians, Hopewell people gained prestige by giving gifts to others, not by accumulating wealth (Hall 1997:156).

In an oft quoted passage, Struever and Houart (1964:88) suggested that Hopewell goods were, "status-specific objects which functioned in various ritual and social contexts within community life"—and eventually were "deposited as personal belongings or contributed goods with the dead, reaffirming the status of the deceased." Hall reminds us that these goods also reaffirmed the status of the *living* and served to maintain the bonds within a dispersed tribal network. The exotic goods were once cited as evidence that the Hopewell were a ranked society with centralized redistribution under the control of 'Big Men' or chiefs (Muller 1986:92; Sahlins 1963; Seeman 1979b). Now they are considered corporate gifts or community, but not personal, valuables (Fortier 1998:358; Hall 1997; Seeman 1995). The Hopewell Interaction Sphere shows us how dispersed, egalitarian societies comprised of social segments of varying scales can have contacts and ties to other groups and still maintain their autonomy (see Service 1971). The monumental earthworks built by Hopewell societies and the flow of exotic goods between the widely spaced centers show us that complex interactions can occur without the strong centralized authority found in chiefdoms and states. Prehistoric tribal societies were also capable of these kinds of accomplishments (see Price and Brown 1985).

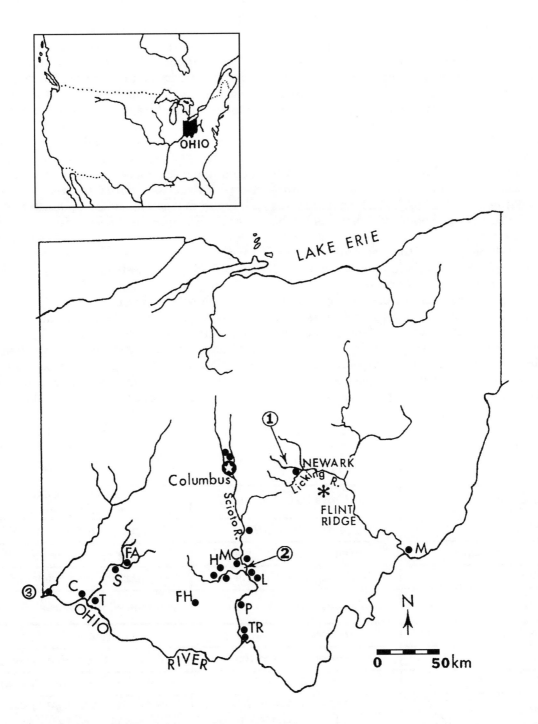

Fig. 1. The location of (1) the Murphy site (33LI212), (2) the McGraw site, and (3) the Jennison Guard site in relation to the major Ohio Hopewell earthworks (black dots). The Newark Earthworks, which include the Hale's House site (33LI252) is shown by the larger black dot. C = Cincinnati, FA=Fort Ancient, FH=Fort Hill, H=Hopewell, L=Liberty (Edwin Harness), M=Marietta, MC=Mound City, P=Piketon, S=Stubbs, T=Turner, TR=Tremper.

Hopewell Social Organization

Were Ohio Hopewell societies really tribal societies? Over thirty years ago at a Society for American Archaeology meeting in Chapel Hill, Struever (1965:212) stated that his comparison of Ohio and Illinois Hopewell revealed that they operated at different levels of social integration. He believed that Ohio Hopewell societies met the criteria for a chiefdom, while Illinois Hopewell groups did not (Sahlins and Service 1960; Service 1962; Struever 1965).

His conclusion was not surprising, given the spectacular array of Ohio Hopewell artifacts, burials, mounds and earthworks. The most elaborate built environment in the prehistoric United States is found in the Ohio Valley, and it is easy to be overawed by these ancient monuments (Clay 1998). For many archaeologists, the magnitude of Hopewell earthwork construction and the abundance of exotic artifacts is difficult to explain in the absence of a hierarchical social structure, well-developed agriculture, craft specialization, and redistribution (Hall 1997:156)—the very elements that define a chiefdom.

However, there is no hard evidence for *any* of these features in Ohio Hopewell Societies. Creamer and Haas (1985) provide some criteria for distin-

guishing tribes from chiefdoms (Table 1). If we apply these criteria to Ohio Hopewell societies, we find that the archaeological evidence for most of their 'domestic' activities is consistent with what would be expected in a tribal society, while their level of labor organization and exchange is more like a chiefdom. Ohio Hopewell settlements are small, similar-looking, and dispersed. There are few or no houses at these small sites with no differentiation in architecture, and no evidence for communal storage (Table 1). The large ceremonial earthworks suggest that labor was organized at the regional level, and the caches of exotic goods found under the mounds suggest that there was extensive exchange, but centralized, ascribed leadership is not necessary to explain Hopewell exchange and earthwork construction. N'omi Greber (1979a, 1979b, 1991) found evidence for a wide range of social complexity in the burial data from several Ohio Hopewell mounds and earthworks, including evidence for ascribed status, achieved status, or both, sometimes within the same burial populations. Greber (1979b:38) described Ohio Hopewell societies as ranked descent groups. Individuals could achieve status through their political, religious, and economic activities. This is consistent with the level of social organization that Fried (1967) and Service (1971) found in non-hier-

Table 1. Archaeological correlates of tribes and chiefdoms, after Creamer and Haas 1985: Table 1.

	TRIBE	**CHIEFDOM**
Settlement Pattern	***similar sites, dispersed***	hierarchy of sites *central places*
Architecture	***no differentiation***	status differentiation
Labor Organization	local community level	***regional level***
Surplus	***little (household level)***	intensive food production
Storage	***no communal storage***	centralized food storage facilities
Specialists	***limited, religious***	craft specialization
Rank	***ranked kin groups***	clear hierarchical levels
Exotics	few exotic goods	***caches or graves with exotics***
Trade	***local exchange of food*** little long-distance trade	***extensive exchange of exotics*** restricted to elites
Boundaries	***defined by artifact styles?***	well-defined defensive features
Stress	evidence for warfare or environmental stress	evidence for intensive warfare
Terms in Bold Italic: seem to be characteristics of Ohio Hopewell		

230

archical, segmentary tribal societies (Creamer and Haas 1985; Greber 1979b, 1991).

Robert L. Hall (1997:156) suggested that the elaborate ceremonial complex of the Ohio Hopewell developed as part of an organizational solution in tribal societies where subsistence was based on hunting, fishing, gathering nuts and wild plants, and sowing and harvesting some native plants that may have been domesticated. Ohio Hopewell subsistence was based on seasonal mobility and dispersed settlements. To avoid becoming isolated, these groups needed some means of social integration. Constructing earthworks and participating in elaborate rituals may have been a way of maintaining ties between the dispersed members of these societies.

Exotic goods and foodstuffs were exchanged at Hopewell ceremonial centers, but the primary function of the earthworks may have been social, rather than economic. Too often we see the earthworks described only in economic terms. They are called *transaction* or *redistribution* centers for Interaction Sphere artifacts and food supplies. For some archaeologists, the rationale for the Hopewell Interaction Sphere and the investment of labor in earthwork and mound construction is that by doing these things, dispersed groups would maintain ties that allowed them to share food during times of scarcity (Brose 1979; Ford 1979; Wymer 1993). Following Hall, Andrew Fortier (1998:357) suggests that Hopewell earthworks were rendezvous centers that operated like the Great Basin Shoshone *fandangos*. Julian Steward (1938:237) observed that the feasting, dancing, and visiting at the fandangos promoted social intercourse without economic motivation (also see Clay 1998 for similar ideas about Adena ceremonial centers).

The Hopewell concern with food shortages and fluctuating resources may have led to the adoption of a mobile, dispersed subsistence system. Small groups may have spread out and traveled to locations where certain resources were abundant during certain seasons of the year.

This solution to the problem of unpredictable and uneven food resources would have led to a situation where the small groups were becoming isolated from each other. Scheduled feasts, adoption ceremonies, and burial rituals held at the earthworks would allow the dispersed groups to maintain ties. This would keep the Hopewell tribes integrated (Hall 1997; Seeman 1995). However, the scale of integration is not clear. Clusters of small Ohio Hopewell settlements have been identified near some of the larger earthworks (Dancey

and Pacheco, eds. 1997), but it is not clear if these clusters were occupied by members of independent tribes or if the clusters were segments of larger tribal 'superclusters.' Lepper (1995) has proposed that two large Ohio Hopewell centers in Newark and Chillicothe were linked by a "Great Hopewell Road." We do not know how far Hopewell groups had traveled when they came to the earthwork centers.

Sedentary Farmsteads?

James Brown once remarked that the contrast between the large Ohio Hopewell ceremonial complexes and the tiny Middle Woodland domestic sites is really striking, and others have also been impressed by this contrast in scale (Aument 1992; Baker 1993; Cowan et al. 1999, 2000; Yerkes 1990, 1994, 2000). There are no large, nucleated Hopewell villages located near the earthworks, and one wonders why did the people who built these earthen monuments disperse into such small and widely scattered habitation sites when they left the ceremonial sites? To account for this disparity, in one model of Ohio Hopewell settlement systems the small sites are called "sedentary farmsteads" (Dancey 1991; Dancey and Pacheco 1997; Pacheco 1996, 1997). However, several archaeologists have questioned the assumption that these small Ohio Hopewell domestic sites were occupied nearly continuously for long periods of time (Clay and Creasman 1999; Weller et al. 1999; Yerkes 1990, 1994). If sedentary sites are stable, formally organized, year round-settlements (Holley 1993:279; Murdock 1967:159), then excavations at such sites should reveal substantial domestic dwellings and numerous storage pits. There should be a diverse artifact assemblage including discarded tools that show evidence of both short-term and long-term use, and the remains of plants and animals that were obtained during several different seasons of the year. Ethnographic studies have shown that sedentary groups construct, larger more complex structures and facilities than mobile groups and invest more labor in the construction of their dwellings (Binford 1983; Clay and Creasman 1999; Fortier 1993; Holley 1993; Kent 1991, 1992; Saunders 1990).

Analysis of radiocarbon dates from two small Hopewell sites located near major earthworks (the Murphy and McGraw sites) revealed that there were several brief occupation episodes at each site, not the single long-term occupations proposed in the dispersed hamlet model (Carr and Haas 1996).

No substantial domestic structures, thick middens, or other evidence for long-term occupation were found at these sites (Fig. 2, see Lepper and Yerkes 1997; Yerkes 1990, 1997). The deep bell-shaped or flat-bottomed storage pits that are so common at villages inhabited by Late Prehistoric (A.D. 1000-1670) agricultural groups like the Fort Ancient (Fig. 3, see Nass 1987; Nass and Yerkes 1995; Wagner 1996) are not found at the small Hopewell sites (Fig. 4). The features found at these small Ohio Valley Hopewell sites include shallow basins, hearths, and earth ovens (Fig. 2). These are the types of features that are quite common at sites occupied by mobile Late Archaic foragers (Kozarek 1997; McElrath et al. 1984; Yerkes 1986).

Gail Wagner (1996:267-268) asks, why did Fort Ancient groups use underground storage pits? She argues that the pits provided "concealed storage" for foods and other goods during the winter season when the villages were abandoned and the Fort Ancient populations dispersed to hunting camps. The concealed storage pits (Fig. 4 d, e) indicate that the Fort Ancient groups planned on coming back to the villages in the spring. The *absence* of concealed storage pits or cache pits at the small Ohio Hopewell sites suggests that these Middle

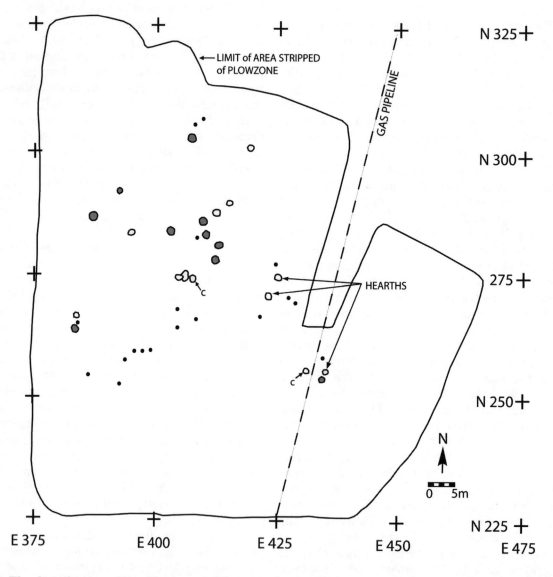

Fig. 2. The distribution of the 43 excavated features in the 6500 square meter area where the plowzone was removed at the Murphy site (33LI212). Note the dispersed pattern of postholes (black dots), earth ovens (shaded), shallow cylindrical pits (C), shallow basins (not shaded), and hearths.

Woodland groups may *not* have intended to return to these sites in the near future.

Sedentary populations were extremely rare in the Ohio Valley during prehistoric and early historic times. Even the Fort Ancient groups that are considered to be "consummate maize agriculturists" (Wagner 1996:256) only spent the warmer months of the year in their circular villages (Fig. 3). Family groups dispersed to hunting camps during the winter (Essenpreis 1978; Wagner 1996). This pattern of seasonal nucleation and dispersal was practiced by many of the historic agricultural tribes of the Ohio Valley-Great Lakes Region such as the Shawnee, Miami, and Potawatomi (Callender 1978; Fitting and Cleland 1969; Mason 1981:32-36).

The development of native North American agricultural systems that included clearing some of the forest, tilling the soil with hoes, and cultivating maize, squash, beans, sunflower, tobacco, and several other plants did not lead to year-round residence at permanent villages (Stoltman and Baerreis 1983:259-262; Hall 1980; Wagner 1996). The relationship between subsistence practices and sedentism is complex. All foragers are not mobile, and all farmers are not sedentary (Baker 1993; Becker 1999:22; Phillips 1998:217). Consuming native domesticated plants does not make the Ohio Hopewell farmers. The presence of domesticated weedy plants at the small settlements is not an archaeological correlate of sedentism.

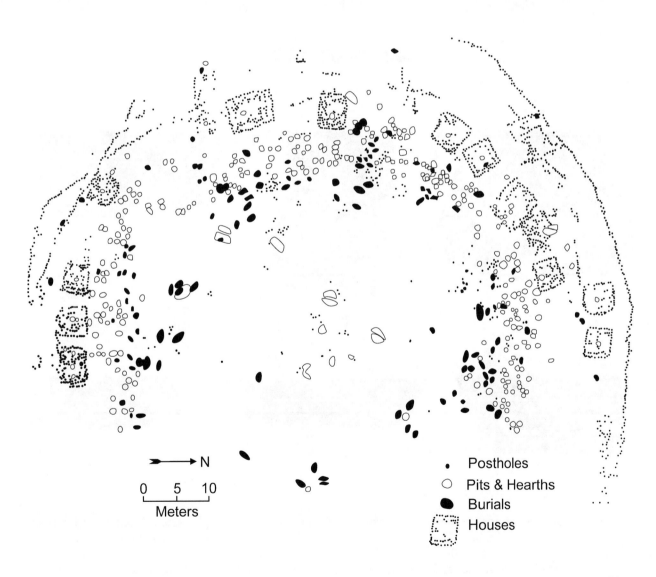

N

0 5 10
Meters

• Postholes
○ Pits & Hearths
● Burials
▢ Houses

Fig. 3. The site plan of the excavated portion of the Sun Watch Fort Ancient Village in Dayton, Ohio (after Nass and Yerkes 1995: Fig. 3-3).

Mobility patterns are usually reconstructed from seasonal patterns in the faunal and floral remains recovered at prehistoric sites (Cross 1988; Monks 1981; Yerkes 1987). However, the degree of sedentism at small Ohio Hopewell sites is not based on sound seasonal proxy data. Kozarek (1997:133) claims that evidence of "multiseasonal" exploitation of animals and the presence of seasonally available species indicate that the small Jennison Guard Hopewell site (located on the Ohio River floodplain near Cincinnati) was a permanent settlement. However, she presented no empirical data in support of her claim. Repeated occupations by Hopewell groups returning to the site at different seasons of the year may give the illusion of a permanent occupation (Becker 1999:2), and it is diffi-

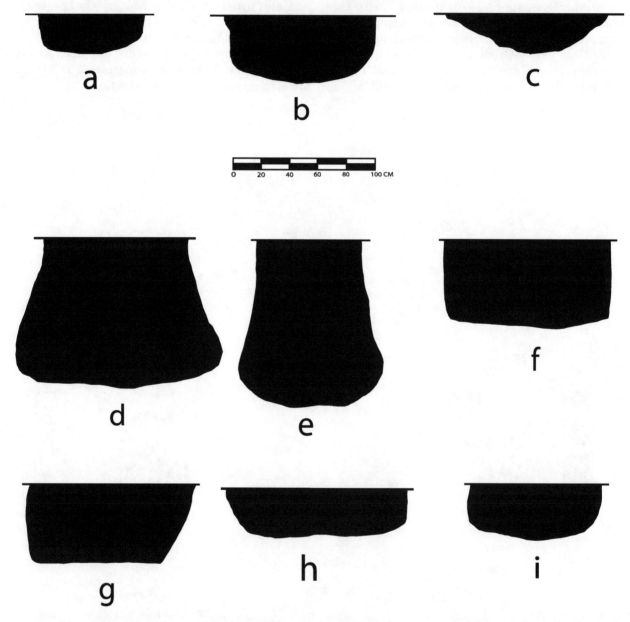

Fig. 4. a-c: Cross-sections of pit features from the Ohio Hopewell Murphy site (33LI212). d-i: Cross-sections of pits at the Fort Ancient Sun Watch site. Note the shallow cylindrical pit (a), earth-oven or roasting pit (b), and shallow basin (c) from The Murphy site (see Fig. 2), and the much deeper bell-shaped pits (d, e) and deeper flat-bottomed pits (f, g) from Sun Watch Village (see Fig. 3). Even the shallower flat-bottomed pits (h) and basin-shaped pits (i) at Sun Watch Village are deeper than the deepest pits at the Ohio Hopewell Murphy site (After Dancey 1991; Nass 1987).

cult to distinguish multiple occupations from continuous ones in the archaeological record (Rocek and Bar-Yosef 1998; Yerkes 1986).

Instead, a number of untested assumptions are made to estimate how long people resided at these small sites. Wymer (1997:160-161) assumes that the only way the Hopewell could have obtained weedy native plants and hazelnuts is if they stayed in the same location all year long (however, she finds the lack of any remains of house structures at small settlements like the Murphy site to be "puzzling"). Others cite the "structure" of activities at site as reflected in the distribution of artifacts and features as archaeological correlates for sedentism (Dancey 1991; Kozarek 1997; Wymer 1997). This is based on the untested assumption that discrete activity areas, few overlapping features, and systematic refuse disposal would characterize sedentary settlements. While no structures have been found at these small sites, it is assumed that they were permanently occupied for extended, and uninterrupted, periods of time. However, if this were the case, why are there not permanent structures, storage pits, or substantial middens at these sites?

In fact, the assumed correlates for sedentism (discrete activity areas, few overlapping features, and systematic refuse disposal) may actually indicate very brief occupation episodes at the small (less than one hectare) Murphy site and the excavated portions of the Jennison Guard site (Dancey 1991; Kozarek 1997). Refitting, microwear, and spatial analysis studies at Old World hunting gathering sites revealed similar patterns of discrete activity areas, few overlapping features, and systematic refuse disposal (Becker 1999; Becker and Wendorf 1993; Cahen et al. 1979), although these sites were shown to be short-term occupations, not permanent settlements.

Pacheco (1988:92-93) listed following archaeological correlates for sedentary Hopewell farmsteads along Raccoon Creek near the Newark Earthworks: the sites are small, functionally similar, structurally identical, and linearly dispersed. However, Stanley Baker (1993:32) noted that these features are also characteristics of sites that were part of mobile, hunting and gathering settlement/subsistence systems.

Hopewell Agriculture

R. Berle Clay and Charles M. Niquette (1989:17) remarked that Woodland agriculture in the Ohio Valley was assumed by archaeologists long before any empirical evidence for farming had been recovered from archaeological contexts. It was once thought that the Ohio Hopewell were maize farmers living in sedentary villages. It was believed that the earthworks and elaborate mortuary rituals of Hopewell required a food surplus and agricultural economy (Thomas 1894:614-620; Willey and Phillips 1958:157-158). There is no evidence to support this view. A more recent model has them living in dispersed farmsteads surrounding "vacant" earthworks, and growing native weedy crops with a system of shifting slash-and-burn cultivation (Dancey and Pacheco 1997; Prufer 1965; Wymer 1993). The evidence for this model isn't particularly strong either. No substantial domestic structures, thick middens, or other evidence for long-term occupation were found at these sites (Yerkes 1990; 1997; also see Clay and Creasman 1999; Cowan n.d.). The mobile settlement-subsistence system employed by the Ohio Hopewell seems to have included regular trips to the earthworks for feasting, adoption, mortuary rituals, exchange and social interaction. Following these visits, small groups dispersed to different locations during different seasons to hunt, fish, gather nuts and wild plants, and harvest the native domesticated plants that they had sown earlier.

The starchy, oily, weedy plants

Dee Anne Wymer (1993, 1997) found that the three most common weedy plants found at the small Ohio Hopewell sites near the Newark Earthworks in Licking County, Ohio, are erect knotweed (*Polygonum erectum*), goosefoot (*Chenopodium* sp.), and maygrass (*Phalaris caroliniana*). Sumpweed (*Iva annua* var. *macrocarpa*) and sunflower (*Helianthus annus*) are present, but less common. These starchy and oily weeds are classified as native domesticated plants by virtue of the observed changes in the morphology of their seeds, or by their presence at archaeological sites that are believed to lie beyond the natural range of the weed. Wymer (1997) argues that forests must have been cleared and gardens must have been maintained year-round in order to grow these weedy plants. However, it has not been demonstrated that these native plants depended on humans for their propagation. Paleoethnobotanists suggest that sunflower, sumpweed, and *Chenopodium* were domesticated between 2500 and 1000 B.C. in Eastern North America. Mobile Late Archaic foragers probably domesticated knotweed and maygrass during same interval (Fritz 1990; Watson 1996:162).

The Hopewell cultural climax has been attributed to an agricultural 'revolution' that led to increased sedentism, intensification in food production, and the concentration of dispersed populations (Seeman 1992:35; Wymer 1997). However, the native domesticates that were the basis of their 'unique' agricultural system had been cultivated for at least 900 years before the beginning of this alleged Hopewell agricultural revolution. Wymer (1997:161) describes the Ohio Hopewell as farmers. If farming is defined as a system of agricultural crop production that employs systematic soil preparation and tillage (Harris 1998), and if agriculture is reserved for contexts where human groups depend on plants for most of their subsistence needs (Bronson 1977:26), then the Hopewell were certainly *not* farmers. The Hopewell may have practiced a form of cultivation, where useful species of wild and/or domesticated plants are sown and harvested with or without tilling the soil (Bronson 1977; Harris 1998; Stoltman and Baerreis 1983:257). It is misleading to view these starchy, oily weeds as agricultural plants that depended on humans for their reproduction. The weedy cultigens were supplements to the wild nuts, plants, fish and game that supported the Hopewell—as they had supported their ancestors (Dunne and Green 1998; Watson 1988, 1989; Yarnell 1993).

There is no evidence for increased cultivation of these native weedy plants by the Hopewell. It is better to view the cultigens as favored species whose propagation was encouraged by mobile foragers.

According to Jack Harlan (1995:13), planting seeds was not uncommon among hunter-gatherers. In North America, the usual pattern was to burn a patch of vegetation in the fall and sow some seeds in the spring. There was no need to remain at the location where the seeds were sown. The foragers only needed to return when the seeds had ripened. Patty Jo Watson (1988:42-43) described these Middle Woodland domesticated weedy seed plants as secondary in importance to forest plant foods (like hickory nuts, acorns, wild berries, etc.).

There was great variability in the kinds and proportions of plants utilized by different groups of Ohio Hopewell. They were probably quite sophisticated in their use of plants, but they did not have to live in sedentary farmsteads in order to sow and harvest them. The relative abundance of the three starchy weeds recovered at the four small Ohio Hopewell sites studied by Wymer (1997) was quite variable (Fig. 5). These sites were located in different microenvironmental zones, and the small floral samples from the four sites may contain the plants that were most common at each location during the season that they were occupied. When

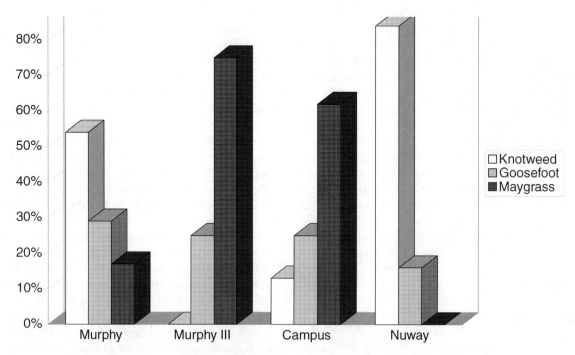

Fig. 5. Percentages of Native Weedy Domesticates at Small Ohio Hopewell sites in Licking County, Ohio. Data from Wymer (1987, 1993, 1997).

Wymer (1987, 1993) studied the plant remains from two larger Late Woodland (A.D. 400-1000) sites near Columbus, Ohio, she found a similar pattern of plant species abundance at both sites (Fig. 6). This may be due to the fact that the late Woodland samples represent the seeds collected over several seasons, rather than a single season. These data reveal that patterns of Ohio Hopewell plant utilization are consistent with the methods employed by hunter-gatherers (summarized in Harlan 1995).

There is no evidence that domesticated plants were the staples in the diets of the Ohio Hopewell societies, or that they invested substantial amounts of labor in food production activities. No prehistoric agricultural tools are associated with the Ohio Hopewell. While later Fort Ancient and Mississippian societies made and used hoes made of chipped stone, shell, and bone (scapulae) and deer-jaw sickles, no comparable farming tools have been found at Ohio Hopewell sites (Brown 1964b; Cobb 1989; Wagner 1996). The tool kit of the Ohio Hopewell is a hunting and gathering tool kit (Cowan n.d., Yerkes 1994).

There is no need to invent a 'unique' system of swidden agriculture with no ethnographic analog to explain Ohio Hopewell subsistence practices. For more than 30 years Robert L. Hall has argued

that there is nothing about Ohio Hopewell societies that could not be explained by the workings of cultural processes that were known from eyewitness accounts of historic Woodland tribal societies (Hall 1980:408; 1997:156). Hall's doctrine of cultural uniformitarianism can help us understand Ohio Hopewell subsistence and to learn why they devoted so much time and energy to the construction of mounds and earthworks and to the exchange of elaborate artifacts. Rather than going back to the days of the Moundbuilder myths and indulging in a form of cultural catastrophism that views the Ohio Hopewell as a society with no analogs, we should affirm their connection with their Native American descendants (Hall 1997). An examination of the ethnohistorical record can provide us with hypotheses about Hopewell behavior that can be tested with archaeological data.

Hopewell Craft Specialization

The Hopewell produced some of the most elaborate prehistoric artifacts found in Eastern North America, and yet the evidence for craft specialization is ambiguous (Yerkes 1994, 2002). Hopewell mounds contained substantial quantities of corner-notched projectile points (Snyders cluster, see

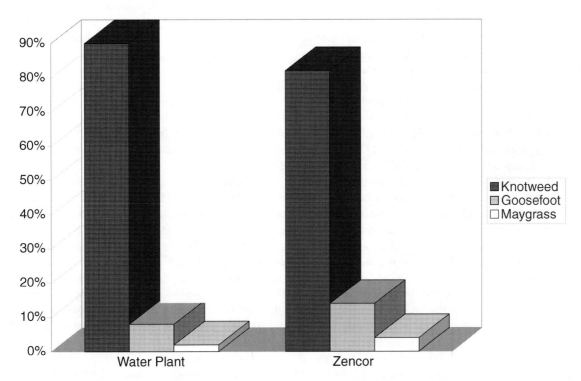

Fig. 6. Percentages of Native Weedy Domesticates at two late Woodland sites in Franklin County, Ohio. Data from Wymer (1987, 1993, 1997).

Justice 1987:210-204), bifacial cache blades, and prepared cores and bladelets (Odell 1994; Seeman 1992); some pottery vessels with distinctive zoned-incised decoration, and other elaborate exotic goods made of mica, copper, textiles, and pipestone.

These items were identified as grave offerings for the tombs of important individuals. However, some exotic artifacts have been found in domestic settings as well as graves (although large quantities of exotic goods have only been found in mounds). Large Hopewell earthwork complexes have been described as regional distribution centers for exotic raw materials and the finished goods that were produced in workshops located in or near the earthworks (Genheimer 1984; Struever and Houart 1972). Some have suggested that craft production was carried out under the auspices of chiefs who controlled the local and long-distance distribution of finished goods and raw materials (Bernhardt 1976; Parry 1994; Seeman 1979b). The exotic Hopewell artifacts seem to be valued commodities that were presented as gifts or exchanged, but there is no evidence for specialized production of these items.

Ohio Hopewell bladelet production and exchange

C. W. Cowan et al. (1981) believe that Hopewell bladelets and cores were produced at small sites for distribution to distant places via a regional exchange network. However, there are no correlates of craft specialization at such sites, such as spatial segregation of production debris or evidence for a high volume of lithic artifact production (cf. Evans 1978; Michaels 1989). Microwear analysis of bladelets from small Ohio Hopewell sites such as the Murphy (Yerkes 1994) and Paint Creek Lake Site #5 (Lemmons and Church 1998), from areas within the Newark Earthworks (Lepper and Yerkes 1997), and from the fill of the east lobes of Capitolium Mound, Marietta (Yerkes 1994) suggests that bladelets were not specialized tools. They were used for the same tasks as flakes and bifaces. Large quantities of bladelets have been found in mounds, but no craft workshops have been identified at habitation sites or earthworks (Yerkes 1994).

The development of Hopewell core-and-bladelet technology is enigmatic. It was not designed to produce specialized tools. There are no new Hopewell activities that required bladelets. They were used the same way that flakes and bifaces were used by earlier Archaic groups and by the ensuing Late Woodland and Late Prehistoric groups (Lem-

ons and Church 1998; Odell 1994; Yerkes 1986, 1990, 1994, 1997). Most of the Ohio Hopewell bladelets were made of either bright colored flint, or black and dark gray chert. The Hopewellian lithic technology was designed to produce large numbers of these distinctive artifacts, but the bladelets were not used for any special tasks, nor were they manufactured by specialists for export to distant locations (Lemons and Church 1998; Odell 1994; Yerkes 1990, 1994, 1997).

Bladelets made of exotic lithic raw materials are common at Hopewell sites near the Newark Earthworks, the supposed distribution center for Flint Ridge Flint. At the Newark Expressway sites, equal numbers of bladelets were made of Flint Ridge Flint and Wyandotte chert, even though the sources for Wyandotte chert are located over 300 km away,[1] (DeRegnaucourt and Georgiady 1998; Lepper and Yerkes 1997; Seeman 1975; Tankersley 1985). At the sites in the Murphy Tract survey near Newark (Pacheco 1997) the ratio of Flint Ridge flint bladelets to Wyandotte chert bladelets is about 2 to 1, but the ratio of flakes and bifaces made of Flint Ridge flint to similar artifacts made of Wyandotte chert is about 10 to 1. If Hopewell bladelets made of Flint Ridge Flint were being produced for export, why were so many exotic bladelets coming to the Newark area?

Members of Ohio Hopewell tribal societies were able to obtain bladelets made of many different types of colorful chert. The distribution pattern of Hopewell bladelets indicates that many of them circulated between sites located within the Ohio Hopewell heartland, but only a few were left at sites located further away near the sources of other exotic raw materials such as mica, copper, and marine shell. This distribution pattern does not support the idea that bladelets were produced for export.

Robert L. Hall suggested an alternative explanation for this distribution pattern. The production of bladelets may relate to Hopewell gift-giving rituals (Hall 1997:10-13, 155-159). Bladelets made of distinctive chert and flint would be presented in ceremonies held at the earthworks. These ceremonies may have included adoption rituals that strengthened the ties between the mobile, dispersed groups. The importance of the bladelets may have been their symbolic value (Seeman 1995). The possession of bladelets may have reminded them of the social connections signified by the gift and the spiritual power embodied by the exotic object itself (Helms 1991), even if they used the bladelets for everyday tasks.

Conclusions

The Ohio Hopewell were mobile foragers that gathered wild foods, hunted, fished, and collected or cultivated some weedy plants as they moved between upland rockshelters, floodplain camps and large earthwork complexes over the course of the year. Robert L. Hall suggests that the Hopewell may have developed their elaborate rituals and exchanged elaborate, exotic goods at their ceremonial centers in order to integrate the members of dispersed, segmented tribal societies, and also to establish and maintain peaceful relationships between unrelated groups by creating fictive kinship ties. Through these ties dispersed groups could depend on neighboring kin groups in time of food shortages. The adoption rituals, gift giving, and mortuary ceremonies would also allow individuals to rise in the eyes of their tribes and to be recognized for their personal achievements (Hall 1997:157-157).

The Hopewell do not reveal their secrets easily, and there are aspects of their behavior that we may never understand. However, their elaborate cultural landscape testifies to their ability to maintain local and individual autonomy within an extensive tribal network for several centuries. The Ohio Hopewell earthworks and the elaborate goods that are found within them were not produced by emerging Middle Woodland chiefdoms that were competing with each other for political and social territories. It is in this regard that they stand in stark contrast to the later Mississippian societies. Such an elaborate ceremonial complex may have been necessary to maintain the ties that linked the small diverse mobile segments of Hopewell tribes (Hall 1997). The Hopewell show us the degree of cultural complexity that can be achieved within the organizational flexibility of tribal networks, even by mobile societies that lacked food surpluses, specialized production, and permanent residences (Baker 1993).

Notes

[1]Some caution may be needed in accepting the identification of all of the dark gray chert found at the sites near the Newark Earthworks as 'exotic' Wyandotte chert. Delaware chert resembles Wyandotte chert, and can be found within 50 km of the Newark Earthworks (Converse 1972; Stout and Schoeblaub 1945:24-32; Vickery 1983:76).

References Cited

Aument, Bruce W.
 1992 Variability in Two Middle Woodland Habitation Sites from the Central Ohio Uplands. Paper presented at the 57th Annual Meeting of the Society for American Archaeology, Pittsburgh.

Baker, Stanley W.
 1993 33PK153: Site Comparison and Interpretation. In *Phase III Re-Examination of Selected Prehistoric Resources and Phase II Testing of Flood Prone Areas Impacted by the Proposed PIK-32-13.55 Project in Seal Township, Pike County, Ohio (PID. 7563).* Cultural Resources Unit, Bureau of Environmental Services, Ohio Department of Transportation, Columbus, OH.

Becker, Mark S.
 1999 Reconstructing Prehistoric Hunter-Gather Mobility Patterns and the Implications for the Shift to Sedentism: A Perspective from the Near East. Unpublished Ph.D. dissertation, Department of Anthropology, University of Colorado, Boulder.

Becker, Mark, and Fred Wendorf
 1993 A Microwear Study of a Late Pleistocene Qadan Assemblage from Southern Egypt. *Journal of Field Archaeology* 20:389-398.

Bernhardt, John
 1976 A Preliminary Survey of Middle Woodland Prehistory in Licking County, Ohio. *Pennsylvania Archaeologist* 46:39-54.

Binford, Lewis R.
 1983 *In Pursuit of the Past: Decoding the Archaeological Record.* Thames and Hudson, New York.

Braun, David P.
 1986 Midwestern Hopewellian Exchange and Supralocal Interaction. In *Peer Polity Interaction and Socio-Political Change,* edited by C. Renfrew and J. F. Cherry, pp. 117-126. Cambridge University Press, Cambridge.

Braun, David P., and Stephen Plog
 1982 Evolution of "Tribal" Social Networks: Theory and Prehistoric North American Evidence. *American Antiquity* 47:504-525.

Bronson, B.
 1977 The Earliest Farming: Demography as Cause and Consequence. In *Origins of*

Agriculture, edited by C. R. Reed, pp. 23-48. Mouton, The Hague.

Brose, David S.
1979   A Speculative Model of the Role of Exchange in the Prehistory of the Eastern Woodlands. In *Hopewell Archaeology: the Chillicothe Conference,* edited by D. S. Brose and N. Greber, pp. 3-8. Kent State University Press, Kent, OH.

Brose, David S., and N'omi Greber (editors)
1979   *Hopewell Archaeology: the Chillicothe Conference.* Kent State University Press, Kent, OH.

Brown, James A.
1964a   The Northeastern Extension of the Havana Tradition. In *Hopewellian Studies,* edited by J. R. Caldwell and R. L. Hall, pp. 107-122. Illinois State Museum Scientific Papers 12. Springfield
1964b   The Identification of a Prehistoric Bone Tool from the Midwest: The Deer-Jaw Sickle. *American Antiquity* 29:381-386.

Cahen, Daniel, Lawrence H. Keeley, and Francis L. van Noten
1979   Stone Tools, Toolkits, and Human Behavior in Prehistory. *Current Anthropology* 20:661-683.

Callender, Charles
1978   Shawnee. In *Handbook of North American Indians,* 15, *Northeast,* edited by B. G. Trigger, pp. 622-635. Smithsonian Institution Press, Washington, D.C.

Carr, Christopher, and Herbert Haas
1996   Beta-count and AMS Radiocarbon Dates of Woodland and Fort Ancient Period Occupations in Ohio 1350 B.C. - A.D. 1650. *West Virginia Archaeologist* 48:19-53.

Caldwell, Joseph R.
1964   Interaction Spheres in Prehistory. In *Hopewellian Studies,* edited by J. R. Caldwell and R. L. Hall, pp. 133-143. Illinois State Museum Scientific Papers 12. Springfield

Caldwell, Joseph R., and Robert L. Hall (editors)
1964   Hopewellian Studies. Illinois State Museum Scientific Papers 12. Springfield.

Clay, R. Berle
1998   The Essential Features of Adena Ritual and their Implications. *Southeastern Archaeology* 17:1-21.

Clay, R. Berle, and Steven D. Creasman
1999   Middle Ohio Valley Late Woodland Nucleated Settlements: "Where's the Beef?" Paper presented at the 1999 Meeting on Kentucky Archaeology, Kentucky Heritage Council, Lexington.

Clay, R. Berle, and Charles Niquette
1989   Cultural Overview, In *Phase III Excavations at the Niebert Site (46MS103) in the Gallipolis Locks and Dam Replacement Project, Mason County, West Virginia,* pp. 10-26. Contract Resource Analysts, Inc. Contract Publication Series 89-06. Lexington, KY.

Cobb, Charles R.
1989   An Appraisal of the Role of Mill Creek Chert Hoes in Mississippian Exchange Systems. *Southeastern Archaeology* 8:79-92.

Converse, Robert N.
1972   Flints Used by Ohio's Prehistoric Indians. *Ohio Archaeologist* 22(2):36-39.

Creamer, Winifred, and Jonathan Haas
1985   Tribe versus Chiefdom in Lower Central America. *American Antiquity* 50:738-754.

Cowan, C. Wesley, B. W. Aument, L. J. Klempay, and L. R. Piotrowski
1981   Variation in Hopewell Settlement Patterns and Lithic Industries in the Vicinity of the Newark Earthworks: Some Preliminary Observations. Paper presented at the 1981 Midwestern Archaeological Conference, Madison, Wisconsin.

Cowan, Frank L.
n.d.   A Mobile Hopewell?: Questioning Assumptions of Hopewell Sedentism. In *Perspectives on Middle Woodland at the Millenium,* edited by J. Buikstra, and J. O'Gorman (in preparation).

Cowan, Frank L., T. S. Sunderhaus, and R. L. Genheimer
1999   Notes from the Field, 1999: More Hopewell "Houses" at the Stubbs Earthwork Site. *The Ohio Archaeological Council Newsletter* 11(2):11-16.
2000   Wooden Architcture in Ohio Hopewell Sites: Structural and Spatial Patterning at *the Stubbs Earthworks Site.* Paper presented at the 65[Th] Annual Meeting of the Society for American Archaeology, Philadelphia.

Cross, John R.
1988   Expanding the Scope of Seasonality Research in Archaeology. In *Coping with Seasonal Constraints,* edited by R. Huss-Ashmore et al., pp. 55-63. MASCA Research Papers in Science and Archaeology 5. University Museum, University of Pennsylvania, Philadelphia.

Dancey, William S.
1991 A Middle Woodland Settlement in Central Ohio: A Preliminary Report on the Murphy Site (33Li212). *Pennsylvania Archaeologist* 61(2):37-72.

Dancey, William S., and P. J. Pacheco (editors)
1997 Ohio Hopewell Community Organization. Kent State University Press, Kent OH

DeRegnaucourt, Tony, and Jeff Georgiady
1998 *Prehistoric Chert Types of the Midwest.* Occasional Monographs in Archaeology 7. Upper Miami Valley Archaeological Research Museum, Arcanum, OH

Deuel, Thorne (editor)
1952 *Hopewellian Communities in Illinois.* Illinois State Museum Scientific Papers 5. Springfield.

Dunne, Michael T., and William Green
1998 Terminal Archaic and Early Woodland Plant Use at the Gast Spring Site (13LA152), Southeast Iowa. *Midcontinental Journal of Archaeology* 23:45-88.

Essenpreis, Patricia S.
1978 Fort Ancient Settlement: Differential Responses at a Mississippian-Late Woodland Interface. In *Mississippian Settlement Patterns,* edited by B. D. Smith, pp. 141-167. Academic Press, New York.

Evans, Robert K.
1978 Early Craft Specialization: An Example from the Balkan Chalcolithic. In *Social Archaeology: Beyond Subsistence and Dating,* edited by C. R. Redman *et al.*, pp. 113-129. Academic Press, New York.

Fitting, James E., and Charles E. Cleland
1969 Late Prehistoric Settlement Patterns in the Upper Great Lakes. *Ethnohistory* 16:289-302.

Ford, Richard I.
1979 Gathering and Gardening: Trends and Consequences of Hopewell Subsistence Strategies. In *Hopewell Archaeology: the Chillicothe Conference,* edited by D. S. Brose and N. Greber, pp. 234-238. Kent State University Press, Kent, OH.

Fortier, Andrew C.
1997 Pre-Mississippian Economies in the American Bottom of Southwestern Illinois,. 3000 B.C.– A.D. 1050. *Research in Economic Anthropology* 19:341-392.

Fried, Morton H.
1967 *The Evolution of Political Society.* Random House, New York.

Fritz, Gayle J.
1990 Multiple Pathways to Farming in Precontact Eastern North America. *Journal of World Prehistory* 4:387-476.

Genheimer, Robert A.
1984 A Systematic Examination of Middle Woodland Settlements in Warren County, Ohio. Report prepared for the Ohio Historic Preservation Office, Columbus.

Greber, N'omi B.
1979a Comparative Study of Site Morphology and Burial Patterns at Edwin Harness Mound and Seip Mounds 1 and 2. In *Hopewell Archaeology: the Chillicothe Conference,* edited by D. S. Brose and N. Greber, pp. 27-38. Kent State University Press, Kent, OH.

1979b Variation in Social Structure of Ohio Hopewell Peoples. *Midcontinental Journal of Archaeology* 4:35-78.

1991 A Study of Continuity and Contrast between Central Scioto Adena and Hopewell Sites. *West Virginia Archaeologist* 43:1-26.

1997 Two Geometric Enclosures in the Paint Creek Valley: An Estimate of Possible Changes in Community Patterns Through Time. In *Ohio Hopewell Community Organization,* edited by W. S. Dancey and P. J. Pacheco, pp. 207-230. Kent State University Press, Kent, OH.

Green, William (editor)
1994 *Agricultural Origins and Development in the Midcontient.* Report 19, Office of the State Archaeologist, University of Iowa, Iowa City.

Griffin, James B.
1964 The Northeast Woodlands Area. In *Prehistoric Man in the New World,* edited by J. D. Jennings and E. Norbeck, pp. 223-258. University of Chicago Press, Chicago.

1997 Interpretations of Ohio Hopewell 1845-1984 and the Recent Emphasis on the Study of Dispersed Hamlets. In *Ohio Hopewell Community Organization,* edited by W. S. Dancey and P. J. Pacheco, pp. 405-426. Kent State University Press, Kent, OH.

Griffin, James B., Richard E. Flanders, and Paul F. Titterington
1970 The Burial Complexes of the Knight and Norton Mounds in Illinois and Michigan. Memoir 2, Museum of Anthropology, University of Michigan, Ann Arbor.

Hall, Robert L.
1979 In Search of the Ideology of the Adena-Hopewell Climax. In *Hopewell Archaeology: the Chillicothe Conference,* edited by D. S. Brose and N. Greber, pp. 258-265. Kent State University Press, Kent, OH.
1980 An Interpretation of the Two-Climax Model of Illinois Prehistory. In *Early Native Americans: Prehistoric Demography, Economy, and Technology,* edited by D. L. Browman, pp. 401-462. World Anthropology Series, Mouton, The Hague.
1997 *An Archaeology of the Soul: North American Indian Belief and Ritual.* University of Illinois Press, Urbana and Chicago.
Harlan, Jack R.
1995 *The Living Fields: Our Agricultural Heritage.* Cambridge University Press, Cambridge.
Harris, David R.
1998 The Origins of Agriculture in Southwest Asia. *The Review of Archaeology* 19(2):5-11.
Helms, Mary W.
1991 *Esoteric Knowledge, Geographical Distance and the Elaboration of Leadership Status: Dynamics of Resource Control.* Anthropological Papers 85, Museum of Anthropology, University of Michigan, Ann Arbor.
Holley, George R.
1993 Observations Regarding Sedentism in Central Silver Creek and the Enduring Significance of the FAI-64 Archaeological Mitigation Program. *Illinois Archaeology* 5:276-284.
Justice, Noel D.
1985 *Stone Age Spear and Arrow Points of the Midcontinental and Eastern United States.* Indiana University Press, Bloomington.
Kent, Susan
1991 The Relationship Between Mobility Strategies and Site Structure. In *The Interpretation of Archaeological Spatial Patterning,* edited by E. M. Kroll and T. D. Price, pp. 33-59. Plenum Press, New York.
1991 Studying Variability in the Archaeological Record: An Ethnoarchaeological Model for Distinguishing Mobility Patterns. *American Antiquity* 57:635-660.
Kozarek, Sue Ellen
1997 Determining Sedentism in the Archaeo-logical Record. In *Ohio Hopewell Community Organization,* edited by W. S. Dancey and P. J. Pacheco, pp. 131-152. Kent State University Press, Kent OH.
Lemons, Reno, and Flora Church
1998 A Use Wear Analysis of Hopewell Bladelets from paint Creek Lake Site #5, Ross County, Ohio. *North American Archaeologist* 19:269-277.
Lepper, Bradley T.
1995 Tracking Ohio's Great Hopewell Road. *Archaeology* 48(6):52-56.
Lepper, Bradley T., and R. W. Yerkes
1997 Hopewellian Occupations at the Northern Periphery of the Newark Earthworks: The Newark Expressway Sites Revisited. In *Ohio Hopewell Community Organization,* edited by W. S. Dancey and P. J. Pacheco, pp. 175-206. Kent State University Press, Kent OH
Mainfort, Robert C., Jr., and Lynne P. Sullivan (editors)
1998 *Ancient Earthen Enclosures of the Eastern Woodlands.* University Press of Florida, Gainesville.
Mason, Ronald J.
1981 *Great Lakes Archaeology.* Academic Press, New York.
McElrath Dale L., Thomas E. Emerson, Andrew C. Fortier, and James L. Phillips
1984 Late Archaic Period. In *American Bottom Archaeology,* edited by C. J. Baeris and J. W. Porter, pp. 34-58. University of Illinois Press, Chicago and Urbana.
Michaels, George H.
1989 Craft Specialization in the Early Postclassic of Colha. *Research in Economic Anthropology,* Supplement 4:139-183.
Monks, Gregory
1981 Seasonality Studies. In *Advances in Archaeological Method and Theory* 4, edited by M. B. Schiffer, pp. 177-240. Academic Press, San Diego.
Muller, Jon
1984 *Archaeology of the Lower Ohio River Valley.* Academic Press, Orlando.
Murdock, George P.
1967 Ethnographic Atlas: A Summary. *Ethnology* 6:109-236.
Murphy, James L.
1989 *An Archaeological History of the Hocking Valley* (revised edition). Ohio University Press, Athens, OH

Nass, John P., Jr.
1987 Use-wear Analysis and Household Archaeology: A Study of the Activity Structure of the Incinerator Site, An Anderson Phase Fort Ancient Community in Southwestern Ohio. Unpublished Ph.D. dissertation, Department of Anthropology, Ohio State University, Columbus.

Nass, John P., Jr., and Richard W. Yerkes
1995 Social Differentiation in Mississippian and Fort Ancient Societies. In *Mississippian Communities and Households,* edited by J. D. Rogers and B. D. Smith, pp. 58-80. University of Alabama Press, Tuscaloosa.

Odell, George H.
1994 The Role of Stone Bladelets in Middle Woodland Society. *American Antiquity* 59:102-20.

Pacheco, Paul J.
1985 Ohio Middle Woodland Settlement Variability in the Upper Licking River Drainage. *Journal of the Steward Anthropological Society* 18:87-117.

1996 Ohio Hopewell Regional Settlement Patterns. In *A View from the Core: A Synthesis of Ohio Hopewell Archaeology,* edited by P. Pacheco, pp. 16-35. Ohio Archaeological Council, Columbus, OH.

1997 Ohio Middle Woodland Intracommunity Settlement Variability: A Case Study from the Licking Valley. In *Ohio Hopewell Community Organization,* edited by W. S. Dancey and P. J. Pacheco, pp. 41-84. Kent State University Press, Kent, OH.

Parry, William J.
1994 Prismatic Blade Technologies in North America. In *The Organization of Prehistoric North American Chipped Stone Tool Technologies,* edited by P.J. Carr, pp. 87-98. International Monographs in Prehistory, Ann Arbor, MI.

Phillips, James L.
1998 Remarks on Seasonality and Sedentism: Archaeological Perspectives from Old and New World Sites. In *Seasonality and Sedentism: Archaeological Perspectives from Old and New World Sites,* edited by T. R. Rocek and O. Bar-Yosef, pp. 217-221. Harvard University, Peabody Museum of Archaeology and Ethnography, Peabody Museum Bulletin 6, Cambridge.

Price, T. Douglas, and James A. Brown (editors)
1985 *Prehistoric Hunter-Gathers: The Emergence of Cultural Complexity.* Academic Press, San Diego.

Price, T. Douglas, and Anne Birgitte Gebauer (editors)
1995 *Last Hunters-First Farmers.* SAR Press, Santa Fe.

Prufer, Olaf H.
1965 *The McGraw Site: A Study in Hopewellian Dynamics.* Cleveland Museum of Natural History Scientific Publications 4(1). Cleveland, OH.

Rocek, Thomas R., and Ofer Bar-Yosef (editors)
1998 *Seasonality and Sedentism: Archaeological Perspectives from Old and New World Sites.* Harvard University, Peabody Museum of Archaeology and Ethnography, Peabody Museum Bulletin 6, Cambridge.

Sahlins, Marshall D., and Elman R. Service (editors)
1960 *Evolution and Culture.* University of Michigan Press, Ann Arbor.

Sanders, Donald
1990 Behavioral Conventions and Archaeology: Methods for the Analysis of Ancient Architecture. In *Domestic Architecture and the Use of Space: An Interdisciplinary Cross-Cultural Study,* edited by S. Kent, pp. 43-72. Cambridge University Press, Cambridge.

Scarry, C. Margaret (editor)
1993 *Foraging and Farming in the Eastern Woodlands.* University Press of Florida, Gainesville.

Seeman, Mark F.
1975 The Prehistoric Chert Quarries and Workshops of Harrison County, Indiana. *Indiana Archaeological Bulletin* 1:47-61.

1979a The Hopewell Interaction Sphere: The Evidence for Interregional Trade and Structural Complexity. *Indiana Historical Society Prehistoric Research Series* 5(2). Indianapolis, IN

1979b Feasting with the Dead: Ohio Hopewell Charnel House Ritual as a Context for Redistribution. In *Hopewell Archaeology: The Chillicothe Conference,* edited by D.S. Brose and N. Greber, pp.39-46, Kent State University Press, Kent, OH.

1992 Woodland Traditions in the Midcontinent: A Comparison of Three Regional

Sequences. *Research in Economic Anthropology, Supplement* 6:3-46.

1995 When Words are not Enough: Hopewell Interregionalism and the Use of Material Symbols at the GE Mound. In *Native American Interactions,* edited by M. S. Nassaney and K. E. Sassaman, pp. 122-143. University of Tennessee Press, Nashville, TN.

Service, Elman R.
1971 *Primitive Social Organization.* Random House, New York.

Steward, Julian H.
1938 Basin-Plateau Aboriginal Sociopolitical Groups. *Handbook of North American Indians.* Bureau of American Ethnology, Smithsonian Institution, Bulletin 120, Washington, D.C.

Stoltman, James B., and David A. Baerreis
1983 The Evolution of Human Ecosystems in the Eastern United States. In *Late Quaternary Environments of the United States, 2, The Holocene,* edited by H. E. Wright, Jr., pp. 252-270. University of Minnesota Press, Minneapolis.

Stout, Wilbur, and R. A. Schoenlaub
1945 *The Occurrence of Flint in Ohio.* Fourth Series, Bulletin 46, State of Ohio, Department of Natural Resources, Division of Geological Survey, Columbus.

Struever, Stuart
1965 Middle Woodland Culture History in the Great Lakes Riverine Area. *American Antiquity* 31:211-223.

Tankersley, Kenneth B.
1985 Mineralogical Properties of Wyandotte Chert as an Aid to Archaeological Finger-Printing. In *Lithic Resource Procurement: Proceedings from the Second Conference on Prehistoric Chert Exploitation,* edited by S. Vehik, pp. 251-264. Southern Illinois University at Carbondale, Center for Archaeological Investigations, Occasional Paper 4, Carbondale, IL.

Thomas, Cyrus
1894 *Report of the Mound Explorations of the Bureau of American Ethnology.* 12th Annual Report of the Bureau of American Ethnology, Washington D.C.

Vickery, Kent D.
1983 The Flint Sources. In *Recent Excavations at the Edwin Harness Mound, Liberty Works, Ross County, Ohio,* by N. Greber, pp. 73-85. Mid-Continental Journal of

Archaeology, Special Paper 5, Kent State University Press, Kent, OH

Wagner, Gail E.
1996 Feast or Famine? Seasonal Diet at a Fort Ancient Community. In *Case Studies in Environmental Archaeology,* edited by E. J. Reitz, L. A. Newsom, and S. J. Scudder, pp. 255-271. Plenum Press, New York.

Watson, Patty Jo
1988 Prehistoric Gardening and Agriculture in the Midwest and Midsouth. In *Interpretations of Culture Change in the Eastern Woodlands during the Late Woodland Period,* edited by R. W. Yerkes, pp. 39-67. Occasional Papers in Anthropology 3, Department of Anthropology, Ohio State University, Columbus, OH.

1989 Early Plant Cultivation in the Eastern Woodlands of North America. In *Foraging and Farming: The Evolution of Plant Exploitation,* edited by D. R. Harris and G. C. Hillman, pp. 555-571. Unwin Hyman, London.

1996 Of Caves and Shell Mounds in West-Central Kentucky. In *Of Caves and Shell Mounds,* edited by K. C. Karstens and P. J. Watson, pp. 159-164. University of Alabama Press, Tuscaloosa.

Weller Von Molsdorff, Ryan J., J.J. Burks, and J. B. Burcham
1999 Phase II Cultural Resource Management Assessment of Sites 33FR1520 and 33FR1521 in Plain Township, Franklin County, Ohio. CRM Report submitted to EMH&T, Inc. by APPLIED Archaeological Services, Inc. Columbus, OH.

Willey, Gordon R., and Phillip Phillips
1958 *Method and Theory in American Archaeology.* University of Chicago Press, Chicago.

Wymer, Dee Ann
1987 The Paleoethnobotanical Record of Central Ohio - 100 B.C. to A.D. 800: Subsistence Continuity amid Cultural Change. Unpublished Ph.D. dissertation, Department of Anthropology, Ohio State University, Columbus, OH.

1993 Cultural Change and Subsistence: The Middle Woodland and Late Woodland Transition in the Mid-Ohio Valley. In *Foraging and Farming in the Eastern Woodlands,* edited by C. M. Scarry, pp. 138-156. University Press of Florida, Gainesville.

1997 Paleoethnobotany in the Licking River Valley, Ohio: Implications for Understanding Ohio Hopewell. In *Ohio Hopewell Community Organization,* edited by W. S. Dancey and P. J. Pacheco, pp. 153-171. Kent State University Press, Kent, OH.

Yarnell, Richard A.

1993 The Importance of Native Crops during the Late Archaic and Woodland Periods. In *Foraging and Farming in the Eastern Woodlands,* edited by C. M. Scarry, pp. 11-26. University Press of Florida, Gainesville, FL.

Yerkes, Richard W.

1986 Late Archaic Settlement and Subsistence on the American Bottom. In *Foraging, Collecting, and Harvesting: Archaic Period Subsistence in the Eastern Woodlands,* edited by S.W. Neusius, pp. 225-245, *Occasional Paper* 6. Center for Archaeological Investigations, Southern Illinois University-Carbondale, Carbondale, IL.

1987 Seasonal Patterns in Late Prehistoric Fishing Practices in the North American Midwest. *Archæozoologia* 1:137-148.

1990 Using Microwear Analysis to Investigate Domestic Activities and Craft Specialization at the Murphy site, a Small Hopewell Settlement in Licking County, Ohio. In *The Interpretative Possibilities of Microwear Studies,* edited by B. Gräslund, H. Knutsson, K. Knutsson, and J. Taffinder, pp. 167-176. Aun 14, Uppsala, Sweden.

1994 A Consideration of the Function of Ohio Hopewell Bladelets. *Lithic Technology* 19:109-127.

2000 Mounds of the Southern United States. In *Arqueologia de las Tierras Bajas,* edited by A. D. Coirolo and R. B. Boksar, pp. 117-134. Ministerio de Educacion y Cultura, Comision Nacional de Arqueologia, Montevideo, Uruguay.

2002 Using Lithic Artifacts to Study Craft Specialization in Ancient Societies. In *Written in Stone: The Multiple Dimensions of Lithic Analysis*, edited by R. W. Yerkes and P. N. Kardulias, pp. 17-34. Lexington Books (Rowman and Littlefield Publishers), Boston. (in press)

13. The Evolution of Tribal Social Organization in the Southeastern United States

David G. Anderson

Introduction

Almost seven thousand years separate the presumably egalitarian hunting gathering bands of the Paleoindian and Early Archaic periods and the hierarchical agricultural chiefdoms of the Mississippian period in the Southeast (Table 1). What kinds of organizational forms occurred during this interval? Where did they occur on the landscape, and how and why did they change through time?

The Southeastern United States is an outstanding laboratory in which to study variability and change in tribal societies, just as it has been for chiefdom research. The later Archaic and Woodland archaeological record from the Southeast exhibits great variation in settlement/subsistence systems, ritual and ceremonial activity, monumental construction, long distance exchange, and warfare. This in turn suggests appreciable organizational variability, both over time and across space at any given moment. In recent years archaeologists have tended to emphasize this variation in their discussions, rather than attempt to place all developments at any given time within monolithic constructs. Thus, phrases like 'multiple pathways' or 'multilinear evolution' are used to describe developmental trends in the region, and 'cultural pluralism', 'diversity', and 'variability' for conditions at given moments in time.

The recognition of variation and change in the organizational structures of later Archaic and Woodland (presumably) 'tribal' level societies is thus a new frontier for research, likely to increasingly attract the kind of detailed research attention currently given to Paleoindian and Mississippian occupations. Such activity is long overdue, given that tribes were the most complex organizational form present for several thousand years, for an appreciable proportion of the human occupation of the region. There is clear evidence for appreciable variability in settlement patterning, social organization, and extent of ceremonial activ-ity and monumental construction in the societies in the region over this interval, as well as for changes in these characteristics. Examination of this information can contribute greatly to our understanding of cultural evolution, specifically the emergence and operation of tribal social organization, and the evolution of complex societies in general.

What is a Tribe?

Archaeologists have tended to call post-band, pre-chiefdom societies 'tribes' or sometimes 'lower level middle range societies' or 'complex hunter-gatherers' (e.g., Feinman and Neitzel 1984; Price and Brown 1985). The latter terms are employed in acknowledgment of problems with the concept of 'tribe' as defined by ethnologists, whose classic cases were often influenced by more complex chiefdom or state level societies (e.g., Fried 1968, 1975).

Tribes are defined in organizational terms, as groupings of numerous smaller, band (or larger) size social segments that have been fused together into something more, a sum greater than the separate parts. As Marshall Sahlins (1961:93–94) has noted:

> A band is a simple association of families, but a tribe is an association of kin groups which are themselves composed of families. A tribe is a segmental organization. It is composed of a number of equivalent, unspecialized multifamily groups, each the structural duplicate of the other: a tribe is a congeries of equal kin group blocks... It is sometimes possible to speak of several levels of segmentation... "Primary tribal segment" is defined as the smallest multifamily group that collectively exploits an area of tribal resources and forms a residential entity all or most of the year.... In most cases the primary segment seems to fall between 50 and 250 people... Small localized—often primary—tribal segments tend to be economically and

Table. 1. A Cultural and Chronological Framework for the Southeastern United States. Calibrations from Stuiver et al. 1998, adapted from Anderson 2001:145-146.

Calibrated B.P. (Intercepts from Calib 4.3 program)	Conventional (dates approximate)	Radiocarbon rcbp	Period	Culture Complex	Climatic Event
					Pronounced Warming
50	AD 1950	0	Modern		
				Industrial Revolution	Little Ice Age Ends
298	AD 1700	250	US National		
524	AD 1475	500		European Colonization	Little Ice Age Begins
				Mississippian	
929	AD 1075	1000			Medieval Warm Period
			Late Woodland	Coles Creek	
1388, 1358, 1354	AD 675	1500			Subatlantic
1948, 1936, 1934	AD 50	2000	Middle Woodland	Hopewell	
					Sub-Boreal
2710, 2629, 2617, 2562, 2542, 2518, 2513	600 BC	2500	Early Woodland	Adena	
3208, 3179, 3169	1200 BC	3000		Poverty Point	
4500, 4490, 4440	2475 BC	4000	Late Archaic	Stallings Island	
5728	3750 BC	5000		Watson Brake	Hypsithermal Ends
6850, 6838, 6825, 6824, 6800, 6764	4800 BC	6000	Middle Archaic	Morrow Mountain	Atlantic
7820, 7807, 7792	5800 BC	7000			Hypsithermal Begins
				Stanly	
8986, 8874, 8825, 8819	6950 BC	8000			
				Bifurcate	Cold Episode
10,189	8240 BC	9000	Early Archaic		
10,736, 10,708, 10,702	8775 BC	9500		Corner Notched	Boreal
11,254, 11,253, 11,234	9300 BC	9900			
11,545, 11,512, 11,400, 11,391, 11,340	9500 BC	10,000			
11,687, 11,677, 11,642	9725 BC	10,100		Early side Notched	Younger Dryas ends/Preboreal
11,930, 11,804, 11,768	9900 BC	10,200	Late Paleoindian		
				Dalton	
12,622 12,472, 12,390	10,550 BC	10,500			
12955 (12889) 12660	10,940 BC	10,800			
				Cumberland/Folsom	
12,944	10,995 BC	10,900			Younger Dryas begins
13,132	11,183 BC	11,100	Middle Paleoindian		Inter-Allerød Cold Period ends
13,155	11,206 BC	11,200		Clovis widespread	
13,411	11,462 BC	11,400			Inter-Allerød Cold Period begins
13,455	11,506 BC	11,500			
				Clovis beginnings??	
13,811	11,862 BC	11,750			Allerød
14,043, 13,923, 13,858	12,000 BC	11,950			Older Dryas ends
14,065	12,116 BC	12,000		Little Salt Springs/ Page-Ladson	
			Early Paleoindian		Older Dryas begins
14,100	12,150 BC	12,100		Monte Verde	
15,084, 14,731, 14,382	12,750 BC	12,500			
15,231, 14,606, 14,449	12,900 BC	12,600			Bølling begins
				Meadowcroft (?) Cactus Hill (?)	
19,091	17,142 BC	16,000			
21,392	19,443 BC	18,000		Initial Colonization (?)	Glacial maximum

politically autonomous. A tribe as a whole is normally not a political organization but rather a social-cultural-ethnic identity. It is held together primary by likenesses among its segments... and by pan-tribal institutions, such as a system of intermarrying clans, of age grades, or military or religious societies, which cross cut the primary segments. Pan tribal institutions make a tribe a more integrated social institution (even if weakly so) than a group of intermarrying bands... pan tribal social institutions are perhaps the most indicative characteristic of tribal society. Such institutions clearly demarcate the borders of a tribe, separating it as a social (and ethnic) entity. (Sahlins 1961:93–94)

If we view tribes in the simplest of perspectives, as grouping of people on a larger scale than that of individual bands, the questions we are exploring in the Southeast can be asked in the following way: "when was the band transcended, why did this change occur, and what replaced it?"

To know what a tribe is, we must also know what its purpose is. Why should people construct and maintain organizational forms that transcend local co-residence and subsistence groups? According to Braun and Plog (1982) 'tribalization' (the process by which tribes came about) was a risk minimization strategy intended to overcome subsistence stress/shortfalls/uncertainty. To Bender (1985) and others, tribalization also encompassed alliance formation at a larger scale than that afforded by band/macroband interaction. Implicit in both approaches is the existence of pressure on resources, something brought about by overpopulation or uncertainty in resource availability. In such formulations, tribal emergence may be inevitable when threshold conditions are reached. While such thresholds are typically unspecified, they would likely be when regional population levels reached the point that dramatic resource shortfalls, when they occurred, could not be buffered by storage or relocation into unoccupied areas.

Less often implicated in the formation and maintenance of tribal societies, at least in the Southeast, is intergroup conflict or warfare. Promotion of group identity/ethnic discreteness at a large scale likely proved an adaptive advantage. The classic and oft cited ethnographic example of the value of (one particular type of) tribal organization is the Nuer, whose segmentary lineage kinship/organizational system gave them a decided military advantage over their neighbors, the Dinka (Kelly 1985; Sahlins 1961). In such a view, the advantages of tribal social organization were such that, once this form of organization appeared anywhere, it was likely to be widely adopted through a process of competitive emulation. Acting 'tribally', quite simply, may have been essential to overcome political as well as environmental stress. The same process, of course, has been used to explain the spread of chiefdoms (Carneiro 1981).

The Emergence of Tribal Societies in the Southeast

When are bands transcended, or replaced by more elaborate organizational forms in the Southeast? The way to approach this question is to look for evidence for the initial emergence of regular intensive interaction between band-sized segments, directed to tasks that could promote 'tribal' solidarity. When does the regional archaeological record appear to be shaped by the result of actions by tribal as opposed to band-level groups? As I argue below, this probably occurred a lot further back into the past then we have traditionally assumed, at least as far back as the Middle Archaic period, and possibly, in some times and places, even earlier.

Exactly when tribal organization emerged in Eastern North America is currently unknown, although I shall argue here that it was probably somewhere around 5000 to 6000 years ago. Determining exactly when the first 'tribe' appeared in the region, however, is a far less interesting or important research question than exploring changes in these organizational forms over the centuries and across the region; that is, how tribal societies actually operated. As we shall see, it appears that tribal societies emerged and then faded away in many areas and times and, even when widely established over the region, only in some cases left behind dramatic material reminders of their presence. Indeed, a cycling between less complex and more complex organizational forms is suggested, much as occurs in chiefdoms and early states (Anderson 1994; Blitz 1998; Marcus 1993; see Parkinson 1999, and this volume, Chapter 18; Fowles, this volume, Chapter 2). Tribal social organization in the Southeast emerged from within a regional backdrop of band-level societies. Tribal cycling might thus be viewed as the emergence and collapse of tribal level social organization amid a regional landscape of band level societies.

As the papers in this volume demonstrate, however, organizational change in tribal societies, once they are widely established on the landscape, operates in a very different manner altogether. Tribes may occasionally fragment, but more typically they fluctuate between periods of greater or lesser integration and hence complexity. The nature and scale of mechanisms integrating groups together are what change, and what make tribal societies geographically diffuse and organizationally flexible entities (see Parkinson 1999, and this volume, Chapter 18; Fowles, this volume, Chapter 2).

That is, it is unlikely that tribal organization, once widely established, ever completely disappeared from a given region (unless the local societies transformed into or were absorbed by chiefdoms or states), just as it is improbable that chiefdoms, once widely established, ever completely disappeared from a given region (unless they transformed into or were absorbed by states). The adaptive advantages of these organizational forms was likely such that, once they appeared widely, they would never completely disappear. The critical phrase here is "appeared widely." In the Southeast, it is increasingly evident that a number of experiments in the formation of complex social organization occurred, both of tribal societies and later in time of chiefdoms, which achieved only localized and comparatively short-term success.

The regional archaeological record has numerous examples of what for their time are seemingly anomalously large centers, suggesting equally complex and unusual organizational forms, as exemplified by sites such as Watson Brake, Poverty Point, Pinson, or Kolomoki (Fig. 1). Explaining these seeming exceptions, as well as understanding what kinds of sites and organizational forms were perhaps more typical, is a major challenge.

Complex tribal level societies are traditionally assumed to have been present in many parts of the Southeast during the Woodland period, from about 3500 to 1000 cal. B.P., and particularly toward the latter end of the period (e.g., Bense 1994:141; B. Smith 1986:45). During the Paleoindian and earlier part of the Archaic period, until about 6000 or so years ago, populations are assumed to have lived in small bands of from 25 to 50 people. These groups met from time to time and interacted with other bands over large areas, but each is assumed to have been essentially autonomous in subsistence production, with no formal leadership positions beyond those individuals could achieve through their own abilities. Tribes are not thought to have been present, although interaction over large ar-

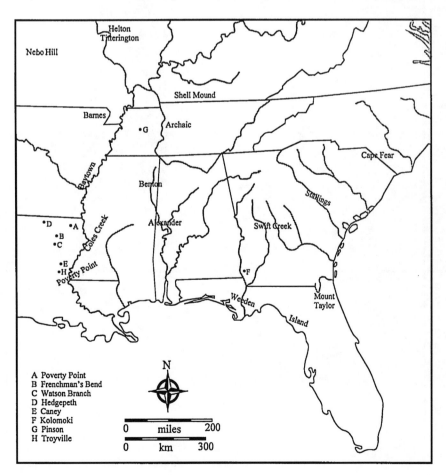

Fig. 1. Location of Archaeological Sites and Cultures Mentioned in the Text.

eas, including periodic aggregation by members of two or more bands into larger groups on a temporary basis is assumed to have occurred, to facilitate information exchange and maintain mating networks (Anderson and Sassaman 1996). Regularly interacting bands formed groupings called macrobands, but these were fluid in composition, and the presence of a band within a particular macroband was determined by regional physiography and resource structure (i.e., conditions promoting interaction, population levels, and the number and proximity of groups to one another), and mating network requirements, than by any overarching organizational structures, which are assumed to have been absent.

The temporary aggregation of large numbers of people thus appears to have appreciable antiquity in the Southeast, extending back into Paleoindian times. But these aggregation events appear to have been between essentially equivalent bands, and do not directed toward the creation

or maintenance of more complex organizational forms, that is, tribal level societies. There is little evidence for unusual ceremony and no evidence for monumental construction during the Paleoindian and Early Archaic periods across much of the region, activities that might hint that these bands were tied together in a more permanent fashion. Essentially egalitarian bands, loosely tied together into macroband scale interaction networks, are all that are thought to have been present during the Paleoindian and Early Archaic periods.

There are hints however, that a more complex society may have developed during the Late Paleoindian era in the central Mississippi Valley, during what has been called the "Dalton efflorescence" from ca. 12,500 to 11,200 cal. B.P. (Morse and Morse 1983:70–97; see Fig. 2). This hunting and gathering culture was apparently characterized by formal cemeteries, such as that found at the Sloan site in northeast Arkansas (Morse 1997), and by the manufacture, exchange, and apparent

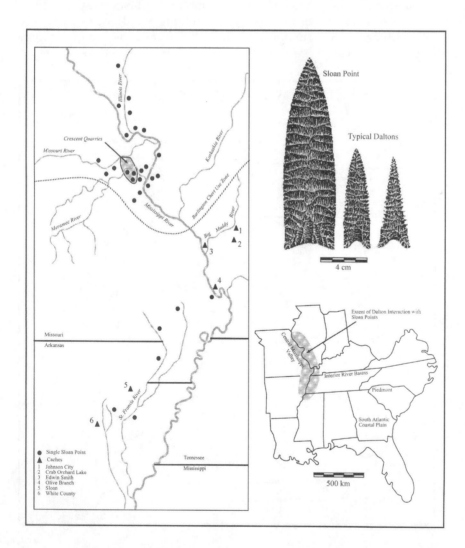

Fig. 2. Sloan points and the Extent of a Hypothesized Dalton Culture Interaction Network in the Central Mississippi Alluvial Valley (adapted from Walthall and Koldehoff 1998:260–261, courtesy The Plains Anthropological Society).

use in ritual context of elaborate stone tools, epitomized by unusually large and elaborate, hypertrophic bifaces, called Sloan points (see Sassaman 1996:62–64 for a discussion of the social implications of technical hypertrophy as expressed in bannerstone distributions in the Middle and Late Archaic Southeast; these include using such items to create and maintain alliances, reinforce status differentiation between individuals and groups and, through their destruction or burial, in helping maintain egalitarian relationships).

A geographically extensive Late Paleoindian interaction and exchange network extending for several hundred kilometers along the Central Mississippi Valley has been postulated, with Dalton point using groups bound together by the ritual use of elaborate stone tools, a so-called "Cult of the Long Blade" (Walthall and Koldehoff 1998). Whether a tribal form of organization was present, however briefly, cannot be determined, although something unusual was clearly happening. This culture, while seemingly atypical, may simply represent the ultimate potential of band-level organization. It emerged in one of the richest ecological settings in the world, along a river system providing perhaps the greatest interaction potential to be found anywhere in Eastern North America (Morse 1975, 1997). Central Mississippi Valley Dalton culture collapsed after ca. 11,450 cal. B.P., however, and nothing comparable in scale, complexity, or ceremony is evident in this or indeed any part of the region for several thousand years thereafter. Dalton Culture in the Central Mississippi Valley may well reflect an early experiment in the development of complex society, or tribalization, but it was not one that took root or spread widely.

When did tribes emerge in the
Southeastern US?

Given the definition of tribal social organization and the reasons for its existence advanced above, it is hard to escape the conclusion that tribal beginnings in the Southeast occur with the first clear evidence for widespread long distance exchange and interaction, monumental construction, intergroup conflict, and territorial marking, as exemplified in marked cemeteries and buffer zones. This happened during the Middle Archaic period, from ca. 9500 to 5800 cal. B.P., or 8000 to 5000 radiocarbon years ago (rcbp). Am I arguing that band-level organization was transcended in the Southeast during the Middle Archaic? Quite sim-

ply, yes, albeit initially only in some areas and for greater or lesser periods.

Beginning in the Middle Archaic, evidence for extensive ceremonial behavior appears in a number of areas of Eastern North America (see summaries in Anderson et al. n.d.; Bense 1994; Phillips and Brown 1983; Sassaman and Anderson 1996; B. Smith 1986; and Steponaitis 1986). Burials with elaborate grave goods of worked shell, bone, stone, and copper appear in many parts of the region, signaling a new emphasis on individual status and in some cases group affiliation. Many of these goods were exchanged over great distances, suggesting increased interaction between groups. Not all of this interaction was positive. Many burials resulted from violent death, as evidenced by broken bones, embedded projectile points, and scalping marks. As populations grew and mobility decreased, competition and interaction between groups appears to have increased, perhaps as people were forced closer and closer together on the landscape. The evidence suggests that this competition took place in a number of arenas. Individuals competed for personal status items acquired as a result of (and contributing to) the growth of exchange networks. The increased evidence for warfare suggests that food or other resources may have been contested by local groups, and/or that success in this arena was itself another means of acquiring status, as it was known to have been in the late prehistoric and early historic Southeast. The construction and use of elaborate mound centers may itself reflect increased competition between individuals or groups, which was expressed through collective ceremonial behavior.

Regarding the latter, it is important to note that massive earthen mound complexes were being constructed at a very early date in parts of the Southeast, well back into the Archaic period prior to 5000 cal. B.P. (Russo 1994a, 1996a). At sites like Caney, Frenchman's Bend, Hedgepeth, and Watson Brake, huge complexes with multiple mounds are present, which in some cases are connected by earthen embankments (see Figs. 3-6; Saunders et al. 1994, 1997; Gibson 1996). One of the most complex sites is Watson's Brake, where the main period of construction occurred between about 5400 to 5000 cal. B.P. (see Fig. 6; Saunders et al. 1997). This site consists of 11 mounds, seven of which are connected by a circular ridge/midden deposit. The largest mound is over 7 meters high, and the entire complex extends almost 300 meters across. Analyses of plant and animal remains from the site suggest seasonal occupation, in the spring, summer, and fall, although it should be noted that only a tiny portion of the site has been investigated to date.

A number of early mound sites also have been found in Florida, where both earth and shell were commonly used as construction material (Russo 1994b, 1996b; see Fig. 7). At the Horr's Island site on the southwest Florida coast, for example, a complex arrangement of mounds was constructed between 4600 and 5000 cal. B.P. (Fig. 7). Analysis of subsistence remains indicates that this site was occupied year round, the earliest evidence for true sedentism in the region. Apparently, the abundant local marine resources allowed this sedentary lifestyle. Other early mounds dating to between ca. 5500 and 4000 cal. B.P. have been found in northeast Florida at Tomoka (Piatak 1994) and Tick Island (Aten 1999; Russo 1994b:106–108), in the lower Missouri River valley at sites of the Nebo Hill culture, and at Helton and Titterington phase

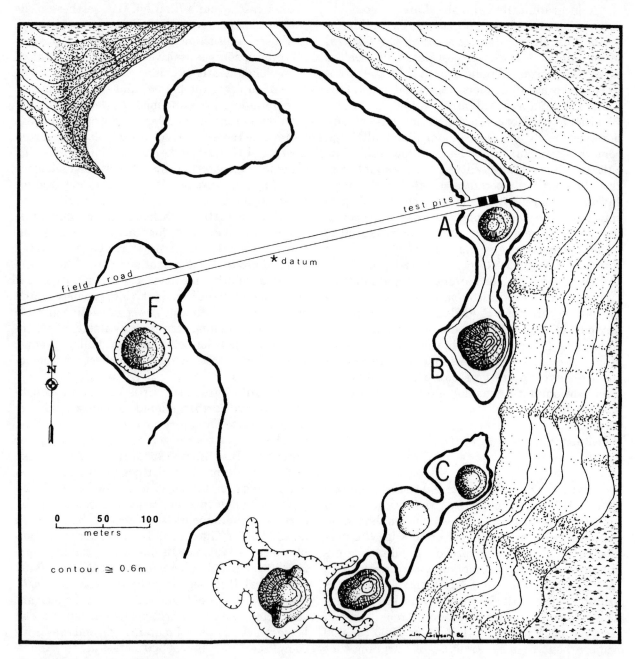

Fig. 3. The Caney Mounds, Louisiana (drawn by Jon Gibson, adopted from Gibson 1994:173, courtesy *Southeastern Archaeology*).

sites of Illinois and Missouri from 5000 to 4000 cal. B.P. (Claassen 1996:243; Russo 1994b:106–108).

Other elaborate Middle and Late Archaic cultures are known from across Eastern North America, among which perhaps the best known archaeologically are the Shell Mound Archaic cultures of the Midsouth and lower Midwest (Claassen 1996; Marquardt and Watson 1983), the Benton Interaction Sphere in the lower Midsouth (Johnson and Brookes 1989), the Stallings Island Culture of Georgia and South Carolina (Sassaman 1993), the Mount Taylor culture of the St. Johns river valley of northeastern Florida (Piatak 1994), and the Old Copper culture of the Great Lakes Region (Stoltman 1986). All appear to have participated in the long distance exchange networks spanning much of the region at this time. While still considered egalitarian societies, it is clear that some individuals had much higher status than others, and likely competed in their own and other societies for recognition and leadership in warfare, exchange, and probably the direction of public construction episodes and ceremony.

During the Middle and Late Archaic periods across much of Eastern North America, appreciable evidence also appears for substantial house construction activity (Sassaman and Ledbetter 1996), the beginnings of violent conflict between groups (Milner 1999; M. Smith 1996), long distance trading networks (Jefferies 1995, 1996; Johnson 1994) and, as noted previously, increasing ceremonialism manifested in large-scale earthwork construc-

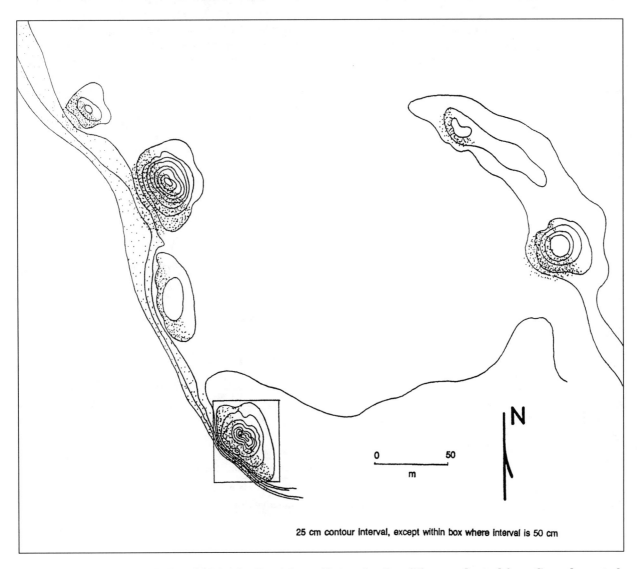

25 cm contour interval, except within box where interval is 50 cm

Fig. 4. The Frenchman's Bend Mounds, Louisiana (drawn by Jon Gibson, adopted from Saunders et al. 1994:139, courtesy *Southeastern Archaeology*).

tion. Wild plants were utilized extensively. By the Late Archaic, local plants such as chenopodium, sunflower, and maygrass were being cultivated for their starchy or oily seeds, and other plants that were likely domesticated elsewhere, such as squash, were adopted (B. Smith 1992). As cultivated crops became more important, they would have likely had the effect of increasing the available food supply and, hence, eventually human population levels. Cultivation would have also likely increasingly tied people to specific tracts of land, where their field were located, resulting in decreased group mobility (Gremillion 1996; B. Smith 1992). The Late Archaic also witnessed the so-called "container revolution" in which vessels of fired clay or stone appeared from Florida through the Carolinas, but this technology did not spread very far until the subsequent Woodland period (B. Smith 1986; Sassaman 1993, 2002). Like agriculture, pottery production is also thought by some researchers to have led to increases in food pro-

cessing capabilities, and hence to increases populations levels and, because of the fragile nature of this technology, to decreased group mobility (Fiedel 2001; Sassaman 1993, 2002).

Monumental construction and the emergence of tribal societies in the Southeastern US

The fact that monumental construction activity, long distance exchange, subsistence intensification, and warfare were all occurring upwards of 5000 years ago in parts of the region suggests that societies more complex than simple bands had emerged (Bender 1985; Saitta 1983). Perhaps the clearest evidence for the emergence of tribal societies during the Archaic period is monumental architecture, the construction of which was likely conducted by a great many cooperating people linked together by common ritual or purpose. Such joint social endeavors as well as the continued use

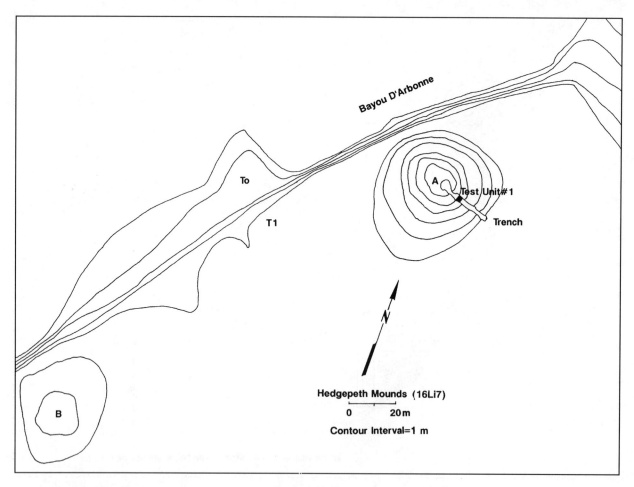

Fig. 5 The Hedgepeth Mounds, Louisiana (adapted from Saunders et al. 1994:146, courtesy *Southeastern Archaeology*).

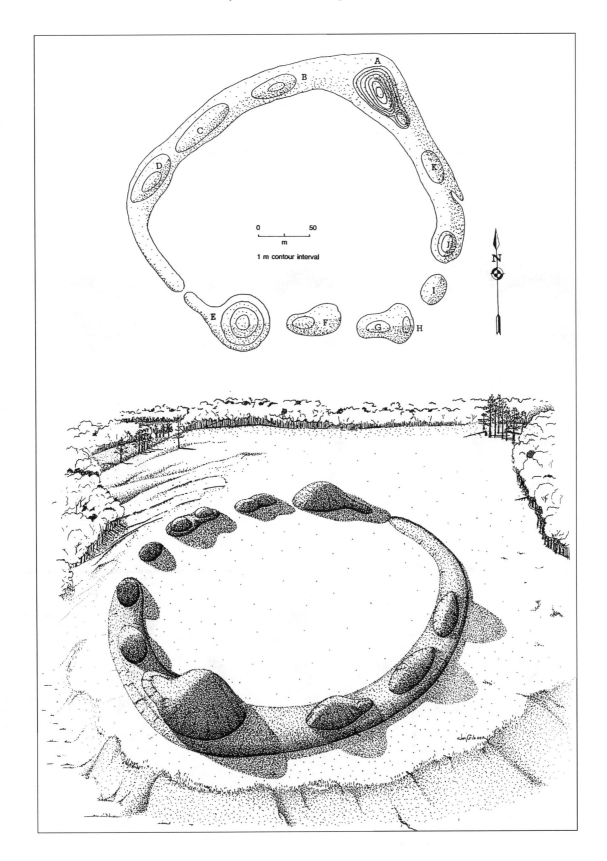

Fig. 6 The Watson Brake Mounds, Louisiana, contours and idealized reconstruction (drawn by Jon Gibson, adopted from Saunders et al. 1994:145, courtesy *Southeastern Archaeology*).

of the sacral-political landscapes they produced created and helped maintain links between these groups. In such a view, the individual mounds at sites like Watson's Brake, or the varying masses of shell and earth at Horr's Island and other early circular or U-shaped coastal middens, may represent the efforts of contemporaneous tribal segments, whose collective activity transformed them into an organizational form larger and more complex than what they had previously (Russo 1999; Russo and Saunders 1999; Widmer 1999). The ringed causeway linking the separate mounds at Watson Brake, in this view, represents the new collectivity.

It has also been variously suggested by southeastern archaeologists like Michael Russo, Rebecca Saunders, Dolph Widmer, and others, that the sizes of the individual mounds, or masses of earth and

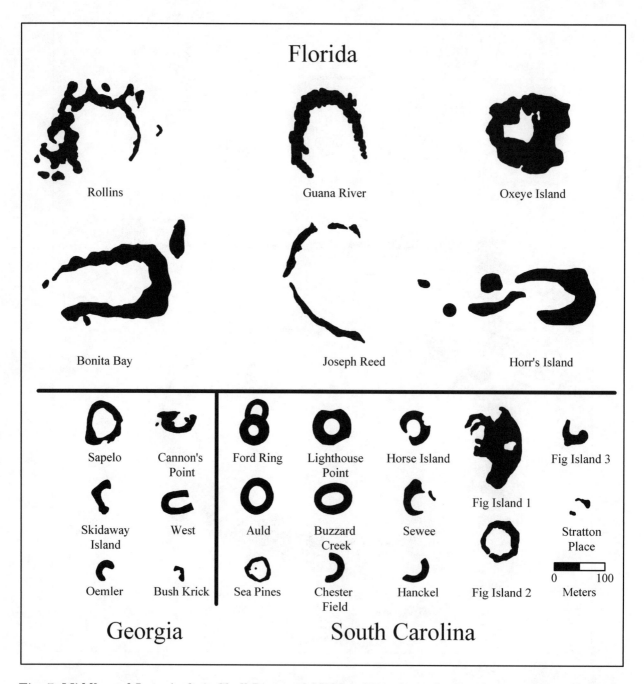

Fig. 7. Middle and Late Archaic Shell Ring and Midden Sites from the Southeastern United States (adapted from Russo and Heide 2001:492, courtesy *Antiquity*).

shell, in these early mound complexes is related to the size and political fortunes or abilities of the groups that formed them, with larger the mounds produced by the largest and most politically savvy groups. Widmer (1999, n.d.), in a particularly elegant argument, has suggested that the emergence of lineage-based collateral kinship systems (i.e., bifurcate merging/Iroquoian, generational/Hawaiian) accompanied the development of the tribal segments creating individual mounds, replacing the less inclusive lineal (i.e., Eskimo) kinship systems typically used by mobile band-level foraging populations. Changes in kinship thus accompanied and facilitated the development of larger corporate groupings, creating and maintaining the labor base essential to large-scale cooperative endeavors.

Widmer (1999, n.d.) further argues that the differential reproductive success of these tribal segments or lineages, something itself shaped by varying environmental productivity and initial population size and density, translated into differential political success, which can be directly measured by the size of the individual mounds, and the status value of associated material remains, in and near individual mounds within multimound complexes. Russo (1999, n.d.), who has made a similar argument, has begun to test these ideas directly, examining the material remains found in different parts of early shell and earthen midden complexes in coastal Florida. In the years to come, we shall increasingly see efforts to test such scenarios, to reconstruct the construction sequence and, hence, political histories of these Archaic societies, much as we now explore the political fortunes of later Woodland and Mississippian centers. Careful archaeological analyses should, for example, suggest the kind of activities other than mound building that may have brought the peoples (future tribal segments?) together. At Watson Brake, for example, there is an unusual lapidary industry centered on the drilling of chert beads (Saunders et al. 1997), suggesting craft activities may have been a loci of competition and a means of fostering interaction and exchange, much as it is assumed to have been in the later Poverty Point culture in the region (Gibson 1996:302, 2000:171ff). Blitz's (1999) fission-fusion process for the formation of multimound centers would thus appear to apply equally well to tribal as well as chiefdom level societies in the region, with a long history, stretching well back into the Archaic.

How to recognize the existence of other possible correlates of pan-tribal social institutions linking tribal segments together over large areas, of course, is a major challenge. This problem is compounded by the likelihood that the earliest tribal forms were also perhaps the most weakly integrated, making their recognition even more difficult. The major centers of the Middle and Late Archaic Southeast, as well as during much of the subsequent Woodland period were, I believe, formed by the actions of tribal level groups, whose segments were ordinarily dispersed across the landscape, but that periodically came together for exchange, ritual, and cooperation in construction. I also strongly suspect that other such tribal-level groups were present in the region during these periods, yet who did not direct their collective energies to mound construction. There are simply too many areas in the Southeast where large numbers of sites have been found, or concentrations of presumed prestige goods like grooved axes, bannerstones, and soapstone bowls, to suggest otherwise (Anderson 1996:163–166; Sassaman 1996:67–71). While band-level groupings may have continued in some areas early on, over time the adaptive advantages of tribal organization would have likely been such that the organizational form was widely adopted, save perhaps in the most marginal areas.

Why did tribal societies emerge in the Middle Archaic Southeastern US?

Why did tribes emerge in the Middle Archaic and not before or after, if this argument is correct? Probably because critical population density and spacing thresholds were reached at this time, and because normal climatic uncertainty may have been exacerbated (Anderson 2001; Anderson et al. n.d.; Hamilton 1999; Sassaman 1995:182–183; Widmer 1999, n.d.). The Middle Archaic appears to have been a time of interrelated environmental stress and population pressure. By the Middle Archaic period, from ca. 8500 to 5500 B.P. there is evidence for more restricted mobility in many parts of the region, something unquestionably brought on, in part, by increasing population levels. Some areas appear to have been abandoned or greatly depopulated, particularly portions of the southeastern Gulf and Atlantic Coastal Plains, where pine forests replaced hardwoods, providing less food for both game animals and the human groups that preyed upon them. What economic conditions were like for human populations over the region, in fact, is the subject of appreciable research and debate. Large sites characterized by dense accumulations of occupational debris, particularly shellfish, for example, appear in a number of the major river valleys in the Southeast and Midwest, and towards the end of the Middle Archaic period large shell middens appear along the coast as well. The occurrence of these sites has long been thought due, in part, to a retrenchment of populations into particularly favored areas during the Mid Holocene (e.g., Brown 1985:219–221; Brown and Vierra 1983:167–168; Sassaman 1995:182–183). Stresses of various kinds — environmental as well as social — thus prompted organizational elaboration in groups whose population levels and densities were such that they could maintain such structures (i.e., following arguments by Carneiro [1967, 2000] about the direct relationship between population size and density and level of organizational complexity).

Settlement nucleation and tribal organization

The archaeological record of the later Archaic and Woodland Southeast provides numerous cases of monumental construction activity, bringing together large numbers of people otherwise scattered over the landscape much of the time. In most areas, however, there is little or no evidence for large nucleated settlements, or sedentary communities, at least until well into the Woodland period (Anderson and Mainfort 2002; Nassaney and Cobb 1991; B. Smith 1986). Complexity in ritual but not in social organization is inferred, although something greater than band level organization is either implicit or explicit in most arguments (Brose 1979; Clay 1998). By the latter part of the Woodland period, however, evidence for sedentary communities is increasingly widespread, and intensive agriculture based on local domesticates appears to have been practiced in some areas. These changes are thought to have resulted in the emergence of fairly complex tribal organizational forms, which themselves were eventually, and in some cases fairly quickly, replaced by chiefdoms in many areas.

The centuries around ca. 1600 cal. B.P./A.D. 400 may have been something of a "trip over" or threshold era for the emergence of complex tribal forms in the Southeast. If Clay (1998:16) is correct, previous tribal organizational processes worked as much to preclude the emergence of more complex organizational forms, by keeping populations scattered. Prior to this era, tribal identity was stymied by mortuary ritual, not enhanced by it (Clay 1998:15). While there may have been quantitative changes in the size of mounds or the number of

participating segments prior to this, little evidence exists of any qualitative or fundamental change in the nature of sociopolitical organization. Centers were typically formed by the intermittent collective action of otherwise dispersed populations. Settlement nucleation, accordingly, may be the single most visible archaeological correlate of more complex tribal organization, as well as of profound changes in the way in which the world was viewed by native peoples in the region; there is little evidence for such settlements prior to the Late Woodland era in most parts of the region (Cobb and Nassaney 2002).

Once again, of course, these changes were not universal. Settlement patterns during the later Woodland period varied appreciably over the region. In some areas, such as in the Ohio and Lower Mississippi River Valleys (New Town and Coles Creek cultures), nucleation was widespread, while in other areas, like the South Atlantic slope, peoples tended to remain dispersed in fairly small groups of "mobile, part-time horticulturalists" until much later in time (Cobb and Nassaney 1995:206ff, 2002). With settlement nucleation, however, intermittent monumental construction was no longer needed to bring peoples together. Monumental construction of course continued in some parts of the region during the Late Woodland and Mississippian periods, for historical reasons among others, but in many of these societies its purpose had changed. Tribal forms of organization and collective ceremony had given way to forms characteristic of chiefdoms. Fostering group identify remained an important aspect of these collective activities, but they were also now directed to maintaining and legitimizing the power and authority of chiefly elites.

Exploring Tribal Organizational Variability: Advantages and Expectations

The scale of tribal societies

Examining the kind of sociopolitical organization Archaic and Woodland peoples had can give us better insight about what we are looking at in the southeastern archaeological record, as well as give us ideas about how to better sample and examine that record. The geographic extent and population levels and densities of tribal societies, for example, are things that should perhaps receive greater consideration in the interpretation of Archaic and Woodland archaeological cultures. Ethnographic tribes were frequently quite extensive, extending over thousands and sometimes tens of thousands of square miles, and often involved extremely large numbers of people, in the thousands, tens of thousands, and occasionally even in the hundreds of thousands (e.g., Feinman and Neitzel 1984; Kelly 1985). We need to be giving at least some consideration to the possibility that the artifacts, sites, and localities that we typically work with may be the remains of cultural systems integrated at comparable scales.

One attempt to explore possible tribal interaction in the Southeast that considered large geographic scales was Dan F. Morse's (1977) adoption of Sahlins' (1961) classic paper "The Segmentary Lineage: An Organization of Predatory Expansion." Morse examined later Woodland developments in the central Mississippi valley, specifically what the changing distributions of Barnes and Baytown pottery on sites over time may have represented. In his view, the grog-tempered Nuer equivalent Baytown peoples were expanding into the territory of the less complex sand tempered Dinka equivalent Barnes peoples. However questionable this scenario may seem to some—and Morse's equations of ceramic distributions and phases with prehistoric polities has had his share of critics (e.g., O'Brien 1995; O'Brien and Dunnell 1998)—these are exactly the kind of organizational dynamics and geographic and temporal scales we must start considering, if we hope to develop a better understand what was occurring in the later Archaic and Woodland periods in the Southeast. Most importantly, Morse offered possible archaeological correlates for the tribal expansion he postulated, notably the rapid replacement of one type of pottery assemblage by another.[1]

Another archaeological example from the Southeast of a geographically extensive tribal form of organization may be the Swift Creek culture in the South Appalachian area (see summaries in Stephenson et al. 2002 and Williams and Elliott 1998). Swift Creek appears to have encompassed a number of diverse adaptations to coastal, coastal plain, and interior upland environments, each with somewhat distinctive centers and patterns of outlying site distribution. Centers included ring midden/burial areas on the coast (Bense 1998), small mound/shrines in the interior uplands (Williams and Freer 1998), and a few major centers with platform or other mounds that appear to have been tied in to pan-regional Hopewellian interaction (Anderson 1998). Yet for all these apparent differences, Swift Creek is a distinct archaeological entity identified by a common ceramic series

that occurs over a vast area, encompassing much of Georgia as well as portions of adjacent states (ca. 75,000 square kilometers). Design motif analyses document appreciable interaction over large portions this area, with both pots and paddles moving long distances (Snow and Stephenson 1998). Much of what we think of as Swift Creek, accordingly, may be a single tribal society, with segments of differing size, adaptation, and local complexity unified by a common iconography, technology, and interaction network.[2] This is certainly an idea that should be considered, and we should also begin to think about other southeastern archaeological cultures like Weeden Island, Baytown, or Alexander the same way.[3]

The Swift Creek case gets us into questions of how we recognize tribal entities/totalities, as well as tribal segments, and how these social constructs likely interacted with one another. One result of such research might be the construction of regional political geographies for the later Archaic and Woodland periods, much as we now attempt for the Mississippian period (e.g., Anderson 1991; Milner et al. 2001; Scarry and Payne 1986). This is not a sterile exercise, since the effort of attempting such reconstructions will help highlight where people were on the southeastern landscape, and what they were likely doing. When actual site data are mapped at a regional scale, we often find our preconceptions about where people were on the landscape are quite simply wrong (Anderson 1996) (Figs. 8 and 9). Middle and Late Archaic site concentrations, for example, occur in places where there are well known archaeological cultures dating to these periods, such as along the major river systems of the Midsouth. But these distributions also reveal large numbers of sites in places where no such archaeological cultures are known, or at least where little research directed toward understanding their nature has occurred. Sassaman (1996), as noted previously, made a similar finding when plotting the distribution of unusual artifacts like bannerstones, grooved axes, and soapstone vessels over the southeastern landscape—nodes or concentrations of these artifacts, possibly indicative of centers of production or consumption, were sometimes found in altogether unexpected areas, well away from the centers of the well known archaeological cultures of the period (Fig. 10). Something we must always consider, accordingly, is how our preconceptions about what is going on over the landscape actually compares with the information available about the southeastern archaeological record. By focusing on the elaborate, mound or shell midden building sites and cultures of the later Archaic, for example, we may well be missing where the vast majority of the people were living, and opportunities to explore how they were organized.

Understanding elaborate burial ceremonialism in tribal societies

Another archaeological example of the value of "thinking tribally" centers on the interpretation of the elaborate burial ceremonialism characteristic of some societies in the region, particularly during the Middle Woodland period, from ca. 2300 to 1600 cal. B.P. During the early part of the Woodland period after about 3500 cal. B.P. pottery, which had appeared about 1000 years earlier in Florida and the Carolinas, was widely adopted and used across the region (Sassaman 1993). Long distance exchange declined markedly in many areas when compared with the preceding Late Archaic period,

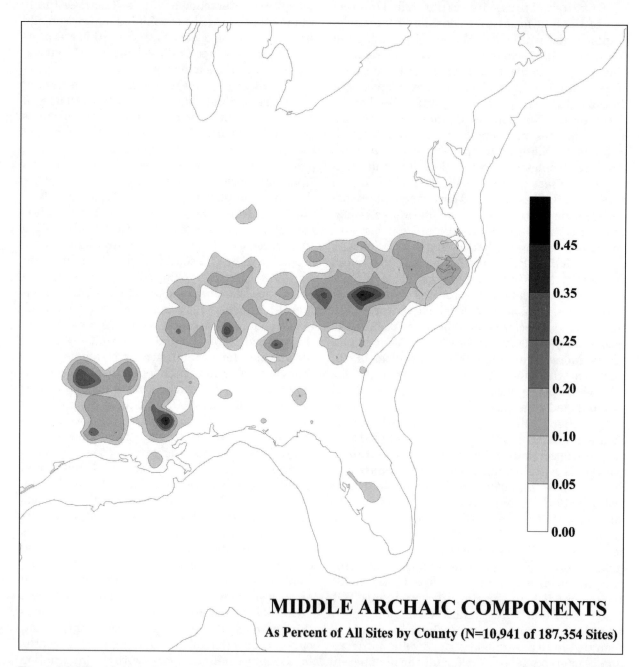

MIDDLE ARCHAIC COMPONENTS

As Percent of All Sites by County (N=10,941 of 187,354 Sites)

Fig. 8. Middle Archaic Components in the Southeastern United States, as percent of all Sites by County (n=10,941 of 187,354 sites; modified from Anderson 1996:161, courtesy University Press of Florida).

and for the most part people appear to have been living in small, more-or-less egalitarian groups, with community size on the order of a few dozen people, or several families. Earthen burial mounds occur in many areas. Mortuary facilities were often located away from settlements, suggesting they served to bring together peoples from a number of communities, a pattern we now know dates well back into the Archaic (see summaries of Woodland period archaeology in the Southeast by Anderson and Mainfort 2002; Bense 1994:109–182; Smith

1986:35–57; Nassaney 2000).

By the Middle Woodland period, long distance exchange networks had reemerged, spectacular mounds and earthwork complexes were built in many areas, similarities in iconography and ritual behavior are evident between many societies, and some individuals were buried in elaborate tombs within or under massive mounds. This behavior has come to be known as Hopewellian interaction, after the type site and archaeological culture in southern Ohio (Brose and Greber 1979; Pacheco

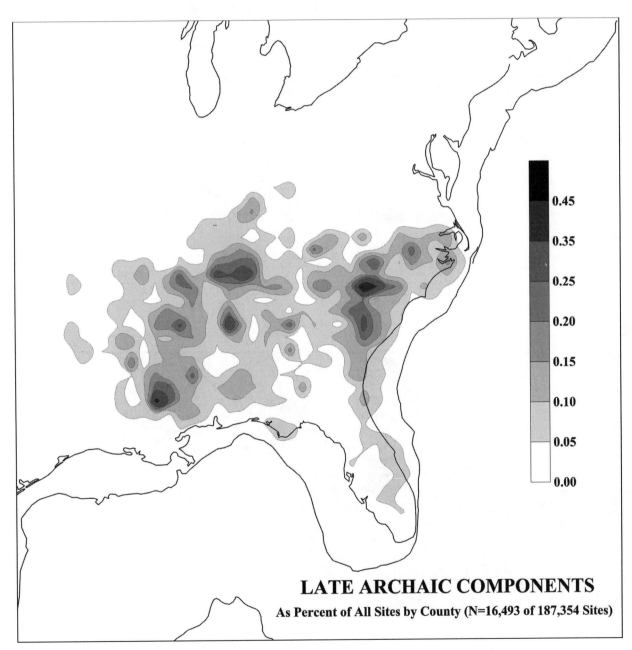

LATE ARCHAIC COMPONENTS

As Percent of All Sites by County (N=16,493 of 187,354 Sites)

Fig. 9. Late Archaic Components in the Southeastern United States, as percent of all Sites by County (n=16,493 of 187,354 sites; modified from Anderson 1996:162, courtesy University Press of Florida).

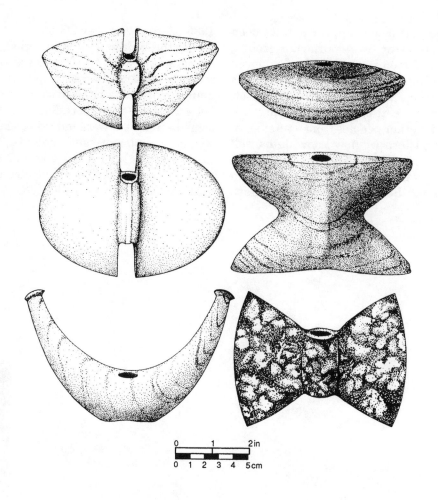

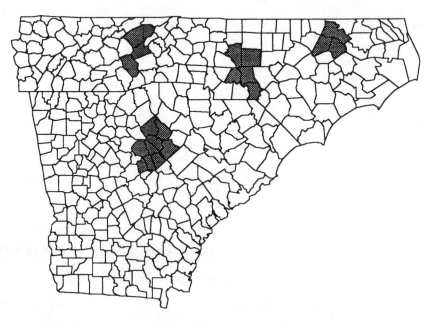

Fig. 10. Elaborate bannerstones and bannerstone distribution in the South Appalachian area (adopted from Sassaman 1996:61, 64, courtesy University Press of Florida).

1996). Many differing societies were actually present within the region, of course, whose participation in this interaction network varied greatly. Native cultigens are thought to have played a major role in the diet some areas, although this remains to be well documented. Maize, while present, was not used extensively. Tribal societies are assumed to have been present, since there is no evidence for the hereditary leadership positions found in chiefdom societies. Besides enhancing individual status, long distance interaction and exchange likely helped reduce the possibility of warfare and subsistence uncertainty for everybody, by creating ties between different groups.

The spectacular individual burials and associated grave assemblages that occur at some Middle Woodland sites in the Southeast are assumed to commemorate highly successful individuals, who were able to enlist the help of their communities in the pursuit of their social and ritual agendas. These have been called 'Big Man' societies (B. Smith 1986), a form of social organization best known from Melanesia. It must be noted, however, that the ethnographic examples offered of Big Man societies are nowhere near as complex as some of the Hopewellian societies of the Eastern Woodlands appear to have been (Sahlins 1963, 1972:248–255). Monumental construction, for example, is absent or minimal in most of the ethnographic cases. Likewise, in ethnographic cases, Big Men typically had reputations for generosity and gift giving, while many of the Eastern Woodlands folks apparently "took it with them" when they died.[4] Even if Big Men (and Women, after Bense [1994:141]) were present, how these individuals participated in the collective ceremony and monumental construction that characterize Middle Woodland societies needs to be determined. These same kinds of questions need to be asked in every period where there is evidence for both collective monumental construction and prestige goods-based individual status competition.

It is probable, for example, that the same people that accumulated great wealth and prestige through their involvement in exchange networks also oversaw, or at least used their assets and abilities to encourage and support collective ceremony and monumental construction activities. Successful practitioners of such strategies likely came from specific clans or lineages, that themselves enjoyed greater demographic success and controlled disproportionately more resources than other such groups (Widmer 1999). Continued success could mean that, over time, these kinship

groupings acquired higher status, as well as became increasing embued with sacred value, which could eventually lead to the emergence and legitimization of ranking (i.e., Friedman 1975; Friedman and Rowlands 1977; Kelly 1993). Archaeological correlates of this are indicated by the uneven sizes of mounds at multimound Archaic and early Woodland ceremonial centers (Russo 1999, 2002; Widmer 1999, n.d.). Thus, even within so called egalitarian tribal societies, some groups were clearly better off than others, with greater access to resources, status goods, and probably control over positions of ceremony ceremonial and leadership positions.

We also need to be thinking about the kinds of social organization, burial ceremonialism (or lack thereof), and exchange and interaction that may have been present in parts of the region where obvious archaeological correlates of complex social organization like mounds or earthworks are lacking. As noted above, Middle and Late Archaic site distributions in the Southeast (Figs. 8 and 9) show many of the well known archaeological cultures but, somewhat surprisingly, they also document other site concentrations that are as just as extensive but are all but unknown and unrecognized archaeologically (Anderson 1996). The Pee Dee and Cape Fear Rivers in North and South Carolina, for example, have just as many late Archaic sites as the Savannah and Ogeechee Rivers, yet lack the massive shell middens and fiber tempered pottery that have made the Stallings culture so well known. Was this area—only one example among many that could be offered through inspection of these maps— occupied by a group that was just as complex but whose social energies were directed into something other than piling up shell or earth, or making elaborately decorated pottery?

Sassaman's (1996) finding of nodes or concentrations in the regional occurrence of classic Archaic period artifact types like bannerstones and grooved axes is excellent evidence supporting this possibility. Some of these nodes correspond to well known cultures, but others do not. Again, equally populous or powerful societies may be indicated, who signaled group affiliation in less archaeologically visible ways than by building mounds or producing elaborately decorated pottery. On the other hand, Sassaman (1991, 1995, 2001:229–232) has argued that the Middle Archaic Morrow Mountain point using peoples of the Carolina Piedmont, due to their marginal location within the overall region and a consensus strategy, were able to opt out of the warfare and intense status competition occurring in the Midsouth. Did such resistance characterize some peoples and areas in later Archaic and Woodland times as well? Probably, but saying it and proving it are two different things. We need to be thinking about what mechanisms may have bound less archaeologically visible peoples into larger social entities, if indeed they were so organized. We also need to explore whether traditions of resistance indeed exist, how they may have formed, and how they may have been shaped by their position within the regional political and physiographic landscape (e.g., Clark and Blake 1994; Sassaman 1991, 1995, 2001). Resistance to domination would appear to be as important a theme in the Southeast, for example, as its imposition.

Causes and Processes of Evolutionary Change in Southeastern Tribal Societies

The Southeast did not become saturated with complex tribes overnight. Thousands of years are involved, and over this interval appreciable variation and change in organizational form occurred. Likewise, there were broad changes in climate and resource structure that must be considered, as well as technological innovations as well as social conditions that affected the abilities of societies to exploit these conditions. Early on, ca. 5000 to 6000 B.P., there may have been some short-lived developments of 'tribal' societies in a few areas. The mound centers in eastern Louisiana and southern Florida are possible examples, although given the labor represented in their construction, these societies appear more to represent the culmination, rather than the onset, of tribal organization. Careful examination of the local archaeological record in these areas, and particularly the construction history of specific mound centers, is essential to determine how they were formed and used, and whether one or more such centers were contemporaneous or succeeded one another.

In the Lower Mississippi Valley and along the major river systems of the Midsouth, areas with high interaction potential, change likely occurred more rapidly than in marginal areas (Clark and Blake 1994). That these societies likely came and went like blinking Christmas tree lights, an image used to describe Mississippian chiefdoms in the region, is probable. Whether these societies had a greater or lesser duration than Mississippian societies, however, is something that has yet to be explored. The occupation spans at major centers

such as Pinson, Poverty Point (Figs. 11-12), and Horr's Island, where fairly extensive excavations have occurred, suggest use over several hundred years, not the few generations characteristic of many Mississippian chiefdoms (Hally 1993). Tribal societies in the region may have been more stable than chiefdoms, although the fortunes of individual segments may have changed appreciably over time. Particular tribal societies may have been long lived, but their organizational properties may have been manifest in different ways at different times, reflecting what Parkinson (1999, and this volume, Chapter 18) and Fowles (this volume, Chapter 2) describe as a hallmark of these societies, their organizational flexibility, or ability to adopt differing structural poses (after Gearing 1958) as circumstances dictate.

Middle Archaic societies inhabited a different social and political landscape than their Late Archaic and Woodland successors, with major differences also apparent in climate and biota. These conditions, of course, changed over time. Regional population levels are thought to have increased markedly during the Late Archaic and Woodland periods, and likely helped drive major changes in sociopolitical organization. Population growth, like subsistence intensification, was not unilineal or universal, however, but appears to have fluctuated appreciably in different parts of landscape, just as agriculture itself was adopted in some areas and not in others. Nonetheless, a broad upward trend in population appears to have occurred, punctuated by periods of more rapid growth or decline brought on by technological innovations in food production or warfare, or broad (i.e., global scale) climatic trends.[5] The effects of these differing variables, of course, changed over time. Innovations in subsistence technology, for example, may have first alleviated stress by providing new sources of food and then, through resulting population increase, led to increased levels of stress. Climate changes likewise may have initially induced stress, but people would eventually adapt to the new conditions.

The degree to which political consolidation occurs also depends on circumstances external to the tribe itself. Historical trends, for example, are critical. In the Nuer case, Sahlins noted that:

> social structure is shaped by historical conditions... who settled an area first and who must expand against existing populations.... The first peoples into an area will tend to be less able to organize collectively, and have minimal systems promoting fusion (i.e., complementary

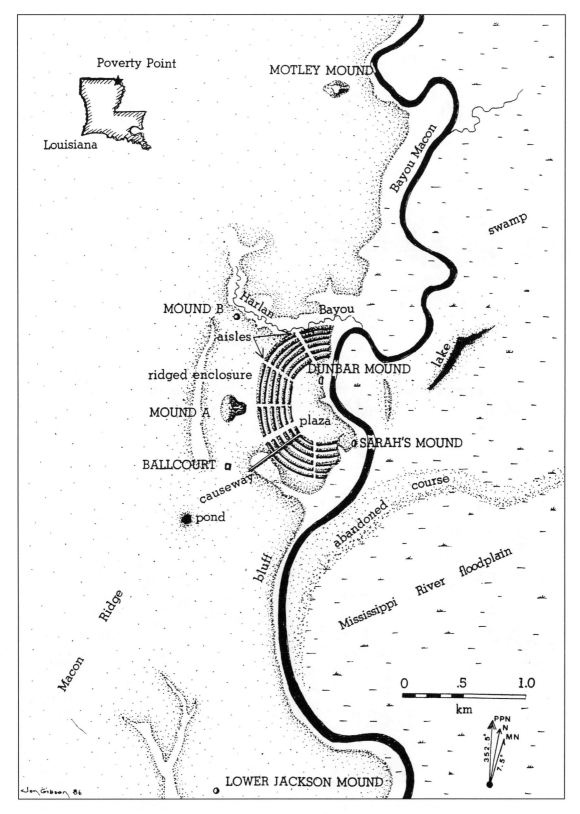

Fig. 11. The Poverty Point Site, Louisiana (drawn by Jon Gibson, from Gibson 2000:82, courtesy University Press of Florida).

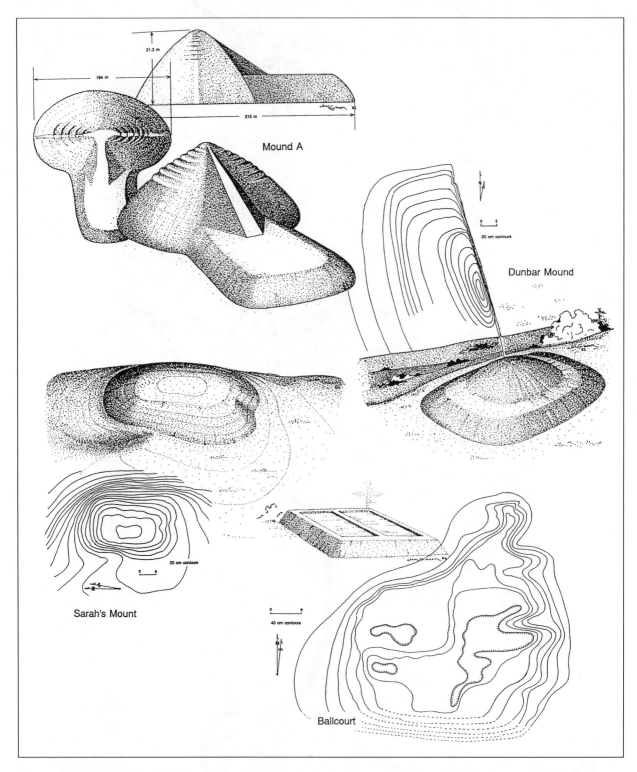

Fig. 12. Mounds at the Poverty Point Site, Louisiana (drawn by Jon Gibson, from Gibson 1994:171, courtesy *Southeastern Archaeology*).

opposition).... The segmentary lineage system is self liquidating" (Sahlins 1961:114–115, 118) That is, once the threat is gone, or expansion ceases, the system withers away (see Kelly 1985 for a detailed study of the Nuer/Dinka case, and the reasons behind Nuer expansion). There is no question that there is appreciable variability in the tribal societies of the prehistoric Southeast. The Lower Mississippi Alluvial valley, the Ohio and Tennessee River valleys, and the southern Atlantic and Gulf coastlines, for example, have much longer and more visible histories of elaborate monumental construction or participation in long-distance exchange, than are evident in most other parts of the region. Interaction potential likely shaped some of these developments (i.e., being near major transportation/communication arteries), but so too did prior historical conditions.

Tribes and chiefdoms can occur contemporaneously within larger regions (Creamer and Haas 1985), just as appreciable variability can occur within smaller regions dominated by one or the other of these general levels of organization (Anderson 1994; Hally 1993; Muller 1997). Recognition of this fact is important, but we must also ask what the conditions were that allowed such diversity to occur. The regional political geography and historical trajectories of each group must be considered in the study of Archaic and Woodland tribal formulations just as they are now routinely considered in Mississippian chiefdom research (e.g., Bender 1985:53–54). Sassaman (1991, 1995, 2001), as noted, has argued that some Middle and Late Archaic groups, specifically those in the Piedmont portion of Georgia and the Carolinas, consciously opted out of or resisted complex society formation. The highly mobile Middle Archaic foraging populations of the South Atlantic Slope were certainly organized differently than their contemporaries in the Midsouth. Claassen (1996) has also noted that shell middens and bead use are unevenly distributed through the Southeast during the Later Archaic. Site distribution maps, however, clearly indicate many of the areas where beads and shell middens are lacking were nonetheless intensively occupied. The groups in these areas may well have opted out of involvement in activities like personal status competition, monumental construction, or warfare.

Processes of change in tribal societies are thus scale dependent and multivariate. When examining change through time, we must be aware that different processes occur at differing scales. One means of dealing with this reality is to adopt a perspective similar to Braudel's (1972/73) model of longue durée, conjunctures, and evenments, which for simplicity's sake might be considered the examination of trends at century to millennial, decadal to century, and momentary to annual scales, respectively (Sherratt 1992; Fowles, this volume, Chapter 2). Short of Pompeii-like situations, archaeology is best suited to documenting long term patterns of land use and change (Binford 1983). Just as a multiscalar perspective must be adopted to our examination of temporal trends, a similar approach must be adopted to examine changes over space. That is, we must recognize that cultural processes may act or be acted out at superregional, regional, subregional, locality, and site/locational scales, and that what constitutes satisfactory explanations will likely vary depending on the area under examination (Neitzel 1999; Neitzel and Anderson 1999)

Organizational change is also dependent upon and shaped by resource structure and physiography. Sufficient subsistence resources must be present in an area to support tribal scale interaction/solidarity enhancing activities. Resource predictability or unpredictability is also crucial, as it directly influences population levels and technological (food production) capabilities. There appears to be a greater chance for the formation of tribes and for conflict between tribes when resources are extensive yet finite and to some extent unpredictable. Physiographic structure, specifically the location of rivers, coastlines, and mountain ranges and passes, shapes interaction potential and, hence, the likelihood that complex societies will form in a given area (Clark and Blake 1994). Not surprisingly, evidence for the first complex societies in the Southeast appears in resource rich areas like the Lower Mississippi Alluvial valley of Louisiana, coastal Florida, and the major river systems of the midcontinent. The growth of organizational complexity was fueled by resource availability, population levels, and interaction potential.

The Archaeological Recognition of Southeastern Tribal Societies

Tribes are admittedly difficult to recognize archaeologically (Braun and Plog 1982). Nonetheless, a number of specific attributes, when examined, can help to determine the existence and extent of tribal societies. These include: (1) ceramic assemblages/series, especially those that are widely shared (i.e., Swift Creek, Baytown, Weeden Island, Stallings); (2) projectile point types or styles, again when widely shared; (3) raw material distributions, such as stone, metal, or shell; (4) prestige or unusual goods distributions (i.e., nodes of distinctive goods, such as bannerstones, grooved axes, soapstone bowls, shell beads, worked copper, bone pins, etc.) (5) settlement distributions (i.e., size classes of habitation vs. ceremonial site types); (6) monumental construction activity, particularly that with characteristics indicative of the actions of multiple tribal segments (i.e., mounds of differing sizes at centers); and (7) evidence for buffer zones (i.e., where people are and aren't found on the landscape can indicate the extent of areas occupied or controlled by them). None of these characteristics is unique or sufficient to determine if tribal societies were present, of course, but they do give us an indication of what we should being looking at.

If tribal boundaries were strictly defined by their members, for example, artifact distributions may exhibit sharp discontinuities rather than gradual transitions from one society to the next Sassaman and his colleagues (1988) examined raw material use on diagnostic Early, Middle and Late Archaic projectile points along the length of the Savannah River, and the nature of the fall-off curves for each material from the source areas suggested a change from fairly fluid to restricted settlement mobility from the Middle to the Late Archaic periods. The Late Archaic may have thus been the time when more complex organizational forms emerged locally. Likewise, architectural correlates of complexity need to be considered. Brown (1979), for example, notes that societies with charnel houses were likely to be more complex, as manifest in the existence of ritual specialists, than societies where simple interment or the use of crypts to 'process' the dead occurred. Finally, specific artifact distributions can indicate interaction zones, as has been demonstrated with bone pins (Jefferies 1995, 1996); Benton points (Johnson and Brookes 1989); and Late Archaic and Woodland pottery types (see Sassaman 1993, 2002).

We must also carefully examine the developmental histories of individual sites and monuments if we are to accurately interpret the organizational systems of the groups that produced them (Clay 1998). As recent work at Adena and Hopewell centers has shown, massive earthworks and ceremonial precincts may well be the product of numerous small episodes, or a few major episodes widely separated in time, that cumulatively added up to an impressive architectural record. As Clay (1998:4) put it: "Adena burial mounds become less important [as] monuments to the dead than the tangible and variable records of social interaction worked out in mortuary events." The same is likely the case at many Archaic and Woodland mound centers in the Southeast. Interaction occurred between peoples spanning large areas, and impressive monumental construction occurred in some times and places as a result, but the size and internal organization of the constituent groups appears to have been relatively uncomplicated.

Conclusions

Evidence for long-distance prestige good exchange, warfare, and monumental construction indicate that band level society was transcended during the Mid-Holocene some 6000 years ago in parts of the Southeast. While appreciable variation in organizational complexity occurred over the next several thousand years a common pattern also characterized many of these societies: populations dispersed over the landscape in fairly small groups most of the time periodically came together for brief intervals in much larger numbers to engage in a range of activities that varied from society to society, but included such things as engaging in communal ceremony, ritual, and monumental construction, promoting social identities, buffering subsistence uncertainty, or facilitating the aggrandizing behavior of individuals. While the presence, nature, and scale of monumental construction, long distance exchange, ritual activity, and mortuary treatment varied tremendously over time and space, the overall pattern of dispersed to temporarily nucleated to dispersed settlement—and associated periods of lesser to greater to lesser social integration and organizational complexity—appears to have been widespread, and remarkably stable, for thousands of years.

The tribal societies of the Archaic and Woodland Southeast were characterized by fairly fluid organizational systems that fluctuated between periods of greater or lesser integration, and by relatively impermanent centralized authority structures. Indeed, authority appears to have been centralized and pronounced only when people came together; the public offices and organizational structures evident or implied by activities occurring during periods of nucleation may have been all but nonexistent the rest of the time. Not until late in the Woodland period do nucleated population/ceremonial centers occupied for much or all of the year appear in some areas, replacing the earlier pattern of occasional nucleation by dispersed populations. These more permanently occupied communities served as the ceremonial and organizational centers for hierarchical, chiefdom level societies, whose level of internal integration remained fairly constant, at least within certain upper and lower limits. In these societies, authority was manifest in the hereditary position of the chief and in his/her relationships with other members of society. While the fortunes of specific individuals and societies were often in flux, the institution of chiefly leadership was itself stable. Tribal societies, in contrast, were more variable in centralization

Tribes did not appear everywhere or overnight in the Southeast, nor is it likely that the initial tribal forms were particularly stable, long lived, or complex. While current evidence pretty conclusively indicates tribal organization emerged in the latter part of the Middle Archaic period, it is possible that tribal societies were present much earlier in time, although their recognition is likely to prove difficult. Tribal formations in the Southeast once established, varied dramatically, from the peoples who built the massive mounds and earthworks at Archaic sites like Watson Brake, Poverty Point, or at Woodland centers like Kolomoki, Pinson, and Troyville, to the peoples who built the shell middens at Stallings Island and Indian Knoll, to less visible social groups like the people who made Barnes pottery in northeast Arkansas, or scattered Late Archaic projectile points across the landscape near the North Carolina/South Carolina border. An impressive amount of variation is evident over the thousands of years tribes were present in the region. Some were innovative in the ways in which they directed their social energies, while others were more likely imitative, emerging and operating through processes of competitive emulation. Neither sedentism nor agriculture was essential to the emergence of tribal level organization in the Southeast, although they did play an important role in the subsequent changes observed in the region's societies. Over much of the several thousand year record of tribal societies in the region, in fact, what one sees is the cyclic emergence and decline of ritual/ceremonial centers formed by dispersed populations, rather than a pattern of ever increasing sedentism and organizational complexity. This patterns appears to have changed dramatically only in the later Woodland with the widespread appearance of nucleated settlements. Over much of the interval tribal societies are assumed to have been present in the region, however, there appears to have been little *qualitative* change in organization.

What is also interesting is that over the several thousand years tribes are assumed to have been present in the Southeast, there is little evidence for the long term continuity within specific areas of societies engaging in complex behavior (i.e., monumental construction, long distance exchange). That is, while centers with appreciable monumental construction might have been reused by later peoples, at no center and apparently in no area is monumental construction continuous throughout the period tribal societies are assumed to have been present. There are breaks or gaps in the record in each area, for greater or lesser periods. In the lower Mississippi Valley, for example, some Late Woodland Coles Creek and Mississippian mound centers were built on or near Poverty Point mounds, but in no case does mound construction appear to have continued unabated over the entire 3500 year span between the earliest and latest occupations. Individual tribal societies were thus capable of immense feats, but they were also over the long term, fairly ephemeral, although perhaps not as fleeting as the individual chiefdoms that succeeded them in many areas in the Late Woodland and Mississippian periods. As one reviewer of this paper noted, the Southeast "displays many cases in which pockets of tribal societies emerged against a backdrop of band level societies and then faded out before they caught on. Likewise there are examples of chiefdoms that emerged in a predominantly tribal level world and then faded." We need to put great thought to how tribal societies formed and developed in the Archaic and Woodland Southeast.

Given all this, there is, to my mind, one obvious answer to Brown and Vierra's (1982) classic question, "What Happened in the Middle Archaic?" Tribes.

Notes

[1] I like the ideas Morse advances, and agree that it is possible that a replacement of Barnes ceramic using populations by Baytown (and later, by initial Mississippian) ceramic using groups was occurring (see also Morse and Morse 1983, 1990). I do think, however, that Baytown pottery is dispersed far too widely across the central and lower Mississippi Alluvial Valley to be a good diagnostic indicator of any one particular social group.
[2] While arguing that Swift Creek ceramics may be the archaeological signature of a single tribal society may seem extreme, given the settlement vari-

ability over their range of occurrence, the geographic extent is certainly within the limits of ethnographic tribal societies, such as the Nuer (Kelly 1985). Even given the observed settlement variability, do I believe that Swift Creek, and similar archaeological cultures in the Woodland Southeast, particularly those that share common or identical ceramic assemblages, may well represent the occurrence of one or no more than a few closely related tribal societies. The geographic scale of tribal societies, it should be noted, does not seem to be constrained by span of control or distance parameters, unlike the situation in chiefdom and early state societies, where a ca. 20 km radius around centers tends to delimit the area under direct control (e.g., Hally 1993; Renfrew 1974, 1975). Tribal societies integrate people over large areas, yet lack the authority structures by which their constituent populations are under the direct control of any one group or segment, save in temporary circumstances such as in warfare or collective ceremonial activity.

[3]Similar thinking about the scale and operation of tribal societies is starting to appear in the Midwest (e.g., Emerson 1999).

[4]Richard Yerkes, in commenting on an earlier version of this paper, suggested instead of "taking it with them" elaborate grave goods found with Hopewellian burials were "given to them" by members of the community. Destruction through burial of elaborate goods would help maintain the need for interaction and exchange, and also could tend to reinforce egalitarian relationships, by ensuring wealth accumulated in life was not passed on.

[5]Interest in global climate change and its impact on human societies has a long history, particularly in Eastern North America (e.g., Griffin 1960, 1961), and the Southeast in particular (Anderson 2001). Widmer (1999, 2002), for example, has argued that fluctuation in sea level over time profoundly effected marsh and floodplain resource productivity, both along the coast and inland, and hence the fortunes of later Archaic and Woodland tribal societies dependent upon these resources. Similar arguments have been advanced by other researchers, who have argued that changes in stream gradients or fluctuations in sea level would effect the distributions of shellfish and other wild game (e.g., Brooks; Little 2001; Walker 2000). An apparent Late Mid-Holocene onset of increasing severe El Nino events has been advanced as a source of stress prompting organizational change, specifically the creation of larger social groups and alliance networks (i.e., tribal societies), to buffer presumably increased uncertainty in resources (Hamilton 1999). Fidel (2001) has argued that a global cooling event resulted in appreciable population decline and relocation during the Early Woodland period in the northeast. Gunn (2000) and his colleagues make a case that a similar cooling episode occurred in the sixth century A.D., during the initial Late Woodland period, that likewise resulted in population changes within the region. Our research on these matters is still far from complete or conclusive. I for one strongly believe that the impact of climate change on the cultures within the region was profound (Anderson 2001)

Acknowledgements

This paper was originally presented in the session "The Archaeology of Tribal Societies" organized by William Parkinson and Sev Fowles, at the 64th Annual Meeting of the Society for American Archaeology, 25 March 1999, Chicago, Illinois. Bill and Sev provided valuable comments to successive drafts of the manuscript, and have my heartfelt thanks. A somewhat different version of this paper was subsequently presented in the session "Big Mound Power! Or, Power, Who Needs It? Midlevel Societies in the Real Old South" organized by Phil Carr and Jon Gibson, at the 56th annual meeting of the Southeastern Archaeological Conference, 12 November 1999, Pensacola, Florida. A workshop subsequently held at Poverty Point in the fall of 2000 by the symposium participants greatly assisted me in refining my thinking. I thanks the organizers, Phil Carr and Jon Gibson, and all the participants. Many of the ideas herein are derived from extended conversations from John E. Clark, Jon Gibson, Michael Russo, Kenneth E. Sassaman, Joe Saunders, and Randolph E. Widmer; any good points the reader may find herein owes a great deal to their commentary. The author, of course, assumes sole responsibility for any problems or errors in the argument.

References Cited

Anderson, David G.
1991 Examining Prehistoric Settlement Distribution in Eastern North America. *Archaeology of Eastern North America* 19:1–22.
1994 *The Savannah River Chiefdoms: Political Change in the late Prehistoric South-*

east. The University of Alabama Press, Tuscaloosa

1996 Approaches to Modeling Regional Settlement in the Archaic Period Southeast. In *Archaeology of the Mid-Holocene Southeast*, edited by Kenneth Sassaman and David Anderson, pp. 157–176. University Press of Florida, Gainesville.

1998 Swift Creek in a Regional Perspective. In *A World Engraved: Archaeology of the Swift Creek Culture*, edited by J. Mark Williams and Daniel T. Elliott, pp. 274–300. The University of Alabama Press, Tuscaloosa.

2001 Climate and Culture Change in Prehistoric and Early Historic Eastern North America. *Archaeology of Eastern North America* 29:143–186.

Anderson, David G., and Robert C. Mainfort, Jr.
2002 An Introduction to Woodland Period Archaeology in the Southeast. In *The Woodland Southeast*, edited by David G. Anderson and Robert C. Mainfort, Jr., pp. 1-19. The University of Alabama Press, Tuscaloosa.

Anderson, David G., and Robert C. Mainfort, Jr. (editors)
2002 *The Woodland Southeast*. The University of Alabama Press, Tuscaloosa.

Anderson, David G., and Kenneth E. Sassaman (editors)
1996 *The Paleoindian and Early Archaic Southeast*. The University of Alabama Press, Tuscaloosa.

Anderson, David G., Michael Russo, and Kenneth E. Sassaman
n.d. Mid-Holocene Cultural Dynamics in Southeastern North America. Manuscript under review. Originally presented at the International Conference on Climate and Culture at 3000 B.C., University of Maine, Orono, 1998.

Bender, Barbara
1985 Emergent Tribal Formation in the American Midcontinent. *American Antiquity* 50(1):52–62.

Bense, Judith A.:
1994 *Archaeology of the Southeastern United States: Paleoindian to World War I*. Academic Press, San Diego.

1998 Santa Rosa–Swift Creek in Northwest Florida. In *A World Engraved: Archaeology of the Swift Creek Culture*, edited by J. Mark Williams and Daniel T. Elliott,

pp. 247–273. University of Alabama Press, Tuscaloosa.

Blitz, John
1999 Mississippian Chiefdoms and the Fission: Fusion Process. *American Antiquity* 64:577–592.

Braudel, F.
1972/73 *The Mediterranean and the Mediterranean World in the Age of Philip II* (2 vols.). Harper and Row, New York.

Braun, David, and Stephen Plog
1982 Evolution of 'Tribal' Social Networks: Theory and Prehistoric North American Evidence. *American Antiquity* 47:504–25.

Brooks, Mark J., Peter A. Stone, Donald J. Colquhoun, Janice G. Brown, and Kathy B. Steele
1986 Geoarchaeological Research in the Coastal Plain Portion of the Savannah River Valley. *Geoarchaeology* 1:293–307.

Brooks, Mark J., Kenneth E. Sassaman, and Glen T. Hanson
1990 Environmental Background and Models. In *Native American Prehistory of the Middle Savannah River Valley: A Synthesis of Archaeological Investigations on the Savannah River Site, Aiken and Barnwell Counties, South Carolina*, edited by Kenneth E. Sassaman, Mark J. Brooks, Glen T. Hanson, and David G. Anderson, pp. 19–66. Savannah River Archaeological Research Papers, no. 1. University of South Carolina, South Carolina Institute of Archaeology and Anthropology, Columbia.

Brose, David S., and N'omi Greber, (editors)
1979 *Hopewell Archaeology: The Chillicothe Conference*. Kent State University Press, Kent, Ohio.

Brown, James A.
1985 Long Term Trends to Sedentism and the Emergence of Complexity in the American Midwest. In *Prehistoric Hunter-Gatherers, The Emergence of Cultural Complexity*, edited by T. Douglas Price and James A. Brown, pp. 201–231. Academic Press, Orlando.

Brown, James A., and Robert K. Vierra
1983 What Happened in the Middle Archaic? Introduction to an Ecological Approach to Koster Site Archaeology. In *Archaic Hunters and Gatherers in the American Midwest*, edited by James L. Phillips and

James A. Brown, pp. 165–195. Academic Press, New York.

Carneiro, Robert L.

1967 On the Relationship Between Size of Population and Complexity of Social Organization. *Southwestern Journal of Anthropology* 23:234–243.

1981 The Chiefdom: Precursor of the State. In *The Transition to Statehood in the New World*, edited by Grant D. Jones and Robert R. Kautz, pp. 37–79. Cambridge

2000 *The Muse of History and The Science of Culture*. Kluwer Academic/Plenum Publishers, New York

Claassen, Cheryl P.

1994 A Consideration of the Social Organization of the Shell Mound Archaic. In *Archaeology of the Mid-Holocene Southeast*, edited by Kenneth Sassaman and David Anderson, pp. 235–258. University Press of Florida, Gainesville.

Clay, R. Berle

1998 The Essential Features of Adena Ritual and their Implications. *Southeastern Archaeology* 17:1–21

Clark, John E., and Michael Blake

1994 The Power of Prestige: Competitive Generosity and the Emergence of Rank Societies in Lowland Mesoamerica. In *Factional Competition in the New World*, edited by Elizabeth M. Brumfiel and John W. Fox, pp. 17–30. Cambridge University Press, Cambridge.

Cobb, Charles R., and Michael S. Nassaney

1995 Interaction and Integration in the Late Woodland Southeast. In *Native American Interactions: Multiscalar Analyses and Interpretation in the Eastern Woodlands*, edited by Michael Nassaney and Kenneth E. Sassaman, pp. 174–204. University of Tennessee Press, Knoxville.

2002 Domesticating Self and Society in the Woodland Southeast. In *The Woodland Southeast*, edited by David G. Anderson and Robert C. Mainfort, Jr., pp. 525-539. The University of Alabama Press, Tuscaloosa.

Creamer, Winifred and Jonathan Haas

1985 Tribe versus Chiefdom in Lower Central America. *American Antiquity* 50:738–754.

Emerson, Thomas E.

1999 The Langford Tradition and the Process of Tribalization on the Middle Mississip-

pian Borders. *Midcontinental Journal of Archaeology* 24:3–56.

Feinman, Gary and Jill Neitzel

1984 Too Many Types: An Overview of Sedentary Prestate Societies in the Americas. In *Advances in Archaeological Method and Theory*, edited by Michael B. Schiffer, pp. 39–102. Academic Press.

Fiedel, Stuart J.

2001 What Happened in the Early Woodland? *Archaeology of Eastern North America* 29:101–142.

Fried, Morton

1968 On the Concepts of "Tribe" and "Tribal Society". In *Essays on the Problem of Tribe*, edited by June Helm, pp. 3–20. American Ethnological Society. Proceedings of the 1967 Annual Spring Meeting. University of Washington Press.

1975 *The Notion of Tribe*. Cummings Publishing Company, Menlo Park California

Friedman, Jonathan

1975 Tribes, States, and Transformations. In *Marxist Analyses and Social Anthropology*, edited by M. Bloch, pp. 161–202. Tavistock, New York.

Friedman, Jonathan, and Michael J. Rowlands

1977 Notes toward an Epigenetic Model of the Evolution of "Civilization." In *The Evolution of Social Systems*, edited by Jonathan Friedman and Michael J. Rowlands, pp. 201–276. University of Pittsburgh Press, Pittsburgh.

Gearing, Fred

1958 The Structural Poses of 18th-century Cherokee Villages. *American Anthropologist* 60:1148–1156.

Gibson, Jon L.

1994 Before Their Time? Early Mounds in the Lower Mississippi Valley. *Southeastern Archaeology* 13:162–186.

1996 Poverty Point and Greater Southeastern Prehistory: The Culture That Did Not Fit. In *Archaeology of the Mid-Holocene Southeast*, edited by Kenneth E. Sassaman and David G. Anderson, pp. 288–305. University Presses of Florida, Gainesville.

2000 *The Ancient Mounds of Poverty Point: Place of Rings*. University Press of Florida, Gainesville.

Gremillion, Kristen J.

1996 The Paleoethnobotanical Record for the Mid-Holocene Southeast In *Archaeology of the Mid-Holocene Southeast*, edited by Kenneth Sassaman and David Anderson, pp. 99–114. University Presses of Florida, Gainesville.

Griffin, James B.
1960 Climatic Change: A Contributory Cause of the Growth and Decline of Northern Hopewellian Culture. *Wisconsin Archaeologist* 41(1):21–33.
1961 Some Correlations of Climatic and Cultural Change in Eastern North American Prehistory. *Annals of the New York Academy of Sciences* 95:710–717.

Gunn, Joel D. (editor)
2000 *The Years Without Summer: Tracing A.D. 536 and its Aftermath*. British Archaeological Reports International Series 872, Archaeopress, London.

Haas, Jonathan, and Winifred Creamer
1993 Stress and Warfare among the Kayenta Anasazi of the Thirteenth Century A.D. *Fieldiana Anthropology*, new series, no. 21. Chicago.

Hally, David J.
1973 The Territorial Size of Mississippian Chiefdoms. In *Archaeology of Eastern North America Papers in Honor of Stephen Williams*, edited by James B. Stoltman, pp. 143–168. Archaeological Report No. 25. Mississippi Department of Archives and History, Jackson.

Hamilton, Fran E.
1999 Southeastern Archaic Mounds: Examples of Elaboration in a Temporally Fluctuating Environment? *Journal of Anthropological Archaeology* 18:344–355.

Jefferies, Richard W.
1995 Late Middle Archaic Exchange and Interaction in the North American Midcontinent. In *Native American Interaction: Multiscalar Analyses and Interpretations in the Eastern Woodlands*, edited by Michael S. Nassaney and Kenneth E. Sassaman, pp. 73–99. University of Tennessee Press, Knoxville.
1996 The Emergence of Long-Distance Exchange Networks in the Southeastern United States. In *Archaeology of the Mid-Holocene Southeast*, edited by Kenneth E. Sassaman and David G. Anderson, pp. 222–234. University Presses of Florida, Gainesville.

Johnson, Gregory
1978 Information Sources and the Development of Decision-making Organizations. In *Social Archaeology beyond Subsistence and Dating*, edited by C. L. Redman, M. J. Berman, E. V. Curtin, W. T. Langhorne, Jr., N. M. Versaggi, and J. C. Wanser, pp. 87–112. Academic Press, New York.
1982 Organization Structure and Scalar Stress. In *Theory and Explanation in Archaeology: The Southampton Conference*, edited by Colin Renfrew, M. J. Rowlands, and Barbara A. Seagraves, pp. 389–421. Academic Press, New York

Johnson, Jay K., and Samuel O. Brookes
1989 Benton Points, Turkey Tails and Cache Blades: Middle Archaic Exchange in the Southeast. *Southeastern Archaeology* 8:134–145.

Kelly, Raymond S.
1985 *The Nuer Conquest: The Structure and Development of an Expansionist System*. University of Michigan Press, Ann Arbor.
1993 *Constructing Inequality: The Fabrication of a Hierarchy of Virtue among the Etoro*. University of Michigan Press, Ann Arbor.

Little, Keith J.
2000 Late Holocene Climate Fluctuations and Culture Change in the Southeastern United States: Evidence from the Tennessee Valley. MA thesis, Department of Anthropology, The University of Alabama.

Marcus, Joyce
1993 Ancient Maya Political Organization. In *Lowland Maya Civilization in the Eighth Century A.D.*, edited by Jeremy A. Sabloff and J. S. Henderson, pp. 111–172. Dunbarton Oaks Research Library and Collection, Washington, D.C.

Marquardt, William and Patty Jo Watson
1983 The Shell Mound Archaic of Western Kentucky. In *Archaic Hunters and Gatherers in the American Midwest*, edited by James Phillips and James Brown, pp. 323–339. Academic Press, New York.

Milner, George R.
1999 Warfare in Prehistoric and Early Historic Eastern North America. *Journal of Archaeological Research* 7:105–151.

Milner, George R., David G. Anderson, and Marvin T. Smith
2002 The Distribution of Eastern Woodlands Peoples at the Prehistoric Historic Interface. In *Societies in Eclipse: Eastern*

North America at the Dawn of History, edited by David S. Brose, C. Wesley Cowan, and Robert C. Mainfort, Jr., pp. 9-18. Smithsonian Institution Press, Washington, D.C.

Morse, Dan F.
1975 Paleoindian in the Land of Opportunity: Preliminary Report on the Excavations at the Sloan Site (3GE94). In *The Cache River Archaeological Project: An Experiment in Contract Archaeology*, assembled by Michael B. Schiffer and John H. House, pp. 93–113. Research Series 8. Arkansas Archaeological Survey, Fayetteville.

1977 The Penetration of Northeast Arkansas by Mississippian Culture. In *For the Director: Research Essays in Honor of James B. Griffin*, edited by Charles E. Cleland, pp. 186–211. Anthropological Papers, no. 61. University of Michigan, Museum of Anthropology, Ann Arbor.

1997 An Overview of the Dalton Period in Northeastern Arkansas and in the Southeastern United States. In *Sloan: A Paleoindian Dalton Cemetery in Arkansas*, edited by Dan F. Morse, pp. 123–139. Smithsonian Institution Press, Washington, D.C.

Morse, Dan. F. (editor)
1997 *Sloan: A Paleoindian Dalton Cemetery in Arkansas*. Smithsonian Institution Press, Washington, D.C.

Morse, Dan F., and Phyllis A. Morse (editors)
1983 *Archaeology of the Central Mississippi Valley*. Academic Press, New York.

Morse, Dan F., and Phyllis A. Morse
1990 Emergent Mississippian in the Central Mississippi Valley. In *The Mississippian Emergence*, edited by Bruce D. Smith, pp. 153–173. Smithsonian Institution Press, Washington, D. C.

Nassaney, Michael S.
2000 The Late Woodland Southeast. In *Late Woodland Societies: Tradition and Transformation across the Midcontinent*, edited by Thomas E. Emerson, Dale L. McElrath, and Andrew C. Fortier, pp. 713–730. University of Nebraska Press, Lincoln.

Nassaney, Michael S., and Charles R. Cobb, (editors)
1991 *Stability, Transformation, and Variation: The Late Woodland Southeast*. Plenum Press, New York.

Neitzel, Jill E. (editor)
1999 *Great Towns and Regional Polities in the Prehistoric American Southwest and Southeast*. Amerind Foundation New World Studies Series 3, University of New Mexico Press, Albuquerque.

Neitzel, Jill E., and David G. Anderson
1999 Multiscalar Analyses of Middle Range Societies: Comparing the Late Prehistoric Southwest and Southeast. In *Great Towns and Regional Polities in the Prehistoric American Southwest and Southeast*, edited by Jill E. Neitzel, 243–254. Amerind Foundation New World Studies Series 3, University of New Mexico Press, Albuquerque.

O'Brien, Michael J.
1995 Archaeological Research in the Central Mississippi Valley: Culture History Gone Awry. *The Review of Archaeology* 16:23–36.

O'Brien, Michael J., and Robert C. Dunnell (editors)
1998 *Changing Perspectives on the Archaeology of the Central Mississippi Valley*. University of Alabama Press, Tuscaloosa.

Pacheco, Paul J. (editor)
1996 *A View from the Core: A Synthesis of Ohio Hopewell Archaeology*. The Ohio Archaeological Council, Inc., Columbus, OH.

Parkinson, William A.
1999 The Social Organization of Early Copper Age Tribes on the Great Hungarian Plain. Unpublished Ph.D. dissertation, Department of Anthropology, University of Michigan, Ann Arbor.

Phillips, James L., and James A. Brown (editors)
1983 *Archaic Hunters and Gatherers in the American Midwest*. Academic Press, New York.

Piatak, Bruce J.
1994 The Tomoko Mound Complex in Northeast Florida. *Southeastern Archaeology* 12:109–118.

Renfrew, Colin
1974 Beyond a Subsistence Economy: The Evolution of Prehistoric Social Organization in Prehistoric Europe. In *Reconstructing Complex Societies*, edited by C. B. Moore, pp. 69–95. Bulletin Supplement, no. 20. American Schools of Oriental Research, Cambridge, Massachusetts.

1975   Trade as Action at a Distance: Questions of Integration and Communication. In *Ancient Civilization and Trade*, edited by J. A. Sabloff and C. C. Lamborg-Karlovsky, pp. 1–60. Albuquerque: University of New Mexico Press.

Rogers, Rhea J.
1995   Tribes as Heterarchy: A Case Study from the Prehistoric Southeastern United States. In *Heterarchy and the Analysis of Complex Societies*, edited by R. M. Ehrenreich, Carole L. Crumley, and Janet E. Levy. Archeological Papers of the American Anthropological Association No. 6:7–16.

Russo, Michael
1991   Archaic Sedentism on the Florida Coast: A Case Study from Horr's Island. Unpublished Ph.D. dissertation, Department of Anthropology, University of Florida. University Microfilms, Ann Arbor, Michigan.

1994a   A Brief Introduction to the Study of Archaic Mounds in the Southeast. *Southeastern Archaeology* 13:89–93.

1994b   Why We Don't Believe in Archaic Ceremonial Mounds and Why We Should: The Case from Florida. *Southeastern Archaeology* 13:93–109.

1996a   Southeastern Preceramic Archaic Ceremonial Mounds. In *Archaeology of the Mid–Holocene Southeast*, edited by Kenneth E. Sassaman and David G. Anderson, pp. 259–287. University Presses of Florida, Gainesville.

1996b   Southeastern Mid-Holocene Coastal Settlements. In *Archaeology of the Mid-Holocene Southeast*, edited by Kenneth E. Sassaman and David G. Anderson, pp. 177–199. University Presses of Florida, Gainesville.

1999   Bigger, Longer, and Uncut: Thresholds of Power at Florida Archaic Shell Rings? Paper presented at the 56th Annual Meeting of the Southeastern Archaeological Conference, Pensacola, Florida.

n.d.   In *Big Mounds, Big Power* (tentative title), edited by Phil Carr and Jon L. Gibson. The University of Alabama Press, Tuscaloosa. Manuscript under review.

Russo, Michael, and Gregory Heide
2001   Shell Rings of the Southeast US. *Antiquity* 75:491–492.

Russo, Michael, and Rebecca Saunders
1999   Identifying the Early Use of Coastal Fisheries and the Rise of Social Complexity in Shell Rings and Arcuate Middens on Florida's Northeast Coast. Project report submitted to the National Geographic Society.

Sahlins, Marshall
1961   The Segmentary Lineage: An Organization of Predatory Expansion. *American Anthropologist* 63(2):332–345.

1963   Poor Man, Rich Man, Big Man, Chief: Political Types in Melanesia and Polynesia. *Comparative Studies in Society and History* 5(3):285–303.

1968   *Tribesmen*. Prentice-Hall, Inc., Englewood Cliffs, N.J.

1972   *Stone Age Economics*. Aldine Publishing Company, New York.

Saitta, Dean J.
1983   On the Evolution of "Tribal" Social Networks. *American Antiquity* 48:820–24.

Sassaman, Kenneth E.
1991   Adaptive Flexibility in the Morrow Mountain Phase of the Middle Archaic Period. *South Carolina Antiquities* 23:31–41.

1993   Early Pottery in the Southeast: Tradition and Innovation in Cooking Technology. University of Alabama Press, Tuscaloosa.

1995   The Cultural Diversity of Interactions Among Mid-Holocene Societies of the American Southeast. In *Native American Interactions: Multiscalar Analyses and Interpretation in the Eastern Woodlands*, edited by Michael Nassaney and Kenneth E. Sassaman, pp. 174–204. University of Tennessee Press, Knoxville.

1996   Technological Innovations in Economic and Social Contexts. In *Archaeology of the Mid-Holocene Southeast*, edited by Kenneth E. Sassaman and David G. Anderson, pp. 57–74. University Presses of Florida, Gainesville.

2001   Hunter-Gatherers and Traditions of Resistance. In *The Archaeology of Traditions: Agency and History before and After Columbus*, edited by Timothy R. Pauketat, pp. 218-236. University Press of Florida, Gainesville.

2002   Woodland Ceramic Beginnings. In *The Woodland Southeast*, edited by David G. Anderson and Robert C. Mainfort, Jr., pp. 398-420. The University of Alabama Press, Tuscaloosa.

Sassaman, Kenneth E., and David G. Anderson (editors)

1996 *Archaeology of the Mid-Holocene Southeast*. University Presses of Florida, Gainesville.

Sassaman, Kenneth, and Jerald Ledbetter

1996 Middle and Late Archaic Architecture. In *Archaeology of the Mid-Holocene Southeast*, edited by Kenneth Sassaman and David Anderson, pp. 75–96. Gainesville: University Press of Florida, Gainesville.

Saunders, Joe, Thurman Allen, and Roger Saucier

1994 Four Archaic? Mound Complexes in Northeast Louisiana. *Southeastern Archaeology* 13:134–153.

Saunders, Joe W., Rolfe D. Mandel, Roger T. Saucier, E. Thurman Allen, C. T. Hallmark, Jay K. Johnson, Edwin H. Jackson, Charles M. Allen, Gary L. Stringer, Douglas S. Frink, James K. Feathers, Stephen Williams, Kristen J. Gremillion, Malcolm F. Vidrine, and Reca Jones

1997 A Mound Complex in Louisiana at 5400–5000 Years Before the Present. *Science* 277:1796–1799.

Scarry, John F., and Claudine Payne

1986 Mississippian Polities in the Fort Walton Area: A Model Generated from the Renfrew-Level XTENT Algorithm. *Southeastern Archaeology* 5:79–90.

Service, Elman R.

1962 *Primitive Social Organization*. Random House New York.

1975 *Origins of the State and Civilization*. W.W. Norton and Company, New York.

Sherratt, Andrew.

1982 What can Archaeologists learn from Annalistes? In *Archaeology, Annales, and Ethnohistory*, edited by B. Knapp, pp. 135–142.

Smith, Bruce D.

1986 The Archaeology of the Southeastern United States: From Dalton to De Soto, 10,500–500 B.P. *Advances in World Archaeology* 5:1–92.

1992 *Rivers of Change: Essays on Early Agriculture in Eastern North America*. Smithsonian Institution Press, Washington, D.C.

Smith, Maria O.

1996 Biocultural Inquiry into Archaic Period Populations of the Southeast: Trauma and Occupational Stress. In *Archaeology of the Mid-Holocene Southeast*, edited by Kenneth Sassaman and David Anderson, pp. 134–154. University Presses of Florida, Gainesville.

Snow, Frankie, and Keith L. Stephenson

1998 Swift Creek Designs: A Tool for Monitoring Interaction. In *A World Engraved: Archaeology of the Swift Creek Culture*, edited by J. Mark Williams and Daniel T. Elliott, pp. 99–111. The University of Alabama Press, Tuscaloosa.

Stephenson, Keith L., Judith A. Bense, and Frankie Snow

2002 Some Aspects of Deptford and Swift Creek of the South Atlantic and Gulf Coastal Plains In *The Woodland Southeast*, edited by David G. Anderson and Robert C. Mainfort, Jr., pp. 318-351. The University of Alabama Press, Tuscaloosa.

Steponaitis, Vincas P.

1986 Prehistoric Archaeology in the Southeastern United States, 1970-1985. *Annual Review of Anthropology* 14:363–404.

Stuiver, Minze, Paula J. Reimer, Edouard Bard, J. Warren Beck, G. S. Burr, Konrad A. Hughen, Bernd Kromer, Gerry McCormac, Johannes van der Plicht, and Marco Spurk

1998 INTCAL98 Radiocarbon Age Calibration, 24,000–0 cal BP. *Radiocarbon* 40(3).

Upham, Steadman (editor)

1990 *The Evolution of Political Systems*. Cambridge University Press, New York.

Walker, Karen J.

2000 A Cooling Episode in Southwest Florida During the Sixth and Seventh Centuries A.D. In *The Years Without Summer: Tracing A.D. 536 and its Aftermath*, edited by Joel D. Gunn, pp. 119–127. British Archaeological Reports International Series 872, Archaeopress, London.

Walthall, John A., and Brad Koldehoff

1998 Hunter-gatherer Interaction and Alliance Formation: Dalton and the Cult of the Long Blade. *Plains Anthropologist* 43:257–273.

Widmer, Randolph

1999 Explaining Sociopolitical Complexity in the Foraging Adaptations of the Southeastern United States. Paper presented at the 56th Annual Meeting of the Southeastern Archaeological Conference, Pensacola, Florida.

n.d.   Explaining Sociopolitical Complexity in the Foraging Adaptations of the Southeastern United States: The Role of Demography, Kinship, and Ecology in Sociocultural Evolution. In *Big Mounds, Big Power* (tentative title), edited by Phil Carr and Jon L. Gibson. The University of Alabama Press, Tuscaloosa. Manuscript under review.

Wright, Henry T.
1984   Prestate Political Formations. In *On the Evolution of Complex Societies, Essays in Honor of Harry Hoijer 1982*, edited by Tim K. Earle, pp. 43-77. Undena Publications, Malibu, CA.

Williams, J. Mark, and Daniel T. Elliott (editors)
1998   *A World Engraved: Archaeology of the Swift Creek Culture*. The University of Alabama Press, Tuscaloosa.

Williams, J. Mark, and Jennifer Freer Harris
1998   Shrines of the Prehistoric South Patterning in Middle Woodland Mound Distribution In *A World Engraved: Archaeology of the Swift Creek Culture*, edited by J. Mark Williams and Daniel T. Elliott, pp. 36–47. The University of Alabama Press, Tuscaloosa.

14. Mesoamerica's Tribal Foundations

John E. Clark and David Cheetham

Archaeological definition of tribal social systems in Mesoamerica has never been attempted. In the absence of good settlement pattern studies all that can be done here is to assume that cultural complexes characterized by sedentary agricultural settlements but lacking community stratification had a tribal social structure. (Sanders and Price 1968:110)

Generally speaking, it is archaeologically a poorly defined stage in the evolution of Mesoamerican society—perhaps because the development of chiefdoms entailed a rapid growth, and the tribal stage would therefore have been of brief duration in many areas. (Sanders and Price 1968:112)

Mesoamerica is the anthropological wasteland of tribal studies. The concept of 'tribe' is not even on the radar screens of most Mesoamericanists, and no adequate case study of an archaeological tribal society from there has yet been published. The profound ironies implicated in this abysmal state of affairs are pivotal because all debates concerning the origins of Mesoamerican civilizations presume tribal foundations and institutions of diverse sorts. But postulated tribal substrates are presumed rather than demonstrated, and cherished tribal assumptions are not subject to archaeological investigation. To our knowledge, Sanders and Price's (1968) exploratory essay on the evolution of Mesoamerican civilization and its eight paragraphs devoted to tribes, their definition, identification, and possible ephemeral existence (epigraphs), was the first and last word on tribal matters. Our purpose here is to revisit some of the issues they raised, and for related reasons of trying to understand evolutionary development.

As with Sanders and Price's exegesis, our efforts here must necessarily confront primordial issues of the whats, whens, wheres, and whys of tribal societies in the geographic segment of Middle America that would later become Mesoamerica, a term that implies a region of cultural practices and beliefs characteristic of chiefdom and state societies. As analytical concepts implicating evolutionary development and cultural practices, the notions of tribes and Mesoamerica are mutually exclusive and complementary. Mesoamerican societies evolved from tribal ones, and to the degree that [Mesoamerican] practices of stratified society expanded, tribalism in Middle America receded. Thus, there has been a logically-necessary, historical and structural complementarity between tribalism and Mesoamerican practices throughout the history of Mesoamerica. How the latter arose from and replaced the former, however, remains to be determined. Before such issues can eventually be addressed adequately, it is first necessary to treat tribes in their own right as viable social formations and not merely as preludes to, or footnotes of, civilized life.

Our purpose here is to organize the extant information and initiate discussion of proto-Mesoamerican tribal societies. In the body of our essay we will be concerned with delimiting the tribal era, identifying possible tribal territories at the close of this period, and exploring mechanisms of tribal social integration. To facilitate comparisons with information from older reports, all chronological considerations are with uncalibrated radiocarbon dates (indicated by lower case bc). The groundwork for addressing questions of social integration comes from our consideration of claims made for four possible tribal societies, representative of the ecological and historical diversity of proto-Mesoamerica. Three are well publicized within the current limits of their datasets (namely, highland Mexico, Valley of Oaxaca, and Coastal Chiapas), and we will only briefly recount claims made for them. We draw the fourth case from the Maya Lowlands of present-day northern Guatemala and Belize, and we treat it in greater detail because it has not been considered previously from a tribal vantage.

Our intent here is to provide a basic database and arguments for future discussions of tribal issues in Middle America. We hope our summaries of the data and proposed interpretations serve as a springboard for more nuanced interpretations in the future. Our effort begins with definitions and a short historical overview of tribal issues in Mesoamerica, followed by four sections of data presentation, and concluding with our preliminary attempt to delimit tribal institutions of social integration as manifested in the four case studies.

Problems with Identifying Proto-Mesoamerican Tribes

Prior to Sanders and Price's (1968) path-breaking book, *Mesoamerica: The Evolution of a Civilization*, the concept of 'tribe' had not been used in Mesoamerican studies in a technical way. And it has rarely been evoked since. The opening epigraphs constitute nearly the entire corpus of methodological and theoretical statements on tribes for this region. As a concept, 'tribe' is inherently sloppy, but even with Sanders and Price's simplified clarification of 'tribal' to mean "sedentary agricultural settlements but lacking community stratification [sic]," few plausible archaeological candidates have ever been suggested, and only two candidates (the Valley of Oaxaca and the Chiapas coast, as discussed below) have been outlined based upon diachronic regional settlement data, as they recommended.

Of the nine possible tribes postulated for all Mesoamerica by Sanders and Price in 1968, only three currently remain possibilities (Ajalpan in the Tehuacán Valley, Cotorra in central Chiapas, and Arévalo in Highland Guatemala); recent archaeological investigations demonstrate that the other six societies were more complex than initial reports of their material remains had suggested. In a case of particular relevance here, Sanders and Price (1968:111) proposed that the Lowland Maya had a tribal organization during the Mamom and early Chicanel phases of the Middle and Late Preclassic periods (ca. 800-100 bc). The emerging consensus now is that the Mamom era saw the emergence of paramount chiefdoms, with the earliest and largest Maya state being in place by 300-200 bc (Clark and Hansen 2000, 2001; Clark et al. 2000; Hammond 2000; R. Hansen 1998; cf. Sharer 1994:117).

Confusing a state or paramount chiefdom for a tribe borders on the spectacular, but given the circumstances of the database in the late 1960s, it was an understandable understatement. Part of the problem of misidentification arises from definitions and expectations, the rest concerns issues

of preservation and sampling of early remains, especially in the tropical climes involved, and the rules of acceptable inference with fuzzy datasets. Tribes are partially defined negatively in terms of what they are not—as much as what they are. Thus, the failure to find, identify, or securely infer clear evidence of social ranking and/or stratification carries the interpretive consequence of making the cultures involved, by default, appear egalitarian and tribal. But finding such evidence, particularly at the beginning of a research project, is rare. With this definitional logic, the absence of any evidence for social ranking or stratification is accorded equal analytical weight as positive evidence for sedentism or agriculture. The inappropriate logical leap of making positive inferences from the absence of information has been the cause of most misidentifications of tribal societies in Mesoamerica, under whatever label.

A further word about the archaeological record of Middle America sets the stage for our treatment of possible tribes. Although there is scattered evidence of early big-game hunters throughout the length and breadth of the region that would become Mesoamerica (Gonzalez Jácome 1987; Hester 2001; MacNeish 1986, 2001b, 2001c; MacNeish and Nelken-Terner 1983; Mirambell 2000; Stark 1981; Zeitlin and Zeitlin 2000), towards the end of the hunting and gathering period (ca. 3500-1800 bc), the heavy reliance on chipped stone tools (bifaces and scrapers) dropped out in most regions. This leads to another irony that obscures identification of tribal groups. With the notable exception of groups who lived in what is now northern Belize (see below), the tail end of the Late Archaic, the critical prelude to the Early Formative period, was basically a post-stone projectile points and pre-pottery era, so these sites are exceptionally difficult to identify because durable diagnostic artifacts in any medium are lacking. Roughly-shaped ground stone tools and fire-cracked cobbles are sometimes present but are not diagnostic in and of themselves. The trend towards archaeological invisibility, due to the replacement of formal chipped stone tools by perishable tools and the move to open-air sites, is surely significant in its own right as an indicator of subsistence and technological changes that were taking place during the period from 2500 to 1600 bc. Importantly, the various highland caves that provide the general Middle America Archaic sequence reveal almost no traces of use for this critical period—and the absence of evidence in these dry caves cannot be explained by the lack of non-perishable artifacts. The meager evidence for all proto-Mesoamerica suggests, in fact, a dramatic shift in settlement at this time (MacNeish 1986).

Towards A Working Definition of Tribal Societies

Issues of definition must be resolved before headway can be made on identifying tribes in the proto-Mesoamerican archaeological record. In prior drafts of this paper we were frustrated in our attempts to identify tribes because we made two operational decisions that undermined our objective at the start. First, we pursued the concept of tribe as outlined by Sanders and Price (epigraph) because their definition makes pragmatic allowance for problems with the thin archaeological record in question. In their working definition, the three pillars of tribalism are the presence of agriculture, sedentism, and egalitarianism. Societies having these characteristics are clearly tribal, but this definition sets tribal membership too high to be useful for our current project as it only provides space for complex tribes or village tribalism. Numerous tribal societies known cross-culturally are not sedentary, and others lack agriculture, so these criteria cannot serve as universal characteristics of tribalism. The only common characteristic all ethnographic tribes share with Sanders and Price's 'tribes' is the presence of 'egalitarianism' (meaning achieved rather than ascribed social statuses), but in Sanders and Price's usage, egalitarianism is a negative trait better understood as the absence of social stratification. This definition is too inclusive because it fails to distinguish between social stratification and hereditary rank.

We compounded our first misstep with another by approaching the task of identifying tribes as if they were unitary phenomena, believing that the impoverished data from proto-Mesoamerican preceramic sites would not allow us to move beyond simple distinctions. Our monolithic thinking created a nest of problems that we could only resolve by fragmenting the tribal concept into possible sub-types. In the real world, tribal social formations cover an impressive array of social complexity, as essays in this book attest. And the principal identifying attributes vary according to the spatial and temporal scales involved, as Fowles and Parkinson note in their opening essay (this volume). We explore various temporal and spatial scales here for possible proto-Mesoamerican tribal societies. For current purposes we proceed with the assumption that the analytical category of 'tribe'

is intermediate between others representing groupings of lesser and greater social complexity. Critical to these distinctions are mechanisms and practices of social integration (Service 1971). As such, analytical isolation of an archaeological tribe involves the dual tasks of differentiating it from simpler band and more complex, chiefdom forms. Distinguishing tribes from chiefdoms is not entirely straightforward (cf. Marcus and Flannery 1996:76, 92-110), but it is the easier of the two tasks as it involves a qualitative distinction between egalitarian and non-egalitarian or ranking systems. We take the presence of institutionalized, hereditary inequalities among adult males, or what are variously described as rank or simple chiefdom societies, to signal the end of tribalism in any given archaeological sequence. The distinction between bands and tribes at the other end of the social continuum is much more difficult to make or to identify archaeologically as both involve small-scale, egalitarian societies. But its very difficulty calls into question the analytical utility of making this tough distinction.

The emergence of tribal societies from bands has not been addressed in the Mesoamerican literature, and given the difficulty of making the distinction and the minor interpretive gain, it is not critical for our analysis that we achieve razor precision on this question. In reality, the data for the time periods involved are so scant that theoretical arguments over the precise dawn of tribalism will have no practical effect on our analysis. For current purposes we consider tribal societies to be larger and more integrated than bands, the latter essentially being nomadic, nuclear or extended family groups. Tribes represent a shift in organization and thus are more than momentary amalgamations of small bands into macro-band groups. Here we consider minimal tribes to be integrated above the level of extended families, perhaps consisting of 30 or more people. Such groups would have been smaller than many postulated macro-bands; however, the issue is not transitory group sizes but institutions of long-term social integration.

Following this logic, we suggest that distinctions among types of tribal groups accord with their scale and/or institutions for achieving social cohesion. Compared to band societies, tribes represent an advance in scale and integration of egalitarian groups, and they are identified archaeologically by evidence of either or both. Thus, nucleated villages are by definition evidence of integration and scale, and one need only determine whether they operated on egalitarian or ascription principles to decide whether they were tribal villages or chiefdoms.

The link between tribes and agriculture is less obvious. We follow distinctions made by others for increasing levels of subsistence commitment, from plant tending, cultivation, and horticulture, to agriculture (see Piperno and Pearsall 1998:6-7). Strictly defined as "larger scale field systems," we think that agriculture signals the presence of at least tribal-level societies, given group commitments to land, crop tending, creation of surplus, storage, and so on. On the other hand, we do not see any necessary connection between the beginnings of plant manipulation or domestication with tribalism. We associate different scales of tribalism with subsistence practices in a scheme analogous to Madsen's (1982) nomadic foragers to sedentary collectors continuum for the Great Basin groups of the American West. His analysis was brought to our attention after we tumbled onto the current distinctions, so any similarities in the typologies and their purported meanings are strictly accidental.

Our claim that tribal societies have been ignored in the Mesoamerican literature rests on a technical distinction that we need to clarify before proceeding to consider data issues. We refer to the use of this particular analytical category of evolutionary analysis and not to questions of any past reality of tribal societies in proto-Mesoamerica or to archaeological discussions of these past societies under different labels and schema. The same social entities considered 'tribes' following Service's (1971) early views, have just as fruitfully been considered from other theoretical perspectives as 'egalitarian' (Fried 1967; Service 1975), as 'agricultural villages' or 'tribal villages' (Piña Chan 1975:65), as 'egalitarian agricultural societies' (Matos 2000), as 'permanent villages' (McClung de Tapia and Zurita 2000), as 'autonomous villages' (Marcus and Flannery 1996), 'egalitarian villages' (Marcus and Flannery 2001), or even as 'primitive communities [*comunidad primitiva*]' (Nalda 1981). The notion of 'tribe' puts a premium on social characteristics while the other concepts emphasize politics and/or economics. Each category derives from explanatory schemes that privilege certain causal factors in the evolutionary process. Sanders and Price's (1968) proposal for studying tribal societies never got off the ground because Mesoamerican scholars continued to favor concepts derived from Lewis Henry Morgan's *Ancient Society* or Marxism which have emphasized the economic base or modes of production. These are more easily operationalized archaeologically, and Nalda (1997) argues that they provide better theoretical grounding than the category of 'tribe' and are also superior in their historical perspective (vs. the synchrony of tribes). In sum, the theoretical preference in the Mesoamerican literature has privileged, and continues to privilege, subsistence practices and technologies over tribes—the transition from hunter-gatherer societies to agricultural societies (Stark 1981, 1986). However, these categories roughly parallel aspects of the 'tribal' concept; therefore, it is possible to extract from the literature evidence of tribal societies that are not described as such.

Delimiting the Tribal Era

Distinctions and definitions of past social entities aside, we have to deal with the contours of extant archaeological data for inferring the presence of tribes in proto-Mesoamerica and their duration. Most evidence considered here concerns the end of the tribal era about 1200 bc, with its beginnings being much more nebulous at 5000-3000 bc, depending on the region. There are different plausible beginning dates for proto-Mesoamerican tribes depending on the principal distinguishing criterion one champions as critical. The most likely possibilities are listed in Table 1. Here we take as our surrogate measure, or secondary indicator, of tribalism the significant investment in horticulture, as roughly indicated by the clear presence of domesticated plants such as corn in the archaeological record about 5000 bc. The tending and manipulation of plants long antedate this era in many places of the neotropics (Piperno and Pearsall 1998), but these activities most likely were part of band-level, hunting-and-gathering subsistence strategies. Consequently, we do not think it appropriate to bind tribal beginnings to the earliest evidence of cultivated and/or domesticated plants. As argued by Piperno and Pearsall (1998), the 5000 bc date represents a noticeable shift in subsistence and land-use patterns and dependency on cultivated crops. We take it as the earliest plausible date for tribal beginnings in proto-Mesoamerica.

The next significant shift in the Late Archaic record occurred at about 2500 bc all across the lowlands. The evidence largely comes from sediment cores that show consistent changes in vegetation communities characteristic of deforestation (reduction in the arboreal pollens), massive burning (a dramatic increase in the percentage of carbon particulates), and greater reliance on clearly domesticated plants such as corn, manioc, and sweet potato (for summaries see Fedick 2001; Piperno and Pearsall 1998; Pohl et al. 1996; Pope et al. 2001; Rue 1989). These data are interpreted as evidence of slash-and-burn [swidden] agriculture and agricultural intensification—practices that continued until the rise of permanent villages about 1600-1400 bc. It is worth noting that this final period of the Late Archaic is poorly known in the Mexican

Highlands as few occupations have been found in the numerous known caves. This shift away from natural shelters, presumably to open sites, implies a basic change in subsistence and settlement patterns for the highlands during this period. The known lowland sites and occupational traces are small and dispersed, suggesting a practice of shifting cultivation and small hamlets. Increased population and group size, greater settlement perma-

Table 1. Chronological variability in prehistoric Mesoamerican tribal societies.

Region	Preceramic, Early Corn, bc	Youngest Late Archaic, bc	Oldest Pottery, bc	Earliest Ranking, bc	Village Tribal Period
1. West Mexico	1500 Patzcuaro	1700 lower Ceboruco 1500 Patzcuaro	1400-1000 Capacha & El Opeño	1000 San Felipe 1100-800 El Opeño ?	600-400
2. Valley of Mexico	5090 pollen, kernels Tlapacoya	2000 Zohapilco	1550 Tlalpan	1150 Tlapacoya	400
3. Puebla-Tlaxcala	5000-2500, pollen? Tlaxcala	2500? Texcal Cave	1500 Tzompantepec	1150? Las Bocas	350?
4. South Puebla	3500? San Marcos Cave	2500-2000 Abejas Cave	1600 Purrón	>850 sites Tr 369, Tr 363	<750
5. Central Guerrero	no data	no data	1400 Cacahuananche	1000 Teopantecuanitlán	400
6. Valley of Oaxaca	7300, pollen Guilá Naquitz	2000 Martínez shelter	1550 Espirdión	1200-1150 San José Mogote	300
7. North Veracruz & South Tamaulipas	2200, corn cob	1800-1400 Romero Cave	1600 Chajil	1100 Altamirano	500
8. North Central Veracruz	no data	2400 Santa Luisa	1600 Raudal	1100 Santa Luisa	500
9. Central Veracruz	no data	2400 Colonia Ejidal	1500 unnamed	1100 El Viejón	400
10. Southern Veracruz	2250, pollen Laguna Pompal	2000 Laguna Pompal	1500 Ojochi	1300 San Lorenzo	200
11. Tabasco	4800, pollen San Andrés cores	2100 San Andrés	1400 Molina	1100 Zapata	300
12. Central Chiapas	4500, pollen Santa Marta	1600-1450? Camcum shelter	1450 Lato & Aripi	1100 Mirador-Miramar	350
13. Coastal Chiapas	2500, phytoliths Tlacuachero	1800 Chantuto	1600 Barra	1400 Paso de la Amada	200
14. Coastal Guatemala	3500, phytoliths Sipacate SIP001	2500 pollen, burning Sipacate SIP99E	1600 Madre Vieja	1300 Grajeda	300
15. Highland Guatemala	no data	1000? Quiché Basin	950 Arévalo	800 Kaminaljuyú	150
16. Lowland Guatemala	3600 disturbance, Petén Lakes	1500-900 Petén Lakes	900 Eb	850 Tikal and Uaxactun?	50
17. Belize	3500, pollen Cob & Cobweb	1500-1100 Colhá	1000 Cunil	900 Cahal Pech	100
18. Northern Honduras	3000, pollen Lake Yojoa core	1700? Puerto Escondido	1600 Barrahona	1300 Puerto Escondido	300
19. Western Honduras	2200, pollen Petapilla core 2	1700 Copán	1450 Rayo	1000 Copán	350
20. El Salvador	no data	2000 La Periquita	1550 Bostán	1000 Chalchuapa	550

nence, and smaller collecting ranges are all implicated in the changing patterns (see Piperno and Pearsall 1998).

The beginning of the end for tribalism was the emergence of nucleated agricultural villages about 1600-1400 bc in most of proto-Mesoamerica. Because these early villages lack any of the clear markers of hereditary rank or social stratification (i.e., elite burials, special residential architecture, or abnormal clumps of wealth), they are presumed to have been egalitarian and hence tribal. In all cases, villages are associated with the first use of pottery, and vice versa. Thus, pottery serves as a handy surrogate measure of the rise of village life in the data listed in Table 1. For some areas of Mesoamerica, such as Tehuacan and Guerrero, pottery was thought to long antedate the first villages, but as Clark and Gosser (1995) argue, these earliest dates for ceramics cannot withstand close scrutiny. The best data indicate the co-occurrence of ceramics and village life.

Excluding the 11 pollen traces, the 54 Late Archaic occupational sites known for proto-Mesoamerica (see Appendix 1B) were seasonal habitation sites such as rock shelters, or specialized open air sites such as shell middens or chert sources (Hester et al. 1996; Voorhies 1996). Many may represent small hamlets of shifting cultivators (Piperno and Pearsall 1998) who made logistic forays from semi-permanent base-camps and small hamlets to specialized sites to procure resources such as chert, obsidian, game animals, or shellfish.

The favored beginning date for tribes in proto-Mesoamerica depends on one's theoretical leanings, primary definitions, and interpretations of anemic evidence. We take the moderate view here that tribalism began with a significant reliance on domestic plants and horticulture about 5000 bc and ended with the rise of rank societies about 1400-1100 bc, thereby bracketing a tribal period of approximately four millennia. Different kinds of tribalism were involved, with increases in social complexity and scale through time, until the emergence of rank societies. A more conservative reading of the data would shorten the tribal period by starting it at 3000-2500 bc to correspond with the onset of shifting slash-and-burn agriculture and small hamlets of collectors or semi-sedentary farmers. An even more conservative view would be to return to Sanders and Price's original prescription and consider only egalitarian villagers as tribal. This was our initial bias in collecting the data, but we now consider it an indefensible position. The events and processes that culminated in the way of

life that appears archaeologically as permanent villages of ceramic-using agriculturalists represented another significant shift from previous practices, but we believe it was to more complex forms of tribal organization from simpler ones, rather than from non-tribal to tribal organization. Most groups in proto-Mesoamerica adopted pottery and village life by about 1400 bc and had developed or adopted social ranking or chiefdom organization by 1000 bc. Thus, the period we consider as advanced tribalism (i.e., village tribes) lasted only four centuries or less in most regions. Our coarse-grained overview of the tribal era and possible changes in scale and complexity through time suggest that sedentary village life was antithetical to tribal lifeways because group egalitarianism did not long survive after the emergence of villages in any known region of proto-Mesoamerica.

A Census of Proto-Mesoamerican Tribal Societies

The tribal challenge for Middle America is how to interpret scant evidence, or its shadows. Data from lake and swamp sediment cores demonstrate that much more was going on at 2500-1600 bc than is clearly evident in any recovered artifacts (Table 1). We have plotted all verified Late Archaic sites and pollen traces in Fig. 1 (see Appendix 1:A-D for documentation and critical commentary for Table 1 and Figs. 1-3). With the exception of northern Belize, proto-Mesoamerica was a sparsely populated place during the terminal Late Archaic period (MacNeish 1986; Stark 1981, 1986, 2000; Voorhies 1996; Zeitlin and Zeitlin 2000). This impression is corroborated by the low frequency of subsequent early pottery sites as well (Fig. 2). One possible explanation for the paucity of Late Archaic sites, therefore, is that there are not that many out there to find. Of course, a related problem is the lack of diagnostic, non-perishable artifacts for this period in all areas except northern Belize (see Hester et al. 1996; Iceland 1997; Zeitlin 1984). There are few sites, and the ones known have almost no significant depth. If these remains indeed represent residues left by past tribal societies, tribes were few and widely dispersed.

The sites and traces of human occupations shown in Fig. 1 are more or less contemporaneous and convey an impression of population distribution and density during the terminal Archaic (earlier Archaic sites are not shown). These sites represent the 'pre-ceramic,' Late Archaic. In contrast,

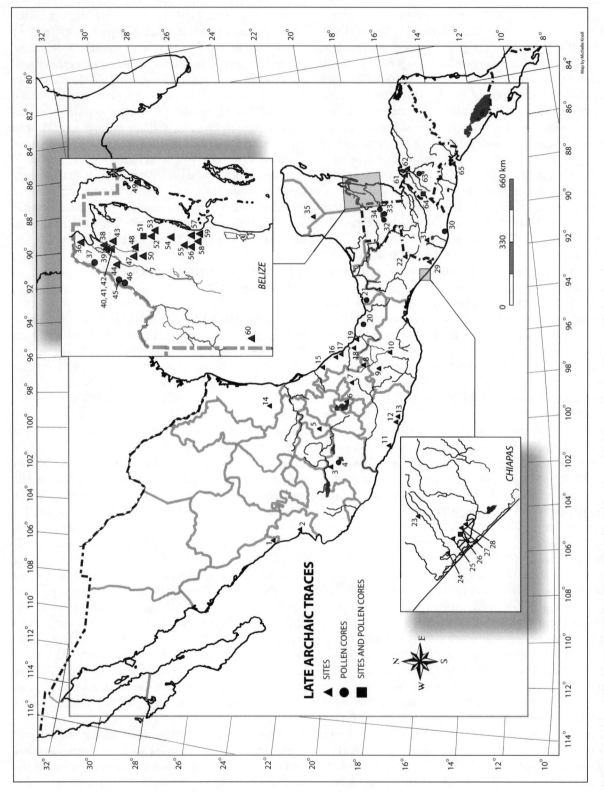

Fig. 1 Map of proto-Mesoamerica showing the distribution of the youngest Late Archaic sites.

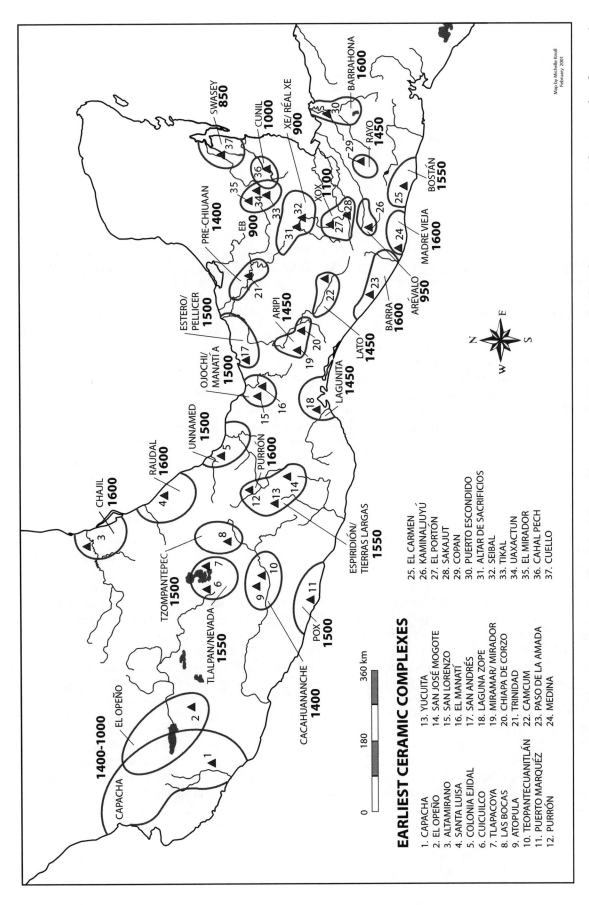

EARLIEST CERAMIC COMPLEXES

1. CAPACHA	13. YUCUITA
2. EL OPEÑO	14. SAN JOSÉ MOGOTE
3. ALTAMIRANO	15. SAN LORENZO
4. SANTA LUISA	16. EL MANATÍ
5. COLONIA EJIDAL	17. SAN ANDRÉS
6. CUICUILCO	18. LAGUNA ZOPE
7. TLAPACOYA	19. MIRAMAR/ MIRADOR
8. LAS BOCAS	20. CHIAPA DE CORZO
9. ATOPULA	21. TRINIDAD
10. TEOPANTECUANITLÁN	22. CAMCUM
11. PUERTO MARQUÉZ	23. PASO DE LA AMADA
12. PURRÓN	24. MEDINA

25. EL CARMEN	
26. KAMINALJUYÚ	
27. EL PORTÓN	
28. SAKAJUT	
29. COPAN	
30. PUERTO ESCONDIDO	
31. ALTAR DE SACRIFICIOS	
32. SEIBAL	
33. TIKAL	
34. UAXACTUN	
35. EL MIRADOR	
36. CAHAL PECH	
37. CUELLO	

Fig. 2 Map of proto-Mesoamerica showing the distribution of the earliest pottery for each ceramic complex. Outlined areas represent the area of each ceramic complex.

285

Fig. 2 displays the distribution of early ceramic complexes and their most probable dates. We consider the style zones of the earliest pottery in each region to be the best indicators of possible tribal territories at the close of the tribal era. As mentioned, early pottery also serves as an indirect measure of village sedentism (see Arnold 1999 for a speculative critique of the supposed link between pottery use and sedentism for early Mesoamerica). As mapped in Fig. 2, delimited zones of early pottery use do not represent contemporaneous phenomena but rather a temporal series for the spread and adoption of ceramic technology. Of particular interest here are a pair of facts: First, pottery was adopted *simultaneously* in the different corners of proto-Mesoamerica about 1600-1500 bc (see Clark and Gosser 1995), and second, the Maya Lowlands was the last major sector of proto-Mesoamerica to adopt pottery. We explore implications of the Maya case in following discussion, but for now we observe that one reason for the significantly greater number of Late Archaic sites in northern Belize may be that the Late Archaic (i.e., aceramic) period there persisted 600 years longer than elsewhere and is not deeply buried under recent alluvium. In fact, the Late Preceramic period (1500-900 bc; Iceland 1997) in Belize aligns with the first three to five pottery phases along the Pacific and Gulf Coasts and in the central Mexican highlands, regions that during this interval included scores of small villages and hamlets and some capital centers (Clark 1997). A strictly contemporaneous comparison of population distribution at 1200-1000 bc would show Belize as sparsely populated compared to other occupied regions of Mesoamerica. This temporal lag in social developments is clearly evident in Table 1. Most areas of Mesoamerica had chiefdom societies before the peoples of the Maya Lowlands brought themselves to accept pottery and other civilizing ways.

Fig. 3 provides visual confirmation of the temporal progression and spread of social practices. Note the succession of dates for the earliest evidence of social ranking from region to region. By 'ranking' we refer to evidence for hereditary rank, or social practices most would attribute to simple chiefdom societies. We have not attempted to be exhaustive in our listings in Table 1 and Fig. 3 of all rank societies in Mesoamerica; rather, we attempt broad coverage of proto-Mesoamerica to provide a simplified picture of the origin and growth of Mesoamerica as a region of high culture. Assessments of the beginnings of ranking are particularly difficult when data are scarce, so many of our

identifications will be viewed by some as either overly generous or stingy. All we are attempting here is the best precision allowed by the nature of the extant evidence and its measuring devices so that broad patterns will still become clear despite some fuzzy data points. In all cases the pattern is the familiar one of early events having subsequent effects in time and space. All three phenomena listed in Table 1 (early corn, pottery, and ranking) follow this pattern. As detailed in the accompanying appendices, we have trimmed or restored a century here and there to various original claims for absolute chronology to bring phenomena in line with recent findings. More temporal refinements will be necessary, and will occur, but for now the data listed are as current and chronologically accurate as we can make them.

The distributions in Figs. 1-3 provide the essential information concerning the territorial presence and duration of tribal societies in proto-Mesoamerica, and for their spread and later usurpation. These data, as well as those listed in Table 1, bracket the tribal era, beginning with the appearance of horticulture and ending with the emergence of simple chiefdom or rank societies. In comparing Figs. 1-3, what is noteworthy is the *displacement* of the first ceramic-using villagers from the places favored by Late Archaic peoples. With few exceptions, Late Archaic remains do not underlie those of the earliest Formative (see MacNeish 1986:122). The three sites with aceramic deposits directly or shallowly beneath those of ceramic-bearing layers (Appendix 1B: 22. Camcum, 23. Vuelta Limón, and 61. Puerto Escondido) are problematic as the deposits are only hypothesized to be Late Archaic because pot sherds are absent in the very lowest levels, but these may merely be aceramic, Early Formative deposits. At most other sites with underlying Archaic levels there is a significant depositional discontinuity of nearly a millennium between Late Archaic deposits and later, overlying ceramic ones, so no continuity of occupation is implicated. In fact, the discontinuity is so striking in most instances that it can only be by chance rather than social memory that the superimposition occurred (Appendix 1B: 6. Zohapilco/Tlapacoya, 15. Santa Luisa, 18. Colonia Ejidal, 29. San Carlos, and 64. Copán). This superimposition highlights the second discontinuity evident in Table 1. There is a substantial chronological gap in most regions between the latest Late Archaic and the earliest Early Formative. This gap corresponds precisely to the missing period in most highland cave sequences.

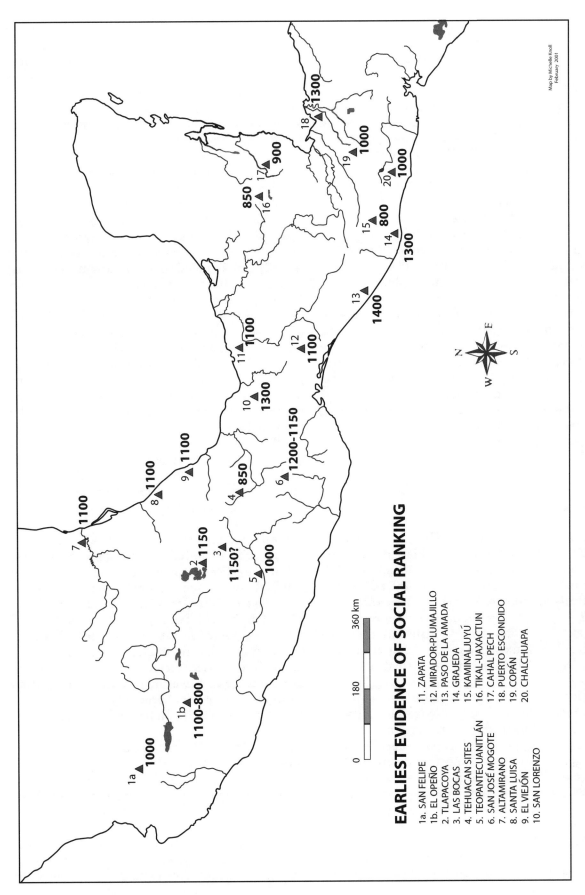

EARLIEST EVIDENCE OF SOCIAL RANKING

1a. SAN FELIPE
1b. EL OPEÑO
2. TLAPACOYA
3. LAS BOCAS
4. TEHUACAN SITES
5. TEOPANTECUANITLÁN
6. SAN JOSÉ MOGOTE
7. ALTAMIRANO
8. SANTA LUISA
9. EL VIEJÓN
10. SAN LORENZO

11. ZAPATA
12. MIRADOR-PLUMAJILLO
13. PASO DE LA AMADA
14. GRAJEDA
15. KAMINALJUYÚ
16. TIKAL-UAXACTUN
17. CAHAL PECH
18. PUERTO ESCONDIDO
19. COPÁN
20. CHALCHUAPA

Map by Michelle Knoll
February 2001

Fig. 3 Map of Mesoamerica showing the earliest rank centers in each area.

Early Formative and terminal Late Archaic sites seldom are found in the same locations, so excavation of one type of site rarely reveals evidence of the other. We believe the spatial and temporal disjunctions between these sites signal different subsistence and settlement pursuits and priorities. The gap at the end of the Archaic period implies a shift in tribal strategies and possibly of integrative mechanisms. We noted the widespread evidence in the lowlands of Middle America for significant forest clearance and cultivation of corn (and other cultigens) about 2500 bc. Viewed in broader context, these linked phenomena give rise to three important observations.

First, the earliest occurrence of cultigens in the archaeological record about 7000 bc did not correspond to any obvious shift in hunting-and-gathering lifestyles. There are no positive archaeological indications of changes in group size or habitation permanence, nor any notable impact on the environment corresponding to the first appearance of cultigens. The first evidence of a minor change is with the adoption of horticulture about 5000 bc, thus our preference for making this the earliest plausible date for the beginnings of minimal tribal societies in proto-Mesoamerica.

Second, the peoples who started burning and clearing forests for agricultural fields and/or hunting practices about 3000-2500 bc are almost archaeologically invisible in terms of artifacts. Our knowledge of them comes from paleobotanical data that indicate that corn, manioc, sweet potatoes, and other managed plants had become much more significant in peoples' diets by this time (Piperno and Pearsall 1998). The very artifactual invisibility of these peoples, coupled with the pollen and soot trails of their shifting cultivation and forest clearance, suggest a change from more mobile lifeways to exploitation of different resource patches. We think this dark period of prehistory (2500-1600 bc) was the heyday of tribalism across proto-Mesoamerica as slash-and-burn agriculture and cultigens spread and became more important. The temporal discontinuities suggest exploitation of different resource patches, and in different ways.

Third, we previously acknowledged the spatial disjunction between Late Archaic sites and the permanent hamlets and villages of the earliest pottery-users. These ceramic-users were sedentary villagers and, in most instances, dependent on agriculture for a livelihood. Presumably they chose the best overall locations to settle down and plant their favored crops, whether cereals or tubers. That earlier peoples had not occupied the same ground is therefore significant for tribal questions. If these ghostly Archaic lowlanders were sedentary, they chose to park themselves elsewhere—presumably exploiting a different suite of natural resources than during subsequent periods of increasing reliance on agriculture, or following a different strategy for incorporating horticultural pursuits within their mixed economies.

In contradistinction to the Late Archaic-to-Formative spatio-temporal disjunction and its entailed shift in cultural practices, the transition from early hamlets to ranked villages was one of spatial *continuity*. Most sites shown in Fig. 3 were also the earliest villages in their regions and the epicenters of distinct ceramic complexes and styles (Fig. 2) that signaled zones of intimate social and economic contact. In reductionist terms, it looks like early villages grew into big villages—that tribal village societies invented or adopted institutions of ascribed ranking. This observation falls well short of being an explanation, but it does appear obvious that sedentism and agriculture were integral to the basic process of institutionalizing social inequality and that these twin practices became common towards the end of the period we consider the tribal era.

We drew attention to the continuity between early pottery-using villages and the rise of social ranking or, put differently, of the 'tribal demise,' but we abstained from attributing the process of tribal usurpation to ecological factors or to natural social growth. The data in Table 1 (Figs. 1-3) show that ranking spread through time and space, meaning that history mattered in the dispersal of these cultural practices. Rank societies in coastal Chiapas and highland Oaxaca and Mexico arguably could have developed under pristine conditions (Clark 1997), but those in the Maya Lowlands were surely derivative or secondary (Cheetham 1998). The early Lowland Maya were among the last peoples in proto-Mesoamerica to forego their tribal ways. The same tardiness, however, cannot be claimed for the emergence of tribal practices themselves, as a consideration of individual tribal histories shows.

Diverse Tribal Histories and Adaptations

Information concerning the development and organization of tribal societies is available from four distinct environmental regions of proto-Mesoamerica. From case to case the data are extremely uneven and incomplete, but they are all that are currently available for cobbling together a picture

288

of possible proto-Mesoamerican tribal institutions. Here we briefly review well-published cases from the highland valleys of Mexico and Oaxaca and coastal Chiapas, Mexico, and we devote more space to making a case for the Lowland Maya of Belize. Unlike the other three cases, we consider two descending regional scales of analysis for the Lowland Maya. Our principal interest in reviewing these tribal histories is to draw out evidence proposed by various scholars of integrative, egalitarian social practices in proto-Mesoamerica.

Lacustrine tribal adaptations in the Valley of Mexico

A 50 meter-long trench excavated in 1969 by Christine Niederberger (1976, 1979, 1987, 1996) through stratified fossil beaches at the site of Zohapilco-Tlapacoya (Fig. 1:6), located on the shore of Lake Chalco-Xochimilco in the southern Basin of Mexico, provides the best information for an Archaic-to-Formative sequence for the temperate highlands of Mexico. Although there are no adequate Archaic settlement pattern data for this highland basin, information from Zohapilco (the Archaic component) and Tlapacoya (the Formative component) provide critical diachronic data for addressing tribal issues.

Starting at 5500 bc with the Playa phase (5500-3500 bc), there was a nearly continuous occupation at this lake shore site; the two significant interruptions (at 3500-2500 and 2000-1450 bc) relate to rises in lake levels and/or devastating effects of local volcanic eruptions. Niederberger (1996, 2000) argues for a slow, local evolutionary process from proto-agriculture to the rise of rank societies at Tlapacoya (about 1150 bc) and for early sedentism and horticulture. Zohapilco was a favorable location for human occupation through time because of "splendid landscapes and abundant resources" and an "extraordinary ecological bounty" that provided food resources during all seasons of the year (Niederberger 1996:83).

Studies of ancient landscapes and faunal, pollen, and archaeological remains have shown that the shores of the freshwater Chalco-Xochimilco lake at Tlapacoya-Zohapilco was occupied year-round by pre- or protoagricultural communities as early as the sixth millennium B.C. (Niederberger 1987). Its inhabitants had access to nearby and diversified ecological zones. They exploited a lacustrine environment rich with fishes, turtles, and amphibians or resident aquatic birds, such as coots and Mexican ducks, as well as migratory geese, grebes,

and ducks, including pintails, mallards, shovelers, teals, and red-heads. On riverine fertile alluvial soils, horticultural experiments were already underway; they also took advantage of the resources of the neighboring pine-oak-alder forests, habitat of small and large mammals such as the white-tail deer.

During the third millennium B.C., agricultural practices with such plants as maize, amaranth, green tomato, squash, chayote, and chili pepper were fully implemented. Zohapilco's inhabitants then used larger and more standardized stone-grinding tools (Niederberger 1996:84).

In terms of our more general concern with the emergence of tribal societies in Mesoamerica, Zohapilco at 5500 bc provides the earliest evidence of sedentism (pre-ceramic) and horticulture, the latter involving the minor use of cereals that would become significant staples for later peoples. Of particular interest is the possibility of "marked territorial stability" at this early date, based largely on naturally-available resources (Niederberger 1979:141). Most of the information, however, concerns paleo-environments and subsistence practices rather than mechanisms of social integration. We do not know how extensive Zohapilco was during any given occupation or how it related to other settlements or camps in the same region. De Terra (1959) reports two other possible, contemporaneous Middle Archaic sites near the shores of the various connected lakes in the Basin of Mexico. One deposit dating to about 4500 bc was recovered beneath the Formative levels at Tlatilco, to the west, and an occupation surface with two stone-lined hearths, an adult burial, and a variety of cutting and grinding stone tools was recovered to the north on Lake Texcoco at San Vicente Chicoloapan.

On the map of early pottery distributions (Fig. 2), we represent the earliest ceramics at Tlapacoya and the Basin of Mexico as the Nevada complex, although it is younger than the postulated and poorly-known Tlalpan complex from across the lake at Cuicuilco (Appendix 1C:6). The distribution of Nevada pottery is largely hypothetical pending more data from other early sites. It is important to point out that this early pottery relates most closely to that from highland Oaxaca, to the southeast, and there is some evidence of early trade between these two highland regions (Niederberger 2000). Unfortunately, the Nevada phase (ca. 1400-1250 bc) at Tlapacoya is poorly represented, so we lack details of village tribalism beyond the artifacts themselves, which consist principally of potsherds, a few ceramic figurine fragments, and stone tools. At the neighboring center of Tlatilco located across the lake, for the following Ayotla phase (ca. 1250-1000 bc) archaeologists have found numerous burials with vessel and figurine offerings, including occasional ceramic masks and rattles (García Moll et al. 1991), both of which may relate to dancing and public rituals.

It is not clear, however, how many inferences about antecedent tribal institutions one can squeeze from data concerning subsequent rank systems. The earliest evidence of significant social distinctions and possibly of inherited leadership in Tlapacoya and neighboring regional centers are Ayotla phase ceramic figurines that depict adult males in towering headdresses and elaborate shaman and/or ballplayer's garb (Bradley and Joralemon 1993)—perhaps indicating that the source of some of their legitimacy came from participation in these public activities and rituals. Some of the costume items depicted on the human male figurines, such as mirrors and jade jewelry, were included in high-status burials at Tlatilco and Tlapacoya (Niederberger 1996, 2000). Information from other contemporaneous regions of proto-Mesoamerica support the idea that both shamanism and ball-playing were tribal institutions deeded to later Mesoamerican societies and were important mechanisms of tribal social integration. Ceramic masks for covering the lower-half of one's face are known from Tlatilco (also portrayed on early figurines) and have been interpreted as evidence of dance societies; they certainly do indicate public rituals and occasions of some kind that likely go back to the tribal era (see Lesure 1997, 1999).

Riverine tribal adaptations in the Valley of Oaxaca

In contrast to the site-specific information from the Basin of Mexico, the Valley of Oaxaca provides the best diachronic and synthetic data for evaluating tribal societies in Middle America. The Oaxaca sequence extends back to 9000 bc and is continuous until the present-day (Flannery et al. 1981; Marcus and Flannery 1996). Early occupations in this semi-arid highland valley are known from caves, rockshelters, and a few open-air sites; later occupations hug the banks of the few small rivers that bisect the three, long branch valleys that comprise the greater Valley of Oaxaca. Only two possible sites (Cueva Blanca and the Martínez rockshelter in the Mitla area; see Fig. 1:10) have been reported for the critical period of 3000-1500

bc, just before the advent of egalitarian village life and the use of ceramics; the evidence from these two sites is remarkably thin (Marcus and Flannery 1996:59). This interval is also the most poorly-known period in the neighboring Tehuacán Valley sequence (MacNeish 1972; cf. Niederberger 1979). Even with this critical gap in the sequence, however, the Oaxaca data provide a rich record of village tribalism from about 1450 bc until the advent of rank societies around 1150-1000 bc. Settlement survey data for sequential ceramic periods, coupled with extensive excavation data from houses and house compounds, provide information on possible institutions of social integration at the end of tribal times during the Early Formative period.

The Oaxaca and Tehuacán data indicate the persistence of band-level societies well past our proposed 5000 bc date for the beginnings of tribalism. It is important to stress here that the spread of tribal institutions in proto-Mesoamerica was neither uniform nor synchronous. It is very likely, for a number of plausible historical and ecological reasons, that groups in the semi-arid valleys of Tehuacán and Oaxaca adopted horticulture and tribal ways much later than did groups living in the lowlands (see Piperno and Pearsall 1998:314). Unlike the lake-dwellers of the temperate Valley of Mexico and the hunter-fisher-gatherers of the lowland neotropics, Archaic peoples of the Valley of Oaxaca (and Tehuacán) followed a more nomadic foraging pattern dictated by the availability of seasonal foods. Flannery and Marcus follow MacNeish's (1964, 1972) Tehuacán Valley interpretation of small campsites and occupational surfaces in caves and rockshelters and see them as seasonal microband camps left by 4-6 people. During certain seasons of the year, several small bands came together as a macroband of 15 to 25 people to harvest abundant resources (Marcus and Flannery 1996:52). The interpretation of seasonal aggregations and dispersals of small bands mapping on to environmental resources takes Jennings's (1957) proposed Desert Archaic adaptation—based on Steward's (1938, 1955) Great Basin Shoshone study—as its model. Occupational surfaces in the Oaxaca caves and rockshelters represent seasonal use by small, mixed groups of men, women, and children. Flannery and his colleagues interpret the data for Oaxaca from 8000-3000 bc as evidence of band societies (Flannery et al. 1981:57:table 3-1; cf. MacNeish 1972 for Tehuacán), with an important shift from foraging to collecting strategies occurring about 3000 bc (Marcus and Flannery 1996:61). In particular, the limited Late Archaic evidence from Cueva Blanca suggests that it was a logistical camp of male deer-hunters rather than a microband camp typical of earlier periods. If so, this signals an important shift in subsistence strategies and mobility from foraging sites to base camps/logistical camps (ibid.) that might indicate the beginnings of tribal organization. Marcus and Flannery (1996:53) estimate the total Late Archaic population of the 2000 km² Valley of Oaxaca at 75-150 people.

As discussed, the third millennium bc in proto-Mesoamerica witnessed significant changes in subsistence strategies, most apparent in the lowlands with the appearance of swidden agriculture and a greater commitment to maize agriculture. There are divergent ways to interpret the Oaxaca record compared to those of its neighbors in proto-Mesoamerica, but we think they indicate that tribal institutions were adopted in highland Oaxaca about two millennia after their appearance in other regions such as the Basin of Mexico and the lowlands (see below). The period we hypothesize for the beginnings of tribalism in the Valley of Oaxaca (3000-1500 bc) is only poorly represented. Of itself, this fact implies a change in subsistence-settlement patterns and mobility from earlier times, with most sites being open-air logistic camps or base camps.

One early open-air site is of particular interest because it sheds light on possible egalitarian institutions. Gheo-Shih, a Middle Archaic site (5000-4000 bc) 1.5 ha in extent and located on the valley floor, is thought to represent a summer macroband camp for exploiting mesquite pods that produced "180-200 kg of edible portions per ha" during June-August (Flannery et al. 1981:62). A cleared rectangular space 20 x 7 m in the middle of the site, lined on it long sides by small boulders, is thought to have been a "dance ground" (Flannery 2001; Flannery et al. 1981:62; Marcus and Flannery 1996:58). Evidence of small rustic shelters or windbreaks surround the demarcated, cleared area; and there is possible evidence for the special manufacture of stone pebble beads in this habitation zone.

> No similar ornament-making area has been found at any of the smaller sites of the Archaic. Like the boulder-lined 'dance ground', this area for ornament manufacture implies that when temporary abundance allowed Archaic foragers to get together in camps of 15-25 persons, they engaged in social, ritual, and craft activities not carried out at smaller camps. (Marcus and Flannery 1996:59)

All these data suggest several band-level integrative mechanisms for promoting group cohesion at the dawn of tribalism. Other activities thought to have been undertaken during seasonal reunions at sites such as Gheo-Shih include "group ritual, gift-giving, exchange, and perhaps even initiation and courtship" (Marcus and Flannery 1996:53). Many of these same activities continued as basic practices of social interaction in later time periods. With the rise of autonomous village groups, however, two other beliefs and practices are thought to have been critical. "One was a belief in descent from a common ancestor. The other was membership in fraternal orders to which one had to be initiated" (Marcus and Flannery 1996:25). These practices segregated along public and private domains.

The evidence for these remarkable inferences come from analyses of village life for the Tierras Largas phase (1400-1150 bc) and the first half of the following San José phase (1150-850 bc). Earlier pottery and a domestic structure were found for an ephemeral Espirdión complex (1550-1400 bc, *our beginning estimate*), but these sherds are currently limited to one small excavation from the site of San José Mogote, the principal Early Formative site of the Valley (Marcus and Flannery 1996:75). Tierras Largas pottery is the first easily recognizable and widely dispersed ware in the region. Settlement during the Tierras Largas phase extended to all three narrow arms of the Oaxaca Valley, with 19 sites being known. An estimated 463-925 persons occupied these branch valleys towards the close of this phase (Marcus and Flannery 1996:78). Most lived in widely dispersed hamlets one to three ha in size, with San José Mogote being the exception to the rule at seven ha. During Tierras Largas times the population at this large site was loosely distributed in "nine discrete residential areas," with an estimated population of 71-186 people (Marcus and Flannery 1996:78). Each residential sector of San José Mogote was about the size of one of the small outlying hamlets, thought to have housed about 25-50 people each. Hamlets comprised 5-10 comfortably-spaced, small households of 4-5 people, each household with its own yard and subterranean storage pits. Over 50 percent of Valley population, however, was dispersed around the large village of San José Mogote in the northern branch valley (Etla), the location of the most favorable soil and ecological conditions for growing beans, squash, corn, and chili, as well as the best access to the adjacent mountain slopes for procuring a variety of raw materials and foodstuffs (Marcus and Flannery 1996:81-82).

Near the western edge of the San José Mogote village cluster, Flannery and his associates uncovered a stratified series of small public buildings dating to Tierras Largas times and lasting into the San José phase (Flannery and Marcus 1976:210-11). The superimposed buildings' special construction, form, orientation, treatment, and features distinguish them from residential structures. Marcus and Flannery (1996:87) see these sequential buildings as the ancient Oaxacan equivalent of Men's Houses, "initiates temples," or *kivas* known ethnographically in which ceremonies were carried out for a select group of villagers. "Periodically each such building was razed, and a new one was built on virtually the same spot. Measuring no more than 4 x 6 m, these buildings could only have accommodated a fraction of the community" (ibid.). They may have served as "limited-access structures where a small number of fully initiated men could assemble to plan raids or hunts, carry out agricultural rituals, smoke or ingest sacred plants, and/or communicate with the spirits" (ibid.). All of these practices and rites would have served to diffuse social tensions (at least among the leading males of the community) and promote social cohesion, as is thought to be the case for the practices carried out in the ethnographic analogous structures from which Marcus and Flannery draw their inspiration.

Ancestor veneration and a lineage principle have been inferred from early ceramic figurines and slightly later ceramic vessels carved with designs of supernatural creatures thought to represent Earthquake (earth) and Lightening (sky), dual forces of nature still important to the Zapotec descendants of the early inhabitants of the Valley of Oaxaca (Marcus and Flannery 1996:95). Ancestor veneration was critical to social integration because:

> An individual is integrated into a large group of relatives by shared descent; the spirits of the ancestors are invited to take part in descendants' activities; the continued presence of the ancestors, either as burials or curated skeletal parts, makes farming and warfare successful, reinforcing one's right to a particular plot of land. (Marcus and Flannery 1996:78)

With the exception of one baked-clay, female human figurine found at Zohapilco (Niederberger 1979) in 2200 bc preceramic levels, human ceramic figurines first appear in other regions of proto-Mesoamerica with the first evidence of nucleated villages and pottery. The three co-occur with great consistency. For Tierras Largas phase villagers, Marcus and Flannery (1996:87) "consider most of these figurines to represent female ancestors, and

to be part of a woman's ritual complex centered in the home. ...there was a separate men's ritual complex, focused on Men's Houses at some distance from the household." Fragments of figurines, predominantly of women, are ubiquitous in household refuse, but none have been found in the special structures thought to be Men's Houses. Likewise, burials occur associated with houses, or under their floors, but not with the special public buildings (Marcus and Flannery 1996:87-88). As noted, burial of one's ancestors around the house constituted a clear property claim. It must also have been a fundamentally important ritual act for restoring group cohesion after the loss of one of its members. Marcus and Flannery (1996:84) make the important point that the unstandardized mortuary treatment and orientations of graves show that each person meriting social recognition and burial was treated as an individual rather than according to social roles. This changed in the following phase with the emergence of hereditary social ranks and stereotypic interments in special cemeteries (Marcus and Flannery 1996:96).

The postulated Earth and Sky Clan distinctions among Early Formative groups living in Oaxaca date to the period in which leadership at San José Mogote became hereditary rather than to the Tierras Largas phase of village egalitarianism. Nonetheless, these clan distinctions are thought to predate the origins of rank and only to have become materialized in specially-carved ceramic vessels at this later time (Flannery and Marcus 1994:387; cf. Clark 1997 and Lesure 2000). Similar dichotomous distinctions among contemporaneous groups, as evident in distributions of similarly decorated ceramic vessels, are thought to have been in force all across proto-Mesoamerica (Marcus 1999). It is important to stress that the claims made for the meaning of the designs and their distributions have not been demonstrated. Their interpretation as clan insignia is logically implausible, however, and therefore unacceptable, regardless of how well they might fit professional preconceptions of tribal and early rank societies. It distends credibility to claim that all early Mesoamerican societies split into moieties, and that they were the same two thought to have existed in early Oaxaca (ibid.). Rather, the distribution of excised and inscribed ceramic vessels with supernatural creatures relates to the spread of institutions of hereditary rank from an outside source rather than to indigenous developments within the Valley of Oaxaca (see Clark 1997), so the designs should not be taken as evidence of pre-rank

Oaxacan tribal institutions unless, and until, more compelling evidence is forthcoming.

In their overall appraisal of the evidence of village egalitarianism (our tribalism) in highland Oaxaca, Marcus and Flannery draw on three famous ethnographic models taken from the America Southwest, New Guinea, and Highland Burma. They see the transitional stage of egalitarianism in the Valley of Oaxaca, most clearly evident at San José Mogote and its environs, as one of groups organized around competing charismatic leaders (analogous to New Guinea big-men) that evolved into rank systems similar to those reported for Highland Burma. Their composite model explains many of the activities reconstructed for Tierras Largas times, as well as the evolution of hereditary leadership during the San José phase.

> San José Mogote must...have had a succession of self-selected, socially ambitious leaders who knew how to turn their hard-won agricultural surplus into prestigious public works. Such men, the ethnographic record tells us, accumulate more than their share of wives, kinsmen, and affines, as well as a body of followers who do their bidding in return for favors and reflected glory. It was probably this kind of leadership, and not simply Class I land, that attracted nine clusters of families to San José Mogote during the Tierras Largas phase. (Marcus and Flannery 1996:88)

A similar process of competitive leadership appears to have occurred among the early ceramic-using villagers of coastal Chiapas, Mexico, but at an earlier time period.

Coastal tribal adaptations in Chiapas

In no other region of proto-Mesoamerica is the spatial disjunction between terminal Late Archaic and Early Formative village societies as stark as for the earliest societies of the Chiapas coast. Archaic shell middens known from the mid-coast date from 5000 to 1800 bc, and the earliest villages and ceramics (1600 bc) are from the Mazatan region located 60 km down the coast to the southeast; a broad freshwater swamp system separates the two regions. Although environmental conditions of both sectors of the coast differ drastically from those of the highland valleys already considered, the developments and transformations of tribalism in coastal Chiapas parallel those postulated for these other regions.

The shell middens in the Chantuto area of the Chiapas coast (Fig. 1:23-28) have been subject to investigation off and on for the past 50 years (Drucker 1948; Lorenzo 1955), with systematic investigations undertaken the past 30 years by Barbara Voorhies (1976, 1996, 2001) and her associates (Kennett and Voorhies 1996; Michaels and Voorhies 1999; Voorhies et al. 1991). It has always been clear that the Late Archaic exploitation of aquatic resources in the mangrove estuaries and lagoons of this coastal zone represented specialized and perhaps seasonal activities that were an integral part of a broader subsistence system that included inland sites and terrestrial pursuits. Only one inland site in the Chantuto region has been located and investigated to date (Voorhies 1996), so our understanding of the Late Archaic system remains tilted towards specialized exploitation of shellfish and related aquatic resources, with the remaining part of the subsistence-settlement pattern being hypothesized rather than demonstrated.

Understandings of the earliest villages located on the low coastal plain in the Mazatan region (Fig. 2:23) suffer from the same deficiencies because Late Archaic antecedents to village life there remain undiscovered and unknown. Based on the inferred contours of the earliest sedentary village life, Clark and Blake (1994) speculate about the necessary nature of antecedent, Late Archaic societies, but their ideas on these matters remain to be tested against actual archaeological evidence. Despite these mammoth deficiencies in the data for the coastal Late Archaic, we do have some secure data that shed light on possible tribal institutions and their antiquity in this region.

The earliest evidence of human occupation of the Chiapas coast comes from the recently investigated Middle Archaic shell midden at Cerro de las Conchas, dating to 5000-3000 bc (Blake et al. 1995; Voorhies 1996). Recovered food remains show exploitation of a mangrove estuary and lagoon environment. The only formal artifacts are perforated large bivalve shells [*anadara grandis*], large turtleshell fishhooks, and an occasional heating stone. Unlike the later shell middens reported by Voorhies (1976) for the Late Archaic (3000-1800 bc), a variety of shellfish were exploited at Cerro de las Conchas rather than the monotonous mounds of small marsh clams evident at these later shell heaps. Other than the different types of shells constituting the middens, other estuarine resources exploited appear to have been similar.

In a recent study of seasonality based on oxygen isotope analysis of the growth layers of marsh clams from early and late shell middens, Kennett and Voorhies (1996) demonstrate that later shell middens were used exclusively during the rainy season (May-October), whereas the earlier shell midden evinces use throughout the year. In the grand scheme of things, Kennett and Voorhies interpret these data to indicate a shift in subsistence strategies between 5000 and 3000 bc, from foraging to collecting. This hypothesized change, and its timing, accord well with others seen throughout proto-Mesoamerica for the same period.

Two other interpretations of the late shell middens are of interest. The principal implication of the late shell middens as seasonal specialized activity areas—or logistic camps—is that base camps were located elsewhere. One possible inland base camp has been located (Vuelta Limón, Appendix 1B. 23), but the occupation layer is thin and provides few clues to the activities, or their seasonality, once carried out there. Presumably, corn and root crop agriculture would have been a principal activity around inland base camps. Second, activities effected at shell middens involved specialized procurement and production, such as drying fish, shellfish, or even shrimp. Some of these dried food products may have been items of regional and long-distance exchange. The first evidence of obsidian exchange from the distant Guatemala highlands dates to the Late Archaic (Nelson and Voorhies 1980); products from the shell middens may have been items circulated in this Archaic exchange system (Clark 1994b).

One early feature from Tlacuachero, a seasonal shell midden in the estuary lagoon system, was a 20 cm thick, 20 by 50 meter clay living surface that included posthole impressions of several small structures (Voorhies et al. 1991:31). The clay was canoed into the site from upriver and would have constituted a major labor investment. The oval shape (8 x 10 m) of the primary structure and its proportions are similar to those known for the earliest Formative residences from the Mazatan region, thereby indicating continuity of culture and peoples from Archaic to Formative times between these two regions (Clark 1994b). The only other demonstrable continuity between these cultures is the large quantities of fire-cracked rocks used for cooking. The frequency of fire-cracked rock, and by implication Archaic food preparation practices, continued for several centuries after the initial adoption of ceramic technology and production of fancy, fired-clay vessels (Clark and Gosser 1985).

About 1600 bc, the inland occupations of Chiapas peoples became much more visible archaeologically with the construction of permanent villages and the first use of ceramic vessels; the shell middens ceased to be visited slightly before this time (Blake et al. 1995). In the Mazatan region, the earliest ceramics (Barra complex, ca. 1600-1450 bc) were some of the most elaborate. By 1400 bc, there was clear evidence of rank societies in this region. The emergence of institutionalized hereditary inequality just two centuries or less after the appearance of sedentary villages and ceramics suggests the prior presence of sophisticated, aceramic tribal groups in the region for which there is currently no direct concrete evidence (Clark 1994b; Clark and Blake 1994).

We will not pursue here the wisdom of imagining undiscovered inland Late Archaic Chiapas coastal societies; rather, we consider postulated tribal institutions supported by real evidence for village tribalism. Barra villages are rather evenly spaced across the region. In Clark's (1994b) survey, 38 Barra-phase sites were identified, with the largest at Paso de la Amada taking up 10.85 ha of occupied space. Paso de la Amada at this time was a dispersed village consisting of different occupational clusters. "There appear to have been at least 10 units of comparable size in the village cluster. The various pockets of occupation, with their associated special residence, appear as neighborhoods or barrios and could possibly represent groups of related kin" (Clark 1994b:380). Population for early Paso de la Amada is estimated at 270-380 people, with over 600 people calculated for the 200 km² region. This is a comparable population to the Tierras Largas population of the Valley of Oaxaca, but in a zone a tenth its size. In the following phase, Paso de la Amada quadrupled in size while the population in the region increased ten-fold (Clark 1994b:212). This phenomenal population growth followed the emergence of rank societies in the region, with Paso de la Amada being the seat of the largest chiefdom. The principal evidence for the emergence of hereditary inequality are the multiple, two-tiered settlement hierarchies for the various neighboring chiefdoms and elite architecture at their central villages. At Paso de la Amada, successive refurbishment and amplification of the chiefly residence at Mound 6 indicates hereditary leadership and privilege (Blake 1991; Clark 1994b).

Clark and Blake (1994) speculate that the principal institutions of Barra-phase, egalitarian villages included ritual feasting and drinking, gift-giving, public rituals, and long-distance exchange. As claimed for the Basin of Mexico, the Mazatan region would have been especially favorable to collector-horticulturalists. The natural abundance of this swampy sector of the Chiapas coastal plain, buttressed by a significant commitment to raising crops—probably manioc and sweet potatoes, with some maize (Clark 1994b)—allowed production of surpluses that were deployed by aggrandizers for social ends. This interpretation of tribal practices parallels the most recent model for highland Oaxaca, as summarized above.

During their final season of excavation at Paso de la Amada, Warren Hill and Michael Blake discovered a clay-surfaced ballcourt dating to the beginning of the site (Hill et al. 1998). The ballcourt's antiquity and its construction history suggest that the well-known Mesoamerican ballgame was a tribal institution of special significance. Other evidence of early ballplaying in proto-Mesoamerica and South America, such as the male figurines of ballplayers in highland Mexico, support this conclusion (Hill 1999). The "dance ground" at Gheo-Shih, for example, could have been a simple playing court (Taube 1992). Hill and Clark (2001) argue that construction of a formal ballcourt at Paso de la Amada, and promotion of ballgame matches among rival villages, helped foster a transition to rank society among Chiapas coastal groups. Important side features of gaming would also have included gambling and feasting (ibid.). Interestingly, ballplayer figurines have not been found in the Mazatan region (see Clark 1994b; Lesure 1997, 1999), although they are known for Gulf Coast societies, the Basin of Mexico, and Western Mexico for the Early Formative (Hill 1999).

Material traces of basic tribal institutions noted for other regions are also present in the Mazatan Early Formative, namely, ceramic human figurines and distinct, fancy ceramic vessels. It is not clear, however, whether figurines were used in the same way, or had analogous meanings, to those from Oaxaca and highland Mexico (see Lesure n.d.). Thus far, no burials have been recovered for the Barra phase, the postulated tribal village period. Interments from the following Locona phase (1450-1300 bc), representing the shift to rank society, have been found associated both with individual residences and with public space. Evidence for construction of some public spaces, such as the ballcourt, with communal work-groups precedes evidence for hereditary ranking. We think communal building efforts would have been an important means of social integration—and not just evidence for integrated activity (Hill and Clark 2001).

Before leaving the Chiapas case, we must address an issue raised by Marcus and Flannery (1996:88-92) in their comparative evaluation of village egalitarianism in other regions of proto-Mesoamerica. They suggest that the superimposed series of large, oval buildings at Mound 6 at the southern end of Paso de la Amada, Chiapas, would have served as "initiates' temples" in a manner similar to the small public buildings at San José Mogote, Oaxaca. Their proposal is at odds with Blake's (1991) and Clark's (1994b, 1997; Clark and Blake 1994) interpretation of these structures as chiefly residences, and as the most compelling evidence for inherited inequalities within one family line. We will not rehearse the original arguments of the primary investigators here. It should be sufficient to point out some of the striking differences between the two series of buildings in light of Marcus and Flannery's (1996:87) observations and criteria for distinguishing public buildings from residences. In contrast to the swept and cleaned Men's Houses at San José Mogote, the various instantiations of the special building at Paso de la Amada are associated with truck-loads of domestic refuse, including the highest concentration of female figurines at the site, as well as sub-floor burials of infants and patio burials of women. Clearly, the Paso de la Amada buildings were not Men's Houses. On the other hand, they were not run-of-the-mill residences either, nor strictly domestic. The argument here is really over analytical categories rather than archaeological data. The public-versus-private distinction for structures is a false dichotomy, as anyone who has thrown a party in her home knows. The special residences at Mound 6, Paso de la Amada, were obviously built for show and also for accommodating large crowds, especially in the ample northern patio area. Such multiple uses of residential space probably extend back into tribal times.

Tribal territories in the Maya Lowlands, a synchronic view

Evidence for integrative institutions for the Maya Lowlands are much less clear than for the Chiapas coastal lowlands given the paltry data involved. Consequently, our approach for the Maya region requires a wider net and longer temporal scale to capture and depict possible Maya tribal practices. Evidence for occupation in the Lowlands goes back to Paleolithic times, but there is no clear evidence for continuous occupation throughout the Archaic. Claims for a continuous sequence are founded on projectile point styles and postulated dates for each style based on general form, but these claims have not been verified with dated excavations (see MacNeish 1986, 2001a). Our evaluation here of the Maya case relies on excavated data. We suspect that tribes were present in the Lowlands at the time that the earliest Archaic inhabitants show up there about 3000 bc. Tribes persisted until 900-700 bc, the period that witnessed the spread of social ranking across the Maya Lowlands (see below). Thus, the Maya area presents an interesting case of prolonged tribalism. Tribalism was more successful and long-lived here than elsewhere in proto-Mesoamerica. Perhaps a more appropriate way to view this case, tribal societies were more resistant to the supposed allurements of the rank societies that flanked them on the west and south centuries earlier (Fig. 3). Why was tribalism so successful in the Maya Lowlands, and what were the consequences of its success for subsequent historical developments of Maya civilization? Data are still too scarce to address these questions, but we can start this project by making a case for Maya tribalism going back to the Middle Archaic period and ending in the Middle Preclassic.

The baseline for understanding early social developments in the Maya Lowlands is the Mamom period and ceramic horizon that dates from 800 to 300 bc (Fig. 4). Mamom pottery was first discovered in the Maya Lowlands at Uaxactun, central Peten, Guatemala (Ricketson and Ricketson 1937), and was the first evidence of a village period preceding Maya high civilization. Mamom pottery has since become the hallmark of the Middle Preclassic Lowland Maya. Subsequent investigations have found this diagnostic waxy, predominantly deep-red monochrome pottery all across the Lowlands, and in most places it is still the earliest pottery. In a few select regions of northern Guatemala and Belize, earlier pottery has been found; it is referred to as "pre-Mamom" because the Mamom horizon is the natural marker for assessing relative stratigraphy in the Lowlands. In contrast to the consistent, lustrous Mamom monochromes, pre-Mamom pottery is stylistically diverse. These older assemblages are generally small and have rarely received

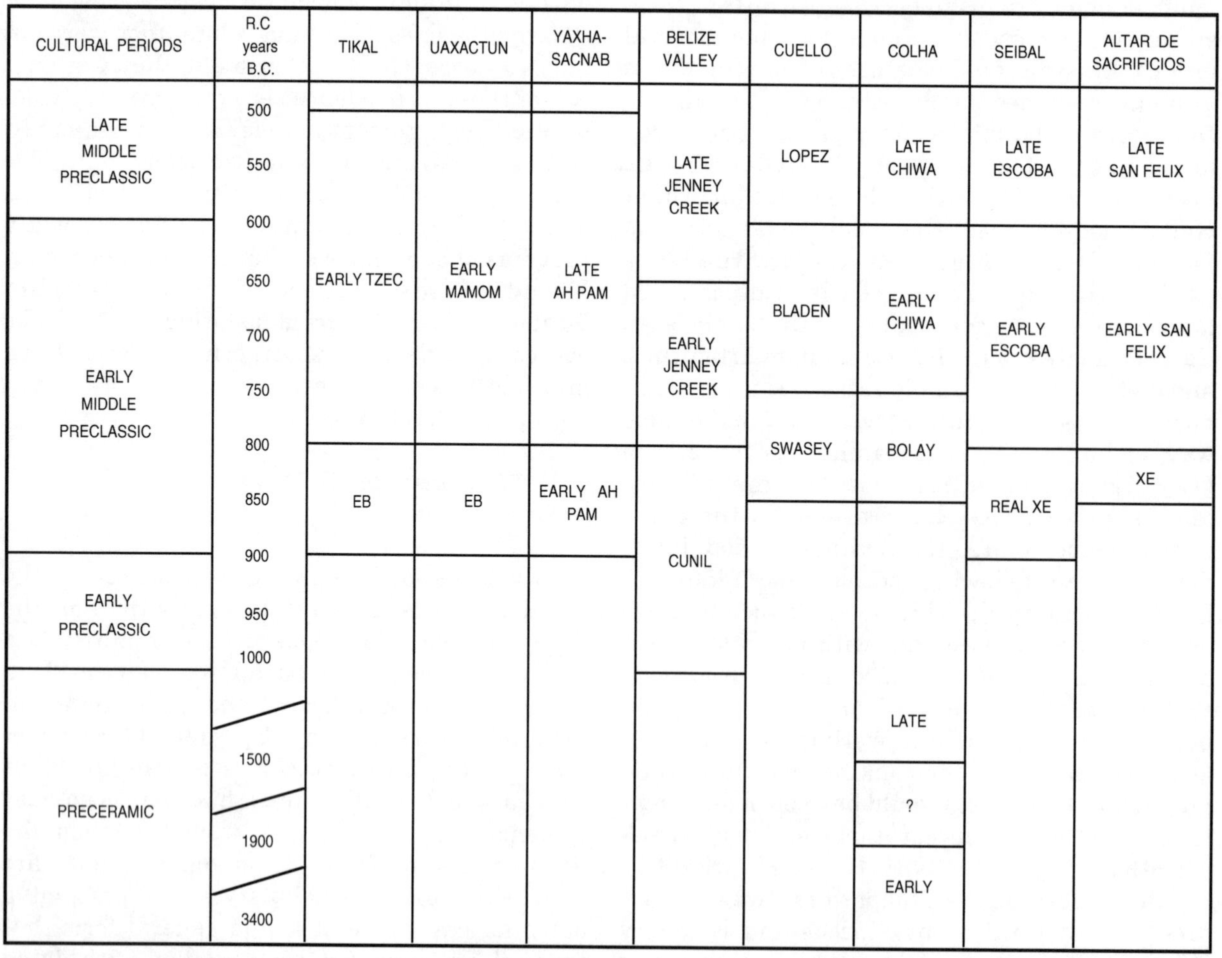

CULTURAL PERIODS	R.C years B.C.	TIKAL	UAXACTUN	YAXHA-SACNAB	BELIZE VALLEY	CUELLO	COLHA	SEIBAL	ALTAR DE SACRIFICIOS
LATE MIDDLE PRECLASSIC	500 550 600				LATE JENNEY CREEK	LOPEZ	LATE CHIWA	LATE ESCOBA	LATE SAN FELIX
EARLY MIDDLE PRECLASSIC	650 700 750 800	EARLY TZEC	EARLY MAMOM	LATE AH PAM	EARLY JENNEY CREEK	BLADEN	EARLY CHIWA	EARLY ESCOBA	EARLY SAN FELIX
						SWASEY	BOLAY		
	850 900	EB	EB	EARLY AH PAM	CUNIL			REAL XE	XE
EARLY PRECLASSIC	950 1000								
PRECERAMIC	1500 1900 3400						LATE ? EARLY		

Fig. 4 Early Cultural Phases of the Maya Lowlands.

detailed study or reporting. Sanders and Price (1968:111) suggested that Mamom peoples were probably tribal. Their interpretation is now no longer tenable; any Maya tribes must predate this period.

Over the past several years we have assembled and compiled the various scraps of pre-Mamom pottery from the Maya Lowlands to evaluate them independently of the original reports and to assess their chronological placement and cultural significance. All the pre-Mamom assemblages of the central Lowlands can be grouped into the four ceramic complexes shown in Fig. 5. Much detailed typological analysis has gone into extracting the data summarized in these simple distributions, but we will not rehearse the details here (see Appendix 3) as they are more appropriate for a different forum. Non-specialist readers need only know that we have examined almost all the early Maya pottery in question—and most of the contemporaneous and earlier assemblages from adjacent regions in neighboring Tabasco and Chiapas, Mexico, to the west, and in highland Guatemala and Honduras, to the south. Of course, personal knowledge of the sherds does not mean that we have mastered their significance. Our reason for trying to impose some order on the small collections of pre-Mamom pottery from an inter-regional perspective is that we think they hold the key for resolving questions of Maya tribes and subsequent developments of Maya civilization.

Pre-Mamom pottery in the Maya Lowlands falls into four complexes distributed territorially across northern Guatemala and Belize (Fig. 5). We consider these zones as probable tribal territories and designate each by the name of its defined ceramic complex. These complexes are, from southwest to northeast, Xe, Eb, Cunil, and Swasey. They were all contemporaneous during the latter half of the ninth century bc (Fig. 4). Of the four, only Swasey has achieved any level of notoriety in the discipline and popular press as the precursor of Maya civilization. It turns out, however, that Swasey hype was based on an erroneous placement 1200 years too early (see Appendix 3D), due to a series of circumstances still not clearly understood. Claims for a Swasey complex prior to the ninth century bc are untenable in terms of the documented history of pottery forms, modes, and designs in Mesoamerica (see Webster 2001; Zeitlin 1989). The Cunil complex, just recently defined (Awe 1992; Cheetham 1998; Cheetham and Awe n.d.), is the earliest of the four beginning at 950-1000 bc, with Swasey now known to be the latest at 850 bc, instead of its original 2050 bc (Hammond 1977; Hammond et al.

1979), or its more recent revisions at 1200 cal. BC (Hammond 2000, 2001; Kosakowsky and Pring 1998). Pushing Swasey back to the ninth century bc substantially alters the picture of the early Maya and their involvement in general developments in Mesoamerica.

The four reconstructed ceramic assemblages show various degrees of similarity and difference in the forms of individual vessels, their sizes, frequencies, and decorations. A few salient points are apparent in comparing the illustrations of these complexes (Figs. 6-9). There are significant differences in vessel forms that are easily recognized and sufficient affinities and commonalities to demonstrate contemporaneity and interaction among the makers and users of these early pots (cf. Kowokowsky and Pring 1998). In short, the four assemblages represented competing vessel inventories. Makers and users of each were probably aware of what their neighbors were doing and crafted their vessels accordingly. The known distribution area of each assemblage was roughly comparable, about 5000 km^2 (see Fig. 5). If we are correct in our suspicion that these earliest pottery zones represent linguistic tribal territories of constituent smaller tribal units of similar language and culture, then these ranges were about the same size—suggesting a minimal base population for a viable tribal organization comprising a dozen or more small sedentary villages and a comparable population distribution or settlement dispersion.

One critical fact not apparent in the illustrations is that none of the pre-Mamom ceramic complexes in the Maya Lowlands has any logical, local or extra-local antecedent (see Cheetham 1998:27; Clark and Gosser 1995:217; Pyburn 1994). This is the first pottery in the Maya Lowlands, and it is stylistically distinct from pottery in probable donor regions in Mesoamerica, Central America, or South America. As evident in Table 1 and Fig. 2, the Maya were the last major group in Mesoamerica to adopt pottery; neighboring groups had been making and breaking pots for at least 500 years before their pyro-technology made it to the Maya Lowlands. But none of the adjacent neighbors to the south in highland Guatemala or Honduras, or to the west in Chiapas or Tabasco, Mexico, had pottery similar to Xe, Eb, Cunil, or Swasey. Inter-regional resemblances are either generic or modal. This fact suggests a complicated borrowing process for the introduction of pottery into the Maya Lowlands and/or the possibility that we still have not recovered the very earliest pottery, but we doubt this. One conclusion is patent from our reconstructions of neighboring ceramic assemblages: a clear case *cannot be made* for late colonization of the Maya Lowlands by ceramic-users from either the Guatemalan highlands to the south or from Chiapas/Tabasco to the west, as speculated by many (Adams 1971:154; Andrews 1990; Lowe 1977:198; Willey 1977:400), because none of the known pottery types from likely donor areas show up in the hypothesized colonized zones. The pre-Mamom Maya ceramic assemblages appear to have had their own individual histories of parallel and complementary development.

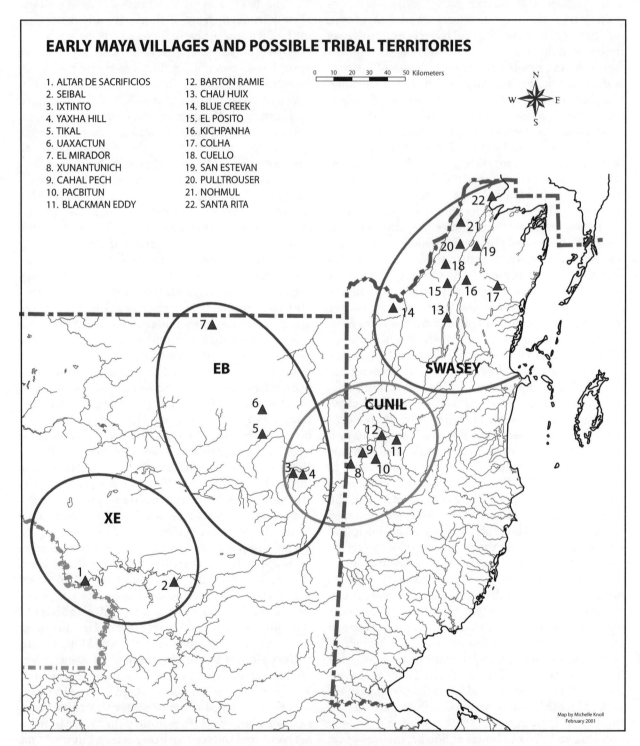

EARLY MAYA VILLAGES AND POSSIBLE TRIBAL TERRITORIES

1. ALTAR DE SACRIFICIOS
2. SEIBAL
3. IXTINTO
4. YAXHA HILL
5. TIKAL
6. UAXACTUN
7. EL MIRADOR
8. XUNANTUNICH
9. CAHAL PECH
10. PACBITUN
11. BLACKMAN EDDY
12. BARTON RAMIE
13. CHAU HUIX
14. BLUE CREEK
15. EL POSITO
16. KICHPANHA
17. COLHA
18. CUELLO
19. SAN ESTEVAN
20. PULLTROUSER
21. NOHMUL
22. SANTA RITA

Map by Michelle Knoll
February 2001

Fig. 5 Distribution of Lowland Maya villages and estimated boundaries of tribal territories, *ca.* 850 bc.

Fig. 6 Reconstruction of Réal Xe Maya (900-800 bc) ceramic vessels from the Pasión River area (drawing by Ayax Moreno).

Fig. 7 Reconstruction of Eb Maya (900-800 bc) ceramic vessels from the central Petén (drawing by Ayax Moreno).

Data are too scarce to speculate much about earlier histories for pre-Mamom ceramic complexes, but viewing these complexes in their most likely chronological context suggests that the four Maya macro-groups had independent histories. We summarize their similarities and differences in Appendix 3 and portray them in Figs. 6-9. The basic inter-regional pattern of the four ceramic complexes is that the most significant similarities between neighboring groups are in the slipped serving vessels. In contrast, the most significant differences are in the forms and sizes of the utilitarian pottery, and their handles. In addition, special pot forms are confined to each group. The upshot of this pattern is that the distinctions we made in defining possible territories (Fig. 5) were largely based on utilitarian forms. The fancy serving bowls and plates were broadly similar, thus signaling a

Fig. 8 Reconstruction of Cunil Maya (1000-800 bc) ceramic vessels from the Belize Valley (drawing by Ayax Moreno).

Fig. 9 Reconstruction of Swasey Maya (850-750 bc) ceramic vessels from northern Belize (drawing by Ayax Moreno).

broader region of interaction. With the exception of Swasey vessels, most slipped pots were characterized by a uniformly dull, non-waxy, monochrome finish. Color frequencies were generally similar across the region as well, with a preference for red. There is little doubt that the popularity of slipped red pottery was an important precursor to the succeeding Mamom complex, an important implication being that makers of pre-Mamom pottery were also Maya by direct genealogical connection.

Vessel forms are also another important indicator of cultural uniformity within the Lowland region. Chief among these was the wide everted-rim plate or dish. These unique incised vessels, virtually absent in other regions of Mesoamerica at this time, were produced in all proposed tribal territories except Swasey. Another telling indicator of territorial interaction for this time are simple designs cut or scratched into fancy vessels after they were fired brick-hard, most notably everted-rim plates and dishes. Designs varied from simple

lines to complex motifs such as crosses and a possible bird wing motif (Fig. 8). Curiously, these designs are absent on Swasey pottery (Fig. 9).

A parallel line of evidence corroborating the territorial distinctions is the distribution of hand-modeled anthropomorphic figurines (Fig. 10). Figurine frequencies varied widely among early Maya groups, with almost none being found with Swasey (see Hammond 1991). Figurine use in the Cunil and Eb spheres was more frequent than in other territories.

Viewed through time, the early period of pottery use in the Maya Lowlands represents a trend from stylistic autonomy of domestic pottery to convergence. By 800 bc, all four regions shown in Fig. 5, as well as many others, were incorporated into the Mamom sphere or horizon, and all the peoples in this interaction sphere made and employed a similar suite of ceramic vessels, albeit in different frequencies (Ball 1977). Similarities among slipped serving vessels in the four pre-Mamom assemblages

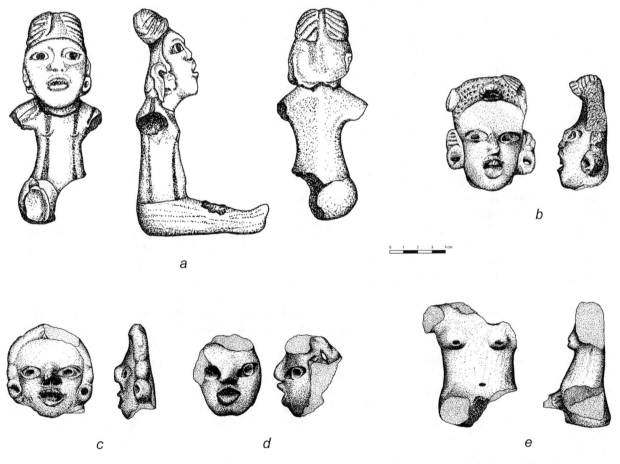

Fig. 10 Pre-Mamom Maya ceramic figurines. (a) Seated male or adolescent female with body paint or tattoos, Eb phase, Tikal (redrawn from Laporte and Fialko 1993:Fig. 7); (b-e) Solid heads and seated female torso, Cunil phase, Cahal Pech (redrawn from Awe 1992:Figs. 71c, 72c, 73a, 78b).

show a trend towards this later homogenization, probably as a consequence of increasing social intercourse. On stylistic and cultural grounds, we expect utilitarian pottery to change less rapidly than that designed for ostentation, given the audiences, messages, and social functions involved. Thus, we find counter-intuitive the contradiction in ceramic styles during the early village period of Maya development. We suspect that the differences in utilitarian wares demonstrate older tribal territories that likely pre-date the adoption of pottery. If true, this implies that the groups were in place well before the adoption of pottery, a possibility suggested by the sediment core and pollen evidence.

If we are correct in our inferences thus far, two additional points are implicated. First, the classes of differences evident in the four pre-Mamom ceramic assemblages that we attribute to separate tribal groups may have been more *de facto* markers of significant cultural differences and distinctiveness due to divergent histories and development than anything overtly or actively marked. Differences in domestic wares suggest greater isolation among these early groups than their current shallow ceramic histories allow (cf. Kosakowsky and Pring 1998:64). This would certainly be the case if adoption of ceramic technology followed a pattern of "dependent invention" described by Clark and Gosser (1995; cf. Pyburn 1994) for the earliest ceramic assemblages of Middle America. In this process, the first ceramic vessels produced by a borrowing group mimic forms of perishable containers already in use by them at the time. The consequence of reproducing old forms in a new medium is stylistic diversity among pottery assemblages of peoples residing in adjacent areas, from the very outset of the local application of the borrowed technology, because the first ceramic forms fossilize particular perishable container forms and decorations which themselves had a longer, divergent history.

Second, the shared characteristics of fancy ceramic vessels indeed represent the beginnings of a consolidation of styles and greater cultural interaction among these lowland groups. Consequences of this interaction were soon to lead to the rise and/or promulgation of rank societies all across the Maya Lowlands during the Mamom period, or just before. We believe this interaction and development was already well underway during pre-Mamom times when village sedentism first began to leave an indelible mark on the landscape. In short, by the time Maya tribes show up archaeologically with pots and pans, they were already

being transformed. If there are such things as stable tribal societies, in the ancient Maya Lowlands they must be sought in the pre-ceramic era, a task to which we now turn.

Tribal territories in Northern Belize, a diachronic view

Due to the recent flurry of research activity in northern Belize the past 15 years, this region now boasts the best record of Late Archaic period settlement anywhere in Middle America. It is the only region in which the transition from Late Archaic settlements to the earliest villages has been traced, without spatial or temporal disjunction, from one period to the other. Consequently, it is possible to evaluate changes in settlement patterns from the Late Archaic to Preclassic times. The data for the earliest agricultural villages, however, are still thin, so the northern Belize data cannot answer all our questions concerning past tribal lifeways and their transformation. But with their longer record they do provide another view of processes not evident in the other three cases previously considered.

The keys for understanding the Belize data are recent excavations at Colha and Pulltrouser Swamp (Fig. 1:51, 44). Colha is a resource area of large nodules of high-quality chert that were exploited for making chipped-stone tools, beginning during the Preceramic period and continuing throughout pre-Columbian times. Recent excavations at Colha have revealed, dated, and defined two preceramic components for the Late Archaic and their artifactual content (Hester et al. 1996; Iceland 1997; Iceland et al. 1995). Minor excavations to the northwest of Colha at Pulltrouser Swamp have verified the early dating of some of the diagnostic stone tools in a habitation rather than a production context (Pohl et al. 1996). Sediment cores taken from Pulltrouser Swamp, as well as Cobweb Swamp located just 300 m from the principal Late Archaic components identified at Colha, have also provided rich pollen records that reveal significant changes in subsistence activities that parallel the archaeological record (see Hester et al. 1996; Pohl et al. 1996). Based on these data, Iceland (1997) defines Early and Late Preceramic chipped-stone tool complexes, each with diagnostic tools. These identified diagnostics now allow one to sort through the troublesome claims made for the Belize Archaic period by MacNeish (1986). Of the over 150 Archaic sites (see Zeitlin 1984) claimed for the Belize Archaic

Archaeological Reconnaissance project (BAAR), less than two dozen have been confirmed through the presence of diagnostic artifacts and/or excavated remains. Here we follow recent identifications and evidence and ignore earlier BAAR claims for the antiquity of stone tools made solely on typological grounds.

As already confessed, our considerations of the earliest Maya Preclassic has had to pass through a similar gauntlet to separate fact from fiction regarding the earliest villages and ceramics. Our appraisal of early Maya history arises from a preemptive disagreement with Hammond's views concerning the dating and significance of the Swasey ceramic complex and associated remains (Appendix 3D). The early pronouncements of Swasey's deep antiquity at 2050 bc, based on the most complete series of radiocarbon dates at the time, rather than 850 bc caught everyone off guard, and it adversely affected all studies carried out during the decade that it was held to be possibly true, including MacNeish's (1986) study of the Belize Archaic. Data from Colha establish the dating of the Preceramic era as well as the following Swasey period (see Hester et al. 1996; Iceland 1997).

Excavations at specialized chipped-stone tool production sites such as Colha and Kelly have documented an Early Preceramic period (ca. 3000-1900 bc) that corresponds with the first clear evidence of cultivated crops and human manipulation of the environment, as recorded in the pollen record. As synthesized by Pohl and her associates (Pohl et al. 1996), the overall picture of northern Belize reconstructed from sediment core data points to three significant watershed eras. Dated pollen and carbon particulate profiles reveal that the first evidence of domestic maize and manioc dates to just before 3000 bc; evidence of forest clearance from burning (presumably due to slash-and-burn agriculture) becomes pronounced beginning by 2500 bc; and, an intensification of wetland agriculture is evident about 1500-1300 bc, towards the end of the Belize Late Preceramic.

Excavations at Colha, Kelly, and Pulltrouser have identified at least two types of sites—reminiscent of the distinctions between sites made for the Chiapas and Oaxaca Late Archaic. Some Belize sites were specialized resource exploitation camps at which locally-available chert nodules were knapped into a variety of tools. Other sites were probably hamlets where, among other things, the same stone tools were used. This distinction suggests logistically-organized activities at quarry-production sites that were organized from basecamps

or semi-permanent hamlets of swidden agriculturalists. Colha was an unusual place in this regard as it was both a specialized stone-extraction, tool-production site as well as an agricultural hamlet for wetland (swamp edge) agriculture. Used and refurbished stone tools are found among manufacturing rejects (Iceland 1997:107). However, no clear evidence of permanent residences or household features have been recovered in the excavations. Primary occupation refuse at Colha has only been recovered from a few excavations around the *aguada* (water hole) adjacent to Cobweb Swamp, but "constricted unifaces have been found in excavations in all four quadrants over a considerable portion of the site, suggesting the possibility of a Preceramic community of considerable size" (Iceland 1997:209). Based on the site map, the Late Preceramic remains extended well over 300 ha. This suggests both a loosely aggregated community and, perhaps, recurrent use of the general area over the two millennia of the Preceramic era. The recently reported site at Caye Coco just northeast of Colha was at least 150 m^2 in extent (Rosenswig and Masson 2002), and the neighboring Fred Smith site has a documented scatter of Preceramic lithics of over 400 m^2 in extent (Rosenswig, personal communication, 2001). These are the only data currently available for assessing the size of a Late Preceramic settlement in the Maya Lowlands. At the regional scale, consideration of the distribution of chipped-stone artifacts for the Early and Late Preceramic allow an overall assessment of settlement before the advent of sedentary, ceramic-using villages.

> The varied environments exploited during the early Preceramic in northern Belize suggest that the inhabitants may have followed a subsistence strategy similar to that proposed for the Chantuto [Chiapas], with permanent or semi-permanent settlements with access to upland and swamp margin resources, such as Colha and Pulltrouser Swamp, serving as residential bases, while resources at specialized locations in the lowland pine ridge and coastal areas were exploited on a seasonal basis....This combination of chert production and wetland cultivation dominates the early Preceramic archaeological record at Colha/Cobweb Swamp, and their presence must have encouraged sedentism to control permanent resources at a time when population densities were surely rising. (Iceland 1997:287-88)

Recent studies have identified diagnostic Late Archaic chipped-stone tools. As verified through excavation, large, stemmed bifacially-flaked spear points, termed Lowe points, are characteristic of the Early Preceramic period (ca. 3000-1900 bc) (Iceland 1997; T. Kelly 1993). MacNeish (1986) identified these points as "Pedernales-like" and assigned them to an earlier period. Sites where these have been found are shown in Fig. 11 (see Appendix 2 for documentation). T. Kelly (1993:215) proposes that these massive tanged bifaces, averaging 9.3 cm long and 6.0 cm wide, may have been used on thrusting spears or harpoons. Iceland (1997:203) is uncomfortable with this interpretation given the points' distribution across a variety of environmental zones, but he does not offer a better alternative. To us, Lowe points look like the durable portion of hafted knives, a possibility that could be verified by a detailed use-wear analysis.

The points we have been able to examine personally all evince alternate-opposite retouch (see T. Kelly 1993:210) which results in beveled edges and rhomboid transverse cross-sections for the blade portion of these stemmed bifaces. These beveled-edged bifaces appear to have been retouched while still in their hafts, thus they have standard bases for hafting but vary widely in length and blade width below the notched base. The heavy patina on many of these tools, however, makes striations difficult to detect with low magnification, but the micro-chipping wear patterns on some are consonant with their use as knives. Other stone tools characteristic of the Early Preceramic period include massive macroblades up to 25 cm long, large cores, pointed blades, and small flake-blades (Iceland 1997:29). The pointed blades were used as

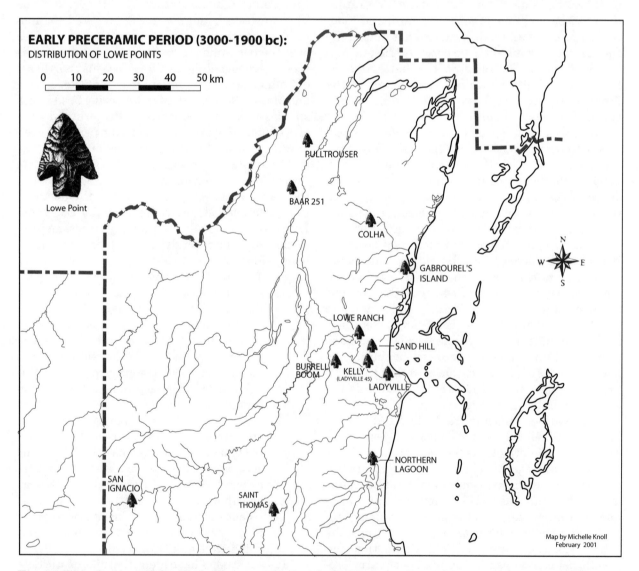

Fig. 11 Distribution of the Early Preceramic sites in Belize as indicated by reported Lowe points.

scrapers, perhaps for working wood, or as expedient quarrying tools (Iceland 1997:190).

The most diagnostic chipped stone artifacts for the following Late Preceramic period (1500-1000/850 bc) are "snowshoe-shaped," constricted unifaces (Gibson 1991; Iceland 1997). Their distribution is shown in Fig. 12. Studies of use-wear traces on these tools reveal that they functioned as adzes and woodworking tools, and occasionally as hoes (Gibson 1991; Hudler and Lohse 1994; Iceland 1997:229). All these uses may relate to forest clearance and field preparation and relate to the period of agricultural intensification evident in sediment cores. Other stone tools in the later assemblage include cores and macroblades, bifaces, and trimmed blades (Iceland 1997:28-29), forms and

tools useful for a multitude of cutting and scraping tasks. Surprisingly absent from these Archaic inventories are any grinding stones for processing the cultivated maize and manioc thought to be important at this time. Absence of grinding and pounding tools, however, may be due to the special contexts represented in the archaeological sample, as most of the excavations were of chipped-stone tool production areas rather than farmsteads. Stone mortars and "stone bowls" are associated with constricted unifaces in some of the reported BAAR sites (Zeitlin 1984; cf. Iceland 1997:183), so they may eventually be attributed to the Late Archaic. Pohl et al. (1996:365-66) report that mano and metate fragments were found in Late Preceramic deposits in four of their excavations.

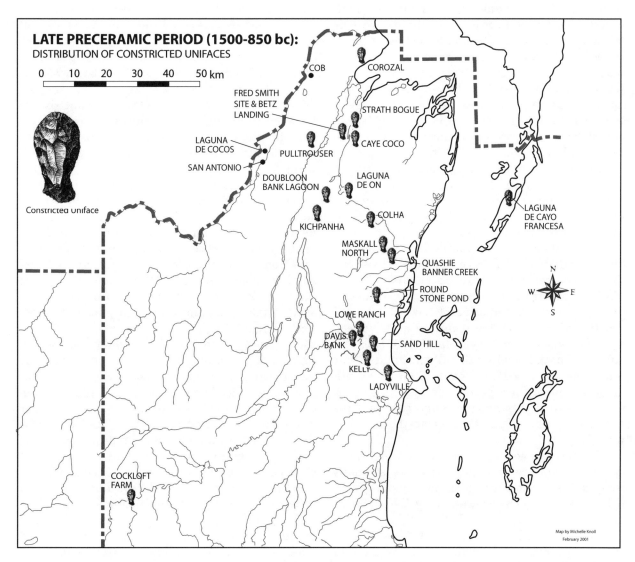

Fig. 12 Distribution of Late Preceramic sites in northern Belize as indicated by reported constricted unifaces and pollen traces.

As apparent in Figs. 11 and 12, the distribution of Early and Late Preceramic sites is nearly identical, suggesting continuity and stability of Late Archaic populations in northern Belize and exploitation of the same range of natural resources. As to pending chronological controversies, this continuity further indicates that the time interval between the Lowe-point and constricted-uniface periods was probably brief, as suggested for the late dating of Lowe points, rather than the millennia required for MacNeish's (1986) interpretation of projectile point styles (Iceland 1997; T. Kelly 1993). The pollen and carbon particulate records from sediment cores taken from some of the sites listed suggest a dramatic shift during this period to intensive agriculture which involved cultivation of maize and manioc. It is interesting that agricultural intensification did not entail any clear shift in settlement location as it is thought to have done in the other regions of proto-Mesoamerica previously considered. It is well to remember, however, that the other regions also show a marked shift in settlement at 3000-2500 bc by becoming virtually invisible. Belize represents the mirror image of this pattern. Its invisible era is the pre-3000 bc period, with recognizable diagnostic artifacts and site visibility at 3000 bc marking "an important transition in the scale and organization of human society in this region" (Iceland and Hester 1996:9). Belize does differ from the other regions in that Preceramic sites such as Colha continued to be occupied into the ceramic era.

Fig. 13 displays these continuities by comparing the distribution of Preceramic stone tools and the earliest ceramic spheres in northern Belize. The known distribution of Swasey pottery conforms precisely to the distribution of Lowe points and constricted unifaces. These continuities have been described and explored by Iceland (1997) who argues for spatial, temporal, cultural, and ethnic continuity (see also Hester et al. 1996). The continuity of some rather special stone-working strategies is sufficient to make a sound case that the Late Preceramic populations of northern Belize were Mayan.

The correspondence between the Cunil ceramic sphere with pre-ceramic stone artifacts is equally remarkable as it conforms to the nearly empty area to the southwest of Swasey territory. Whether this apparent emptiness means that the region was only sparsely occupied during the Late Preceramic or only that Archaic peoples of this region, as did other peoples of proto-Mesoamerica, left few obvious, durable and diagnostic artifacts to be recovered remains to be determined. We suspect the latter. The territorial complementarity evinced between Cunil and Swasey goes back to Preceramic times before either group adopted ceramic technology. That Swasey postdates Cunil pottery by at least a century makes the clear stylistic differences between them all the more remarkable. Social marking and claims to distinct social identities appear to have been clearly intended. Pyburn's (1994:430) comments appear apropos:

> ...the people who made Swasey pottery were trying to communicate something with it, and considering the distance that Swasey style traveled, they were probably trying to express something across or about cultural boundaries.
>
> It is no accident that the earliest assemblages of material culture we recognize as Maya consist mainly of Swasey pottery. Swasey was created, in some part, to proclaim "We are Maya," and it set the stage for the growth of interaction between sites, and the eventual regionalization and rise of complex society in the Maya Lowlands. (Pyburn 1994:432)

Given what appears to be clear regional rivalry between Cunil and Swasey during their brief period of contemporaneity, the messages of both were probably more specific as to their particular way of being Maya.

The adoption of pottery in the Cunil territory corresponds to the first clear signs of village sedentism and, thus, advanced tribalism. The evidence of social ranking follows so close on the heels of the first evidence of pottery that it calls into question our working assumption that early ceramic villages were egalitarian and tribal. Awe (1992) makes a plausible case for the presence of social ranking during the Cunil phase at Cahal Pech, Belize; he estimates its start at about 1000 bc, the beginning of the phase, but his data for presumed privileged consumption of foreign goods such as jade and obsidian, and for special domestic architecture, actually demonstrate social ranking within Cahal Pech towards the end of the phase, thus our more conservative estimate of 900 bc (Table 1) for the presence of ranking and hereditary social inequality at this village. Subsequent excavations at Cahal Pech recovered evidence of three additional sequences of domestic buildings and associated refuse that strengthen Awe's claims for ranking, and our chronology for it, by showing differential consumption of jade artifacts and special incised pots, and distinctions in domestic architecture that parallel the consumption patterns (Cheetham 1996, 1998). This time period around 900 bc represents

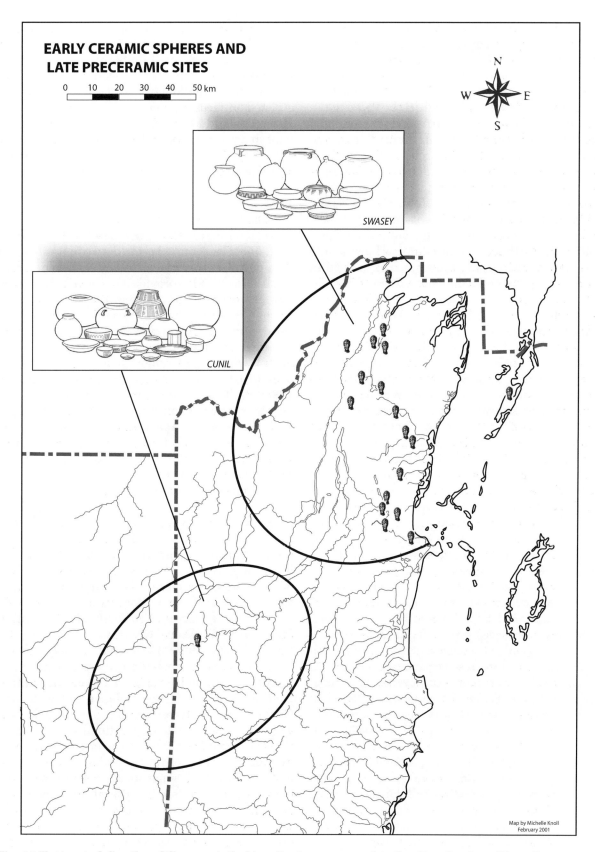

EARLY CERAMIC SPHERES AND LATE PRECERAMIC SITES

SWASEY

CUNIL

Map by Michelle Knoll
February 2001

Fig. 13 Estimated Cunil and Swasey tribal territories compared to the distribution of Late Preceramic artifacts.

307

the final curtain for tribalism in the western Belize region. The beginnings of tribalism are more hypothetical, given the thin record of traces.

One of the consequences of the reassessment of MacNeish's Archaic materials and claims for a continuous cultural sequence from the Paleoindian through the Archaic has been a foreshortening of the estimated Archaic period, limiting it principally to the Late Archaic (Marcus 1995). In effect, Lowe points represent the first substantial population that left discernible evidence in the region; other than a few early projectile points there is no evidence currently of significant human presence in Belize between 9000 and 3500 bc (Iceland 1997:175). We think that Late Archaic Lowe points [sic] were multipurpose knives, perhaps used in processing game and fish, among other things. In contrast, chipped-stone tools characteristic of the Late Preceramic appear designed for more agricultural pursuits. There appears to have been substantial population continuity from this Early Preceramic era to ceramic times (Cunil and Swasey), with the pollen record showing increasing reliance on cultivated plants. We believe that tribalism was already in place beginning with the first evidence of the Preceramic about 3000 bc and that it continued until the latter half of the Cunil phase, about 900 bc. Tribalism persisted several centuries longer in northern Yucatan. As summarized by Iceland et al. (1995:15), the data from Colha provide the best picture of the Late Archaic.

> It seems clear that fairly intensive stone quarrying and production activities were taking place at various locations in the northern Belize chert-bearing zone going back, possibly continuously, to at least 3000 B.C. Even at this early date, stoneworking shows evidence of standardization and skill.... These lithic activities, moreover, coincided with the initial appearance of cultigens and possible gradual intensification of agriculture in some parts of the region. At Colha, where they occur together, the combination of cultivation and chert exploitation provide some evidence of population size, concentration, and permanence of residence beyond that of hunter-foragers. It may be that together, the year-round potential for cultivating and gathering resources on the swamp margin and exploiting the lithic raw material of the nearby uplands provided the initial incentives for sedentism, territoriality, social differentiation, and eventual adoption of Mesoamerican cultural traditions in this corner of the eastern Maya lowlands.

Given the truncated village tribal era for northern Belize, our knowledge of possible integrative mechanisms is scant. Limited data for the Late Preceramic era indicate low-level craft specialization in chert implements and exchange of constricted unifaces to peoples living in northernmost Belize (Iceland 1997:208). As we saw for other cases, long-distance exchange began by the end of the Late Archaic all across proto-Mesoamerica—thus signaling significant contact among peoples and, consequently, knowledge of others' cultural practices.

The picture of village tribalism in Belize comes from 10 test excavations in Plaza B at Cahal Pech (Fig. 5:9). Consequently, the data are limited, but they parallel other cases already reviewed and, in some respects, also provide some intriguing ambiguities worth special consideration. To date, excavations have revealed remains of four sequences of residential structures at Cahal Pech. This small hill-top hamlet is estimated to have been .75 ha in extent, with other small hamlets located on adjacent hill tops within a 2 km area (Cheetham 1998:20). This loose arrangement of settlement parallels the pre-rank village clusters at both Paso de la Amada, Chiapas, and San José Mogote, Oaxaca. A total of 75-150 persons are estimated for greater Cahal Pech during Cunil times, a cipher that compares favorably with that for Tierras Largas phase San José Mogote.

The evidence for rank society at Cahal Pech consists of differences in consumption of special goods and elaboration of domestic architecture. No human burials for this time have been found. One of the four residences is much fancier than the others, and many more special goods were found there than elsewhere. Exotic artifacts include jade mosaic pieces, marine shell beads, obsidian flakes imported from highland Guatemala (Awe 1992:341; Awe and Healy 1994), and special incised pots with crosses, possible bird-wing designs, and other motifs (Cheetham 1998; Fig. 8). The motifs on these pots share a family resemblance to those from Oaxaca and elsewhere in 1000 bc Mesoamerica and are solid evidence of foreign influence and connections at Cahal Pech. That these incised pots show up almost exclusively at the elaborate residences and not the others suggests controlled access and perhaps benefits deriving therefrom (Cheetham 1995, 1998). As with the Oaxaca and Mazatan cases, the evidence of privileged consumption of foreign goods, and of items with borrowed symbols, suggest the presence of charismatic leaders (aggrandizers or big men types) in the Maya Lowlands by 1000 bc.

The most elaborate residence in question is Structure B-IV 10c-sub, and it was preserved by being encased in later building amplifications. Structure B-IV has a lengthy history as its 13 construction episodes span the entire occupational sequence at Cahal Pech, from 1000 bc to AD 900, and it may even cap a thin layer of Late Archaic deposit as its lowermost level appears to be aceramic (Cheetham 1995:27, 1998:21). In its later instantiations, Structure B-IV was a modest temple in a formal plaza, but our interest here is in the earliest buildings underneath the later superimposed temples. Structure B-IV appears to have begun as an insignificant residential structure that was rebuilt and elaborated through time, with the location eventually deemed a worthy site for a public shrine. The size and elaboration of the final Structure B-IV Cunil residences are reminiscent of the public buildings described for the Valley of Oaxaca. Therefore, the argument that these buried Cunil buildings represent special residences of the village hereditary leader rather than ritual structures merits special attention here.

> The most elaborate example of Cunil phase architecture (Structure B-IV 10c-sub)...consisted of a lime-plastered pole-and-thatch building set on a 20 cm high lime-plastered platform with the door side (or long axis) oriented slightly west of magnetic north. The interior floor of this building, which is also lime-plastered, is 20 cm lower than the platform on which the building sat. A 65 cm wide lime-plastered "bench" abuts the east interior wall; a similar bench probably borders the west interior wall as well. The exterior walls...were decorated "barber-pole" style with vertical bands of dull red paint.... (Cheetham 1998:22)

In contrast, other Cunil residences discovered below the leveled area of Plaza B were built on low platforms, with tamped floors of a mixture of earth, clay, and marl. Superstructures were of pole and thatch. Lime plaster was not used in or on these buildings, nor were their exterior walls painted (Cheetham 1996, 1998:21). Nonetheless, residents of these dwellings had access to jade and marine shell beads, as well as obsidian, albeit in lesser quantities than their neighbors residing in 10c-sub (Cheetham 1996).

The distinctions among these buildings fit those described by Marcus and Flannery (1996) for San José Mogote in their argument for Men's Houses and Initiates Temples. Was Cahal Pech Structure B-IV 10c-sub such a ritual building, or was it a

residence? Awe's (1992:341) initial appraisal was that "The large quantity and variety of the artefacts, plus the exotic source of several items (jade, obsidian, and marine shell) within Cache 1 (found on the floor of Structure B-IV 10c-sub) indicates that Str. B-4 was either the dwelling of a wealthy family, or that the structure was used for important ritual functions." He decided in favor of the former, and we concur. We interpret the structure as a residence—and evidence of hereditary inequality by this time—rather than a public ritual building. The similarities in the Belize and Oaxaca buildings turn out to be superficial.

In terms of archaeological indicators of past use, the Cahal Pech buildings share more similarities to the chiefly residence at Paso de la Amada, Chiapas, than to the San José Mogote buildings. That temples were constructed over Structure B-IV residences is intriguing and would seem to favor a ritual use for the earlier buildings, but history does not work backwards like this, despite optimistic claims of direct historicists. History evaluated in a forward direction requires documenting the earliest buildings and then determining subsequent changes in form and possibly function through time. The earliest structures beneath 10-sub were similar to the three Cunil residences described for other parts of the site, having tamped marl-clay-earth floors, pole-and-thatch superstructures, and normal domestic refuse is associated with these buildings (Floors 13-sub, 12, and 11 of Str. B-IV) (Awe 1992:205-208). The later buildings (10 a-sub, 10b, 10c, and 10d) also involved more than one structure. Cheetham (1996, 1998) suggests that the normal domestic unit comprised a main dwelling and one or more out-buildings. The fact that these earlier residences are not elaborate gives us confidence that rank society did not begin with the founding of Cahal Pech and that it began as a tribal hamlet.

Aside from cleanliness issues and associated domestic refuse, including figurines and food remains, the Cahal Pech Cunil-phase Structure B-IV buildings also differ from the postulated Oaxaca Men's Houses in basic building biographies. No two sequential structures of the B-IV sequence were exactly the same. There was a consistent elaboration and amplification through time—with an eventual change in form and function (Awe 1992:133-36; Cheetham 1996). In this regard, it is of interest that the penultimate Cunil residence on this spot was purposely burned down, and at least one cache of objects was left on the floor (Awe 1992:121-23); not all of the floor was exposed in the excavation unit, but a short tunnel revealed that the cache was limited to the excavated portion. Awe (1992:135, 341) considers the cache of 133 items a consequence of a termination ritual. Cache 1 included special items that may have been costume elements or parts of a mask, such as three carved jade mosaic elements, one drilled canine tooth, a perforated peccary scapula, and 19 marine shell beads. We think that the termination ritual may have included torching the house as part of a mortuary ritual commemorating the death of the village leader who once occupied this spot, with subsequent superimposed buildings being shrines to his memory and eventually temples. This would be a natural sequence for ancestor veneration thought to have been practiced in Oaxaca and in the Maya Lowlands in slightly later times (McAnany 1995). The cached materials may have been some of the leaders' personal belongings, with some items suggestive of costuming and perhaps shamanistic functions.

These last speculations carry us afield from our main point. The compelling logic for the identification of Men's Houses in Oaxaca is the rigid history of form and imputed function involved. In fact, what we are presented with is the lack of history as played out over time. The buildings represent constancy of form and, supposedly, function. Superimposed buildings maintained the same size, shape, internal features, and elaborated construction materials, such as plaster floors and white-washed walls. In contrast, the Cahal Pech B-IV structures evince development and change from building to building, beginning with a common residence, transformation to a special residence, and later transformation to a shrine and temple.

The processes leading to the transformation of tribalism at Cahal Pech are not yet clear, but they seem to have involved some of the same sort of social strivers we have seen before. The special artifacts found associated with Str. B-IV 10c-sub show that this household was involved in long-distance exchange, accumulation, and perhaps ceramic innovation. A case can also be made for involvement in ritual activity and shamanism (see Cheetham 1998). For the moment, all the proto-Mesoamerican cases considered here suggest that involvement in ritual was a fundamental aspect of tribal village leadership, and perhaps part of its eventual undoing and transformation to rank society.

Proto-Mesoamerican Prescriptions for Tribal Integration

We have proposed three types of tribal societies for proto-Mesoamerica that correspond roughly to horticulture-foragers (ca. 5000-2500 bc), collector-horticulturalists (ca. 2500-1500 bc), and village-agriculturalists (ca. 1500-1100 bc.) Data adduced to make our case are still underwhelming for all issues, so our remarks are necessarily more speculative than substantive. To move beyond naive efforts of trying to identify past tribal societies from the calculated square-footage of their scattered garbage, we will need information on social activities and practices. Here in our concluding considerations of possible tribal institutions, we focus on some of the more important integrative mechanisms proposed for proto-Mesoamerica in its waning moments of village tribalism.

Our proposal of an era of minimal tribes (horticulture-foragers) is just a guess, with the best information for its timing and content coming from the poorly-known Basin of Mexico case. By 2500 bc, however, the evidence for all regions of proto-Mesoamerica for the existence of collector-horticulture tribes is much more convincing. Greater reliance on a partially-produced food supply and of shifts in settlement indicate that a significant change had occurred. We attribute these changes, as do others (Piperno and Pearsall 1998; Pohl et al. 1996), to more productive cultigens such as maize and manioc, greater reliance on shifting cultivation in the tropical lowlands, and formation of larger and more permanent groups: tribes. We have few clues as to how these tribes functioned, but in the long temporal view, they appear to have been stable social groups, persisting for at least a 1000 years in most regions of proto-Mesoamerica (e.g., Oaxaca and Chiapas), and for at least 2000 years in the Maya Lowlands. How much of this presumed stability was due to smart social practices, or how much to ecological constraints to producing a more ample food surplus that could support larger groups, remains an open question. We have necessarily linked the early developments of tribalism to issues of the food quest. Ecological opportunities and constraints of various regions for providing food for foragers, coupled with environmental possibilities for growing the various domestic plants to sweeten ecological potentials through horticulture, explain the general timing of collector tribes in proto-Mesoamerica.

Although we have portrayed developments as general and pervasive, the tribalization of Middle America was not a homogeneous or synchronous process. The physical and cultural landscapes were heterogeneous, and this antecedent diversity had a limiting effect on the development and historic spread of tribal institutions in the region. The slow developments in the domestication of various sorts of plants, and their spread to appropriate growing regions had a great deal to do with the rise of collector-horticulturalists. The ability to manage part of one's food supply and supplement a region's natural bounty transformed the conditions of possibility for forming and remaining in larger groups throughout the year. The widespread changes in settlement patterns at 2500 bc in proto-Mesoamerica demonstrate that most peoples took advantage of basic techniques of food production and the consequent opportunities to reside in larger, less nomadic groups.

In some unusual circumstances, such as the famous Tehuacán Valley case (MacNeish 1964, 1972, 1992, 2001c), local conditions without agriculture may have been comfortable enough, and the addition of early maize horticulture marginal enough (see Piperno and Pearsall 1998:314), that peoples persisted in their pre-tribal ways longer than in other areas. The magnitude of the local horticultural opportunity failed to provide sufficient motivation or opportunity for change. We suspect an analogous situation obtained for the Lowland Maya and their collector-horticulture adaptation. Of the many ways to interpret the data, perhaps one of the fairer ways is to suppose that the early Maya had established a workable adaptation that served them well, and they were under-motivated to adopt pottery and village sedentism, given their comfort levels, when their neighbors did. What appears in the comparative historical record as laggard behavior may, in fact, be evidence of a robust adaptation to local conditions extremely favorable for semi-nomadic lifeways.

The rise of sedentary village tribes, or what we consider complex tribalism, beginning about 1600-1400 bc does not appear to accord with any obvious changes in agricultural techniques or improved varieties of domesticated plants (it may correspond to climatic changes). Village life does correspond to the adoption of ceramic-vessel technology (contra Arnold 1999). Nucleated village living necessitated a major advance in social integration to attract and hold people together with minimal blood-shed, but tribal village life appears to have been relatively unstable as it lasted less than two centuries in many regions (Table 1). In fact, the usurpation of tribal life appears to have been a village affair, perhaps because of an unhealthy conjunction of circumstances: tight and tethered living in a confined space, the production of dependable surpluses, the need periodically to use aging surpluses to make room for new ones, and the presence of social strivers who knew how to put stale surpluses to good use in sponsoring public functions. Charismatic leaders and aggrandizers appear to have been the principal beneficiaries in the transformation of village tribes into rank societies, a transformation that occurred about 1300-1000 bc in most regions of proto-Mesoamerica. In the process, tribal institutions were also transformed to serve the interests of the new hereditary village leaders, Mesoamerica's first chiefs.

What were the institutions that served proto-Mesoamerican tribes for over two millennia? They were cultural practices and institutions for promoting larger group size and locational permanence. Our review of four cases provided a roster of possible late tribal practices. The Oaxaca case contributes arguments for dance grounds, gift-giving, Men's Houses (and associated initiation rites that may have included ingestion of narcotics), ancestor veneration, and the clan principle. The more limited data from highland Mexico suggest the importance of shamanism, possible social occasions involving costumed dancers and music, and playing ball. Chiapas coastal societies are thought to have sponsored feasts, ritual drinking, gaming, gambling, communal work projects of various sorts, gift-giving, and to have engaged in shamanistic practices. For the Lowland Maya we have suggested some shamanistic practices and ancestor veneration. In all cases, charismatic leaders, or aggrandizers, are thought to have been those who held achieved leadership positions and who planned and sponsored the sundry activities that brought people together, logistically and socially. Whether this current consensus concerning village tribalism and charismatic leaders will be supported by future data, or prove to be merely a passing scholarly fad, remains to be seen. Clearly, this list of tribal institutions is fabulously incomplete; nonetheless, the postulated and inferred practices are sufficient to support several important observations.

Proto-Mesoamerican tribes, as do all tribes, faced the dilemma of aggregation. Tribal peoples

311

had manifold reasons for getting together with others, but crowds are trouble. Social tensions and problems multiply with simple additions of members to a group. In our simplified view of things, tribes had motive and opportunity to get people together, but not the direct means. Tribal societies are similar to lame-duck administrations, the social equivalents of *responsibility without authority*. Absent authority to command, how did tribal leaders coax people together and persuade them to behave decorously? They managed this marvel of social physics in the same way that similar structurally-wounded organizations work today: by manipulating incentive structures, and/or changing peoples' perceptions of incentive structures, to draw them along paths of least resistance towards desired ends. Thus characterized, the tribal dilemma and its solutions are basic politics writ small. If our list of probable tribal institutions from proto-Mesoamerica is correct enough to undergird analysis, then tribal leaders there pursued the two obvious solutions for promoting aggregation: enticing people to congregate by giving them what they wanted, and giving them what they needed while persuading them to want it.

Tribal leaders in proto-Mesoamerica appealed to base motives of self-gratification and higher, spiritual motives. In modern terms, tribal institutions oscillated between the ancient equivalents of spring break and midnight mass. Diversionary institutions of the first sort, such as gaming, gambling, drinking, gift-giving, and feasting were self-recruiting and required minimal supervision or discipline. Serious institutions of the second order, such as male initiations, ancestor worship, marriage, burial, or other life-crisis rites occurred under the sanction of the ultimate controlling supernatural authority. Sin and sacraments became an unbeatable pair for promoting group cohesion. In sum, a wide range of social practices provided an assortment of good reasons for getting together and sharing a good time, or a critical time.

Most practices inferred for village tribal societies persisted long after tribes transformed themselves into rank societies. Our basic chronology of possible forms of tribalism demonstrates that village tribalism was indeed ephemeral (Table 1), as Sanders and Price suggested in the epigraph, compared to the more stable and long-lived forms of horticultural tribes. The brief career of village tribalism reveals a basic instability, probably because of unforeseen, long-term consequences of short-term decisions for maintaining group cohesion. It is not clear how the transition to village tribalism

occurred, but it everywhere appeared flanked by agriculture and ceramic technology, and nearly always with ceramic figurines. These appear to have been a package deal, and given our analysis, they should be seen as fundamental tribal institutions. Referring to structural contradictions rather than vitalism, we propose that tribal village life carried the seeds of its own transformation. Village life only became stable in later times with the advent of social stratification and sanctioned means of enforcing social discipline.

Mesoamerica was clearly an outgrowth of tribal lifeways and practices. But these practices were transformed with the emergence of hereditary privilege and the institutionalization of supra-community governance. Although it is possible to trace their histories back to tribal times, institutions did not function in the same way, nor mean the same thing, for peoples of different eras. Beliefs in natural forces, for example, through time crossed the tribal-rank divide and eventually became, with the emergence of social stratification and civilization, beliefs in gods. Figurines that once may have represented ancestors in domestic rituals became transmogrified, once across the social divide, into images of rulers. Even something as innocuous as tribal games became the competitive Mesoamerica ballgame associated with high ritual and human sacrifice. The game was transformed from an integrative institution for participants to a divisive one for participants, but integrative for spectators. Examples of transformed institutions could be multiplied. Our point is that the multitude of Mesoamerican institutions need, eventually, to be traced to their tribal roots.

If as scholars we are ever to understand the evolution of Mesoamerican civilizations, we must trace its basic institutions back to their tribal lair. As demonstrated here, Mesoamerica's tribal foundations were deep and diverse, as varied as the stunning landscapes in which tribes arose and thrived. The general storyline for Mesoamerican civilization should be how social singularity grew out of tribal diversity. How were divergent tribal histories, practices, and trajectories combined, amalgamated, homogenized, and repackaged as a coherent set of fundamental Mesoamerican beliefs and practices? Current controversies concerning early Mesoamerica have the tribal contribution to its early stratified societies upside-down. Rather than seeing commonalities arising from diversity through historic interactions among various contributors over long periods of time, some scholars imagine the commonalities as deriving from an earlier, pan-Mesoamerican substrate of common practices, beliefs, and symbols. Such lapses in logic dodge responsibility for addressing issues of Archaic tribes while at the same time claiming sanctuary in imaginative reconstructions of tribal lifeways, in the absence of evidence. The time is long past for such efforts. As should be apparent, research on tribal issues is desperately needed for all regions of Mesoamerica. We hope that it is equally clear that such research will be of fundamental importance and be warmly received by the profession.

Acknowledgments

This paper is a project in progress; some arguments have a blurred history while others are still weeping wounds. Over the years we have greatly benefitted from the generosity of our colleagues and their shared comments on prior work with early ceramics, the origins of rank, and Archaic sites, their permissions to view artifact collections, and their liberality in allowing us on occasion to cite unpublished data. We are particularly grateful for the comments, instruction, access, and aid received from Pierre Agrinier, Paul E. Amoroli, Barbara Arroyo, María Aviles, Jaime Awe, Francisco Estrada Belli, Michael Blake, Fred Bové, Laura Castañeda, Donaldo Castillo V., Michael D. Coe, T. Patrick Culbert, Ann Cyphers, Annick Daneels, Laura Finsten, Vilma Fialko, Kent V. Flannery, Severin Fowles, Donald W. Forsyth, James Garber, Joaquin García Bárcena, Angel García Cook, Rebecca González L., Gillet Griffin, Thomas H. Guderjan, Norman Hammond, Richard D. Hansen, Marion Popenoe de Hatch, Paul F. Healy, John S. Henderson, Bernard Hermes, Thomas R. Hester, Warren D. Hill, Harry B. Iceland, Joel Janetski, Kevin Johnston, Rosemary Joyce, Douglas J. Kennett, Laura Kosakowsky, Juan Pedro Laporte, Lisa LeCount, Thomas A. Lee, Jr., Richard G. Lesure, Richard Leventhal, Michael W. Love, Gareth W. Lowe, Patricia A. McAnany, Guadalupe Martínez Donjuán, Joyce Marcus, Ray T. Matheny, Leonor Merino Carrión, Joseph B. Mountjoy, Jesus I. Mora-Echevarría, Carlos Navarrete, Hector Neff, Christine Niederberger, Patricia Ochoa, Arturo José Oliveros, Ponciano Ortiz, William A. Parkinson, Jeffrey R. Parsons, Tomas Peréz S., Mary D. Pohl, Helen Pollard, Kevin O. Pope, Terry Powis, Mary E. Pye, Anne K. Pyburn, Eugenia J. Robinson, María del Carmen Rodríguez, Robert M. Rosenswig, Diana Santamaria, Paul Schmit, Robert J. Sharer, Barbara Stark, Juan Luis Velásquez, René Viel, Christopher von Nagy, Barbara Voorhies, Phil C. Weigand, S. Jeffrey K. Wilkerson, Marcus Winter, and Robert N. Zeitlin. We are also grateful to the directors of the Peabody Museum at Harvard and the directors of the National Museums of Anthropology in Guatemala and Mexico City for allowing us to view ceramic collections in storage. We are especially grateful to Nora López Olivares, Director of Prehispanic and Colonial Monuments of the Institute of Anthropology and History (IDAEH) in Guatemala, for permission to view the collections of early pottery from Tikal. Our particular thanks go to Michelle Knoll for the illustrations.

Appendix 1: Data for Table 1

A. Evidence of Early Corn and Agriculture (numbers correspond to Table 1)

1. **Lake Patzcuaro**, Michoacán, Mexico: 1500 bc, pollen in lake core (Watts and Bradbury 1982).

2. **Zohapilco/Tlapacoya**, Mexico, Mexico: 5090 bc, pollen (Lorenzo and Gonzalez 1970; McClung de Tapia 1992:149; Niederberger 1979); 3000 bc, pollen (Mirambell 1978:228).

3. **Tlaxcala**, Mexico, Mexico: 5000-2500 bc, possible pollen evidence (Werner 1997:115; he cites a report of a pollen profile published in German that we have not been able to find).

4. **San Marcos Cave**, Tehuacán Valley, Puebla, Mexico: 3500 bc, cobs (Long et al. 1989:1037; Fritz 1994, 1995).

5. **Guerrero**, no data available.

6. **Guilá Naquitz**, Valley of Oaxaca, Mexico: 7300 bc, pollen (Flannery 1986:8).

7. **Valenzuela Cave**, SW Tamaulipas, Mexico: 2200 bc, Flacco phase (MacNeish 1958, 1971:574; McClung de Tapia 1992:150).

8. **North Central Veracruz**, no data available.

9. **Central Veracruz**, no data available.

10. **Laguna Pompal**, Southern Veracruz, Mexico: Lake core, 2250 bc, evidence from the same core showing the early presence of corn indicates that forest clearance was minor and, therefore, that cultivation was not intense (Goman 1992:33, cited in Arnold 2000:122 and Stark and Arnold 1997:20).

11. **San Andrés** and **La Venta**, Tabasco, Mexico: 4800 bc, pollen from three sediment cores (Pope et al. 2001; see also Rust and Leyden 1994, Rust and Sharer 1988).

12. **Santa Marta rock shelter**, Chiapas, Mexico: 4500 bc, pollen (García Bárcena 1976, 2001; MacNeish and Eubanks 2000:6).

13. **Tlacuachero**, Chiapas, Mexico: 2500 bc, phytoliths; possible 5500 bc phytolith at Cerro de las Conchas (Jones and Voorhies n.d.).

14. **Sipacate**, Guatemala: 3500 bc, "significant quantitiies" of phytoliths from sediment core SIP001 originally reported at 7000 bc, but more securely to 3500

bc; early corn pollen dating to 3500 bc was recovered in sediment core SIP99E just below a level indicating significant burning (Neff et al. 2000).

15. **Guatemala Highlands**, no data available.

16. **Petén Lakes**, Petén, Guatemala: 3600-3000 bc evidence of forest clearing; maize not present but inferred (Islebe et al. 1996). Maize pollen at 2000 bc (Cowgill and Hutchinson 1966:122; see Deevey 1978; Deevey et al. 1979; Tsukada 1966).

17. **Cob** and **Cobweb Swamps**, Belize: 3500 bc, pollen (Jones 1994; Pohl et al. 1996:263).

18. **Lake Yojoa**, Honduras: ca. 3000 bc, pollen from sediment core (Rue 1989).

19. **Copán**, Honduras: 2200 bc, pollen from the Petapilla Core 2 (Webster et al. 2000:117).

20. **El Salvador**, no data available.

B. Evidence of the latest Archaic (numbers correspond with Fig. 1)

1. **El Calón**, Sinaloa, Mexico: 1750 bc, constructed shell pyramid 25 m high (Scott 1985; Scott and Foster 2000:130).

2. **Matanchén**, Nayarit, Mexico: Coastal shell mound, 2100-1700 bc (Mountjoy 2001b; Mountjoy et al. 1972). The infrequency of Archaic remains in Western Mexico is not from lack of looking. In his various intense surface surveys, Mountjoy (1998) has only found the one site listed here.

3. **Los Portales Cave**, Michoacán, Mexico: Highland cave site, 2500-2200 bc (Michelet et al. 1989:80; Pollard 2001:459).

4. **Pátzcuaro**, Michoacán, Mexico: Highland lake shore, pollen cores 1500 bc (Watts and Bradbury 1982; see also O'Hara et al. 1993 for corroborating erosion evidence).

5. **San Nicolás** tradition, Querétero, Mexico: Highland cave site near San Juan del Río (MacNeish and Nelken-Terner 1983:81).

6. **Zohapilco/Tlapacoya**, Mexico, Mexico: Lake edge, 2000 bc (Mirambell 1978; Niederberger 1976, 1979, 1987, 1996; Watts and Bradbury 1982).

7. **Texcal Cave**, Puebla, Mexico: Highland cave, latest pre-ceramic phase, Texcal II, runs from 5000 to 2500 bc, dating determined by comparative analysis to other sequences, no radiocarbon dates for this phase (Mora and García Cook 1996:274; García Moll 1977:62).

8. **Abejas Cave**, Tehuacán Valley, Puebla, Mexico: Highland cave in semi-arid region, estimated at 2000 bc by Flannery (1983:28) to bring the original estimated date of 2500 bc (Johnson and MacNeish 1972:25) for the end of this phase and occupation in line with more recent evidence for the first pottery in Tehuacán and Oaxaca.

9. **Yazanú**, Yanhuitlán-Nochixtlán Valley, Oaxaca, Mexico: semiarid highland valley, 2000 bc (Flannery 1983:28; Lorenzo 1958).

10. **Martínez Rock Shelter**, Mitla Valley, Oaxaca, Mexico: Highland rock shelter, 2000 bc (Flannery 1983:28; Flannery et al. 1981:62).

11. **CG-1**, Guerrero, Mexico: Estuary Shell Midden, one of 11 in the Laguna de Tetitlán, 1220 ± 280 bc (Gonzáles-Quintero and Mora-Echevarría 1978:57). This is an aceramic site that could represent the end of the Archaic period or be an aceramic site during the start of the Early Formative period. Our revision of the early Pox pottery of the Guerrero coast (see section C) would put the first pottery at about this same time.

12. **Coyuco de Benítez**, Guerrero, Mexico: Estuary shell midden, no dates (Schmidt and Litvak King 1986:36).

13. **Puerto Marquéz & Zanja**, Guerrero, Mexico: Estuary shell mounds, 2300 bc (Brush 1965).

14. **Romero Cave**, Tamaulipas, Mexico: Highland cave, 1800-1400 bc (MacNeish 1971:574).

15. **Santa Luisa**, Veracruz, Mexico: Lowland riverine, 2400 bc (Wilkerson 1975, 1981, 2001a, c).

16. **Trapiche**, Veracruz, Mexico: Lowland riverine, no date, late pre-ceramic (García Payón 1971:512).

17. **El Viejón**, Veracruz, Mexico: Lowland riverine, no date, late pre-ceramic (García Payón 1971:512).

18. **Colonia Ejidal**, Veracruz, Mexico: Lowland riverine, 2400 bc, radiocarbon date (Daneels 1997:213).

19. **Cerro de las Conchas,** Veracruz, Mexico: Coastal shell midden with aceramic layers (Lorenzo 1961:16).

20. **Laguna Pompal**, Veracruz, Mexico: Lowland, mountain lake, 2000 bc (Goman 1992, cited in Arnold 2000, and in Stark and Arnold 1997:20).

21. **San Andrés & La Venta**, Tabasco, Mexico: Lowland Estuary/ swamp, 2100 bc (Pope et al 2001; Rust and Leyden 1994; Rust and Sharer 1988).

22. **Camcum rock shelter**, Chiapas, Mexico: Highland valley rock shelter near fresh water spring and river, no date, aceramic levels below the ceramic levels, no depositional break in the stratigraphy. If it is truly Late Archaic rather than merely aceramic, then it represents the very end of the period, estimated at 1600-1450 bc (Lee and Clark 1988).

23. **Vuelta Limón**, Chiapas, Mexico: Coastal riverine 1800 bc (Voorhies 1996, 2001).

24. **Islona Chantuto**, Chiapas, Mexico: Estuary shell middens, 1800 bc (Blake et al. 1995; Voorhies 1976, 1996, 2001).

25. **Campón**, Chiapas, Mexico: Estuary shell middens, 1800 bc (Blake et al. 1995; Voorhies 1976, 1996, 2001).

26. **Tlacuachero**, Chiapas, Mexico: Estuary shell middens, 1800 bc (Blake et al. 1995; Voorhies 1976, 1996, 2001).

27. **El Chorro**, Chiapas, Mexico: Estuary shell middens, 1800 bc (Blake et al. 1995; Voorhies 1976, 1996, 2001).

28. **Zapotillo**, Chiapas, Mexico: Estuary shell middens, 1800 bc (Blake et al. 1995; Voorhies 1976, 1996, 2001).

29. **San Carlos**, Chiapas, Mexico: Lowland riverine, 2200 bc, 1-3 m below lowest ceramic levels (Barra levels), separated by river sand (Clark 1994; Voorhies 1996).

30. **Grajeda**, Sipacate, coastal Guatemala; 7000-2500 bc, data from two sediment cores (Neff et al. 2000).

31. **Quiché Basin** sites, Guatemala, Highland valley: These are surface sites with patinated, basalt flake tools that have not been dated, and their hypothetical terminal date was calculated by estimating the first appearance of pottery. This late date of 1000 bc is therefore

based on the supposed date for the adoption of pottery in this region, but it has not been independently confirmed (see Brown 1980; Weeks 2001).

32. **Petenxil**, Guatemala: Lake shore, 2000 bc (Deevey et al. 1979).

33. **Quexil**, Guatemala: Lake shore, 1500-900 bc (Deevey et al. 1979).

34. **Sacnab**, Guatemala: Lake shore, 1500-900 bc (Deevey et al. 1979).

35. **Loltún**, Yucatan, Mexico: 1800 bc, Lowland cave site (Velázquez Valadéz 1980).

36. **Corozal**, Belize: Lowland coast, surface find of constricted uniface (Iceland and Hester 1996).

37. **Cob**, Belize: Lowland riverine (Pohl et al. 1996).

38. **Strath Bogue (PR 10)**, Belize: Upland site west of Progresso Lagoon; the base of a constricted uniface was recovered with patinated chert flakes in aceramic levels (Rosenswig and Masson 2002).

39. **Subop 7 (PR 9)**, Belize: Upland site west of Progresso Lagoon; patinated chert flakes found in orange soil horizons, but no diagnostic artifacts were recognized (Rosenswig and Masson 2002).

40. **Fred Smith Site (PR 11)**, Belize: Site on the shore of Progresso Lagoon; numerous patinated flakes recovered in aceramic, orange soil horizon (Rosenswig and Masson 2002).

41. **Betz Landing**, Belize: Lowland riverine (Zeitlin 1984:364).

42. **Patt Work Site (PR 12)**, Belize: Upland site west of Progresso Lagoon; patinated chert flakes found in orange soil horizons, but no diagnostic artifacts were recovered (Rosenswig and Masson 2002).

43. **Caye Coco (PR1)**, Belize: Island in Progresso Lagoon, northern Belize. Patinated chert flakes and a constricted uniface were found in orange soil horizon. The documented extent of the Archaic deposits is 150 m² (Rosenswig 2001, 2002; Rosenswig and Masson 2002).

44. **Pulltrouser**, Belize: Lowland riverine, swamp (Bower 1994; Pohl and Pope 2001; Pohl et al. 1996).

45. **Laguna de Coco,** Belize: Lowland riverine, swamp (B. Hansen 1990).

46. **San Antonio**, Belize: Lowland riverine, swamp (Pohl et al. 1990; Pohl et al. 1996).

47. **Doubloon Bank Lagoon**, Belize: Site on the shore of Progresso Lagoon; a constricted uniface and patinated flakes were recovered. (Rosenswig and Masson 2002; Iceland 1997:206).

48. **Laguna de On (LO1)**, Belize: Island in the lagoon; patinated chert flakes found in aceramic levels, and a constricted uniface found in mixed context with Postclassic artifacts (Rosenswig and Masson 2002; Rosenswig and Stafford 1998).

49. **Laguna de Cayo Francesa**, Belize: Lowland peninsula, surface find of constricted uniface (Iceland 1997:215; see Guderjan 1993 for location).

50. **Kichpanha**, Belize: Lowland, constricted uniface found on the surface (Gibson 1991:229).

51. **Colha & Cobweb**, Belize: Lowland riverine, swamp, 1500-1100 bc (Hester et al. 1996; Iceland 1997), the acceptable sigma ranges on the younger dates overlap

with the appearance of pottery, so there was no interval between the terminal Archaic and the earliest Formative, in this case the Middle Formative as evaluated in the broader region.

52. **Maskall North,** Belize: Lowland interior (Gibson 1991; Hester et al. 1996; Iceland 1997:206).

53. **Quashie Banner Creek**, Belize: Lowland interior (Gibson 1991; Hester et al. 1996; Iceland 1997:206).

54. **Rockstone Pond**, Belize: Inland riverine (Iceland 1997:211).

55. **Lowe Ranch (BAAR 35, BAAR 31)**, Belize: Lowland interior (Gibson1991; Hester et al. 1996; Iceland 1997:206; Zeitlin 1984).

56. **Davis Bank**, Belize: Lowland interior (Gibson1991; Hester et al. 1996; Iceland 1997:206; Zeitlin 1984).

57. **Sand Hill**, Belize: Lowland interior (Gibson1991; Hester et al. 1996; Iceland 1997:206; Zeitlin 1984).

58. **Kelly Site,** Belize: Lowland interior (Gibson1991; Hester et al. 1996; Iceland 1997:206; Zeitlin 1984).

59. **Ladyville (1 & 32)** Belize: Lowland interior (Iceland 1997:213).

60. **Cockloft Farm**, Belize: Lowland riverine (Iceland 1997:206).

61. **Puerto Escondido**, Sula Valley, Honduras: Lowland riverine; this is slim evidence coming from an aceramic deposit under the lowest levels of the site, separated by a thin sterile sand and clay layer from the overlying Barrahona deposits (Henderson and Joyce 1998:13; Joyce and Henderson 2001).

62. **Rio Pelo**, Honduras: Lowland riverine, no date (Rue 1989; Wonderly 1991; Wonderly and Caputi 1984). Lorenzo (1961:17) cites the coastal shell midden site of **Jericó** as Archaic, based on an early report by Stone (1941), but the site is not Archaic (Healy 1984:230; Rosemary Joyce, personal communication, 2001).

63. **Lake Yojoa**, Honduras: Lake shore, dated sediment core and pollen, 3000 bc (Rue 1989).

64. **Copán**, Honduras: Inland riverine, swamp, 1700 bc from Petapilla Core 2 (Webster et al. 2000:116-117). The evidence of Late Archaic occupation under the site of Copán comes from pre-radiocarbon era excavations (Longyear 1948) and has not been dated or investigated since (cf. Schortman and Urban 2001).

65. **La Periquita**, El Salvador: shell midden/ island in the western Gulf of Fonseca, ca. 2000 bc (Paul Amaroli, personal communication, 1999).

C. Earliest Pottery Complexes (site numbers correspond with Fig. 2)

Capacha: 1. Capacha, Colima, western Mexico: (I. Kelly 1980; see also Baus de Czitrom1989; Mountjoy 1994, 2001a) This complex is tied to the El Opeño question (see below) as ceramics of each type have been found in association in early tombs (Cabrera 1989; Oliveros 1989; Mountjoy 1989; Weigand 1985:61-63, 2000, 2001). We tentatively accept an early beginning date of 1600-1400 bc date for these two complexes (proposed by Kelley 1980) and an ending date of about 1000-800 bc. Both of these complexes relate to the Tlatilco complex in the Basin of Mexico that dates to about 1200-1000 bc, and this is also the high point of the El Opeño and Capacha complexes. The range of dates for both complexes stretch back earlier than ceramic cross-ties would allow, as noted by Mountjoy (1994, 2000, 2001a; see Grove 2000b). This corresponds to Oliveros and de los Ríos Paredes' (1993:47) later radiocarbon dates of about 1200-800 bc for El Opeño, and thus for both complexes, following the evidence and reasoning of Mountjoy (1989:14, 1994, 1998:254). We cannot dismiss the earlier dates, but given the long period of the phase, the detailed ceramic cross-ties are accommodated without belying the early dates. We bracket the dates here as 1400-1000 bc.

El Opeño: 2. El Opeño, Michoacan/Jalisco, western Mexico: 1200-800 bc (Noguera 1939; Oliveros 1974, 1989; Oliveros and de los Ríos Paredes 1993; Williams 2001); see preceding commentary.

Chajil: 3. Altamirano, Veracruz, Mexico: 1600 bc, the date proposed by the investigators appears reasonable to us on the basis of internal evidence, radiocarbon sequences, and relationships and cross-ties of other early complexes (Castañeda 1989, 1992; Clark and Gosser 1995; Merino and Garcia Cook 1987, 1989; personal observation JEC)

Raudal: 4. Santa Luisa, Veracruz, Mexico: 1600 bc, this is slightly younger than Wilkerson's (1981:182) estimate of 1700 bc. We have lowered his estimate to bring this early assemblage in line with all the other assemblages that it resembles. Further documentation, larger samples, and more dates will be required to establish the earlier date.

Unnamed: 5. Colonia Ejidal, Veracruz, Mexico: 1500 bc is our estimate of what are described as Ocós-like sherds (Daneels 2000); these would align with Ojochi and Locona pottery described for southern Veracruz and coastal Chiapas.

Tlalpan & Nevada: 6. Cuicuilco, Mexico, Mexico; 7. Tlapacoya, Mexico, Mexico; 1550 bc for Cuicuilco (Tolstoy 1978:245, 252-53; personal observation JEC & DC). **Tlalpan** is minor complex of questionable authenticity, but we have examined a collection of sherds and think that the hypothetical early date is probable. We estimate this as a very thin phase pending better documentation. The following **Nevada** phase defined at Tlapacoya is more secure at 1450 bc (Nichols 2001; Niederberger 1976. 1987, 2000; Tolstoy 1978). Nevada lines up stylistically with the Tierras Largas complex from the Valley of Oaxaca. The distribution of early pottery in the Basin of Mexico is based upon the distribution of Nevada pottery. Grove (2000b) argues for two different ceramic complexes for the Basin of Mexico with affinities to adjacent regions, but these date to the period following the Nevada phase.

Tzompantepec: 8. Las Bocas, Puebla, Mexico: 1500 bc, we have shaved a century from García Cook's (1981; García Cook and Merino C. 1988) rounded bi-century estimates for his early phase of the Puebla/Tlaxcala region. No carbon dates are reported, and his estimates were based on cross-ties to complexes that were originally estimated as older than they really are. Tolstoy (1978) reports early pottery at the site of Las Bocas.

Cacahuananche: 9. Atopula, Guerrero, Mexico; 10. Teopantecuanitlán, Guerrero: Mexico: 1400 bc for the Atopula site (Henderson 1979). We have extended this identification to cover the early complex at nearby Teopantecuanitlán. We have avoided the issue of Xochipala (Gay 1972) because we are not convinced that it is Early Preclassic; none of the early figurines and objects have been recovered in scientific excavations (Paul Schmit, personal communication); thermoluminesence dating of some of the figurines yield an early date of 1500 bc (Gillet Griffin, personal communication), and other objects such as carved stone bowls would fit into the Early Formative pattern. If so, developments in Guerrero would be comparable to those in neighboring regions.

Pox: 11. Puerto Marquéz, Guerrero, Mexico: 1500 bc. We have listed this date much later than originally reported and popularly repeated because the ceramics are similar to those from the Tierras Largas phase from Oaxaca (see Clark and Gosser 1995 for detailed arguments about the radiocarbon dates and ceramic cross-ties).

Espiridión & Tierras Largas: 12. Purrón, Puebla, Mexico; 13. Yucuita, Oaxaca, Mexico; 14. San José Mogote, Oaxaca, Mexico: We have included the famous **Purrón** complex from the Tehuacán Valley, Puebla, with the **Espiridión** materials from the Valley of Oaxaca in a wider ceramic sphere. These first two complexes are only poorly known, so the distribution shown in Fig. 2 corresponds to the succeeding well attested **Tierras Largas** complex that dates to about 1450 bc (Flannery and Marcus 1994; personal observation JEC).We have down-graded the exaggerated claims for the antiquity of the Purrón complex to 1600 bc based on its similarities with the better contextualized materials from Oaxaca (see Flannery and Marcus 1994), for reasons given by Clark and Gosser (1995), rather than the oft-cited estimates of 2500 bc (MacNeish et al. 1970:21, 2001c; Johnson and MacNeish 1972). The Espiridión ceramics align with the late Purrón pottery from the Tehuacán Valley (Flannery and Marcus 1994; Marcus 1983a; Marcus and Flannery 1996). Our estimate of 1550 bc for Espiridión is consistent with this logic and ceramic cross-dating.

Ojochi & Manatí A: 15. San Lorenzo, Veracruz, Mexico; 16. El Manatí, Veracruz, Mexico: 1500 bc (Coe and Diehl 1980; Ortíz and Rodriguez 1994:75-77, 1999:228; personal observation JEC).

Estero & Pellicer: 17. San Andrés, Tabasco, Mexico: 1500 bc, based on stylistic similarities to other complexes (Sisson 1976; see also, Lowe 1978, von Nagy 1997; von Nagy et al. 2000).

Lagunita: 18. Laguna Zope, Oaxaca, Mexico: 1450 bc, based on similarities to pottery from San Lorenzo and the Chiapas coast (Zeitlin 1978, 1979, 2001).

Aripi: 19. Miramar/Mirador, Chiapas, Mexico: 20. Chiapa de Corzo, Chiapas, Mexico: 1450 bc (Agrinier, Cheetham, and Lowe 2000, personal observation JEC).

Pre-Chiuaan: 21. Trinidad, Tabasco, Mexico: 1400 bc, based on ceramic cross-ties to Chiapas sequences (Lowe

1978; Rands 1987).

Lato: 22. Camcum, Chiapas, Mexico: 1450 bc (Clark 1990; Clark et al. n.d.); Lato sherds also found at other open sites in the region.

Barra: 23. Altamira, Paso de la Amada, and San Carlos, Chiapas, Mexico: 1600 bc (Blake et al. 1995; Ceja 1985; Gosser 1994; Lowe 1975, 1978; redefined by Clark).

Madre Vieja: 24. Medina, Guatemala: 1600 bc, related to and contemporaneous with the Barra complex (Arroyo 1994; personal observation JEC).

Bostán: 25. El Carmen, El Salvador: 1550 bc (Arroyo 1995, personal observation JEC)

Arévalo: 26. Kaminaljuyú, Guatemala: This is a phantom phase that remains to be anchored in time with a sufficient collection, stratigraphy, and dates. The estimate of 950-800 bc is much recent than normally published (see Shook and Hatch 1999; cf. Lowe 1978); this dating is based on preliminary ceramic cross-times of a special collection of materials from near the ancient Miraflores lake in the possession of Marion Popenoe de Hatch. Clark places this probable Arévalo collection to this time frame based on similarities to pottery from the Chiapas and Guatemalan coasts (personal observation 2000, JEC). The following Las Charcas phase remains to be adequately dated, too, but its beginning placement to about 800 bc is firm based upon stylistic similarities to the pottery of its neighbors. The distribution of early highland Guatemala pottery conforms to the Las Charcas sphere. Recent finds of early pottery at the site of Piedra Parada in the Valley of Guatemala (Hermes and Velásquez 2001) corresponds to the Arévalo complex (personal observation 2001, JEC) and underlies Las Charcas pottery.

Xox: 27. El Portón, Guatemala; 28. Sakajut, Guatemala: 1100 bc, based on ceramic cross-ties to pottery from coastal Chiapas and Guatemala (see Sharer and Sedat 1978).

Rayo: 29. Copán, Honduras: 1450 bc (Viel 1993a, b; Webster et al. 2000:21-22; personal observation JEC).

Barrahona: 30. Puerto Escondido, Honduras: 1600 bc (Henderson and Joyce 1998; Joyce and Henderson 2001; personal observation JEC).

Xe: 31. Altar de Sacrificios, Guatemala (Adams 1971; personal observations DC & JEC): 900 bc, our beginning date based on ceramic cross-ties with Seibal and other Maya sites to the east.

Réal Xe: 32. Seibal, Guatemala (Willey 1970; personal observations DC & JEC): 900 bc, our beginning date based on ceramic cross-ties with Maya sites to the east (Tikal and Cahal Pech).

Eb: 33. Tikal, Guatemala; 34. Uaxactun, Guatemala; 35: El Mirador, Guatemala: 900 bc, this dating is based on ceramic similarities to the Cunil complex as determined by Cheetham's recent observations (2001; Cheetham et al. 2002) of a large collection of Eb pottery from two cultuns from the Lost World at Tikal described by Laporte and Fialko (1993a). Our date corresponds with Laporte and Fialko's (1999) but predates Culbert's (1993) most recent chronology by a century. Observations for Uaxactun are based on material from Plazas E and A (O. Ricketson 1937; Smith 1937, 1955:13-14) and

housed in the Harvard Peabody Museum and the National Museum of Archaeology in Guatemala City (personal observations, DC & JEC).

Cunil: 36. Cahal Pech, Belize: 1000 bc (Cheetham 1998; Cheetham and Awe n.d.).

Swasey: 37. Cuello, Belize (Kosakowsky 1983; Kosakowsky and Pring 1998; Pring 1977): 850 bc, our logic for this controversial call is based on the reevaluation of radiocarbon dates (Andrews and Hammond 1990; see Table 2) and the frequent Mamom-like attributes of Swasey Ceramics (personal observations, DC, JEC, & Donald Forsyth; see Appendix 3).

D. Evidence of Early Social Ranking by Region and Site (numbers correspond to Table 1 and Fig. 3)

1a. **San Felipe**, Jalisco, Mexico: 1000 bc. First verified complex architecture; it is associated with shaft tombs during the San Felipe phase, thought to begin by 1000 bc (Beekman 2000, Weigand 1985, 1989, 1993, personal communication).

1b. **El Opeño**, Michoacán, Mexico: 1100-800 bc. Possible high status burials with imported jade objects and special symbolic objects and sets of human figurines, some depicted playing the ballgame (Noguera 1939; Oliveros 1974, 1989; Oliveros and de los Ríos Paredes 1993; Mountjoy 1989:13, 1998; Weigand 1985:61, 2000). Rank is not definitive because this culture is only well known through mortuary remains; possible occupational remains have just recently been identified for it (Phil Weigand, personal communication 2001). The El Opeño tombs cover a broad time period, so we are supposing that the most elaborate, largest tombs (Weigand 2000) with special offerings date towards the end of the phase.

2. **Tlapacoya**, Mexico, Mexico: 1150 bc. This is our extrapolation of Niederberger's (1996, 2000) assignment of capital centers (Tlapacoya and Tlatilco) to the Ayotla phase (1200-1000) based on special public platforms and special burials of adults with high status goods.

3. **Las Bocas**, Puebla, Mexico: 1150 bc. This is an unverified guess based on artifact comparisons with Tlapacoya and Tlatilco in the Basin of Mexico which both seem to represent early rank societies (see #2).

4. **Tr 369 & Tr 363**, Tehuacán Valley, Puebla, Mexico: 850 bc. This is the beginning of the early Santa Maria phase which saw a change in settlement patterns to one based upon a site hierarchy with villages with platforms and plazas (MacNeish et al. 1972:391). Given the research focus of the Tehuacán project on early domesticates in dry caves rather than open sites, this is probably a conservative estimate for the first social ranking in this region.

5. **Teopantecuanitlán**, Guerrero, Mexico: 1000 bc. This is an extrapolation of Martínez Donjuán's (1986, 1994) data for the early architecture and Olmec-style bas-relief stone monuments at this impressive site. Ceramic crossties are closest with the Manantial complex from Tlapacoya, and the sculpture is Middle Formative in style, or related to La Venta rather than the San Lorenzo style (see Grove 1994, 2000a, b; Reilly 1994).

6. **San José Mogote**, Oaxaca, Mexico: 1200-1150 bc,

San José phase, site hierarchy, monumental architecture, differential burial offerings (Marcus and Flannery 1996:93).

7. **Altamirano**, Veracruz, Mexico: 1100 bc., Chacas phase, planned settlement and small, circular pyramids (Castañeda 1992:Chpt. 7).

8. **Santa Luisa**, Veracruz, Mexico: 1100 bc., Ojite phase, possible platform mound, evidence of extensive interaction with the San Lorenzo Olmec, the first phase in which corn grinding stones became common (Wilkerson 1981:188, 191).

9. **El Viejón**, Veracruz, Mexico: 1100 bc. This is an unverified guess (i.e., no buildings or burials of this period have yet been excavated) based on the presence of a special early sculpture in the round at this site dating to the San Lorenzo horizon (see Wilkerson 1981:193), on stylistic grounds (Clark and Pye 2000:229). All other such sculptures have been found in association with chiefdom level societies (see Clark 1997).

10. **San Lorenzo**, Veracruz, Mexico: 1300 bc., hierarchical settlement pattern and large village by Bajío/Chicharras times and the beginnings of monumental stone sculpture (Coe and Diehl 1980; Cyphers 2000).

11. **Zapata (EPS-15)**, Tabasco, Mexico: 1100 bc. Evidence of construction of large earthen mounds (von Nagy 1997:269). This is much earlier than evidence of social ranking at **La Venta**, Tabasco, Mexico, because this center was not yet founded. Based on comparative ceramic studies, we believe 900 bc represents the founding of La Venta as a center. The settlement was laid out and planned from the very beginning to establish the pyramid/plaza center. Some of the sculpture probably dates to this earliest occupation (Clark and Hansen 2001; Clark and Pye 2000). The earlier dates reported for the eastern slope of La Venta Island (Rust 1992:124; Rust and Leyden 1994:183; Rust and Sharer 1988) do not represent a continuous occupation that led to the establishment of the ritual center.

12. **Mirador-Miramar & Plumajillo**, Chiapas, Mexico: 1100 bc. The presence of rank society here is inferential on the basis of it being an Olmec-related specialized site for the manufacture of iron-ore cubes, most of which were exported to San Lorenzo. This community in Chiapas may have been an Olmec colony (see Agrinier 1975, 1981; Clark 1994a; Lowe 1998:77). Chiapa de Corzo is the major Middle Formative site in this region, but there is no clear evidence of social ranking at this site until the Chiapa II or Dili pottery horizon, which is closely linked to La Venta styles. The first evidence of public architecture and site planning at Chiapa de Corzo dates to the latter part of this period (see Agrinier 2000; Clark and Hansen 2001; Clark et al. 2000).

13. **Paso de la Amada**, Chiapas, Mexico: 1400 bc. This is based upon settlement hierarchies, special domestic architecture, planned public architecture and plazas, and special mortuary offerings with children (Clark 1991, 1994, 1997; Clark and Blake 1994; Hill and Clark 2001).

14. **Grajeda**, Sipacate, Guatemala: 1300 bc, equivalent to the Ocós phase, special platform mound (Barbara Arroyo, personal communication 2001).

15. **Kaminaljuyú**, Guatemala: 800 bc. This date is based on our adjustment of the ceramic phases at this site to

Table 2. Uncalibrated radiocarbon dates from Cuello, Belize (after Hammond et al. 1995:124, figure 2, table 1; Housley et al. 1991:516, 518, table 2).

Laboratory No.	Date	Context	Date B.P.	Date bc
OxA-2103	"Middle" Swasey	Burial 62, fraction "a"	2840±100	890±100
OxA-2017	Bladen	Burial 7	2560±70	610±70
OxA-2016	Bladen	Burial 123	2390±70	440±70
OxA-4542	Bladen	paleosol (charcoal)	2650±60	700±60
OxA-4452	Bladen	paleosol, carbonized manioc root	2540±70	590±70
OxA-4453	Bladen	paleosol (charcoal), 20-25 cm above bedrock	2485±70	535±70
OxA-4454	Bladen	paleosol (charcoal), 15-20 cm above bedrock	2800±70	850±70
OxA-4455	Bladen	charcoal, chultun (F361)	2745±75	795±75
OxA-4456	Bladen	seed, chultun (F361)	2535±70	585±70
OxA-4457	Bladen	charcoal, chultun (F361)	2625±75	675±75
OxA-4458	Bladen	Burial 176	2600±75	650±75
OxA-4459	Bladen	Burial 177	2545±70	595±70
OxA-4460	Bladen	Burial 178	2620±75	670±75
OxA-4461	Swasey(?)	Burial(s) 179-180	3040±80	1090±80
OxA-5037	Bladen	Burial 174	2715±75	765±75

fit recent chronological refinements in neighboring regions. Clear evidence of social ranking is apparent in the Las Charcas phase in terms of differential mortuary practices, site planning and architecture, and the first monumental sculpture (Shook and Hatch 1999:297). The evidence is clear for the end of the phase, but it must have begun earlier (Clark et al. 2000).

16. **Tikal & Uaxactun**, Guatemala: 850 bc. This is inferential based on Cunil pottery from Cahal Pech and the presence of early modest structures at these sites, including the oldest documented E-Group in the Maya Lowlands at the Mundo Perdido at Tikal (Fialko 1988; Laporte and Fialko 1993a, b, 1995, 1999). The earliest evidence of complex chiefdoms in the Maya Lowlands presently comes from Nakbe, but there is no compelling, reliable evidence from this site indicative of early ranking, and the site postdates the beginning of both Tikal and Uaxactun. We believe that the quick spread of the Mamom ceramic horizon signals a shift to social ranking and site hierarchy all across the Lowlands but not to its very beginning. Clear evidence for monumental architecture appears during the late Mamom period in the Mirador Basin at Nakbe and other sites (Clark et al. 2000; Clark and Hansen 2000, 2001; Hansen 1998).

17. **Cahal Pech**, Belize: 900 bc, clear evidence of permanent ranking differences date to the middle of the first ceramic phase, Cunil, and is in the form of clear distinctions in domestic architecture, use of pots with special designs, and jade (Cheetham 1996, 1998).

18. **Puerto Escondido**, Honduras: 1300 bc. The evidence here is the special domestic architecture recovered for the Ocotillo phase (1400-1150 bc), which we conservatively date to the middle of the phase (Henderson and Joyce 1998; Joyce and Henderson 2001).

19. **Copán**, Honduras: 1000 bc. This is an interpretation of the data for differential mortuary practices for the Gordon phase. Some individuals were buried with impressive numbers of jade artifacts and pots with pan-Mesoamerican symbols (Fash 1985, 1991:67-71). The only real question here is when to date the Gordon complex. We agree with Joyce and Henderson (2001) that it falls in the end of the Early Preclassic and aligns with the San Lorenzo Olmec horizon rather than the La Venta horizon.

20. **Chalchuapa**, El Salvador: 1000 bc. This estimate gives the benefit of the doubt to this site that has special stone sculpture by 800 bc and a very large pyramid by 700 bc (Sharer 1994:58, 75). More rudimentary forms of social ranking must have come earlier and probably align with those seen for neighboring Copán.

Appendix 2: Distribution of Lowe Points in Belize (ca. 3000-1900 bc) (data for Fig. 11)

1. **Pulltrouser**, (T. Kelly 1993:206).
2. **BAAR 251**, (T. Kelly 1993:206).
3. **Colha**, (Iceland 1997:192).
4. **Gabrourel's Island**, (Iceland 1997:193).

5. **Lowe Ranch**, (T. Kelly 1993:206).
6. **Sand Hill**, (T. Kelly 1993:206).
7. **Burrell Boom**, (T. Kelly 1993:206).
8. **Kelly (Ladyville 45)**, (T. Kelly 1993:206).
9. **Ladyville**, (T. Kelly 1993:206).
10. **Northern Lagoon**, (T. Kelly 1993:206).
11. **San Ignacio**, (Iceland 1997:192).
12. **Saint Thomas**, (Patricia McAnany, personal communication 2001).

Appendix 3: Dating the Early Lowland Maya Ceramic Complexes

1. Xe/Réal Xe Ceramic Complex

The first pre-Mamom ceramic complex reported on at length for a Maya Lowland site, Xe (Adams 1971:79-84), was collected during the Peabody Museum's investigations at Altar de Sacrificios between 1959-1963. About 3,000 sherds were found on the old ground surface below Plaza B and Mounds 6, 24, 25, and 38, but contemporary architecture was not discovered (Adams 1971:79-80; Willey 1973:22-23). A single *uncalibrated* radiocarbon date of 745±185 bc is reported (Willey 1973:23). Adams (1971:117; see also Willey 1970:326) suggests that Xe is slightly later than Réal Xe at the nearby site of Seibal, and based on the single radiocarbon date and personal observations of the Xe pottery collection in 2000, we partially agree with this assessment and think that some Xe ceramics should be placed in an Early Mamom-related phase (Early San Felix at Altar) with a temporal span of about 800/750-600 bc. The occasional presence of diagnostic Cunil, Eb, and Réal Xe ceramic traits (matte slips, post-slip incising), however, indicates a brief, pre-Mamom Xe phase occupation at Altar de Sacrificios.

Most of the approximately 3,700 Réal Xe phase pot sherds collected during the 1964-1968 Peabody Museum excavations at Seibal come from the old ground level below Plaza A where, as at Altar de Sacrificios, contemporary architecture is lacking (Willey 1970:321). Based on comparison with Xe phase pottery from Altar de Sacrificios, Willey (1970:318, Fig. 2) dated the phase to 800-600 bc, though he believed it to be slightly older given the prevalence of non-waxy, matte slips and presence of fine-line incising. Having viewed the collection of Réal Xe sherds, we fully agree and believe a phase span of 900-800 bc is appropriate.

Willey (1970; see also Sabloff 1975) classified Réal Xe ceramics into two wares, five groups, and 15 types, all of which are calcite-tempered. Uaxactun Unslipped Ware jars (63% of complex), the most frequent form, are similar to Eb specimens—large, with tall outcurved necks. Unlike Eb, however, wide strap-handles were sometimes applied to vessel shoulders, and red daub was not used. Also lacking are chalice censers, censer stands, and colanders. These absences may be due to relative sample sizes rather than cultural practices. The only attribute connecting Réal Xe and Cunil phase jars is the use of wide strap-handles, though tecomates with direct or exterior-thickened rims were produced in both areas. Other Uaxactun Unslipped Ware forms at Seibal include bowls with incurved sides and bowls and dishes with outsloping sides and direct, exterior-thickened, or narrow horizontally-everted rims. Decoration is limited to different kinds of impressions (fingernail gouging, appliqué-impressed fillets) on bowls and dishes. A rare form shared with Eb and Cunil is the hourglass-shaped mushroom stand with fingernail impressions on the upper surface.

Rio Pasión Slipped Ware (37% of complex), unlike most slipped Xe ceramics from Altar de Sacrificios, has the dull or matte surfaces typical of all other Cunil-related ceramic complexes. Red (22.8% of complex) is the most frequent slip, followed by white (11.1%) and black (2.9%), with red-and-white and red-and-black bichromes lagging behind at 0.3 percent. Absent are orange and black-and-white slips. This, and the frequency of white-slipped vessels, occasional use of fluted decoration, and serving vessels with angled sides distinguish Réal Xe from Cunil and Eb, though other shared attributes certainly demonstrate close ties. For example, the most frequent vessel forms (tecomates, dishes, plates, and bowls) often have exterior-thickened rims, and slip preservation is often poor. Serving vessels with outsloping (dishes) or rounded (bowls) sides were also popular, and the ubiquitous Cunil era wide horizontally-everted rim dish occurs in all slip colors (e.g., Willey 1970:Figs. 10m, 24n-p), including specimens with the thickened or "beaded" lip noted for Eb (see below). The surface of a few "white-slipped" Réal Xe sherds from dishes with exterior-thickened rims and deep bowls with slightly barrel-shaped sides are identical to unslipped burnished pottery at Tikal. Another significant tie between Réal Xe and Cunil/Eb is post-slip incised decoration (about 4% of Réal Xe ceramic complex), which Willey (1970:328) describes as "fine-line" and "ragged." Tecomate exteriors and the superior surface of everted rim plates, among other vessel surfaces, received this kind of decoration, and motifs found in Eb and Cunil have been identified in the collection of unpublished Réal Xe sherds now housed at the Peabody Museum.

2. Eb Ceramic Complex

Eb phase ceramics at Tikal were first recognized during the University of Pennsylvania investigations from 1958-1970 (W. R. Coe 1965a, 1965b). A total of 5,811 sherds were discovered in three loci: bedrock underlying the North Acropolis, a subterranean storage chamber 1.5 km east of the site center, and Mundo Perdido Str. 5C-54. This material was sorted into early (n=4,213) and late (n=1,598, from Mundo Perdido) facets by Culbert (1977:33-34), who aptly equated Late Eb with Mamom pottery from Uaxactun (E. Ricketson 1937:230-254; Smith 1955:111-116; Smith and Gifford 1966). Based on an *uncalibrated* radiocarbon date of 588±53 bc and "sheer guesswork," Culbert (1977:28-30) suggested a starting date of 700 bc for Early Eb (later changed to 800-600 bc [Culbert 1993]), the origins of which he considered external to Tikal but unrelated to other early Lowland Maya ceramic complexes then avail-

able for comparison (Xe, Réal Xe, Early Jenney Creek). Some similarities were, however, noted with early Mamom sherds from Uaxactun (now known to be pre-Mamom [personal observation 2000, DC]), and thus the complete analysis (Culbert n.d.) is not entirely free of Mamom ceramic group and type names (e.g., Juventud, Chunhinta, Savanna). This has served to mask both the antiquity and pre-Mamom characteristics of Early Eb pottery.

The Proyecto Nacional Tikal discovered additional Early Eb phase pottery in two subterranean storage pits (Problematical Deposits 6 and 12) during the 1979-1982 investigations of the Mundo Perdido group (Laporte and Fialko 1993a, 1995). Totaling some 23,384 sherds, this is the largest collection of pre-Mamom pottery currently known in the Maya lowlands. Culbert's (n.d.) group and type names were used in the preliminary classification (Laporte and Fialko 1993b; see also Hermes 1993), which included illustrations of a few common vessel forms from Problematical Deposit 6. In 1999, David Cheetham and Donald Forsyth viewed the ceramics from both deposits, and in 2001 Cheetham and Clark were permitted to study the saved sherds from the Mundo Perdido deposits. Cheetham's ongoing analysis differs from previous studies in three important ways. First, the Early/Late Eb phase division is changed to reflect the marked differences between ceramics of the pre-Mamom Early Eb (now called Eb) and early Mamom-related Late Eb (now called Early Tzec) phases (see Fig. 4). Second, Eb pottery is no longer puzzling or unique. Identical and closely-related types and vessel forms have been identified in the Cunil ceramic complex of the Belize Valley, as well as contemporary complexes from Uaxactun, Seibal (Réal Xe), Altar de Sacrificios (Xe), and the Lakes Yaxha-Sacnab area (Early Ah Pam). Finally, based on these similarities the Eb phase is assigned a shortened time span (ca. 900-800 B.C.), the beginning date of which corresponds with Laporte and Fialko's (1999) most recent Tikal chronology.

The Eb ceramic complex consists of two wares, eight ceramic groups, and 13 types. The most popular cooking and storage vessels of Uaxactun Unslipped Ware are large thick-walled jars with medium-tall outcurved necks and flat bottoms that resemble Réal Xe phase jars from Seibal. Unlike contemporary utilitarian vessels of the Belize Valley, handles were seldom applied, the few examples being narrow and loop-shaped. Less frequently, tecomates were produced and red daub was applied to vessel exteriors—a decorative trait shunned by the Cunil and Réal Xe Maya. Rare, unslipped Eb vessel forms include red-rimmed colander bowls, chalice-shaped censers, and ceramic "stools," all of which were also produced by Cunil Maya in the Belize Valley. Eb pottery also includes a class of highly burnished (but unslipped) buff-colored storage and serving vessels, including large, slightly barrel-shaped vases and plates and dishes with the wide horizontally-everted rim style present in all Cunil-related ceramic complexes. Although these burnished pots were not produced in the Belize Valley, a few probable trade sherds have been identified

320

at the site of Xunantunich (personal observation 2000, DC).

Because all Eb slips are non-waxy and most are dull, the six slipped ceramic groups are classified as Belize Valley Dull Ware. Unlike its Cunil counterpart, however, this calcite tempered pottery is less prone to surface erosion. The dominant Eb slip is red (28% of complex), followed by black (6.3%), brown (4.6%), cream (.15%), orange (.10%), and black-and-white (.05%). Slipped vessel forms include tecomates with exterior-thickened rims and small jars with tall necks, but the most frequent form is a deep dish with a flat base, thin outsloping sides, and direct rim. Other prominent serving vessels are flat bottom plates and dishes with vertical or slightly outsloping sides and exterior-thickened rims, and the ubiquitous Cunil era plates with wide, horizontally-everted rims that occasionally have a thickened or "beaded" lip. Special Eb forms include hourglass-shaped "mushroom stands" with fingernail-impressed tops, a form present in the Belize Valley and at Seibal. As with Cunil, about 4 percent of Eb vessels were incised after firing (and on slipped vessels, after slipping and firing), with tecomates and everted rim plates especially targeted for this kind of adornment. Designs vary from simple rim encircling lines to complex Olmec style motifs, many of which are also found in the Cunil and, to a lesser extent, Réal Xe complexes.

3. Cunil Ceramic Complex

Cunil pottery was first recognized during Trent University's investigations (1988-1995) at the Belize Valley site of Cahal Pech, in a small pit penetrating a lengthy sequence of Preclassic period building platforms below Str. B-4 of the site core (Awe et al. 1990). Subsequent excavations into the summit B-4 3-sub (a well-preserved Late Preclassic temple that was stripped and restored) cut through 6.5 meters of superimposed building surfaces (Awe 1992:106-143; Cheetham 1992, 1998:21-24), including several Cunil constructions located below raised temple platforms containing Early Jenney Creek sherds (see Sharer and Kirkpatrick 1976; Willey et al. 1965). The temporal span of 1000-800 bc for the Cunil phase portion of this sequence is supported by five *uncalibrated* radiocarbon dates (Healy and Awe 1995) ranging from 980±50 bc to 760±120 bc, including a date of 790±70 bc from a carbonized post associated with the penultimate Cunil building. Some 250 of the approximately 1,200 Cunil sherds obtained from these excavations were briefly described by Awe (1992:226-231). Subsequent excavations directly in front of Str. B-4 (Cheetham 1995) and across Plaza B (Cheetham 1996) exposed four additional Cunil phase residential units (one an ancillary Str. B-4 building) and increased the ceramic sample to 2,357 sherds and three whole or partial vessels. A type-variety analysis of all Cunil ceramics was initiated in 1995 (Cheetham 1998:24-28; Cheetham and Awe 1996), and is now being finalized for publication (Cheetham and Awe n.d.).

Pure Cunil deposits have also been found on bedrock below the principal temple at the nearby site of Xunantunich (Strelow and LeCount 2001), and small numbers of weathered Cunil sherds mixed with Early Jenney Creek material have been identified in collections of pottery from basal deposits at several settlement clusters in the periphery of Cahal Pech, as well as the Belize Valley sites of Blackman Eddy, Barton Ramie, and Pacbitun (personal observations 1994-95, 2000, DC). Cunil sherds are also present at several sites in the vicinity of Lakes Yaxha-Sacnab area of eastern Petén (see Rice 1979), including Yaxha Hill and Ixtinto (personal observation 2000, DC), where they were produced along with ceramics characteristic of the contemporary Eb phase.

The Cunil ceramic complex is comprised of two wares, eight ceramic groups, and 14 types. Belize Valley Coarse Ware (75.1% of complex) is a utilitarian pottery tempered with calcite and sand. The surface of most cooking and storage vessels (jars and tecomates) are brown (Sikiya Unslipped) or black-brown (Pat Black-brown) and often burnished to a slip-like consistency on the upper shoulder and neck. Typical medium-size jars have rounded bottoms, short vertical necks, and wide vertical strap-handles—a form quite different from those of neighboring groups. The undulating appliqué-impressed fillet decoration of later, early Jenney Creek phase jars (e.g., Sharer and Kirkpatrick 1976:figure 18) is lacking, and jars with outcurved necks are extremely rare. Less frequent unslipped vessel forms include incurved bowls, flat-bottom plates with wide horizontally-everted rims, flat bottom dishes or bowls with vertical sides, colander bowls with rounded bases and sides, and chalice-shaped censers. Less common Coarse Ware types include Ardagh Orange-brown, the precursor of Early Jenney Creek Jocote Orange-brown pottery (see Sharer and Kirkpatrick 1976:63-68) once thought to have originated in Western El Salvador (Sharer and Gifford 1970), Branch Mouth Black, a glossy slipped pottery consisting of multicolored (black, white, and reddish-orange) jars or tecomates with very thin (1-4 mm) walls, and Duende Orange, a rare type with burnished orange surfaces that were occasionally carved.

Belize Valley Dull Ware (24.9% of complex), encompasses four ceramic groups of serving vessels with red (Uck, 16.3% of complex), black (Chi, 4.4%), cream (Cocoyol, 1.7%), or black-and-white (Puc, 0.2%) slips, and one small group of orange pottery (Cu, 2.2%) with abraded to moderately burnished surfaces. Brown slips are not unknown, but occur on a rare bichrome variant of red-slipped pottery. Other rare slip combinations include red-and-black, black-and-brown, and red-on-buff. Most slips are uniformly dull, but on a small number of specimens fired at relatively high temperatures, they are hard and slightly glossy. Dull Ware pottery was tempered with volcanic ash, which yielded distinctive buff or yellow-orange (Cu Group only) pastes that are usually quite soft and gritty. This resulted in a ineffective bonding surface for the slip, which is poorly preserved on many specimens. Ash temper was used to produce vessels as far west as Lakes Yaxha-Sacnab (see Rice 1979:13), and a probable Cunil trade sherd of the Cu Orange type has been identified among Eb phase sherds at Tikal (personal observation 2001, DC).

Flat-bottom dishes and plates with slightly outsloping sides and exterior-thickened rims are the most common form of slipped serving vessel. The most distinctive form, however, is the flat-bottom plate with outsloping sides and wide, horizontally-everted rim—a form characteristic of all Cunil-related complexes in the Maya Lowlands. Other Dull Ware forms include bowls with rounded sides (sometimes with hollow tubular legs), tecomates with direct or exterior-thickened rims, vases with exterior-thickened rims, bowls, dishes, and miniature vessels with vertical sides, small spouted vessels or "cream pitchers," and saucers. Cunil potters created a pseudo bichrome effect on most monochrome pots by leaving the exterior unslipped.

Slightly less than four percent of all Cunil pottery was decorated with thin (1-2 mm) incisions after both slip application and firing, a practice that created "jagged" lines and revealed the light-colored paste. The designs vary from single and multiple lines encircling vessel rims, to geometric and curvilinear shapes, to complex "Olmec-style" motifs. Although most serving vessel forms sometimes received such "post-slip" incised designs, the most complex motifs were usually executed on the exterior of tecomates, round-sided bowls, and the superior surface of wide, horizontally-everted rims. Rare forms of decoration include red-slipped, "glyph-like" abstract designs and carved motifs.

4. Swasey Ceramic Complex

Swasey phase pottery gathered during nine seasons of excavations (1975-80 [Hammond ed. 1991], 1990 [Hammond et al. 1991], and 1992-93 [Hammond et al. 1992, 1995]) at the northern Belize site of Cuello forms the most controversial early Maya ceramic complex. The initial collection of about 1,500 sherds has been published (see Pring 1976, 1977, 1979; Pring and Hammond 1982; Kosakowsky 1982, 1983, 1987; Kosakowsky and Pring 1991), and excavations in the 1990s have yielded an undisclosed number of additional sherds. The beginning date of 2500-2000 B.C. first proposed for Swasey (Hammond 1977; Hammond et al. 1976, 1977, 1979) was soon challenged based on a suite of unacceptable radiocarbon dates from the 1975-1980 excavations (Andrews 1990:18; Andrews and Hammond 1990) and overall ceramic attributes (Andrews 1990:5-7; Coe 1980:24-35; Marcus 1983b:459-460, 1984; Zeitlin 1989), the consensus—notwithstanding protestation from Hammond—being that Swasey began sometime early in the first millennium before Christ, perhaps by 800 bc (Andrews 1990:6). A similar beginning date has been proposed for other sites in northern Belize with Swasey-related phases, including Colha (Adams and Valdez 1980; Potter et al. 1984; Valdez 1987, 1994; Valdez and Adams 1982) and Santa Rita (Chase and Chase 1987).

Subsequent AMS dates from human bone, charcoal, and other Bladen phase (the subsequent phase at Cuello) materials gathered at Cuello during the early 1990s (Hammond et al. 1995; Housley et al. 1991) form the basis of the latest phase span for Swasey (1200-900 B.C., *calibrated*), which is accepted by the project's cerami-

cists (Kosakowsky and Pring 1998). However, when presented in *uncalibrated* form—as must be done to facilitate comparison with most other early Maya phases and all other extraregional sequences—a different picture emerges (see Table 2). The average date of Bladen samples (650±70 bc) conforms well with the Early Mamom-related Bladen phase time span proposed here (ca. 750-600 bc), as does the average date for Bladen Burials 176-178 (638±73 bc) and the pottery itself (D. Cheetham, D. Forsyth, and J. Clark, personal observation 2000). The most "acceptable" (Housley et al. 1991:518) ^{14}C date for middle Swasey Burial 62 (890±100 bc), the earliest burial at the site (Housley et al. 1991:516), falls at the beginning of our proposed Swasey phase span (ca. 850-750 bc). In fact, the only Swasey date not conforming to this time frame (from Burial 179/180, a woman holding a child [1090±80 bc]) is suspect since these burials were "closely spaced" in a 2 x 2 m area with Bladen Burials 176-178, suggesting that all were part of "an intentional grouping...likely to have been interred within a short period" (Hammond et al. 1995:126).

Swasey ceramics provide additional evidence that the phase does not date much earlier than 800 bc. In the most recent classification (Kosakowsky and Pring 1998:57-58; see also Kosakowsky 1987) the complex consisted of three wares, five groups, and 10 types. The two unslipped wares (Unspecified and Fort George Orange) comprise about 38 percent of the complex. Jars with short outcurved necks, thickened rims, and squared lips are the most frequent form. Most have lip-to-shoulder, double- or triple-strand handles, a style occasionally found in post-Cunil deposits at Cahal Pech and the Xe phase at Altar de Sacrificios. Other utilitarian Swasey forms include odd, amphora-like jars or bottles—a form not produced by Cunil, Eb, or Xe potters—that persisted into much later phases. Swasey lacks several rare unslipped forms of the Cunil-related complexes, including chalice censers, censer stands, mushroom stands, and colander bowls. Tecomates were produced, but unlike the exterior-thickened and rounded rim specimens made by Cunil, Eb, and Xe potters, most have the distinctive squared and thickened rim noted for the jars, and they are relatively rare.

Rio Nuevo Glossy Ware (62% of complex) of the Swasey phase includes three ceramic groups with red, buff, and black slips. Red-slipped Consejo pottery *from Swasey levels* includes dull, slightly glossy, and occasional waxy finishes (Cheetham, Forsyth, and Clark, personal observation 2000). Although rare, the presence of waxy pottery—a distinctive surface treatment after 800/750 bc throughout the lowlands—indicates that Swasey was a relatively late, ephemeral phase in Northern Belize that began during late Cunil/Eb times. Many Consejo sherds (of all finishes) also have a distinctive white or light color underslip that sets them apart from red-slipped pottery of the Cunil, Eb, and Réal Xe complexes. Such sherds have been found in post-Cunil deposits at Cahal Pech and in post-Eb Problematical Deposits at Tikal (personal observation 2001, DC). Swasey also includes red-and-cream vessels that closely replicate the color and form of Early Mamom Muxanel red-and-cream pottery. This color combination is lacking in Cunil/Eb, where red-on-*unslipped* pottery is present, but rare. Typical Swasey serving vessel forms include incurved bowls and flat-bottom plates and dishes with outsloping sides, exterior-thickened rims, and rounded lips—all of which are good Cunil/Eb markers. Many other vessels, however, have squared lips and angled or recurved sides that are quite different. Vessels with recurved sides, in particular the cuspidor form, are virtually unknown in the Belize Valley and Central Petén until Early Mamom times. Perhaps the most notable difference in terms of form, however, is the complete absence of plates with wide horizontally-everted rims. Finally, although post-slip incised decoration is rare in Swasey (most being preslip) it is an important link with the Cunil-related complexes. The designs, however, are very simple and the complex "Olmec-style" motifs noted for other pre-Mamom complexes are completely lacking.

References Cited

Adams, Richard E. W.
  1971 The Ceramics of Altar de Sacrificios. *Papers of the Peabody Museum of Archaeology and Ethnology*, Vol. 63(1). Harvard University, Cambridge.

Adams, Richard E. W., and Fred Valdez, Jr.
  1980 The Ceramics of Colha, Belize: 1979 and 1980 Seasons. In *The Colha Project, Second Season, 1980 Interim Report*, edited by T. R. Hester, J. D. Eaton, and H. J. Shafer, pp 15-40. Center for Archaeological Research, University of Texas, San Antonio.

Agrinier, Pierre
  1975 Un Complejo Cerámico, Tipo Olmeca, del Preclásico Temprano en El Mirador, Chiapas. In *Balance y Perspectiva de la Antropología de Mesoamérica y el Norte de México*, Vol. 2:21-34. Sociedad Mexicana de Antropología.
  1981 *The Early Olmec Horizon at Mirador, Chiapas, Mexico*. Papers of the New World Archaeological Foundation, No. 48. Provo, Utah.
  2000 *Mound 27 and the Middle Preclassic Period at Mirador, Chiapas, Mexico*, Pierre Agrinier. Papers of the New World Archaeological Foundation, No. 58. Provo, Utah.

Agrinier, Pierre, David Cheetham, and Gareth W. Lowe
  2000 Appendix 1: Three Early Ceramic Complexes from Miramar, Chiapas, Mexico. In *Mound 27 and the Middle Preclassic Period at Mirador, Chiapas, Mexico*, by Pierre Agrinier. Papers of the New World Archaeological Foundation, No. 58. Provo, Utah.

Andrews, E. Wyllys, V.
  1990 The Early Ceramic History of the Lowland Maya. In *Vision and Revision in Maya Studies*, edited by F. Clancey and P. D. Harrison, pp. 1-19. University of New Mexico Press, Albuquerque.

Andrews, E. Wyllys, V, and Norman Hammond
  1990 Redefinition of the Swasey Phase at Cuello, Belize. *American Antiquity* 55:570-584.

Arnold, Philip J., III
  1999 *Tecomates*, Residential Mobility, and Early Formative Occupation in Coastal Lowland Mesoamerica. In *Pottery and People: A Dynamic Interaction*, edited by J. M. Skibo and G. M. Feinman, pp. 157-170. University of Utah Press, Salt Lake City.
  2000 Sociopolitical Complexity and the Gulf Olmecs: A View from the Tuxtla Mountains, Veracruz, Mexico. In *Olmec Art and Archaeology in Mesoamerica*, edited by J. E. Clark and M. E. Pye, pp. 117-135. National Gallery of Art, Washington.

Arroyo, Barbara
  1994 The Early Formative in Southern Mesoamerica: An Explanation for the Origins of Sedentary Villages. Unpublished Ph.D. dissertation, Department of Anthropology, Vanderbilt University, Nashville, Tennessee.
  1995 Early Ceramics from El Salvador: The El Carmen Site. In *The Emergence of Pottery: Technology and Innovation in Ancient Societies*, edited by W. K. Barnett and J. W. Hoopes, pp. 199-208. Smithsonian Institution Press, Washington.

Awe, Jaime Jose
  1992 Dawn in the Land between the Rivers: Formative Occupation at Cahal Pech, Belize and its Implications for Preclassic Development in the Maya Lowlands. Unpublished Ph.D. dissertation, Institute of Archaeology, University of London.

Awe, Jaime J., and Paul Healy
  1994 Flakes to Blades? Middle Formative Development of Obsidian Artifacts in the Upper Belize River Valley. *Latin American Antiquity* 5:193-205.

Awe, Jaime J., Mark D. Campbell, Cassandra Bill zzzz and David Cheetham

1990 Early Middle Formative Occupation in the Central Maya Lowlands: Recent Evidence from Cahal Pech, Belize. *Papers from the Institute of Archaeology* 1:1-6. University College London.

Ball, Joseph W.

1977 The Rise of Northern Chiefdoms: A Sociopolitical Analysis. In *The Origins of Maya Civilization*, edited by R. E. W. Adams, pp. 101-132. University of New Mexico Press, Albuquerque.

Baus de Czitrom, Carolyn

1989 Panorama Actualizado del Preclásico en Colima y Regiones Cercanas. In *El Preclásico o Formativo: Avances y Perspectivas: Seminario de Arqueología "Dr. Román Piña Chan"*, edited by M. Carmona Macias, pp. 27-38. INAH and the Museo Nacional de Antropología, Mexico City, Mexico.

Beekman, Christopher S.

2000 The Correspondence of Regional Patterns and Local Strategies in Formative to Classic Period West Mexico. *Journal of Anthropological Archaeology* 19:385-412.

Blake, Michael

1991 An Emerging Early Formative Chiefdom at Paso de la Amada, Chiapas, Mexico. In *The Formation of Complex Society in Southeastern Mesoamerica*, edited by W. R. Fowler, pp. 27-46. CRC Press, Boca Raton.

2001a Mazatan Region. In *Archaeology of Ancient Mexico and Central America: An Encyclopedia*, edited by S. T. Evans and D. L. Webster, pp. 451-453. Garland Publishing, Inc., New York & London.

2001b Paso de la Amada (Chiapas, Mexico). In *Archaeology of Ancient Mexico and Central America: An Encyclopedia*, edited by S. T. Evans and D. L. Webster, pp. 583-584. Garland Publishing, Inc., New York & London.

Blake, Michael, John E. Clark, Barbara Voorhies, George Michaels, Michael W. Love, Mary E. Pye, Arthur Demarest, and Barbara Arroyo

1995 A Revised Chronology for the Late Archaic and Formative Periods Along the Pacific Coast of Southeastern Mesoamerica. *Ancient Mesoamerica* 6:161-183.

Bower, B.

1994 Maya Beginnings Extend Back at Belize Site. *Science News* 145:279.

Brown, Kenneth L.

1980 A Brief Report on Paleoindian-Archaic Occupation in the Quiche Basin, Guatemala. *American Antiquity* 45:313-324.

Brush, Charles F.

1965 Pox Pottery: Earliest Identified Mexican Ceramic. *Science* 149:194-95.

Cabrera, Rubén

1989 La Costa de Michoacán en la Época Prehispánica. In *Historia General de Michoacán: Volumen I: Escenario Ecológico, Epoca Prehispánico*, pp. 137-153. Gobierno de Michoacán.

Castañeda, Laura Adriana

1989 La Cerámica de la Planicie Costera. In *El Preclásico o Formativo: Avances y Perspectivas: Seminario de Arqueología "Dr. Román Piña Chan"*, edited by M. Carmona Macias, pp. 119-142. INAH and the Museo Nacional de Antropología, Mexico City, Mexico.

1992 Altamirano: Un Sitio del Formativo al Noreste de México. Thesis of Licenciada, Escuela Nacional de Antropología e Historia, Mexico City, Mexico.

Ceja, Jorge Fausto

1985 *Paso de la Amada: An Early Preclassic Site in the Soconusco, Chiapas, Mexico.* Papers of the New World Archaeological Foundation, No. 49. Provo, Utah.

Chase, Arlen F., and Diane Z. Chase

1987 Putting Together the Pieces: Maya Pottery of Northern Belize and Central Peten, Guatemala. In *Maya Ceramics: Papers from the 1985 Maya Ceramic Conference*, edited by P. M. Rice and R. J. Sharer, pp. 47-72. *BAR International Series* 345(i). Oxford.

Cheetham, David

1992 Cahal Pech, Str. B-4 Excavations: 1988-1991. Unpublished Ms., Department of Archaeology, Belmopan, Belize.

1995 Excavations at Structure B-4, Cahal Pech, Belize: 1994 Operations. In "Belize Valley Preclassic Maya Project: Report on the 1994 Field Season," edited by P. F. Healy and J. J. Awe, pp. 18-44. *Trent University, Occasional Papers in Anthropology*, No. 10. Peterborough.

1996 Reconstruction of the Formative Period Site Core of Cahal Pech, Belize. In "Belize

Valley Preclassic Maya Project: Report on the 1995 Field Season," edited by P. F. Healy and J. J. Awe, pp. 1-33. *Trent University, Occasional Papers in Anthropology*, No. 12. Peterborough.

1998 Interregional Interaction, Symbol Emulation, and the Emergence of Socio-Political Inequality in the Central Maya Lowlands. Unpublished Master's thesis, Department of Anthropology and Sociology, University of British Columbia, Vancouver.

2001 Cunil: A Pre-Mamom Horizon of the Southern Maya Lowlands. Paper presented at the 66th Annual Meeting of the Society for American Archaeology, New Orleans.

Cheetham, David, and Jaime J. Awe

1996 The Early Formative Cunil Ceramic Complex at Cahal Pech, Belize. Paper presented at the 61st Annual Meeting of the Society for American Archaeology, New Orleans.

n.d. The Cunil Ceramic Complex, Cahal Pech, Belize. Ms. in possession of the authors.

Cheetham, David, Donald W. Forsyth, and John E. Clark

2002 La Cerámica Pre-Mamom de la Cuenca del Rio Belice y del Petén Central: Las Corresponencias y sus Implicaciones. Paper presented at the XVI Simposio de Investigaciones Arqueológicas en Guatemala, Guatemala City.

Clark, John E.

1990 La Fase Lato de la Cuenca Superior del Río Grijalva: Implicaciones por el Despliegue de la Cultura Mokaya. In *Primer Foro de Arqueología de Chiapas: Cazadores-Recolectores-Pescadores, Agricultores Tempranos*, pp. 107-110. Serie Memorias Chiapas, No. 4. Tuxtla Gutierrez, Chiapas, Mexico.

1991 The Beginnings of Mesoamerica: Apologia for the Soconusco Early Formative. In *The Formation of Complex Society in Southeastern Mesoamerica*, edited by W. R. Fowler, pp. 13-26. CRC Press, Boca Raton.

1994a El Sistema Económico de los Primeros Olmecas. In *Los Olmecas en Mesoamérica*, edited by J. E. Clark, pp. 189-201. Editorial Equilibrista and Citibank, Madrid.

1994b The Development of Early Formative Rank Societies in the Soconusco, Chiapas, Mexico. Unpublished Ph.D. dissertation, Department of Anthropology, University of Michigan, Ann Arbor.

1997 The Arts of Government in Early Mesoamerica. *Annual Review of Anthropology* 26:211-234.

2000 Towards a Better Explanation of Hereditary Inequality: A Critical Assessment of Natural and Historic Human Agents. In *Agency in Archaeology*, edited by M. Dobres and J. Robb, pp. 92-112. Routledge, London.

Clark, John E., and Michael Blake

1994 The Power of Prestige: Competitive Generosity and the Emergence of Rank Society in Lowland Mesoamerica. In *Factional Competition and Political Development in the New World*, edited by E. M. Brumfiel and J. W. Fox, pp. 17-30. Cambridge University Press, Cambridge.

Clark, John E., Barbara Arroyo, and David Cheetham

n.d. Early Preclassic Ceramics. In *Ceramic Sequence of the Upper Grijalva Region, Chiapas, Mexico*, edited by D. D. Bryant, J. E. Clark, and D. Cheetham. Papers of the New World Archaeological Foundation, Provo, Utah.

Clark, John E., and Dennis Gosser

1995 Reinventing Mesoamerica's First Pottery. In *The Emergence of Pottery: Technology and Innovation in Ancient Societies*, edited by W.K. Barnett and J.W. Hoopes, pp. 209-221. Smithsonian Press, Washington, DC.

Clark, John E., and Richard D. Hansen

2000 Preclásico Tardío (400 a.C.- 200 d.C.). *Arqueología Mexicana* 8(46):12-19.

2001 The Architecture of Early Kingship: Comparative Perspectives on the Origins of the Maya Royal Court. In *The Maya Royal Court*, edited by T. Inomata and S. D. Houston, pp. 1-45. Westview Press, Boulder, Colorado.

Clark, John E., Richard D. Hansen, and Tomás Pérez Suárez

2000 La Zona Maya en el Preclásico. In *Historia Antigua de México: Volumen 1: El México antiguo, sus áreas culturales, los orígenes y el horizonte Preclásico*, edited by L. Manzanilla and L. López Luján, pp. 437-510. INAH, Mexico City, Mexico.

Clark, John E., and Mary E. Pye
  2000 The Pacific Coast and the Olmec Problem. In *Olmec Art and Archaeology in Mesoamerica*, edited by J. E. Clark and M. E. Pye, pp. 217-251. National Gallery of Art, Washington.
Coe, Michael D.
  1980 *The Maya* (2nd Edition). Thames and Hudson, London.
Coe, Michael D., and Richard A. Diehl
  1980 *In the Land of the Olmec*. University of Texas Press, Austin.
Coe, William R.
  1965a Tikal, Guatemala, and Emergent Maya Civilization. *Science* 147:1401-1419.
  1965b Tikal: Ten Years of Study of a Maya Ruin in the Lowlands of Guatemala. *Expedition* 8:5-56.
Cowgill, Ursula M., and G. Evelyn Hutchinson
  1966 The History of the Petenxil Basin. In "The History of Laguna de Pentenxil: A Small Lake in Northern Guatemala," by U. M. Cowgill, G. E. Hutchinson, A. A. Racek, C. E. Goulden, R. Patrick, and M. Tsukada, pp. 121-126. *Memoirs of the Connecticut Academy of Arts and Sciences*, No. 17. New Haven.
Culbert, T. Patrick
  1977 Early Maya Development at Tikal, Guatemala. In *The Origins of Maya Civilization*, edited by R. E. W. Adams, pp. 27-43. University of New Mexico Press, Albuquerque.
  1993 The Ceramics of Tikal: Vessels from the Burials, Caches and Problematical Deposits. Tikal Report No. 25, Part A. *University Museum Monograph* 81. University of Pennsylvania, Philadelphia.
  n.d. Descriptions of the Preclassic Ceramics, Tikal, Guatemala (Eb Ceramic Complex: Eb Complex Collections). Unpublished manuscript, Department of Anthropology, University of Arizona, Tucson.
Cyphers, Ann
  2000 Early Settlement at San Lorenzo. Paper presented at the Meeting to honor Gareth W. Lowe, Tucson, Arizona, November.
Daneels, Annick
  1997 Settlement History in the Lower Cotaxtla Basin. In *Olmec to Aztec: Settlement Patterns in the Ancient Gulf Lowlands*, edited by B. L. Stark and P. J. Arnold, III, pp. 206-252. The University of Arizona Press, Tucson.

  2000 La Relacción entre la Costa del Golfo y la Costa Pacífica de Centroamérica, Vista desde Veracruz. Paper presented at the XIV Simposio de Investigaciones Arqueológicas en Guatemala, 17-21 July, Guatemala City.
Deevey, Edward S. Jr.
  1978 Holocene Forests and Maya Disturbance Near Quexil Lake, Peten, Guatemala. *Polskie Archiwum Hydrobiologii* 25:117-129.
Deevey, E. S., Don S. Rice, Prudence M. Rice, H. H. Vaughan, Mark Brenner, and M. S. Flannery
  1979 Maya Urbanism: Impact on a Tropical Karst Environment. *Science* 206:298-306.
De Terra, Helmut
  1959 A Successor of Tepexpan Man in the Valley of Mexico. *Science* 129:563-564.
Drucker, Philip
  1948 Preliminary Notes on an Archaeological Survey of the Chiapas Coast. *Middle American Research Records* 1:151-169.
Fash, William L.
  1985 La Sequencia de Ocupación del Grupo 9N-8, Las Sepulturas, Copán, y sus Implicaciones Teóricas. *Yaxkin* VIII (1-2):135-140.
  1991 *Scribes, Warriors and Kings: The City of Copán and the Ancient Maya*. Thames and Hudson, London.
Fedick, Scott L.
  2001 Agriculture and Domestication. In *Archaeology of Ancient Mexico and Central America: An Encyclopedia*, edited by S. T. Evans and D. L. Webster, pp. 7-15. Garland Publishing, Inc., New York & London.
Fialko, Vilma
  1988 Mundo Perdido, Tikal: Un Ejemplo de Complejos de Conmenoración Astronómica. *Mayab* 4:13-21.
Flannery, Kent V.
  1983 Tentative Chronological Phases for the Oaxaca Preceramic. In *The Cloud People: Divergent Evolution of the Zapotec and Mixtec Civilizations*, edited by K. V. Flannery and J. Marcus, pp. 26-29. Academic Press, New York.
  1986 The Research Problem. In *Guilá Naquitz: Archaic Foraging and Early Agriculture in Oaxaca, Mexico*, edited by K.V. Flannery, pp. 3-18. Academic Press, New York.
  2001 Gheo-Shih (Oaxaca, Mexico). In *Archaeology of Ancient Mexico and Central America: An Encyclopedia*, edited by S. T. Evans

and D. L. Webster, p. 299. Garland Publishing, Inc., New York & London.

Flannery, Kent V., and Joyce Marcus
1976 Evolution of the Public Building in Formative Oaxaca. In *Culture Change and Continuity: Essays in Honor of James Bennett Griffin*, edited by C. E. Cleland, pp. 205-221. Academic Press, New York.
1994 *Early Formative Pottery of the Valley of Oaxaca, Mexico*. Memoirs of the Museum of Anthropology, University of Michigan, No. 27. Ann Arbor, Michigan.

Flannery, Kent V., Joyce Marcus, and Stephen A. Kowalewski
1981 The Preceramic and Formative of the Valley of Oaxaca. In *Handbook of Middle American Indians: Supplement 1: Archaeology*, edited by J. A. Sabloff, pp. 48-93. University of Texas Press, Austin.

Fried, Morton H.
1967 *The Evolution of Political Society: An Essay in Political Anthropology*. Random House, New York.

Fritz, Gayle J.
1994 Are the First American Farmers Getting Younger? *Current Anthropology* 35:305-309.
1995 New Dates and Data on Early Agriculture: The Legacy of Complex Hunter-Gatherers? *Annals of the Missouri Botanical Garden* 82:3-15.

García Cook, Angel
1981 The Historical Importance of Tlaxcala in the Cultural Development of the Central Highlands. In *Handbook of Middle American Indians: Supplement 1: Archaeology*, edited by J. A. Sabloff, pp. 244-276. University of Texas Press, Austin.

García Cook, Angel, and B. Leonor Merino Carrión
1988 Notas sobre la Cerámica Prehispánica en Tlaxcala. In *Ensayos sobre Alfarería Prehispánica e Histórica: Homenaje a Eduardo Noguera*, edited by M. C. Serra Puche and C. Navarrete, pp. 275-342. Universidad Nacional Autónoma de México, Mexico City.

García Bárcena, Joaquin
1976 *Excavaciones en el Abrigo de Santa Marta, Chiapas*. Informes del Departamento de Prehistoria, INAH. Mexico City.
2001 Santa Marta Cave (Chiapas, Mexico). In *Archaeology of Ancient Mexico and Central America: An Encyclopedia*, edited by S. T. Evans and D. L. Webster, p. 653. Garland Publishing, Inc., New York & London.

García Moll, Roberto
1977 *Analisis de los Materiales Arqueológicos de la Cueva del Texcal, Puebla*. Colección Científica, No. 56. INAH, Mexico City, Mexico.

García Moll, Roberto, Daniel Juárez Cossío, Carmen Pijoan Aguade, María Elena Salas Cuesta, and Marcela Salas Cuesta
1991 *Catálogo de Entierros de San Luis Tlatilco, Mexico: Temporada IV*. Serie Antropología Física-Arqueología. INAH, Mexico City.

García Payón, José
1971 Archaeology of Central Veracruz. In *Handbook of Middle American Indians: Volume 11, Part Two: Archaeology of Northern Mesoamerica*, edited by G. F. Ekholm and I. Bernal, pp. 505-542. University of Texas Press, Austin.

Gay, Carlo T. E.
1972 *Xochipala: The Beginnings of Olmec Art*. The Art Museum, Princeton University.

Gibson, Eric C.
1991 A Preliminary Functional and Contextual Study of Constricted Adzes from Northern Belize. In *Maya Stone Tools: Selected Papers from the Second Maya Lithic Conference*, edited by T. R. Hester and H. J. Shafer, pp. 229-237. Prehistory Press, Madison, Wisconsin.

González Jácome, Alba, editor
1987 *Orígenes del Hombre Americano (Seminario)*. Secretaría de Educación Pública, Mexico City, Mexico.

González-Quintero, Lauro, and Jesus I. Mora-Echevarría
1978 Estudio Arqueológico-Ecológico de un Caso de Explotación de Recursos Litorales en el Pacífico Mexicano. In *Arqueolobotánica: Métodos y Aplicaciones*, pp. 53-73. INAH Colección Científica, No. 63. Mexico City.

Goman, Michelle
1992 Paleoecological Evidence for Prehistoric Agriculture and Tropical Forest Clearance in the Sierra de los Tuxtlas, Veracruz, Mexico. Unpublished M.A. thesis, Department of Geography, University of California, Berkeley.

Gosser, Dennis C.
1994 The Role of Ceramic Technology during the Late Barra and Early Locona Phases at Mound 5, Paso de la Amada, Chiapas, Mexico. Unpublished M.A. thesis, Department of Anthropology, Brigham Young University, Provo, Uath.

Grove, David C.
1994 Chalcatzingo. In *Los Olmecas en Mesoamérica*, edited by J. E. Clark, pp. 165-173. Citibank, Mexico City.
2000a Faces of the Earth at Chalcatzingo, Mexico: Serpents, Caves, and Mountains in Middle Formative Period Iconography. In *Olmec Art and Archaeology in Mesoamerica*, edited by J. E. Clark and M. E. Pye, pp. 277-295. National Gallery of Art, Washington.
2000b The Preclassic Societies of the Central Highlands of Mesoamerica. In *The Cambridge History of the Native Peoples of the Americas: Volume II: Mesoamerica, Part 1*, edited by R. W. Adams and M. J. Macleod, pp. 122-155. Cambridge University Press, Cambridge.
2001 Formative (Preclassic) Period (2000 BCE–250 CE). In *The Oxford Encyclopedia of Mesoamerican Cultures: The Civilizations of Mexico and Central America*, edited by David Carrasco, pp. 236-243. Oxford University Press, Inc., New York.

Guderjan, Thomas H.
1993 *Ancient Maya Traders of Ambergris Caye*. Cubola Publishers, Benque Viejo del Carmen, Belize.

Hammond, Norman (editor)
1991 *Cuello: An Early Maya Community in Belize*. Cambridge University Press, Cambridge.

Hammond, Norman
1977 The Earliest Maya. *Scientific American* 236:116-133.
1991 Ceramic, Bone, Shell and Ground Stone Artifacts. In *Cuello: An Early Maya Community in Belize*, edited by N. Hammond, pp. 176-191. Cambridge University Press, Cambridge.
2000 The Maya Lowlands: Pioneer Farmers to Merchant Princes. In *The Cambridge History of the Native Peoples of the Americas: Volume II: Mesoamerica, Part 1*, edited by R. W. Adams and M. J. Macleod, pp. 197-249. Cambridge University Press, Cambridge.

2001 Cuello (Orange Walk, Belize). In *Archaeology of Ancient Mexico and Central America: An Encyclopedia*, edited by S. T. Evans and D. L. Webster, pp. 196-97. Garland Publishing, Inc., New York & London.

Hammond, Norman, Amanda Clarke, and Francisco Estrada Belli
1992 Middle Preclassic Maya Buildings and Burials at Cuello, Belize. *Antiquity* 66:955-964.

Hammond, Norman, Amanda Clarke, and Sara Donaghey
1995 The Long Goodbye: Middle Preclassic Maya Archaeology at Cuello, Belize. *Latin American Antiquity* 6:120-128.

Hammond, Norman, Amanda Clarke, and Cynthia Robin
1991 Middle Preclassic Maya Buildings and Burials at Cuello, Belize: 1990 Investigations. *Latin American Antiquity* 2:353-363.

Hammond, Norman, Sara Donaghey, Rainer Berger, Suzanne de Atley, V. Roy Switzer, and Alan P. Ward
1977 Maya Formative Phase Radiocarbon Dates from Belize. *Nature* 267:608-610.

Hammond, Norman, Duncan C. Pring, Rainer Berger, V. Roy Switser, and Alan. P. Ward
1976 Radiocarbon Chronology for Early Maya Occupation at Cuello, Belize. *Nature* 260:579-581.

Hammond, Norman, Duncan C. Pring, Richard Wilk, Sara Donaghey, Frank P. Saul, Elizabeth S. Wing, A. V. Miller, and Lawrence H. Feldman
1979 The Earliest Lowland Maya? Definition of the Swasey Phase. *American Antiquity* 44:92-110.

Hansen, Barbara C. S.
1990 Pollen Stratigraphy of Laguna de Cocos, Albion Island, Rio Hondo, Belize. In *Ancient Maya Wetland Agriculture: Excavations on Albion Island, Northern Belize*, edited by M. Pohl, pp. 155-187. University of Minnesota Publications in Anthropology and Westview Press, Boulder, Colorado.

Hansen, Richard D.
1998 Continuity and Disjunction: The Pre-Classic Antecedents of Classic Maya Architecture. In *Function and Meaning in Classic Maya Architecture*, edited by S. D. Houston, pp. 49-122. Dumbarton Oaks, Washington DC.

Hatch, Marion Popenoe de
2001 Kaminaljuyu (Guatemala, Guatemala). In *Archaeology of Ancient Mexico and Central America: An Encyclopedia*, edited by S. T. Evans and D. L. Webster, pp. 387-390. Garland Publishing, Inc., New York & London.

Healy, Paul F.
1984 Northeast Honduras: A Precolumbian Frontier Zone. In *Recent Developments in Isthmian Archaeology: Advances in the Prehistory of Lower Central America: Proceedings of the 44th International Congress of Americanists, Manchester, 1982*, edited by F. W. Lange, pp. 227-241. B.A.R. International Series 212. Oxford.

Healy, Paul F., and Jaime J. Awe
1995 Radiocarbon Dates from Cahal Pech, Belize: Results from the 1994 Season. In *Belize Valley Preclassic Maya Project: Report on the 1994 Season*, edited by P. F. Healy and J. J. Awe, pp. 198-215. *Trent University, Occasional Papers in Anthropology*, No. 10. Peterborough.

Henderson, John S.
1979 *Atopula, Guerrero, and Olmec Horizons in Mesoamerica*. Yale University Publications in Anthropology, No. 77. Department of Anthropology, Yale University, New Haven.
2001 Puerto Escondido (Cortés, Honduras). In *Archaeology of Ancient Mexico and Central America: An Encyclopedia*, edited by S. T. Evans and D. L. Webster, p. 617. Garland Publishing, Inc., New York & London.

Henderson, John S., and Rosemary Joyce
1998 Investigaciones Arqueológicas en Puerto Escondido: Definición del Formativo Temprano en el Valle Inferior del Río Ulúa. *Yaxkin* 17:5-35.

Hermes, Bernard, and Juan Luis Velásquez
2001 La Cerámica del Sitio Piedra Parada. In Informe del Proyecto de Investigación y Salvamento Arqueológico, en un Area Adyacente al Sitio Arqueológico Piedra Parada, Guatemala, O. R. Román, director and editor, pp. 30-75. Report submitted to the National Institute of Sport, Ethnology, and Archaeology (IDAEH), Guatemala City.

Hester, Thomas R.
2001 Paleoindian Period. In *Archaeology of Ancient Mexico and Central America: An Encyclopedia*, edited by S. T. Evans and D. L. Webster, pp. 577-581. Garland Publishing, Inc., New York & London.

Hester, Thomas R., Harry B. Iceland, Dale B. Hudler, and Harry J. Shafer
1996 The Colha Preceramic Project: Preliminary Results from the 1993-1995 Seasons. *Mexicon* 18:45-50.

Hermes, Bernard
1993 Dos Reportes del Laboratorio Cerámico: Vasijas Miniatura y Adiciones Tipológicas para la Epoca Preclásica. In *Tikal y Uaxactún en el Preclásico*, edited by J. P. Laporte and J. A. Valdés, pp. 47-52. Universidad Nacional Autónoma de México, Mexico City.

Hill, Warren D.
1999 *Ballcourts, Competitive Games and the Emergence of Complex Society*. Unpublished Ph.D. dissertation, Department of Anthropology and Sociology, University of British Columbia.

Hill, Warren D., Michael Blake, and John E. Clark
1998 Ball Court Design Dates Back 3,400 Years. *Nature* 392:878-879.

Hill, Warren D., and John E. Clark
2001 Sports, Gambling, and Government: America's First Social Compact? *American Anthropologist* 103(2):1-15.

Hoopes, John W.
1994 Ford Revisited: A Critical Review of the Chronology and Relationships of the Earliest Ceramic Complexes in the New World, 6000-1500 B.C. *Journal of World Prehistory* 8:1-49.

Housley, Rupert M., Norman Hammond, and Ian A. Law
1991 AMS Radiocarbon Dating of Preclassic Burials at Cuello, Belize. *American Antiquity* 56:514-519.

Hudler, Dale B., and John Lohse
1994 Replication and Microscopy: Determining the Function of Unifacial Chert Tools from Belize. Unpublished manuscript on file with the Texas Archaeological Research Laboratory, Austin.

Iceland, Harry B.
1997 The Preceramic Origins of the Maya: The Results of the Colha Preceramic Project in Northern Belize. Unpublished Ph.D. dissertation. Department of Anthropology, University of Texas, Austin.

Iceland, Harry B., and Thomas R. Hester
  1996 The Colha Preceramic Project: A Status Report. Paper presented at the 61ˢᵗ Annual Meeting ot the Society of American Archaeology, New Orleans.
Iceland, Harry, Thomas R. Hester, Harry J. Shafer, and Dale Hudler
  1995 The Colha Preceramic Project: A Status Report. *Newsletter of the Texas Archaeological Research Laboratory* 3:11-15.
Islebe, Gerald A., Henry Hooghiemstra, Mark Brenner, Jason J. Curtis, and David A. Hodell
  1996 A Holocene Vegetation History from Lowland Guatemala. *The Holocene* 6(3):265-271.
Jennings, Jesse D.
  1957 *Danger Cave.* Memoirs of the Society for American Archaeology 14.
Johnson, Frederick, and Richard S. MacNeish
  1972 Chronometric Dating. In *The Prehistory of the Tehuacán Valley: Volume 4: Chronology and Irrigation*, edited by F. Johnson, pp. 3-55. University of Texas Press, Austin.
Jones, John G.
  1994 Pollen Evidence for Early Settlement and Agriculture in Northern Belize. *Palynology* 18:205-211.
Jones, John G., and Barbara Voorhies
  n.d. Dietary Reconstructions: Human-Plant Interactions. Chapter prepared for volume on the Archaic period of southern Chiapas, Mexico, edited by B. Voorhies.
Joyce, Rosemary, and John S. Henderson
  2001 Beginnings of Village Life in Eastern Mesoamerica. *Latin American Antiquity* 12:5-23.
Kelly, Isabel
  1980 *Ceramic Sequence in Colima: Capacha, an Early Phase.* Anthropological Papers of the University of Arizona, No. 37. The University of Arizona Press, Tucson.
Kelly, Thomas C.
  1993 Preceramic Projectile-Point Typology in Belize. *Ancient Mesoamerica* 4:205-227.
Kennett, Douglas J., and Barbara Voorhies
  1996 Oxygen Isotopic Analysis of Archaeological Shells to Detect Seasonal Use of Wetlands on the Southern Pacific Coast of Mexico. *Journal of Archaeological Science* 24:1051-1059.
Kosakowsky, Laura J.
  1982 A Preliminary Summary of Formative Ceramic Variability at Cuello, Belize.

Cerámica de Cultura Maya 12:26-42. Temple University, Philadelphia.
  1983 *Intra-site Variability of the Formative Ceramics from Cuello, Belize: An Analysis of Form and Function.* Unpublished Ph.D. dissertation, University of Arizona.
  1987 Prehistoric Pottery at Cuello, Belize. *Anthropological Papers of the University of Arizona*, No. 47. University of Arizona Press, Tucson.
Kosakowsky, Laura J., and Duncan C. Pring
  1991 Ceramic Chronology and Typology. In *Cuello: An Early Maya Community in Belize*, edited by N. Hammond, pp. 60-69. Cambridge University Press, Cambridge.
  1998 The Ceramics of Cuello, Belize: A New Evaluation. *Ancient Mesoamerica* 9:55-66.
Laporte, Juan Pedro, and Vilma Fialko
  1993a El preclásico de Mundo Perdido: Algunos aportes sobre los orígenes de Tikal. In *Tikal y Uaxactún en el Preclásico*, edited by J. P. Laporte and J. A. Valdés, pp. 9-46. Universidad Nacional Autónoma de México, Mexico City.
  1993b Análisis Cerámico de Tres Depósitos Problemáticos de Fase Eb, Mundo Perdido, Tikal. In *Tikal y Uaxactún en el Preclásico*, edited by J. P. Laporte and J. A. Valdés, pp. 53-69. Universidad Nacional Autónoma de México, Mexico City.
  1995 Un Reencuentro con Mundo Perdido, Tikal, Guatemala. *Ancient Mesoamerica* 6:41-94.
  1999 El Preclásico en las Tierras Bajas Mayas Centrales. In *Historia General de Guatemala, Volume I: Epoca Precolumbina*, edited by Marion Popenoe de Hatch, pp. 339-350. Asociación de Amigos del País, Fundación para la Cultura y el Desarrollo, Guatemala City.
Lee, Thomas A., Jr., and John E. Clark
  1988 Oro, Tela, Y Xute: Investigaciones Arqueológicas en la Región Camcum, Colonia Las Delicias, Chiapas. *Arqueología* 4:7-46.
Lesure, Richard G.
  1997 Figurines and Social Identities in Early Sedentary Societies of Coastal Chiapas, Mexico, 1550-800 b.c. In *Women in Prehistory: North America and Mesoamerica*, edited by C. Claassen and R. A.

Joyce, pp. 225-248. University of Pennsylvania Press, Philadelphia.

1999 Figurines as Representations and Products at Paso de la Amada, Mexico. *Cambridge Archaeological Journal* 9:209-220.

2000 Animal Imagery, Cultural Unities, and Ideologies of Inequality in Early Formative Mesoamerica. In *Olmec Art and Archeology in Mesoamerica*, edited by J. E. Clark and M. E. Pye, pp. 193-215. National Gallery of Art, Washington DC.

n.d. The Goddess Diffracted: Thinking about the Figurines of Early Villages. Ms.

Long, Austin, B. F. Benz, D. J. Donahue, A. J. T. Jull, and L. J. Toolin

1989 First Direct AMS Dates on Early Maize from Tehuacán, Mexico. *Radiocarbon* 31:1035-1040.

Longyear, J. M., III

1948 A Sub-pottery Deposit at Copán, Honduras. *American Antiquity* 13:248-249.

Lowe, Gareth W.

1975 *The Early Preclassic Barra Phase of Altamira, Chiapas: A Review with New Data*. Papers of the New World Archaeological Foundation, No. 38. Provo, Utah.

1977 The Mixe-Zoque as Competing Neighbors of the Early Lowland Maya. In *The Origins of Maya Civilization*, edited by R. E. W. Adams, pp. 197-248. University of New Mexico Press, Albuquerque.

1978 Eastern Mesoamerica. In *Chronologies in New World Archaeology*, edited by R. E. Taylor and C. W. Meighan, pp. 331-393. Academic Press, New York.

1998 *Mesoamérica Olmeca: Diez Preguntas*. INAH Colección Científica, No. 370. Mexico City.

Lorenzo, José Luís

1955 Los Concheros de la Costa de Chiapas. *Anales del Instituto de Antropología, Boletín* 7:41-50.

1958 *Un Sitio Precerámico en Yanhuitlán, Oaxaca*, Publ. 6. INAH, Mexico City.

1961 *La Revolución Neolítica en Mesoamérica*. Departmento de Prehistoria, INAH, Mexico City.

Lorenzo, José Luís and Lauro Gonazales Q.

1970 El más Antiguo Teosinte. *Boletín, INAH* 42:41-43. Mexico City.

McAnany, Patricia A.

1995 *Living with the Ancestors: Kinship and Kingship in Ancient Maya Society*. University of Texas Press, Austin.

MacNeish, Richard S.

1958 *Preliminary Archaeological Investigations in the Sierra de Tamaulipas, Mexico*. Transactions of the American Philosophical Society, Vol. 48, Part 6. The American Philosophical Society, Philadelphia.

1964 Ancient Mesoamerican Civilization. *Science* 143:531-537.

1971 Archaeological Synthesis of the Sierra. In *Handbook of Middle American Indians: Volume 11, Part 2: Archaeology of Northern Mesoamerica*, edited by G. F. Ekholm and I. Bernal, pp. 573-581. University of Texas Press, Austin.

1972 The Evolution of Community Patterns in the Tehuacan Valley of Mexico and Speculations about the Cultural Processes. In *Man, Settlement, and Urbanism*, edited by P. J. Ucko, R. Trigham, and G. W. Dimbleby, pp. 67-93. Duckworth, London.

1986 The Preceramic of Middle America. *Advances in World Archaeology* 5:93-129.

1992 *The Origins of Agriculture and Settled Life*. University of Oklahoma Press, Norman.

2001a Archaic Period (c. 8000-2000). In *Archaeology of Ancient Mexico and Central America: An Encyclopedia*, edited by S. T. Evans and D. L. Webster, pp. 30-33. Garland Publishing, Inc., New York & London.

2001b Early Development and the Archaic Period (before 2600 BCE). In *The Oxford Encyclopedia of Mesoamerican Cultures: The Civilizations of Mexico and Central America*, edited by David Carrasco, pp. 226-236. Oxford University Press, Inc., New York.

2001c Tehuacán Region. In *Archaeology of Ancient Mexico and Central America: An Encyclopedia*, edited by S. T. Evans and D. L. Webster, pp. 705-710. Garland Publishing, Inc., New York & London.

MacNeish, Richard S., Mary W. Eubanks

2000 Comparative Analysis of the Río Balsas and Tehuacán Models for the Origin of Maize. *Latin American Antiquity* 11:3-20.

MacNeish, Richard S., Frederick A. Peterson, and Kent V. Flannery

1970 *The Prehistory of the Tehuacán Valley: Volume 3: Ceramics*. University of Texas Press, Austin.

MacNeish, Richard S., Frederick A. Peterson, and James A. Neely

1972 The Archaeological Reconnaissance. In *The Prehistory of the Tehaucan Valley: Volume 5: Excavations and Reconnaissance*, edited by R.S. MacNeish, M.L. Fowler, A. García Cook, F.A. Peterson, A. Nelken-Terner, and J.A. Neely, pp. 341-495. University of Texas Press, Austin.

MacNeish, Richard S., and Antoinette Nelken-Terner

1983 The Preceramic of Mesoamerica. *Journal of Field Archaeology* 10:71-84.

McClung de Tapia, Emily

1992 The Origins of Agriculture in Mesoamerica and Central America. In *The Origins of Agriculture: An International Perspective*, edited by C. W. Cowan and P. J. Watson, pp. 143-171. Smithsonian Institution Press, Washington.

McClung de Tapia, Emily, and Judith Zurita Noguera

2000 Las Primeras Sociedades Sedentarias. In *Historia Antigua de México: Volumen 1: El México antiguo, sus áreas culturales, los orígenes y el horizonte Preclásico*, edited by L. Manzanilla and L. López Luján, pp. 255-295. INAH, Mexico City, Mexico.

Madsen, David B.

1982 Get it Where the Gettin's Good: A Variable Model of Great Basin Subsistence and Settlement Based on Data from the Eastern Great Basin. In *Man and Environment in the Great Basin*, edited by D. B. Madsen and J. F. O'Connell, pp. 207-226. SAA Papers, No. 2, Society for American Archaeology.

Marcus, Joyce

1983a The Espiridión Complex and the Origins of the Oaxacan Formative. In *The Cloud People: Divergent Evolution of the Zapotec and Mixtec Civilizations*, edited by K.V. Flannery and J. Marcus, pp. 42-43. Academic Press, New York.

1983b Lowland Maya Archaeology at the Crossroads. *American Antiquity* 48:454-482.

1984 Reply to Hammond and Andrews. *American Antiquity* 49:829-833.

1995 Where is Lowland Maya Archaeology Headed? *Journal of Archaeological Research* 3:3-53.

1999 Men's and Women's Ritual in Formative Oaxaca. In *Social Patterns in Pre-Classic Mesoamerica*, edited by D. C. Grove and R. A Joyce, pp.67-96. Dumbarton Oaks, Washington, DC.

Marcus, Joyce, and Kent V. Flannery

1996 *Zapotec Civilization: How Urban Society Evolved in Mexico's Oaxaca Valley*. Thames and Hudson, London.

2001 Cultural Evolution in Oaxaca: The Origins of the Zapotec and Mixtec Civilizations. In *The Cambridge History of the Native Peoples of the Americas, Volume II: Mesoamerica, Part 1*, edited by R. E. W. Adams and M. J. Macleod, pp. 358-406.

Martínez Donjuán, Guadalupe

1986 Teopantecuanitlán. In *Arqueología y Etnohistoria del Estado de Guerrero*, 55-80. INAH and the Gobierno del Estado de Guerrero. Mexico City, Mexico.

1994 Los Olmecas en el Estado de Guerrero. In *Los Olmecas en Mesoamérica*, edited by J. E. Clark, pp. 143-163. Citibank, Mexico City.

Matos Moctezuma, Eduardo

2000 Mesoamérica. In *Historia Antigua de México: Volumen 1: El México antiguo, sus áreas culturales, los orígenes y el horizonte Preclásico*, edited by L. Manzanilla and L. López Luján, pp. 95-119. INAH, Mexico City, Mexico.

Merino Carrión, B. Leonor, and Angel García Cook

1987 Proyecto Arqueológica Huaxteca. *Arqueología* 1:31-72.

1989 El Formativo en la Cuenca Baja del Río Pánuco. In *El Preclásico o Formativo: Avances y Perspectivas: Seminario de Arqueología "Dr. Román Piña Chan"*, edited by M. Carmona Macias, pp. 101-118. INAH and the Museo Nacional de Antropología, Mexico City, Mexico.

Michaels, George H., and Barbara Voorhies

1999 Late Archaic Period Coastal Collectors in Southern Mesoamerica: The Chantuto People Revisited. In *Pacific Latin America in Prehistory: The Evolution of Archaic and Formative Cultures*, edited by M. Blake, pp. 39-54. Washington State University Press, Pullman, Washington.

Michelet, D., M. C. Arnauld, and M. F. Fauvet Berthelot

1989 El Proyecto del CEMCA en Michoacan: Etapa I: Un Balanace. *Trace* 16:70-87.

Mirambell Silva, Lorena

1978 Tlapacoya, a Late Pleistocene Site in Central Mexico. In *Early Man in America*, edited by A. L. Bryan, pp. 221-230. Department of Anthropology, University of Alberta, Edmonton.

2000 Los Primeros Pobladores del Actual Territorio Mexicano. In *Historia Antigua de México: Volumen 1: El México antiguo, sus áreas culturales, los orígenes y el horizonte Preclásico*, edited by L. Manzanilla and L. López Luján, pp. 223-254. INAH, Mexico City, Mexico.

Mora, Raziel, and Angel García Cook

1996 Restos Precerámicos y Acerámicos en el Área. In *Antología de Tlaxcala, Volumen 1*, edited by L. Mirambell, pp. 269-280. INAH and the Gobierno del Estado de Tlaxcala, Mexico City.

Mountjoy, Joseph B.

1989 Algunas Observaciones sobre el Desarrollo del Preclásico en la Llanura Costera del Occidente. In *El Preclásico o Formativo: Avances y Perspectivas: Seminario de Arqueología "Dr. Román Piña Chan"*, edited by M. Carmona Macias, pp. 11-26. INAH and the Museo Nacional de Antropología, Mexico City, Mexico.

1994 Capacha: Una Cultura Enigmática del Occidente de México. *Arqueología Mexicana* II (9):39-42.

1998 The Evolution of Complex Societies in West Mexico: A Comparative Perspective. In *Ancient West Mexico: Art and Archaeology of the Unknown Past*, edited by R. F. Towsend, pp. 251-265. The Art Institute of Chicago and Thames and Hudson, London.

2000 Prehispanic Cultural Development along the Southern Coast of West Mexico. In *Greater Mesoamerica: The Archaeology of West and Northwest Mexico*, edited by M. S. Foster and S. Gorenstein, pp. 81-106. University of Utah Press, Salt Lake City.

2001a Capacha (Colima, Mexico). In *Archaeology of Ancient Mexico and Central America: An Encyclopedia*, edited by S. T. Evans and D. L. Webster, pp. 95-96. Garland Publishing, Inc., New York & London.

2001b Matanchén (Nayarit, Mexico). In *Archaeology of Ancient Mexico and Central America: An Encyclopedia*, edited by S. T. Evans and D. L. Webster, p. 416. Garland Publishing, Inc., New York & London.

Mountjoy, Joseph B., R. E. Taylor, and Lawrence H. Feldman

1972 Mantanchén Complex: New Radiocarbon Dates on Early Coastal Adaptation in West Mexico. *Science* 175:1242-43.

Nalda, Enrique

1981 México Prehispánico: Origen y Formación de las Clases Sociales. In *México: Un Pueblo en la Historia*, edited by E. Semo, pp. 51-177. Editorial Nueva Imagen, Universidad Autónoma de Puebla, Mexico.

1997 La Organización Social en el México Prehispánico: Un Recuento desde la Perspectiva de la Arqueología. In *Homenaje al Profesor César A. Sáenz*, edited by A. García Cook, A. G. Mastache, L. Merino, and S. Rivero T., pp. 91-102. INAH, Colección Científica, No. 351. Mexico City.

Neff, Hector, Barbara Arroyo, Deborah Pearsall, John G. Jones, Dorothy E. Freidel, and Cesar Veintimilla

2000 Medioambiente y Ocupación Humana en la Costa Sur de Guatemala. Paper presented at the XIV Simposio de Investigaciones Arqueológicas en Guatemala, 17-21 July, Guatemala City.

Nelson, Fred W., and Barbara Voorhies

1980 Trace Element Analysis of Obsidian Artifacts from Three Shell Midden Sites in the Littoral Zone, Chiapas, Mexico. *American Antiquity* 45:540-50.

Nichols, Deborah L.

2001 Tlapacoya (México, Mexico). In *Archaeology of Ancient Mexico and Central America: An Encyclopedia*, edited by S. T. Evans and D. L. Webster, pp. 757-758. Garland Publishing, Inc., New York & London.

Niederberger, Christine

1976 Zohapilco: Cinco Milenios de Ocupación Humana en un Sitio Lacustre de la Cuenca de México. INAH Colección Científica: Arqueología, No. 30. Mexico City, Mexico.

1979 Early Sedentary Economy in the Basin of Mexico. *Science* 203:131-142.

1987 *Paleopaysages et Archeologie Pre-urbaine du Bassin de Mexico*. Centre d'Etudes Mexicaines et Centraméricaines, Mexico.

1996 The Basin of Mexico: A Multimillennial Development Toward Cultural Complexity. In *Olmec Art of Ancient Mexico*, edited by E. P. Benson and B. de la Fuente, pp. 83-93. National Gallery of Art, Washington, DC.

2000 Ranked Societies, Iconographic Complexity, and Economic Wealth in the Basin of Mexico toward 1200 B.C. In *Olmec Art and Archaeology in Mesoamerica*, edited by J. E. Clark and M. E. Pye, pp. 169-191. National Gallery of Art, Washington, DC.

Noguera, Eduardo

1939 Exploraciones en El Opeño, Michoacán. *XXVII Congreso Internacional de Americanistas* 1:574-86. Mexico City.

O'Hara, Sarah L., F. Alayne Street-Perrott, and Timothy P. Burt

1992 Accelerated Soil Erosion around a Mexican Highland Lake caused by Prehispanic Agriculture. *Nature* 362:48-51.

Oliveros, José Arturo

1974 Nuevas Exploraciones en El Opeño, Michoacán. In *The Archaeology of West Mexico*, edited by B. Bell, pp. 182-201. Sociedad de Estudios Avanzados del Occidente de México, A.C., Ajijic, Jalisco, Mexico.

1989 Las Tumbas más Antiguas de Michoacán. In *Historia General de Michoacán: Volumen I: Escenario Ecológico, Epoca Prehispánico*, pp. 123-134. Gobierno de Michoacán, Mexico.

Oliveros, José Arturo, and Magdelena de los Ríos Paredes

1993 La Cronología de El Opeño, Michoacán. *Arqueología* 9-10:45-48.

Ortíz C., Ponciano, and María del Carmen Rodríguez

1994 Los Espacios Sagrados Olmecas: El Manatí, un Caso Especial. In *Los Olmecas en Mesoamérica*, edited by J.E. Clark, pp. 69-91. Citibank and Editorial Equilibrista, Madrid, Spain.

1999 Olmec Ritual Behavior at El Manatí: A Sacred Space. In *Social Patterns in Pre-Classic Mesoamerica*, edited by D. C. Grove and R. A. Joyce, pp. 225-254. Dumbarton Oaks, Washington, DC.

Paradis, Louise I.

2001 Guerrero Region. In *Archaeology of Ancient Mexico and Central America: An Encyclopedia*, edited by S. T. Evans and D. L. Webster, pp. 311-321. Garland Publishing, Inc., New York & London.

Piña Chan, Román

1975 El Periodo Agrícola Aldeano: Consideraciones Generales. In *Del Nomadismo a los Centros Ceremoniales*, edited by R. Piña Chan, pp. 64-79. INAH, Mexico City, Mexico.

Piperno, Dolores R., and Deborah M. Pearsall

1998 *The Origins of Agriculture in the Lowland Neotropics*. Academic Press, San Diego.

Piperno, Dolores R, Anthony J. Ranere, Irene Holst, and Patricia Hansell

2000 Starch Grains Reveal Early Root Crop Horticulture in the Panamanian Tropic Forest. *Nature* 407:894-897.

Plunket Nagoda, Patricia, and Gabriela Uruñela

2001 Puebla-Tlaxcala Region. In *Archaeology of Ancient Mexico and Central America: An Encyclopedia*, edited by S. T. Evans and D. L. Webster, pp. 611-617. Garland Publishing, Inc., New York & London.

Pohl, Mary D., Paul R. Bloom, and Kevin O. Pope

1990 Interpretation of Wetland Farming in Northern Belize: Excavations at San Antonio Río Hondo. In *Ancient Maya Wetland Agriculture: Excavations on Albion Island, Northern Belize*, edited by M. D. Pohl, pp. 187-278. Westview Press, Boulder, Colorado.

Pohl, Mary, and Kevin Pope

2001 Pulltrouser Swamp (Orange Walk, Belize). In *Archaeology of Ancient Mexico and Central America: An Encyclopedia*, edited by S. T. Evans and D. L. Webster, pp. 617-618. Garland Publishing, Inc., New York & London.

Pohl, Mary D., Kevin O. Pope, John G. Jones, John S. Jacob, Dolores R. Piperno, Susan D. deFrance, David L. Lentz, John A. Gifford, Marie E. Danforth, and J. Kathryn Josserand

1996 Early Agriculture in the Maya Lowlands. *Latin American Antiquity* 7:355-72.

Pollard, Helen P.

2001 Michoacán Region. In *Archaeology of Ancient Mexico and Central America: An Encyclopedia*, edited by S. T. Evans and D. L. Webster, pp. 458-464. Garland Publishing, Inc., New York & London.

Pope, Kevin O., Mary E. D. Pohl, John G. Jones, David L. Lentz, Christopher von Nagy, Francisco Vega Vera, and Irv Quitmeyer

2001 Origin and Environmental Setting of

Ancient Agriculture in the Lowlands of Mesoamerica. *Science* 292:1370-1373.

Potter, D. R., Tom R. Hester, S. L. Black, and Fred Valdez Jr.
1984   Relationships Between Early Preclassic and Early Middle Preclassic Phases in Northern Belize: A Comment on "Lowland Maya Archaeology at the Crossroads." *American Antiquity* 49:628-631.

Pring, Duncan C.
1976   *Illustrations for Preclassic Ceramic Complexes in Northern Belize.* Cambridge University, Centre of Latin American Studies. Cambridge.
1977   *The Preclassic Ceramics of Northern Belize.* Unpublished Ph.D. dissertation, University of London.
1979   The Swasey Complex of Northern Belize: A Definition and Discussion. In *Studies in Ancient Mesoamerica, IV*, edited by J. A. Graham, pp. 215-229. Contributions of the University of California Archaeological Research Facility, No. 41. Berkeley.

Pring, Duncan C., and Norman Hammond
1982   The Stratigraphic Priority of Swasey Ceramics at Cuello, Belize. *Cerámica de Cultura Maya* 12:43-48. Temple University, Philadelphia.

Pyburn, K. Anne
1994   The Origin of Ancient Maya Pottery: Special Products and Specialist Production. *Terre Cuite et Société: La Céramique, Document Technique, Économique, Culturel.* XIVe Rencontres Internationales d'Archéologie et de l'Historie d' Antibes, Éditions APDCA, Juan-les-Pins.

Rands, Robert L.
1987   Ceramic Patterns and Traditions in the Palenque Area. In *Maya Ceramics: Papers from the 1985 Ceramics Conference*, edited by P. M. Rice and R. J. Sharer, pp. 203-238. BAR International Series, Oxford, England.

Reilly, F. Kent, III
1994   Cosmología, Soberanismo y Espacio Ritual en la Mesoamérica del Formativo. In *Los Olmecas en Mesoamérica*, edited by J. E. Clark, pp. 239-259. Citibank, Mexico City.
2001   Teopantecuanitlán (Guerrero, Mexico). In *Archaeology of Ancient Mexico and Central America: An Encyclopedia*, edited by S. T. Evans and D. L. Webster, p. 722. Garland Publishing, Inc., New York & London.

Rice, Prudence M.
1979   Introduction and the Middle Preclassic Ceramics of Yaxha-Sacnab, Guatemala. *Cerámica de Cultura Maya* 10:1-36. Temple University, Philadelphia.

Ricketson, Oliver G., Jr.
1937   Part I: The Excavations. In *Uaxactun, Guatemala, Group E—1926-1931*, pp. 1-180. Carnegie Institution of Washington Publication 477. Carnegie Institution, Washington.

Ricketson, Oliver G., and Edith B. Ricketson
1937   *Uaxactun, Guatemala, Group E—1926-1931.* Carnegie Institution of Washington Publication 477. Carnegie Institution, Washington.

Ricketson, Edith B.
1937   Part II: The Artifacts. In *Uaxactun, Guatemala, Group E—1926-1931*, by O. G. Ricketson and E. B. Ricketson, pp. 183-292. Carnegie Institution of Washington Publication, No. 477. Washington, DC.

Rosenswig, Robert M.
2001   Preceramic Evidence from Northern Belize and Caye Coco. In *Belize Postclassic Project 2000: Investigations at Caye Coco and the Shore Settlements of Progreso Lagoon*, edited by R. M. Rosenswig and M. Masson, pp. 87-95. Institute of Mesoamerican Studies, Occasional Paper No. 6. The University of Albany-SUNY.
2002   Excavations of Preceramic Components at Caye Coco and the Fred Smith Site. In *The Belize Postclassic Project 2001: Investigations and Analysis at Progreso Lagoon*, edited by R. M. Rosenswig and M. Masson, pp. xx-xx, Institute of Mesoamerican Studies, Occasional Paper No. 7. The University of Albany-SUNY.

Rosenswig, Robert M., and Marilyn A. Masson
2002   Seven New Preceramic Sites Documented in Northern Belize. Manuscript submitted to *Mexicon*.

Rosenswig, Robert M., and T. W. Stafford, Jr.
1998   Archaic Component Beneath a Postclassic Terrace at Subop 19, Laguna de On Island. In *Belize Postclassic Project 1997: Laguna de On, Progreso Lagoon, Laguna Seca*, edited by M. A. Masson and R. M. Rosenswig, pp. 81-89. Institute

of Mesoamerican Studies, Occasional Paper No. 2. The University of Albany-SUNY.

Rue, David J.
1989 Archaic Middle American Agriculture and Settlement: Recent Pollen Data from Honduras. *Journal of Field Archaeology* 16:177-184.

Rust, William F., III
1992 New Ceremonial and Settlement Evidence at La Venta, and its Relation to Preclassic Maya Cultures. In *New Theories on the Ancient Maya*, edited by E. C. Danien and R. J. Sharer, pp. 123-129. The University Museum, University of Pennsylvanian, Philadelphia.

Rust, William F., III, and Barbara W. Leyden
1994 Evidence of Maize Use at Early and Middle Preclassic La Venta Olmec Sites. In *Corn and Culture in the Prehistoric New World*, edited by S. Johannessen and C. Hastorf, pp. 181-201. Westview Press, Boulder, Colorado.

Rust, William F., III, and Robert J. Sharer
1988 Olmec Settlement Data from La Venta, Tabasco. *Science* 242:102-104.

Sabloff, Jeremy A.
1975 Excavations at Seibal, Department of Peten, Guatemala: Ceramics. *Memoirs of the Peabody Museum of Archaeology and Ethnology, Harvard University*, Vol. 13(2). Cambridge.

Sanders, William T., and Barbara J. Price
1968 *Mesoamerica: The Evolution of a Civilization*. Random House, New York.

Schmidt, Paul, and Jaime Litvak King
1986 Problemas y Perspectivas de la Arqueología en Guerrero. In *Arqueología y Etnohistoria del Estado de Guerrero*, pp. 27-51. INAH and the Gobierno del Estado de Guerrero. Mexico City.

Schortman, Edward M., and Patricia A. Urban
2001 Southeast Mesoamerica. In *Archaeology of Ancient Mexico and Central America: An Encyclopedia*, edited by S. T. Evans and D. L. Webster, pp. 675-684. Garland Publishing, Inc., New York & London.

Scott, Stuart D.
1985 Core versus Marginal Mesoamerica: A Coastal West Mexican Perspective. In *The Archaeology of West and Northwest Mesoamerica*, edited by M. S. Foster and P. C. Weigand, pp. 181-192. Westview Press, Boulder.

Scott, Stuart D., and Michael S. Foster
2000 The Prehistory of Mexico's Northwest Coast. In *Greater Mesoamerica: The Archaeology of West and Northwest Mexico*, edited by M. S. Foster and S. Gorenstein, pp. 107-135. University of Utah Press, Salt Lake City.

Service, Elman R.
1971 *Primitive Social Organization: An Evolutionary Perspective*, second edition. Random House, New York.
1975 *Origins of the State and Civilization: The Process of Cultural Evolution*. W. W. Norton and Company, New York.

Sharer, Robert J.
1994 *The Ancient Maya*, fifth edition. Stanford University Press, Stanford.

Sharer, Robert J., and James C. Gifford
1970 Preclassic Ceramics from Chalchuapa, El Salvador, and Their Relationships with the Maya Lowlands. *American Antiquity* 35:441-462.

Sharer, Robert J., and Muriel Kirkpatrick
1976 The Jenney Creek Ceramic Complex: Type Descriptions. In "Prehistoric Pottery Analysis and the Ceramics of Barton Ramie in the Belize Valley," by J. C. Gifford, pp. 63-83. *Memoirs of the Peabody Museum of Archaeology and Ethnology, Harvard University*, Vol. 18. Cambridge.

Sharer, Robert J., and David W. Sedat
1978 *Archaeological Investigations in the Northern Maya Highlands, Guatemala: Interaction and the Development of Maya Civilization*. University of Pennsylvania, Philadelphia.

Shook, Edwin M., and Marion Popenoe de Hatch
1999 Las Tierras Altas Centrales: Períodos Preclásico y Clásico. In *Historia General de Guatemala: Volumen 1: Epoca Precolombina*, edited by M. P. Hatch, pp. 289-318. Asociación de Amigos del País, Fundación para la Cultura y el Desarrollo, Guatemala City.

Sisson, Edward B.
1976 *Survey and Excavation in the Northwestern Chontalpa, Tabasco, Mexico*. Unpublished Ph.D. dissertation, Department of Anthropology, Harvard University, Cambridge, Massachusetts.

Smith, Robert E.
1937 *A Study of Structure A-1 Complex at Uaxactun, Peten, Guatemala*. Carnegie

Institution of Washington Publication 456, pp. 189-230. Carnegie Institution, Washington.

1955 Ceramic Sequence at Uaxactun, Guatemala, Volume I. *Middle American Research Institute, Tulane University, Publication* 20. New Orleans.

Smith, Robert E., and James C. Gifford

1966 Maya Ceramic Varieties, Types, and Wares at Uaxactun. Supplement to "Ceramic Sequence at Uaxactun, Guatemala." *Middle American Research Institute, Tulane University, Publication* 28:125-174. New Orleans.

Stark, Barbara L.

1981 The Rise of Sedentary Life. In *Handbook of Middle American Indians: Supplement 1: Archaeology*, edited by J. A. Sabloff, pp. 345-372. University of Texas Press, Austin, Texas.

2000 Framing the Gulf Olmecs. In *Olmec Art and Archaeology in Mesoamerica*, edited by J. E. Clark and M. Pye, , pp. 31-53. National Gallery of Art, Washington, DC.

Stark, Barbara L., and Philip J. Arnold, III

1997 Introduction to the Archaeology of the Gulf Lowlands. In *Olmec to Aztec: Settlement Patterns in the Ancient Gulf Lowlands*, edited by B.L. Stark and P.J. Arnold, III, pp. 3-39. The University of Arizona Press, Tucson.

Steward, Julian H.

1938 *Basin-Plateau Aboriginal Sociopolitical Groups*. Smithsonian Institution Bureau of American Ethnology, Bulletin 120. United States Government Printing Office, Washington, DC.

1955 *Theory of Cultural Change*. University of Illinois Press, Urbana.

Stone, Doris

1941 *The Archaeology of the North Coast of Honduras*. Memoir of the Peabody Museum of Archaeology and Ethnology, Harvard University, Vol. 9(1). Cambridge.

Strelow, Duane, and Lisa LeCount

2001 Regional Interaction in the Formative Southern Maya Lowlands: Evidence of Olmecoid Stylistic Motifs in a Cunil Ceramic Assemblage from Xunantunich, Belize. Poster presented at the 66th Annual Meetings of the Society for American Archaeology, New Orleans.

Taube, Karl A.

1992 Uses of Sport: Review of The Mesoamerica Ballgame. *Science* 256:1064-1065.

Tolstoy, Paul

1978 Western Mesoamerica before A.D. 900. In *Chronologies in New World Archaeology*, edited by R. E. Taylor and C. W. Meighan, pp. 241-284. Academic Press, New York.

Tsukada, Matsuo

1966 The Pollen Sequence. In "The History of Laguna de Pentenxil: A Small Lake in Northern Guatemala," by U. M. Cowgill, G. E. Hutchinson, A. A. Racek, C. E. Goulden, R. Patrick, and M. Tsukada, pp. 63-66. *Memoirs of the Connecticut Academy of Arts and Sciences*, No. 17. New Haven.

Valdez, Fred, Jr.

1987 *The Prehistoric Ceramics of Colha, Northern Belize*. Unpublished Ph.D. dissertation, Harvard University, Cambridge.

1994 The Colha Ceramic Complexes. In "Continuing Archaeology at Colha, Belize," edited by T. R. Hester, H. J. Shafer, and J. D. Eaton, pp 15-40. *Studies in Archaeology* 16. Texas Archaeological Research Laboratory, The University of Texas at Austin.

Valdez, Fred, Jr., and Richard E. W. Adams

1982 The Ceramics of Colha after Three Field Seasons: 1979-1981. In *Archaeology at Colha, Belize: The 1981 Interim Report*, edited by T. R. Hester, H. J. Shafer, and J. D. Eaton, pp. 21-30. Center for Archaeological Research, University of Texas, San Antonio.

Viel, René

1993a Copán Valley. In *Pottery of Prehistoric Honduras: Regional Classification and Analysis*, edited by J. S. Henderson and M. Beaudry-Corbett, pp. 12-18. Monograph 35, Institute of Archaeology, University of California, Los Angeles.

1993b *Evolución de la Cerámica de Copán, Honduras*. Co-published by the Instituto Hondureño de Antropología e Historia and the Centro de Estudios Mexicanos y Centroamericanos, Tegucigalpa, D.C., Honduras, and Mexico City.

Velázquez Valadéz, R.

1980 Recent Discoveries in the Caves of Loltun, Yucatan, Mexico. *Mexicon* 2(4):53-55.

von Nagy, Christopher

1997 The Geoarchaeology of Settlement in the Grijalva Basin. In *Olmec to Aztec: Settlement Patterns in the Ancient Gulf Lowlands*, edited by B. L. Stark and P. J. Arnold, III, pp. 253-277. The University of Arizona Press, Tucson.

von Nagy, Christopher, Maria B. Tway, Mary D. Pohl, and Kevin Pope

2000 Informe: Estudios sobre la cerámica y otros artifactos del sitio San Andrés (Barí 1), Municipio de Huimanguillo, Tabasco, México. Anexo al informe general del año 1999. Report of field work submitted to INAH, Mexico City.

Voorhies, Barbara

1976 The Chantuto People: An Archaic Period Society of the Chiapas Littoral, Mexico. *Papers of the New World Archaeological Foundation*, No. 41. Provo, Utah.

1996 The Transformation from Foraging to Farming in Lowland Mesoamerica. In *The Managed Mosaic: Ancient Maya Agriculture and Resource Use*, edited by S. L. Fedick, pp. 17-29. University of Utah Press, Salt Lake City.

2001 Soconusco-South Pacific Coast and Piedmont Region. In *Archaeology of Ancient Mexico and Central America: An Encyclopedia*, edited by S. T. Evans and D. L. Webster, pp. 667-671. Garland Publishing, Inc., New York & London.

Voorhies, Barbara, George H. Michaels, and George M. Riser

1991 Ancient Shrimp Fishery. *National Geographic Research and Exploration* 7(1):20-35.

Watts, W. A., and J. Platt Bradbury

1982 Paleoecological Studies at Lake Patzcuaro on the West-Central Mexican Plateau and at Chalco in the Basin of Mexico. *Quaternary Research* 17:56-70.

Webster, David L.

2001 Maya Culture and History. In *Archaeology of Ancient Mexico and Central America: An Encyclopedia*, edited by S. T. Evans and D. L. Webster, pp. 424-430. Garland Publishing, Inc., New York & London.

Webster, David, AnnCorinne Freter, and Nancy Gonlin

2000 *Copán: The Rise and Fall of an Ancient Maya Kingdom*. Harcourt Brace & Company, Orlando.

Weeks, John M.

2001 Guatemala Highlands Region. In *Archaeology of Ancient Mexico and Central America: An Encyclopedia*, edited by S. T. Evans and D. L. Webster, pp. 306-311. Garland Publishing, Inc., New York & London.

Werner, Gerd

1997 Las Consecuencias de la Agricultura de los Últimos Tres Mil Años en los Suelos de Tlaxcala. In *Antologia de Tlaxcala, Volumen IV*, edited by A. García Cook and B. L. Merino C., pp. 114-134. INAH and the Gobierno del Estado de Tlaxcala. Mexico City.

Weigand, Phil C.

1985 Evidence for Complex Societies During the Western Mesoamerican Classic Period. In *The Archaeology of West and Northwest Mesoamerica*, edited by M. S. Foster and P. C. Weigand, pp. 47-91. Westview Press, Boulder, Colorado.

1989 Architecture and Settlement Patterns within the Western Mesoamerican Formative Tradition. In *El Preclásico o Formativo: Avances y Perspectivas: Seminario de Arqueología "Dr. Román Piña Chan"*, edited by M. Carmona Macias, pp. 39-64. INAH and the Museo Nacional de Antropología, Mexico City, Mexico.

1993 *Evolución de una Civilización Prehispánica*. El Colegio de Michoacán, Zamora, Michoacán.

2000 The Evolution and Decline of a Core of Civilization. In *Greater Mesoamerica: The Archaeology of West and Northwest Mexico*, edited by M. S. Foster and S. Gorenstein, pp. 43-58. University of Utah Press, Salt Lake City.

2001 West Mexico. In *Archaeology of Ancient Mexico and Central America: An Encyclopedia*, edited by S. T. Evans and D. L. Webster, pp. 819-824. Garland Publishing, Inc., New York & London.

Wilkerson, S. Jeffrey K.

1975 Pre-Agricultural Village Life: The Late Preceramic Period in Veracruz. *Contributions of the University of California Archaeological Research Facility*, No. 27 (Studies in Ancient Mesoamerica III): 111-122. University of California, Berkeley.

1981 The Northern Olmec and Pre-Olmec

Frontier on the Gulf Coast. In *The Olmec & Their Neighbors: Essays in Memory of Matthew W. Stirling*, edited by E.P. Benson, pp. 181-194. Dumbarton Oaks, Washington, DC.

2001a Gulf Lowlands: North Central Region. In *Archaeology of Ancient Mexico and Central America: An Encyclopedia*, edited by S. T. Evans and D. L. Webster, pp. 324-329. Garland Publishing, Inc., New York & London.

2001b Gulf Lowlands: North Region. In *Archaeology of Ancient Mexico and Central America: An Encyclopedia*, edited by S. T. Evans and D. L. Webster, pp. 329-334. Garland Publishing, Inc., New York & London.

2001c Santa Luisa (Veracruz, Mexico). In *Archaeology of Ancient Mexico and Central America: An Encyclopedia*, edited by S. T. Evans and D. L. Webster, pp. 651-653. Garland Publishing, Inc., New York & London.

Williams, Eduardo
2001 Opeño, El (Michoacán, Mexico). In *Archaeology of Ancient Mexico and Central America: An Encyclopedia*, edited by S. T. Evans and D. L. Webster, p. 558. Garland Publishing, Inc., New York & London.

Willey, Gordon R.
1970 Type Descriptions of the Ceramics of the Réal Xe Complex, Seibal, Peten, Guatemala. In "Monographs and Papers in Maya Archaeology," edited by W. R. Bullard, Jr., pp. 313-355. *Papers of the Peabody Museum of Archaeology and Ethnology, Harvard University*, Vol. 61. Cambridge.

1973 The Altar de Sacrificios Excavations: General Summary and Conclusions. *Papers of the Peabody Museum of Archaeology and Ethnology, Harvard University*, Vol. 64(3). Cambridge.

1977 The Rise of Maya Civilization: A Summary View. In *The Origins of Maya Civilization*, edited by R. E. W. Adams, pp. 383-423. University of New Mexico Press, Albuquerque.

Willey, Gordon R., William R. Bullard, Jr., John B. Glass, and James C. Gifford
1965 Prehistoric Maya Settlements in the Belize Valley. *Papers of the Peabody Museum of Archaeology and Ethnology, Harvard University*, Vol. 54. Cambridge.

Wonderly, Anthony
1991 The Late Preclassic Sula Plain, Honduras: Regional Antecedents to Social Complexity and Interregional Convergence in Ceramic Style. In *The Formation of Complex Society in Southeastern Mesoamerica*, edited by W. R. Fowler, Jr., pp. 143-169. CRC Press, Boca Raton, Florida.

Wonderly, Anthony, and Pauline Caputi
1984 1983 Excavations at Río Pelo (YR 125), Sula Plain, northwestern Honduras. Ms. on file, Instituto Hondureño de Antropología e Historia. Centro Regional del Norte, La Lima, Honduras.

Zeitlin, Robert N.
1978 Long-Distance Exchange and the Growth of a Regional Center on the Southern Isthmus of Tehuantepec, Mexico. In *Prehistoric Coastal Adaptations: The Economy and Ecology of Maritime Middle America*, edited by B. L. Stark and B. Voorhies, pp. 183-210. Academic Press, New York.

1979 Preclassic Exchange on the Southern Isthmus of Tehuantepec, Mexico. Unpublished Ph.D. dissertation, Department of Anthropology, Yale University.

1989 Review of "Preclassic Maya Pottery at Cuello Belize" by Laura J. Kosakowsky. *The Latin American Anthropology Review* 1(1):17-18.

1984 A Summary Report on Three Seasons of Field Investigations into the Archaic Period Prehistory of Lowland Belize. *American Anthropologist* 86:358-369.

2001 Oaxaca and Tehuantepec Region. In *Archaeology of Ancient Mexico and Central America: An Encyclopedia*, edited by S. T. Evans and D. L. Webster, pp. 537-546. Garland Publishing, Inc., New York & London.

Zeitlin, Robert N., and Judith F. Zeitlin
2000 The Paleoindian and Archaic Cultures of Mesoamerica. In *The Cambridge History of the Native Peoples of the Americas: Volume II: Mesoamerica, Part 1*, edited by R. E. W. Adams and M. J. Macleod, pp. 45-121. Cambridge University Press, Cambridge.

15. Early Neolithic Tribes in the Levant

O. Bar-Yosef and D. E. Bar-Yosef Mayer

The Scope of the Paper

Classifying social systems for the purpose of studying cultural evolution is not an easy task. The recorded variability in today's world and the recent historical past has caused some major disagreements among scholars, particularly when attempting to define the terms 'bands', 'tribes', and the like (Wolf 1984; Giddens 1984). This situation stems from the mosaic of organizational systems across the globe from the surviving foragers to the overarching complex meta-populations.

To categorize social systems, cultural anthropologists and ethnographers employ a suite of oral, visual, biological, and economic information that is ultimately amalgamated in published reports and summaries (Kelly 1995; Johnson and Earle 2000). Part and parcel of these investigations are studies of kinship, languages and dialects, songs, myths, and the daily and annual social interactions during the anthropological field studies. No less important is the entire array of material culture, predominantly manufactured of perishables. However, most of this cultural data is unavailable to us, the archaeologists. Instead, the best we can do is to use our field observations, and the results of laboratory research in variable domains, to reconstruct the sequence of cultural evolution of past societies, as punctuated by changes. In doing so, we venture into the realm of social anthropology from which we derive our inferences, while constantly facing the constraints of our own empirically based information, and our paradigmatic biases.

In considering the disadvantages of archaeology versus historically documented social systems, it is correct to point out that the explanation of 'how past systems and institutions came into being' is often unknown—as recognized by E. Wolf who noted "that in a majority of cases the entities studied by anthropologists owe their development to processes that originate outside them and reach well beyond them..." (Wolf 2001:314). This is where prehistoric archaeology becomes a useful tool.

It is true that we build our referential models by employing the knowledge of complex hunter-gatherers, farmers and horticulturists, as well as pastoral nomads, whether defined as 'tribal', 'local groups', and/or chiefdoms (Arnold 1996; Flannery 1999; Johnson and Earle 2000). In such an endeavor we are yielding to the 'tyranny of ethnography' (Wobst 1978) while trying to explain cultural evolution and the emergence of social forms as can be recognized in archaeological records (Hayden 1995). In this sense, this paper is not different than others on the same subject. What differs is the region, the time, and the approach to the social interpretation of the archaeological evidence.

Most studies of social evolution, departing from the so-called 'small scale' or 'intermediate societies' of hunter-gatherers, accept that agricultural systems flowed into various regions of the world either by diffusion or colonization. In such cases, the cultural change did not germinate from inside but was triggered by the outside world. However, the emergence of agriculture as a new subsistence system was different as this emergence occurred in 'core areas'. Limiting us to Eurasia and Africa, it suffices to say that most experts today agree that the Neolithic Revolution took place in two focal areas, namely, the Levant and the middle Yangzeh river valley (Smith 1998). This means that except for complex foraging societies (a social structure that appeared and disappeared in a cyclical manner during the Upper Paleolithic) the formation of larger and more complex social organizations were first established in these two regions. We therefore thought that instead of imposing any of the existing classifications of social organizations on the wealth of information retrieved from early Holocene sites in southwestern Asia, it would be best to summarize the evidence and then propose an interpretation. This approach may allow the

Neolithic archaeology of southwestern Asia to tell an interesting story about the evolution of complex social structures, prior to the emergence of states, and that these could fall under the general category of 'tribal or ranked societies' (Flannery 1999; Fowles, this volume, Chapter 2; Parkinson, this volume, Chapter 1).

The last decade brought a wealth of new data but, as illustrated by various scholars (Fig. 1; Aurenche and Kozlowski 1999; Braidwood and Braidwood 1986; Harris 1998a, 1998b; Cauvin 2000a; Mellaart 1975), all are amenable to diverse socio-economic interpretations and classifications. Traditionally Near Eastern Neolithic archaeology centered on reporting the finds (architecture, lithics, fauna, botanical remains, etc.), establishing chronological correlations, and dealing with the aspects of the origin and evolution of agricultural systems. Much less effort and contemplation was dedicated to presenting alternative social interpretations. This lacuna, as noted by Kuijt (2000) is now being rapidly filled by new publications (Cauvin 2000a, 2000b; Kuijt 2000). We therefore, in the following pages, bring the information and published interpretations to our proposed paleo-social reconstruction of early Neolithic societies.

As a general background, we have briefly summarized the chronology and cultural sequence of the region as well as what is known concerning climatic changes during this time span. The Epi-Paleolithic and early Neolithic cultural entities, which persisted through the Terminal Pleistocene and very early Holocene, are fully described in the literature (Aurenche and Kozlowski 1999; Bar-Yosef 1998; Goring-Morris and Belfer-Cohen 1997; Henry 1998). The Early Neolithic period (ca. 11,500-8,200 cal. B.C. is traditionally subdivided into Pre-Pottery Neolithic A (PPNA) and Pre-Pottery Neolithic B (PPNB). We decided to select the richest archaeological records of the PPNB which lasted for about 2,000 years or slightly longer by a few centuries, as indicated by calibrated radiocarbon chronology (Stuiver et al. 1998; Fig. 1)—and to focus on these records as the bases of our discussion.

The PPNB is traditionally subdivided, on the combined bases of stratified assemblages and radiocarbon dates, into four phases, as follows: Early PPNB (EPPNB), Middle (MPPNB), Late (LPPNB), and Final. The last phase, during which a different core reduction strategy was practiced (and exemplified by several publications, is also known as PPNC; e.g., Rollefson 1997; Rollefson et al. 1992). With the progress in dating many Neolithic sites one may expect that this subdivision or an alternative one, will enable us to use in the future a time scale of a few centuries, instead of a couple of millennia.

The archaeology of the period is presented in a series of sections. First, we present the data concerning the economic basis of sites across the region, followed by the inter- and intra-site variability, and the evidence for ceremonial centers and rituals. Foragers who continued to survive in the semi-arid belt and apparently played an important role within the PPNB interaction sphere, receive our attention and the nature of their mutual interactions with the farming communities is summarized. By incorporating all these data sets, we proceed to reconstruct the social structures of the PPNB Neolithic tribal societies that we interpret to represent non-literate ranked societies in southwestern Asia. The evolution of these socially complex entities served as a stepping-stone for the formation of the more famous and better known civilizations of the ancient Near East.

Neolithic Entities and the Emergence of Agriculture

During the terminal Pleistocene and the early Holocene, southwestern Asia and more particularly the Levant and Anatolia witnessed a series of socio-economic changes. These changes found their expression in prehistoric entities that began with the Natufian cultural complex (commonly referred to as an Epi-Paleolithic entity) and ended with the collapse of the early Neolithic civilization. As mentioned above, we chose the PPNB period (ca. 10,500-8,200 cal. B.P.) due to the richness of archaeological records, which seem amenable to the interpretation of past social structures as expressions of tribal societies. In the future, a similar analysis could be conducted for the earlier PPNA for which new data is now rapidly accumulating (Stordeur 2000a, 2000b). The PPNA was the period in which the initial phases of the Neolithic Revolution took place, and the available summaries can be found in the literature (Bar-Yosef and Meadow 1995; Cauvin 2000a; Goring-Morris and Belfer-Cohen 1997; Harris 1998a, 1998b; Mellaart 1975; Moore 1989; Smith 1998).

In brief, current investigations demonstrate that the Neolithic Revolution took place in the Western Wing of the Fertile Crescent, the region known as the 'Levant' (Aurenche and Kozlowski 1999; Kozlowski 1999; Bar-Yosef 1998; Bar-Yosef and Belfer-Cohen n.d.; Goring-Morris and Belfer-Cohen 1997; Harris 1998b; Moore and Hillman

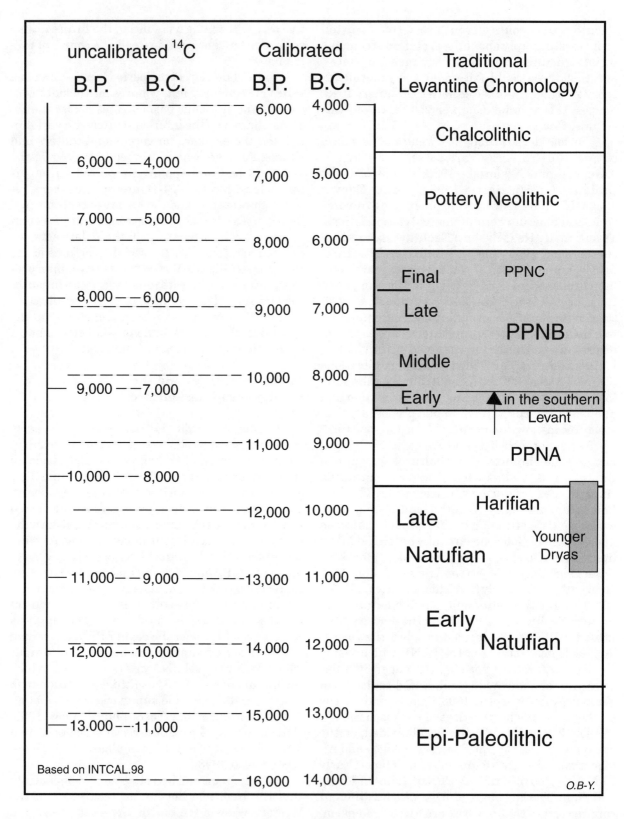

Fig. 1. A chronological chart of calibrated and uncalibrated dates from the late Epi-Paleolithic through the Chalcolithic periods in the Levant. The reader is advised to keep in mind that the horizontal lines do not indicate precise dates, but an average that disregards the standard deviation of the calibrated dates as well as the ambiguities caused by the dendrocalibration.

1992). This region stretches from the foothills of the Taurus Mountains in southeast Turkey (in the arc that combines the upstream of the Euphrates and the Balikh), to the southern tip of the Sinai peninsula (Fig. 2). It is characterized today by north-south-oriented vegetational belts. Contrary to numerous past publications that dealt with the issue of agricultural origins, the paleo-botanical evidence represents a different geographic spread of vegetational associations (Fig. 2). It indicates that the recent spatial distribution of phytogeographical areas (Zohary 1973) only reflects the climate of the late Holocene and the cumulative effects of human activities, especially since the Bronze Age (Baruch and Bottema 1999; Hillman 1996; van Zeist and Bottema 1991). Pollen cores and carbonized plant remains from various sites indicate that during the Younger Dryas the plant belt contracted and only expanded due to the wetter conditions of the early Holocene (Fig. 2) (Bar-Mathews et al. 1997, 1999). The impact on carrying capacity, which can only be roughly estimated, was undoubtedly noticed by humans living during the early Holocene who witnessed rapid expansion of arable land. In the course of adopting the cultivation of cereals and legumes, a suite of founder crops became domesticated (Hillman 1996; Kislev 1997; Zohary 1989; Zohary and Hopf 2000). Unfortunately, time estimates required for the domestication of various species of cereals and legumes are widely diverse.

The earliest phase of farming communities, often called PPNA, is still rather poorly known due to the meager number of excavated and published sites. The evidence from hamlets and/or villages such as Mureybet (Cauvin 1977), Jerf el Ahmar (Stordeur and Jammous 1995; Stordeur 2000a, 2000b), Netiv Hagdud (Bar-Yosef and Gopher 1997), Jericho (Kenyon and Holland 1981), Gilgal (Noy 1989), Dhra (Kuijt 1995), and W16 in Wadi Feinan (Mithen and Finlayson 2000), seems to reflect the initial phases of a complex house society. However, the overall cultural picture is rather schematic and therefore proposed reconstructions of social organizations can be made only generally. This situation, which undoubtedly is temporary as additional fieldwork and publications are in progress, is due not only to the paucity of data but primarily to the particular characteristics of each of the known sites.

By the time of the PPNB (ca. 10,500-8,200 cal. B.P.), systematic cultivation of Einkorn, Emmer wheat, barley, a suite of legumes, and flax was practiced. The increasing number of inhabitants per village surpassed by up to twenty times the largest Early Natufian hamlet reflecting an unprecedented prehistoric population growth within about 2,500 years (note the geographic distribution in Figs. 3-4). Evidence for central public buildings, which followed the few cases known from the PPNA such as the tower in Jericho (Bar-Yosef 1986), and the rounded 'kiva' type in Jerf el Ahmar (Stordeur 2000a, 2000b), were already uncovered in almost every village site reflecting the emergence of social complexity (Bar-Yosef 2001; Cauvin 2000a; Kuijt 2000, and papers therein).

The Economic Basis of PPNB Societies

This overview briefly summarizes both farming and foraging communities. Among the first farmers, agricultural activities became a common practice and through time the incipient phases of goat and sheep domestication that took place in the Taurus-Zagros arc were followed by their introduction into neighboring territories (Fig. 5). Contemporary foragers continued to hunt and gather plant food while developing intricate relationships with farming communities. Traditionally, the entire Levant is considered an interaction sphere of both the 'sown land and the desert'. Thus it is interesting to follow the evolving dichotomy between farmers-herders and foragers. By the end of the PPNB (ca. 8,500-8,200 cal. B.P.) while farmers occupied the Mediterranean vegetational belt and part of the steppic zone, foragers were spread from the steppic through the arid belt and in the north through the mountainous areas and portions of the Anatolian plateau. The evidence for interactions between the practitioners of the two economic systems will be presented below. That these mutual relationships could have ranged from friendly encounters to violent conflicts is well known from historical examples (Spielmann and Eder 1994).

The identification of the economic basis of the interactions emanates from a few archaeobotanical assemblages and numerous animal bone collections. Carbonized seeds were better preserved in sites located mostly in the northern and central Levant and their taphonomy which allowed for particular preservation, is discussed in several papers (de Moulins 1997; Harris 1998a; Hillman et al. 1997; Kislev 1992, 1997; Miller 1996, 1997; van Zeist and de Roller 1995; van Zeist et al. 1986; van Zeist and Waterbolk-van Rooijen 1985; Zohary and Hopf 2000).

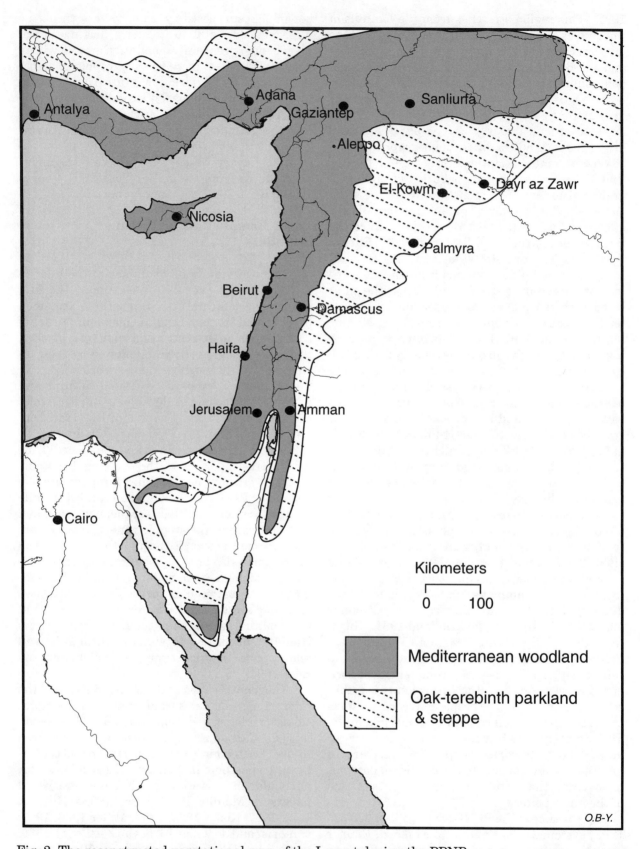

Fig. 2. The reconstructed vegetational map of the Levant during the PPNB.

When the range of activities of early farmers (males, females, and children) are considered we generally would like to have the information concerning fields, tilling techniques if any, the average amount of winter precipitation or whether irrigation was practiced, the techniques and timing of harvesting, storage methods, the use of fodder when animals were penned and tended, and finally, perhaps the most enigmatic aspect, food preparation procedures.

Given the 10,000-year history of agriculture in the Levant and adjacent regions, it is difficult today, even with air photography, to identify prehistoric fields. Long periods of alluviation probably caused the burial of these early fields (Goldberg and Bar-Yosef 1990; Wilkinson and Tucker 1995)

although it is not impossible that some exposures along wadi courses may one day reveal a prehistoric field or an irrigation canal. van Zeist suspected that either winter precipitation was higher during the PPNB or that irrigation was practiced in the marginal eastern belt (van Zeist and Waterbolk-van Rooijen 1985). Using stable carbon isotope analysis, Araus and associates tested seeds from the PPNB deposits of Tel Halula (located in the Euphrates valley) to examine water availability (Araus et al. 1998, 1999). The results suggest that the prehistoric crops enjoyed better water supplies than available today through winter rain. However, without direct evidence for surface irrigation or dug-up canals, and/or the seeds of wild weeds that grow in periodically irrigated fields,

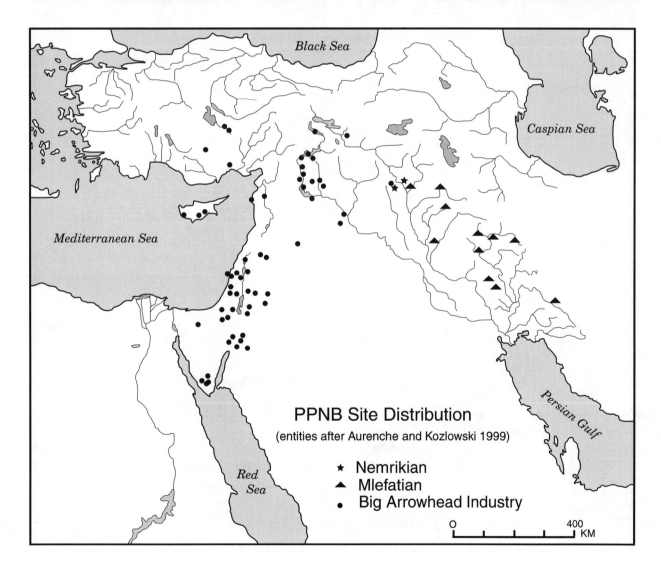

Fig. 3. Distribution of the PPNB sites after Aurenche and Kozlowski (1999) and their entities as defined on the basis of lithic studies (see also Gopher 1994; Kozlowski 1999).

345

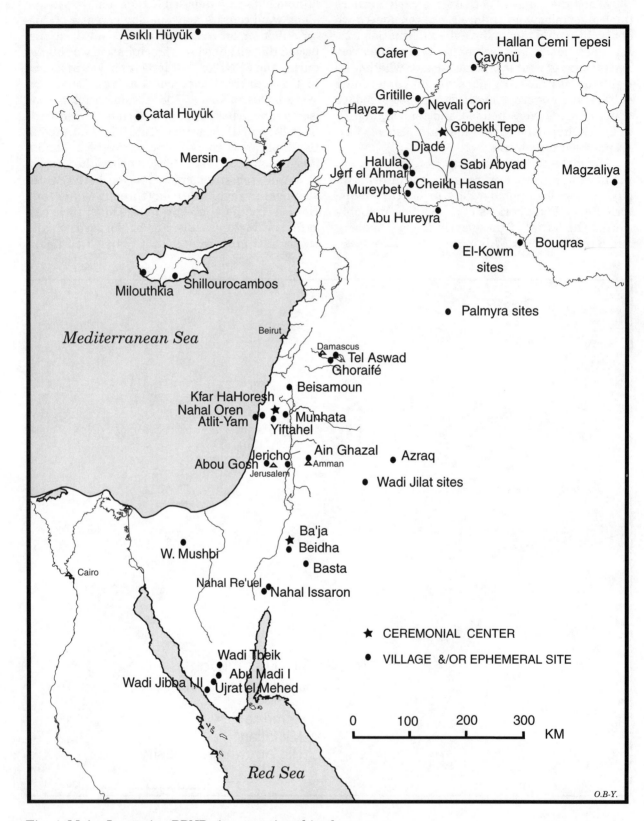

Fig. 4. Major Levantine PPNB sites mentioned in the text.

346

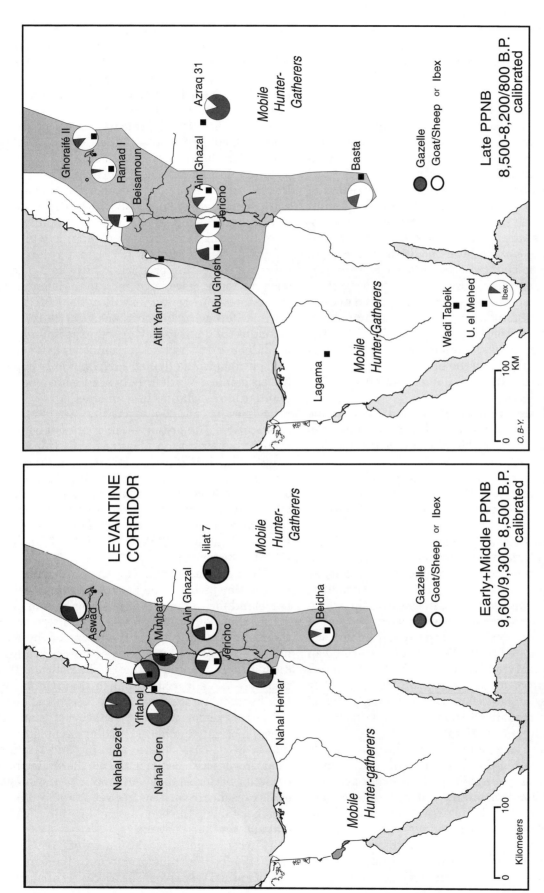

Fig. 5. The acquisition of herding goats and sheep during the PPNB in the southern Levant (after Bar-Yosef 2000). A. the situation during the MPPNB. B. The expanding of herding during the LPPNB.

347

one cannot confirm the practice of irrigation. Experimental investigation demonstrated that cereal phytoliths in today's irrigated fields are different from those of dry farming because they are multi-celled, and thus can serve as a tool to identify ancient irrigation (Miller-Rosen and Weiner 1994). However, the paleo-climatic proxy data from carbonate accumulations in caves and pollen cores already point to a generally higher annual precipitation than today during this period.

The tool-kits of the early farmers included axes/adzes, which in the central and southern Levant were bifacially shaped with transverse blows producing a sharp cutting edge (also known as Tahunian axes) and later modified by a certain amount of polishing. In the villages in the northern Levant and Anatolia polished celts were standard. All these tools were mostly employed in wood working including felling trees, clearing bushes, shaping wooden objects, and on occasion tilling the land (Cauvin 2000a; Yamada 2000). There is no evidence for the use of the plough, which probably followed long after the domestication of cattle (Sherratt 1983).

Harvesting equipment evolved from simple sickles to V-shaped bone tools for stripping seed heads from straw, and later to the *tribulum* (Anderson 1998; M.-C. Cauvin 1973).

Storage facilities were of variable shapes and are known from special built-in installations within the houses, or in courtyards as well as specific rooms that were filled with grain (Akkermans and Duistermaat 1996). The changes in storage facilities could mark the shift from nuclear family consumption to larger social units and perhaps, as found in some PPNB sites, to an institutionalized control of public granaries. In this domain, which borders both public and private property, we should mention the water wells. The earliest known water wells—dated to EPPNB—were uncovered in Cyprus in Mylouthkia and Shillourocambos (Peltenburg et al. 2000) and the latest, a finely constructed well was found in Atlit-Yam, a coastal LPPNB site that lies 8-10 m under the current sea level (Galili and Nir 1993).

In identifying the division of labor and the role of gender within the daily, monthly and annual cycle of farming, we have made no major progress except by employing ethnographic evidence and observations of modern peasant societies. We envision prehistoric males and females as carrying out a variety of tasks. We imagine that males were responsible for manufacturing the tools and assume that the females were in charge of twining

and basketry. The earliest, flimsy if direct, evidence for cordage and basketry was uncovered in PPNA Netiv Hagdud (Schick 1997). In PPNB contexts, the knife handle cover from Çayönü is known as well as a wealth of other various remains (baskets, boxes, head-gear) from Nahal Hemar cave (Schick 1988; 1989). Certain items were produced from annuals (members of the Cerealia family) while more elaborate objects such as the headgear and a 'napkin' were twined from linen. The production of linen required a considerable amount of work beginning with sawing linseeds, weeding during the growing season, pulling, rippling, retting, bracking, scutching, hackling, and finally spinning (McCorriston 1997, and references therein). Hence the production of twined objects such as those discovered in Nahal Hemar cave raises questions as to who within the PPNB society invested in this labor intensive activity?, was it done at the domestic level?, were the items made for daily use?, or perhaps as components for spiritual paraphernalia that saw daylight only in public ceremonies? We definitely need more evidence in order to respond to these queries.

Somewhat simpler seems the case of animal exploitation. The preservation of animal bones is commonly better than plant remains. Due to the length of the PPNB period, and the slow process of introducing herd animals into village economies, one notices how the boundaries between villages with goats and sheep and those without, shifted through time (Fig. 5; Bar-Yosef 2000; Horwitz et al. 1999; Martin 1999; Peters et al. 1999; Vigne et al. 1999; Zeder 1999).

Most scholars agree that the bulk of current information points to the Taurus-Zagros arc as the homeland for the incipient penning and possible subsequent domestication of goats and sheep. In the mountain ranges and the plains of the foothills, these two herd animals were already hunted during the millennia of the Epi-Paleolithic. It is therefore not surprising that in this region, the familiarity of foragers and early farmers as hunters in this region with the behavior of goat and sheep, motivated under particular circumstances (not to be discussed here) penning and tending. That this practice began in the northern Levant is becoming better established in recent years, in spite of the presence in very low frequencies of wild goats and ibex among the bone assemblages in the central and southern Levant.

Current reports indicate an age of Early PPNB (EPPNB) for the transformation in the exploitation of animal resources. The process of husbandry began with sheep during the EPPNB with some hints that goats were also included (Peters et al. 1999). Later, during the middle and late PPNB (MPPNB and LPPNB), either goats and/or sheep, were herded into the central and southern Levant (Fig. 5; Bar-Yosef 2000; Martin 1999). It is not inconceivable that this transfer developed with long-distance exchange lines that evolved rapidly during this period. With such an activity one can envisage local foragers, as well as mobile farmers, playing the important role of the 'middle-man'.

A clear example of the dislocation of goat, sheep, cattle and pigs (as well as the wild Fallow deer) is documented in the PPNB Cypriote site of Shillouro-cambos (Vigne et al. 1999, 2000). These animals, not original species of the island, must have been imported via boats or rafts, whatever was the sea-faring vehicle of the colonists. Zooarchaeological analysis of bone assemblages demonstrated the similarity between the earliest goats in Cyprus and those considered the wild population on the mainland. Hence, the expected morphological changes entailed in the process of domestication, and occurred slowly over a long period of time (Peters et al. 1999). The implications for the continental sites are simple. At the sites located in the natural habitat of caprovines, such as PPNB Çafer Hüyük, the absence of size changes cannot be assumed to be due to continued hunting by farmers, because the practice of penning had most likely already started. In areas where bones of wild goats were rarely found in older (Epi-Paleolithic and PPNA) contexts, the sudden shift to high frequencies of caprovines within a faunal spectrum is the best indication for the onset of herding (Davis 1982). In the semi-arid sites of the Syro-Arabian desert, goats became part of the economy only by 8,000/7,500 cal. B.P. and later (Martin 1999; Figs. 5a-5b).

Indeed, the boundaries between farmers-herders (who continued to hunt and gather wild plants), and foragers who essentially subsisted in the semi-arid region, were far from stable during the PPNB. By about 7,500 cal. B.P. the economic dichotomy between farmers-herders and pastoral nomads emerged and was established in the following millennia. Members of both economic regimes continued to hunt and trap, as well as gather wild plants, seeds, and fruits for various purposes including those used for medicinal purposes.

Goats and sheep were originally exploited as sources of meat and hides. Only later is there evidence for the use of hair, wool, and milk. Cattle and pigs appear during the MPPNB and LPPNB pe-

riod. The penning of aurochs and their ensuing domestication appears to have been first motivated by religious reasons ('the 'bull-cult'; Cauvin 2000a). Similar to other animals, cattle (mostly bulls) were sacrificed, possibly during ceremonial feasts. The subsequent use of the cattle as a source of milk and as draft animals is an achievement in what Sherratt (1981) named the Secondary Products Revolution.

In the Levant, pigs were probably the last animals to be incorporated into the Neolithic household. While it has been proposed that there is evidence of the penning of pigs in Hallan Çemi during the late Epi-Paleolithic, further analysis suggested that it was not a case of domestication (Peters et al. 1999). Early husbandry of pigs is reported from the MPPNB sites (Hongo and Meadow 2000).

In sum, the fully developed Neolithic economy with domesticated species of plants and animals appears to have emerged earlier in the northern Levant. Due to geographic proximity, new inventions and innovations did not escape the inhabitants of the central and southern Levant. This regional network formed the body of the PPNB interaction sphere.

The PPNB Inter-and-Intra Site Variability: The Domestic Aspects

In order to define territories within which sites can be classified as central villages, subsidiary villages, hamlets, seasonal stations and the like, we need to have the most basic information about location, potential routes, sizes and contents. Essentially we seek the kind of documents that are required for spatial analysis or landscape archaeology. Today, most of the data sets, even when incomplete, are primarily available from farming communities, due to the number of excavations and site reports. From these the following picture concerning location, ancient routes, site size, domestic architecture will be discussed below and serve as population estimates (Fig. 6).

It is quite obvious that the largest village sites are located in the river valleys and their tributaries, intermontane valleys or inland basins that accommodated lakes, ponds, and springs. Many of these sites are currently covered by artificial lakes, the results of modern dam construction.

The particular location of these villages reflects their proximity to arable land, fresh water sources, and to routes along river valleys or mountain passes. We note that ceremonial centers (see the following section) are situated either at the top of a hill visible from a considerable distance (Göbekli

Tepe) or a well-hidden narrow valley (Kfar HaHoresh and Ba'ja).

There is a clear size hierarchy among PPNB settlements in spite of the limitations imposed by small, excavated surfaces in most sites (Bar-Yosef and Meadow 1995; Hole 2000; Kuijt 2000). Although ethnoarchaeological studies (Kramer 1982, 1983; Watson 1978, 1979) indicate that the measurable surface of mounds cannot be translated by a simple formula to a number of inhabitants, the size distribution of PPNB sites seems to reflect absolute differences in the number of people. We assume that the largest tested sites accommodated, based on population estimates of 100-150 people per hectare, a viable biological unit of at least 400-500 people (Bar-Yosef and Belfer-Cohen 1989). This estimate could be higher if we consider 12.0 hectare as the size of the largest villages. Hence, tribal territories were perhaps inhabited by 1,500-2,500 people or more, depending on the area within the Levant.

Large and medium size villages are assumed to be major demographic centers and some may have even served as central places for annual gatherings. The better known sites in the Taurus foothills and the Levant include Çayönü (Özdogan 1999), Çafer Hüyük (Cauvin et al. 1999), Navali Çori (Hauptmann 1999), Göbekli Tepe (Schmidt 1999), Tel Halula (Molist 1998), Abu Hureira (Moore 1975), Bouqras (Akkermans et al. 1983), Beisamoun (Lechevallier 1978), Yiftah'el (Garfinkel 1987), Kfar HaHoresh (Goring-Morris 2000), Munhata (Gopher and Orelle 1995), 'Ain Ghazal (Rollefson 1997, 2000), Jericho (Kenyon and Holland 1981), Beidha (Kirkbride 1966), and Basta (Nissen et al. 1987).

In each site, the domestic buildings often reflect a multi-generational use of the same basic social units. In a recent analysis, Byrd (2000) suggested that nuclear families were a stable social entity in the southern Levant from the Natufian through the PPNB. These families occupied the independent rectangular buildings that vary in size, type and construction, from site to site and sometimes within the same site (Hole 2000). However, the presence of larger compounds such as in Bouqras may denote the accommodation of extended families. Such an interpretation is born by today's Near Eastern traditional villages where neighboring or attached houses are generally those of kin-related nuclear families.

In most PPNB sites during the MPPNB, houses were subdivided into smaller rooms (known as the 'cell plan'), a process that stipulated the addition of a second floor. The small, cramped units, served as cellars and storage facilities. This suggestion relies on the well-preserved houses with two floors uncovered mainly in the LPPNB sites such as Basta and Ghwair in Jordan as well as the corridor houses in Beidha (Byrd 2000; Kirkbride 1966; Simmons and Najjar 2000). In these sites employing stones and building material for the walls ensured better preservation. In addition, the custom of filling abandoned habitation units (Özdogan and Özdogan 1998) saved them for future archaeologists. Larger houses versus smaller ones, possibly reflect unequal wealth and social status as suggested by size differences in Çayönü, where the largest excavated exposure is available (over 5,000 square meters).

The Evidence for Ceremonial Centers

The geographic distribution of the PPNB material elements, as mentioned above, reflects territorial subdivisions within the Levant and Anatolia. Assuming that the territorial social structure was loose and kinship-based, we may expect to uncover the evidence for religious activities. Such activities, aimed at maintaining, regulating, and codifying the social structure to ensure the biological and cultural survival of the group would generate both perishable and non-perishable remains. Perishable remains, which often represent a unique event or a series of events, would include food and drinks consumed during religious feasts, of which only animal bones may survive. Chewing hallucinogenic plant substances and/or drinking alcoholic beverages are an integral part of conducting rituals in forager and peasant societies. There is evidence that the human experience of preparing plant foods for consumption led them to recognize the advantages of fermenting wheat and barley into beer (Katz and Voigt 1986) and enhanced the process of intentional cultivation. However, we do not yet have direct evidence for the use of these substances.

The non-perishable, sturdy elements that survived the vagaries of time and physically embody the relationships between humans and their gods are reflected in three types of sacred locales. The first are special sites where the religious activities seem to have been the central focus, including, Göbekli Tepe, Kfar HaHoresh, and Ba'ja (Gebel and Hermansen 1999; Goring-Morris 2000; Hauptmann 1999). The second type is a unique building in each village that stands out among domestic architecture, and served the local community as a shrine or 'meeting house'. In both types of sites/buildings the investment and survival is for a multi-generational period. Examples of this type of structure were uncovered in Beihda, 'Ain Ghazal, Navali Çori and Çayönü. The third category is sacred localities, which perhaps marked territorial ownership, such as Nahal Hemar cave.

Other material expressions of the Neolithic realm of beliefs are mortuary practices, figurative expressions such as the reliefs on the T-shaped pillars and stelae at Göbekli Tepe and Navali Çori (Hauptmann 1999; Schmidt 1998, 1999), the plaster statues (Fig. 7) and modeled skulls in the southern Levant (Goring-Morris 2000; Rollefson 2000, and references therein; Strouhal 1973), and the various types of small clay figurines of humans and animals found in every site (Voigt 1991, and references therein; Voigt 2000). These represent the ideology, artistic concepts, and techniques of production at the time of creation, although they could have been used by many ensuing generations.

We begin by mentioning the impressive site of Göbekli Tepe that spans a surface of about 35-40 hectares. The excavated areas exposed a series of superimposed rounded and rectangular structures (large rooms) supported by T-shaped pillars that served for mounting the roof. Floors are often plastered. Most amazing are the carvings of various animals on the pillars including snakes, cranes, ducks, foxes, rams, bulls, boar and lions (Fig. 7). Human figures appear from the earliest layer but become, in the current sample, the dominant images in the upper layers (Schmidt 1999). Göbekli Tepe is still under excavation, and a fuller picture will emerge in due course. The faunal remains from the earliest layers are predominantly gazelle, wild cattle, wild ass, wild sheep, and boar (Peters et al. 1999). It is worth noting that more than 60% of the wild cattle remains are those of bulls (as noted by the investigators, in a regular village site just a few kilometers away, the ratio of males to females among the cattle bones is 1:5). This finding supports the observation that male animals were the preferred sex for sacrificed animals in the ancient Near East. Hence the remains from feasting during ceremonies supports Cauvin's suggestion to see the Woman and Bull as the ruling divinities of the Neolithic cultures. His proposal relies on the finds of figurines and bucrania in the Mureybetian sites in the mid-Euphrates river valley, where recently supportive evidence was revealed in the site of Jerf el Ahmar (Stordeur 2000a, 2000b).

A different type of a central site is the small village of Kfar HaHoresh (Goring-Morris 2000; Goring-Morris et al. 1994-5) where the main features were graves, rectangular plastered floored structures, and caches of special tools, artifacts and animal bones, which reflect the range of activities from the mundane to the sacred. The lithic industry includes all the common types found in every village, with blades removed from naviform cores, bifacial tools, and the suite of arrowheads known from other MPPNB sites. Imported precious materials include obsidian and cinnabar (originating in Anatolia) as well as marine shells mostly from the Mediterranean Sea but a few from the Red Sea. Among the special finds are a plastered skull associated with a headless gazelle skeleton, and a pit that contained the remains of eight aurochs, six of which were adults. Aside from well-defined burials, including adults with jaws and no crania, the entire excavated area was littered with human remains. Among the game animals, besides the aurochs, were gazelle, goat, wild boar, deer, hare, and fox. Thus, as noted by the excavator, the unique characteristic of the site is the joint burial of humans and animals. Certain burials seem to have been sealed by the plaster floors. Small limestone slabs are categorized as 'tomb stones' or stelae. The information from Kfar HaHoresh illuminates the complex ceremonial aspects associated with funerary rites (see below, Goring-Morris 2000, and references therein).

A somewhat similar site is Ba'ja, situated in a small closed valley in southern Jordan, where the surrounding cliffs left only a narrow wadi canyon as the sole entrance (Gebel and Hermansen 1999; Gebel et al. 1997). The exposed buildings are seen by the excavators as multi-room courtyard houses of the LPPNB age. Most houses had a second story and an intact staircase was discovered in one of them. Rooms of the first floors are interpreted as accommodating domestic activities, and specialized crafts, such as the production of stone rings. While the evidence for the special status of the site as a ceremonial center is still meager, its unique topographic situation is very promising.

The evidence from Göbekli Tepe and Kfar HaHoresh begs for alternative interpretations. On one hand we can claim that these sites are just central villages where annual aggregation took place, and during the rest of the year the local community had the same life style as in every other village. Alternatively it suggests that these sites were occupied by a special sect of this society (possibly a segmentary tribe), who due to their 'spiritual role' in conducting religious ceremonies and rituals had a different status. This proposal re-

O. Bar-Yosef and D. E. Bar-Yosef Mayer

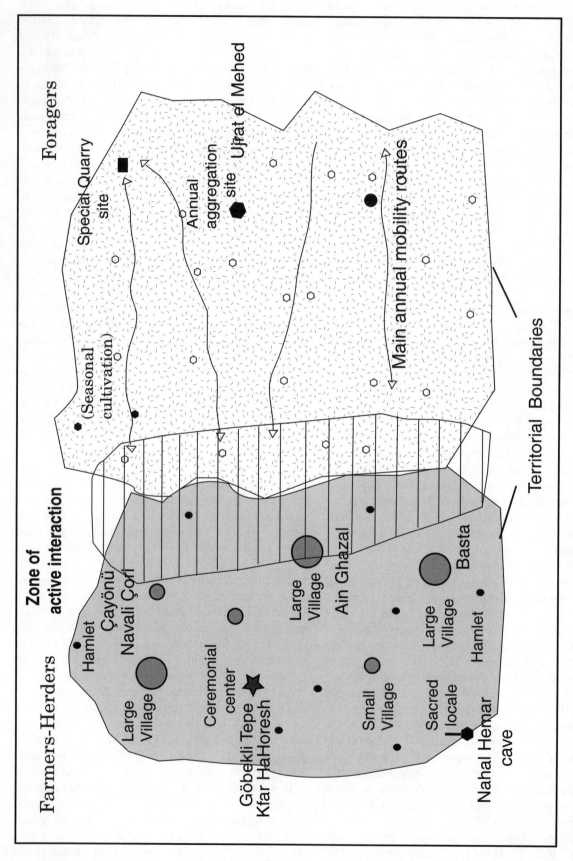

Fig. 6. A schematic model of farmer-herder interactions with foragers and their subsequent settlement pattern. Names of sites are given as examples. Only the main interaction zone is marked on this map, however, this does not imply that foragers did not periodically occupy larger areas of the farmers' land.

sembles Mellaart's earlier proposal concerning the area he excavated at Çatal Hüyük (Mellaart 1975). With the telling evidence from Göbekli Tepe such interpretations seem more credible. In addition, the evolutionary distance from this kind of segmentary tribe to the rise of a sect of priests is not far. The situation, as archaeologically documented, definitely differs from a hunting-gathering society where almost every member could be a shaman, as common among known modern foragers (Lewis-Williams 2000).

The last example for a unique locality that could have served also as a territorial marker is Nahal Hemar cave, a small dark chamber, with an entrance less than a meter wide, located at the confluence of two major wadis, which descend to the Dead Sea (Bar-Yosef and Alon 1988; Bar-Yosef and Schick 1989). Despite an intensive survey in the immediate area, no site that could have been a habitation site was found in the immediate environment.

The interior of the Nahal Hemar cave was occupied by a series of huge blocks that did not allow for the formation of leveled living floors. The cave was filled with limestone rubble mixed with coprolites, twigs, and numerous Neolithic objects radiocarbon dated to the MPPNB. The assemblages of the three main layers contained objects that could have been used in domestic activities, such as a sickle, the special Nahal Hemar flint knives, bone spatulas, baskets, and asphalt-coated containers. However, the large number of the Nahal Hemar knives (over 200) and other items such as stone masks, adorned skulls, fragments of plaster human statues (Goren et al. 1993), bone figurines shaped with asphalt, white plaster, red ochre and green mineral, as well as twined decorated head gear, numerous painted wooden beads, and plaster weights for what possibly was a straw skirt, are reminiscent of other discoveries of cached ceremonial objects (Bar-Yosef and Alon 1988; Bar-Yosef and Schick 1989; Schick 1989).

In certain cases such objects, when losing their active role and/or due to breakage (random and/or intentional) are buried in pits (known as 'favissa') in order to preserve their value as non-domestic items. The collection of Nahal Hemar cave does not seem to fall in this 'favissa' category for several reasons (*contra* Garfinkel 1994). Among others, objects that lost their holy value were buried outside the sacred building (which in Neolithic times and later periods is generally a shrine or a temple). This does not apply to Nahal Hemar cave, which was probably a storage facility next door to an open-air gathering locale, heretofore undiscovered, that probably occupied the wide bank of the wadi. In addition, we found evidence for breakage and damage during Neolithic times caused by a fire that occurred inside the cave, as well as ibex using the cave as a refuge in winter, hyena occupations, and modern plundering. In conclusion, it seems that the original assemblage stored at Nahal Hemar cave, does not represent the property of a household but a community.

The last category is the village 'shrines' or 'temples'. These were noticed by the excavators of Beihda, 'Ain Ghazal, Navali Çori, and Çayönü. In each case, the structure often differs from the common domestic buildings. Such is the 'Terrazzo building' in Çayönü , the only structure with a plaster floor. In Navali Çori, the benches, pillars and sculptures announced the particular features of the building (Hauptmann 1999). In 'Ain Ghazal, one structure was built according to a rounded plan and plastered, in contrast to the surrounding rectangular houses. Another is a typical house, but contained several stelae and an altar-like installation (Rollefson 1998, 2000). In Beidha the squarish large building stands out among the common 'corridor-type' houses (Byrd 2000; Kirkbride 1968). The presence of a special structure within a settlement was heralded earlier in Early Natufian ('Ain Mallaha) and PPNA sites (Jericho and Jerf el Ahamar; Goring-Morris 2000).

In sum, the hierarchical variability represented in villages by ceremonial central sites, cult buildings, or sanctuaries, as well as special sites such as Nahal Hemar cave, reflect an unprecedented territorial cultural complexity, which we feel, indicates the presence of a segmentary and non-egalitarian social structure. This issue will be further discussed below.

Mortuary Practices and Mobile Objects: Additional Evidence for Cosmology and Social Differentiation

Mortuary practices are a well-known source for evaluating the social status of individuals and groups within human societies. Besides the number of the buried individuals, information concerning the position of the skeletons, whether a primary or secondary burial, as well as the presence and value of grave goods, are the criteria employed for estimating social ranking. Examining this kind of observations among PPNB sites follow the same path.

During the PPNB period we notice a reduction in the number of on-site burials in spite of the increase in the number of excavated sites. Thus, in spite of the degree of conservatism in mortuary practices a change is noticed when compared to the PPNA (Aurenche and Kozlowski 1999). Burying the dead on site in abandoned houses, courtyards, and below the house floors continued but finding cemeteries beyond the living space of the village is expected. In addition, mass burials in special buildings have been discovered in a few sites. There are rare examples of grave goods with the human relics.

The most distinctive feature of PPNB mortuary practices was the removal of adult skulls while leaving intact the full skeleton of children. The removal of adult skulls started in the Late Natufian but became a standard procedure in the PPNA villages, and seems to reflect the different social status attributed to each age class. It has been suggested that secondary burials (including skull caches) and the lack of grave goods are sound indications for negotiating equality and codifying social cohesion within communities (Kuijt 1996, 2000). Apparently, this strategy was adopted as the economic changes caused by the rapidly increasing role of agricultural products and accumulation of surplus threatened to break past social alliances. However, the different treatment applied to children and adults tells us that they were not equal members of society. Hence, what may seem to be an effort to keep the southern society egalitarian, hardly applies to the northern region. Moreover, graves with offerings were uncovered in Neolithic sites in the Zagros and its foothills and a similar phenomenon was documented among the burials in Çatal Hüyük (Mellaart 1967, 1975), indicating social ranking among colonizers and/or locals who adopted agriculture. Finally, a change in ideology is recorded among late PPNB contexts in the Levant where most adult burials were left untouched.

In several sites special buildings produced massive accumulations of skeletal remains. One example of a 'house of the dead' was uncovered in Çayönü (Özdogan 1999). In what the excavators named the 'skull building' secondary burials of more than 300 individuals were uncovered, with 76 isolated skulls above the post-cranial elements, all packed into three cells, at the back of a large room that could have served as a sanctuary. Another case is Dja'de (Coqueugniot 1998) where in a 'cell house' the remains of about 40 individuals, including detached skulls, were exposed. This phenomenon resembles the PPNB skeletons that were

buried in the narrow staircase passage of the Jericho PPNA tower (Kenyon 1957).

In many cases the removed skulls were reburied in various contexts including special pits, thus creating 'skull caches' (Kuijt, 2000 p. 137-164). Similar secondary burial of disarticulated or partially articulated skeletons was also practiced (Goring-Morris 2000; Kuijt 1996; Özdogan 1999).

A small number of the skulls were given a spectacular treatment as manifested by the plaster modeled and painted skulls from Jericho, 'Ain Ghazal, Kfar HaHoresh, Beisamoun, Ramad, Mureybet IVB, and Nevali Çori (Aurenche and Kozlowski 1999; Cauvin 1972; Contenson 1971; Goring-Morris 2000; Hauptmann 1999; Lechevallier 1978; Rollefson 2000; Strouhal 1973). A different case are those modeled with some sort of a collagen mixture found in Nahal Hemar cave (Yakar and Hershkovitz 1988). Collectively, skulls are interpreted to represent one facet of the 'cult of the ancestors'. In addition, all of the plastered skulls had their face shaped and painted (often red and green) sometimes with shells in their eye-sockets. It is worth noting that in the Ugaritic literature (mid-second millennium B.C.) the acts of pouring plaster on the skull of the dead god *Aqht* and the avulsion of his teeth (as noticed on most of the plastered skulls), by the goddess *Anat* are done in the context of funerary activities when *Aqht* departs to the netherworld. This description is interpreted as a mythological reminder of an old practice which Margalit (1983) believes was known in the Late Bronze Age to people from accidental finds of archaeological specimens while constructing their own houses on ancient mounds.

Even without the implication of plastering the skull of a dead god, it seems that the small number of adult skulls that were plastered indicates that these were revered members of the group, perhaps the elite of the village. Their final deposition in particular loci, commonly interpreted as burial pits, means that they were considered holy objects and disposal was not permitted in the regular dumps, as occurred for example with many clay figurines.

One may wonder if the differential treatment of the deceased reflects their social status. If it did, then what we see is ranking by age and selection among the adults. Did this tripartite division mark the social ranking within each village? The positive response needs further support from intra-village structure, information we have only from the excavations of Çayönü.

No less relevant to the issue of cosmology is the collection of human plaster statues unearthed in

'Ain Ghazal, Jericho (over 30 items), and a few small fragments in Nahal Hemar cave (Goren et al. 1993; Rollefson 2000). Their archaeological context in the villages testifies to the intentional burial of cult objects. The breakage of such items prior to their interment is a well-known phenomenon from later, historic periods. The human fully standing statues and busts of males, females, and children frequently display asphalt circled eyes and line paintings, as well as two-tiered size, and the presence or absence of hands. Therefore, by employing archaeological analogies, the statues seem to represent a group of deities of a Neolithic pantheon. The fundamental, primordial belief, that gods bear the same physical image as humans, is an old one. Creating humans in the form of gods is recorded in the depiction of the creation of Man in the Akkadian epic of Gilgamesh (Amiran 1962). The two-tiered hierarchy among the complete specimens from 'Ain Ghazal may reflect the ranking within the human society.

The more common finds are the clay figurines of animals and humans, some of which could have been toys or teaching devices. It is only through careful attention to the contexts, as demonstrated by Voigt (1991, 2000) that we will be able to decipher their social and religious meanings. The clay figurines are not as numerous in the Levant, the homeland of the PPNB civilization, as in the two neighboring eastern and western regions where the impact of this civilization was felt within a short time, namely in western Iran and the Anatolian plateau (Haji Firuz and Çatal Höyük; Voigt 1983). In Voigt's latest interpretation (2000), which takes into account both sculptures and wall paintings, the figurines seem to represent a gender-balanced view and/or sending a message of abundance and fertility. The efforts involved in manufacturing the clay figurines are minimal, and once out of use, they could have been discarded or given to children—as indicated by one study of a pastoral Asian society (Süger et al. 1991).

In the context of simple 'temples' or 'shrines' the representation of incised and carved animals and humans on pillars and stelae, sculptures, and as plastered statues, embody the range of symbols that formed the religious world of this civilization. Not surprisingly, their overall distribution resembles almost the entire array of deities and sacred figures known from the ancient Near East. The mixture of nature's agencies, physical and animal, as well as humans were key elements in all the old religions prior to the emergence of monotheism in this region.

In sum, when ceremonial centers, cult buildings, sanctuaries, 'houses of the dead', reliefs on pillars and stelae, undecorated stelae, mobile objects that were employed in rituals and plays (whether in public, in sacred domains, or in the course of intimate encounters of the nuclear and/ or extended family) are taken into account, three major conclusions may be reached: (a) there is significant evidence to indicate the existence of territorially organized, non-egalitarian societies that would fall under the category of 'tribes'; (b) we can begin to grasp what Cauvin refers to as the 'birth of the gods' (Cauvin 2000a); and (c) mythological epics recorded during the Bronze Age and later guard the Neolithic ideologies and their material realization and crystallization may cautiously serve as sources for interpreting the PPNB and Chalcolithic beliefs (Amiran 1962; Cauvin 2000a; Margalit 1983)

Cauvin's early book (1972) was the pioneering study that showed the road to a better understanding of Neolithic cosmology, a point which did not escape researchers such as Eliade in the history of religion and who thought that "the history of religious ideas and beliefs is one with the history of civilization" (Eliade 1978, p. 44). Eliade clearly expressed his view that there was a social evolutionary continuum from the early Neolithic to the city-state of Mesopotamia. Hence, the Neolithic cosmology and religious practices—even if the various interpretations mentioned above or in the cited references remain tentative—undoubtedly encompass a large array of physical expressions for the shared ethos of Neolithic communities, and indicate that rituals were conducted in both public and household spheres. When compared to the pre-Neolithic societies in the Near East such as the Natufian (Bar-Yosef 1997), the PPNB civilization within each of its territories, produced to date a much richer and more telling portrait of the suite of changes incorporated under the term 'the Neolithic Revolution'. It is obvious that a certain amount of this richness resulted from the cultural growth and continuity from the preceding period, the PPNA. It is expected that the spade of the active archaeologists will reveal in the near future more data from this period.

PPNB Foragers in the Semi-Arid Belt

In the pursuit of social geography across the Near East, we now turn to the PPNB foragers in the marginal zone, where small-scale societies persisted for a very long time and interacted with farmers-herders (Fig. 6). They are known from a series of excavations in Jordan, the Negev and Sinai and their sites are smaller by comparison to the villages, with the largest ones extending over ca. 1,000 square meters (Bar-Yosef 1984; Garrard 1998; Garrard et al. 1994, 1996; Gopher et al. 1994).

Animal bones, some plant remains, and large collections of grinding slabs indicate a subsistence based on hunting and gathering (Garrard 1999; Martin 1999). Employing various criteria such as topography and exposure to winds, building techniques, seasonal procurement strategies, ratios of cores to debitage and shaped items, suggest a classification of sites into winter and summer camps.

For example, sites considered winter camps (Bar-Yosef 1984) were excavated in southwestern Sinai (Wadi Jibba I and II, about 300-350 m above sea level, 25 km from the shores of the Gulf of Suez), as well as in the highland area some 1,000 m above sea level, where metamorphic rocks and sandstones meet (Wadi Tbeik; Gopher 1989). Despite differences in altitude, these sites have common features. First, they are sheltered from northwestern winds. Second, they are compounds of small rooms (2.0-3.0 meters in diameter with stone built walls). When the collapsed rocks are taken into account the original walls stood to 0.80-1.30 meter high, and the super-structure was probably brush.

Wadi Tbeik for example, was 250 square meters and contained over 1,000 identifiable bones (Tchernov and Bar-Yosef 1982). The assemblage is dominated by male ibex (MNI of 33 versus 16 females), which may indicate that males were hunted during winter, when females were calving. Female meat during winter is lean and is considered inedible by hunters (Speth and Spielmann 1983). The lack of horn cores and vertebrae could perhaps be related to the selection of parts brought to camp.

Four sites interpreted as summer camps were excavated in the valleys of the highlands of southern Sinai, at an altitude of ca. 1,600 m above sea level. All were located in areas open to prevailing winds and therefore would have not been selected, given the low temperatures and cold, harsh winds, as winter shelters. The sites ranged in size from ca. 250 m2 to ca. 20-25 m2.

The excavations in Ujrat el Mehed exposed a unique site with flimsy structures, rich lithic industries with low frequencies of unretouched debitage indicating that most stone objects were carried into this area (Gopher 1994). The faunal remains from this large excavation comprised more

than a 1,000 identifiable bones, and were mainly ibex, gazelle, hare and fox (Dayan et al. 1986). Bones of quail (*Coturnix coturnix*) indicate a late spring-summer occupation as these birds migrate across the Mediterranean into the Sinai in large flocks, and until recently, were net-trapped along the northern Sinai coast. The quail generally arrive in southern Sinai by April-May. Additional indications of late spring-summer occupation were the unfused distal humeri of ibex bones, as it has been suggested that they were hunted six to eight months after birth. Today most ibex births take place during late March or early April. Assuming the same birthing cycle during the PPNB, these young antelopes could have been hunted during October and November. Occupation of Ujrat el Mehed from early spring to fall would also coincide with the season for the collection of seeds (late April through July) and fruits (August through November in places above the valley floors). Moreover, this season would be suitable for holding social gatherings, which included ritual burials, exchange of artifacts, and other activities that enhance the social cohesion of the group (e.g., mating arrangements, dancing, and participation in public ceremonies).

The centrality of Ujrat el Mehed is reflected in the richness of its malacological assembly. Marine shells used for making beads and pendants (Bar-Yosef Mayer 1997) were retrieved from every PPNB site, both winter and summer camps. Predominantly they were collected from the Red Sea shores, though a few originated in the Mediterranean. However, the variability of the shell species in Ujrat el Mehed is the highest indicating that they were brought in via a larger geographic network than in any of the other sites.

Another special feature of Ujrat el Mehed is a series of small, carefully-built, oval and bell-shaped underground pits that originally could have served for the storage of grain or other foodstuff. While only one of these pits contained arrowheads, shell beads, unworked shells and a few other objects, four contained skulls and long bones of 16 adult skeletons in secondary burials (Hershkovitz et al. 1994). An additional skeleton was uncovered in a pit dug in the center of a rounded room and filled with reddish-purple clay. A few slabs were placed in upright position on top of it, covering the remains of a baby.

Hence, Ujrat el Mehed with its topographic location reveals evidence for its particular position among the local settlement pattern as a focal site for annual aggregations (Fig. 8). The secondary burials of adults in underground storage pits rep-

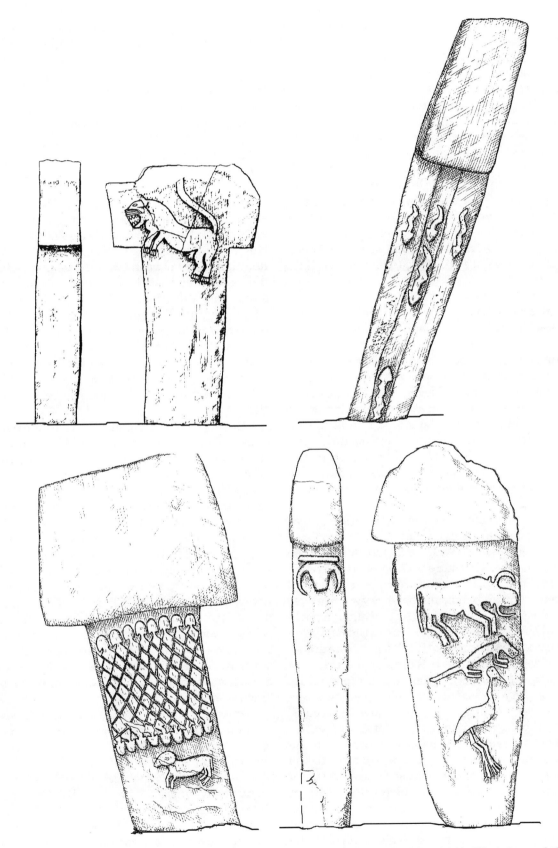

Fig. 7. A selection of T-shaped pillars from Göbekli Tepe (after Schmidt 1998). The sizes of these partially exposed pillars are top left 1.45 m, top right 3.15 m, bottom left 3.15, bottom right 3.15 m.

resent a different belief system than that of the farmers, as described above. These conclusions are supported by lithic analysis that demonstrates that most if not all the lithics were transported from elsewhere. About 40,000 pieces, including 6,000 projectile points, were found with only two dozen cores (Gopher 1989).

A somewhat similar picture of seasonal variability was exposed among four sites in Jordan, some 450 km northeast of southern Sinai but only 60-80 km from farming villages. The climate and topography in central Jordan is not as harsh as in the Sinai. The excavations exposed the remains of habitations, rich lithic and groundstone assemblages, fauna, marine shells, and carbonized plant residues (Garrard et al. 1994, 1996; Garrard 1998; Martin 1999).

Thus, among the PPNB sites, Jilat 7 was a summer camp with flimsy hut structures. It contains evidence for cultivation of emmer wheat, wild and domesticated barley, which are present as grains and chaff, and a large number of grinding and pounding stone tools (as a ratio of excavated volume per number of objects). Jilat 26 was essentially a winter occupation as demonstrated by the thickness of the walls, the orientation of the entrances, and the cluster of storage facilities and hearths. The inhabitants could have been mobile farmers but the bulk of the evidence, we feel, indicates that they were foragers who practiced seasonal farming.

Among the Late Neolithic sites, Jilat 25 was probably a summer camp but Jilat 13 produced conflicting data sets, which may indicate that the site was used during more than one season. In this context it is worth noting that observations of Bedouin campsites indicate that every group moves from one ecozone to another. As a result, if a packing order exists, then a winter location for one group may become a summer site for a neighboring group. The absence of distinct topographic features like these in the southern Sinai, and the possibility that mobility across the Jordanian plateau incorporated larger areas, should be taken into account.

Without going into further detail, the entire array of excavated and published sites from the semi-arid region may in general conform to the image of forager 'egalitarian societies'. This is a somewhat misleading label which still prevails in the literature on hunter-gatherers and reflects the notion that there was equality in food sharing, minimal ownership of material elements, and the like. The increasing number of recently published papers stresses the non-egalitarian components of every human society, including among the hunter-gatherers (Kelly 1995; Lewis-Williams 2000; Speth 1990). Looking at the overall social organization of foragers, whether classified as 'egalitarian' or 'non-egalitarian' (also known as complex small scale societies) in the Near East, it seems to have been vastly different from the Neolithic tribes.

Interactions Between Farmers and Foragers

Interaction between Neolithic farmers-herders and their contemporary mobile foragers played an important role not yet fully researched (Fig. 6). Human societal interactions are in constant flux. Relationships between two societies, especially if their economic basis is somewhat or entirely different, may interchange. They could be amicable, which may lead to intermarriage (generally of women who marry up into economically better communities), they could ignore each other (if the spatial organization over the landscape such as separation by high mountain ranges would permit), or they may have physical conflicts with each other.

During the early Neolithic, trade or exchange relationships are clearly expressed in the presence of marine shells from the Red Sea among the inland farming communities. Another case of non-perishables is the 'down the line' movement of obsidian from Central Anatolia into the Levant (Renfrew and Dixon 1977). The exchange of commodities (such as grain) between the two groups was suggested but not yet fully demonstrated. To judge from ethnographic examples, we know that foragers in return for their products, obtain carbohydrates from farmers. Transport of edibles is demonstrated in the case of Nahal Hemar cave, where evidence of fruits and seeds of plants that grow some 15-150 km away were found. Even under wetter climatic conditions, acorns and colocynth originated in the coastal plan some 50-60 km away (Kislev 1988).

Among the other archaeological markers for the mutual interactions between farmers and foragers are the special type of game drives known as the 'desert kites' (Meshel 1974). These were probably laid-out by PPNB foragers (Betts 1998) in order to hunt *en masse* either gazelles or onagers (Perevolotsky and Baharav 1991). Employing this technique, which is also known from other locations in the world, means that there was a need for the meat, hides and horns from more than a single animal. It was suggested that the simple construction of two stone lines converging to a small enclosure and the ensuing communal efforts in hunting were a response to demands created by large farming communities (Bar-Yosef 1986). The latter, it seems preferred to keep their flocks as capital to be carefully consumed on special occasions. In one Jordanian site (Jilat 26; Garrard et al. 1994), the foundation of a rectangular house in a foragers' camp littered with rounded structures is seen as the "merchant's temporary home", an interpretation that needs further testing.

From peaceful interactions we move on to the inter-communal conflicts. As argued by Keeley (Keeley 1996), archaeologists during the last three decades "have increasingly pacified the past" (p.18), mostly because concrete evidence for warfare has not been recovered. One of us is blamed (Otterbein 1997) for suggesting that the PPNA tower in Jericho and the wall on its outside perimeter, were not elements of a defense system against human aggression. It is rather bizarre to claim that archaeologists who grew up in this region are unfamiliar with the fact that warfare is inevitable for human groups competing for territory. The case of Jericho, as elsewhere (Bar-Yosef 1986), shows that there was probably only one tower in this settlement, which functioned differently from Bronze Age or Medieval towers. The latter, were built outside the perimeter of the wall in order to shoot the climbing attackers and not inside the village. Supportive evidence comes from PPNB sites where a simple terrace wall was built in order to protect the mound accumulations from causing collapse of houses and erosion. Such walls were exposed in Beidha, where a series of steps built on its outer face was uncovered Kirkbride (Kirkbride 1966), in 'Ain Ghazal, in the eastern field (Rollefson 2000), in Tel Halula (Molist 1988), and in Magzalia (Bader 1989).

Historical records concerning past tribes, indicate that pre-state societies were engaged from time to time in warfare for various reasons. Among these are obtaining booty, vengeance and glory, but not for political control (Hallpike 1988). It seems, in spite of the poor evidence, we can expect that this type of conflict existed among hunter-gatherers and farming communities in the Near East (Ember and Ember 1997; Ferguson 1997).

Concluding Remarks: Identifying the Social Territories and the Collapse of the PPNB Civilization

Innovations and inventions characterized the new social environment of the Near Eastern Neolithic in creating constant feedback that ended with the emergence of socially ranked societies. In the continuum from the latest bands of foragers (ca. 11,500 B.P.) in the core area to chiefdoms and states, the tribal 'zone' would be a critical formative period. It was a long one. From the early days of the PPNA to the first chiefdoms in southwestern Asia, ca. 7,500–7,000 B.P. four millennia had passed (Flannery 1999). During the long time span a considerable number of organizational and economic shifts are archaeologically recognized, while the basic elements of the regional cosmology remained the same (Cauvin 2000b). Viewing the social forces within each society as energizing the observable changes, Cauvin named the process as the Revolution of Symbols. While this is an attractive proposal, we do not feel that one can easily decouple the social realm from the economic arena. As human history tells us, economic decisions will have social implications, as much as decisions on social issues will have an impact on the economy of the society. Holding the view that one aspect is more important than the other characterizes the endless debates among historians as well as archaeologists on what determines the trajectory of the cultural evolution. In the 20th century search for the reasons and mechanisms behind the ancient origins of agriculture in the Near East, it has been easier to retrieve the physical evidence for early farming and ensuing animal domestication. However, with the proliferation of accurate information gained from paleo-climatic investigations, radiocarbon dating, genetics of founder crops and the like, it becomes clearer that social decisions were made in the course of anguishing situations, some of which were the 'climatic surprises' (Glantz et al. 1998). Today, as in the past, in face of a natural disaster, decisions must be made to protect society. The same would be true in times of food abundance when personal and/or group conflicts transpired as a major crisis. In such events, temporary and/or hereditary leaders resolved (or not) current conflicts through traditional alliance building, verbal negotiations, communal feasts, and the like—that hardly leave any physical evidence. What could be an easy solution for a band of hunter-gatherers (such as fissioning) will be more complex at the ranked, tribal level and increasingly so in chiefdoms and states.

One of the relevant issues, which is not fully explored in papers on the Near Eastern Neolithic, is the rapid population growth. This phenomenon evident from site sizes, characterized the villages during the PPNA and more particularly in the

PPNB, and resulted in a combination of mounting total fertility of females, their reduced mobility, availability of weaning foods, and increasing investments in adolescents. It is expected in such situations, as shown by ethnic studies, that a population increase ignites a tendency among groups toward inclusive identity (Glazer and Moynihan 1975, and papers therein). Large villages, as mentioned above, were biological descent groups that developed the means for safeguarding and transmitting their own culture. Hence, recurring elements in material culture, mortuary practices, clay figurines, and the like, facilitate the tentative delineation of the original homelands, and the ensuing direction of colonization and/or diffusion.

We therefore turn to mapping the proposed tribal territories within the PPNB interaction sphere. We employ the information as summarized above to circumscribe territories, an effort to tentatively recreate the spatial distribution of PPNB social units. Among the prominent markers are the distribution of ceremonial centers, architectural house types, technical aspects of heavy duty tools such as axes and adzes, frequencies of variable types of projectile points, modeled skulls, and the like (Fig. 8). However, the reader is reminded that the PPNB period lasted for at least two thousand years and cultural changes and territorial shifts were expressed through time. In the multigenerational processes (Fowles, this volume, Chapter 2) this is not a surprising observation.

On the whole when we consider the long duration of the Epi-Paleolithic, it seems that the rhythm of changes had accelerated since the incipience of intentional cultivation in the Levantine Corridor at the end of the Younger Dryas (ca. 11,600 cal. B.P.). Within the newly formed interaction sphere one can identify similar beliefs and the overall ruling cosmology as described by Cauvin (2000a). Special elements such as the few modeled skulls found in various sites, may hint to the presence of elite members or chiefly families. However, no unique tombs were discovered to date and thus we cannot as yet classify one or more of these PPNB entities as a chiefdom. With ongoing fieldwork, this may change in a few years. In accordance with Flannery's view (1999), that the Samarran sites reflect a ranked society prior to the establishment of the Halafian chiefdoms, we suggest that the social precursors of this process were already in operation during the PPNB.

Evidence for what should have been an organized effort and not just a family affair was the colonization of Cyprus. The construction of seafaring craft, the sea crossing by several groups, and transport of land animals to the island, as shown by the discovery of several early PPNB sites, speaks for the presence of leaders.

The rare engraved flat pebbles and 'shaft straighteners' in the PPNA and more frequently stamps in the PPNB, are markers of personal property (of individuals or extended families?). The signs on these objects, as noted by Cauvin (2000a, 2000b) resemble the pictographs of early writing of later time. One may add here the study of the tokens that are currently believed to be the elements of a counting system (Schmandt-Besserat 1990).

Traded or exchanged items indicate a much wider interaction sphere where sources and producers were located beyond the permeable boundaries of the PPNB civilization. Among the better-known exchanged materials were the obsidian, chlorite bowls, asphalt, cinnabar, and marine shells.

During the two millennia of the PPNB only few settlements survived for many centuries. Various reasons account for the abandonment of houses in a living village, from the death of the head of the family to the outcome of verbal and physical conflicts (Cameron and Tomka 1993, and papers therein). However, when the entire village is abandoned, the causes could be more complex, from over-exploitation of the immediate environment or conflicts with neighboring villages to the impact of a series of droughts. Under any circumstances, the abandonment of one village or several may precipitate societal restructuring. It is therefore critical to document the timing of abandonment, and whether it was a local event or a regional phenomenon.

Following Fowles (this volume, Chapter 2), we have attempted to determine whether it is possible to identify intra-generational, multi-generational, or long term processes within this period. Some aspects of Neolithic life represent a moment in time, and among those one can think of the actual moment of plastering a skull, or hunting an animal, etc. At the same time the material culture left behind also represents aspects of multi-generational practices (worshipping a specific skull, continuation in hunting of the same animals). Trade is yet another representation of multiple time-frames: in this period, trade is based on personal or group relationships, and depending on the nature and strength of the relationship it could be either a single event or a continuous effort that may span generations.

Construction of ceremonial centers, on the one hand, and the more mundane houses, storage facilities, granaries, and wells also represent an entire sequence from the moment of their initial construction, to the end of their use (but probably not throughout the two thousand years of the period).

Several aspects discussed above concern religious practices. Those are represented by skulls modeled in plaster, the construction of ceremonial centers such as Kfar HaHoresh, and by burial practices. Being rigid and conservative aspects of life it is impossible to differentiate them within the PPNB, or to subdivide them within this period. The burial of a single individual is usually a mani-

festation of on-going long term traditions that pertain to the entire community. Moreover, these traditions are some of the best indicators of continuity, and change in burial practices often indicate to the archaeologist the onset of a new period and/or new culture.

The one Neolithic trait that we are unable to attribute to a certain moment is that of the gradual process of animal domestication. It should be attributed to the entire period, since to date it is impossible to identify the 'first domesticator'.

The stratigraphic gap between the PPNB layers and those labeled as Pottery Neolithic is well

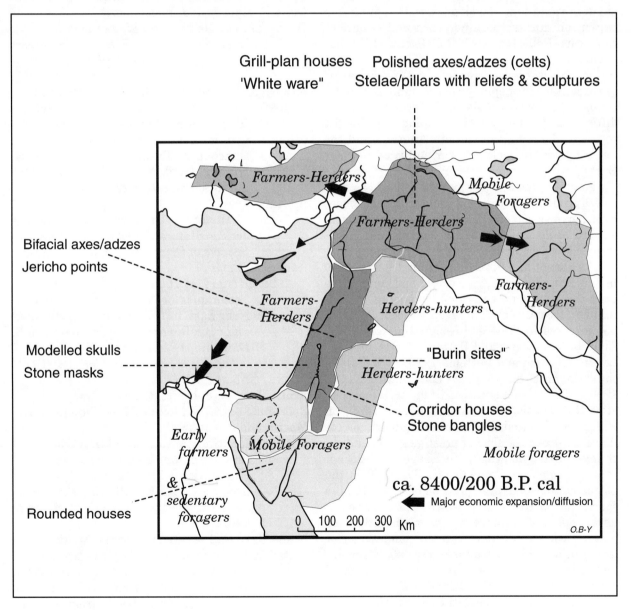

Fig. 8. Tentative map of tribal entities in the Levant and adjacent areas. A few suggested cultural markers are labeled on the map.

established in the Levant and eastern Anatolia (Aurenche and Kozlowski 1999; Gopher and Gophna 1993). Further support for the observation concerning the abandonment of PPNB villages was gleaned from the establishment of new hamlets and farmsteads across the southern Levant. The cultural gap is also evidenced in the northern Levant (Akkermans et al. 1983; Akkermans & Duistermaat 1996; Özdogan & Basgelen 1999), as well as on the Anatolian plateau.

The proposal, to explain the collapse of a major village such as 'Ain Ghazal was derived from comparisons between contemporary ecological hardships caused by the Industrial Revolution and the ensuing rapid land development and population expansion during the nineteenth and twentieth centuries (Rollefson 1990; Rollefson and Köhler-Rollefson 1989; Rollefson et al. 1992). Over-exploitation of pastures and tree felling were suggested as reasons for the depletion of the immediate environment of this large village. However, it would be difficult to employ the same explanation for the regional abandonment in both Anatolia and the Levant given the ecological variability of the Near East.

Another perspective views the collapse as a result of economic over-exploitation of poorer villages by richer ones. Unfortunately, we have no conspicuous archaeological evidence for raiding and enslaving of certain communities by chiefly villages.

An abrupt climatic change around 8,400–8,200 B.P, is recorded in the ice cores, and could have been the culprit for the rapid worsening of environmental conditions. This event is documented in pollen cores in Greece (Rossignol-Strick 1995), Anatolia (van Zeist and Bottema 1991), and the Levant (Baruch and Bottema 1999) as well as in the stalagmites of Soreq Cave (Bar-Mathews et al. 1999). Affected by a series of droughts, tribal societies that subsisted on farming and herding, in which the demands of better-off individuals (or families) drove the flow of prestige goods and exchange of commodities with foragers, could not continue to accumulate surplus. The shift in the pattern of seasonal precipitation necessitated the search for pastures further away and resulted in lower yields of summer harvests. The economic deterioration would accelerate the competition for leadership within such a ranked society (Carneiro 1990; Flannery 1999) resulting in an organizational change expressed in the disappearance of previously large villages and the establishment of smaller villages, hamlets and farmsteads. The new conditions probably increased the reliance on the more flexible subsistence strategy of pastoral nomads, which seem to appear in the archaeological record sometime around or after 7,000 cal. B.P. However, as the Mesopotamian evidence of the Hassuna/Samarra culture indicates, the recovery of the social systems took only one to three centuries, and the local populations were on the road from ranked tribal societies to early chiefdoms.

References Cited

Akkermans, P. A., J. A. K. Boerma, A. T. Clason, S. G. Hill, E. Lohof, C. Meiklejohn, M. le Mière, G. M. F. Molgat, J. J. Roodenberg, W. Waterbolk-van Rooyen and W. van Zeist
   1983   Bouqras Revisited: Preliminary Report on a Project in Eastern Syria. *Proceedings of the Prehistoric Society* 49:335-372.

Akkermans, P. M. M. G. and K. Duistermaat
   1996   Of Storage and Nomads. The Sealings from Late Neolithic Sabi Abyad, Syria. Commentaires de R. Bernbeck, S. Cleuziou, M. Frangipane, A. Le Brun, H. Nissen, H. T. Wright et réponse des auteurs. *Paléorient* 22(2):17-44.

Amiran, R.
   1962   Myths of the Creation of Man and the Jericho Statues. *Bulletin of the American Schools of Oriental Research* 167:23-25.

Anderson, P. C.
   1998   History of Harvesting and Threshing Techniques for Cereals in the Prehistoric Near East. In *The Origins of Agriculture and Crop Domestication*, edited by A. B. Damania, J. Valkoun, G. Willcox and C. O. Qualset, pp. 145-159. ICARDA, Aleppo, Syria.

Araus, J. L., A. Febrero, R. Buxó, M. O. Rodríguez-Ariza, F. Molina, M. D. Camalich, D. Martín and J. Voltas
   1997   Identification of Ancient Irrigation Practices based on the Carbon Isotope Discrimination of Plant Seeds: a Case Study from the South-East Iberian Peninsula. *Journal of Archaeological Science* 24(8):729-740.

Araus, J. L., A. Febrero, M. Catala, M. Molist, J. Voltas and I. Romagosa
   1999   Crop Water Availability in Early Agriculture: Evidence from Carbon Isotope Discrimination of Seeds from a Tenth Millennium BP Site on the Euphrates. *Global Change Biology* 5:201-212.

Arnold, J. E.
1996 *Emergent Complexity: The Evolution of Intermediate Societies*. International Monographs in Prehistory. Archaeological Series 9. University of Michigan, Ann Arbor.

Aurenche, O. and S. K. Kozlowski
1999 *La Naissance du Néolithique au Proche Orient ou Le Paradis Perdu*. Editions Errance, Paris.

Bader, N. O.
1989 *Earliest Cultivators in Northern Mesopotamia: The Investigations of Soviet Archaeological Expedition in Iraq at Settlements Tell Magzaliya, Tell Sotto, Kül Tepe*. Nauka, Moscow.

Bar-Mathews, M., A. Ayalon and A. Kaufman
1997 Late Quaternary Paleoclimate in the Eastern Mediterranean Region from Stable Isotope Analysis of Speleothems at Soreq Cave, Israel. *Quaternary Research* 47:155-168.

Bar-Mathews, M., A. Ayalon, A. Kaufman and G. J. Wasserburg
1999 The Eastern Mediterranean Paleoclimate as a Reflection of Regional Events: Soreq Cave, Israel. *Earth and Planetary Science Letters* 166:85-95.

Bar-Yosef Mayer, D. E.
1997 Neolithic Shell Bead Production in Sinai. *Journal of Archaeological Science* 24(2):97-112.

Bar-Yosef, O.
1984 Seasonality Among Neolithic Hunter-Gatherers in Southern Sinai. In *Animals and Archaeology, 3. Herders and Their Flocks*, edited by J. Clutton-Brock and C. Grigson, pp. 145-160. 202. British Archaeological Reports International Series, Oxford.
1986 The Walls of Jericho: An Alternative Interpretation. *Current Anthropology* 27:157-162.
1997 Symbolic Expressions in Later Prehistory of the Levant: Why are they so few? In *Beyond Art: Pleistocene Image and Symbol*, edited by M. W. Conkey, O. Soffer, D. Stratmann and N. G. Jablonski, pp. 161-187. vol. 23. Memoirs of the California Academy of Science, San Francisco.
1998 The Natufian Culture in the Levant—Threshold to the Origins of Agriculture. *Evolutionary Anthropology* 6(5):159-177.

2000 The Context of Animal Domestication in Southwestern Asia. In *Archaeozoology of the Near East IV A: Proceedings of the Fourth International Symposium on the Archaeozoology of Southwestern Asia and Adjacent Areas*, edited by M. Mashkour, A. M. Choyke, and F. Poplin. ARC Publicatie 32, Centre for Archaeological Research and Consultancy; Groningen Institute for Archaeology; Rijksuniversiteit. Groningen.
2001 From Sedentary Foragers to Village Hierarchies: The Emergence of Social Institutions. In *The Origin of Human Social Institutions*, edited by G. Runciman, pp. 1-38. vol. 110. Proceedings of the British Academy, London.

Bar-Yosef, O. and D. Alon
1988 Excavations in the Nahal Hemar Cave. *Atiqot* 18:1-30.

Bar-Yosef, O. and A. Belfer-Cohen
1989 The Origins of Sedentism and Farming Communities in the Levant. *Journal of World Prehistory* 3(4):447-498.
n.d. Facing Environmental Crisis: Societal and Cultural Changes at the Transition from the Younger Dryas to the Holocene in the Levant. In *The Transition from Foraging to Farming in Southwestern Asia*, edited by U. Baruch, R. Cappers, and S. Bottema. Ex Oriente, Berlin.

Bar-Yosef, O. and A. Gopher (editors)
1997 *An Early Neolithic Village in the Jordan Valley, Part I: The Archaeology of Netiv Hagdud*. Peabody Museum of Archaeology and Ethnology, Harvard University, Cambridge.

Bar-Yosef, O. and R. H. Meadow
1995 The Origins of Agriculture in the Near East. In *Last Hunters, First Farmers: New Perspectives on the Prehistoric Transition to Agriculture*, edited by T. D. Price and A. B. Gebauer, pp. 39-94. School of American Research Advanced Seminar Series, D. W. Schwartz, general editor. School of American Research Press, Santa Fe.

Bar-Yosef, O. and T. Schick
1989 Early Neolithic organic remains from Nahal Hemar cave. *National Geographic Research* 5(2):176-190.

Baruch, U. and S. Bottema
1999 A New Pollen Diagram from Lake Hula: Vegetational, Climatic, and Anthropo-

genic Implications. In *Ancient Lakes: Their Cultural and Biological Diversity*, edited by H. Kawanabe, G. W. Coulter and A. C. Roosevelt, pp. 75-86. Kenobe Productions, Belgium.

Betts, A. V. G.
1998   Holocene Cultural Ecology and Environments of the Northeastern Badia. In *The Prehistoric Archaeology of Jordan*, edited by D. O. Henry, pp. 151-161. BAR S705, Oxford.

Braidwood, L. and R. Braidwood
1986   Prelude to the Appearance of Village-Farming Communities in Southwestern Asia. In *Ancient Anatolia: Aspects of Change and Cultural Development (Essays in Honor of Machleld J. Mellink)*, edited by J. V. Vorys, E. Porada, B. S. Ridgeway and T. Stech, pp. 3-11. University of Wisconsin Press, Madison.

Byrd, B. F.
2000   Households in Transition: Neolithic Social Organization within Southwest Asia. In *Life in Neolithic Farming Communities: Social Organization, Identity, and Differentiation*, edited by I. Kuijt, pp. 63-98. Plenum Press, New York.

Cameron, C. M. and S. A. Tomka
1993   *Abandonment of Settlements and Regions: Ethnoarchaeological and Archaeological Approaches. New Directions in Archaeology*. Cambridge University Press, Cambridge.

Carneiro, R. L.
1990   Chiefdom-level Warfare as Exemplified in Fiji and the Cauca Valley. In *The Anthropology of War*, edited by J. Haas, pp. 190-211. Cambridge University Press, Cambridge.

Cauvin, J. C.
1972   *Les Religions Néolithiques de Syro-Palestine*. Maisonneuve, Paris.
1977   Le Moyen-Euphrate au VIIIᵉ millénaire d'apres Mureybet et Cheikh Hassan. In *Le Moyen Euphrate: Zone de Contacts et d'Echanges*, edited by J. C. Margueron, pp. 21-34. E. J. Brill, Leiden.
2000a   *The Birth of the Gods and the Origins of Agriculture*. Translated by T. Watkins. Cambridge University Press, Cambridge.
2000b   The Symbolic Foundations of the Neolithic Revolution in the Near East. In *Life in Neolithic Farming Communities: So-cial Organization, Identity, and Differentiation*, edited by I. Kuijt, pp. 235-251. Plenum Press, New York.

Cauvin, J., O. Aurenche, M.-C. Cauvin and N. Balkan-Atli
1999   The Pre-Pottery Site of Cafer Höyük. In *Neolithic in Turkey: Cradle of Civilization. New Discoveries*, edited by M. Özdogan and N. Basgelen, pp. 87-104. Arkeoloji ve Sanat Yayinlari, Istanbul.

Cauvin, M.-C.
1973   Problèmes d'Emmanchement des Faucilles du Proche-Orient: Les Documents de Tell Assouad (Djezireh, Syrie). *Paléorient* 1:101-106.

Contenson, H. D.
1971   Tell Ramad, a Village of Syria of the 7th and 6th millennia B.C. *Archaeology* 24:278-83.

Coquegniot, E.
1998   Dja'de el Mughara (moyen-euphrate), un Village Néolithique dans son Environnement Naturel à la Veille de la Domestication. In *Espace Naturel, Espace Habité: en Syrie du Nord (10e-2e millénaires av. J-C.). Actes du colloque tenu à l'Université Laval (Québec) du 5 au 7 mai 1997*, edited by M. Fortin and O. Aurenche, pp. 109-114. Canadian Society for Mesopotamian Studies, Toronto, Ontario.

Davis, S. J. M.
1982   Climatic Change and the Advent of Domestication of Ruminant Artiodactyls in the Late Pleistocene-Holocene Period in the Israel Region. *Paléorient* 8(2):5-16.

Dayan, T., E. Tchernov, O. Bar-Yosef and Y. Yom-Tov
1986   Animal Exploitation in Ujrat el Mehed, a Neolithic Site in Southern Sinai. *Paléorient* 12(2):105-116.

de Moulins, D.
1997   *Agricultural Changes at Euphrates and Steppe Sites in the Mid-8th to the 6th Millenium B.C.* British Archaeological Reports, BAR International Series 683, Oxford.

Eliade, M.
1978   *A History of Religious Ideas*. University of Chicago Press, Chicago.

Ember, C. R. and M. Ember
1997   Violence in the Ethnographic Record: Results of Cross-Cultural Research on

War and Aggression. In *Troubled Times: Violence and Warfare in the Past*, edited by D. L. Martin and D. W. Frayer, pp. 1-20. War and Society. vol. 3. Gordon and Breach Publishers; Overseas Publishers Association, Amsterdam.

Ferguson, R. B.
1997 Violence and War in Prehistory. In *Troubled Times: Violence and Warfare in the Past*, edited by D. L. Martin and D. W. Frayer, pp. 321-355. War and Society. vol. 3. Gordon and Breach Publishers; Overseas Publishers Association, Amsterdam.

Flannery, K.V.
1999 Chiefdoms in the Early Near East: Why it's so Hard to Identify Them. In *The Iranian World. Essays on Iranian Art and Archaeology*, edited by A. Alizadeh, Y. Majidzadeh, and S.M. Shahmirzadi, pp. 44-61. Iran University Press.

Galili, E. and Y. Nir
1993 The Submerged Pre-Pottery Neolithic Water Well of Atlit-Yam, Northern Israel, and its Paleoenvironmental Implications. *The Holocene* 3(3):265-270.

Garfinkel, Y.
1987 Yiftahel: A Neolithic Village from the Seventh Millennium B.C. in Lower Galilee, Israel. *Journal of Field Archaeology* 14:199-212.
1994 Ritual Burial of Cultic Objects: The Earliest Evidence. *Cambridge Archaeological Journal* 4(2):159-188.

Garrard, A. N.
1998 Environment and Cultural Adaptations in the Azraq Basin: 24,000-7,000 BP. In *The Prehistoric Archaeology of Jordan*, edited by D. O. Henry, pp. 139-150. BAR S705, Oxford.
1999 Charting the Emergence of Cereal and Pulse Domestication in South West Asia. *Environmental Archaeology* 4:67-86.

Garrard, A. N., D. Baird, S. Colledge, L. Martin and K. Wright
1994 Prehistoric Environment and Settlement in the Azraq Basin: An Interim Report on the 1987 and 1988 Excavation Seasons. *Levant* 26:73-109.

Garrard, A. N., S. Colledge and L. Martin
1996 The Emergence of Crop Cultivation and Caprine Herding in the "Marginal Zone" of the Southern Levant. In *The Origins and Spread of Agriculture and Pastoral-*

ism in Eurasia, edited by D. Harris, pp. 204-226. UCL Press, London.

Gebel, H. G. and B. D. Hermansen
1999 Ba'ja Neolithic Project 1999: Short Report on Architectural Findings. *Neo-Lithics* 3:18-21.

Gebel, H. G., K., Z. Kafafi and G. O. Rollefson (editors)
1997 *The Prehistory of Jordan, II. Perspectives from 1997*. Volumes 4 and 5. Ex Oriente, Berlin.

Giddens, A.
1984 *The Constitution of Society: Outline of the Theory of Structuration*. University of California Press, Berkeley.

Glantz, M. H., D. G. Streets, T. R. Stewart, N. Bhatti, C. M. Moore and C. H. Rosa
1998 *Exploring the Concept of Climate Surprises: A Review of the Literature on the Concept of Surprise and How it is Related to Climate Change*. U. S. Department of Energy, Office of Energy Research.

Glazer, N. and D. P. Moynihan (editors)
1975 *Ethnicity: Theory and Experience*. Harvard University Press, Cambridge, MA.

Goldberg, P. and O. Bar-Yosef
1990 The Effect of Man on Geomorphological Processes Based upon Evidence from the Levant and Adjacent Areas. In *Man's Role in Shaping the Eastern Mediterranean Landscape*, edited by S. Bottema, G. Entjies-Nieborg and W. Van Zeist, pp. 71-86. Balkema, Rotterdam.

Gopher, A.
1989 Neolithic Arrowheads in the Levant: Results and Implications of a Seriation Analysis. *Paléorient* 15(1):57-64.
1994 *Arrowheads of the Neolithic Levant: A seriation analysis*. Dissertation Series 10. Eisenbrauns, Winona Lake, Indiana.

Gopher, A. and R. Gophna
1993 Cultures of the Eighth and Seventh millennium BP in Southern Levant: A Review for the 1990s. *Journal of World Prehistory* 7(3):297-351.

Gopher, A., A. N. Goring-Morris and D. Gordon
1994 Nahal Issaron: The Lithics of the Late PPNB Occupation. In *Neolithic Chipped Stone Industries of the Fertile Crescent: Proceedings of the First Workshop on PPN Chipped Lithic Industries*, edited by H. G. Gebel and S. K. Kozlowski, pp. 479-494. Ex Oriente, Berlin.

Gopher, A. and E. Orelle
1995   *The Groundstone Assemblages of Mun-
       hata, a Neolithic Site in the Jordan Val-
       ley, Israel: A Report.* Association Palé-
       orient, Paris.
Goren, Y., I. Segal and O. Bar-Yosef
1993   Plaster Artifacts and the Interpretation
       of the Nahal Hemar Cave. *Journal of the
       Israel Prehistoric Society* 25:120-131.
Goring-Morris, A. N.
2000   The Quick and the Dead: The Social
       Context of Aceramic Neolithic Mortuary
       Practices as Seen from Kfar HaHoresh.
       In *Life in Neolithic Farming Communi-
       ties: Social Organization, Identity, and
       Differentiation*, edited by I. Kuijt, pp. 103-
       136. Plenum Press, New York.
Goring-Morris, A. N. and A. Belfer-Cohen
1997   The Articulation of Cultural Processes
       and Late Quaternary Environmental
       Changes in Cisjordan. *Paléorient* 23(2):
       71-94.
Goring-Morris, A. N., Y. Goren, L. K. Horwitz, I.
Hershkovitz, R. Lieberman, J. Sarel, D. Bar-Yosef
1994-5 The 1992 Season of Excavations at the
       Pre-Pottery Neolithic B Settlement of
       Kefar HaHoresh. *Journal of the Israel
       Prehistoric Society* 26:74-121.
Hallpike, C. R.
1988   *The Principles of Social Evolution.*
       Clarendon Press, Oxford.
Harris, D. R.
1998a The Origins of Agriculture in Southwest
       Asia. *The Review of Archaeology* 19(2):5-
       12.
1998b The Spread of Neolithic Agriculture from
       the Levant to Western Central Asia. In
       *The Origins of Agriculture and Crop Do-
       mestication*, edited by A. B. Damania, J.
       Valkoun, G. Willcox and C. O. Qualset,
       pp. 65-82. Report No. 21 of the Genetic
       Resources Conservation Program, Divi-
       sion of Agriculture and Natural Re-
       sources. ICARDA, Aleppo, Syria.
Hauptmann, H.
1999   The Urfa Region. In *Neolithic in Turkey:
       Cradle of Civilization. New Discoveries*,
       edited by M. Özdogan and N. Basgelen,
       pp. 65-86. Arkeoloji ve Sanat Yayinlari,
       Istanbul.
Hayden, B.
1995   Pathways to Power: Principles for Cre-
       ating Socioeconomic Inequalities. In
       Foundations of Social Inequality, edited

by T. D. Price, and G. M. Feinman, pp.
       15-86. Plenum Press, New York.
Henry, D. O. (editor)
1998   *The Prehistoric Archaeology of Jordan.*
       Archaeopress, Oxford.
Hershkovitz, I., O. Bar-Yosef and B. Arensburg
1994   The Pre-Pottery Neolithic Populations of
       South Sinai and their Relations to other
       Circum-Mediterranean Groups: Anthro-
       pological Study. *Paléorient* 20(2):59-84.
Hillman, G.
1996   Late Pleistocene Changes in Wild Plant-
       Foods Available to Hunter-Gatherers of
       the Northern Fertile Crescent: Possible
       Preludes to Cereal Cultivation. In *The
       Origins and Spread of Agriculture and
       Pastoralism in Eurasia*, edited by D.
       Harris, pp. 159-203. UCL Press, London.
Hillman, G. C., A. J. Legge and P. A. Rowley-
Conwy
1997   On the Charred Seeds from Epipalaeo-
       lithic Abu Hureyra: Food or fuel? *Cur-
       rent Anthropology* 38(4):651-659.
Hole, F.
2000   Is Size Important? Function and Hierar-
       chy in Neolithic Settlements. In *Life in
       Neolithic Farming Communities: Social
       Organization, Identity, and Differentia-
       tion*, edited by I. Kuijt, pp. 191-209. Ple-
       num Press, New York.
Hongo, H. and R. H. Meadow
2000   Faunal Remains from Prepottery Neo-
       lithic Levels at Çayönü, Southeastern
       Turkey: A Preliminary Report Focusing
       on Pigs (*Sus* sp.). In *Archaeozoology of
       the Near East IV A: Proceedings of the
       fourth international symposium on the
       archaeozoology of southwestern Asia and
       adjacent areas*, edited by M. Mashkour,
       A. M. Choyke and F. Poplin, pp. 121-140.
       vol. ARC Publicatie 32. Centre for Ar-
       chaeological Research and Consultancy;
       Groningen Institute for Archaeology;
       Rijksuniversiteit Groningen, Groningen.
Horwitz, L. K., E. Tchernov, P. Ducos, C.
Becker, A. von den Driesch, L. Martin and A.
Garrard
1999   Animal Domestication in the Southern
       Levant. *Paléorient* 25(2):63-80.
Johnson, A.W. and T. Earle
2000   *The Evolution of Human Societies: From
       Foraging Group to Agrarian State*, Sec-
       ond Edition. Stanford University Press,
       Stanford.

Katz, S. H. and M. M. Voigt
  1986 Bread and Beer: The Early Use of Cereals in the Human Diet. *Expedition* 28(2):23-34.
Keeley, L. K.
  1996 *War Before Civilization.* Oxford University Press, New York.
Kelly, R.
  1995 *The Foraging Spectrum: Diversity in Hunter-Gatherer Lifeways.* Smithsonian Institution Press, Washington.
Kenyon, K.
  1957 *Digging Up Jericho.* Benn, London.
Kenyon, K. and T. Holland
  1981 *Excavations at Jericho, Vol. III: The Architecture and Stratigraphy of the Tell.* British School of Archaeology in Jerusalem, London.
Kirkbride, D.
  1966 Five Seasons at the Pre-Pottery Neolithic Village of Beidha in Jordan. *Palestine Exploration Quarterly* 98:5-61.
  1968 Beidha: Early Neolithic Village life south of the Dead Sea. *Antiquity* XLII:263-274.
Kislev, M. E.
  1988 Dessicated Plant Remains from Nahal Hemar: An Interim Report. *Atiqot* 18:76-81.
  1992 Agriculture in the Near East in the VIIth Millennium B.C. In *Préhistoire de l'Agriculture: Nouvelles Approches Experimentales et Ethnographiques.*, edited by P. C. Anderson-Gerfaud, pp. 87-93. Monographie du CRA, no. 6. CNRS, Paris.
  1997 Early Agriculture and Paleoecology of Netiv Hagdud. In *An Early Neolithic Village in the Jordan Valley Part I: The Archaeology of Netiv Hagdud*, edited by O. Bar-Yosef and A. Gopher, pp. 209-236. Peabody Museum of Archaeology and Ethnology, Harvard University, Cambridge.
Kozlowski, S. K.
  1999 *The Eastern Wing of the Fertile Crescent: Late Prehistory of Greater Mesopotamian Lithic Industries.* British Archaeological Reports International Series 760, Oxford.
Kramer, C.
  1982 *Village Ethnoarchaeology.* Academic Press, New York.
  1983 Spatial Organization in Contemporary Southwest Asian Villages. In *The Hilly Flanks and Beyond*, edited by T. C. Young, Jr., P. E. L. Smith and P.

Mortensen, pp. 347-368. Studies in Ancient Civilization No. 36. The Oriental Institute, Chicago.
Kuijt, I.
  1995 Pre-Pottery Neolithic A Settlement Variability: Evidence for Sociopolitical Developments in the Southern Levant. *Journal of Mediterranean Archaeology* 7(2):165-192.
  1996 Negotiating Equality through Ritual: A Consideration of Late Natufian and Prepottery Neolithic A Period Mortuary Practices. *Journal of Anthropological Archaeology* 15:313-336.
  2000 People and Space in Early Agricultural Villages: Exploring Daily Lives, Community Size, and Architecture in the Late Pre-Pottery Neolithic. *Journal of Anthropological Archaeology* 19(1):75-102.
Lechevallier, M.
  1978 *Abou Gosh et Beisamoun. Deux Gisements du VIIe Millenaire avant l'Ere Chretienne en Israel.* Mémoires et Travaux du Centre de Recherches Préhistoriques Français de Jérusalem, 2. Association Paléorient, Paris.
Lewis-Williams, J. D. (editor)
  2000 *Stories that Float from Afar.* Texas A & M University Press, College Station, TX.
Margalit, B.
  1983 The "Neolithic Connexion" of the Ugarit poet of Aqht. *Paléorient* 9(2):93-98.
Martin, L.
  1999 Mammal Remains from the Eastern Jordanian Neolithic, and the Nature of Caprine Herding in the Steppe. *Paléorient* 25(2):87-104.
McCorriston, J.
  1997 The Fiber Revolution: Textile Extensification, Alienation, and Social Stratification in Ancient Mesopotamia. *Current Anthropology* 38(4):517-549.
Mellaart, J.
  1967 *Çatal Hüyük, a Neolithic Town in Anatolia.* Thames and Hudson, London.
  1975 *The Neolithic of the Near East.* Thames and Hudson, London.
Meshel, Z.
  1974 New Data about the "Desert Kites". *Tel Aviv* 1:129-143.
Miller, N. F.
  1996 Seed Eaters of the Ancient Near East: Human or Herbivore? *Current Anthropology* 37(3):521-528.

1997 The Macrobotanical Evidence for Vegetation in the Near East, c. 18 000/16 000 BC to 4 000 BC. *Paléorient* 23(2):197-208.

Miller-Rosen, A. and S. Weiner
1994 Identifying Ancient Irrigation: A New Method Using Opaline Phytoliths from Emmer Wheat. *Journal of Archaeological Science* 21(1):125-132.

Mithen, S. and C. Finlayson
2000 WF16, a New PPNA site in Southern Jordan. *Antiquity* 74(283):11-12.

Molist, M.
1998 Espace collectif et espace domestique dans le néolithique des IXème et VIIIème millenaires B.P. au nord de la Syrie: apports du site de Tell Halula (Valée de l'Euphrate). In *Espace Naturel, Espace Habité: en Syrie du Nord (10e-2e millénaires av. J-C.). Actes du colloque tenu à l'Université Laval (Québec) du 5 au 7 mai 1997,* edited by M. Fortin and O. Aurenche, pp. 115-130. Canadian Society for Mesopotamian Studies, Toronto, Ontario.

Moore, A. M. T.
1975 The Excavation of Tell Abu Hureyra in Syria: A Preliminary Report. *Proceedings of the Prehistoric Society* 41:50-77.
1989 The Transition from Foraging to Farming in Southwest Asia: Present Problems and Future Directions. In *Foraging and Farming: The Evolution of Plant Exploitation,* edited by D. R. Harris and G. C. Hillman, pp. 620-631. Unwin Hyman, London.

Moore, A. M. T. and G. C. Hillman
1992 The Pleistocene to Holocene Transition and Human Economy in Southwest Asia: The Impact of the Younger Dryas. *American Antiquity* 57(3):482-494.

Nissen, H. J., M. Muheisen, H. G. Gebel, C. Becker, R. Neef, H. J. Pachur, N. Qadi and M. Schultz
1987 Report on the First Two Seasons of Excavation at Basta (1986-1987). *Annual of the Department of Antiquities of Jordan* 31:79-119.

Noy, T.
1989 Gilgal I: A Pre-Pottery Neolithic site, Israel. *Paléorient* 15(1):11-18.

Otterbein, K.
1997 The Origins of War. *Critical Review* II(2):251-277.

Özdogan, A.
1999 Çayönü. In *Neolithic in Turkey: Cradle of Civilization. New Discoveries,* edited by M. Özdogan and N. Basgelen, pp. 35-64. Arkeoloji ve Sanat Yayinlari, Istanbul.

Özdogan, M. and N. Basgelen (editors)
1999 *Neolithic in Turkey: The Cradle of Civilization. New Discoveries.* 3. Arkeoloji ve Sanat Yayinlari, Istanbul, Turkey.

Özdogan, M. and A. Özdogan
1998 Buildings of Cult and the Cult of Buildings. In *Light on top of the Black Hill. Studies presented to Halet Çambel,* edited by G. Arsebük, M. Mellink, J. and W. Schirmer, pp. 581-601. Ege Yayinlari, Istanbul.

Perevolotsky, A. and D. Baharav
1991 The Distribution of Desert Kites in Eastern Sinai and Sub-Regional Carrying Capacity: An Ecological Perspective. *Journal of Arid Environments* 20:239-249.

Peters, J., D. Helmer, A. von den Driesch and M. S. Segui
1999 Early Animal Husbandry in the Northern Levant. *Paléorient* 25(2):27-47.

Peltenburg, E., S. Colledge, P. Croft, A. Jackson, C. McCartney, and M.A. Murray.
2000 Agro-Pastoralist Colonization of Cyprus in the 10th millennium BP: Initial Assessments. *Antiquity* 74(286):844-853.

Renfrew, C. and J. Dixon
1977 Obsidian in Western Asia: A Review. In *Problems in Economic and Social Archaeology,* edited by G. de G. Sieveking, I. H. Longworth, and K. E. Wilson, pp. 137-150. Westview Press, Boulder.

Rollefson, G. O.
1990 The Uses of Plaster at Neolithic 'Ain Ghazal, Jordan. *Archeomaterials* 4(1):33-54.
1997 Changes in Architecture and Social Organization at Neolithic 'Ain Ghazal. In *The Prehistory of Jordan, II. Perspectives from 1997,* edited by H. Gebel, Z. Kafafi and G. Rollefson, pp. 287-308. Studies in Early Near Eastern Production, Subsistence and Environment, Gebel and Neef, general editor. Ex Oriente, Berlin.
1998 'Ain Ghazal (Jordan): Ritual and Ceremony III. *Paléorient* 24(1):43-58.
2000 Ritual and Social Structure at Neolithic 'Ain Ghazal. In *Life in Neolithic Farming Communities: Social Organization,*

Identity, and Differentiation, edited by I. Kuijt, pp. 165-190. Plenum, New York.

Rollefson, G. O. and I. Köhler-Rollefson
1989 The Collapse of Early Neolithic Settlements in the Southern Levant. In *People and Culture in Change: Proceedings of the Second Symposium on Upper Palaeolithic, Mesolithic and Neolithic Populations of Europe and the Mediterranean Basin*, edited by I. Hershkovitz, pp. 73-89. BAR S508(i), Oxford.

Rollefson, G. O., A. H. Simmons and Z. Kafafi
1992 Neolithic cultures at 'Ain Ghazal, Jordan. *Journal of Field Archaeology* 19:443-470.

Rossignol-Strick, M.
1995 Sea-land Correlation of Pollen Records in the Eastern Mediterranean for the Glacial-Interglacial Transition: Biostratigraphy versus Radiometric Time-Scale. *Quaternary Science Reviews* 14:893-915.

Schick, T.
1988 Nahal Hemar Cave - Cordage, Basketry and Fabrics. *Atiqot* 18:31-43.

1989 Early Neolithic Twined Basketry and Fabrics from the Nahal Hemar Cave in Israel. In *"Tissage, Corderie, Vannerie": actes des IX rencontres internationales d'Archeologie et d'Histoire d'Antibes, 20-22 Octobre 1988.*, pp. 41-52, Ville d'Antibes.

1997 Miscellaneous Finds: A Note on the Perishable Finds from Netiv Hagdud. In *An Early Neolithic Village in the Jordan Valley*, edited by O. Bar-Yosef and A. Gopher, pp. 197-200. vol. I. Peabody Museum, Cambridge, MA.

Schmandt-Besserat, D.
1990 Accounting in the Prehistoric Middle East. *Archeomaterials* 4:15-23.

Schmidt, K.
1998 Frühneolithische Tempel Ein Forschungsbericht zum präkeramischen Neolithikum Obermesopotamiens. *Mitteilungen der Deutschen Orient-Gesellschaft zu Berlin. Sonderdruck* 130:17-49.

1999 Boars, Ducks, and Foxes - the Urfa-Project 99. *Neo-Lithics* 3:12-15.

Sherratt, A.
1981 Plough and Pastoralism: Aspects of the Secondary Products Revolution. In *Pattern of the Past: Studies in Honor of David Clarke*, edited by I. Hodder, G. Isaac and N. Hammond, pp. 261-306. Cambridge Univeristy Press, Cambridge.

Sherratt, A.
1983 The Secondary Exploitation of Animals in the Old World. *World Archaeology* 15(1):90-104.

Simmons, A. H. and M. Najjar
2000 Preliminary Report of the 1999-2000 Excavation Season at the Pre-Pottery Neolithic Settlement of Ghwair I, Southern Jordan. *Neo-Lithics* 1/00:6-8.

Smith, B. D.
1998 *The Emergence of Agriculture*. 2nd edition. Scientific American Library, New York.

Speth, J. D.
1990 Seasonality, Resource Stress, and Food Sharing in So-Called 'Egalitarian' Foraging Societies. *Journal of Anthropological Archaeology* 9(2):148-188.

Speth, J. D. and K. A. Spielmann
1983 Energy Source, Protein Metabolism, and Hunter-Gatherer Subsistence Strategies. *Journal of Anthropological Archaeology* 2:1-31.

Spielmann, K. and J. Eder
1994 Hunters and Farmers: Then and Now. *Annual Review of Anthropology* 23:303-323.

Stordeur, D.
2000a New Discoveries in Architecture and Symbolism at Jerf el Ahmar (Syria), 1997-1999. *Neo-Lithics* 1/00:1-4.

2000b Jerf el Ahmar: et l'Emergence du Néolithique au Proche Orient. In *Premiers Paysans du Monde: Naissances des Agricultures*, edited by J. Guilaine, pp. 31-60. Collection des Hesperides. Editions Errance, Paris.

Stordeur, D. and B. Jammous
1995 Pierre à Rainure à Décor Animal Trouvée dans l'Horizon PPNA de Jerf el Ahmar (Syrie). *Paléorient* 21(1):129-130.

Strouhal, E.
1973 Fire Plastered Skulls from Pre-Pottery Neolithic B Jericho. *Paléorient* 1:231-247.

Stuiver, M., P. J. Reimer, E. Bard, J. W. Beck, G.S. Burr, K. A. Hughen, B. Kromer, G. McCormac, J. van der Plicht, M. Spurk
1998 INTCAL98 Radiocarbon Age Calibration, 24,000–0 cal. BP. *Radiocarbon* 40 (3): 1041-1084.

Süger, H., S. Castenfeldt, and M. Fentz
1991 Small Functional Items and Regeneration of Society, Dough Figurines from the

369

Kalash People of Chitral, Northern Pakistan. *Folk* 33:37-66.

Tchernov, E. and O. Bar-Yosef
1982 Animal Exploitation in the Pre-Pottery Neolithic B period at Wadi Tbeik, Southern Sinai. *Paléorient* 8:17-37.

van Zeist, W. and S. Bottema
1991 *Late Quaternary Vegetation of the Near East.* Beihefte zum Tübinger Atlas des Vorderen Orients, Reihe A (Naturwissenschaft) Nr.18. Dr. Ludwig Reichert Verlag, Weisbaden.

van Zeist, W. and G. J. de Roller
1995 Plant Remains from Asikli Höyük, a Pre-Pottery Neolithic site in Central Anatolia. *Vegetation History and Archaeobotany* 4:179-185.

van Zeist, W., P. E. L. Smith, R. M. Palfenier-Vegter, M. Suwjin and W. A. Casparie
1986 An Archaeobotanical Study of Ganj Dareh Tepe, Iran. *Paleohistoria* 26 (1984):201-224.

van Zeist, W. and W. Waterbolk-van Rooijen
1985 The Palaeobotany of Tell Bouqras, Eastern Syria. *Paléorient* 11(2):131-147.

Vigne, J.-D., H. Buitenhuis and S. Davis
1999 Les Premiers Pas de la Domestication Animale à l'Ouest de l'Euphrate: Chypre et l'Anatolie Centrale. *Paléorient* 25(2): 49-62.

Vigne, J.-D., I. Carrére, J.-F. Saliége, A. Person, H. Bocherens, J. Guilaine and F. Brios
2000 Predomestic Cattle, Sheep, Goat, and Pig during the late 9th and the 8th Millenium cal. BC on Cyprus: Preliminary Results of Shillourokambos (Parekklisha, Limassol). In *Archaeozoology of the Near East IV A: Proceedings of the fourth international symposium on the archaeozoology of southwestern Asia and adjacent areas*, edited by M. Mashkour, A. M. Choyke and F. Poplin, pp. 83-106. ARC Publicatie 32. Centre for Archaeological Research and Consultancy; Groningen Institute for Archaeology; Rijksuniversiteit Groningen, Groningen.

Voigt, M. M.
1983 *Hajji Firuz Tepe, Iran: The Neolithic Settlement.* Hasanlu Excavations Reports I. The University Museum, Philadelphia.
1991 The Goddess from Anatolia: An Archaeological Perspective. *Oriental Rug Review* 11(2):32-39.

2000 Çatal Höyük in Context: Ritual at Early Neolithic Sites in Central and Eastern Turkey. In *Life in Neolithic Farming Communities: Social Organization, Identity, and Differentiation*, edited by I. Kuijt, pp. 253-293. Plenum Press, New York.

Watson, P. J.
1978 Architectural Differentiation in some Near Eastern Communities, Prehistoric and Contemporary. In *Social Archaeology*, edited by C. L. Redman et al, pp. 131-158. Academic Press.
1979 *Archaeological Ethnography in Western Iran.* University of Arizona Press, Tucson.

Wilkinson, T. J. and D. J. Tucker
1995 *Settlement Development in the North Jazira: A Study of the Archaeological Landscape.* British School of Archaeology in Iraq; Department of Antiquities and Heritage, Baghdad; Aris and Phillips, Warminster.

Wobst, M. H.
1978 The Archeo-Ethnology of Hunter-Gatherers or the Tyranny of the Ethnographic Record in Archaeology. *American Antiquity* 43: 303-309.

Wolf, E. R.
1984 Culture: Panacea or Problem? *American Antiquity* 49: 393-400.
2001 *Pathways of Power: Building an Anthropology of the Modern World.* University of California Press, Berkeley.

Yakar, R. and I. Hershkovitz
1988 The Modelled Skulls of Nahal Hemar. *Atiqot* 18:59-63.

Yamada, S.
2000 Development of the Neolithic: Lithic Use-Wear Analysis of Major Tool Types in the Southern Levant. Unpublished Ph.D. dissertation, Harvard University.

Zeder, M. A.
1999 Animal Domestication in the Zagros: A Review of Past and Current Research. *Paléorient* 25(2):11-25.

Zohary, D.
1989 Domestication of the Southwest Asian Neolithic Crop Assemblage of Cereals, Pulses, and Flax: The Evidence from the Living Plants. In *Foraging and Farming: The Evolution of Plant Exploitation*, edited by D. R. Harris and G. C. Hillman, pp. 358-373. One World Archaeology. Unwin Hyman, London.

Zohary, D. and M. Hopf
2000 *Domestication of Plants in the Old World.* Second Edition ed. Clarendon Press, Oxford.

Zohary, M.
1973 *Geobotanical Foundations of the Middle East.* Springer Verlag, Stuttgart.

16. A Neolithic Tribal Society in Northern Poland

Peter Bogucki

The lowlands of northern Poland are part of the larger geographical unit known as the North European Plain, which stretches from Holland to Russia. The North European Plain was covered either by ice during the Weichsel Glaciation or with glacial outwash south of the ice sheets. When the ice retreated, it left behind a landscape of moraines, outwash plains, sub-ice meltwater channels ('tunnel valleys') with slow-flowing streams, and lakes. The northward-flowing rivers, most prominently the Oder and the Vistula, and the great east-west meltwater valleys, between Warsaw and Berlin and between Toruń and Eberswalde, divide the region into smaller physiographic provinces.

One such province is the flat region of clay ground moraine and sandy outwash dissected by glacial tunnel valleys in north-central Poland known as Kuyavia (*Kujawy*, in Polish). Kuyavia (Fig. 1) is bounded on the east by the Vistula river, on the north by the Toruń-Eberswalde meltwater valley, and in the south by the Warsaw-Berlin meltwater valley. In the west it connects with the similar region of Great Poland (*Wielkopolska*, in Polish) through a zone of many small lakes. Kuyavia

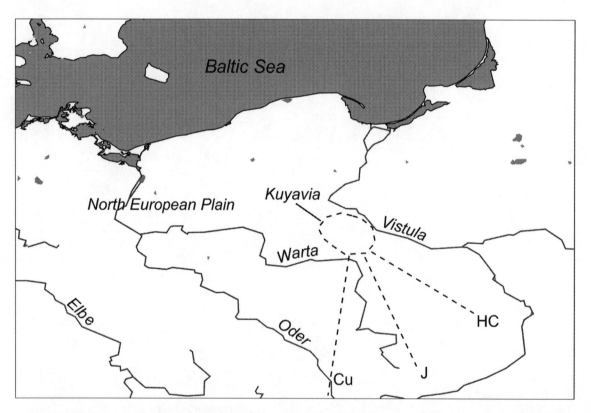

Fig. 1 Map of north-central continental Europe showing location of the Kuyavia region on the North European Plain. Key: HC - Holy Cross Mountains in central Poland, source of the "chocolate" flint; J - source area of Jurassic flint in southern Poland; Cu - general direction from which copper reached Kuyavia. Width of map approximately 600 kilometers.

has some of the most fertile soils in Poland and today is a productive agricultural area for wheat, potatoes, sugar beets, and rapeseed. Bottomlands in the tunnel valleys contain lush meadows.

Neolithic farmers were drawn to Kuyavia in the initial agricultural colonization of central Europe (see Bogucki 1996a and 2000 for an overview of this process; Fig. 2 provides a chronological chart). It was one of the first areas outside the loess basins of central Europe to see farming settlement. Sites of the Linear Pottery culture, dating between 5400 and 5000 B.C. (recalibrated dating) are found primarily on low fingers of land along tunnel valleys or shallow lakes. The Linear Pottery settlements in the lowlands have a 'pioneer' character, with dense deposits of rubbish but sparse structural remains. Only recently have some ostensible rectangular longhouses been reported (Czerniak 1994, 1998), but large Linear Pottery settlements on the scale of Bylany or Köln-Lindenthal have yet to be found.

A pattern of relatively small Early Neolithic settlements persisted in this area during the first half of the fifth millennium B.C. The Linear Pottery culture had been succeeded by local variants of the Stroke-Ornamented Pottery (*Stichbandkeramik*) Culture and the early phases of the Lengyel Culture. The Lengyel Culture, named after a site in southern Hungary, was the principal Neolithic culture of the fifth millennium B.C. in east-central Europe (Bogucki and Grygiel 1993b). It takes numerous local forms in Hungary, Austria, Slovakia, Moravia, Bohemia, and southern Poland, (see articles in Koštuřík 1994 for a review of recent knowledge about the numerous Lengyel variants.) During the second half of the fifth millennium B.C., these regional entities became further differentiated along a variety of trajectories.

Around 4500 B.C. in Kuyavia, one such group of late Lengyel communities emerged with a coherent set of characteristics. These include:
-trapezoidal longhouses;
-burials within the settlement following a distinctive ritual;
-intensive land use for agriculture, livestock, hunting, fishing, timber, and fuelwood; and,
-acquisition of copper and flint from distant sources.
These characteristics—along with distinctive mica-tempered, minimally decorated ceramics—distinguish the Brześć Kujawski Group, named after a settlement first investigated in the 1930s and then between 1976 and 1984 (Jażdżewski 1938; Bogucki and Grygiel 1983, 1993a). Other major sites of the

Brześć Kujawski Group include Biskupin 15a (Maciejewski, Rajewski, and Wokrój 1954); Krusza Zamkowa (Czerniak 1980); Osłonki, investigated between 1989 and 1994 (Grygiel and Bogucki 1997); Miechowice, where excavations have been conducted since 1995; and recently Konary (see Fig. 3). The major settlements uniformly display the characteristics listed above. In addition, a variety of minor settlements, such as Falborz and Kuczyna,

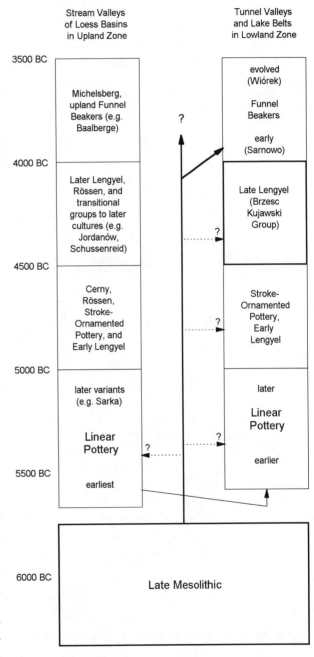

Fig. 2 Chronological chart of principal cultural units of the early and middle Neolithic in north-central Europe.

have yielded habitation traces of the Brześć Kujawski Group without major elements like longhouses and burials.

The settlements of the Brześć Kujawski Group are found in areas covered by large expanses of relatively flat glacial boulder clay, broken by the traces of tunnel valleys and kettle lakes. These glacial relic landforms attracted early farming settlements, and sites of the Brześć Kujawski Group are almost uniformly associated with such terrain features. In many cases, they are on the same spots as earlier Linear Pottery settlements, reflecting some common element in patterns of land-use. Streams that flowed in these channels or linked lakes were almost certainly important communication routes. The Bachorza and Notec valleys were important arteries through Kuyavia.

The longhouse settlements of the Brześć Kujawski Group clearly reflect its 'Danubian' cultural heritage from the Linear Pottery culture in the sixth millennium B.C. and its successors such as Stroke-Ornamented Pottery and Rössen earlier in the fifth millennium B.C. The question still remains whether the inhabitants of the Brześć Kujawski Group settlements were the local descendants of the earlier Linear Pottery farming settlers of the Polish lowlands 40 generations earlier or whether they represent fresh immigrants to this

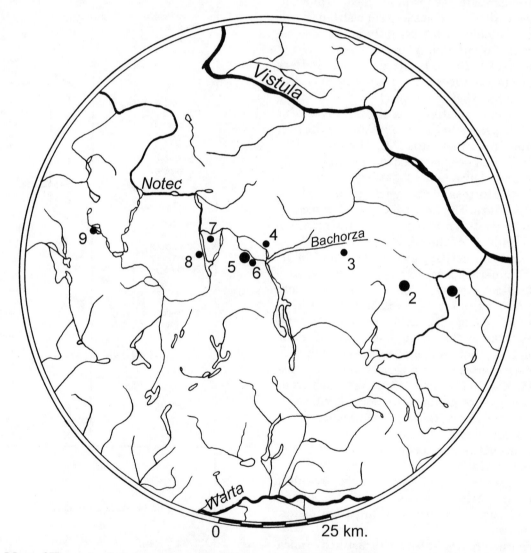

Fig. 3. Map of Kuyavia showing principal settlements of the Brześć Kujawski Group with longhouses. Larger dots indicate sites with multiple excavated longhouses, while small dots indicate sites at which one or two longhouses have been excavated. Key: 1 - Brześć Kujawski; 2 - Osłonki-Miechowice-Konary; 3 - Dobre; 4 - Łojewo; 5 - Krusza Zamkowa; 6 - Przedbojowice; 7 - Kościelec Kujawski; 8 - Dobieszewice; 9 - Biskupin (after Grygiel 1986, with addition of Osłonki-Miechowice-Konary sites).

area from points to the south. Their use of copper (discussed further below) clearly reflects connections to the south, as does their use of flint imported from southern Poland. At the same time, the nearby outwash plains and meltwater valleys had been occupied by indigenous foraging peoples well after 5000 B.C., and some role for these groups in the formation of the Brześć Kujawski Group cannot be completely discounted.

Even a millennium after the initial establishment of farming communities in the Polish lowlands, the settlements of the Brześć Kujawski Group were still on the frontier of agricultural settlement in central Europe. To the northwest, in the coastal areas of the western Baltic basin, lay settlements of the Ertebølle Culture, late Mesolithic sedentary foragers who did not adopt agriculture until about 4000 B.C. We now know that Ertebølle communities had contacts with central European farmers, as indicated by finds of 'Danubian' ground stone axes (Fischer 1982) and jadeite and copper axes (Klassen 2000). Between the Brześć Kujawski Group and Ertebølle were other late Mesolithic inland foragers, still relatively poorly known. An important unresolved research question is the degree to which its frontier location between foragers and farmers contributed to the distinctive character of the Brześć Kujawski Group. A hint of possible connections is provided by the prevalence of antler 'T-axes' at Brześć Kujawski Group settlements, especially in male burials. These are not typical 'Danubian' antler forms, yet they are characteristic Ertebølle types, suggesting some measure of interaction across the North European Plain.

Distinctive Features of the Brześć Kujawski Group

The large settlements of the Brześć Kujawski Group typically contain four main types of features: longhouses, burials, clay-extraction pits, and smaller pits. The longhouses and the burials each have their own specific characteristics that are discussed below. Clay extraction pits were the quarries from which the clay subsoil was dug for plastering houses. They are immense excavations that can be up to two meters deep and with irregular sides and bottoms that drop off into deep hollows and basins. They often contain very few artifacts and faunal materials. Smaller pits, on the other hand, tend to be round or oval. Round ones often have bell-shaped profiles, while the oval ones resemble a bathtub. Such features often yield the densest concentrations of animal bones and artifacts.

The longhouses were built using a bedding-trench technique, with the southern end wider than the northern (Fig. 4). They can be up to 40 meters in length, although 20-25 meters is more common, and about 4-6 meters wide at the wider, southern end and 2-3 meters wide at the narrower, northern end. At the moment, there is no convincing explanation for the trapezoidal ground plan, nor are we certain where the entrances were. Impressions in the bottoms of the bedding trenches indicate that split timbers formed the upright structural members. There is evidence of rebuilding, often after fires, sometimes to enlarge earlier structures. A very common feature is an oval interior pit, 2-3 meters long, oriented parallel to the axis of the house but offset to the right side (Fig. 5).

Inhumation burials are found among the longhouses. During the period between ca. 4500 and 4200 B.C., when these settlements were at their largest, the burials followed a strict ritual: contracted inhumations, in specially dug burial pits, heads oriented towards the south-southeast. Males are always on their right sides, females always on their left sides. Many of the burials form small groupings of up to seven individuals. (In the final phases of several of these settlements, the burial rite was relaxed and corpses were interred in existing rubbish pits, with no attention to body orientation; this is clearly in sequence with the earlier rite, not a contemporaneous alternative form.) At Brześć Kujawski, studies of isolated houses suggest that burials are those of the inhabitants of a nearby house (Grygiel 1986); at Osłonki, the patterning of the burials and houses is complex, so unraveling such associations will take time.

The grave goods that accompany these burials are significant. Rarely are ceramic vessels interred with the dead. The most common objects found in the graves are bone and antler tools, flint tools, tooth and shell beads, bone armlets, and copper ornaments. Antler 'T-axes' occur exclusively in male burials (Fig. 6). T-axes, so named due to their presumed shape when hafted, are beams of red deer antler from which the tines and base have been removed and a beveled edge has been produced at one end by cutting, snapping, and grinding (Grygiel and Bogucki 1990). Danish experimental work indicates that these could have been used for woodworking (Jensen 1991), and finds of repaired axes suggest that they were indeed used for working some material (Grygiel 1986; Grygiel and Bogucki

1990). They are always found held in the hand or near the head. Bone points are also associated with males. At Osłonki a male was buried with a quiver of antler projectile points along his lower back.

A particularly distinctive feature of the richest burials are bone armlets (or 'brassards') found on some skeletons, most frequently of females, as in two remarkable burials at Krusza Zamkowa (Czerniak 1980; see Fig. 7), although it appears that at Biskupin a burial with such armlets may be

that of a male. These were made from ribs of large animals (probably cattle), softened and bent, then carved with chevrons in bands. Other bone artifacts in burials include perforated animal teeth worn as pendants and bone points and awls.

Flint blades are found exclusively in male burials. Although local flint often was used and discarded in rubbish deposits, the finest blades found in burials were made from 'chocolate' flint from the Holy Cross Mountains about 200 kilometers dis-

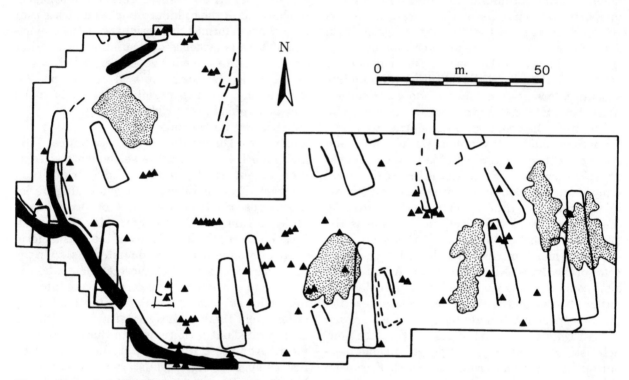

Fig. 4. Plan of 1989-1994 excavations at Osłonki, showing trapezoidal longhouses, burials (triangles), clay borrow pits (stippled), and fortification ditch.

Fig. 5. Trapezoidal house at Kościelec Kujawski (after Czerniak 1979). Note interior pits along east wall of house, a chracteristic feature of many Brześć Kujawski Group longhouses. Contour lines at 20 cm. intervals; excavation grid in 10-meter squares.

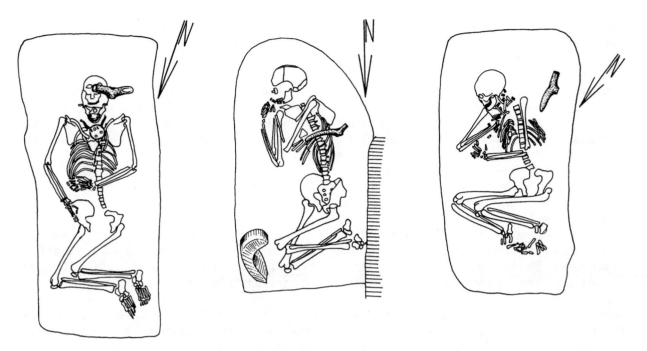

Fig. 6. Male burials from Brześć Kujawski with antler T-axes (after Grygiel 1986).

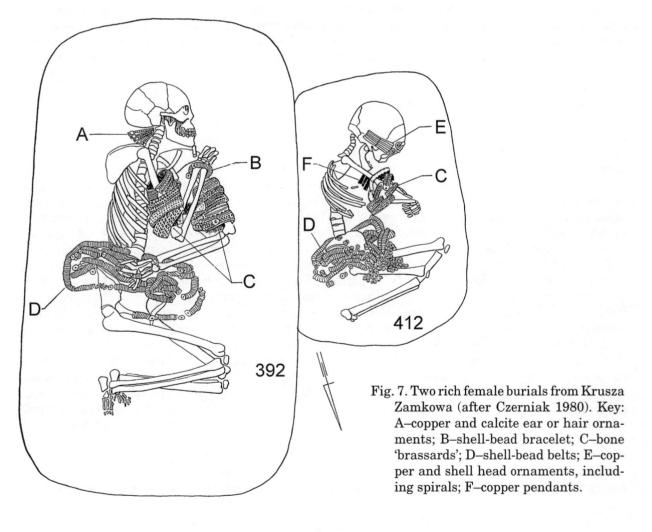

Fig. 7. Two rich female burials from Krusza Zamkowa (after Czerniak 1980). Key: A–copper and calcite ear or hair ornaments; B–shell-bead bracelet; C–bone 'brassards'; D–shell-bead belts; E–copper and shell head ornaments, including spirals; F–copper pendants.

tant and from Jurassic flint from about 300 kilometers away (see locations on Fig. 1). These two types of flint have superb flaking qualities and few interior flaws (Domański and Webb 2000) and were used widely throughout the Vistula and Oder valleys during the early and middle Neolithic.

Copper artifacts, among the earliest in north-central Europe, are body ornaments: beads, bracelets, pendants, and composite head decorations characterized as 'diadems'. All are made by hammering, rolling, and repoussé technique. The source of the copper is still to be determined, but the nearest known is at least 700 kilometers distant. Copper ornaments are found in both male and female graves, although the greatest quantities are found with females. The distance from which the copper was obtained would have made it quite costly to acquire. Yet in several burials there are lavish displays of this material. One of the most remarkable was excavated in 1990 at Osłonki (Grygiel and Bogucki 1997). In this grave, a woman wore a headdress consisting of 49 strips of copper, curled at the ends. In addition, one wider strip of copper ribbon, about 1.5 cm wide and wrapped around itself on a bias three times, apparently formed the central element in this diadem. These strips were apparently formed around a belt of perishable material, perhaps cloth or leather. Nineteen of the smaller strips and the large central strip have repoussé ornament: rows of raised dimples. This individual also wore five copper plaques and numerous copper beads. Other burials these sites have similar, although not quite so dramatic, displays of copper.

Shell beads, although produced from mundane, locally available freshwater clamshells, are significant for the quantities in which they occur. Since each bead was cut out individually, their manufacture in quantities sufficient for, in some cases, belts of 5,000 to 8,000 beads, would have been a non-trivial investment of effort for a society in which labor was a key resource. Shell beads are known from male and female graves; with males, they occur around the neck, which females often have several belts around their waists.

Longhouse construction made great demands on local oak and pine forests, as did the need for fuel for the settlements' fires. The subsistence economy of the Brześć Kujawski Group was based on the cultivation of cereals, keeping livestock (cattle, sheep, goat, and pig), hunting (deer and waterfowl), and fishing. Evidence for deforestation can be seen in pollen and sedimentation profiles of basins near Osłonki (Bogucki 1999). The overall

impression from the detailed study of materials from Brześć Kujawski and Osłonki is that the consumption of natural resources from the catchments of these large sites was considerable and may not have been sustainable (Bogucki 1996b). The acquisition of copper and flint also must have made demands on the resources of these communities, although it is unclear what items moved south in exchange.

Households of the Brześć Kujawski Group

The four principal types of features described above are elements of the household clusters of the Brześć Kujawski Group (Bogucki and Grygiel 1981; Grygiel 1986, 1994). Each such cluster has a house, one or two clay extraction pits, several smaller pits, and several burials. The household clusters are considered to be the material traces of a residential group corresponding to a farming household. These households made fundamental decisions about the acquisition, allocation, consumption, and disposal of resources. Each settlement was composed of several contemporaneous households, up to about a dozen in the case of Brześć Kujawski. The frequent rebuilding of the houses contributes to an impression of much larger and denser agglomerations of population.

Household cluster studies in the early 1980s at Brześć Kujawski indicated that burials were integral parts of the domestic complex of the house and associated features (Bogucki and Grygiel 1981; Grygiel 1986, 1994). The household context of the burial is significant, for it indicates that such a domestic unit was a central organizing principle of this society even in death. Ancestors continued to be part of the domestic unit and were *not* relegated to a distant cemetery. Burials, then, tell us something of the story of these households. Getting at this is easier where we can assign them to specific household clusters, as in several cases at Brześć Kujawski, but it is much more difficult at sites like Osłonki where there are many more houses and a denser palimpsest of features.

Households of the Brześć Kujawski Group would have differed in the number of members, their access to resources and accumulation of property, and the skill with which they were managed. Relations of kinship, friendship, and trust would have developed with some households both near and far, while with others there would have been animosity, distrust, and spite. They would have needed to work out access rights to arable land, grazing, and timber among themselves. Each would have been in a competitive relationship with the others, with relations of status and power being characterized by ephemeral asymmetries.

It is also clear, however, that these households saw some benefit in aggregating into larger settlements such as Osłonki, Brześć Kujawski, and Krusza Zamkowa. The inhabitants of these settlements were probably in close contact along the network of streams and lakes that ran through the postglacial landscape as well as through a network of paths and trails. The contemporaneous settlements of Brześć Kujawski and Osłonki are under ten kilometers apart, and there must have been regular contact between them. Konary and Miechowice are separated from Osłonki by under a kilometer, forming a dense concentration of households around the shores of several small lake basins. Such a concentration might be termed a 'hamlet' in the sense that the term is used by Cancian (1996) to refer to institutionalized alliances of domestic groups, in which their affiliation is demonstrated through residential proximity.

Households and Transegalitarian Societies

The household is increasingly used as an analytical unit in anthropology and archaeology, but it is not without its critics. Many researchers, myself included, have until now treated households as single-interest units of decision-making, a convenient but unrealistic view. Ethnographers who study households note the differing, and often divergent, interests of spouses and other household members, which shift as the household moves through its developmental cycle (Bryceson 1995, Holtzman 1997). Rather than being a simplification, the introduction of the household as an analytical unit entails new complexities that have to be taken into account.

In her study of households and gender in rural Zambia, Kate Crehan (1997:93-95) makes the following observation:

> One characteristic that is general... is that households are always both collective entities and made up of separate individuals. They are sites within which conflictual and supportive relationships are always entwined; disentangling the specific relations of subordination and domination that exist within this dense, and emotionally saturated, knot is not straightforward. It is important neither to romanticize the household—assuming that it can be treated

as a single entity with a single set of interests, aims, and within which resources are unproblematically shared—nor, in reaction to such romanticization, to move so far in the other direction as to see households as no more than sites of an unrelenting struggle between warring autonomous individuals.

A particularly important distinction lies among different forms of prestige and power within the household, specifically between the political agenda of the household in the community and its economic activities. For example, men might be dominant in the sphere of public politics in a community, yet in terms of economic organization spouses may constitute relatively autonomous units, engaging in his and her own productive activities. At a certain point, however, their interests converge, and a household identity emerges.

At any moment, the households of a settlement are in different stages of their cycle of demographic and economic development and decline. They expand, accumulating property and members, and contract. As a result, some households are in the ascendance of their accumulation cycle, while others are in eclipse. There are thus inherent inequalities within any agrarian community composed of households. In Neolithic societies, these patterns of social relationships are very difficult to perceive archaeologically, since they are ephemeral and not cumulative. Such societies might be called 'transegalitarian' (Hayden 1995; Blake and Clark 1999), in that they are neither completely egalitarian nor ranked in any permanent or formal manner. Competition among households produces short-term asymmetries in wealth and power. Clearly these asymmetries contribute to the construction of identities within specific households.

The individual identities that grow out of household activities have particular relevance for the construction of gender. Henrietta Moore (1994:92-3) has pointed out that the differentiation of tasks by gender, the negotiations between spouses about resource allocation and the use of income, and the negotiations with children about their postmarital residence are a set of practical activities, which are the outcome of local ideas about the proper behavior of men and women. So, she notes, what makes households important is that they produce specific sorts of persons with specific social identities. The archaeological challenge is to somehow get inside the household to try to get a sense of this, an ambitious goal that we are nowhere near approaching.

Identity and Gender in Brześć Kujawski Households

Biological sex was clearly a fundamental distinction made by the Brześć Kujawski Group. This is seen clearly in the consistent position of males lying on their right sides and females on their left. Among the grave goods, we can see that there are some clear markers of maleness, specifically antler axes, other bone tools, and flint tools. There are no corresponding implements that mark femaleness. All other grave goods are body ornaments. The presence of head decoration, bone armlets, and belts of shell beads is typically correlated with a female burial, while tooth and shell beads around the neck are characteristic of males. There is almost no ambiguity in these associations, and they appear to reinforce the biological differences recognized by the body orientation.

The next question, then, is whether this fundamental distinction between the sexes informs us about the culturally defined construction of gender in this Neolithic society. Julia Hendon (1996) points out that gender is a symbolic system that structures social and economic relations within the household and the larger community. Frequently these are sought in inferences about the contribution of different individuals to household production and craft specialization. The most distinct evidence that we have for household craft production among these communities (not necessarily specialization) is the antler-working atelier at Brześć Kujawski where antler axes were made and repaired, whose refuse is found in Pit 892 (Grygiel 1986). Since antler axes are such a vivid symbol of maleness in the burials, we confidently can attribute this activity to men. Otherwise, at the moment we have only the standard archaeological evidence of tool production, animal butchery, and grain preparation, although as we proceed with post-excavation analysis of material from Osłonki and Miechowice additional dimensions of domestic life may come into focus.

Yet it is clear that a central activity of the Neolithic households at these sites was the extraction from the environment of all sorts of resources: crops, livestock, wild animals and plants, fish, shellfish, turtles, waterfowl, shed antlers, timber and fuelwood, clay, local stone and flint. This labor-intensive activity not only supported the household but also fueled the acquisition of copper and flint, and the more labor a household could command translated into greater opportunity to acquire these exotic materials. While the non-local flint was superior to local flint in its flaking qualities, the local material was perfectly adequate for most tasks. The copper was simply used for personal ornamentation, certainly of the dead, perhaps also of the living. They did not need these exotic materials, but they wanted them. One might even depict the inhabitants of these sites as having embraced an 'ideology of accumulation'.

We are confident that the Neolithic society described here did not have genealogically-based differences in status and wealth, for aside from the burials, there is remarkable consistency and homogeneity among the household remains. Instead, the lavish displays of copper, shell beads, and bone armlets in burials capture something of the success of individual households at particular moments in their developmental cycle. If household economies were characterized by the pooling of contributions from their individual members, then perhaps the displays of personal ornament in the graves can be taken as a reflection of the value of that individual's contribution to the success of the household at a moment in its cycle of development and accumulation.

At the same time, it is probable that the rich deposits in female graves are not an accurate measure of the social power enjoyed by these individuals in their lifetime, for in most agrarian societies known ethnographically there is a marked asymmetry in favor of men. Perhaps we can see here women being accorded recognition in death that they may have been denied in life, a recognition of their contribution to the success of the household economy, by the willingness of their survivors to commit such valuables to the grave.

The burial rite of the Brześć Kujawski Group can be interpreted as a set of fundamental underlying beliefs about individual and collective identity, upon which the consequences of the competition among households for accumulation of property were superimposed. Collectively, the orientation of the corpses' heads toward the south-south-east—parallel with the houses, I might add—reflects a value shared by the entire society. Moreover, the consistent distinction between males and females in the orientation of the body indicates a common value system that dictated this strict rule. Variation in the richness, variety, and type of grave goods results both from the inclusion of fairly clear symbols of maleness (antler axes, flint blades, bone points) and from the results of individual households' ability to convert the fruits of their labor into expensive and exotic materials, namely shell beads, carved bone armlets, flint and, especially, copper. The speculation offered here is that this provided some recognition of the contribution made by individuals towards the household's accumulation strategy.

The Tempo of Brześć Kujawski Society

The foregoing discussion of individual identity and gender highlights the interplay between intragenerational and multigenerational processes in communities of the Brześć Kujawski Group. Personal identity would have been dynamic and changing, depending in large measure on the fortunes of the household of which the individual was a member and the position of that individual within the household. At death, the individual took his or her identity into the grave, leaving the survivors to reconstruct their relationships and their household's position in the community. On the other hand, the burial rite itself, as well as the fundamental social configuration that is represented by the household clusters, persisted over many generations.

Composed as they were of individual households, the settlements of the Brześć Kujawski Group were changing continually on intragenerational and multigenerational time scales. Intragenerational processes included the destruction and rebuilding of individual houses, the digging and filling of the adjacent pits, and the progressive accumulation of burials as household members died. The arrangement of burials in small groups clearly reflects some sort of memory about their location, possibly even grave markers on the surface. On a multigenerational time scale, the size and spatial extent of the settlement changed. This is seen most clearly at Osłonki, where a large fortification ditch cut through earlier house sites and left others outside the enclosed area, presumably abandoned. It seems clear that the settlement had existed first in a non-fortified form, then as a somewhat more densely settled enclosed form. We can only speculate on the reasons for this, but it presumably involves the development over time of conflict and warfare, either with other Brześć Kujawski communities or with nearby forager populations.

Although the intergenerational and multigenerational processes gave the Brześć Kujawski Group is distinctive identity, it must be kept in mind that it is part of a long-term sequence of Neolithic cultural development on the North European Plain. The characteristics of longhouse construction and contracted burial clearly associ-

ate the Brześć Kujawski Group with its Linear Pottery and Lengyel precursors, although the pattern of burial within the settlement is different from the separate cemeteries observed in earlier times (compare the Linear Pottery cemeteries discussed in Jeunesse 1997, for example.) Thus the domestic architecture and ritual traditions have very deep roots, but their convergence in the shorter-term household processes of the Brześć Kujawski Group gives them a distinctive character.

In the long run, however, the intensive patterns of land use and settlement density that characterize the Brześć Kujawski Group were not sustainable (Bogucki 1996b). Around 4100/4000 B.C., the intensive pattern of household aggregation and accumulation was replaced by the more extensive, dispersed pattern of settlement that characterizes the Funnel Beaker Culture of the Polish lowlands. Yet the Funnel Beaker Culture developed its own distinctive burial pattern that involved the construction of enormous earthen long barrows (Midgley 1985), the so-called 'Kuyavian megaliths'. Since almost all of them have been destroyed by agriculture over the past several centuries, we do not know how many barrows originally existed. Since flat cemeteries (e.g. Pikutkowo) are also known, and since each long barrow holds only a few bodies, it seems likely that such burial was not available to all members of society. Scholars beginning with V. Gordon Childe have pointed out the similarities between the Kuyavian earthen long barrows of the Funnel Beaker Culture and the trapezoidal longhouses of the Brześć Kujawski Group (Childe 1949, Midgley 1992). Midgley (1992:481) makes a compelling argument that these similarities are not coincidental. Thus the transformation of domestic architecture into élite funerary architecture was part of the long-term processes seen among the Neolithic societies of the North European Plain.

The Brześć Kujawski Group was a relatively short-lived phenomenon within a much longer Neolithic sequence. At most, it lasted 500 years, but probably less. In many respects, it is anomalous in the archaeological visibility of its longhouses and graves and its conspicuous accumulation of exotic materials, but it is also clear that these characteristics merely represent exaggerated examples of long-term developmental trends in Neolithic society. Its compact nature and richness of data make the Brześć Kujawski Group an excellent 'laboratory' for studying many sorts of characteristics of tribal societies on a variety of analytical scales.

Acknowledgement

Information compiled by Thalia Gray for her 1995 M.A. thesis at New York University was very useful in preparing this paper, although all interpretations remain the responsibility of the author. Parts of this paper were presented at the 1998 Society for American Archaeology meetings in Seattle under the title of "Identity and Gender in a Neolithic Society."

References Cited

Blake, Michael, and John Clark
1999 The Emergence of Hereditary Inequality: The Case of Pacific Coastal Chiapas, Mexico. In *Pacific Latin America in Prehistory: The Evolution of Archaic and Formative Cultures,* edited by Michael Blake, pp. 55-73. Washington State University Press, Pullman.
Bogucki, Peter
1996a The Spread of Early Farming in Europe. *American Scientist* 84:242-253.
1996b Sustainable and Unsustainable Adaptations by Early Farming Communities of Northern Poland. *Journal of Anthropological Archaeology* 15:189-311.
1999 Neolithic Settlement and Landscape at Osłonki, Poland. In *Settlement and Landscape: Proceedings of a Conference in Århus, Denmark, May 4-7 1998*, edited by Charlotte Fabech and Jytte Ringtved, pp, 108-110. Jutland Archaeological Society, Moesgård.
2000 How Agriculture Came to North-Central Europe. In *Europe's First Farmers*, edited by T. Douglas Price, pp. 197-218. Cambridge University Press, Cambridge.
Bogucki, Peter, and Ryszard Grygiel
1981 The Household Cluster at Brześć Kujawski 3: Small-Site Methodology in the Polish Lowlands. *World Archaeology* 13:59-72.
1983 Early Farmers of the North European Plain. *Scientific American* 248(4):104-112.
1993a Neolithic Sites in the Polish Lowlands: Excavations at Brześć Kujawski, 1933-1984. In *Case Studies in European Prehistory*, edited by Peter Bogucki, pp. 147-180. CRC Press, Boca Raton.

1993b The First Farmers of North-Central Europe. *Journal of Field Archaeology* 20(3):399-426.
Bryceson, Deborah F.
1995 Gender Relations in Rural Tanzania: Power Politics or Cultural Consensus?. In *Gender, Family, and Household in Tanzania*, edited by Colin Creighton and C.K. Omari, pp. 37-69. Avebury, Aldershot, UK.
Cancian, Frank
1996 The Hamlet as Mediator. *Ethnology* 35:215-228.
Childe, V. Gordon
1949 The Origin of Neolithic Culture in Northern Europe. *Antiquity* 23:129-135.
Crehan, Kate
1997 *The Fractured Community. Landscapes of Power and Gender in Rural Zambia.* University of California Press, Berkeley.
Czerniak, Lech
1979 Osada Kultury Lendzielskiej w Kościelcu Kujawskin, gm. Pakość, Stan. 16. *Pomerania Antiqua* 8:73-109.
1980 *Rozwój Społeczeństw Kultury Póżniej Ceramiki Wstęgowej na Kujawach.* Adam Mickiewicz University (Archaeological Series 16), Poznań.
1994 *Wczesny i Środkowej Okres Neolitu na Kujawach, 5400-3650 p.n.e.* Polish Academy of Science, Institute of Archaeology and Ethnology, Poznań.
1998 The First Farmers. In *Pipeline of Archaeological Treasures*, edited by M. Chłodnicki and L. Krzyżaniak, pp. 23-36. Poznańskie Towarzystwo Prehistoryczne, Poznań.
Domański, Marian, and John Webb
2000 Flaking Properties, Petrology and Use of Polish Flint. *Antiquity* 74:822-853.
Fischer, Anders
1982 Trade in Danubian Shaft-Hole Axes and the Introduction of Neolithic Economy in Denmark. *Journal of Danish Archaeology* 1:7-12.
Gray, Thalia
1995 Variability and Patterning: Social and Gender Organization Visible in the Lengyel Burials of Osłonki. Unpublished Masters thesis, Department of Anthropology, New York University.
Grygiel, Ryszard
1986 The Household Cluster as a Reflection of the Fundamental Social Unit of the

Brześć Kujawski Group of the Lengyel Culture in the Polish Lowlands. *Prace i Materiały Muzeum Archeologicznego i Etnograficznego* 31:43-334.

1994 Untersuchungen zur Gesellschaftsorganisation des Früh- und Mittelneolithikums in Mitteleuropa. In *Internationales Symposium Über die Lengyel-Kultur 1888-1988*, edited by P. Košturík, pp. 43-77. Masaryk University-Museum of Archaeology and Ethnography, Brno-Łódź.

Grygiel, Ryszard, and Peter Bogucki
1990 Neolithic Manufacture of Antler Axes at Brześć Kujawski, Poland. *Archaeomaterials* 4:69-76.

1997 Early Farmers in North-Central Europe: 1989-1994 Excavations at Osłonki, Poland. *Journal of Field Archaeology* 24:161-178.

Hayden, Brian
1995 Pathways to Power. Principles for Creating Socioeconomic Inequalities. In *Foundations of Social Inequality*, edited by T. Douglas Price and Gary M. Feinman, pp. 15-103. Plenum Press, New York.

Hendon, Julia
1996 Archaeological Approaches to the Organization of Domestic Labor: Household Practice and Domestic Relations. *Annual Review of Anthropology* 25:45-61.

Holtzman, Jon D.
1997 Gender and the Market in the Organization of Agriculture among Samburu Pastoralists. *Research in Economic Anthropology* 18:93-113.

Jażdżewski, Konrad
1938 Cmentarzyska Kultury Ceramiki Wstęgowej i Związane z Nimi Ślady Osadnictwa w Brześciu Kujawskim. *Wiadomości Archeologiczne* 15:1-105.

Jensen, Gitte
1991 Ubrugelige Økser? Forsøg med Kongemose- og Ertebøllekulturens Økser of Hjortetak. In *Eksperimentel Arkæologi*, edited by Bo Madsen, pp. 9-21. Historical-Archaeological Experimental Center, Lejre.

Jeunesse, Christian
1996 Pratiques Funéraires au Néolithique Ancien. Sépultures et Nécropoles des Sociétés Danubienne (5500-4900 av. J.-C.). Editions Errance, Paris.

Klassen, Lutz
1999 Waterborne Exchange and Late Ertebølle Social Structure. In *Schutz des Kulturerbes unter Wasser. Veränderungen europäischer Lebenskultur durch Flu- und Seehandel. Beiträge zur Vor- und Frühgeschichte in Mecklenburg-Vorpommern*, vol. 35, pp. 43-51. Archäologisches Landesmuseum Mecklenburg-Vorpommern, Lübstorf.

Košturík, Pavel (editor)
1994 *Internationales Symposium Über die Lengyel-Kultur 1888-1988*. Masaryk University-Museum of Archaeology and Ethnography, Łódź.

Maciejewski, F.; Z. Rajewski; and F. Wokrój
1954 Ślady Osadnictwa Kultury tzw. Brzesko-Kujawskiej w Biskupinie, pow. Żnin. *Wiadomości Archeologiczne* 20:67-79.

Midgley, Magdalena
1985 *The Origin and Function of the Earthen Long Barrows of Northern Europe*. BAR International Series 259, Oxford, UK.

1992 *TRB Culture. The First Farmers of the North European Plain*. Edinburgh University Press, Edinburgh.

Moore, Henrietta L.
1994 *A Passion for Difference. Essays in Anthropology and Gender*. Polity Press, Cambridge, UK.

17. Some Aspects of the Social Organization of the LBK of Belgium

Lawrence H. Keeley

Introduction

The goal of this volume's editors is extraordinarily ambitious—to achieve some 'positive' and archaeologically-visible definition of a tribe. Unfortunately, many difficulties stand in their path.

The first problem is that the old anthropological classification of societies into bands, tribes, chiefdoms, states and empires involves a host of variables (demographic, economic, political, social and religious/ideological) that are merely correlated, sometimes strongly, sometimes weakly. For example, ethnographic tribes varied widely in population, from over 60,000 to as few as 1500 members. Some integrated their memberships by means of lineal kinship groups (e.g., the Tiv of Nigeria) while others used sodalities (e.g., the Cheyenne of the Great Plains). Some tribes were pastoralists, some fisher-foragers, some extensive farmers, etc. Yet there are no obvious correlations between these variables in ethnology. There is no one trait or even a single collection of traits that could be used to distinguish all tribes from, say, all bands or chiefdoms.

The second difficulty is that this social classification scheme is evolutionary and accretional. It subdivides a continuum of increasing scale and complexity. In statistical terms, this evolutionary sequence is a Guttman Scale. Each larger and more complicated step represents only an addition to or elaboration of already existing features. 'Ancestral' or 'primitive' features are almost never abandoned. For example, reciprocal exchanges, social obligations to 'close' kin, and achieved statuses are regularly found even among the hereditary nobility of empires.

The third possible problem is that demographic, economic, political and social variability may be largest in the 'middle range' of so-called tribes and chiefdoms and less at the extremes of family bands and empires. This point has not been demonstrated

by cross-cultural research and is impressionistic. If this is so, the task of defining features that characterize all tribes is even more difficult.

All of these aspects of anthropology's standard (evolutionary) classification of societies would mean that defining some exclusive (i.e., 'positive') characteristic of tribes is neither possible nor scientifically useful. Claiming that the only positive characteristic of tribal organization is that it is 'flexible' exactly begs the question. Indeed, is any social organization that endures for more than a few generations not 'flexible?' The real question about any evolutionary, Guttman-scaled variability is: "flexible within what limits?"

Any such limiting or distinguishing characteristics can and should be both positive and negative. After all, in any classification scheme, noting an absent trait is as useful as noting a present one. Tribal organizations are defined by the features they share with bands but not chiefdoms, as well as some shared with chiefdoms but not bands. I will however mention one archaeologically-visible feature of tribes that much ethnology has mentioned: "A tribe is the unit that assembles in the event of warfare" (Hunter and Whitten 1976:394; see also Ember and Ember 1990:239-242). In the case I describe below, this feature of tribal organization seemed to have played an important role.

In this chapter I want simply to recount the archaeologically-visible features of the social and economic organization of the Linear Band Keramik (LBK) colonists that occupied NE Belgium almost 7000 (calibrated; ca. 6300 standard C14) years ago. I will especially focus upon the LBK villages of the Upper Geer Settlement Cluster that my colleague Daniel Cahen and I (and a number of other Belgian prehistorians) have investigated. It is important to note that these Belgian LBK sites are at the northwestern periphery of the trans-European distribution of LBK culture that stretches from northern France to the Ukraine. Also, our sites are late in the grand sequence of the LBK.

The LBK is characterized by a large complex of traits that involve all aspects of archaeologically-visible life and culture, including house form, burial, ceramics, flaked and groundstone lithics, settlement patterns and subsistence economy. Briefly, LBK people were: 1) mixed farmers raising wheat, legumes and flax, domestic cattle, sheep-goats and sometimes pigs; 2) clearing forests on (almost exclusively) loess soils for their fields and pastures; 3) settling along secondary and tertiary streams; 4) living in hamlets and villages of NW/NNW-SW/SSW-oriented rectilinear wattle-and-daubed long-houses; 5) burying their dead in NW-SE oriented oval pits in a semi-flexed position; 6) crafting distinctive pottery types, the fineware of which are decorated with incised/impressed bands; 7) knapping and using broad blades with the most common tools being sickles and endscrapers; 8) making and using saddle querns, groundstone 'shoe-last' adzes and flatter axes. In our region (Belgium), as in most areas of *later* LBK settlement, all of these traits, both functional and stylistic, were completely novel, meaning they were completely unknown among the local Late Mesolithic fisher-foragers. There are longstanding claims, ambiguous in my opinion, that LBK farmers were more gracile and somewhat smaller than the 'native' Late Mesolithic foragers. (If such a physical difference should be demonstrated, it may be a consequence of the more sedentary lifestyle and less carnivorous diet of village farmers compared to seasonally mobile foragers than of genetic differences between natives and newcomers.) Several centuries before it colonizes Belgium, the earliest (älteste=Oldest) LBK appears in the Hungarian Plain/Carpathian Basin and the Older (ältere) LBK reaches western Germany but all the LBK in Belgium is Late LBK (jüngere=Younger).

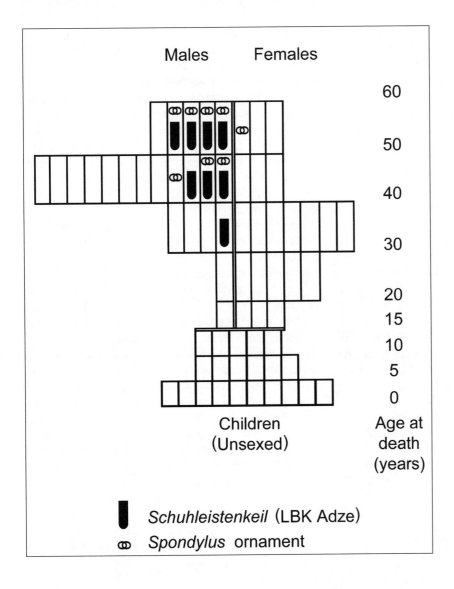

Fig. 1. Schematic of Nitra LBK Cemetery.

However interesting, the facts and controversies regarding LBK origins and the spread of the Early LBK (see Grönenborn 1999) are irrelevant for this paper.

Status of Individuals

Determining whether the status of individuals were achieved or ascribed among the LBK farmers of northeast Belgium is so far impossible as no LBK cemeteries have yet been excavated there. Immediately to the east, in the Netherlands Limburg and the Lower Rhineland of Germany, cemeteries have been found but the bones in the burials have not survived in the acid soils. Thus, the age/sex determinations so essential to the analysis of status at burial were not possible there.

Far to the east in the famous LBK Cemetery at Nitra in Slovakia, the burials (N=72) indicated that, in the LBK culture, status was only achieved (Fig. 1). Grave goods, especially of exotic materials, were found only in the burials of the older men and women, with the oldest adults buried with the most grave goods and the youngest adults usually with none. At Nitra there was no evidence of inherited wealth or status, nor of what might be called chiefs. At a few other LBK cemeteries where bone is preserved, burials of infants or very young children are absent or rare, and usually without grave goods. Many authors (including myself) have generalized from the Nitra evidence, and a few similar Earliest and Early period LBK burial sites, that LBK burials were relatively egalitarian and that LBK statuses were only achieved.

Surveying a number of well-preserved LBK cemeteries excavated during the past two decades, Christian Jeunesse (1997) has mustered evidence that clearly indicates that Nitra does not epitomize all LBK cemeteries and that many of the generalizations based upon it are wrong. In fact, infants and young children were interred at LBK cemeteries accompanied by grave goods, sometimes with offerings as numerous and diverse as those buried with adults, especially during the later periods. In later LBK cemeteries there were also a few adult burials very rich in grave goods, especially items with a 'military' allure (i.e., symbols of power). Jeunesse (1997:117) concludes that, by the end of the LBK, some dead infants and children were given wealthy burials accompanied by the highest attributes of prestige and power, and that these were members of a hereditary elite. However, he notes that even in late LBK cemeteries, the great majority of the interments reflect the older Nitra 'egalitarian' model while only a few reflect a more hierarchical social organization (Jeunesse 1997:118). Nevertheless, it is now clear that LBK societies were not always strictly egalitarian and that some of LBK social groups developed ascribed statuses. Interestingly some of the symbols of status were weapons.

Household Variability

LBK long houses show very little variability in construction or width, only in length. LBK houses always consist variously of from one to three modules: a center, a head and a foot. The smallest and *rarest* forms of LBK house consisted of only a center module. A very common type of LBK house was comprised of a head module joined to a center one. The largest but most (?) common form had all three modules. Some evidence indicates that the center module was domestic in function because the hearth or hearths were located there. The closely spaced central support postholes of the foot section (each posthole usually held two large deep-set posts) left almost no floor space for any prosaic domestic activities. Half of these foot section twin posts probably, like those in the other two modules, supported the house roof but their 'twins' probably supported a heavily burdened internal platform. Thus, the foot module is interpreted as a storage area. The function of the head modules of LBK houses is more obscure. They had almost as much, but always less, floor space as the central modules. But heads were usually the only section of an LBK house, even the longest forms, with wall trenches, meaning the outer walls of the head were especially strongly anchored. The heads of all LBK houses face the locally prevailing northwesterly and northerly winter winds, which may explain the strength of the modules' walls but not their function. Some have argued (Modderman 1986) that the head modules were livestock stables, especially during the winter, but no archaeological evidence, directly or indirectly, supports this hypothesis. It seems that the smallest LBK house represented only a domestic unit, the medium sized house a domestic unit plus a stable, and the longest type a domestic unit, a stable and a storage space. In any case, there is no evidence that the length of an LBK house bears any relationship to the size of the household inhabiting it.

As noted, the smallest form is the rarest. In the Upper Geer sites, none have been found. In another area not too distant, the Aldenhovener Platte (Germany), the longest form was most common (more than 80%). In the household refuse found in the daub pits immediately adjacent to all Upper Geer cluster houses, sickle blades and endscrapers are ubiquitous and the two most common retouched tool types recovered. The sickle blades indicate that some of a house's residents harvested grain, and the endscrapers that some scraped hides. It would appear that all LBK households, whatever the size of their house, harvested grain and had equal access to livestock hides for treatment into rawhide. As bone does not survive in the acid soils found at most LBK habitation sites, house-to-house comparisons of faunal consumption cannot be made. The surviving evidence, however, indicates that all LBK houses (at least on the Upper Geer) were the residences of farmer-herders. In our sample of houses (N=20) on the Upper Geer, all households apparently had equal access to fineware and coarseware pottery, as these are also ubiquitous. Indeed, ceramics show no statistically significant differences between houses *at the same site* either in density (kg/pit) and ratio (fineware/coarseware, by weight). In a larger sample of LBK houses from the Aldenhoverner Platte, the only significant difference found between the refuse of the longest LBK houses (the most common type) and the smaller forms involved grain cleaning debris, in the form of chaff and weed seeds. It seems that grain cleaning occurred at the longest houses, that is, those with a (putative) storage module, but not at the minority (approx. one-fifth) of smaller houses lacking such storage space. If the largest LBK houses are supposed to have been the domiciles of wealthy 'Big Men' or chiefs, then the LBK had far too many 'chiefs' and almost no 'Indians'!

Hamlet-Village Variability

There is evidence from northeastern Belgium that there were some consistent differences in the frequency of certain craft productions between LBK hamlets and villages. (Keeley and Cahen 1989; Cahen et al. 1990; Jadin 1990; Sliva and Keeley 1994; Keeley 1996:151-152).

At the site of Darion, literally massive amounts of debitage from blade production were found. Yet at the site of Oleye, just 6 km. away, where blades and blade tools were equally common as at Darion, very little flaking waste of any kind was found. Ratios between various kinds of blade production waste flakes (e.g., primary flakes, crest blades, core rejuvenation flakes, etc.) vs. blades/blade tools were from five to twenty times higher at Darion than at Oleye. The less extensively excavated site of

Waremme, located almost exactly halfway between Darion and Oleye, while not as rich in debitage as Darion, nevertheless produced plentiful evidence that its inhabitants produced their own blades. Oleye showed a wider variety of flint types than either Darion or Waremme. Oleye's sickle blades and endscrapers (types equally ubiquitous in rubbish pits at all three sites) were more heavily worn and/or resharpened than those at Darion or Waremme. Oleye not produced few of its own blades but received most of them from elsewhere while Darion produced far more blades than were used there. Waremme appears to have been more or less self-sufficient in blade production. Very short distances separate these three sites (ca. 3 km.) and the flint types used were equally available to all three in the Chalk that underlies them all. Such differences in flint blade production were apparently 'arbitrary,' that is, not predicated on geographical propinquity.

Inter-village variability in ceramic production between these Upper Geer sites is less clear but suggestive. Two pots made by the same potter, probably in the same firing, were found at Darion and Oleye (Van Berg 1987, 1988). Although slightly different in size, both had the same shape and construction, both had received the same unusual firing, both had identical decoration designs and, the clincher, both had been decorated with the same broken five-toothed comb. Where these two pots were made cannot be determined but they are evidence that pots were exchanged between LBK settlements. Unlike Darion or Waremme, Oleye has yielded evidence of ceramic production. Several Oleye pits had dense layers of sherds from the same complete pots that could represent 'wasters.' Other pits contained vitrified earth that had been heated far higher than the more common burned daub produced by burned houses (which, alas for simplicity's sake, were very common at Oleye). But one Oleye pit (OZ-87046) contained a dump layer from a potter's workshop. This layer contained three broken pots filled with washed clay, a pottery-burnishing pebble, a sack-shaped concentration of grog (ground pottery) temper, an unusual grinding palette, and a ground-down brick of exotic mineralized sandstone. [The yellow mineral, glauconite, streaking this sandstone brick has been identified in the sand grit temper of some pots from Waremme (J. Stoltman, pers. comm.)] Nothing like this pit's peculiar ceramic workshop debris has been found at any other LBK site. The only evidences of ceramic production at Darion or Waremme are a handful of pottery burnishing pebbles. Access to clays washed naturally by the Geer stream or artificially from the local loess soils, grog ground from old pots, and temper from peculiar sandstone (ca. 20 km. away) was no different at Oleye than at Darion or Waremme.

Twenty-five kilometers to the west-northwest of the Upper Geer LBK cluster are two LBK hamlet sites, Wange and Overhespen, a few hundred meters apart along on the Petite Gette stream (Lodewijlckx 1990). In terms of their house forms, ceramics and many other features, the Petite Gette LBK sites were extremely similar to those of the Upper Geer and typical of the Late LBK of NE Belgium. However, their lithic assemblages have some distinctive features when compared with

those of the Upper Geer sites. Most of the Petite Gette sites blade tools were made of flint types typical of the Upper Geer sites, especially Darion, yet flaking waste from these exotic flints types was rare. Wange and Overhespen, on the other hand, had considerable manufacturing waste from flaking adzes made of Phtanite, an easily recognizable black silicified siltstone. The source of Phtanite is a unique outcrop approximately equidistant (ca. 65 km to the SW as the crow flies) from both the Petite Gette sites and those on the Upper Geer (see Fig. 2). While over 80% of the groundstone adzes found at Upper Geer sites are made of Phtanite, unlike the Petite Gette sites, they have yielded no manufacturing waste of this material.

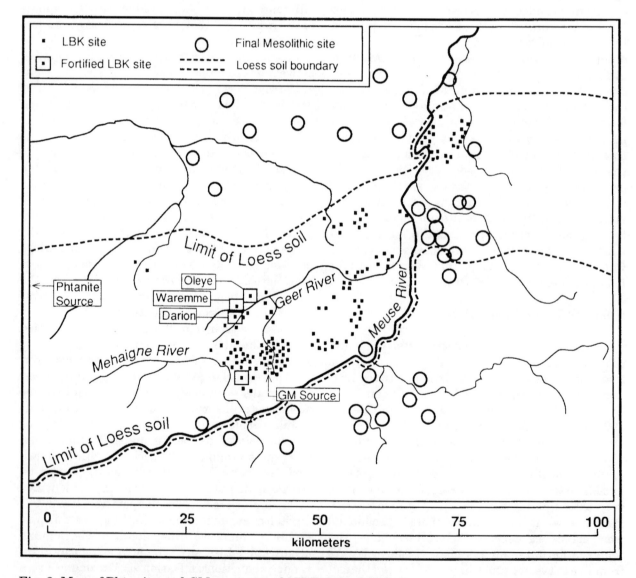

Fig. 2. Map of Phtanite and GM sources and NE Belgian LBK sites.

The Petite Gette sites converted Phtanite blocs into adzes and exchanged them to the villagers of the Upper Geer. In return the former may have received flint blades made of Upper Geer flint.

There also is evidence of a part-time village specialization in the production and use of an unusual hide-working tool called a frit. Frits are large burin spalls that were used, drawknife fashion, to prepare hides in a mode different from and rarer than the hide work done with the ubiquitous endscrapers. At Darion, with only four houses, over 200 frits were found along with debris from their manufacture. At Oleye (at least 13 houses) and Waremme (at least two houses) only 9 frits were recovered altogether.

These apparent craft specializations were village wide because they have not been associated with just one or a few houses on site. They were also part-time because all households harvested grain (sickles) and treated rawhide (endscrapers). Most strikingly, these specializations were geographically arbitrary in the sense that all villages had equal or equally distant access to flint, adze materials, clay and hides. A similar pattern of arbitrary village specializations is known ethnographically from some South American tribes (e.g., Xingu and Yanomamö). In these cases, such part-time, arbitrary, village-wide craft specialization functions to support military alliances between villages (Keeley 1996:151-152).

Some of the LBK villages of the Upper Geer cluster were surrounded by fortifications consisting of a ditch backed by a palisade. All of these fortified villages are located on the very limit of the cluster (Fig. 2). The presence of these fortifications is not correlated with village size, permanency or craft specialization. Of interest here is that fort construction required manpower almost impossible for the some of resident village populations, especially Darion, to have mustered. Thus, their construction would have required in some cases cooperation with other villages nearby. Also, the fortifications would have required many more defenders than the resident village populations could have mustered. Hence, these constructions are clear evidence that LBK villages were not autonomous. As these villages were purposely interdependent economically, they also were so militarily.

The great majority of LBK sites found across Europe apparently were hamlets of 2-5 houses. More rarely there are sites with many more houses (12 to 30+) but not all these houses were of same house generation. Thus some villages were larger and occupied for more generations.

Variability between Clusters

In the Geer region, no one has yet detected any demonstrable consistent variability in ceramics or house form between Upper Geer and the adjoining Yerne clusters. On the other hand the Upper Geer and the Yerne cluster do show dramatic differences in adze-axe raw materials. In the Upper Geer cluster sites over 80% of all adzes were made of Phtanite, a black silicified siltstone, from a source 90 km away (Fig. 2). As mentioned above, it seems that these Phtanite adzes were manufactured 25 km away at Petit Gette sites. In the immediately adjoining Yerne cluster, over 80% of the adzes were made of the local Gres Micaceous, a gray micaceous indurated sandstone. This Gres Micaceous come from a source within the Yerne cluster. However, this outcrop is only a minimum of 6 km and maximum of 15 km from any of the Upper Geer sites, in other words, much closer than the Phtanite source and even the Petite Gette sites. These facts indicate that there is some sort of socio-economic boundary between the Upper Geer and the Yerne clusters. Also there was some form of 'pooling' for adze material acquisition among the various hamlets and villages of each cluster. Such 'pooling' is regarded as being a characteristic of the redistributive economies of chiefdoms.

Thus, regarding the Upper Geer Cluster of LBK:

1) By extrapolation from admittedly very far away, the status of LBK individuals was primarily achieved and wealth was not hereditary. Although there is some slight evidence of ascribed wealth and status at the end of LBK times, LBK burials point to more egalitarian society than those designated chiefdoms and states.

2) LBK households were apparently equal in size (inhabitants), subsistence economy and in access to exotic or labor expensive items. Such egalitarianism is characteristic of bands and tribes while chiefdoms and states evidence household inequalities in these variables.

3) LBK specialized craft production was part-time, varied between villages (not households) and was not determined by geographic propinquity to raw materials. This peculiar pattern was found ethnographically (as far as I can determine) only in a few tribes and was directly related to the maintenance of military alliances.

4) The Upper Geer and Yerne clusters 'pooled' their villages' acquisition of adze materials. Such pooling, the centralized negotiation for acquisition, and the necessary redistribution

this implies, is claimed to be a distinguishing characteristic of chiefdoms and states.

5) Fortification of some hamlets and villages involved the cooperation of nearby unfortified settlements within the cluster for construction and manning. Military cooperation between otherwise mostly self-sufficient habitation groups is a characteristic of tribes, chiefdoms and states but not bands. Fortifications have been claimed to be an exclusive characteristic of chiefdoms and states but this is not true ethnographically: many known tribes fortified their villages. It is true that fortifications were unknown in bands, rare in tribes but almost universal in chiefdoms and states.

The LBK colonists of the Upper Geer showed some social traits characteristic of bands and tribes (only achieved statuses, egalitarian households), one trait that *may* be characteristic of tribes (part-time arbitrary village specialization), and some traits characteristic of chiefdoms ('pooling' exchange and fortifications). The Upper Geer cluster could be described as 'a chiefdom without a chief.' The LBK inhabitants of the Upper Geer cluster were not autonomous, autarkic village bands, nor were they a stratified, hierarchic chiefdom. In short, they were a tribe.

But so what? The old Sahlins-Service evolutionary typology has its only utility as a simplistic shorthand for communication between anthropologists that indicates where a subject society can be roughly located on longest axes of social variation and social evolution (or, it is important to note, devolution!). Over the next 4000 years, in the later Neolithic, Bronze Age and Iron Age, the LBK tribes of the Upper Geer were superceded by more complex tribes, petty chiefdoms, grand chiefdoms, petty states and, eventually, the Roman Empire.

References Cited

Cahen, D., L. Keeley, I. Jadin and P-l. Van Berg
1990 Trois Villages Fortifés du Rubané Récent en Hesbaye Liègois. *Rubané et Cardial.* Pp. 125-146. ERAUL 39, Liège.

Ember, C and M. Ember
1990 *Cultural Anthropology*, 6th Edition. Prentice Hall, Englewood Cliffs, NJ.

Flannery, Kent V. (editor)
1976 *The Early Mesoamerican Village*. Academic Press, New York.

Grönenborn, D.
1999 A Variation on a Basic Theme. *Journal of World Prehistory* 13:123-210.

Hunter, D. and P. Whitten
1976 *Encyclopedia of Anthropology*. Harper & Row, New York.

Jadin, I.
1990 Economie de production dans le Rubane Recent en Hesbaye Liegeoise. In *Rubané et Cardial,* edited by D. Cahen and M. Otte, pp. 147-154. ERAUL, Liège.

Jeunesse, C.
1997 *Pratiques Funéraires au Néolithique Ancien*. Éditions Errance, Paris.

Keeley, Lawrence
1996 *War Before Civilization*. Oxford University Press, New York.

Keeley, Lawrence, and Daniel Cahen
1989 Early Neolithic Forts and Villages in NE Belgium. *Journal of Field Archaeology* 16:157-176.

Lenneis, E.
1997 Houseforms of the Central European Linearpottery Culture and of the Balkan Early Neolithic. *Porocilo o Raziskovanju Paleolitika, Neolitika in Enolitika v Sloveniji* 24:143-150.

Lodewijlchx, Marc
1990 Les Deux Sites Rubanés de Wange et d'Overhespen. In *Rubané et Cardial,* edited by D. Cahen and M. Otte, pp. 105-116. ERAUL, Liège.

Modderman, P.J.R.
1986 On the Typology of Houseplans in their European setting, *Památky Archeologické* LXXVII, 383–394.

Sliva, R. and L. Keeley
1994 Frits and Specialized Hide Preparation in the Belgian Early Neolithic. *Journal of Archaeological Science* 21:91-100.

Van Berg, P.-L.
1987 Rubané Récent de Hesbaye: Signatures Récurrentes de Maitres Potiers. *Bulletin de la Société Royale Belge d'Anthropologie et de Préhistoire* 98:197-222.

1988 *Le Poinçon, le Peigne et le Code*. Thèse de Doctorat, Université de Liège (four volumes).

1990 Céramique du Limbourg et Néolithisation en Europe Nord-Ouest. In *Rubané et Cardial, edited by* D Cahen and M. Otte. Pp. 161-208, ERAUL, Liège.

18. Integration, Interaction, and Tribal 'Cycling': The Transition to the Copper Age on the Great Hungarian Plain

William A. Parkinson

Introduction

This chapter explores long-term processes in the social organization of tribal societies by analyzing the social transformations that occurred on the Great Hungarian Plain at the end of the Neolithic. The chapter begins by outlining a methodology for identifying and tracking changes in tribal social organization over long periods of time. This methodology then is used to model the changes in social organization that occurred during the transition from the Late Neolithic (ca. 5,000–4,500 BC) to the Early Copper Age (ca. 4,500–4,000 BC) in the Körös River Valley in the eastern half of the Carpathian Basin (Fig. 1). By modeling tribal social organization along two analytical dimensions—*integration* and *interaction*—it is possible to identify specific changes in structural organization within cultural trajectories and to compare them within a cross-cultural framework. Although designed primarily to deal with prehistoric archaeological contexts where it is difficult to compare temporal periods of several hundred years or less, the methodology developed in this paper also can be employed in ethnohistoric contexts that deal with shorter time frames.

The information from prehistoric Hungary suggests that during the Late Neolithic, communities on the Great Hungarian Plain were organized into complexly-structured integrative units that interacted intensively within well-defined, spatially discrete geographic areas. This pattern gave way in the Early Copper Age to one dominated by more diffuse, less complexly-structured integrative units that interacted less intensively over a much larger area. When the temporal scope of analysis is extended further back and forward in time, a similar process seems to have occurred at least twice—from the Early Neolithic through the Middle Bronze Age—on the Great Hungarian Plain. This process is somewhat reminiscent of the 'cycling' often associated with chiefdoms (Anderson

1990) and archaic states (Marcus 1993), but in the case of tribal societies it occurs in the absence of any institutionalized central authority and on a much smaller spatial scale. This quality—of societies occasionally to rework their methods of social organization within certain structural bounds—is characteristic of tribal societies, and has been documented not only in other archaeological contexts (e.g., Braun and Plog 1982; Emerson 1999; Feinman et al. 2000), but in ethnohistoric and ethnographic contexts as well (see O'Shea 1989; Parkinson 1999:85-89). As such, this phenomenon of 'tribal cycling' may itself be a criterion useful for distinguishing tribes from other decentralized, segmentary, societies (i.e., 'bands'), which tend not to exhibit such patterning. Since these 'cycles' tend to occur gradually—over several generations—they frequently go undocumented in ethnographic and ethnohistoric descriptions of tribal societies, which are of necessity usually too limited in their temporal depth to detect such subtle patterns.

Setting the Scene: The Neolithic–Copper Age Transition

The transition from the Late Neolithic (ca. 5,000–4,500 BC) to the Early Copper Age (ca. 4,500–4,000 BC) on the Great Hungarian Plain is marked by dramatic changes in the archaeological record (Fig. 1). These changes in material culture indicate that the population of the Great Hungarian Plain underwent a significant social transformation about 4,500 BC. This transformation affected not only intergroup relationships, as indicated by changes in trade networks and settlement organization, but also intragroup relationships, as indicated by changes in house form and mortuary customs. Throughout both of the periods in question there is no evidence of institutionalized social ranking, nor is there any evidence that the farmers and herders who inhabited the villages across the Plain were impinged upon by more complex social forms,

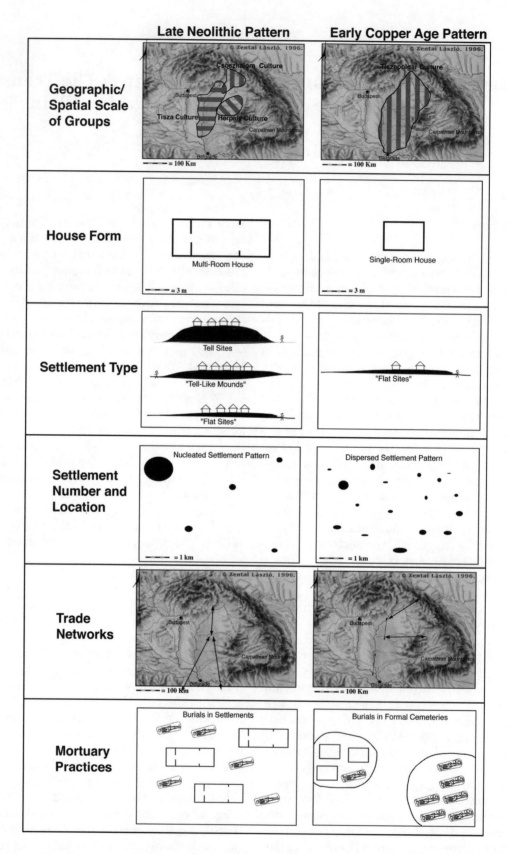

Fig. 1. Patterns of change from the Late Neolithic (ca. 5,000-4,500 BC) to the Early Copper Age (ca. 4,500–4,000 BC).

such as chiefdoms or states. Previous suggestions that these changes can be attributed to large-scale population replacement recently have fallen out of favor (Bánffy 1994, 1995). The social reorganization that took place in the middle of the fifth millennium BC on the Great Hungarian Plain must be understood in terms of the wide range of variability that occurs *within* tribal methods of social organization (see Fowles, this volume, Chapter 2; Parkinson 1999, and this volume, Chapter 1).

The transition from the Late Neolithic to the Early Copper Age on the Great Hungarian Plain coincides with the inception of several technological developments that changed the trajectory of social evolution in Eastern Europe for several millennia. The copper ore sources in the Carpathian and Balkan mountains began to be intensively mined and smelted during this time (Jovanović 1971, 1982). Domestic animals, and especially cattle, began to be exploited not only for their meat, but also for 'secondary products' such as milk and cheese (Chapman 1983; Sherratt 1981, 1983a), and the plow also was introduced into Eastern Europe about this time (Milisauskas and Kruk 1991), permitting the heavier alluvial soils of the Plain to be brought under cultivation.

Roughly contemporary with these technological innovations was a radical change in the way life itself was organized on the Plain (Fig. 1). The changes documented in the archaeological record include:

Changes in the spatial scale of 'cultural groups'. The three geographically-discrete 'cultural groups' that subdivided the Great Hungarian Plain during the Late Neolithic were replaced by a single, relatively homogeneous 'culture' that extended across the entire Plain during the Early Copper Age—the Tiszapolgár Culture. The Late Neolithic 'cultural groups' (Tisza-Herpály-Csőszhalom or Tisza-Herpály/Csőszhalom, see Raczky et al. 1994, 1997 for a more detailed discussion), as they are known in Hungarian literature, are each associated with distinct ceramic assemblages, and differences in settlement type, settlement location and economic strategies (see Kalicz and Raczky 1987a). No such subdivisions are readily identifiable during the Early Copper Age (see Parkinson 1999: 356-364; Sherratt 1983b, 1984, contra Bognár-Kutzián 1972).

Changes in house form. The large, probably multifamily, domestic structures of the Late Neolithic (ca. 10–20 m long) were replaced by much smaller (ca. 5 m long), less substantial dwellings in the Early Copper Age (Bognár-Kutzián 1972;

Goldman 1977; Kalicz and Raczky 1987a; Siklódi 1982, 1983).

Changes in settlement type and organization. The Late Neolithic settlement system, which combined the habitation of large, long-occupied 'tell' sites (up to 6 ha) with more ephemerally occupied 'flat' sites (up to 11 ha), was replaced during the Early Copper Age by a settlement system that consisted almost exclusively of smaller (ca. 0.5–1 ha), more ephemeral settlements with very little vertical stratigraphy (Bognár-Kutzián 1972:164-172; Chapman 1994, 1997; Kalicz and Raczky 1987a; Parkinson 1999:270-275; Sherratt 1983b, 1984).

Changes in settlement number and location. In addition to being smaller than Late Neolithic settlements, Early Copper Age sites were less nucleated and more evenly dispersed across the landscape. In addition, most regions experience a nearly tenfold increase in the number of sites dating to the Early Copper Age (Bognár-Kutzián 1972; Parkinson 1999:281-284; Sherratt 1983b, 1984).

Changes in trade networks. The long-distance trade networks of the Neolithic, which brought goods from as far away as the Aegean, were restructured and redirected in the Early Copper Age to bring copper, gold, and chert from the Carpathians onto the Plain (Biró 1998; Sherratt 1987).

Changes in mortuary practices. Large formal cemeteries were established in the Early Copper Age. These cemeteries—the first of their kind in Europe—frequently were isolated in the landscape and replaced the Neolithic pattern of burying the dead in and around settlement sites (Bognár-Kutzián 1963, 1972; Chapman 1994, 1997b; Derevenski 1997).

These dramatic changes cannot simply be explained in the context of 'traditional' cultural evolutionary scenarios. No chiefdoms emerged suddenly out of the Late Neolithic tribal pattern, and no states colonized the region at the beginning of the Early Copper Age. Indeed, the various mortuary analyses that have been conducted on Early Copper Age cemeteries support the general notion that the grave good associations are more indicative of gender and age distinctions and personal identities (see Bognár-Kutzián 1963, 1972; Chapman 1997b, Derevenski 1997, 2000; Meisenheimer 1989; Némeskeri and Szathmári 1987; Skomal 1980, 1983), rather than vertical (i.e., rank-based) ones. Thus, the transition from the Late Neolithic to the Copper Age on the Great Hungarian Plain makes an ideal setting for exploring the wide range of variability that can characterize social organization within tribal societies. By attempting to understand the long term social processes that led to and resulted in the organization of the Late Neolithic and Early Copper Age, respectively, it may even become possible to generate some more general hypotheses regarding the changes in social organization that occurred within tribal societies elsewhere in the world.

In order to understand the various changes that occurred during the transition from the Neolithic to the Copper Age on the Great Hungarian Plain, it first is necessary to delineate precisely which aspects of social organization were reorganized at the beginning of the Copper Age, and those that continued essentially unchanged from the Neolithic. Only after having identified the specific relationships between the social structures exhibited during each period will it be possible to understand the causal factors that led to their reorganization. In order to identify the patterns of continuity and discontinuity between the Late Neolithic and the Early Copper Age it is useful to model social organization along two discrete, but interrelated, analytical dimensions—integration and interaction.

Theoretical Considerations: Modeling Integration and Interaction in Tribal Societies

The acephalous, decentralized, segmentary nature of tribal societies has forced archaeologists to model tribal social organization by looking at changing patterns of integration and interaction over time (e.g., Adler 1989; Braun 1977; Braun and Plog 1982; Caldwell 1964; Emerson 1999; Flannery 1968b; Haas 1990; Hegmon 1989; Longacre 1966; Plog 1976, 1978; Plog and Braun 1984; Saitta 1983; Struever 1964; Whallon 1968). Unfortunately, we seldom are provided with precise definitions for these terms, which often are used interchangeably throughout the literature.

Integration is usually understood to be a group-level phenomenon, and the term usually refers to processes that bring individuals together into more-or-less formalized units (e.g., Service 1971). *Interaction*, on the other hand, usually refers to more general processes that can occur at both the group and/or individual level (e.g., Caldwell 1964). While interaction usually indicates some kind of social contact (i.e., economic, ritual, political)—whether direct (e.g., face-to-face) or indirect (e.g., down-the-line)—it generally does not indicate anything specific about the relationships between those in con-

tact. The members of one group can trade ceramics with the members of another group, or entire groups can interact with each other, for example during raiding and warfare.

Both of these concepts are intimately intertwined, but it is important to distinguish between them methodologically, since different types of archaeological information tend to speak more to one process than the other. By separating these traditionally ambiguous and overlapping concepts into discrete analytical dimensions, it becomes possible to measure the specific archaeological variables that relate predominantly to one dimension or the other, and to more precisely distinguish processes of integration from processes of interaction.

In keeping with the way these terms have been used traditionally (e.g., Caldwell 1964; Steward 1951), I suggest that the term *integration* should be restricted to refer to *social processes that incorporate individuals into specific organizational (i.e., decision-making) units*. In this sense, societies can be envisioned as being composed of various integrative units—households, neighborhoods, settlements, settlement clusters, etc. *Interaction*, on the other hand, *refers to more diffuse social processes that operate between individuals and groups*. Thus, while individuals and groups may interact (e.g., trade, marry, fight, perform rituals) with each another, they are not necessarily incorporated into integrative units. In the context of this research, the dimension of integration refers to the size, scale, and organization of the basic social segments (the households, neighborhoods and villages), and the dimension of interaction refers to the ways in which these social segments, and their members, interact with each other.

These two analytical dimensions—interaction and integration—are by no means mutually exclusive. Nevertheless, by treating each as an independent line of evidence, it is possible to generate models that more accurately represent the size, scale, and organization of particular elements of social structure. These models then can be used to track diachronic changes within different cultural contexts, and eventually to compare the various trajectories followed by different tribal societies over time. By gradually building up a comparative database that allows the cross-cultural analysis of different tribal trajectories, it will be possible to gain an understanding of the variability—and flexibility—that characterizes social organization in tribal societies (see Fowles, this volume, Chapter 2; Parkinson 1999: chapter 2, and this volume, Chapter 1).

Integration: latent and actualized structure

Most archaeological attempts at dealing with integration in tribal societies have employed the concept of integration as Service (1971) used it—as a classificatory criterion that refers to the presence of pan-residential social institutions that distinguish tribes from 'bands'—rather than as Steward (1951) intended it—as a methodological tool useful for facilitating cross-cultural analysis at multiple scales. Tribes are therefore frequently defined as 'regionally-integrated social networks' (e.g., Bender 1985; Braun and Plog 1982; Emerson 1999; Voss 1980). While this use of the concept—as a criterion for distinguishing tribes from less complex societies (i.e., 'bands')—is acceptable in the context of Braun and Plog's argument, there has been a growing tendency within the discipline to understand integration as a sort of binary social characteristic that distinguishes tribes and other more complex societies from bands, which curiously are understood not to be integrated at all, or at least not as integrated as tribes.

Although tribal societies may indeed be more integrated than bands, they are not *just* integrated. The members of all societies integrate at a variety of different levels, and into a variety of different social units (see Gearing 1958; Steward 1951). This ability for a single community to assume several different 'structural poses', as Gearing called them, or, in Steward's terms, to integrate at several different levels, results in a sort of social flexibility that is essentially built into the structure of most societies. In the context of most tribal societies, this feature is combined with the absence of an institutionalized central authority that in more complex societies tends to hold the system together into more discretely defined social units. This results in a built-in flexibility that allows tribal groups to constitute and reconstitute themselves on an extremely wide variety of different scales—and to incorporate different numbers of members—given different socioenvironmental situations (see Fowles 1997).

In order to deal with the wide range of variability that characterizes social organization in tribal societies, it is useful to distinguish between what I call *latent structure*—the cognized social structure of a group, which outlines the relationship of members of that group to others within and outside the group; and *actualized structure*—the actual structure of the group that interacts regularly to perform specific duties (see Parkinson 1999:49). Latent structure is encoded in a group's cosmol-

ogy, myths, rituals, and kinship. It is a map of the relationships—whether maintained or not—perceived to exist between individuals inside and outside the group. Actualized structure may or may not bear resemblance to latent structure. It refers to the actual structure of how the members of a group interact on a daily, weekly, monthly, or yearly basis. This idea builds upon Julian Steward's (1951) concept of 'levels of sociocultural integration' and Fred Gearing's (1958) concept of 'structural poses'. I simply have tried to endow these well-worn concepts with emic (latent) and etic (actualized) aspects (see Harris 1979) that attempt to differentiate 'cognized models' from 'operational models' (see Rappaport 1979:97).

I see this dichotomization between latent and actualized structure as a way to deal with what Braun and Plog (1982) cumbersomely referred to as the 'non-decomposability' of tribal systems. The idea of non-decomposability suggests that the dynamics of only some hierarchical levels of a system may be observable over a given amount of time (Simon 1973; see also Braun and Plog 1982; Plog and Braun 1984; Saitta 1983). In the theoretical framework proposed here, this idea is reflected in the notion that the members of societies may recognize particular latent structural principles that are seldom, if ever, actualized. The existence of these latent structural principles offers the members of the society a form of legitimized flexibility that can be accessed given the appropriate socioenvironmental conditions.

Despite the archaeologist's inability to observe all of the hierarchical, or structural, levels within tribal societies, different levels nevertheless frequently emerge as being relatively more important than others. While these archaeologically visible levels may not reflect the entire cognized structure recognized by different members of the society at hand, the very fact that particular levels are 'actualized' in some societies at particular times and are 'latent' in others is itself a very meaningful observation. Even more importantly, the various levels that are detectable in a single society can change over time, providing an avenue for tracking the trajectories of changing levels of integration. For these reasons, the concept of integration is treated in the context of this research not as a unified trait that differentiates tribal societies from 'bands', but rather as an analytical dimension that can be modeled by measuring patterns in material variables that were created by the operation of prehistoric social processes. These processes characterize the actualized structure(s) of the society at hand and, in turn, are understood to have been molded by more latent structural principles.

Reconstructing units of integration

The first step necessary for modeling social organization in prehistoric contexts is to determine the size, scale, and organization of the basic social segments—the constituent elements of the society in question. In archaeological contexts this is possible by assessing the size of coresidential units that are indicative of different units of integration.

By measuring the size and organization of domestic structures and how they are organized into neighborhoods and settlements it becomes possible to reconstruct these basic integrative units. Beyond the settlement, it frequently is possible to identify settlement clusters throughout the landscape that correspond to even larger integrative units. Not only can the spatial relationship between settlements be used as a method of discerning integrative units that operated over the long term, but frequently the relationship between settlement sites and other special purpose sites, such as cemeteries or shrines, can also effectively be used to define the location of different boundaries in the social landscape that may have been produced by different integrative units (see Stark 1998). The patterns that emerge from any such analyses then can be compared to patterns of interaction to determine whether they represent the presence or absence of specific social boundaries over the long term. By assessing the degree to which such boundaries were actively maintained or passively transcended, as indicated by patterns of interaction across them, it is possible to generate some conclusions regarding the nature of the relationship between the groups at hand. Such combined analyses eventually can reveal the operation of more latent structural principles over long periods of time.

Coresidential units of integration

By defining the size, scale, and organization of integrative units using empirical data from coresidential units, it is possible to construct a structural model that essentially builds itself from the bottom up. Each unit is understood to correspond to a cognized social unit (e.g., household, clans, sub-tribe), which may or may not be inferentially identifiable through its material correlates.

In general, four coresidential units characterize integration within tribal societies: 1) households, 2) neighborhoods, 3) settlements, and 4) settlement clusters. Not all tribal societies are expected to exhibit all of these units. But by delineating which levels are exhibited in different societies over varying periods of time, and by determining the size, scale and organization of each of those levels, it is possible to track how the structure of such units transformed over time. Furthermore, by tracking how each unit changes with respect to the others, it is possible to delineate precisely those aspects of social organization that are transformed over time, and to infer a variety of different social mechanisms that can be held accountable for those changes. As I will demonstrate below, when this methodology is conducted in concert with analyses of interaction, it is a very effective method of delineating long-term changes in the social organization of prehistoric tribal societies.

The household unit

The household unit frequently, but by no means exclusively, corresponds to a nuclear or extended family group or lineage. The archaeological correlates of this unit include the size, shape, and organization of discrete domestic structures (e.g., wigwams, houses, pithouses, longhouses). This unit normally subsumes the basic unit of production and pooling of resources within tribal societies (Sahlins 1972). Cross cultural analyses also suggest that the size and organization of domestic structures may also be indicative of postmarital residence patterns. For example, Divale (1977) and Ember and Ember (1995) suggested that houses with floor areas bigger than ca. 60 m^2 are correlated very highly with matrilineal social patterns. The shape of domestic structures (e.g., round versus square; see Flannery 1968a) also may reflect something about the structural relationship between household units, since square dwellings lend themselves more readily to agglomeration and accretion than do round dwellings—implying that the tendency to build square or rectangular houses may be indicative of a more fluid relationship between households. Changes that occur within the scale and organization of the household unit may reflect changes in the organization of resource production and pooling within the 'domestic mode of production'.

The neighborhood unit

A neighborhood unit is defined as any structural level that exists between the household and the settlement. The archaeological correlates of this unit include any structural subdivision that occurs between the household unit (the house or longhouse) and the settlement (the village or hamlet), these include room blocks, house clusters, and longhouse clusters. Depending upon the cultural context, such units may not be exhibited at all, or may exist at different scales, reflecting various levels of internal structure within a particular settlement. Such units are likely to indicate the operation of middle-level social groupings, such as kin groups (e.g., extended lineages, clans, or moieties [see Lowell 1996; Marcus and Flannery 1996]). Whereas the household is assumed to bear the majority of the burden of day-to-day food production activities, the neighborhood is less likely to operate as a food-producing unit on a daily basis. Although some degree of productive cooperation and resource pooling is likely to occur within neighborhoods, the greater social contribution of such units is their tendency to facilitate the interactions of individuals living in large settlements into smaller units. These units also are likely to serve as a basis for the mobilization of manpower for conducting communal activities within the settlement, such as building earthlodges or longhouses. Neighborhood units also frequently form the basic units of fission and fusion within tribal societies. They are more likely to form when settlements are large, and require internal organization, especially when previously independent groups nucleate at a large settlement. Conversely, they frequently are the social units that break off to form independent settlements, either seasonally or permanently (see, for example, Carneiro 1987; Chagnon 1983:130). In much the same way that changes in the scale and organization of the household unit are likely to be indicative of shifts within the basic economic organization of the group, changes in the neighborhood unit are likely to reflect more subtle shifts in the nature of intragroup relations. As such, their presence or absence, and their internal organization, provide a rough measure of the degree of structural complexity within settlements.

The settlement unit

The settlement—the farmstead, camp, hamlet, or village—can vary considerably in size, scale, and organization, and as such corresponds to a wide variety of social levels—from individual nuclear families (e.g., farmsteads) to entire tribal societies (e.g., the 'combined' historic Pawnee village near Genoa, Nebraska [see Hyde 1974; O'Shea 1989]). While individuals who live in a settlement

are likely to interact with each other on a daily basis, for the most part the day-to-day routine of most individuals is more likely to be structured by the various social units in which they participate—as members of economic, political, and religious groups—rather than as members of a village or hamlet (see Gearing 1958). The degree to which settlement members interact with one another also depends upon the size of the settlement, the number of integrative units that it is composed of, and the size of each of those units. Obviously, the members of a small isolated hamlet consisting of only one or two households are much more likely to interact with each other on a regular basis than the members of a large settlement composed of several extended lineages. Precisely for this reason, a common feature among tribal societies is some sort of ritual activity that serves, among other things, to unite the members of a settlement behind a given task, simultaneously reaffirming their membership within the settlement itself. Village feasts, seasonal rituals, and even periodic warfare all serve to reproduce the settlement, its constituent units, and their individual members. Changes in the size, scale, and internal reorganization of the settlement itself often corresponds to the actualization of more latent structural transformations within a society. These causes frequently are external, and can relate to factors such as the organization of warfare or subsistence practices (see Hollinger 1995). But just as frequently, changes in the settlement can relate to problems of scalar stress upon internal organizational structures (e.g., McGuire and Saitta 1996).

The settlement cluster

The settlement cluster generally forms the largest spatially-discrete coresidential unit in prehistoric tribal societies. It can correspond to any number of social groups—from extended families to entire societies—depending upon the number and organization of lower-order units integrated within it. The archaeological correlates of this unit include spatially discrete groups of settlements in the landscape, or groups of settlements organized around or separated by special purpose sites, such as cemeteries or shrines. Some pooling of resources may rarely occur at this level, but the integrative processes that unite these larger units are more likely to be ritual in nature, such as communal feasts, funerals, or dances. In some cases, settlement clusters can form even larger groupings—or 'superclusters'—across the landscape. Superclusters are defined as groups of settlement clusters that form discrete units on the landscape. Given the size of this coresidential unit, it is more likely to be indicative of higher-order social units (e.g., 'bands', sub-tribes, tribes). Changes within the organization of settlement clusters and superclusters generally correspond to the actualization of latent structural principles, and usually can be expected to relate to deep-seated changes in the fabric of society.

'Focal' units of integration

In addition to providing a convenient method for parsing apart the actualized social structures of prehistoric societies, the analysis of social organization along these different integrative units allows the researcher to identify particular 'focal units' of integration within each actualized configuration. These focal units refer to the level at which particular societal processes—such as aggression, competition, and mobilization—assume primary roles within the various structural configurations assumed by different societies. For example, if the members of a society are organized into nuclear family groups (household unit) that live in small autonomous hamlets (settlement), that are dispersed evenly across the landscape (settlement cluster), the nature of aggression and competition within that society is likely to operate on a much different scale than if the societal members lived in extended family groups (household units) organized into large, nucleated villages (settlement) that formed discrete, territorially-bounded clusters (settlement clusters). Different structural configurations result in differential roles being assumed by each of these processes.

This implies that, to some extent, the structural configuration of the society at hand lends itself to accommodating different sorts of social processes. For example, as the actualized integrative structure of a society becomes more complex—incorporating more individuals into more elaborately organized coresidential units—processes that occur between the various units, such as economic and political competition, also tend to operate at increasingly higher levels. As such, the degree of complexity exhibited by the actualized integrative structure of a society has particular implications with regards to the degree of social, political, and economic inequality possible within that society. In general, societies that exhibit relatively simple actualized integrative structures are also less likely to exhibit significant degrees of inequal-

ity, since inequality is itself a relative concept that refers to differential access to resources, materials, or social power between the members of a particular group. If the settlement also constitutes the focal unit of pooling within a society, then it is nearly impossible for an individual to achieve some degree of economic inequality within that unit. Similarly, given more complex structural configurations, the nature of warfare is likely to operate at a higher level—including more individuals and focusing more at the inter-village level, than at the inter-family level.

This is not to say that the actions of individuals are completely prescribed by external structural forces beyond their control, for it is the individuals who, through their very actions, create and modify their own social structure (see Giddens 1984). But by their actions, and through practice, individuals do produce and reproduce social structures that to varying degrees mold their behavior within socially acceptable bounds (see also Bordieu 1977).

Modeling interaction in tribal societies

The concept of interaction has a similarly jaded history in the discipline. At various times, the concept has been used to refer to everything from 'interaction' spheres that extend halfway across North America (e.g., Caldwell 1964), to systems of long-distance exchange that brought prestige goods from south America to northern Mexico (Flannery 1968b), to the intimate interaction of a daughter learning how to make pottery from her mother (MacEachern 1998). In order to operationalize this concept for studying social organization in tribal societies, it is important to define the temporal and spatial scales of analysis independently, and to develop a methodology for modeling interaction within those bounds.

Defining the temporal and spatial scales of analysis

The first task necessary in any attempt to reconstruct the nature of interaction in prehistoric societies is to determine the temporal and spatial scales of analysis. In most archaeological contexts, the temporal scale will be determined largely by the nature of the data at hand. The chronological precision of various material sequences will determine at what temporal scale such analysis can occur. For example, in the American Southwest, where dendrochronology provides very precise dating for ceramic sequences, it is frequently possible to discuss prehistoric interaction at a similar scale of temporal precision—at the decadal or generational level. In other parts of the world, where ceramic sequences can be related only to much longer periods of time, perhaps hundreds of years, it is possible to discuss interaction only as a generalized process that occurred over a much longer temporal scale. In these cases, it is important to be aware that any patterns of interaction will refer not to specific interactive spheres, but to the operation of a palimpsest of interactive spheres that operated sequentially or simultaneously over long periods of time.

Since the nature of tribal society is such that social boundaries are fluidly restructured over time (Barth 1969), and since the configurations of actualized structural patterns can vary dramatically over the landscape, it is necessary to define the spatial scope of analysis in geographic, rather than social terms. In other words, the spatial scope of analysis should be determined by specific geographic and topographical features, and not by social features, such as the geographic extent of a particular material 'culture'. By defining the spatial scale in this independent manner, it is possible to generate models of interaction that then can be compared to each other to delineate trajectories of social change within a region.

Within a geographically defined region, interaction, like integration, typically occurs at a variety of levels within prehistoric tribal societies. Nevertheless, just as some integrative units assume focal, or primary roles, patterns of interaction also operate at varying degrees of intensity between and within those integrative units over time. As such, any attempt to model social interaction in prehistoric contexts must be able to deal with this dynamic quality.

Modeling interaction through
stylistic variables

One method that has proven to be particularly effective for modeling interaction in prehistoric contexts is the analysis of stylistic variables within ceramic and lithic assemblages. By articulating such stylistic analyses with the analysis of integrative units, it becomes possible to generate models that more accurately describe the degree of interaction that occurred at different levels within a society over a given amount of time. Such analyses must focus upon the stylistic (and technological) variability exhibited both within and between the integrative units (see Hegmon 1995; Plog 1980, 1990).

In concert with most recent comprehensive treatments of this complex topic (e.g., Carr and Neitzel 1995; Hegmon 1992, 1995, 1998; Plog 1995; Stark 1998), which generally agree that it is necessary to consider several different kinds of stylistic variation, the present analysis approaches the data at several different levels and assesses several different attributes that may have functioned differentially within different social contexts. In order to determine which dimensions of stylistic variability are likely to indicate different dimensions of social interaction, it is particularly useful to focus upon two qualities that are helpful in determining the role a specific attribute may have played within a particular social context. These are: 1) the relative visibility of the attribute, and 2) its social and geographic distribution (see Carr 1995; Voss and Young 1995).

Table 1 synthesizes several of the interpretations proposed by Carr (1995) and Voss and Young (1995) for the distribution of high (in Carr's terms 'visible') and low (in Carr's terms 'obscure') visibility characteristics given different spatial distributions. I have attempted to include those interpretations that will be most applicable for discussing the patterns in ceramic assemblages dealt with in this chapter.

The attribute distributions—uniform, discrete, clinal, and random—relate to the relative occurrence of different attributes at different sites within the study area. A basic assumption underlying the various relationships drawn in the table is that homogeneity, or uniformity, within a single cluster is likely to be indicative of a high degree of interaction—active or passive—between the sites in that cluster, regardless of the visibility of the attribute (see Sackett 1977, 1985, 1998; Weissner 1985, 1990; Wobst 1977). Regarding the relationships between site clusters, I follow the relationships proposed by Carr (1995) and Voss and Young (1995). The interpretations overlap a great deal, and they certainly are susceptible to alternate explanations in different social contexts. Nevertheless, they provide a rough outline for indicating which ceramic attributes are most likely to reveal different patterns of active and passive interaction throughout the study area. While the distribution of high-visibility attributes is more likely to indicate active interaction between groups, boundary-marking, and to a lesser extent, individual creativity; the distribution of low-visibility attributes is more likely to indicate passive interaction through learning, intermarriage, or enculturation (for a more detailed discussion, see Parkinson 1999:164-188).

Table 1. Possible interpretations of stylistic attribute distributions within and between clusters in the study area (based on Carr [1995], Voss and Young [1995], and Parkinson [1999]).

Visibility of Attribute	Distribution Within Cluster	Distribution Between Clusters	Degree of Interaction within Cluster	Degree of Interaction between Clusters	Possible Interpretations of Pattern
High	Uniform	Discrete	High	Low	Marking well-maintained group boundaries between clusters. Little trade or intermarriage between groups.
High	Uniform	Clinal	High	Moderate	Marking permeable group boundary near or within study area. Some trade and/or intermarriage between groups.
High	Uniform	Uniform	High	High	Marking group unity or cooperation across study area. Extensive trade and/or intermarriage between groups.
High	Clinal	Clinal	Moderate	Moderate	Marking very permeable group boundaries between and within clusters. Continuous trade and/or intermarriage throughout area.
High	Discrete	Discrete	Low	Low	Marking settlements as group boundary. Little or no trade between settlements.
High	Random	Random	?	?	Marking individual creativity?
Low	Uniform	Discrete	High	Low	No shared learning or passive interaction between clusters? No intermarriage or trade between clusters?
Low	Uniform	Clinal	High	Moderate or Low	Some shared learning between clusters? Some intermarriage or trade between groups?
Low	Uniform	Uniform	High	High	Much shared learning between clusters. Intermarriage or trade between clusters.
Low	Clinal	Clinal	Moderate	Moderate	Shared learning between clusters. Intermarriage or trade between clusters.
Low	Discrete	Discrete	Low	Low	No shared learning between settlements. No intermarriage or trade between settlements?
Low	Random	Random	?	?	Individual competency?

By assessing the distribution of a battery of different ceramic attributes within and between different clusters within the study area, it will be possible to assess the relative kinds and degree of interaction that occurred within and between sites located in different clusters throughout the study area.

The Study Area–The Körös Region of Eastern Hungary

The study area encompasses an area of approximately 2000 km² in northern Békés County in the eastern Great Hungarian Plain (Fig. 2). The area—known as the Körös-Berettyó Region—is named after the complex river systems that dominate its topography and produced its subtle, yet very complex, surface geomorphology. The Körös River valley is the main east-west corridor that link the center of the Great Hungarian Plain with the rich copper and gold resources in Transylvania and in the Carpathian Mountains beyond. As such, the region would have been centrally involved with the various technological changes that occurred during the Late Neolithic, when 'native' copper began to be exploited, and during the Early Copper Age, when copper ores began to be smelted.

Prior to hydrological regulation, the region was prone to biannual floods—one in early spring, and the other in early summer. In those areas that were high enough to avoid annual flooding, the study area is covered by alkaline loess that was redeposited by the various streams that have meandered their way across the region since the end of the Pleistocene. In the areas that were seasonally inundated, meadow clays and silty loess predominate. A few dispersed pockets of relatively pristine loess sand can still be found in the easternmost part of the study area, and the late Pleistocene Maros alluvial fan covers a large portion of the area in the south. Kosse (1979:47-50) notes that tartar maple-oak forest (*Galatello-Quercetum roboris*) would have been found on the alkaline soils between floodplains and the higher loess plateaus. The floodplains would have contained willow and poplar groves, in addition to marsh grasses. Although the majority of the region is today under industrial production of sunflower and corn, prior to irrigation large tracts were given over to pasture (see Pécsi 1970; Pécsi and Sarfálvi 1964).

For the last thirty years the Körös Region has been the focus of intensive archaeological survey and excavation by Hungarian and British research teams (e.g., Ecsedy et al. 1982; Jankovich et al. 1989; Sherratt 1983b,1984). As part of an ambitious project to document all of the known sites in different counties, the Institute of Archaeology of the Hungarian Academy of Sciences and various regional museums joined forces to publish a series of volumes, known as the *Magyarország Régészeti Topográfiája*, the Archaeological Topography of Hungary (MRT). This series combines the comprehensive documentation of known sites and private collections with intensive surface survey directed explicitly at locating new sites. Beginning in 1998, the author revisited and conducted systematic surface collections at several of the Early Copper Age settlements identified during the MRT surveys (see Parkinson 1999:196-210).

In addition to the intensive surface surveys that have been conducted throughout the study area, two important sites with Early Copper Age settlement features that previously had been excavated within the study area—Vésztő-15 (Vésztő-Mágor [see Ecsedy et al. 1982:183-187; Hegedűs 1972, 1973, 1974, 1975, 1976, 1977a, 1977b, 1982, 1983, 1987; Hegedűs and Makkay 1987; Makkay 1986]) and Örménykút 13 (Örménykút-Makonczai-Domb [see András 1996; Juhász 1991; Jankovich et al. 1989:344])—were available for the present research. The former is a large Late Neolithic tell site that was abandoned at the end of the Late Neolithic and, after a hiatus, was reinhabited during the Early and Middle Copper Ages. The latter is a medieval cemetery that yielded several settlement features, mostly pits, that date to the Early Copper Age. This material forms the basis for the analyses conducted in the following sections.

Reconstructing Integrative Units

This section brings together the relevant information for measuring integrative units during the Late Neolithic and the Early Copper Age. The section treats each integrative unit separately, beginning with the most basic, and discusses each period independently.

Household units

Due to the lack of a sufficient number of excavated Late Neolithic and Early Copper Age settlements in the Körös Region, it is necessary to look beyond the study area to gain an understanding of how household units were organized during the periods in question. In general, Late Neolithic houses tend to be larger and more complexly organized than their Early Copper Age counterparts.

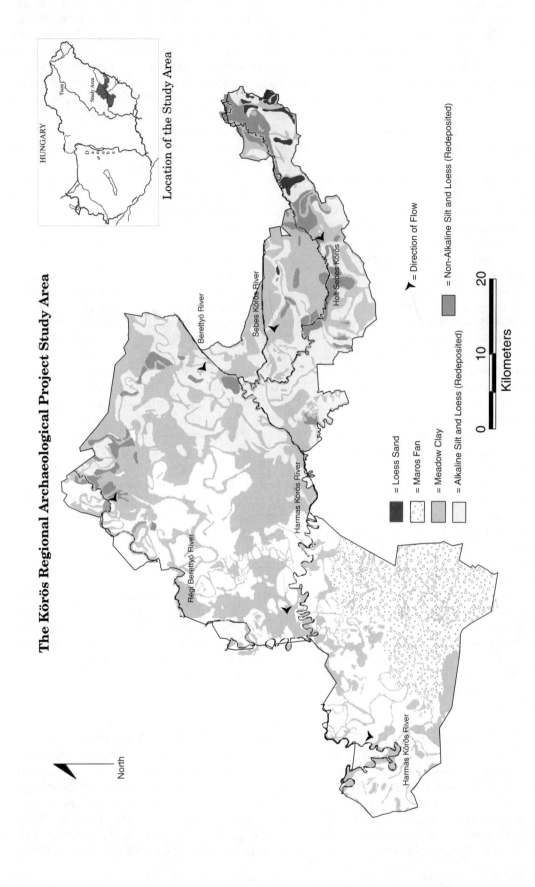

Fig. 2 Surface sediments in the Körös Regional Archaeological Project study area.

Late Neolithic houses

Late Neolithic houses have been excavated at several sites across the Great Hungarian Plain (see Kalicz and Raczky 1987a). In general, they tend to be large rectangular 'longhouses' of timber-framed wattle-and-daub construction, frequently with plastered clay floors. They exhibit a high degree of variability in size, shape, and organization. Some of this variability may be related to traditions inherent to each of the two or three 'cultural groups' that occupied the Plain during this period (i.e., Tisza, Herpály, and Csőszhalom). For example, House Complex 2 at Hódmezővásárhely-Gorzsa (Tisza Culture) is a large (ca. 20 m x 13 m) structure with six internal subdivisions, each with an oven (see Horváth 1987). By contrast, the houses at the site of Polgár-Csőszhalom (Csőszhalom Group) tend to be 8–12 x 4–5 m with a single internal subdivision (Raczky et al. 1997). The houses at Berettyóújfalu-Herpály, on the other hand, are 10–12 x 4–5 m with internal subdivisions, some of which may have been two-storied (Kalicz and Raczky 1987b).

Table 2 lists the areas of several Late Neolithic houses across the Plain. In sites where the exact sizes of individual houses were not available because the sites have not yet been fully published (e.g., Polgár-Csőszhalom), the maximum and minimum sizes listed by the authors were used to generate ranges for house areas. Despite the small number in the sample (*n*=18), the houses are generally large (mean = 59 m^2, median = 37.5 m^2), often with internal subdivisions. There are two outliers—House Complex 2 from Hódmező-vásárhely-Gorzsa (area = 259 m^2), and the maximum size listed for houses at Öcsöd-Kováshalom (area = 148 m^2). House Complex 2 at Hódmező-vásárhely-Gorzsa includes a total of six individual rooms (ca. 3.6–6.2 x 3.6–6.2 m), each with its own oven (see Horváth 1987:35 and figure 6). This large structure likely resulted from the accretion of several additional rooms to a smaller, albeit still quite large (ca. 100 m^2), internally-divided structure.

Early Copper Age houses

Due to the lack of attention that has been paid to Tiszapolgár settlement sites, only nine Early Copper Age Tiszapolgár houses can be included in the analysis. Three of these were identified at Vésztő 20 and Körösladány 14 in surface contexts conducted by the Körös Regional Archaeological Project during fieldwork in 1998 (see Parkinson 1999:197-210). At both sites, the houses were identified as daub concentrations with significant amounts of Tiszapolgár ceramics in their matrix. The remaining Tiszapolgár structures were found in excavated contexts at Tibava (Andel 1961), Lucsky-Vinicky (Šiška 1968), Szerbkeresztúr (Bognár-Kutzian 1972:168; Milleker 1893), Tiszaföldvár-Újtemető (Siklódi 1983), Kenderes-Kulis (Bognár-Kutzián 1972:165), and Bélmegyer-Mondoki (Goldman 1977). Although Bognár-Kutzián (1972:164-70) mentions a few other Early Copper Age houses, for example at Kenderes-Telekhalom and Crna Bara, the floor areas for these structures were not available and could not be included in the present analysis.

In contrast to the Late Neolithic, Early Copper Age houses are generally smaller in area (mean = 26 m^2, median = 22 m^2) and lack internal subdivisions. Also in contrast to the Late Neolithic, the ovens associated with Early Copper Age houses usually are located outside the house (*see* Goldman 1977; Siklódi 1983). Early Copper Age houses also lack the plastered clay floors that frequently are found in Late Neolithic houses. In general, they are of a lighter construction than their Late Neolithic predecessors. They are without exception of simple wattle-and-daub architecture. In some cases (e.g., at Crna Bara), the vertical beams of the walls were fitted into logs laid in foundation trenches. In other cases (e.g., at Kenderes-Kulis), the presence of postholes suggests that the walls were supported by posts.

Changes in the household unit

Despite the small sample size and the large geographic area from which the examples are drawn, a definite trend towards smaller domestic structures can be demonstrated during the transition to the Early Copper Age on the Great Hungarian Plain. The addition of more instances to the sample would almost certainly augment the difference exhibited in this small sample. While this pattern must admittedly be considered preliminary, it is nevertheless useful to explore its implications with regards to the scale and organization of household units during each period.

Throughout the Late Neolithic, the organization of household units on the Great Hungarian Plain most likely was comprised of multi-unit social groups that lived primarily in 'longhouses' with internal divisions. Frequently, as is the case with House Complex 2 at Hódmezővásárhely-Gorzsa,

Table 2. Late Neolithic and Early Copper Age house sizes on the Great Hungarian Plain.

Site	Feature	Context	Location	Phase	Length (m)	Width (m)	Area (m²)	Reference
Hódmezővásárhely-Gorzsa	House complex 2	Level 10, Phase C	Alföld	LN	20.1	12.9	259	Horváth 1987
Hódmezővásárhely-Gorzsa	Room 1	Level 10, Phase C	Alföld	LN	3.6	7	25	Horváth 1987
Hódmezővásárhely-Gorzsa	Room 2	Level 10, Phase C	Alföld	LN	6.2	5.8	36	Horváth 1987
Hódmezővásárhely-Gorzsa	Room 3	Level 10, Phase C	Alföld	LN	6.2	5.8	36	Horváth 1987
Hódmezővásárhely-Gorzsa	Room 4	Level 10, Phase C	Alföld	LN	5.9	5	30	Horváth 1987
Hódmezővásárhely-Gorzsa	Room 5	Level 10, Phase C	Alföld	LN	8.4	4.6	39	Horváth 1987
Hódmezővásárhely-Gorzsa	Room 6	Level 10, Phase C	Alföld	LN	3.6	3.6	13	Horváth 1987
Szegvár-Tuzköves	House K	Level 2	Alföld	LN	14	5.1	71	Korek 1987
Szegvár-Tuzköves	House E	Level 3	Alföld	LN	7	3.4	24	Korek 1987
Szegvár-Tuzköves	House N	Level 4	Alföld	LN	6	3.75	23	Korek 1987
Öcsöd-Kováshalom	Max	N/A	Alföld	LN	18.5	8	148	Raczky 1987b
Öcsöd-Kováshalom	Min	N/A	Alföld	LN	7	3.5	25	Raczky 1987b
Vésztő-Mágor	Trenches IV-VIII	level 3a	Alföld	LN	12.5	6	75	Hegedűs and Makkay 1987
Vésztő-Mágor	Trenches IV-VIII	Level 4	Alföld	LN	13	5.4	70	Hegedűs and Makkay 1987
Herpály	Max	N/A	Alföld	LN	12	5	60	Kalicz and Raczky 1987b
Herpály	Min	N/A	Alföld	LN	10	4	40	Kalicz and Raczky 1987b
Polgár-Csőszhalom	Max	N/A	Alföld	LN	12	5	60	Raczky et al. 1997
Polgár-Csőszhalom	Min	N/A	Alföld	LN	8	4	32	Raczky et al. 1997
Tibava	Feature C	Phase A	Slovakia	TP	11.5	4.5	52	Andel 1961; Siska 1968
Bélmegyer-Mondoki	House 1	Tiszapolgár	Alföld	TP	2.85	2.5	7	Goldman 1977
Tiszaföldvár-Újtemető	House 1	Tiszapolgár	Alföld	TP	5	4	20	Siklódi 1983
Kenderes-Kulis	N/A	Tiszapolgár	Alföld	TP	5.25	4.15	22	Bognár-Kutzián 1972
Lucska-Vinicky	Feature 7	Tiszapolgár	Slovakia	TP	3.6	1.8	6	Šiška 1968
Szerbkeresztúr	N/A	Layer 2	Serbia	TP	4.25	3	13	Bognár-Kutzián 1972
Körösladány 14	Feature 1	Surface	Alföld	TP	8	6	48	Parkinson 1999:201-202
Vésztő 20	Feature 3	Surface	Alföld	TP	11	3.5	39	Parkinson 1999:208-210
Vésztő 20	Feature 4	Surface	Alföld	TP	7.5	3.8	29	Parkinson 1999:208-210

each of the internal divisions was furnished with its own oven. One or more storage pits are usually found inside or directly outside the longhouses. The presence of ovens and storage pits in multiple numbers within each subdivided structure implies the coresidence of smaller individual social units—probably nuclear family groups. The organization of the household unit within Late Neolithic contexts likely constituted of two (e.g., at Öcsöd-Kováshalom and Polgár-Csőszhalom) to five or six (at Hódmezővásárhely-Gorzsa) nuclear family groups. While it is likely that the vast majority of resource production and food preparation occurred within the individual nuclear family groups, as is the case with most societies operating at the 'domestic mode of production' (Sahlins 1972), the coresidence of multiple units within Late Neolithic structures suggests that pooling of resources likely occurred to some extent throughout the entire household.

By the Early Copper Age, this pattern seems to have given way to one in which the smaller groups—probably nuclear families—lived separately, in smaller houses. The tendency of ovens to be located outside Early Copper Age houses further suggests that while resource production was probably still carried out by the members of these smaller groups, food preparation likely was carried out within a larger social unit that included more than one household. The implications of this subtle, yet important, shift are better appreciated in light of their structural context within larger integrative units—neighborhood units and settlements.

Neighborhood units

The material correlates of neighborhood units—house clusters and neighborhood clusters—frequently occur on Late Neolithic settlements throughout the Great Hungarian Plain. They are presently unknown from the few Early Copper Age settlements that have been excavated.

Late Neolithic neighborhoods

During the Late Neolithic, there is evidence for house clusters at several sites. Most notable among these are the sites of Öcsöd-Kováshalom and Polgár-Csőszhalom. The Late Neolithic site at Öcsöd-Kováshalom was divided into five house compounds on tell-like settlements that were separated by a wooden fence. Each compound enclosed a few houses, their associated storage pits, and

activity areas. Raczky (1987b) estimates that four to six houses would have been in use within each compound at any given time. These compounds were surrounded by a larger, thinner, horizontal settlement that extended over an area of approximately three to five ha. Raczky reasonably suggests that this thinner settlement stratum was created by periodic horizontal shifts around the central settlement mounds, suggesting that the area simultaneously occupied did not exceed 2–3 ha (Raczky 1987b:63). This basic pattern of discrete house clusters within a site is repeated at the site of Kökénydomb (see Korek 1972; Raczky et al. 1985), and at the site of Szegvár-Tzköves (Korek 1987:52). While the size and organization of house clusters at the site of Hódmezővásárhely-Gorzsa cannot be precisely defined, their existence can be inferred by the occasional reconstruction of fortification ditches across the site during the Late Neolithic (see Horváth 1987:36).

The type site of the Csőszhalom group—Polgár-Csőszhalom—also exhibits the clustering of domestic structures, albeit in an organizational scheme different than that of the Tisza group. Although the familiar pattern of a large horizontal settlement centered around a smaller tell continues at Csőszhalom (see Raczky et al. 1994), the size of the horizontal settlement is much larger than that estimated for most Tisza sites (ca. 28 ha). As Raczky notes, "… it may be considered unlikely that the entire 28 ha large settlement was inhabited at any given time. Meanwhile, it must be emphasized that the features excavated at this site all represent a more-or-less homogeneous and unified time period" (Raczky et al. 1997:42). Within this larger horizontal settlement, Raczky notes that the longhouses were organized into east-west oriented groups, which often were associated with auxiliary buildings and wells. While house clusters are exhibited at the site of Csőszhalom, they do not seem to have been separated from each other by fences or ditches, as commonly occurs in Tisza contexts.

It is unclear whether settlements of the Herpály group were divided into house clusters. At the type site—Berettyóújfalu-Herpály—Kalicz and Raczky (1987b:107) note that during the earliest phase (Tisza I/II) it consisted of at least two small settlement nuclei surrounded by a quadrangular fence. During later phases, the settlement appears to have been more concentrated on the central part of the tell (ca. 2.5–3 ha), which came to be surrounded by a fortification ditch. This area was densely packed with houses, some of which were two-storied, organized around a small open space, or court. During the later phases of occupation (i.e., Proto-Tiszapolgár) this tightly-packed organization of houses gave way to a looser arrangement of smaller buildings (Kalicz and Raczky 1987b:111).

In general, it would appear that house clusters were a common feature on the Late Neolithic settlements of the Great Hungarian Plain. The vast majority of those sites that have yielded evidence for such features are large settlements with substantial vertical stratigraphy (i.e., tells or tell-like settlements). These also tend to be the kind of sites that have been selected for excavation. This research bias towards larger sites undoubtedly has increased the frequency with which such features are found on Late Neolithic settlements. Whether such features occur on smaller Late Neolithic sites remains a question for future research.

It is unclear to what extent the various house clusters that have been identified on Late Neolithic sites were contemporaneous with each other. At the two sites for which there is the best evidence—Öcsöd-Kováshalom and Polgár-Csőszhalom—the information is somewhat at odds with itself. At the site of Öcsöd-Kováshalom, Raczky (1987b) has argued for three to five compounds that were inhabited more intensively, around which a less intensive habitation periodically shifted in an area of about 5 ha. At the site of Csőszhalom, where over 36 houses have been excavated, the picture is much more complicated. Although the large horizontal site that surrounds the small tell at Csőszhalom is over 28 ha in areal extent, Raczky contends that the material from the site is representative of a "more-or-less homogeneous and unified time period" (Raczky et al. 1997:42). Since the 36 houses were excavated in an area of less than 3 ha, Csőszhalom was either an exceptionally large settlement, or the houses were rebuilt and relocated very frequently during its occupation. Given the exceptional nature of the Csőszhalom site in other respects, including the multi-ditched 'roundel' reminiscent of the Lengyel culture at its center and the 'cult assemblage' found within (see Raczky et al. 1994), either or both of these scenarios is entirely possible. Most other Late Neolithic sites on the Plain exhibit layouts more similar to that found at Öcsöd-Kováshalom (e.g., Kökénydomb and Szegvár-Tzköves).

Early Copper Age neighborhoods

In contrast to Late Neolithic settlements, no clusters have been identified at the few Early Copper Age settlements that have been excavated.

Rather, Early Copper Age settlements seem to have consisted of only a few small houses that possibly shared the use of an outside oven. This conclusion must be considered preliminary, given both the small number of Early Copper Age settlements that have been excavated, and the small areas that were exposed during excavation. Nevertheless, the organization of houses in settlements appears to have changed drastically during this period.

The Early Copper Age settlements that have been excavated produced only the poorly-preserved remains of a few small houses. At most excavated Tiszapolgár settlements, only one house was encountered during excavation (see Bélmegyer-Mondoki [Goldman 1977], Kenderes-Kulis [Bognár-Kutzián 1972:165], and Tiszaföldvár-Újtemető [Siklódi 1983]). At other sites, such as Kenderes-Telekhalom (Bognár-Kutzián 1972:166) and Vésztő-Mágor (Hegedűs 1974, 1975), more than one house was identified, but no apparent spatial patterning could be discerned. The site of Szerbkeresztúr in the Serbian Banat also produced Tiszapolgár structures that may be interpreted as houses (Bognár-Kutzián 1972:168). These features, which were found at roughly 10–30 m intervals, were interpreted initially as fireplaces (Milleker 1893) and are poorly dated. While they exhibit some spatial patterning, they do not seem to have been organized into clusters, or groups on the site.

Two sites that were revisited during fieldwork in 1998 produced the remains of Early Copper Age domestic structures in surface contexts—Körösladány 14 and Vésztő 20. The former produced one structure, the latter two. The two structures at Vésztő 20 were located roughly 15 m apart. It is possible that these two settlements were contemporary with each other (see Parkinson 1999:208-210). If this is the case, then it also is possible that the two sites, which are now separated by an irrigation canal, comprised discrete residential foci within a single large settlement. Excavations are currently being conducted by the Körös Regional Archaeological Project at Körösladány 14 and Vésztő 20, in an attempt to clarify the nature of settlement organization at those sites (see Parkinson et al. 2002).

Thus, no definite house clusters have as yet been identified on Early Copper Age settlements. While Early Copper Age sites frequently are surrounded by small ditches, for example at Tiszaug-Kisrétpart (Siklódi 1983) and at Bélmegyer-Mondoki (Goldman 1977), the occurrence of these features does not seem to be related to defense, or to the definition of house compounds, as it had during the Late Neolithic. Although it is possible that the trenches of the Tiszapolgár settlements were used as bedding trenches for fences, or possibly for irrigation, their shallow cross-section likely indicates a function different than that of their Late Neolithic predecessors.

Changes in the neighborhood unit

The change in house size exhibited during the transition to the Early Copper Age on the Great Hungarian Plain can be interpreted as an indication of changes in the size and organization of the household unit, and most likely indicates concurrent changes in basic economic organization. Similarly, changes in the actualized organization of the neighborhood unit can be interpreted as changes in the internal complexity of settlements. The paucity of the data on the organization of this unit during the Early Copper Age precludes our ability to assess this change accurately. Nevertheless, the lacuna of clearly defined house compounds on Tiszapolgár sites suggests a shift to a less complexly structured process of integration during the Early Copper Age.

The subdivision of villages into house clusters throughout the Late Neolithic can be interpreted in several ways. To a large extent, the accuracy of such an interpretation depends upon defining precisely the chronological relationships between the various clusters within a single village. In several cases, clusters within a settlement are of varying vertical and horizontal scales, suggesting varying lengths of occupation for each of the cluster. It is therefore likely that such house clusters constituted the actual units of residential mobility during the Late Neolithic. The additional subdivision of individual house clusters by fences and trenches also may indicate that husbanded animals (e.g., cattle and pigs) were communally pooled within these intermediate units.

The corresponding lack of house clusters at Early Copper Age settlements may therefore suggest a decrease in the complexity of village structure during that period, and a shift from resource pooling within house clusters to pooling throughout the entire settlement.

Settlement units

The size and organization of Late Neolithic and Early Copper Age settlements within the study area is based upon the extensive information presented in the MRT volumes (see Ecsedy et al. 1982;

Jankovich et al. 1989), and on fieldwork conducted by the Körös Regional Archaeological Project in 1998 (see Parkinson 1999:197-210).

Late Neolithic settlements

The 34 Late Neolithic sites within the study area range in areal extent from less than 0.1 ha to more than sixty hectares (see Parkinson 1999:338). This range is somewhat deceptive, for the two largest sites each have significant Early Neolithic (Körös Culture) habitations, which frequently occur as dispersed low-density sherd scatters spread over very large areas. While the mean size of the Late Neolithic sites (including the two large outliers) is 5.25 ha, the median size—which is less affected by the large outliers—is only 1.95 ha. If the two large sites are excluded from the analysis (Fig. 3A), then the mean drops to 2.28 ha and the median to 1.51 ha. These figures are surprisingly low for the Late Neolithic, especially given the sort of size exaggeration one would expect based upon Raczky's investigations at Öcsöd-Kováshalom (Raczky et al. 1985), which suggests that surface scatters should be deceptively larger than the actual sizes of the subsurface distributions.

Although the distribution of Late Neolithic settlement size estimates is not strongly bimodal, there is a break in the distribution between sites smaller than four hectares and those larger. Makkay (1982, Chapter 11) has suggested that an integrated site hierarchy may have existed during the Late Neolithic in regions such as Szarvas. Sherratt (1997b) has argued for a similar pattern in Dévaványa. It is possible that such a hierarchical distribution may exist for four or five regions within the study area, and while a size hierarchy may exist within each of these individual regions, no such hierarchy can be argued as a general pattern that extends across the entire study area. This is most likely due to the fact that tell sites, which are not very large in areal extent, tend to function in a manner similar to larger 'supersites'. This is discussed further below.

Early Copper Age settlements

Surprisingly, the patterns in site size established during the Late Neolithic change very little during the Early Copper Age, despite an order-of-magnitude increase in the number of sites within the study area (from 34 to 243). The dramatic increase in the number of Early Copper Age sites notwithstanding (n=243), the mean size is 2.9 ha, and the median is 1.54 ha. If the two large outliers, which have substantial Early Neolithic habitations, are excluded from the analysis, then the mean drops to 2.52 and the median to 1.48 (Fig. 3B). In neither case are these numbers significantly different from those of the Late Neolithic. There is a small break in the size distribution just below 4 ha—at a point similar to that witnessed during the Late Neolithic, suggesting perhaps a bimodal distribution. However, the small size of the gap in the distribution (ca. 0.25 ha) during both periods suggests that the bimodality is more likely the result of sampling and/or recording strategies rather than an actual social difference. Rank/size graphs maintain similar profiles during both periods, retaining a distinctively primate shape (see Parkinson 1999:340).

A small number of Early Copper Age sites within the study area are single component (*n*=28) and allow a more accurate estimation of site size for this period. If only the single component sites are included in the analysis, the mean size drops to 0.87 ha, and the median to 0.61 ha (std. dev. = 0.82 ha). The only outlier is just over 4 ha in size. While this distribution may lead one to suggest that the size of Early Copper Age sites is, on average, much smaller than that indicated by the entire sample, including multi-period sites, it must be kept in mind that larger sites are also more likely to have other periods represented on their surface. In other words, the reason that the single component Early Copper Age sites are smaller may simply be because the larger Early Copper Age sites are more likely to have other periods represented.

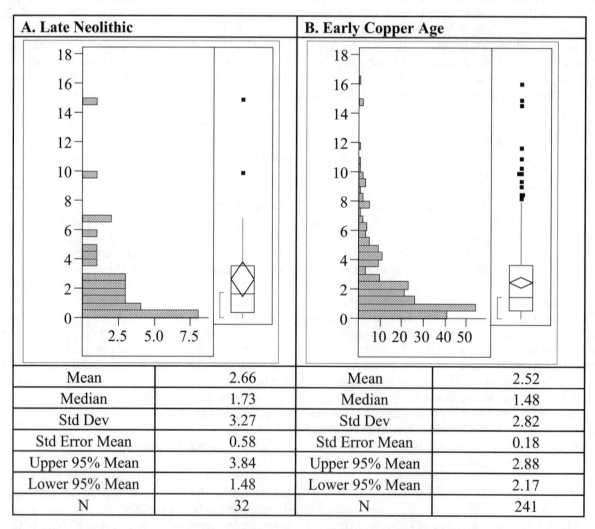

A. Late Neolithic		B. Early Copper Age	
Mean	2.66	Mean	2.52
Median	1.73	Median	1.48
Std Dev	3.27	Std Dev	2.82
Std Error Mean	0.58	Std Error Mean	0.18
Upper 95% Mean	3.84	Upper 95% Mean	2.88
Lower 95% Mean	1.48	Lower 95% Mean	2.17
N	32	N	241

Fig. 3. Histogram of site sizes by period in the study area in hectares. Sites over 20 ha excluded. Means diamonds indicate mean and 95% confidence intervals. Quantile boxes indicate median and upper and lower quantiles.

Changes in settlement organization

The various changes in settlement organization that differentiate Late Neolithic from Early Copper Age sites suggest not a shift in site size, but rather a change in the intensity and duration of site use during the two periods. Although Late Neolithic sites are not considerably larger in horizontal extent, they likely were more intensively occupied than Early Copper Age sites. Not only were Late Neolithic settlements more densely packed with houses and settlement clusters, they also seem to have been occupied for longer periods of time. In this sense, they tend to exhibit a sort of temporal hierarchy in site size, with those sites that were repeatedly occupied for long periods of time developing into tells, and those occupied for shorter periods of time remaining small horizontal (or 'flat') settlements. Although in some regions a site hierarchy based upon site size can be discerned during the Late Neolithic (see, for example, Makkay 1982, Chapter 11), tells are not always large in areal extent. While they were certainly exceptional features of the Late Neolithic landscape, tell sites frequently are much smaller (in horizontal extent) than their 'flat' contemporaries. As will be demonstrated in the following section, Late Neolithic settlement clusters are just as frequently located around tell sites as they are around large 'horizontal' settlements, or 'supersites' (see Sherratt 1997:306).

During the Early Copper Age, the critical shift in settlement organization does not seem to have been related to a change in the overall size of the settlements, but to a change in this dynamic system of site occupation strategies and intensity. In contrast to the Late Neolithic, Early Copper Age sites were occupied less intensively, by fewer co-residential units, and for shorter periods of time. All of this points to a more mobile site use strategy during the Early Copper Age.

Settlement clusters and superclusters

The definition of settlement clusters within the study area was approached in two ways, using two analytical methods that gave precedence to different types of information. The first of these gave priority to the spatial distribution of sites within the study area. Having identified patterns in the spatial distribution of the sites in the study area, patterns were then identified based upon those groupings. The second method gave site size high-

est priority. Having ranked the sites based upon size, patterns were then identified based upon the distribution of sites of different rank. The first method proved far more effective in generating settlement clusters that correspond to credible, realistic units.

Within the spatially-biased method, clusters were defined initially by calculating the relative densities of sites across a grid the size of the study area. This was accomplished by calculating the nonparametric bivariate density of the east (x) and north (y) coordinates of the site centroids (in meters) of different period sites, regardless of size, or type (see, for example, Fig. 4). The relative densities then were generated for each point (i.e., each x and y value) on a grid by calculating the weighted average of points in the neighborhood, where the weights decline with distance. Estimates calculated in this manner are called kernel smoothers (see Sall and Lehman 1996:302).

The result is a contour map that shows those areas where the points (in this case, the sites) are most dense. The contours are calculated according to the quantiles, where a certain percent of the data fall outside each contour curve. In this case, the contours are calculated at 10% intervals. Thus, the outermost contour line circumscribes 90% of the sample, the next 80%, etc. While this method does not take into account changes in landform, and therefore would not be reliable in an area with extreme changes in vertical topography, it works quite well in the flat floodplain of the Alföld.

Having calculated modal density clusters for each period according to the method described above, these were then plotted using a vector-based GIS program (MapInfo 4.0) containing surface information entered from the 1:100,000 soil maps associated with the MRT surveys (Ecsedy et al. 1982; Jankovich et al. 1989) to discern whether they related to any geomorphological features. The site size and type information was then analyzed for each cluster, and the clusters were then redefined based upon their distribution within particular geomorphological microregions (e.g., river drainages or soil types), the distribution of site sizes within each cluster, and the distribution of different site types (e.g., tells, roundels, cemeteries), within each cluster. This method, which tempers a purely objective statistical approach with a more subjective (and thereby better-informed) interaction with the data, proved quite effective in defining settlement clusters in the prehistoric landscape.

William A. Parkinson

Late Neolithic settlement clusters

The Late Neolithic sites in the study area distribute into two large superclusters separated by the 90% density contour (Figs. 4 and 5). The distance separating the eastern and western groups is roughly 30 km, and only one site is located between the superclusters. Interestingly, Jankovich et al. (1989:219) note that the material collected from this site dates either to the late Szakálhát (late Middle Neolithic) or to the earliest phase of the Tisza culture, further reinforcing the interpretation. Although there is only one cluster discernible within the western supercluster, two discrete clusters can be defined within the eastern group by the 50–40% contours. This results in three site clusters within two larger groups, or superclusters. If these clusters are examined more closely, it becomes clear that the eastern supercluster can be further subdivided into three or more discrete clusters (Fig. 4). Three of these smaller clusters within the eastern group of Late Neolithic sites contain tell sites that are located in different river valleys, and two of these clusters have sites that contain Late Neolithic burials.

In addition to these three clusters in the southern part of the eastern group, another can be discerned in the northwestern part of the study area around the large site of Dévaványa 9 (Sártó-Sziget)—a large horizontal site that covers some 14 ha (Fig. 5; Ecsedy et al. 1982; Sherratt 1984:35). The sites included in this cluster have been tentatively based upon their co-occurrence on the alkaline loess that forms the core of the Dévaványa plain, in a previous drainage of the Régi-Berettyó. Although no tell site is identifiable in this region, the large site at Sártó seems to stand out from the others in the region, and in many respects shares several of the characteristics of tells. Like the tell sites in the other clusters, it is located nearest to the river, and has substantial earlier occupations. No burials or cemeteries have been recorded within this cluster. While other clusters also appear on the density contour map of the eastern group, they do not exhibit any internal patterning in site size, site form, or geomorphological distribution.

The largest, clearest, and most discretely-defined cluster of the Late Neolithic is located near Szarvas in the western group (Fig. 5). This cluster has received much attention in the past, and frequently is cited as the idealized model for the Late Neolithic settlement patterning in the Great Hungarian Plain (see, for example, Makkay 1982, Chapter 11)—that of several sites organized around a large

'supersite'. Although no tell site has been identified within this cluster, Szarvas 1 seems to assume a role similar to that assumed by the 'supersite' Sártó in the Dévaványa cluster—it is much larger than the other Late Neolithic sites around it, and it is located very near the river. Interestingly, the burials that have been identified within this cluster are from Szarvas 131, the southernmost site in the cluster, and not from Szarvas 1.

Thus, it is possible to distinguish two different settlement patterns for the Late Neolithic within the study area. The first, characterized in the west (Szarvas) and northwestern (Dévaványa) clusters, includes a single, large, horizontal site and five to seven smaller sites. The two clusters of this type are considerably larger than the other clusters, and incorporate more total site area. By contrast, the other three clusters are much smaller, and are organized not around a large horizontal site, but around a smaller 'tell' site. These differences ostensibly could have resulted from post-depositional (erosional) processes, for there is a general tendency for Late Neolithic sites to be larger in the west, where the Körös may have been much more stable and less susceptible to seasonal flooding along shallow, yet widespread watercourses. Nevertheless, it is tempting to suggest that there may have been two different settlement patterns at work during the Late Neolithic—one tell-centered, incorporating a smaller area and fewer sites, and one 'supersite'-centered, incorporating a larger area and more sites. Whether these were contemporary systems that coexisted in the landscape must await future analysis and additional research.

In much the same way that the lower-order coresidential units (i.e., households and neighborhoods) of the Late Neolithic exhibit a high degree of structural complexity, so too do the settlement clusters. At least two degrees of clustering are exhibited by Late Neolithic sites in the study area. At one level, the individual sites themselves group into small clusters that are tethered to a 'supersite' or tell. At another level, these clusters themselves are organized into two discrete superclusters that are separated by a large unoccupied area. The absence of sites in this area does not seem to be related to geomorphology, for the surface sediments in that area are roughly the same as they are elsewhere. And the region certainly was inhabited during the earlier Neolithic and during the later Copper Age (see Jankovich et al. 1989: Maps 1 and 3). It is therefore likely that this region served as some sort of economic or social boundary zone during the Late Neolithic.

Early Copper Age settlement clusters

During the Early Copper Age, the few previously discretely-defined clusters of the Late Neolithic give way to several larger, more diffuse clusters that at first glance appear to bleed together to form an almost incomprehensible smear across the landscape (Figs. 6 and 7). One cause of this dramatic change is the simple increase in number of sites during this period. The 700% increase in site number—from 34 to 243—experienced during the transition to the Copper Age undoubtedly plays a large role in the change in distribution. Nevertheless, upon closer scrutiny several clusters can be

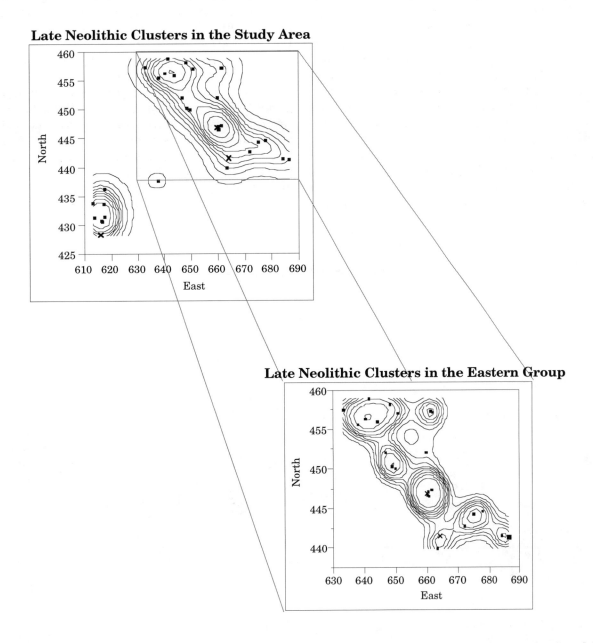

Fig. 4. Nonparametric quantile density clusters for Late Neolithic sites in the study area (top) and in the Eastern Group (bottom right). Each of the contours show paths of equal density. Density is estimated for each point on the grid by taking a weighted average of points in the neighborhood, where the weights decline with distance. The density contours are calculated according to quantiles in 10% intervals. X and Y refer to real kilometers north and east on the 1967 Hungarian Topographic Grid system.

discerned. To some extent, the distribution of these clusters across the Early Copper Age landscape exhibits a degree of internal consistency, but it is only when it is compared with the Late Neolithic pattern that it can be understood fully.

The density contour map of the Early Copper Age (Fig. 6) divides the sites into two large groups that are much less clearly-defined than the Late Neolithic superclusters. Not only are the two groups less dense, but the unoccupied area that separates them is considerably smaller. If each of these groups is analyzed at a finer scale, then the western group can be subdivided into three relatively discrete clusters; and the eastern group into several more diffuse clusters. Although the two clusters that had been identified in the western group distribute into three clusters at this level, the sites in the eastern group fall into at least five clusters that exceed the 70% density contour.

Upon closer inspection, several trends within and between these clusters emerge. The sites in the western group are distributed into three discrete clusters separated by 5–7 km of unoccupied tracts of land (Figs. 6 and 7). Each of these clusters most likely corresponds to a previous meander loop of the Harmas-Körös. The distribution of sites in the eastern group is much more complicated. Although it is possible to discern several smaller clusters that correspond roughly to those indicated by the density contours, several of these do not exhibit any internally coherent patterning in site size, type, or location. While this may, in itself, turn out to be a very interesting aspect of the distribution, it is not a very satisfying analytical result. But if the distribution of Early Copper Age sites is viewed in light of the preceding Late Neolithic clusters, several interesting patterns emerge, and the eastern group can be divided into at least seven diffuse clusters that are separated from each other by only a couple kilometers. Each cluster in that group also seems to be associated with an individual defunct meander loop of the Körös (Fig. 7).

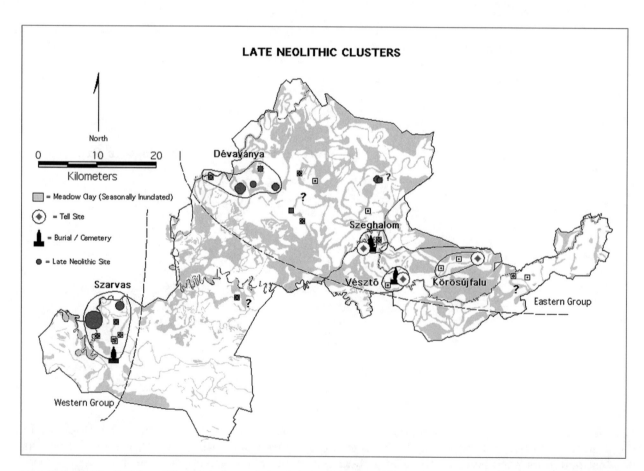

Fig. 5. Late Neolithic settlement clusters in the study area. Sites are represented by dark gray circles and are weighted by size. Note the two superclusters that separate the Eastern and Western Groups, and the tendency for sites to be organized into discrete clusters around tells or 'supersites.'

412

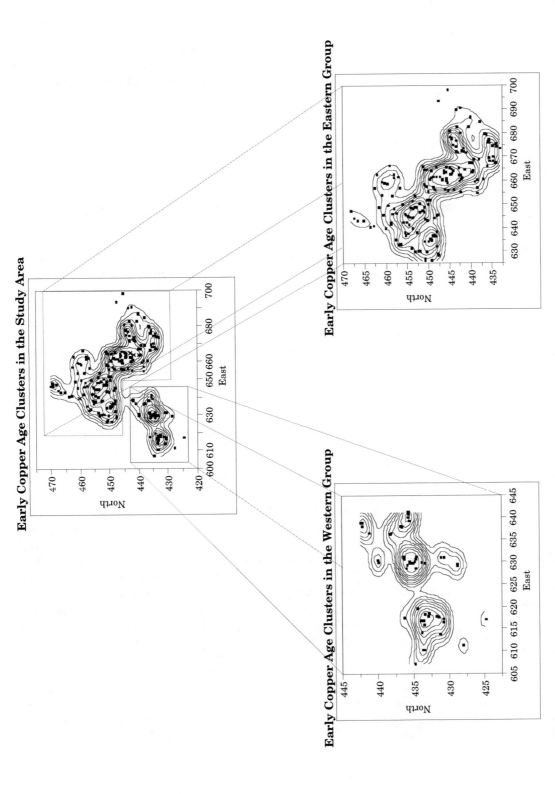

Fig. 6. Nonparametric quantile density clusters for Early Copper Age sites (indicated as dots) in the study area (top) and in the Eastern (bottom right) and Western (bottom left) Groups Each of the contours show paths of equal density. Density is estimated for each point on the grid by taking a weighted average of points in the neighborhood, where the weights decline with distance. The density contours are calculated according to quantiles in 10% intervals. X and Y refer to real kilometers north and east on the 1967 Hungarian Topographic Grid system.

Changes in settlement clusters

Two patterns characterize the settlement pattern of the Early Copper Age: the foundation of new site clusters in previously uninhabited (or sparsely inhabited) microregions, and the expansion of previously-existing Late Neolithic clusters over a larger area. Overlying these two patterns is a more general tendency towards diffusion, making all of the clusters less discrete and closer together.

The foundation of new clusters occurs throughout the entire study area. Within the western group, two new clusters form in Endrd and southern Gyoma. Within the eastern group, the entire Dévaványa plain becomes dotted with sites, and several areas that had previously been uninhabited (e.g., in Okány) are reoccupied for the first time since the Middle Neolithic. The foundation of sites in areas where none existed during the Late Neolithic is to be expected, given the dramatic increase in the number of sites dating to the Early Copper Age. But what is particularly surprising is the tendency of these sites to form definite, albeit somewhat diffuse, clusters.

In addition to the tendency of Early Copper Age sites to form diffuse clusters in areas that previously had been unoccupied, there is also a tendency for those clusters that had been established during the Late Neolithic to persist and expand in size. Almost without exception, those clusters that are located in regions where Late Neolithic clusters had been located tend to be larger than those that are created anew, suggesting that a certain amount of in situ expansion had occurred in those areas.

The distribution of cemeteries and burials during the Early Copper Age is, with a single exception (in North Gyoma), also restricted to those regions that previously had been occupied during the Late Neolithic—the Szeghalom, Vésztő and Dévaványa clusters all contain sites with burials or cemeteries. While this is due largely to the relative intensity of excavation in different parts of the study area, there may have been a tendency for burials and cemeteries to be located in those areas where clusters had been established for a considerable period of time. At least some degree of continuity can be assumed, for each of the Late Neolithic clusters contain at least one site that was reinhabited during the Early Copper Age.

The picture that emerges for the Early Copper Age is, in many ways, much more fluid than it had been during the Late Neolithic. Not only are there more sites and site clusters than there had been during the Late Neolithic, the clusters themselves tend to be larger, and closer together during the Early Copper Age. The essential difference between the two periods seems to be related to a shift in the nature of settlement organization. Whereas the Late Neolithic clusters were each organized around tell sites or large horizontal settlements, no such pattern exists during the Early Copper Age. Although clusters sometimes occur around tell sites, the large 'supersites' of the Late Neolithic generally fall into disuse. The sites included in the more diffuse clusters of the Early Copper Age were not tethered to such focal points in the landscape.

It already has been established that settlement patterns during the Late Neolithic are indicative of a moderate degree of residential mobility (see Whittle [1997] for a discussion of mobility during the Neolithic). Even the tripartite typological scheme that Kalicz and Raczky (1987a) have proposed for Late Neolithic settlements (i.e., 'tells', 'tell-like mounds', and 'horizontal settlements') alludes to the relative frequency with which such mobility occurred during that period. Those sites that were smaller and more intensively occupied for longer periods of time formed tells. Those that were larger and less intensively inhabited formed 'horizontal settlements'. As Raczky (1987) has demonstrated at the site of Öcsöd-Kováshalom (see also Raczky et al. 1985), the degree of residential mobility exhibited at even a single site during the Late Neolithic was highly variable, and different parts of a single settlement may have been inhabited with varying degrees of intensity. This highly dynamic system of mobility and intensity of site use carries over to the regional level as well. But rather than having a few residential foci within sites that are more intensively occupied for longer periods of time, specific sites tend to be more intensively occupied for longer periods of time. The smaller of these, that had been occupied during earlier periods, formed vertically-stratified tells such as Vésztő-Mágor and Szeghalom-Kovácshalom. The larger sites formed horizontal 'supersites', such as Dévaványa-Sártó and Szarvas 1. These intensively occupied sites form the focal point around which residential mobility occurred during the Late Neolithic.

The critical difference between the Late Neolithic pattern and that of the Early Copper Age is, therefore, not the absence of large sites or tell sites, but the failure of such sites to play a central role in the organization of the settlement system across the prehistoric landscape. It is as though the pattern of residential mobility that had characterized the region during the Late Neolithic was expanded in space and increased in frequency. In the absence of a central site that served to tether settlement location and relocation within a defined region, even a slight increase in residential mobility during the Early Copper Age would result in the unconstrained movement of new sites into previously uninhabited regions, forming new clusters in areas where none had existed, and expanding those that had been established previously.

The end result was a system of integration that was considerably less complexly-structured than its Late Neolithic predecessor. The absence of such structural complexity rings through all of the lower-order integrative units of Early Copper Age society (i.e., households, neighborhoods, and settlements), and continues at this regional level.

But while the Early Copper Age pattern is less complexly-structured than the Late Neolithic, it is not entirely without structure. The sites continue to distribute into clusters, as they did during the Late Neolithic. The main difference is that they tend to be larger in spatial extent, to contain more sites, and to be more diffuse. A good deal of this patterning can be attributed to the dramatic increase in site number during the Early Copper Age, and a factor most likely related to an increase in the frequency of site relocation throughout the period. But a certain amount of the Early Copper Age pattern is also due to the absence of a focal site that served to tether settlement relocation to specific places in the landscape.

Integrative units—Discussion

An idealized structural model of Late Neolithic social organization within the study area would include those integrative units outlined in Table 3. The table lists the associated material correlates of each unit, the possible social groups to which they may correspond, and the relative numbers of the units included at each level.

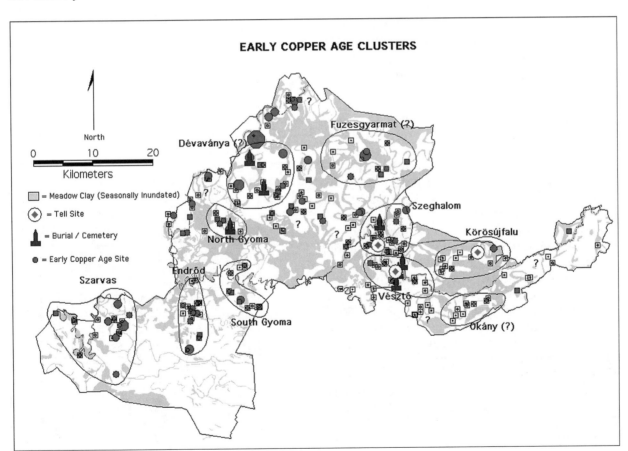

Fig. 7. Early Copper Age settlement clusters in the study area. Sites are represented by dark gray circles and are weighted by size. In contrast to the Late Neolithic, the clusters of this period are more diffuse, and closer together.

415

By comparison to a similar model for the Early Copper Age (Table 4), the Late Neolithic is exceptional in several respects. Not only are more integrative levels represented within the model, but each level tends to exhibit more inherent structural organization, subsuming more—and more complexly-structured—integrative units at each level. From the organization of the household unit, which corresponds to the multi-roomed house or longhouse, to the organization of the superclusters, which include several discrete site clusters, the Late Neolithic is characterized by a high degree of structural complexity. This high degree of structural complexity has several implications with regards to the manner in which different social processes would have occurred within the mixed hunting/fishing/farming/husbanding economy of the period.

That two or more individual family groups, probably nuclear families, lived within each longhouse is indicated by the presence of two or more hearths within each longhouse, and by the presence of ovens in each room of the multi-roomed structures. By contrast, grain-storage pits tend to be associated with the entire structure, or with the house cluster, and not with the particular hearths or ovens. This would suggest that while the preparation of, and most likely the production of, food occurred primarily within each of the smaller units, pooling most likely occurred throughout the entire house or house cluster. Such a system is somewhat reminiscent of the Iroquoian longhouse system, within which paired groups of families resided in cubicles and shared a hearth within a compartment, while grain was stored at either end of the building (Snow 1994:40-51).

The grouping of these houses into clusters at some settlements may indicate the coresidential organization of different extended kin groups, such as lineages, within a single village. Such an organization was more likely lineage-based than moiety-based, since the clusters almost always occur in numbers greater than two (see Lowell 1996; Marcus and Flannery 1996). Similarly, since the clusters normally include only a handful of houses, they are likely not indicative of some larger social grouping, such as a 'band' or sub-tribal grouping.

The house compounds at sites such as Öcsöd-Kováshalom (Raczky et al. 1985; Raczky 1987b) frequently are surrounded by fences, suggesting that although food preparation (and, it is assumed, production) occurred at the domestic level, animals, and possibly some other resources may have been cooperatively kept within the house cluster. Sev-

Table 3. Late Neolithic integrative units.

Integrative Unit	Material Correlate	Possible Social Correlates	Number per Larger Unit
Supercluster	Discrete clusters seperated by large unoccupied areas.	Band or Sub-Tribe	N/A
Settlement Cluster	Discrete groups of sites organized around a "supersite" or tell in a particular river drainage	Band or extended lineage	1-4 per group
Settlement	Tells, tell-like settlements, or horizontal settlements, sometimes fortified, some residential mobility	Lineage or extended lineage	2-7 per settlement cluster
Neighborhood	House clusters at some settlements	Extended family group or lineage	0(?)-5+ per settlement
Household	Multi-roomed house or longhouse	Extended family group or lineage	3-5 per cluster

Table 4. Early Copper Age integrative units.

Integrative Unit	Material Correlate	Possible Social Correlates	Number per Larger Unit
Supercluster	N/A, or larger than study area	N/A	N/A
Settlement Cluster	Diffuse group of sites located in a particular river drainage	Extended family group or lineage	N/A
Settlement	Primarily horizontal settlements, some tells occupied, increased residential mobility	Extended family group or lineage	9-27(?) per cluster
Neighborhood	N/A	N/A	N/A
Household	Small house	Nuclear family group or extended family group	1(?)-3 per settlement

eral clusters at Öcsöd share storage pits that may have been used to keep grain, and some longhouse clusters at Polgár-Csőszhalom share wells (Raczky et al. 1997).

The differential accumulation of house clusters, or 'residential foci', at Öcsöd also alludes to another important characteristic they share. The house compounds seem to have been the units that moved throughout the Late Neolithic. The moderate amount of residential mobility characteristic of the period likely occurred not through the wholesale movement of entire villages, but rather through the periodic movement of house clusters from village to village. This would account not only for the differential accumulation of habitation debris at sites such as Öcsöd, but also for the frequent disassociation between fortifications and settlement remains at sites such as Hódmezővásárhely-Gorzsa (Horváth 1987). In addition, such a system, which would leave large parts of settlements abandoned for long periods of time, also would allow for burials to be placed in unoccupied part of the settlement. Finally, it is likely that the units that had constituted the house cluster during the Late Neolithic became the structural equivalent of settlements during the Early Copper Age. This will be discussed to a greater extent below.

Although the size of Late Neolithic settlements within the study area is—very surprisingly—not significantly larger than their successors, they tend to be much more intensively occupied, and have much more vertical stratigraphy than later settlements. The small number that occur across the landscape speaks to the lengthy duration of their repeated occupation, despite the occasional movement of individual house clusters between settlements, as suggested at Öcsöd-Kováshalom (see Raczky 1985).

Late Neolithic site clusters are organized around tells or supersites, which functioned as focal points in the landscape. These focal sites were repeatedly or even continually occupied, and were without exception located near major watercourses. Such sites frequently yield more evidence of long-distance trade (e.g., cherts, *Spondylus*) than their smaller—or less intensively occupied—contemporaries (Sherratt 1997:307), suggesting that they served as focal points not only for the sites nearby, but also as points of contact from external social arenas. Unfortunately, the inter-annual relationship between such focal sites and others nearby remains unclear. Were the focal sites occupied perennially, and the other settlements in a cluster only seasonally? Or were the sites sequentially occupied, with specific ones returned to more frequently than others? Whatever the case may have been, sites within each cluster were socially tethered to the focal site.

Finally, each of the Late Neolithic clusters within the study area were organized into two superclusters that were separated by ca. 30 km of empty space. These large integrative units most likely corresponded to large social groups, such as 'bands' or sub-tribes. The actualization of such larger social groups into archaeologically identifiable units within the study area suggests an equally complex pattern of social integration, the specific mechanisms of which remain unclear, but which stand out significantly when compared to that of the Early Copper Age.

Early Copper Age integrative units

The situation changes dramatically during the Early Copper Age (Table 4). Nearly every coresidential unit undergoes a significant transformation in scale and organization. Whereas the Late Neolithic pattern was characterized by a high degree of structural complexity—incorporating increasingly complex integrative units—the Early Copper Age pattern is marked by its lack of such complex integration. Such a dramatic shift indicates a more fluid system, within which social boundaries were more permeable and flexible.

At even the most basic level—that of the household unit—the Early Copper Age marks a significant shift in organization. In contrast to the larger multi-roomed structures and longhouses that characterized the Late Neolithic, houses during the Early Copper Age are uniformly smaller and single-roomed. Such structures likely housed individual nuclear family groups, that may have been patrilocal (see Divale 1977; Ember 1973; Ember and Ember 1995; Hollinger 1995). The absence of ovens and hearths within the houses suggests that food preparation likely occurred outside the house, in a more communal environment within the settlement. This, combined with the absence of household clusters within Early Copper Age sites, suggests that food preparation and pooling occurred throughout the entire settlement. It is assumed that resource production was still normally conducted by each household within the settlement. This would all suggest that the Early Copper Age settlement had assumed a role similar to that performed by the Late Neolithic house cluster.

The increase in site number during the Early Copper Age is likely indicative of increased residential mobility. The expansion of settlements into previously unoccupied areas, and the failure of the diffuse Early Copper Age site clusters to exhibit any organization around a particular focal site, both suggest a more mobile system that was, in several respects, more fluidly distributed across the landscape. This fluidity is likely to be attributed to, on the one hand, a breakdown in previously-recognized social boundaries, and to an increase in the degree of residential mobility, on the other hand. While during the Late Neolithic residential mobility occurred within a well-defined area around a focal tell or supersite, during the Early Copper Age such mobility was not so spatially constrained. This points to an ongoing breakdown in social boundary maintenance, and to the lack of integrative units at this localized level.

If it were house clusters, and not entire sites, that formed the residentially-mobile units during the Late Neolithic, it could be that these units essentially had transformed into the settlements of the Early Copper Age. This transformation was likely the result of several processes, but it most likely was associated with a change in the basic mode of economic production, as indicated by the change in the organization of the household unit, and by the suggested relative increase in residential mobility.

The site clusters of the Early Copper age are close together, diffuse, and do not distribute into large superclusters as they did during the Late Neolithic. Unfortunately, the relative contemporaneity of sites within a cluster remains unclear. The clusters range in size from 9–27 sites, and it is unlikely that all were simultaneously occupied. The dramatic increase in number of sites per cluster (from 2–7 during the Late Neolithic), would suggest that much more sequential movement occurred during the Early Copper Age. Rather than periodically returning to the same sites, new sites were founded in areas that had previously been unoccupied.

Taken as a whole, the picture that emerges for the Early Copper Age is that of several small social groups (lineages or extended family groups) living in autonomous settlements that were relocated more frequently and not organized around a particular focal site. All of this suggests a relaxation of structural levels that had been actualized during the Late Neolithic, but which, I argue, became latent during the Early Copper Age. The result is that of a much less complexly-structured system within which social boundaries were more easily transcended. The degree to which interaction occurred across these boundaries is taken up in the following section.

Modeling Interaction During the Early Copper Age

This section uses stylistic information to model the degree of social interaction that occurred between the various integrative units throughout the study area during the Early Copper Age. In contrast to the previous section, which assessed integration *diachronically*, from the Late Neolithic through the Early Copper Age, the approach taken here is *synchronic* in nature, and attempts to assess the degree of interaction that occurred only during the Early Copper Age. While it would, of course, be ideal also to assess interaction during the Late Neolithic, the data for such analyses are currently unavailable. The data included in the analyses derive from two excavated sites—Vésztő-Mágor and Örménykút 13—and from surface contexts at 11 other Early Copper Age sites that were collected systematically during fieldwork in 1998 (see Parkinson 1999:197-216).

The analysis of different stylistic patterns throughout the study area was carried out by analyzing the relative distribution of high- and low-visibility attributes in surface and excavated assemblages from 13 sites located in different clusters throughout the study area. The attributes considered in the following analyses are listed in Table 5, along with their associated visibilities (for a detailed discussion, see Parkinson 1999:355-391). The visibilities assigned to the various attributes are based in part upon Carr's (1995:186) hierarchical model, in part upon Voss' (1982) reasonable assertion that nominal-scale variables are to be equated with highly-visible attributes and continuous variables are to be equated with poorly-visible attributes, and in part upon what is known about stylistic variability in Early Copper Age ceramic assemblages.

The distributions assigned to each attribute are based upon the relative occurrence of the attribute within and between sites from or near different clusters throughout the study area. Potential distributions range from uniform to discrete (Table 5). Although most attributes can be assigned a specific distribution, some attributes occur very infrequently, and their distribution is either ambiguous or unassignable.

Several of the attributes included in the analysis were influenced heavily by chronology and/or sample size and therefore could not be assigned a specific distribution. Nevertheless, an overall pattern that emerges from the data is one of overall homogeneity and uniformity throughout the study area, suggesting a high degree of continuous interaction throughout the entire region during the Early Copper Age. This is indicated by the tendency of most stylistic attributes to distribute uniformly or randomly both within and between clusters. On the other hand, some attributes—such as the frequency of incised decoration (Fig. 8) and everted rim length—allude to significant differences between sites located in the east and west of the study area. While these clinally-distributed patterns are based to a large extent upon the assemblage from the site of Örménykút 13—the sole representative of the western half of the study area—they nevertheless suggest that more active sorts of interaction may have been more spatially confined, and occurred on a more local level.

Finally, the distribution of attributes within the Vésztő cluster, and to some extent within the Okány and North Gyoma clusters, suggests a surprisingly low degree of interaction between sites located within a cluster. This is indicated by the random distribution of attributes between sites that are in very close spatial proximity to one another—a pattern that may be attributed to chronological factors related to periodic shifts in residential mobility between sites within a cluster. This also would suggest that the clusters themselves may have defined territories within which settlements were occasionally relocated.

Uniform and random distributions throughout the study area

Several of the attributes considered in the foregoing analysis exhibit a uniform or random distribution both within particular clusters and throughout the study area (Table 5). Although in several cases a particular attribute could be assigned either a definite uniform distribution or a definite random distribution, the sample sizes frequently were too small to permit an accurate distribution to be assigned. To a large extent, this is due to the fact that few clusters are represented by more than one or two sites. As a result, it frequently is impossible to determine whether a specific attribute patterns randomly or uniformly within (or between) the clusters.

The attributes that exhibit uniform and random distributions are of both high- and low-visibility, and generally relate to those stylistic attributes that also are characteristic of Tiszapolgár assem-

Table 5. Distributions of ceramic attributes included in analysis.

Attribute	Visibility	Distribution Within Clusters	Distribution Between Clusters	Affected by Chronology?
Open Vessel Types	High	Uniform	Uniform	N
Restricted/ Closed Vessl Types	High	Uniform	Uniform	Y?
Pedastalled Vessels	High	Random?	Clinal or Random?	N
Lug Decoration	Low?	Uniform	Uniform	N
Lug Shape	High	Uniform?	Random?	Y?
Lug Cross-Section	High	Uniform?	Uniform?	N?
Lug Height	Low	Uniform	Uniform	Y?
Lug Pierced	Low	Uniform	Uniform	Y?
Lug Location	High	Uniform	Clinal?	Y?
Incised Decoration	High	Uniform?	Clinal	N
Dotted-Incised	High	Uniform?	Clinal	N
Linear-Incised	High	Random?	Random?	Y?
Other Incised	High	Random	Random	N
Encrusted Decoration	High	Random	Random	N
Plastic Decoration	High	Random	Random	N
Pedastal Base Piercing	High	Random	Random	Y?
Base Pierce Size	Low	Random	Random	N?
Everted Rim Diameter	High	Uniform	Uniform?	N
Everted Rim Length	High	Uniform	Clinal?	N
Everted Rim Thickness	Low	Random	Random	N

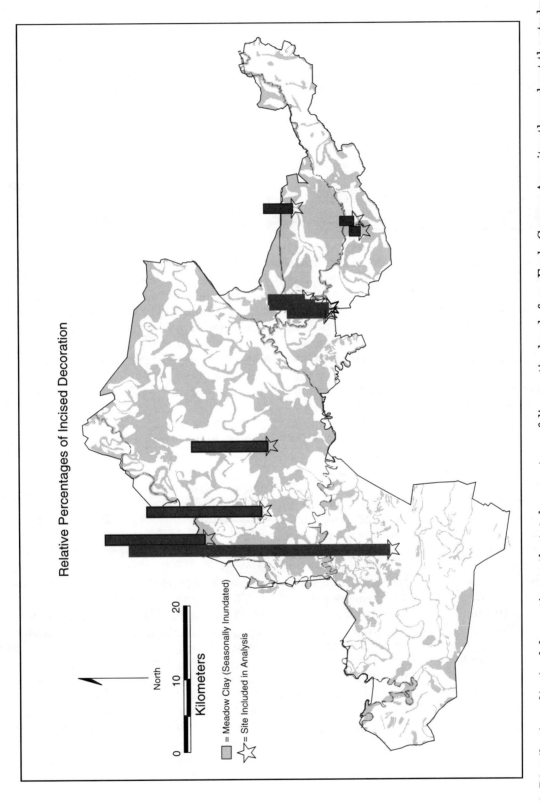

Fig. 8. Distribution of incised decoration as the total percentage of diagnostic sherds from Early Copper Age sites throughout the study area. The maximum percentage represented (i.e., the longest bar) is equal to 70% at Örménykút 13. Note the fall off in frequency of incised decoration to the east.

blages throughout the Great Hungarian Plain (e.g., vessel type). As such, their distribution most likely was generated by the same social processes that simultaneously create and define such large-scale 'horizons' in material culture throughout the world. Namely, by a continuous amount of low-level active interaction via trade, systems of kinship, and other shared cosmological beliefs that result in an expression of unity and cooperation.

Given the widespread distribution of these attributes throughout the entirety of the Great Hungarian Plain, it is perhaps necessary to rethink whether they should have been treated as high-visibility stylistic attributes at all. Their common occurrence would likely have been taken for granted by most of the people who used, saw, and traded them across the landscape.

In light of this, it is perhaps not surprising that nearly all of the low-visibility stylistic attributes were found to be distributed uniformly or randomly throughout the study area. The uniform distribution of low-visibility stylistic attributes, such as the frequency of lug decoration, is indicative of more passive forms of social interaction throughout the region. This includes less-structured contact and shared learning.

Those low-visibility attributes that exhibit random distributions within clusters are somewhat more surprising, and most likely indicate individual traditions of manufacture at a single settlement or a temporal discontinuity between sites. For example, the lug heights at Vésztő 15 are on average three to four mm smaller than those at Vésztő 20 and Körösladány 14. While this may be indicative of a chronological disjuncture, suggesting that Vésztő 20 is slightly earlier than the others, the overall similarity in lug shape and cross-section, between the sites, also can be interpreted as an indication that individually-learned habits of manufacture also may have been responsible.

Overall, the uniform and random distribution of these attributes is very much in line with what one would expect given the size of the study area, and the relatively loose structure of the diffuse integrative units involved, which themselves allude to a high degree of continuous interaction throughout the region.

Clinal and discrete distributions throughout the study area

A few attributes exhibit a distinctly clinal or discrete distribution across the study area, thus adding another level of interaction that can be superimposed above the low-level continuous interaction discussed above. The few attributes with these distributions are without exception high-visibility attributes (e.g., incised decoration, Fig. 8), suggesting that they are particularly well suited to marking expressions of social context and group affiliation. While the definition of these distributions is based in large part upon their relative occurrence at a single site—Örménykút 13—and is hindered by the lack of adequate samples from other sites in the western part of the study area, they nevertheless are striking inasmuch as they differ from the distribution of other attributes, such as lug decoration. Their distribution therefore warrants an interpretation in terms of social process, rather than in terms of chronology.

The high-visibility attributes that distribute clinally or discretely throughout the study area include: the frequency of incised—and in particular dotted-incised—decoration, the frequency of lug location, and variation in everted rim length. All of these attributes exhibit a considerable degree of variability in their distributions at different sites throughout the study area. Nevertheless, when taken as a whole, they may represent a general trend that marks differences between those sites in the eastern half of the study area and those in the western half.

Since the attributes in question cannot be allotted any purely functional qualities, it is unlikely that their distributions can be explained in terms of site function. Similarly, they do not seem to be related to chronology, and therefore are unlikely to be indicative of a temporal distinction. A more likely explanation for their distribution is that they were being used to mark social group identity, and their distribution may therefore be indicative of an interaction zone between two highly interacting, yet somehow socially distinct social groups.

This assertion is based upon the clinal distribution of dotted-incised decoration in assemblages throughout the study area, and assumes that the differences in the other high-visibility decorative attributes would have assumed a similar distribution were they also identifiable at more sites. Since dotted-incised decoration also may be an indication of encrusted decoration in Early Copper Age ceramic assemblages, this would make the absolute visibility of the attribute much more striking to the viewer and would have increased the degree to which vessels decorated in such a manner stood out from undecorated ones. Such high-visibility stylistic attributes are potentially extremely useful for encoding information that is designed to hit

422

a wide audience, and in this case may have been used to indicate either social group membership or other aesthetically-influenced traditions of manufacture that were restricted to neighboring or adjacent groups.

The clinal distribution of dotted-incised sherds in varying frequencies across the study area suggests either that the dotted-incised vessels were being produced somewhere to the west of the study area and either were being traded upstream (from west to east), or that they simply were being produced in significantly fewer quantities further to the east, perhaps because of a general lack of interaction at a further distance (Fig. 8). This latter interpretation could be extended to include patterns of intermarriage between neighboring groups.

In either scenario, the distribution is undoubtedly an indication of a fall-off of interaction at a distance, suggesting by proxy more intensive interaction occurring between neighboring or adjacent groups. While this conclusion is somewhat tentative, and certainly implies several testable hypotheses that need to be followed up in future research, it nevertheless adds a certain amount of dynamism that can used to understand the interactive relationships that existed between the various integrative units within the study area.

Distributions within clusters

Although it would have been ideal to discuss the distribution of attributes throughout several sites within several different clusters throughout the study area, few clusters produced more than one site with a ceramic assemblage large enough to ascertain such patterns. Nevertheless, the Vésztő cluster fortunately yielded three sites within which some general patterns can be established—Vésztő 15, Vésztő 20, and Körösladány 14. Vésztő 20 and Körösladány 14 appear to be more typical Tiszapolgár (i.e., small, 'flat') settlements, and Vésztő 15 (Vésztő-Mágor) is a tell site with an Early Copper Age cemetery that seems to date somewhat later than the settlement occupation levels.

The three sites exhibit overall homogeneity with regards to most high-visibility attributes and a high degree of heterogeneity with regard to some high-visibility attributes. But otherwise the distributions seem to be random between the sites. This is somewhat surprising given the close spatial proximity of the sites, and may be the result of small-scale temporal discontinuities between the occupations.

Although much less likely, the distribution also can be explained by a situation in which settlements that were close together exhibit subtle variations with regards to particular stylistic attributes. Such attributes, since intended for a limited audience, are likely to be much more subtle than the much more obvious ones (such as incised decoration) that are intended for a wider group. For example, the everted rim diameters from Vésztő 15 are on average 5 cm larger than those from Vésztő 20, and are significantly different according to a Student's t-test (t=1.97; Figs. 9 and 10). Since the two sites are less than 2 km from each other and are located on the same river, they almost certainly would have been closely related had they been occupied simultaneously. Therefore if the settlements were occupied simultaneously it is possible that this and other attributes, such as pedestal base pierce size, were subtle expressions of difference between these two closely related local groups, but were generally not recognizable to the greater population of the Körös valley.

It is much more likely that the sites were occupied sequentially by the same social group that over time came to be composed of different people who made their ceramics in slightly different ways yet, in the larger context of the region, maintained several traditions that distinguished them from those made further to the west.

Interaction–Discussion

Unfortunately, a detailed analysis of Late Neolithic interaction throughout the region was far beyond the scope of this chapter, and no direct comparisons can therefore be made between the two periods. Nevertheless, some basic comparisons can be drawn based upon the synthetic work of Kalicz and Raczky (1987a:14), who suggest that the sites in the eastern half of the study area mark the boundary zone between the Tisza and Herpály groups of the Late Neolithic (see Kalicz and Raczky 1987a:9). If this boundary zone can be assumed to have marked a significant break in interaction between the two groups during the Late Neolithic, as indicated by the significant differences expressed in the material culture of each group (see Kalicz and Raczky 1987a; Parkinson 1999:99-140), then the social boundary delineated by the distribution of stylistic attributes during the Early Copper Age may have been a remnant of that earlier one. But rather than being clearly defined and actively maintained, as it had been during the Late Neolithic, the boundary was considerably more diffuse and more permeable during the Early Copper Age. Such an interpretation would be very much in concert with the organization of integrative units during both periods. The implications of these changing patterns of interaction are discussed to a greater extent below.

Conclusions

This chapter set out to achieve two main goals. The primary goal was to gain an understanding of the various social changes that took place on the Great Hungarian Plain during the transition to the Copper Age, about 4,500 BC. The secondary, and more ambitious goal was to outline a theoretical and methodological approach that could be used to model long-term changes in tribal social organization. To this end, it was useful to assume a theoretical perspective that concentrates upon the structural organization of the society in question and attempts to model social organization along two discrete, yet intimately intertwined, analytical dimensions—integration and interaction. Within this approach, the dimension of integration attempts to measure the size, scale, and organization of individual social segments, or integrative units; and the dimension of interaction, on the other hand, attempts to outline the various social relationships within and between those units, thus

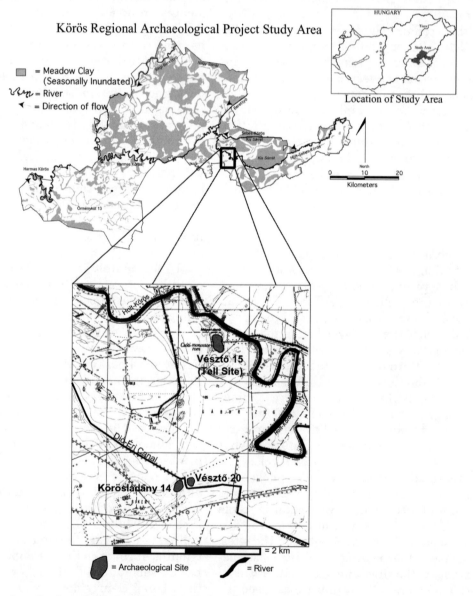

Fig. 9. Map showing the location of sites in the Vésztő Cluster.

adding a more dynamic quality to the model that allows one to demonstrate paths of structural continuity and discontinuity between the two periods. This, in turn, allows the various axes of social change to be identified more precisely.

In order to apply this theoretical and methodological perspective to the Late Neolithic and Early Copper Age of the Great Hungarian Plain, a research design was formulated to explore the dimensions of integration and interaction within a 2,000 km² area in the Körös River valley system. The dimension of integration was then modeled by analyzing the size, organization, and spatial distribution of houses, house-clusters, and settlements during different periods. The dimension of interaction was modeled by analyzing the distribution of a battery of stylistic variables in Early Copper Age ceramic assemblages at different sites throughout the study area.

The goal of the present section is to incorporate the results of those analyses into a coherent model that accurately describes the various social changes that occurred throughout the study area during the transition to the Copper Age, and to relate this to more general trends that occur throughout the region, and to similar processes documented in tribal societies in other geographic and temporal contexts.

Integrating integration and interaction

By comparing the size, scale, and organization of the individual integrative units to their structural equivalents in different periods, it is possible

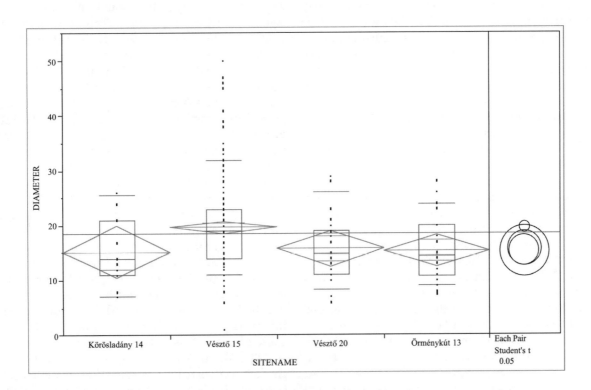

Comparisons for each pair using Student's t – t = 1.97				
Abs(Dif)-LSD	**Vésztő 15**	**Vésztő 20**	**Örménykút 13**	**Körösladány 14**
Vésztő 15	-1.55	0.39	1.14	-0.45
Vésztő 20	0.39	-4.71	-4.06	-5.26
Örménykút 13	1.14	-4.06	-4.13	-5.40
Körösladány 14	-0.45	-5.26	-5.40	-6.81

Fig. 10. Diameter of everted rims by site (in cms) for the three sites in the Vésztő Cluster (Körösladány 14, Vésztő 15, and Vésztő 20) and Örménykút 13, a site in the western half of the study area. Means diamonds show means and 95% confidence intervals. Quantile boxes show medians and quartiles. Note the significant difference between Vésztő 15 and the other two sites in the cluster.

to identify precise patterns of change and continuity in the actualized (i.e., the behaviorally-expressed) structure of the Körös Region during the transition to the Copper Age. By overlaying the patterns of interaction during the Early Copper Age on top of the various integration units that characterize the region, it is possible to gain an even more precise understanding of how the overall organization of the region changed about 4,500 BC.

The transition to the Copper Age is marked by an overall tendency towards fewer structural levels (Table 6). The transformation in the organization of the household unit—from the multi-roomed house or longhouse to the single-roomed house—is most likely associated with a change in the basic unit of production and/or pooling. Combined with the absence of a neighborhood unit during the Early Copper Age, this suggests that the Late Neolithic house clusters—and perhaps even the longhouses and multi-roomed structures themselves—were essentially transformed into the structural equivalent of settlements during the Early Copper Age. The collapsing, or coalescing, of these integrative levels into a single unit—the settlement—indicates that several structural levels that had been expressed during the Late Neolithic became latent and gave way to a less complexly-structured method of integration during the Early Copper Age.

A similar structural coalescence can be detected between the larger integrative units. The discrete clusters and superclusters of the Late Neolithic give way during the Early Copper Age to more, and more diffuse, site clusters throughout the study area. This can be attributed to the absence of a focal settlement—a tell or supersite—that served to tether site locations within a discretely-defined integrated system during the Late Neolithic. The overall result is a more fluid system within which social boundaries were much less concretely expressed and actively maintained.

The analysis of Early Copper Age interaction supports, and in many ways refines, several of these conclusions regarding the organization of integration throughout the study area. The analyses of stylistic attributes in Early Copper Age ceramic assemblages indicate a high degree of active and passive interaction throughout the entire study area. At the same time, the distribution of some attributes—for example, incised decoration—suggests that active interaction occurred more intensively between local groups, and their clinal distribution may be indicative of some sort of social-group boundary in or near the western part of the study area. This boundary may represent the remnants of the same social boundary that separated the Tisza and Herpály Groups during the Late Neolithic. But in its Early Copper Age incarnation, the boundary became less actively maintained and more permeable.

Along with the dissolution and coalescence of the integrative units that served to structure social relations within smaller subregions during the Late Neolithic came a tendency for interaction to occur more freely across those boundaries during the Early Copper Age. This suggests a significant shift in the focal levels of integration at the beginning of the Early Copper Age—from the complex village and subregion during the late Neolithic, to the hamlet and Plain during the Early Copper Age.

The various transformations in social organization that marked the transition to the Copper Age are clarified somewhat by comparison to those that mark the transition to the Middle Copper Age in the region (Table 7; Parkinson 1999:308-318). In contrast to the structural changes that occurred during the Late Neolithic—Early Copper Age transition, which affected the organization of nearly every integrative unit, only the higher-order integrative units seem to have undergone significant reorganization during the Middle Copper Age (Table 8). While the organization of the household and settlement remained essentially the same during that period, there was a subtle, yet marked reversion towards a more complexly-structured system of integration, within which settlements were again organized into clusters and superclusters tethered to specific focal points throughout the landscape. This would suggest the actualization of structural levels that had been latent during the Early Copper Age, and the reemergence of integrative mechanisms that again served to integrate communities at the local level.

The Middle Copper Age bears several formal characteristics to both periods that preceded it. At the more basic level, Middle Copper Age houses, settlements, and cemeteries are organized in a manner similar to their Early Copper Age counterparts. At another scale, the complexly-structured organization of those settlements across the landscape is more reminiscent of the Late Neolithic.

Explaining the transition to the Early Copper Age

Several authors have proposed a variety of causes to explain the transition to the Copper Age in the Carpathian Basin (for a recent discussion,

Table 6. Comparative analysis of integrative units and patterns of interaction - Late Neolithic and Early Copper Age.

Integrative Unit	Late Neolithic Organization	Early Copper Age Organization	Inferred Changes in Social Organization
Supercluster	Discrete settlement clusters separated by large unoccupied areas.	–	Lack of regional integrative mechanism unifying clusters, and in the relaxation of previously-recognized social boundaries.
Settlement Cluster	Discrete groups of sites organized around a supersite or tell in a particular river drainage.	More and more diffuse groups of sites located in a particular river drainage.	Lack of regional integrative mechanism resulting in the foundation of new clusters, and in the relaxation of previously-recognized social boundaries.
Settlement	Tells, tell-like settlements or horizontal settlements, sometimes fortified, thick deposits, suggesting intensive habitation.	Primarily horizontal settlements, some tells occupied, thinner settlements, suggesting less intensive habitation.	More frequent relocation of settlement.
Neighborhood	House Clusters	–	Change in productive and/or pooling unit?
Household	Multi-roomed house or longhouse.	Single-roomed house.	Change in productive and/or pooling unit?
Patterns of Interaction	Intensive interaction over smaller area.	Extensive interaction over larger area.	Relaxation of social boundaries.

Table 7. Comparative analysis of integrative units and patterns of interaction - Early and Middle Copper Age.

Integrative Unit	Early Copper Age Organization	Middle Copper Age Organization	Inferred Changes in Social Organization
Supercluster	–	Diffuse groups of clusters	Possible recognition of regional integrative mechanism resulting in the maintenance and/or creation of social boundaries between clusters.
Settlement Cluster	Diffuse groups of sites located in a particular river drainage.	Fewer, and more discrete groups of sites, possibly organized around a large site	Possible recognition of regional integrative mechanism resulting in the maintenance and/or creation of social boundaries between clusters.
Settlement	Primarily horizontal settlements, some tells occupied.	Primarily horizontal settlements, some tells occupied, 1 multi-ditched "roundel" in study area	–
Neighborhood	–	–	–
Household	Single-roomed house.	Single-roomed house?	–
Patterns of Interaction	Extensive Interaction.	Extensive Interaction?	

Table 8. Comparative analysis of integrative units and patterns of interaction - Late Neolithic through Middle Copper Age.

Integrative Unit	Late Neolithic Organization	Early Copper Age Organization	Middle Copper Age Organization
Supercluster	Discrete settlement clusters separated by large unoccupied areas.	–	Diffuse groups of clusters
Settlement Cluster	Discrete groups of sites organized around a supersite or tell in a particular river drainage.	More, and more diffuse groups of sites located in a particular river drainage.	Fewer, and more discrete groups of sites, possibly organized around a large site
Settlement	Tells, tell-like settlments or horizontal settlements, sometimes fortified, thick deposits, suggesting intensive habitation.	Primarily horizontal settlements, some tells occupied, thinner settlements, suggesting less intensive habitation.	Primarily horizontal settlements, some tells occupied, 1 multi-ditched "roundel" in study area
Neighborhood	House Clusters	–	–
Household	Multi-roomed house or longhouse.	Single-roomed house.	Single-roomed house?
Patterns of Interaction	Intensive interaction over small area?	Extensive interaction over a larger area.	Extensive interaction over a largr area.

429

see Bánffy 1994, 1995; see also Parkinson 1999:430-435). The transition to the Copper Age in the Great Hungarian Plain is frequently associated with an increased reliance upon the domestic cattle (see Bökönyi 1988:115), and with an overall tendency towards a more pastoral economy due in part to the near extinction of wild aurochs within the region (see Bognár-Kutzián 1972:163). Such an explanation is certainly not at odds with the model of social organization proposed here, and would go a long way towards explaining the reorganization of different integrative units during the Early Copper Age.

The transformation in the organization of the immediate coresidential unit to that of a smaller unit (nuclear family?) is itself indicative of a change in the basic productive and/or pooling unit of society. An increased reliance upon an economic system centered more around animal husbandry than around intensive or extensive agriculture could therefore explain such a change. The increase in number and stratigraphically-shallow nature of Early Copper Age settlements are almost certainly indicative of a much higher degree of settlement mobility during the period. This too could be explained by an economic shift towards pastoralism, wherein more frequent settlement relocations may have been necessitated due to overgrazing the steppe grasses (Chang and Koster 1986).

While this economic explanation can account for the organizational changes in these smaller integrative units, it is unclear whether it also can explain the transformations that occurred towards the upper levels of the regional structure—in the reorganization of the settlement clusters and superstructures throughout the region.

The key shift in the organization of settlement clusters during the Early Copper Age seems to be related primarily to the absence of focal settlement—a tell or supersite—that previously served to tether settlement relocation to a few specific locations in the landscape. While an increase in settlement mobility as the result of an economic shift towards pastoralism can explain the increase in the number of sites during the Early Copper Age, it does not necessarily explain their tendency to be relocated in new locations throughout the landscape. Thus, it would seem that this shift may be related to an overall breakdown of higher-order integrative at the regional level. This pattern repeats itself at a larger scale, as reflected by the dissolution of the social boundaries that had subdivided the Plain into two or three groups during the Late Neolithic.

While such patterns indicate less complexly structured integration at the regional level, they may be indicative of more overall integration across the entire Alföld. Although the inferred shift in the basic economic unit—from an extended family unit to a nuclear family unit—can account for the changes in house and settlement form, it is not clear why a shift towards a more pastoral economic base would necessitate such a shift within higher order integrative institutions.

One possible explanation could relate to the differential acquisition and production of 'wealth' within different social structures. Since within a pastoral economic system individual nuclear families can be less dependent upon extended relationships for communal agricultural labor (e.g., clearing fields), they are offered more opportunities to produce and acquire wealth independently of the greater kin group. In such situations, the leaders of individual nuclear families are likely to subvert traditional practices and to assert their independence by setting off on their own. This, in turn, is likely to result in the breakdown of contacts at the local level. Conversely, the breakdown of integrative mechanisms at the local level is more likely to necessitate a greater degree of overall integration at a larger geographic scale. In the absence of a well-structured social network at the local level, it would be necessary to extend alliances further afield to provide some degree of risk buffering—a pattern that is likely to result in the relaxation and less active maintenance of local social boundaries. In terms of material culture, the relaxation of these social boundaries is likely to result in a much more homogeneous region made up of several smaller local areas that vary clinally, but which is not readily distinguishable from the greater whole.

Thus, in much the same way that the fur trade was largely responsible for the breakdown of the longhouse-based system in the eastern United States (see Hollinger 1995; Snow 1996), so too a shift towards increased pastoralism may have been responsible for the social changes that occurred on the Great Hungarian Plain, ca. 4,500 BC.

Long-term perspective on tribal social change

The overall picture that emerges from this analysis of the various social changes that occurred on the Great Hungarian Plain during the transition to the Early Copper Age suggest that of a society whose social organization subsumed within it a considerable degree of structural flexibility. By analyzing this social organization along the two discrete, yet intimately intertwined, dimensions of integration and interaction it has been possible to delineate precisely those structural features that underwent significant transformations over time, and those that did not. The goal has been to provide an approach to modeling long-term social changes in tribal societies that can measure continuity and change in several different social dimensions. The extent to which this method has proven itself more useful than alternative strategies to modeling tribal social organization will be determined by the reader.

The trend I document for the transition to the Copper Age is but a single occurrence in the greater temporal and geographic context of the Carpathian Basin. In fact, the basic pattern—from a few, complexly-structured integrative units interacting intensively over small areas (in the Late Neolithic) to less complexly-structured integrative units interacting extensively over a larger area (in the Early Copper Age)—repeats itself throughout the prehistory of the Plain at least two times from the Neolithic through the Bronze Age. This phenomenon of tribal 'pulsing' or 'cycling', has been documented in tribal societies in a wide variety of historical and geographic contexts, and seems to occur at varying temporal frequencies (Fowles 1997 and this volume, Chapter 2; Parkinson 1999, and this volume, Chapter 1). Although this process is reminiscent of the 'cycling' commonly discussed in chiefdoms (e.g. Anderson 1990) and even states (e.g., Marcus 1993), the absence of any institutionalized central authority allows this process to occur much more fluidly in tribal societies.

Throughout the Early and Middle Neolithic on the Great Hungarian Plain, settlements tend to be small and dispersed. By the end of the Late Neolithic, complexity in regional integration reaches the heretofore unparalleled scale discussed above. At the beginning of the Copper Age, this pattern reverts to a scale of dispersal unknown to the region since the Middle Neolithic, but with one major change—the longhouses that characterize domestic structures throughout the Neolithic are replaced by small, single-family dwellings, indicating a shift not only in settlement pattern, but a shift in the basic productive and/or pooling unit of society. The remainder of the Copper Age is characterized by small dispersed settlements within which single families seem to constitute the basic social segment. During this time, it would appear that the social boundaries that had been actively maintained throughout the Late Neolithic become more diffuse, and more permeable, allowing interaction to occur more freely across the entire Plain. All of this changes at the beginning of the Bronze Age.

During the Early Bronze Age, there is once again a tendency towards nucleation, but unlike the Late Neolithic, the houses that are aggregated onto fortified sites are now single-family structures, not longhouses. Along with this intensive nucleation comes a dramatic decrease in the number of overall sites, and the reconstitution of social boundaries which again subdivide the plain into geographically discrete units, or 'cultural groups' (e.g. Nagy-Rév, Máros, etc.). This pattern persists until the end of the Bronze Age (see O'Shea 1996).

This pattern repeated itself on an astonishingly similar temporal and geographic scale within the confines of the eastern Carpathian Basin (Fig. 11). But it is even more satisfying to note that several authors have described similar processes at work in different cultural contexts (see, for example, Friedman 1975; Parker Pearson 1984; Gunder Frank 1993). For example, O'Shea (1999) has recently argued that the sequence of development in Southeast Spain roughly mirrors that of the Hungarian Plain, and Fowles (1997) research documents this same basic phenomenon occurring to an even more intensive degree, and on a much faster scale, in the precontact Puebloan world (see also Feinman et al. 2000). Other examples can be drawn from a variety of different archaeological and ethnohistoric contexts, ranging from the later prehistory of northern Europe (Bogucki 1996; Kristiansen 1982, 1999; Parker Pearson 1984, 1989), to the prehistoric Midwestern United States (see Braun 1980; Emerson 1999), to the historic Pawnee (see O'Shea 1989; Parkinson 1999:50-55).

While it is tempting to describe such processes as 'cycles', it is important to remember that this term does not accurately represent the phenomenon. Cycling implies a return to an identical state or form. The social processes I, and others, have attempted to describe certainly entail the reworking of the methods of integration and interaction to a form reminiscent of one previously assumed in the society's historical development. But along with historical process come idiosyncratic events that serve, in some cases, to permanently alter the potential trajectories a society can assume during its ontogeny. As several social theorists have pointed out, these events—the social, technological, and environmental changes that affect culture—cause social change, and in so doing create social nuances that frequently, if not always preclude the possibility for a society to return to a state identical to a previous one (see, for example,

William A. Parkinson

Giddens 1984). In this sense, the term 'cycling' is somewhat inappropriate. The term 'trajectory' is perhaps a little better, but bears its own albatross of historical particularism, suggesting a linear sequence of events specific to a single society.

Whatever we choose to call them, the repetition of these processes both within the context of the prehistoric Great Hungarian Plain and in different societies throughout the world would seem to suggest that tribes are not, as Fried (1975:1) suggested, merely 'chimera', or 'societal illusions'. They are real cultural phenomena with measurable attributes that exhibit distinctive patterns. The acephalous character and segmented nature of tribal societies make them particularly difficult to model, especially in prehistoric contexts. Nevertheless, by gradually building up a database of the processes of integration and interaction that characterize historical trajectories in different parts of the world, we may begin to understand the variability—and flexibility—that characterizes social organization in tribal societies.

Acknowledgments

The research in this chapter is based on fieldwork conducted by the Körös Regional Archaeological Project in 1998 with a grant from the National Science Foundation (BSR-9812677). Most of the ideas presented above—many of which derive from my dissertation—were formulated over beers at the Brown Jug with faculty members and fellow graduate students at the University of Michigan. Those ideas were slapped into shape by Alan Sullivan and Vernon Scarborough at the University of Cincinnati, where I had the good fortune to be the Charles Phelps Taft Postdoctoral Fellow from 1999–2000. My thoughts on tribal social organization continue to evolve during conversations with Richard Yerkes and the other archaeologists at Ohio State University, where I had the privilege to be the University Postdoctoral Fellow in Anthropology, and with my new colleagues here at Florida State University.

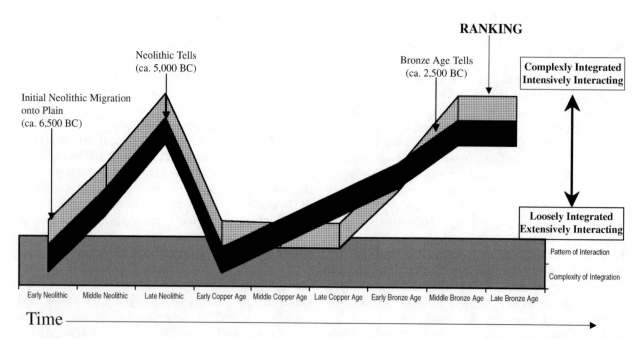

Fig. 11. Changing patterns of integration and interaction throughout the prehistory of the Great Hungarian Plain.

432

References Cited

Adler, Michael
1989 Ritual Facilities and Social Integration in Nonranked Societies. In *The Architecture of Social Integration in Prehistoric Pueblos*, edited by W. Lipe, and M. Hegmon, pp. 35-52. Occasional Paper, No. 1, Crow Canyon Archaeological Center, Cortez, CO.

Andel, Karol
1961 Tibava-Eneolityczny Zespól Osadnicay u Stóp Wyhorlatu. *Acta Archaeologica Carpathica* III(1-2):39-64.

Anderson, David G.
1990 Stability and Change in Chiefdom-Level Societies: An Examination of Mississippian Political Evolution on the South Atlantic Slope. In *Lamar Archaeology: Mississippian Chiefdoms in the Deep South*, edited by M. Williams, and G. Shapiro, pp. 187-252. University of Alabama Press, Tuscaloosa.

András, Liska
1996 X-XI Századi Temeto Örménykúton. *A Békés Megyei Múzeumok Közleményei* 16(1996):175-208.

Bánffy, Eszter
1994 Transdanubia and Eastern Hungary in the Early Copper Age. *A Jósa András Múzeum Évkönyve* XXXVI:291-296.
1995 South-West Transdanubia as a Mediating Area. On the Cultural History of the Early and Middle Chalcolithic. In *Archaeology and Settlement History in the Hahót Basin, SW-Hungary, ANTAEUS: Communicationes ex Instituto Archaeologica Academiae Scientiarum Hungaricae 22*, edited by B. M. Szoke, pp. 157-196. Archaeological Institute of the Hungarian Academy of Sciences, Budapest.

Barth, Fredrik
1969 *Ethnic Groups and Boundaries*. Little, Brown and Co., Boston.

Bender, Barbara
1985 Emergent Tribal Formations in the American Midcontinent. *American Antiquity* 50(1):52-62.

Biró, Katalin
1998 *Lithic Implements and the Circulation of Raw Materials in the Great Hungarian Plain during the Late Neolithic Period*. Hungarian National Museum, Budapest.

Bognár-Kutzián, Ida
1963 *The Copper Age Cemetery of Tiszapolgár-Basatanya*. Archaeologica Hungarica Akadémiai Kiadó, Budapest.
1972 *The Early Copper Age Tiszapolgár Culture in the Carpathian Basin*. Archaeologica Hungarica Akadémiai Kiadó, Budapest.

Bogucki, Peter
1996 Sustainable and Unsustainable Adaptations by Early Farming Communities of Northern Poland. *Journal of Anthropological Archaeology* 15:289-311.

Bökönyi, Sándor
1988 *History of Domestic Mammals in Central and Eastern Europe*. Akadémiai Kiadó, Budapest.

Bordieu, Pierre
1977 *Outline of a Theory of Practice*. Cambridge University Press, Cambridge.

Braun, David
1977 Middle-Woodland-Early Late Woodland Social Change in the Prehistoric Central Midwestern US. Unpublished Ph.D. dissertation, Department of Anthropology, University of Michigan.

Braun, David, and Stephen Plog
1982 Evolution of "Tribal" Social Networks: Theory and Prehistoric North American Evidence. *American Antiquity* 47(3):504-527.

Caldwell, James
1964 Interaction Spheres in Prehistory. In *Hopewellian Studies. Scientific Papers, Volume 12.*, edited by J. Caldwell and R. Hall. Illinois State Museum, Springfield.

Carneiro, Robert L.
1987 Village Splitting as a Function of Population Size. In *Themes in Ethnology and Culture History*, pp. 94-124. Archana Publications, Sadar, India.

Carr, Christopher
1995 A Unified Middle-Range Theory of Artifact Design. In *Style, Society, and Person*, edited by C. Carr, and J. Neitzel, pp. 171-258. Plenum, New York.

Carr, Christopher and Jill Neitzel
1995 Integrating Approaches to Material Style in Theory and Philosophy. In *Style, Society, and Person*, edited by C. Carr and J. Neitzel, pp. 3-26. Plenum, New York.

Chagnon, Napoleon
1983 *Yanomamö: The Fierce People*. Holt, Rinehart and Winston, Inc., Chicago.

Chang, Claudia and H. Koster
  1986 Beyond Bones: Toward an Archaeology
       of Pastoralism. In *Advances in Archaeo-
       logical Method and Theory, Volume 9*,
       edited by M. B. Schiffer, pp. 97-148. Aca-
       demic Press, New York.
Chapman, John
  1983 The "Secondary Products Revolution"
       and the Limitations of the Neolithic.
       *Bulletin of the Institute of Archaeology
       (University of London)* 19(1982):107-22.
  1994 Social Power in the Early Farming Com-
       munities of Eastern Hungary-Perspec-
       tives from the Upper Tisza Region. *A Jósa
       András Múzeum Évkönyve* XXXVI: 79-
       100.
  1997a The Origin of Tells in Eastern Hungary.
       In *Neolithic Landscapes: Neolithic Stud-
       ies Group Seminar Papers 2*, edited by P.
       Topping, pp. 139-164. Oxbow Monograph
       Series, Oxbow, Oxford.
  1997b Changing Gender Relations in the Later
       Prehistory of Eastern Hungary. In *In-
       visible People and Processes: Writing
       Gender and Childhood into European
       Archaeology*, edited by J. Moore, E. and
       Scott, pp. 131-149. Leicester University
       Press, London.
Derevenski, Joanna Sofaer
  2000 Rings of Life: The Role of Early Metal-
       work in Mediating the Gendered Life
       Course. *World Archaeology* 31(3):389-
       406.
  1997 Age and Gender at the Site of Tisza-
       polgár-Basatanya, Hungary. *Antiquity*
       71:875-89.
Divale, W.
  1977 Living Floor Area and Marital Residence:
       A Replication. *Behavior Science Research*
       12:109-115.
Ecsedy, I., L. Kovács, B. Maráz, and I. Torma
(editors)
  1982 Magyarország Régészeti Topográfiája VI.
       Békés Megye Régészeti Topográfiája: A
       Szeghalmi Járás (IV/1). Akadémiai
       Kiadó, Budapest.
Ember, Melvin
  1973 An Archaeological Indicator of Matrilo-
       cal Versus Patrilocal Residence. *Ameri-
       can Antiquity* 38:177-82.
Ember, M. and C. R. Ember
  1995 Worldwide Cross-Cultural Studies and
       their Relevance for Archaeology. *Jour-
       nal of Archaeological Research* 3:87-111.

Emerson, Thomas E.
  1999 The Langford Tradition and the Process
       of Tribalization on the Middle Mississip-
       pian Borders. *Midcontinental Journal of
       Archaeology* 24/1:3-56.
Feinman, Gary, K. Lightfoot, and S. Upham
  2000 Political Hierarchies and Organizational
       Strategies in the Puebloan Southwest.
       American Antiquity 65(3):449-470.
Flannery, Kent V.
  1968a Archaeological Systems Theory and
       Early Mesoamerica. In *Anthropological
       Archaeology in the Americas*, edited by
       B. Meggers, pp. 67-87. Anthropological
       Society of Washington, Washington.
  1968b The Olmec and the Valley of Oaxaca: A
       Model for Interregional Interaction in
       Formative Times. In *Dumbarton Oaks
       Conference on the Olmec*, edited by E.
       Benton, pp. 79-110. Dumbaron Oaks
       Library, Washington.
Fowles, Severin
  1997 Scalar Dynamics in Tribal Society. Un-
       published Manuscript. University of
       Michigan Museum of Anthropology.
Fried, Morton
  1975 *The Notion of Tribe*. Cummings, Menalo
       Park, California.
Friedman, Johnathan
  1979 System, Structure, and Contradiction:
       The Evolution of "Asiatic" Social Forma-
       tions. National Museum of Denmark,
       Copenhagen.
Gearing, Fred
  1958 The Structural Poses of 18th-Century
       Cherokee Villages. *American Anthro-
       pologist* 60:1148-56.
Giddens, Anthony
  1984 *The Constitution of Society: Outline of
       the Theory of Structuration*. University
       of California Press, Berkeley.
Goldman, György
  1977 A Tiszapolgári Kultúra Települése
       Bélmegyeren. *Archeologiai Értesitő*
       104(2): 221-34.
Gunder Frank, Andre
  1993 Bronze Age World System Cycles. *Cur-
       rent Anthropology* 34:383-405.
Haas, Johnathan
  1990 Warfare and the Evolution of Tribal Poli-
       ties in the Prehistoric Southwest. In *The
       Anthropology of War*, edited by J. Haas,
       pp. 171-189. Cambridge University
       Press, New York.

Harris, Marvin
1979 *Cultural Materialism*. Random House, New York.
Hegedűs, Katalin
1973 Vésztő. Archaeological Report. *Régészeti Füzetek* 26:25-6.
1974 Vésztő.. Archaeological Report. *Régészeti Füzetek* 27:21-4.
1975 Vésztő.. Archaeological Report. *Régészeti Füzetek* 28:32-3.
1976a Vésztő.. Archaeological Report. *Régészeti Füzetek* 29:21-2.
1977a Vésztő.. Archaeological Report. *Régészeti Füzetek* 30:15.
1977b A Vésztő.-Mágordombi Újkőkori és Rézkori Temetkezések. Budapest.
1982 Vésztő-Magori-domb. In *Magyarország Régészeti Topográfiája VI. Békés Megye Régészeti Topográfiája: A Szeghalmi Járás (IV/1)*, edited by I. Ecsedy, L. Kovács, B. Maráz, and I. Torma, pp. 184-5. Akadémiai Kiadó, Budapest.
1983 Indications of Social differentiation in the Neolithic of Eastern Hungary. Paper Presented at the Annual Meetings of the Society for American Archaeology.
Hegedűs, Katalin and János Makkay
1987 Vésztő-Mágor: A Settlement of the Tisza Culture. In *The Late Neolithic of the Tisza Region: A survey of recent excavations and their findings*, edited by P. Raczky, pp. 85-104. Szolnok County Museums, Budapest-Szolnok.
Hegmon, Michelle
1989 The Styles of Integration: Ceramic style and Pueblo I integrative architecture in Southwestern Colorado. In *The Architecture of Social Integration in Prehistoric Pueblos*, edited by W. Lipe, and M. Hegmon. Occasional Papers No. 1, Crow Canyon Archaeological Center, Cortez, CO.
1992 Archaeological Research on Style. *Annual Review of Anthropology* 21:517-536.
1995 *The Social Dynamics of Pottery Style in the Early Puebloan Southwest*. Occasional Paper No. 5. Crow Canyon Archaeological Center, Cortez, CO.
1998 Technology, Style and Social Practices: Archaeological Approaches. In *The Archaeology of Social Boundaries*, edited by M. Stark, pp. 264-280. Smithsonian, Washington.
Hollinger, R. E.
1995 Residence Patterns and Oneota Cultural Dynamics. In *Oneota Archaeology: Past, Present, and Future*, edited by W. Green, pp. 141-174. Office of the State Archaeologist, Iowa City.
Horváth, Ferenc
1987 Hódmezővásárhely-Gorzsa: A Settlement of the Tisza culture. In *The Late Neolithic of the Tisza Region*, edited by P. Raczky, pp. 31-46. Szolnok County Museums, Budapest-Szolnok.
Hyde, G.
1974 *The Pawnee Indians*. University of Oklahoma Press, Norman, OK.
Jankovich, D., J. Makkay, and B. Szőke (editors)
1989 *Magyarország Régészeti Topográfiája VIII. Békés Megye Régészeti Topográfiája: A Szarvasi Járás (IV/2)*. Akadémiai Kiadó, Budapest.
Jovanović, Borislav
1982 *Rudna Glava: The Oldest Copper Mining in the Central Balkans*. Institute of Archaeology, Bor-Beograd.
Jovanović, Borislav (editor)
1971 *Metalurgija Eneolitskog Perioda Jugoslavije*. Arheološki Institut, Belgrade.
Juhász, Iren
1991 Örménykút 13. Lelőhely. *Régészeti Füzetek* 43(1991):12.
Kalicz, Nándor and Pál Raczky
1987a The Late Neolithic of the Tisza Region: A Survey of Recent Archaeological Research. In *The Late Neolithic of the Tisza Region*, edited by P. Raczky, pp. 11-30. Szolnok County Museums, Budapest-Szolnok.
Kalicz, Nándor and Pál Raczky
1987b Berettyóújfalu-Herpály: A Settlement of the Herpály culture. In *The Late Neolithic of the Tisza Region*, edited by P. Raczky, pp. 105-125. Szolnok County Museums, Budapest-Szolnok.
Korek, Jozsef
1972 *A Tiszai Kultúra*. Budapest.
1987 Szegvár-Tűzköves: A Settlement of the Tisza culture. In *The Late Neolithic of the Tisza Region*, edited by P. Raczky, pp. 47-60. Szolnok County Museums, Budapest-Szolnok.
Kosse, Krisztina
1979 *Settlement Ecology of the Early and Middle Neolithic Körös and Linear Pottery Cultures in Hungary*. BAR International Series. British Archaeological Reports, Oxford.

Kristiansen, Kristian
   1982   The Formation of Tribal Systems in Later European Prehistory. In *Theory and Explanation in Archaeology: The Southampton Conference*, edited by C. Renfrew, M. Rowlands, and B. Seagraves. Academic Press, New York.
Longacre, William
   1966   Changing Patterns of Social Integration: A Prehistoric Example. *American Anthropologist* 68(1):94-102.
Lowell, J. C.
   1996   Moieties in Prehistory: A Case Study from the Pueblo Southwest. *Journal of Field Archaeology* 23:77-90.
MacEachern, S.
   1998   Scale, Style and Cultural Variation: Technological Traditions in the Northern Mandara Mountains. In *The Archaeology of Social Boundaries*, edited by M. Stark, pp. 107-131. Smithsonian, Washington.
Makkay, János
   1982   A *Magyarországi Neolitikum Kutatásának Új Eredményei*. Akadémiai Kiadó, Budapest.
   1986   *Ásatás a Vésztő-Mágor*. (Napló). Unpublished Manuscript. Institute of Archaeology, Budapest.
Marcus, Joyce
   1993   Ancient Maya Political Organization. In *Lowland Maya Civilization in the Eighth Century A.D.*, edited by J. A. Sabloff, and J. S. Henderson, pp. 111-172. Dumbarton Oaks Research Library and Collection, Washington, D.C.
Marcus, Joyce and Kent V. Flannery
   1996   *Zapotec Civilization: How Urban Society Evolved in Mexico's Oaxaca Valley*. Thames and Hudson, New York.
McGuire, Ran   dall and Dean Saitta
   1996   Although They Have Petty Captains, They Obey Them Badly: The Dialectics of Prehispanic Western Pueblo Social Organization. *American Antiquity* 61:197-216.
Meisenheimer, M.
   1989   *Das Totenritual, Geprägt Durch Jenseitvorstellungen und Gesellschaftsrealität: Theori des Totenrituals eines Kupferzeitlichen Friedhofs zu Tiszapolgár-Basatanya (Ungarn)*. BAR International Series. No. 475. British Archaeological Reports, Oxford.

Milisauskas, Sarunas and J. Kruk
   1991   Utilization of Cattle for Traction During the Later Neolithic in Southeastern Poland. *Antiquity* 65:562-66.
Milleker, B.
   1893   Szerbkeresztúri őstelep. *Archeologiai Értesitő* 1893:300-307.
Némeskeri, J. and Szathmári, L.
   1987   An Anthropological Evaluation of the Indo-European Problem: The anthropological and demographic transition in the Danube Basin. In *Proto-Indo-European. The Archaeology of a Linguistic Problem. Studies in Honor of Marija Gimbutas*, edited by S. N. Skomal and E.C. Polomé. Institute for the Study of Man, Washington, D.C.
O'Shea, John
   1989   Pawnee Archaeology. *Central Plains Archaeology* 1(1):49-107.
   1996   *Villagers of the Maros: A Portrait of an Early Bronze Age Society*. Plenum Press, New York.
   1999   Comparative Trajectories of Change in Prehistoric Europe. Paper Presented at the Annual Meetings of the Society for American Archaeology, Chicago, Illinois.
Parker Pearson, Michael
   1984   Economic and Ideological Change: Cyclical Growth in the Pre-State Societies of Jutland. In *Ideology, Power, and Prehistory*, edited by D. Miller and C. Tilley. Cambridge University Press, Cambridge.
   1989   Beyond the Pale: Barbarian Social Dynamics in Western Europe. In *Barbarians and Romans in North-West Europe from the Later Republic in Late Antiquity*, edited by J. Barett, A.C. Fitzpatrick and L. MacInnes, pp. 102-157. BAR International Series, No. 471., British Archaeological Reports, Oxford.
Parkinson, William A.
   1999   The Social Organization of Early Copper Age Tribes on the Great Hungarian Plain. Ph.D thesis, Department of Anthropology, University of Michigan, Ann Arbor.
Parkinson, William A., Richard W. Yerkes and Atilla Gyucha
   2002   The Neolithic-Copper Age Transition on the Great Hungarian Plain: Recent Excavations at Vésztő-Bikeri, a Tiszapolgar Culture Settlement Site. *Antiquity* 76:619-620.

Pécsi, M.
1970   *Geomorphological Regions of Hungary.* Akadémiai Kiadó, Budapest.

Pécsi, M. and Sárfalvi, B.
1964   *The Geography of Hungary.* Collets, London.

Plog, Stephen
1976   Measurement of Prehistoric Interaction Between Communities. In *The Early Mesoamerican Village*, edited by K. Flannery, pp. 255-72. Academic Press, New York.

1978   Social Interaction and Stylistic Similarity: A Reanalysis. *Advances in Archaeological Method and Theory* 1:383-421.

1980   Stylistic Variation of Prehistoric Ceramics. Cambridge, New York.

1990   Sociopolitical Implications of Southwestern Stylistic Variation in the American Southwest. In *The Uses of Style in Archaeology*, edited by M. Conkey, M. and C. Hastorf, pp. 61-72. Cambridge University Press, Cambridge.

1995   Approaches to Style: Complements and contrasts. In *Style, Society, and Person*, edited by C. Carr and J. Neitzel, pp. 369-392. Plenum, New York.

Plog, Stephen and David Braun
1984   Some Issues in the Archaeology of "Tribal" Social Systems. *American Antiquity* 49(3):619-625.

Raczky, Pál
1985   The Cultural and Chronological Relations of the Tisza Region During the Middle and Late Neolihtic as Reflected by the Excavations at Öcsöd-Kováshalom. *A Szekszárdi Béri Balogh Ádám Múzeum Évkönyve (Szekszárd)* 103-25.

1987b Öcsöd-Kováshalom: A Settlement of the Tisza culture. In *The Late Neolithic of the Tisza Region*, edited by P. Raczky, pp. 61-83. Szolnok County Museums, Budapest-Szolnok.

Raczky, Pál, A. Anders, E. Nagy, K. Kurucz, Zs. Hajdú, and W. Meier-Arendt
1997   Polgár-Csőszhalom dűlő. In *Utak a Múltba: Az M3-as autópálya régészeti leletmentései*, edited by P. Raczky, T. Kovács and A. Anders, pp. 34-44. Magyar Nemzeti Múzeum és az Eötvös Loránd Tudományegyetem Régészettudományi Intézet, Budapest.

Raczky, P., W. Meier-Arendt, K. Kurucz, Zs. Hajdú and Á. Szikora
1994   Polgár-Cs szhalom: A Late Neolithic Settlement in the Upper Tisza Region and its Cultural Connections (Preliminary Report). In *Jósa András Múzeum Évkönyve, XXXVI*, pp. 231-240. A Nyíregyházi Jósa András Múzeum, Nyíregyháza.

Raczky, P., P. Seleanu, G. Rózsa, Cs. Siklodi, G. Kalla, B. Csornay, H. Oravecz, M. Vicae, E. Bánffy, S. Bökönyi and P. Somogyi
1985   Öcsöd-Kováshalom: The Intensive Topographical and Arcaehological Investigation of a Late Neolithic Site. Preliminary Report. *Mitteilungen des Archäologischen Instituts der Ungarischen Akademie der Wissenschaften* 14(1985): 251-278.

Rappaport, Roy A.
1984   *Pigs for the Ancestors: Ritual in the Ecology of a New Guinea People.* Yale University Press, New Haven.

Sackett, James
1977   The Meaning of Style in Archaeology: A General Model. *American Antiquity* 43(3):369-80.

1985   Style and Ethnicity in the Kalahari: A Reply to Wiessner. *American Antiquity* 50(1):154-59.

1998   Style and Ethnicity in Archaeology: The Case for Isochrestism. In *The Archaeology of Social Boundaries*, edited by M. Stark, pp. 32-43. Smithsonian, Washington.

Sahlins, Marshall
1972   *Stone Age Economics.* Aldine, New York.

Saitta, Dean
1983   On the Evolution of "Tribal" Social Networks. *American Antiquity* 48:820-24.

Sall, J. and A. Lehman
1996   *JMP Start Statistics: A Guide to Statistics and Data Analysis Using JMP and JMP-IN Software.* Duxbury Press, New York.

Service, Elman
1971   *Primitive Social Organization: An Evolutionary Perspective.* Second edition. Random House, New York.

Sherratt, Andrew
1981   Plough and Pastoralism: Aspects of the Secondary Products Revolution. In *Pattern of the Past: Studies in Honour of David Clarke*, edited by I. Hodder G. Isaac and N. Hammond. Cambridge University Press, Cambridge.

1983a The Secondary Exploitation of Animals in the Old World. *World Archaeology* 15:90-104.

1983b The Development of Neolithic and Copper Age Settlement in the Great Hungarian Plain, Part I: The Regional Setting. *Oxford Journal of Archaeology* 1(1):287-316.

1984 The Development of Neolithic and Copper Age Settlement in the Great Hungarian Plain, Part II: Site Survey and Settlement Dynamics. *Oxford Journal of Archaeology* 2(1):13-41.

1987 Neolithic Exchange Systems in Central Europe, 5000-3000. In *The Human Uses of Flint and Chert*, edited by G. Sieveking and M. Newcomer. Cambridge University Press, Cambridge.

1997 The Development of Neolithic and Copper Age Settlement in the Great Hungarian Plain - Part II: Site Survey and Settlement Dynamics. In *Economy and Society in Prehistoric Europe: Changing Perspectives*, edited by A. Sherratt, pp. 293-319. Endinburgh University Press, Edinburgh.

Siklódi, Csilla
1982 Előzetes Jelentés a Tiszaug-Kisrétparti Rézkori Telep Ásatásról. *Archeologiai Értesitő* 109(2):231-238.

1983 Kora Rézkori Település Tiszaföldváron. *Szolnok Megyei Múzeum Évkönyv* 1992-1983:11-31.

Simon, H.
1973 The Organization of Complex Systems. In *Hierarchy Theory*, edited by Pattee, H. H., pp. 1-27. Braziller, New York.

Šiška, S.
1968 Die Tiszapolgár-Kultur in der Slowakei. *Slovenská Archeológia (Bratislava)* 16.

Skomal, Susan N.
1980 The Social Organization of the Tiszapolgár group at Basatanya - Carpathian Basin Copper Age. *Journal of Indo-European Studies* 8(1-2):75-82.

1983 Wealth Distribution as a Measure of Prehistoric Change: Chalcolithic to Copper Age Cultures in Hungary. Unpublished Ph.D. dissertation, University of California, Los Angeles.

Snow, Dean
1994 *The Iroquois*. Blackwell, Cambridge, MA.

Stark, Miriam
1998 Technical Choices and Social Boundaries in Material Culture Patterning: An Introduction. In *The Archaeology of Social Boundaries*, edited by M. Stark, pp. 1-11. Smithsonian, Washington.

Steward, Julian
1951 Levels of Sociocultural Integration: An Operational Concept. *Southwest Journal of Anthropology* VII:374-90.

Struever, Stuart
1964 The Hopewell Interaction Sphere in Riverine-Western Great Lakes Culture History. In *Hopewellian Studies. Scientific Papers, vol. 12* edited by J. Caldwell and R. Hall, pp. 85-106. Illinois State Museum, Springfield.

Voss, Jerome
1980 Tribal Emergence During the Neolithic of Northwestern Europe. Unpublished Ph.D. dissertation, Department of Anthropology, University of Michigan, Ann Arbor.

Voss, Jerome and R. Young
1995 Style and the Self. In *Style, Society, and Person*, edited by C. Carr and J. Neitzel, pp. 77-100. Plenum, New York.

Whallon, Robert
1968 Investigations of Late Prehistoric Social Organization in New York State. In *New Perspectives in Archaeology*, edited by S.R. Binford and L.R. Binford, pp. 223-244. Aldine, Chicago.

Whittle, Alasdair
1997 Moving On and Moving Around: Neolithic Settlement Mobility. In *Neolithic Landscapes: Neolithic Studies Group Seminar Papers 2*, edited by Topping, P., pp. 15-22. Oxbow Books, Oxford.

Wiessner, Polly
1985 Style or Isochrestic Variation?: A Reply to Sackett. *American Antiquity* 50(1):160-66.

1990 Is There a Unity to Style? In *The Uses of Style in Archaeology*, edited by M. W. Conkey and C. A. Hastorf, pp. 105-112. Cambridge University Press, Cambridge.

Wobst, Martin
1977 Stylistic Behavior and Information Exchange. In *For the Director: Research Essays in Honor of James B. Griffin*, edited by C. Cleland, pp. 317-342. Anthropological Papers, University of Michigan Museum of Anthropology, Ann Arbor.